# REPUBLIC OF LABOR

**CORNELL UNIVERSITY PRESS** ITHACA AND LONDON

# REPUBLIC OF LABOR

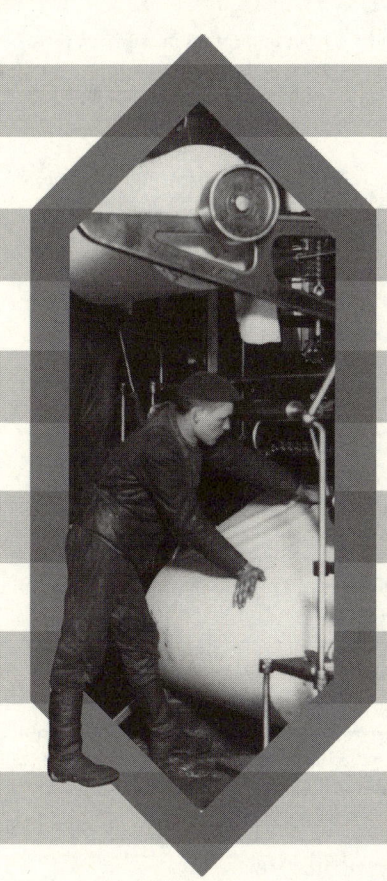

RUSSIAN PRINTERS AND SOVIET SOCIALISM, 1918-1930

## DIANE P. KOENKER

Copyright © 2005 by Cornell University

All rights reserved. Except for brief quotations in a review, this book, or parts thereof, must not be reproduced in any form without permission in writing from the publisher. For information, address Cornell University Press, Sage House, 512 East State Street, Ithaca, New York 14850.

First published 2005 by Cornell University Press
Printed in the United States of America

Design by Scott Levine

Library of Congress Cataloging-in-Publication Data

Koenker, Diane.
  Republic of labor : Russian printers and Soviet Socialism, 1918–1930 / Diane P. Koenker.
     p. cm.
  Includes bibliographical references and index.
  ISBN 0-8014-4308-3 (cloth : alk. paper)
  1. Working class—Soviet Union—History. 2. Labor—Soviet Union—History. 3. Printing industry—Soviet Union—History. 4. Printers—Labor unions—Soviet Union—History. 5. Industrial relations—Soviet Union—History. I. Title.
  HD8526.K59 2005
  331.7′6862′094709042—dc22
                                                     2004030152

Cornell University Press strives to use environmentally responsible suppliers and materials to the fullest extent possible in the publishing of its books. Such materials include vegetable-based, low-VOC inks and acid-free papers that are recycled, totally chlorine-free, or partly composed of nonwood fibers. For further information, visit our website at www.cornellpress.cornell.edu.

Cloth printing     10 9 8 7 6 5 4 3 2 1

FOR HANNAH AND IN MEMORY OF EMMA

# CONTENTS

List of Illustrations — ix
Acknowledgments — xi
Abbreviations — xiii

Introduction: Socialism and the Russian Working Class — 1

## PART I. CIVIL WAR AND THE EVOLUTION OF THE ONE-PARTY TRADE UNION, 1918–1922

1. The Printing Industry in the Era of Revolutionary Transformations — 17
2. The Struggle for a Communist Printers' Union, 1918–1922 — 45
3. The Civil War and Working-Class Culture — 77

## PART II. THE "GOLDEN YEARS" OF THE NEW ECONOMIC POLICY, 1922–1927

4. A New Form of Labor Relations — 109
5. The Working People's Democracy — 143
6. New Cultures of Class — 175

## PART III. THE TWISTING ROAD TO THE FIRST FIVE-YEAR PLAN, 1927–1930

7. The Industry without a Plan: Unemployment and Conflict in the First Five-Year Plan — 215
8. The Twilight of the Socialist Trade Union — 245
9. Class Formation or the Unmaking of the Working Class? — 271

10. Soviet Workers and the Socialist Project: Epilogue and Conclusion — 299

Selected Bibliography — 317
Index — 335

# ILLUSTRATIONS

| | |
|---|---|
| Compositors at their type cases, 1929 | 22 |
| Press department at the *Pravda* print shop, 1922 | 23 |
| Women at work in a pamphlet workshop, 1924 | 24 |
| Comrade Borshchevskii, chairman of the Moscow printers' union and a "patriot of his country" | 95 |
| "For the next contest, I am learning how to set type with both hands" | 129 |
| Masthead of a 1924 issue of *Pechatnik* | 160 |
| "Around Our Print Shops" | 160 |
| Factory committee at the Krasnyi Maiak print shop | 163 |
| "A Physically Uncultured Outburst" | 192 |
| "Drama in the Tarif Grid" | 202 |
| Master and apprentice, 1920s | 204 |
| "Toward the Reelection of the Factory Committee" | 249 |
| Purge meeting at the Fifteenth State Print Shop | 288 |
| Women compositors, 1931 | 303 |

# ACKNOWLEDGMENTS

I take the greatest pleasure in acknowledging the help, advice, and financial assistance that have made this book possible. A number of institutions provided funding and facilities that supported my research and writing: I thank the National Endowment for the Humanities, the International Research and Exchanges Board (including funding from the Title VIII Program of the U.S. Department of State), the Fulbright-Hays Faculty Research Abroad Program of the U.S. Department of Education, the National Council for Eurasian and East European Research, Moscow State University, the Australian National University, the Midwest Universities Consortium on International Affairs, and the University of Illinois Center for Advanced Study. The University of Illinois Research Board has provided valuable support over the years of research and writing.

It is not possible to thank by name all the dedicated and professional archivists and librarians who assisted me in my research, but I owe a huge debt of gratitude to the staffs of the institutions in which I explored the history of Soviet printers: the Russian State Library, the Russian National Library, the State Public Historical Library of Russia, the library of the Scientific Institute for Information in the Social Sciences (INION), the State Archive of the Russian Federation (GARF), the Central State Archive of Moscow Oblast (TsGAMO), the Central State Archive of St. Petersburg (TsGA SPb), the Central State Archive of Historical-Political Documents in St. Petersburg (TsGAIPD SPb), the Russian State Archive of Social and Political History (RGASPI), and the Russian State Archive of Documentary Films and Photographs (RGAKFD). I am also grateful to the directors of the Krasnyi Proletarii firm and the former Sixteenth Print Shop in Moscow, who arranged tours of their plants in 1998 and 1989.

I thank Cornell University Press for permission to reprint in Chapters 1 and 2 material that was originally published, in different form, as "Labor Relations in Socialist Russia: Class Values and Production Values in the Printers' Union," in *Making Workers Soviet: Power, Class, and Identity,* edited by Lewis H.

Siegelbaum and Ronald Grigor Suny (1994). John Ackerman at Cornell has provided thoughtful and incisive advice at key moments during the book's revision: he is a gifted editor. It has been a pleasure to work with Barbara Salazar on the final stages of the process.

Words are insufficient to acknowledge my debt to my *rodnaia* library, the Slavic Library at the University of Illinois. I have the great fortune to work literally next door to one of the world's outstanding Slavic libraries and to have had the benefit of the knowledge and assistance of its extraordinary staff. Marianna Tax Choldin, Larry Miller, and Helen Sullivan have provided immeasurable support, answering any and all reference questions and acquiring the essential trade union journals for this project; the entire staff of the Slavic Library has been an important source of research assistance.

A dedicated succession of research assistants read and digested the daily newspapers used in this book, and for their help, knowledge, and patience I salute Charles Clark, Heather Coleman, Elizabeth Dennison, Kathleen Kennedy, Scott Palmer, Laura Phillips, and Jeffery Sahadeo.

I wish to express my appreciation to my colleagues in the history department at the University of Illinois for many lively discussions on labor history and Russian history. Space permits me to thank only a few by name. Jim Barrett has been a valued colleague and true friend, and his careful and encouraging readings of many drafts of this manuscript have challenged me to think ambitiously and to write parsimoniously. My friend and colleague Mark Steinberg has shared with me his enthusiasm for printers and for popular culture, as well as for Russian history writ large. His own work has provided much inspiration, and his careful reading of several versions of this work has improved it in many ways.

I have also benefited from advice, suggestions, and conversations with scholars and colleagues in North America, Europe, and Russia. Participants at meetings of the Midwest Russian History Workshops have provided valuable comments on several draft chapters. Many friends have offered advice and encouragement: I will not thank them individually but I cannot thank them enough. Lewis Siegelbaum has been a partner in Russian history since we began our dissertation research in Moscow together several regimes ago: he has been a stimulating reader and always a supportive friend. Bill Rosenberg, an exemplary mentor, colleague, and friend, has offered important intellectual and other support at several critical stages of this project, most recently with a careful and constructive reading of the manuscript in its penultimate form. I am happy to share credit with them for the book's completion, but any errors that remain are mine alone.

My family has endured the long process of research and writing with patience and empathy. Roger has lived with these printers for as long as I have, and he has enriched my work with his understanding and insights. I dedicate this book to my daughters, who taught me more about love than I can ever say.

D. P. K.

# ABBREVIATIONS

| | |
|---|---|
| GARF | Gosudarstvennyi Arkhiv Rossiiskoi Federatsii (State Archive of the Russian Federation) |
| TsGA SPb | Tsentral'nyi Gosudarstvennyi Arkhiv Sankt Peterburga (Central State Archive in St. Petersburg) |
| TsGAIPD SPb | Tsentral'nyi Gosudarstvennyi Arkhiv Istoriko-Politicheskikh Dokumentov Sankt Peterburga (Central State Archive of Historical-Political Documents in St. Petersburg) |
| TsGAMO | Tsentral'nyi Gosudarstvennyi Arkhiv Moskovskoi Oblasti (Central State Archive of Moscow Oblast) |
| TsSU | Tsentral'noe statisticheskoe upravlenie (Central Statistical Administration) |
| TsUNKhU | Tsentral'noe upravlenie narodnogo-khoziaistvennogo ucheta |
| *Vestnik vsrpd* | *Vestnik vserossiiskogo soiuza rabochikh pechatnogo dela* (Bulletin of the All-Russian Union of Printing Workers) |
| VSNKh | (Vesenkha) Vysshii sovet narodnogo khoziaistva (Supreme Economic Council) |
| VTsSPS | Vsesoiuznyi tsentral'nyi sovet professional'nykh soiuzov (All-Union Council of Trade Unions) |

# REPUBLIC OF LABOR

# INTRODUCTION

## SOCIALISM AND THE RUSSIAN WORKING CLASS

Workers symbolized the ethos of Soviet socialism. The dictatorship of the proletariat claimed to speak for the vanguard of Russian toiling people, the millions of producers who labored in factories, workshops, and mines across the country. Work and workers shaped the socialist revolution, and the revolution transformed the work cultures and political relations of the old regime. To examine this transformation, this book investigates the experience of workers in the printing trades during the first thirteen years of the Soviet revolution. Starting from the work process, looking at relations among management, state, and labor, and investigating workers' culture, it explores the meaning as well as the politics of socialism in the lives of ordinary workers in the first socialist society in the world. The book will demonstrate the complicated interaction between material reality and ideological dreams, between socialist ideals and Communist Party politics, and between the transformatory promise of socialism and the lived experience of men and women inside and outside the socialist workplace.

The victory in October 1917 of a radical socialist alliance of Bolsheviks and Left Socialist Revolutionaries marked the beginning of a bold effort to create a new, just, and equitable society on the principles of the social ownership of wealth. There were few blueprints for the construction of such a society, and those that designed them had scarcely imagined that socialism would arrive first in a country so devastated by war and so mired in poverty. Three more years of bloody civil warfare and economic destruction further shaped the conditions under which Soviet Russia would conduct its socialist experiment, but these constraints did not diminish the soaring transformatory ambition of Soviet visionaries and officials. In its very totality, the Soviet revolution embraced many dimensions, as it sought to reinvent not only an economy but social relations, ethnic identities, gender roles, personal ethics, intellectual culture, and ultimately the world system. The Soviet experiment consisted of ideas, institutions, and practices, but above all it involved the willing—or unwilling—participation of the citizens of the new republic.

In an earlier work, I argued that the radical socialist outcome of October 1917 reflected genuine beliefs and aspirations of industrial workers, but that it was also the product of specific shocks to their well-being and contingent political choices.[1] I did not assume that this constellation of attitudes would necessarily hold together once the Bolsheviks had come to power. How did workers articulate their political and social aspirations as the revolutionary culture took shape? How did working-class culture change once the revolution had been victorious? These are broad questions, best addressed by investigations of discrete work cultures rather than the entire universe of Soviet Russia's revolutionary workforce. Approaching the question of working-class culture through a local study of one city or one industrial group allows the historian to take full advantage of detailed and multiple sources that reflect the minutiae of the everyday as well as the broad contours of historical processes. A local approach permits the historian to explore particular histories, traditions, and personalities without losing sight of the larger issues at stake.

Workers in the printing industry can serve as a microcosm of the entire Soviet socialist experiment because just about every campaign, policy, and conflict in the postrevolutionary years—from workers' control to rationalization to family reform to purges and denunciation—was reflected in the history of printers and their union. The first workers to organize an industrial trade union, printers had played a significant role in the revolution of 1905. After October 1917, their political support divided quite evenly between the ruling Communists and the opposition Mensheviks. Under Menshevik leadership until 1919, and reflecting considerable Menshevik influence as late as 1923, the printers' union constituted one of the few bastions of resistance to Communist one-party rule, and its leaders offered an articulate alternative for the construction of socialism. As skilled and highly literate workers, printers produced a large vol-

---

1. Diane Koenker, *Moscow Workers and the 1917 Revolution* (Princeton, 1981).

ume of writing through their trade union journals and factory newspapers, which contain a remarkable variety of opinion and reports on production and on trade union concerns, as well as fiction, poetry, and humor. Finally, the role played by gender in the articulation of working-class culture was especially pivotal in this trade, which was dominated by skilled men but in which women accounted for about one-quarter of the workforce.

In some respects, one might argue that printers were not central actors in the drama of the construction of socialism. Their numbers were relatively few: the size of the labor force in printing even by 1930 remained below 75,000, compared with 850,000 workers in the metal industry and 625,000 in the textile industry.[2] The metalworkers, coal miners, and railway workers unquestionably possessed greater economic leverage, and their political commitment to socialism was probably more important to the Communist regime than that of the heterodox printers. The printers' union regularly lamented its status as the "stepson" of Soviet labor organization, but my interest here is not leverage or impact or power alone. I am seeking not to determine how policies came to be decided from the perspective of power but rather to trace how Soviet workers grappled with the challenges of building a socialist working-class culture. Despite their small numbers, printers can be thought of as the canaries in the mine shaft of Bolshevism: their political history and their access to print uniquely positioned them to articulate the safety and the dangers of the socialist experiment.

I am interested above all in the formative years of Soviet socialism, the period in which political leaders and social actors debated and experimented with the forms of socialist culture and practices. The Civil War imposed its particular rigor on the transformation of working-class culture: the years from 1918 to 1920 witnessed the most bitter warfare within the printing industry as Menshevik and Communist trade unions vied for the right to represent these workers. The period of the New Economic Policy (NEP) is often regarded as a period of calm and tolerance, a moment for exploration and open discussion before the reimposition of rigor and industrial discipline with the introduction of the First Five-Year Plan in 1928. By taking this study up to 1930, the midpoint of the First Five-Year Plan, I seek to question the conventional periodization and the discontinuities it represents. My interest is not in the experience of industrialization itself but in the issues and attitudes that printers brought with them to these years of rapid change.

## RUSSIAN PRINTERS AND SOVIET SOCIALISM

Mine is a local study of working-class experience in Soviet Russia's postrevolutionary years, and it engages a number of ongoing discussions about the na-

---

2. Tsentral'noe upravlenie narodno-khoziaistvennogo ucheta [TsUNKhU] Gosplana SSSR, Sektor ucheta truda, *Trud v SSSR. Statisticheskii spravochnik,* ed. A. S. Popov (Moscow, 1936), 94.

ture of the Soviet regime. By privileging the workers' perspective, this study of printers contributes to a reassessment of the relationship between central politics and grassroots support and attitudes: ideological and authoritarian politics indeed structured the possibilities available to members of society, but society talked back, and the experiences of printing industry workers in the 1920s provide considerable evidence of ongoing debate and dissent as well as accommodation. The evolution of what I label participatory dictatorship provided room for the elaboration of so-called Stalinist values of centralism, coercion, and authority, but it also engaged workers in shaping their own environments at many levels.

Issues of industrial organization and labor-management relations were fundamental in developing the ideology and ethics of Soviet socialism, and these issues play a key role in the history of the printers' union and in printers' individual interactions with Soviet power. The Soviet model of labor relations began with an overweening commitment to production and to planning: the printers' case demonstrates how workers altered this model to address their more consumerist vision of socialism. It also reveals the complex influences of custom, market principles, and central planning in printers' understanding of the socialist economy. Utilizing for the first time local records of the trade union movement in the 1920s, this book demonstrates how far from reality were official trade union pronouncements and policies, and how important for local institutional practices were negotiation, resistance, and compromise.[3] As a "school for communism," the trade union could not merely lecture in the style of nineteenth-century pedants: it needed to engage the participation of its audience. Trade union politics on the ground were remarkably vocal and lively in the 1920s.

This book situates socialist worker culture in the broader world context of industrial labor. The postwar political settlements in many countries reflected accommodation with newly empowered working classes, and we should not allow the uniqueness of the Soviet socialist experiment to obscure the common features of the postwar industrial world. Organized labor parties and trade union movements in many countries won new institutional arrangements for collective bargaining, better work conditions, and new welfare schemes such as paid vacations and health insurance. While these gains of labor (and the fear of the Soviet example) generated their own backlash and ensured that labor-management conflict would continue to characterize industrial life in Europe and

---

3. Soviet trade unions have not had their story told. E. H. Carr pays important attention to the institution of the trade unions as part of his ambitious history of the Soviet Union: *A History of Soviet Russia*, 14 vols. (New York and London, 1950–78). Jay B. Sorenson, *The Life and Death of Soviet Trade Unions, 1917–1928* (New York, 1969), is the only historical monograph devoted to the trade union movement; several other studies look briefly and retrospectively at this period: Isaac Deutscher, *Soviet Trade Unions: Their Place in Soviet Labour Policy* (New York, 1950); Emily Clark Brown, *Soviet Trade Unions and Labor Relations* (Cambridge, Mass., 1966); Blair A. Ruble, *Soviet Trade Unions: Their Development in the 1970s* (Cambridge, 1981).

North America, the postwar years ushered in a sufficient level of prosperity to give rise to a new culture of consumerism in both capitalist and socialist worlds.

On the terrain of socialism, printers seized the opportunity to make good on the promise of a revolution in culture, a project launched well before 1917 and embedded in the socialist dream itself. Worker and socialist intellectuals had begun in the last years of the old regime to experiment with forms of expression that would represent collective and social values rather than hierarchical and individual ones.[4] The experience of printers in the 1920s demonstrates quite explicitly the ways in which workers embraced the idea of cultural revolution. Many of the other conflicts and debates surrounding labor, production, and the economy found their representation in style and symbols, from fictional heroes to clothing to the images on the masthead of the trade union journal. Culture also includes everyday life and material culture. Emphasizing the everydayness of socialist experience requires us to look at the routine, the repetitive, and the normal, not only at work but in house and home, getting and spending, swearing, studying, and dancing.[5] The everyday and the exceptional together made up the experience of workers in the construction of a socialist culture. They created ample space for divergent views and interpretations of the meaning of socialism.

The perspective of the everyday also helps to bring questions of gender into focus. Socialist theorists believed that freeing women from their economic dependence on men would create the conditions for a truly equal gender system, but both material shortages and a masculinist work culture made it difficult for the regime to honor the socialist promise of economic emancipation.[6] The creation of a socialist gender system involved not just economics but attitudes, values, and everyday interactions. Gender constituted a fundamental source of difference, and gender identities were crucial to ways in which individuals related to the world around them.[7] Generation was related to gender in important ways. In Soviet trade union practice, women and youth were invariably linked as uncultured and immature, requiring the special solicitude and intervention of the union and party to transform them properly into mature socialist subjects. But just as often, and not only in Soviet Russia, women and young

---

4. The literature is extraordinarily rich. For a discussion, see Michael David-Fox, "What Is Cultural Revolution?" *Russian Review* 58 (1999): 181–201. For an important study of actual practitioners of proletarian culture, see Mark D. Steinberg, *Proletarian Imagination: Self, Modernity, and the Sacred in Russia, 1910–1925* (Ithaca, 2002).

5. Alf Lüdtke, "Introduction: What Is the History of Everyday Life and Who Are Its Practitioners?" in *The History of Everyday Life*, ed. Alf Lüdtke, trans. William Templer (Princeton, 1995), 3–40; N. B. Lebina, *Povsednevnaia zhizn' sovetskogo goroda 1920/1930 gody* (St. Petersburg, 1999).

6. Elizabeth A. Wood, *The Baba and the Comrade: Gender and Politics in Revolutionary Russia* (Bloomington, 1997), chap. 1, offers a valuable survey of these issues.

7. Eric Naiman, *Sex in Public: The Incarnation of Early Soviet Ideology* (Princeton, 1997); Eliot Borenstein, *Men without Women: Masculinity and Revolution in Russian Fiction, 1917–1929* (Durham, 2000).

people were seen as competitors for the livelihoods and status claimed by men.[8] Conflicts over the position of women and young workers in the printing industry, then, drove a wedge into the imagined unity of the Soviet working class.

The study of workers has always involved explorations of worker identity and self-consciousness, and this book investigates the expressions and behaviors that contributed to the articulation of identities, of individuals' sense of place in the world. These identities were multiple and complex. Worker identities under socialism were ascribed by the state in accordance with the state's official ideology, but they also reflected indigenous traditions of urban and work culture.[9] The case of the printers reveals clearly and poignantly the centrality of work and skill in these individuals' sense of themselves, even as individuals sought also to dissolve their personal identities—their individualities—into the larger collective mission of the socialist state.[10] The relation of Soviet workers to one another and to the state, I will argue, was fundamentally ambiguous and complicated, but it is this very ambiguity that makes their experience so emblematic of the making of Soviet socialism. The Soviet printers' story of socialism is both romance and tragedy, both empowering and repressive.

## SOVIET SOCIALISM AND CLASS ANALYSIS

As a way to focus the question of identities and to emphasize the comparative contribution of this exploration of Soviet socialism, I employ the concept of class as a key term. The study of workers conventionally involves the problem of class, but the relationship between "workers" and "class" is far from transparent. In ordinary discussions, "class" follows the adjective "working" almost automatically. This is because the language and theory of the community of scholars who study workers have been saturated with the concept of class, and because, in many historical situations, the concept has infused the language of workers themselves. In Russia, a society in which ideas of class predated the rise of an industrial proletariat, and in which the language of class accompanied the development of worker politics and revolutionary politics, this equivalency is especially pronounced. Class was, in Russia but also elsewhere, constitutive of identity. Class was also a metaphor for a program of action.

The triumph of a socialist regime in Russia complicates the application of

---

8. See Anne E. Gorsuch, *Youth in Revolutionary Russia: Enthusiasts, Bohemians, Delinquents* (Bloomington, 2000); Corinna Kuhr-Korolev, Stefan Plaggenborg, and Monica Wellmann, eds., *Sowjetjugend, 1917–1941: Generation zwischen Revolution und Resignation* (Essen, 2001).

9. Leopold H. Haimson, "The Problem of Social Identities in Early Twentieth Century Russia," *Slavic Review* 47, no. 1 (1988): 1–20. Sheila Fitzpatrick has written extensively on this theme; see, for example, "Ascribing Class: The Construction of Social Identity in Soviet Russia," *Journal of Modern History* 65, no. 4 (1993): 745–70. See also the introduction and many of the essays in Lewis H. Siegelbaum and Ronald Grigor Suny, eds., *Making Workers Soviet: Power, Class, and Identity* (Ithaca, 1994).

10. Jochen Hellbeck, "Fashioning the Stalinist Soul: The Diary of Stepan Podlubnyi (1931–1939)," *Jahrbücher für Geschichte Osteuropas* 44 (1996): 344–73.

class analysis to industrial society, but does not render class analysis irrelevant. To what extent can "class" provide a useful analytic tool for understanding social relations and social identities—the experience of workers—in a socialist system? Does class lose its meaning when the conditions of class struggle allegedly disappear? If not through class, or class alone, then how else did workers come to terms with their collective identities in this liminal period of social transformation? The search for socialist identity was given special urgency in the printers' union by the struggle between Communists and Mensheviks, both of whom appealed to the politics of class. The task of analyzing class identity is complicated by the fact that the socialist regime appropriated the language of class to rationalize its own policies and decisions. It ascribed explicitly class identities even as groups sought to find their own place in the emerging social structure.

The concept of class becomes even more problematic, however, in the light of growing doubts about its utility for analyzing historical relations even in capitalist societies, past and present. William Reddy, for example, argues that class cannot adequately explain political mobilization and conflict, and he questions whether it is possible "to speak of socially distinct sets of individuals, united by some identifiable trait or traits, as having shared intentions."[11] The sociologist John R. Hall summarizes the recent debate by questioning the very primacy of a materialist understanding of social behavior. The development of global capitalism at the end of the twentieth century, the "end of communism as a world-historical social movement," and poststructural critiques all call attention to the inability of class theory "to incorporate understandings of historicity, culture, agency, and social difference."[12] Class theory is in crisis.

Yet how are we to come to grips with the histories of large numbers of individuals, if not by aggregating them in some way, in many ways, into collectivities, into social groups? The history of societies demands that scholars use tools of classification in order to understand the object of study, but scholars must at the same time be sensitive to the potentially distorting or oversimplifying effects of these tools of analysis. Historians have a wide range of classificatory schemes at their disposal for analyzing collectivities: materialist ones such as occupation and standard of living, and behavioral tools such as networks, cohorts, habitus, and clusters.[13] Usages of class analysis incorporate many of these tools.

Class analysis in the Marxist tradition is generally understood to include four elements: structure, formation, struggle, and consciousness.[14] While the first

---

11. William M. Reddy, *Money and Liberty in Modern Europe: A Critique of Historical Understanding* (Cambridge, 1987), 197, 8.

12. John R. Hall, "The Reworking of Class Analysis," in *Reworking Class*, ed. John R. Hall (Ithaca, 1997), 6, 9.

13. As discussed in Haimson, "Problem of Social Identities."

14. Erik Olin Wright, *The Debate on Classes* (London, 1989), 271–72; Ira Katznelson, "Working-Class Formation: Constructing Cases and Comparisons," in *Working-Class Formation*, ed. Ira Katznelson and Aristide R. Zolberg, 3–41 (Princeton, 1986).

does not imply the second, third, or fourth, the fundamental building block of class analysis remains structure, and it is here that many problems have arisen. For Marx, class is constituted in terms of the economic conditions of existence, the relations to the means of production, leading to the "three great classes of modern society" that he begins to enumerate in the unfinished chapter on classes in the third volume of *Capital*.[15] Marx's model has attracted continual challenge, but the enduring appeal of a classification system based on economic interests and unequal power is significant. Modifications to the theory have added more flexibility and complexity to the three great classes.[16] Erik Olin Wright and Pierre Bourdieu introduce concepts of multiple and contradictory locations within class relations, and the notion of multiple assets (skill, cultural capital) possessed by members of a single class.[17] The complicating analytical model offered by Wright seems appropriate for the emerging social structure in the Soviet Union: in some important cultural and rhetorical senses, workers *were* masters of production, and they did indeed occupy contradictory class locations in the social structure. They were subordinate to the bosses, who were themselves subordinate to the relevant trade union and commissariat officials. But workers were also empowered through avenues of educational mobility and ritual denunciatory practices, and even through formal democratic practices, to employ their collective assets to dominate their superiors in certain settings.

But class structure is only the beginning of an exploration of class as an analytical tool. Social historians have tended to emphasize the subsequent levels of class analysis, particularly experience and mobilization. Class is not mere structure, "class in itself," but a conscious experience of collective life, in which groups of people recognize their common bonds as members of a discrete class and seek to organize on its behalf. In the process, they develop practices, culture, and memory that further help to define and consolidate their identities as members of this social class. If class identity initially arises from relations of work, the field of inquiry for class experience extends far beyond the workplace. In fact, the class-identifying nature of the workplace and work process is often taken for granted in ways that some historians have challenged. For Sonya Rose, class is constituted through resistance, and work is not the only or even the major site of contestation.[18] Such a formulation allows the historian to tran-

---

15. Karl Marx, *Capital*, vol. 3, trans. Ernest Untermann (Chicago, 1909), 1031; see also Ralf Dahrendorf, *Class and Class Conflict in Industrial Society* (Stanford, 1959).

16. Much of the challenge has emerged in an effort to explain the middle class: C. Wright Mills, *White Collar: The American Middle Classes* (New York, 1951); Anthony Giddens, *The Class Structure of the Advanced Societies* (New York, 1973); Erik Olin Wright, *Classes* (London, 1985).

17. Erik Olin Wright, "A General Framework for the Analysis of Class Structure" and "Rethinking, Once Again, the Concept of Class Structure," in Wright, *Debate on Classes*, 3–43, 269–348; Pierre Bourdieu, *Distinction: A Social Critique of the Judgement of Taste*, trans. Richard Nice (Cambridge, Mass., 1985), esp. 99–256; Reddy, *Money and Liberty*, 198–200.

18. Sonya Rose, "Class Formation and the Quintessential Worker," in Hall, *Reworking Class*, 133–68.

scend the public/private dichotomy that privileges an "essentialized," normatively male worker and marginalizes women.

Rose's definition of resistance is much broader than political opposition, strikes, or demonstrations: infrapolitics, everyday acts of resistance, and expressive culture can also provide evidence of class-based and class-structuring behaviors that constitute class.[19] For the experience of Soviet workers, this broad definition of resistance offers particular appeal. While strikes did indeed occur in Soviet workplaces, and workers sometimes even organized around political oppositions, their contradictory location as workers and owners made it much more expedient to express opposition and assert their power in more subtle, everyday ways. Their multiple class locations sometimes made it useful to disguise the class nature of their protests.

Everyday practice, better than pure structure, also helps to account for alternate and competing sources of difference in analyzing class. Here concepts of "whiteness," "class-gender" systems, religion, ethnicity, and generation become folded into the broader project of class analysis.[20] Class becomes one element of many, but it does not disappear: the materiality that underlies class analysis exercises a powerful influence on the sensibilities of historical actors. More recently, class analysis has been challenged but also enriched by the linguistic turn in the human sciences.[21] Joan Scott reminds historians of the extent to which class is created not in practice or material reality but in language. For example, it is invented by bureaucrats when they assign categories as part of their own projects of control and domination.[22] William Sewell recognizes the role played by language in constructing meaning: "the relations of produc-

---

19. James C. Scott, *Weapons of the Weak: Everyday Forms of Peasant Resistance* (New Haven, 1985); Robin D. G. Kelley, "'We Are Not What We Seem': Rethinking Black Working-Class Opposition in the Jim Crow South," *Journal of American History* 80, no. 1 (1993): 75–112; Tera W. Hunter, *To 'Joy My Freedom: Southern Black Women's Lives and Labors after the Civil War* (Cambridge, Mass., 1997), 74–97.

20. Rose, "Class Formation," 147; Ava Baron, "An 'Other' Side of Gender Antagonism at Work: Men, Boys, and the Remasculinization of Printers' Work, 1830–1920," in *Work Engendered: Toward a New History of American Labor*, ed. Ava Baron, 47–69 (Ithaca, 1993); Anna Clark, *The Struggle for the Breeches: Gender and the Making of the British Working Class* (Berkeley, 1995); Cynthia Cockburn, *Brothers: Male Dominance and Technological Change* (London, 1983); David Roediger, *Toward the Abolition of Whiteness: Essays on Race, Politics, and Working Class History* (London, 1994); Paul Gilroy, *"There Ain't No Black in the Union Jack": The Cultural Politics of Race and Nation* (London, 1987); Laura Tabili, *"We Ask for British Justice": Workers and Racial Difference in Late Imperial Britain* (Ithaca, 1994).

21. See esp. Lenard Berlanstein's introduction and William H. Sewell Jr., "Toward a Post-materialist Rhetoric for Labor History," in *Rethinking Labor History*, ed. Lenard R. Berlanstein, 15–38 (Urbana, 1993). Bryan Palmer, *Descent into Discourse: The Reification of Language and the Writing of Social History* (Philadelphia, 1990), offers a critique of the linguistic turn.

22. Joan W. Scott, "Statistical Representations of Work: The Politics of the Chamber of Commerce's *Statistique de l'industrie à Paris, 1847–48*," in *Work in France: Representations, Meaning, Organization, and Practice*, ed. Steven Laurence Kaplan and Cynthia J. Koepp, 335–63 (Ithaca, 1986).See also Michael Donnelly, "Statistical Classifications and the Salience of Class," in Hall, *Reworking Class*, 107–31; Ian Hacking, *The Taming of Chance* (Cambridge, 1990).

tion are not only affected but actually constituted by politics and culture." But he insists also that every social relationship is simultaneously constituted by meaning (language), scarcity (material reality), and power.[23]

The Soviet experience has much to contribute to this picture of class analysis. Leopold Haimson stresses the importance of collective self-representation, identities, as a way to understand patterns of collective behavior, shared attitudes, and collective mentalities, but he rejects the possibility of inferring these attitudes solely or largely from class structure.[24] Sheila Fitzpatrick questions the utility of class analysis altogether, given the ways in which the regime appropriated class labels to assign individuals to favored and unfavored places in society. In ascribing class in many of the same ways as the tsarist regime had divided society into *sosloviia*, or estates, the regime erased socially defined class groupings in favor of a "virtual class" imagined by regime statisticians and social controllers.[25] Implicit in this argument, however, is that the *proletariat* remained the one true class whose identity need not be questioned. I will argue that class identity for Russian workers was neither innate nor ascribed, but itself the contingent product of interactions, conflicts, language, and material position.

The theoretical and methodological issues of class analysis provide the foundation for this study. Building upon linguistic interpretations of class, I will propose heuristically that two competing notions of working-class identity provide interpretive power in explaining the political and cultural dynamics of the experience of printers in the years before and during the First Five-Year Plan. "Proletarian" identity consisted of those attributes sanctioned by theory, ideology, and the state: proletarian identity was a normative identity that was used often as a measuring rod to evaluate how far real workers strayed from the socialist ideal. "Worker" identity could coincide with proletarian identity, but it was much more complex and multivalent, and it could include behaviors and practices that contradicted the proletarian ideal. Worker identity permitted the coexistence of the collective "we" and the individual "I." Throughout this book, the term "class" will be used not descriptively but rather interrogatively, and I will be listening above all for the ways in which workers themselves employed the concept to signify their place in the social order.

---

23. Sewell, "Toward a Post-materialist Rhetoric," 26, 27, 33. Margaret Somers challenges more fundamentally the materiality of class experience by stressing the importance of narrative identities, "culturally constructed stories": Somers, "Deconstructing and Reconstructing Class Formation Theory," in Hall, *Reworking Class,* 73–105. See also the work of Marc W. Steinberg, *Fighting Words: Working-Class Formation, Collective Action, and Discourse in Early Nineteenth-Century England* (Ithaca, 1999).

24. Haimson, "Problem of Social Identities," 1, 3, 4; see also William G. Rosenberg, "Identities, Power, and Social Interactions," *Slavic Review* 47, no. 1 (1988): 21.

25. Fitzpatrick, "Ascribing Class."

## THE REPUBLIC OF LABOR

This project began in the early 1980s, and it was shaped initially by research conditions in the Soviet Union at that time. I wanted to investigate the transformation of working-class culture in the postrevolutionary period, to explore the interaction of regime policies and workers' agency. I had noticed in my work on the 1917 revolutions that the journals of the printers' union in the 1920s (which contained numerous reminiscences about the union's revolutionary past) contained fascinating material on shop floor culture, on workers' daily lives, on issues of work discipline, gender relations, recreation, and politics. Although other unions published similar journals, none was as rich and varied as those of the printers, and I believed that the journals alone, in addition to published union proceedings, could serve as a sufficient "archive" for the study of socialist work cultures. These materials were supplemented by the "wall newspapers" that individual enterprises began to publish in the early 1920s: workers in the printing trade could publish these papers in multiple copies, whereas in other industries, the wall newspapers remained typewritten items pinned to bulletin boards. The printed newspapers survived in Soviet libraries, whereas the bulletin boards did not. After 1985, with the initiation of glasnost, the conditions of research on the Soviet period began to change. Archival materials for the Soviet Union gradually became accessible for research by foreign and domestic scholars. By 1989, ordinary trade union records had become available, at both the central and local levels; by the early 1990s, more sensitive materials on political conflicts within the union were opened for research, including the Communist Party records for Leningrad. A final research visit to Russia in 2001 uncovered in the State Archive of the Russian Federation the sensitive materials of the Moscow Communist printers, still accessible only under special conditions.

Much of this archival material reflected the routine business of a large organization. The standard format for recording the proceedings of meetings was laconic and mostly uninformative: in the left-hand column, a list of the points on the agenda, and in the right-hand column, a brief notation of action: "Petition approved," "Referred to the union central committee," or "Situation to be investigated." The archives contain many reports of quarterly or yearly activities and goals, designed to please superiors rather than to inform the historian. But the archival record also contains verbatim reports of many meetings, from stenographic reports of regular all-Russian union congresses, to special meetings of women, youth, and the unemployed, to meetings in local print shops and subunits within the enterprise. These texts, along with the material published in the union journals by worker-correspondents, provide access to the voices of Soviet Russian workers. These voices were of course mediated by official agendas, censorship, self-censorship, and political self-interest. Even among the relatively vocal and literate printers, many voices remained submerged and suppressed. The historian must read these texts with great care, read them against the grain, and read between the lines. It is important to remember that much of what was published was prescriptive rather than descriptive; worker-correspondents' reports were explicitly shaped by central agendas. The advantage of focusing this research on a single industrial group and in several key enterprises makes it possible to evaluate these voices and these texts in their broader context and to note the subtle and sometimes graphic differences among enterprises and across cities. Under this kind of close analysis, the monolithic voice of Soviet centralization begins to break down into many conflicting voices: the center against the provinces, Moscow against Leningrad, Mensheviks against Bolsheviks, women against men, the sober against the slackers. It is precisely in these many eruptions of conflict that the contours of the culture of socialist labor can be traced.

The structure of this book proceeds from my conviction that it is impossible to understand culture, identities, language, or class independent of economic realities. The material relations of production shaped and constrained the daily lives and concerns of printers in specific and measurable ways. The fundamental fact of scarcity—of work, of time, of goods to buy—dominated the concerns of printers throughout this period, more acutely at some moments than others, but never disappearing. Economic conditions and challenges divide the time span covered by this project into three periods, and the book is organized accordingly. The first period, 1918–1921, coinciding with the Russian Civil War, was characterized above all by acute economic deprivation. The material facts of scarcity—industry had shrunk and the cities were starving—shaped the cultural choices available to workers, and they drive the political story of this period. This was a period in which the Menshevik Party waged a fierce and sometimes successful struggle to offer printers an alternative vision of the politics of socialism. Economic recovery in the mid-1920s created a climate of relative prosperity that gives the period from 1922 to 1927 its distinctive shape, a period in which printers were able to negotiate their relations with the state and with their managers from a position of some strength. This moment of prosperity also provided more ample horizons for developing practical political relations and for imagining and implementing cultural choices.

This flirtation with recovery was very short-lived: a growing unemployment crisis took over the industry beginning in 1926, and the pressures of a reserve army of unemployed continued to dominate the printers' union's concerns until late in 1930, when the demand for skilled printers suddenly soared. Nationally, the period from 1927 to 1930 marked the final decisions on and inauguration of the First Five-Year Plan. The plan was intended in part to alleviate the growing crisis in which the printing industry shared, but also to reorient the Soviet economy toward large-scale industrialization, in which printers would play only a limited role. Accompanying this planned economic revolution from above was an increasingly strident political mobilization along so-called class lines, culminating in 1929 and 1930 in the wholesale replacement of the leaders of the Trade Union of Workers in the Printing Industry, who were deemed too soft, too "vegetarian" to conduct the hard-line policies of the First Five-Year Plan.

In each of the book's three sections I begin with a chapter on the economic status of the industry which also considers labor-management relations and workplace conflicts and disputes. Then follows a chapter on the politics of the printers' trade union. Here I trace the changing nature of the political struggles between socialist parties and within the Communist Party, and I also pay attention to the process by which workers engaged in socialist political participation through trade union institutions. The third chapter in each of the book's three sections examines the ways in which workers sought to derive meaning from these experiences; the chapters look closely at the printers' self-representations and at the role played by class in articulating their identities. These chapters also explore how consumption, memory, leisure, and cultural pursuits shaped printers' sense of their place in the revolutionary socialist society. A final chapter serves as an epilogue and conclusion. Even a cursory overview of the fate of the printers' union in the 1930s reveals important continuities with the patterns established in the first years of socialism and suggests that the onset of the First Five-Year Plan did not represent such a sharp break with the first decade of the socialist revolution as the rhetorical label "Great Turn" implies. I then consider what we can learn about class, socialism, and Soviet history from this study of how Soviet printers attempted to construct their "republic of labor."[26]

---

26. The phrase appears in an article about worker indiscipline in one of the leading Moscow print shops: "No one is above the law in our republic of labor": *Moskovskii pechatnik* 11 (22 September 1923): 11. The term was used in the 1922 song "Molodaia gvardiia" [Young guard], by Aleksandr Bezymenskii; see *Russkie sovetskie pesni, 1917–1977* (Moscow, 1977), 50–51: "We are raising the banner,—/Comrades, this way!/Come build with us/The republic of labor!"

# PART I

## CIVIL WAR AND THE EVOLUTION OF THE ONE-PARTY TRADE UNION, 1918–1922

## CHAPTER 1

## THE PRINTING INDUSTRY IN THE ERA OF REVOLUTIONARY TRANSFORMATIONS

*Our life is so hard, we can't speak about a contract, we live from day to day.*

PETROGRAD PRINTER,
MAY 1919

Material scarcity and hardship constituted the birthright of the socialist revolution in Russia, and provided the ineluctable context for the attempts to implement a new society in which the goal would be social ownership of the public wealth. Seven years of international and civil war had halted imperial Russia's hopeful economic progress, cut off supplies and markets, and reduced the economy to the level of bare subsistence. The political emergency of the Civil War produced opposition to the revolutionary Bolshevik government from longtime opponents and increasingly from within the ranks of the supporters of the 1917 revolution. The government responded to economic hardship and political resistance with increasing centralization and repression. The socialism produced by the government's responses to this crisis of shortages would be centralized and coercive, as we shall see, but it also proceeded in response to the very vocal interventions of those who were suffering from the economic collapse.

The legacy of the Civil War would remain imprinted on the style and political culture of the socialist project. Memories of material want would be joined by practices of coercion, centralization, and militancy, symbolized by the Communist official wearing a leather jacket and brandishing a Mauser pistol. The militarized political culture of the Civil War introduced new hierarchies to the egalitarian socialist project, privileging those with guns over those without, leaders over followers, actors over talkers, workers over peasants, and men over women. Such a transformation further sharpened the divisions within the Russian socialist movement, but the Communist political culture that had evolved in this hard world of war and poverty easily rationalized the silencing even of socialist voices that offered alternative visions of the socialist future. This context of revolutionary expectations and wrenching economic hardship provided the setting in which the victorious working class and working-class party would begin to elaborate its understanding of socialism and the practices of a socialist economic structure and political culture.

## WHO WERE THE PRINTERS?

Printers had been the pioneers of labor organization in the Russian empire, and throughout their history they emphasized the distinctiveness and richness of their work traditions and associational life. By the start of the twentieth century, the trade had spawned dozens of assistance funds, burial societies, musical and drama circles, and informal clubs. Workplace rituals helped to instill and transmit a pride of craft and a sense of human dignity, creating a culture that could help its participants negotiate the challenges of modern urban life: printers brought to the revolutionary and trade union movements a collective dignity based on their role as producers but also a particularly refined sense of self.[1] A stratum of highly self-conscious printers labeled themselves not workers (*rabochie*) but "toilers" (*truzheniki*), "free artists of the graphic crafts," and "commanders of the leaden army."[2] These individuals saw themselves, emphasizes Mark Steinberg, as a moral vanguard whose values included self-improvement, pride in craft, and a collective dedication to promoting the dignity and the rights of labor. Such values aligned well with developing ideas about socialism at the beginning of the twentieth century, and these values combined with the resources generated by printers' relatively high standard of living to impel printers to act collectively in defense of their sense of dignity and worth.

1. *Istoriia leningradskogo soiuza poligraficheskogo proizvodstva. Kniga pervaia: 1904–1907* (Leningrad, 1925), 7; Victoria E. Bonnell, *Roots of Rebellion: Workers' Politics and Organizations in St. Petersburg and Moscow 1900–1914* (Berkeley, 1983), 76; Mark D. Steinberg, *Moral Communities: The Culture of Class Relations in the Russian Printing Industry, 1867–1907* (Berkeley, 1992), 49; I. Skachkov, "Ocherk po istorii professional'nogo dvizheniia rabochikh pechatnogo dela v Rossii (1903–1917 gg.)," in *Materialy po istorii professional'nogo dvizheniia rabochikh poligraficheskogo proizvodstva (pechatnogo dela) v Rossii*, comp. I. Skachkov, ed. F. Smirnov, N. Gordon, and A. Borshchevskii (Moscow, 1925), 12.
2. *Istoriia leningradskogo soiuza*, 17.

In 1903, Moscow printers struck successfully for a ten-hour workday and higher wages, and the strike taught a powerful lesson about the importance of solidarity.[3] Printers would build on this history to organize a legal trade union in the 1905 revolution. In St. Petersburg, Moscow, and city after city, printing union organizers rejected the creation of narrow craft-based unions, and instead supported union-building on the industrial principle, one printers' union that would include typesetters, pressmen, lithographers, and bookbinders. This preference for an industrial union flew in the face of Western European and North American tradition, in which trade unions organized along narrow lines of craft specialty. Nowhere else among the leading industrial nations of the world did typesetters and pressmen form a single union.[4] Along with their pride in craft, Russia's printers embraced the class principle early in their organizational life.

This wave of organization drew strength from the ongoing confrontation between employers and workers in the printing industry: printers took advantage of the new climate of organization to press a series of demands that reflected not just their economic grievances but broader moral claims. Above all, the unions demanded the right to bargain collectively with their employers, through the recognition within each workplace of "autonomy commissions" that would be elected to represent workers' interests. They also advocated not just higher wages and a reduction in hours but an end to searches at work, the use of polite address by employers toward their workers, paid two-week vacations, and equal pay for men and women.[5]

The years of reaction after 1907 hindered these unions' ability to engage in active collective bargaining and their organizations remained small. Nevertheless, a remarkable series of journals recorded the activities of these ephemeral union associations.[6] These journals faced the same vulnerabilities as the unions themselves and risked being closed by the police at any moment. The Peters-

3. Steinberg, *Moral Communities*, 130–39; *Istoriia leningradskogo soiuza*, 133–35; V. V. Sher, *Istoriia professional'nogo dvizheniia rabochikh pechatnogo dela v Moskve* (Moscow, 1911), 112–25; Laura Engelstein, *Moscow, 1905: Working-Class Organization and Political Conflict* (Stanford, 1982), 74–75.

4. Elizabeth F. Baker, *Printers and Technology: A History of the International Printing Pressmen and Assistants' Union* (New York, 1957); George E. Barnett, *Chapters on Machinery and Labor* (Cambridge, Mass., 1926); Ellic Howe, ed., *The Trade: Passages from the Literature of the Printing Craft, 1550–1935* (London, 1943); Seymour Martin Lipset, Martin A. Trow, and James S. Coleman, *Union Democracy: The Internal Politics of the International Typographical Union* (Glencoe, Ill., 1956); Sian Reynolds, *Britannica's Typesetters: Women Compositors in Edinburgh* (Edinburgh, 1989); Wayne Roberts, "The Last Artisans: Toronto Printers, 1896–1914," in *Essays in Canadian Working-Class History*, ed. Gregory S. Kealey and Peter Warrian, 125–42 (Toronto, 1976); Sally F. Zerker, *The Rise and Fall of the Toronto Typographical Union, 1832–1972: A Case Study of Foreign Domination* (Toronto, 1982).

5. Steinberg, *Moral Communities*, 172; Sher, *Istoriia*, 173; *Istoriia leningradskogo soiuza*, 137–38.

6. Steinberg, *Moral Communities*, 104–22, 195–96; *Istoriia leningradskogo soiuza*, 81–83, 135.

burg union tried to evade government censorship by publishing a humor journal in 1907, whose motto was "Laughter Is Strength." It was closed after three issues.[7] The union journals of these years before 1917 perfected the format that would characterize the printers' union press after the revolution: leading articles on issues of political and organizational importance, reports from local correspondents in provincial cities and individual enterprises, and artistic contributions: stories, satire, and poetry.[8]

The work of printing had become increasingly important to Russia's economy in the twentieth century. In 1914, according to figures compiled by tsarist agencies, the printing and lithography industries employed 86,130 workers, 89 percent of them men. About one-quarter of these workers, just over 23,000, earned their livings in the two political and commercial centers, St. Petersburg and Moscow. The majority worked in St. Petersburg, the center of the industry in the prerevolutionary period.[9]

The nature of data gathering changed abruptly during the World War and revolutionary years, but there is no question that the number of workers in printing, as in every other branch of industry, fell sharply in the years after 1917. Comparative statistics are not easily produced from otherwise massive collections of censuses, surveys, and compilations. Estimates for the size of the labor force in printing in 1918, for example, range from 24,600 to 57,400. Regardless of the absolute numbers, the key characteristic of these years was an overall shrinking of the labor force in printing and its further concentration in the two capitals of Petrograd and Moscow. In 1918, the two cities accounted for perhaps 70 percent of the country's printers, and by the first half of 1919, 74 percent. By early 1920, this figure had fallen to 65 percent, but more significantly, the new capital, Moscow, had overtaken Petrograd as the industry's center.[10] Petrograd printers' resentment at their loss of status would play a role in the political struggles to come.

Union membership and employment in the industry would remain relatively stable from 1921 until 1925, when the general industrial upturn created increasing numbers of jobs in the industry. Moscow would continue to lead in numbers of printers and union members, followed by Leningrad. No other city employed more than a few thousand printers, and in most cities, the number of printers measured in the hundreds or dozens.[11] Every administrative and eco-

---

7. *Istoriia leningradskogo soiuza,* 330; E. A. Vechtomova, *Zdes' pechatalas' "Pravda"* (Leningrad, 1969), 33.
8. Skachkov, "Ocherk," 65–67; A. Tikhanov, "Rabochie-pechatniki v gody voiny," in *Materialy po istorii professional'nogo dvizheniia,* vol. 3 (Moscow, 1924), 129.
9. Tsentral'noe statisticheskoe upravlenie (hereafter cited as TsSU), *Trudy,* vol. 7, *Statisticheskii sbornik za 1913–1917 gg.* (Moscow, 1921), 10–11; Steinberg, *Moral Communities,* 9.
10. TsSU, *Trudy,* vol. 7, 36; vol. 26, vyp. 2, "Fabrichno-zavodskaia promyshlennost' v period 1913–1918 gg.," 130, 138; vol. 8, *Statisticheskii ezhegodnik 1918–1920 gg.,* 358; vol. 8, pt. 2, 68, 95, 97, 98; vol. 8, pt. 4, 137–38, 175.
11. *Leningradskii pechatnik, 1917–1927 gg.* (Leningrad, 1927), 7; *Fabrichno-zavodskaia promyshlennost' goroda Moskvy i moskovskoi gubernii, 1917–1927 gg.* (Moscow, 1928), 1; *Vtoraia*

nomic center required the services of the printing industry, guaranteeing that printing workers would be found throughout the country, but their concentration outside the capitals was extremely small. Economically and culturally, this was an urban and a metropolitan industry.

## THE PRINTER'S WORK

The technology of printing had shaped patterns of work and the labor process in Russia before the socialist revolution, and this technology changed little in the years after 1917. Work provided the idiom for printers' representations of their self-identity but it was an idiom that expressed both commonality and difference. The structure of printing work, divided into thirty-one specializations, generated tensions between identities common to all printers (their industrial label of "printer") and their separate jobs within the industry.[12] Hierarchies within the structure of work divided printing workers by skill, wage, and gender. Tension also arose between printers' sense of their class identity as workers and their own heightened consciousness of the unique attributes of their craft. Understanding the political and cultural choices made by printers in the 1920s therefore requires a knowledge of the physical layout of the industry and of the jobs performed by its workers.

Most workers in the printing industry were employed in one of four specialties: in typesetting (composing), on printing presses, in lithographic work, or in binding. All four areas required skilled workers. In the composing room, hand compositors (*naborshchiki*) stood at type cases, assembled rows of letters and spaces into galleys, and locked the galleys into page-sized frames. Machine typesetting had been introduced in a few Russian print shops in the early part of the century, promising great gains in productivity: a Linotype operator could set 3,600 letters an hour, compared to a norm of 1,000 letters for a hand compositor. Within the composing room, the work varied by level of difficulty. Setting straight text was the easiest and most appropriate for the Linotype; statistical and foreign-language composition were the most difficult. Newspaper work was a special category, requiring bouts of feverish work and regular night shifts, and newspaper compositors generally commanded the highest wages in the industry as compensation for these difficult conditions.[13]

The composing room was a man's world in Russia, as in most other countries. Women had made major inroads into the occupation during the First World War and Civil War, and although attempts were made to exclude them

---

*vserossiiskaia konferentsiia soiuzov rabochikh pechatnogo dela (14–21 dekabria 1917)* (Moscow, 1918), 10–11.

12. A. Svavitskii and V. Sher, *Ocherk polozheniia rabochikh pechatnogo dela v Moskve (po dannym ankety, proizvedennoi O-vom rabochikh graficheskikh iskusstv v 1907 godu)* (St. Petersburg, 1909), appendix, table 1.

13. B. B. Koiranskii, *Trud i zdorov'e rabochikh tipografii* (Moscow, 1925), 14–15; *Istoriia leningradskogo soiuza*, 22–23, 29–31.

Compositors at their type cases in a large Moscow print shop, 1929. (Rossiiskii Gosudarstvennyi Arkhiv Kinofotodokumentov, 2-31684. Used with permission of the archive.)

again in 1921, they returned gradually during the 1920s. By 1925, women accounted for just over 10 percent of composing room workers, most of them employed as proofreaders. Of the few women skilled compositors, many were employed exclusively on returning type to cases, acknowledged to be one of the most boring and least demanding aspects of the compositor's trade.[14]

Press departments were almost always separate from the composing rooms. The simplest shops relied on pedal-operated job presses and simple flatbed presses; the most technologically advanced plants utilized a combination of flatbed presses and automatic rotary presses. Most printing enterprises relied on skilled labor, not mechanization, to feed and adjust the presses. The boss of the press room was the master pressman (*pechatnik* or *mashinist*), who supervised the work process and set up and adjusted the complex press machinery. He (and it was always he) was assisted by the press feeder (*nakladchik*), the pressman's helper, who supplied paper to the running press. Carriers (*priemshchiki*) took the printed sheets off the press and stacked them on a table. Women were more heavily represented in the press departments than in composing, but

---

14. Koiranskii, *Trud i zdorov'e*, 27–29. In the United States in 1930, women constituted 5.6 percent of all compositors, hand and machine. Florence E. Clark, *The Printing Trades and Their Workers* (Scranton, 1939), 91.

Press department at the *Pravda* print shop, 1922. Note the auxiliary position of women at the machines. (Rossiiskii Gosudarstvennyi Arkhiv Kinofotodokumentov, 2-2053. Used with permission of the archive.)

in strictly auxiliary positions, employed almost exclusively as carriers and press feeders.[15]

Lithographic work, the transfer of color illustrations from the drawing board to the press, constituted a separate set of occupations within the industry. As in the print shop, there were two groups of workers: engravers, inkers, and translators, who prepared the image on a special lithographic stone, and lithographic press operators. Lithographic work occupied about one-quarter of the workers employed in the printing industry in the period before and after the revolution, most of them men.[16]

In the bookbinding process, binders smoothed and folded printed sheets, assembled them into signatures, and sewed them together. Workers then glued the signatures into the book spine, covered the whole thing first with cardboard and then with leather, cloth, or another material, and finally lettered and decorated the cover. Women dominated as folders, a job requiring considerable ex-

15. *Istoriia leningradskogo soiuza*, 30, 45; Koiranskii, *Trud i zdorov'e*, 18, 27–30; Svavitskii and Sher, *Ocherk polozheniia*, 10.
16. Svavitskii and Sher, *Ocherk polozheniia*, table 1, and Koiranskii, *Trud i zdorov'e*, 20–21, 25, 31.

Women at work in a pamphlet workshop, 1924. Mechanization is minimal. (Rossiiskii Gosudarstvennyi Arkhiv Kinofotodokumentov, 4-21165. Used with permission of the archive.)

perience but one that was being mechanized during the 1920s. Most women in binding worked as brochurists, who combined several operations, including assembling and stitching the signatures, but brochurists accounted for less than half of all workers in this specialty.[17]

The four skilled activities of composing, printing, lithography, and binding occupied the vast majority of workers in the printing trade. Skill generally signaled a level of attainment and source of pride common to all craft workers. But skill in the sense of knowledge of a particular craft could also divide one set of skilled workers from another. What was skill, anyway, and how did one acquire it? Russian printers in the 1920s claimed that the basic attributes of "skill" were "responsibility, accuracy, complexity, craftsmanship, difficulty, injuriousness, intensity, severity, and danger."[18] Economists might argue that skill was the accumulation of human capital, acquired through education and training. Sociologists might argue that skill was a social artifact, a construction

17. Koiranskii, *Trud i zdorov'e*, 13–23, 26–40; *Moskovskii pechatnik* 12 (29 May 1925): 3; Mark David Steinberg, "Consciousness and Conflict in a Russian Industry: The Printers of St. Petersburg and Moscow, 1855–1905," Ph.D. diss., University of California, Berkeley, 1987, 323–46.
18. *Zhizn' pechatnika*, 15 July 1923: *otvetstvennost'*, *tochnost'*, *slozhnost'*, *iskusstvo*, *trudnost'*, *vrednost'*, *intensivnost'*, *tiazhest'*, *opasnost'*.

based on status and wage levels rather than pure know-how. Most would agree that skill was a form of property, of capital, an acquisition to be valued, protected, and preserved from excessive competition. Gender also played an important role in the definition of skill, and in most places and times, the acquisition and possession of skill was reserved for men.[19]

For most Russian printers, there were two traditional paths to skill. One was through apprenticeship, which began in the teen years and lasted about four years. Apprentices were assigned to skilled instructors or to skilled craftsmen (*mastery*), who taught them their craft and initiated them into the rituals of the trade. The quality of this training would be a constant complaint in printing industry sources for the 1920s: the prerevolutionary norm for the preparation of apprentices was not to provide systematic training but to use them to run errands, to clean up, to put away type—in short, to serve as cheap common labor for the adult skilled workers.[20] A second method of acquiring skills was the less formal method of "training up." An inexperienced worker began doing menial tasks in the print shop, and by observing the tasks performed around him or her would acquire enough know-how to begin to perform a task, moving up gradually to machine helper and then to machine operator. This was a common path in the industry, and it placed a premium on individual initiative and ability: the newcomer is "placed at a press, and how far he advances along the hierarchical stairway of his given trade depends on his innate dexterity and talent."[21]

Wages rewarded skill. Although there was some variation in skill in the printing industry, the overall average level of wages was high. Before the revolution, printers had ranked among the most highly paid groups of industrial workers in Russia, second only to metalworkers in 1900. By 1914, printers' average level of wages placed them above machine-builders.[22] This lofty economic position had generated its own sense of elite culture among printers. Highly paid compositors referred to themselves as "aristocrats" and "lords" (*bariny*); they came to work by bicycle, wearing starched white shirts and fashionable hair styles; they attended the theater and balls, engaged in ice skating and sledding in the winter, joined clubs, and generally carried a "good tone." At the other end of the scale were the itinerant printers known as "Italians" (named for the type cases they slept on),

---

19. Charles More, *Skill and the English Working Class, 1870–1914* (New York, 1980), 9–24; see also John Rule, "The Property of Skill in the Period of Manufacture," in *The Historical Meanings of Work*, ed. Patrick Joyce, 99–118 (Cambridge, 1987); Diane P. Koenker, "Men against Women on the Shop Floor in Early Soviet Russia: Gender and Class in the Socialist Workplace," *American Historical Review* 100, no. 5 (1995): 1438–64; Reynolds, *Britannica's Typesetters*, 138; Ava Baron, "Contested Terrain Revisited: Gender and the Social Construction of Skill in the Printing Industry, 1850–1920," in *Women, Work, and Technology: Transformations*, ed. Barbara Drygulski Wright et al., 58–83 (Ann Arbor, 1987).

20. Apprenticeship was generally regarded as being longer than necessary for teaching skills alone; it was also a socialization process and a way to exploit cheap labor. See Steinberg, *Moral Communities*, 68–74; Cockburn, *Brothers*, 45–46, 59–60; *Istoriia leningradskogo soiuza*, 62–63; Koiranskii, *Trud i zdorov'e*, 45–49.

21. Sher, *Istoriia*, 57; Svavitskii and Sher, *Ocherk polozheniia*, 9–10.

22. Svavitskii and Sher, *Ocherk polozheniia*, 20; TsSU, *Trudy*, vol. 26, vyp. 1, table 14.

who flitted from job to job, drinking themselves into a stupor in between.[23] Generally a skilled worker earned double the wage of an unskilled worker, a rule of thumb that characterized craft wages across Europe and across time.[24]

The nature of work in the print shop emphasized individual skill and performance, especially in the composing room, but it also involved teamwork and cooperation. Compositors, particularly those working on statistical material, often formed work groups they called "companies" (*kompanii*). These groups would select a leader, or elder, negotiate their labor price with management, assign hours among themselves, and share out their revenue as mutually agreed upon. Such companies could be exclusionary of nonmembers, but they contributed to an especially cohesive work culture. The composing room in general was a noisy, jesting, ribald place of work, without the discipline and rules that were increasingly prevalent in other Russian industrial workplaces.[25] In the press room, the printing press itself created the necessity for teamwork, but here the work culture differed from that of the composing room. Press rooms were noisy and dangerous, and the horseplay of the compositor could lead to serious accidents if practiced around the big rotary or flatbed presses.

The workplace and the nature of printing work thus combined both hierarchy and collectivity, generating social tensions and social glue along a number of axes, both among workers and with their supervisors. Workers themselves ranged along a hierarchical ladder: apprentices took orders from skilled craftsmen, press loaders took orders from the pressman. Standing above the compositors in most establishments was the metteur-en-pages, *metranpazh*, who supervised the assembly of the composed work. His counterpart in the press room was the master printer. Normally, these supervisors had advanced from the ranks of workers, a factor that contributed to what Mark Steinberg has described as a moral community binding "classes" together in the industry.[26] Given this well-established tradition within the industry of mobility from worker to supervisor, and the closely cooperative nature of work as well as work rituals, the practice under socialism of drawing supervisors and even factory managers from among workers would not appear strange to veterans of the printing industry.

## THE SOCIALIZATION OF RUSSIA'S PRINTING INDUSTRY

The term "nationalization" to describe the reorganization of Russian industry after the October 1917 revolution scarcely does justice to the complex, con-

---

23. *Istoriia leningradskogo soiuza*, 15; see also Steinberg, *Moral Communities*, 84–87. In Britain, similar distinctions prevailed: Barnett, *Chapters on Machinery and Labor*, 22–23.

24. *Istoriia leningradskogo soiuza*, 22–23, 28, 43, 45. Also Tsentral'nyi Gosudarstvennyi Arkhiv Moskovskoi Oblasti (hereafter cited as TsGAMO), f. 699, op. 1, d. 4, ll. 37–44 (pay scales for 1918 Moscow tarif); op. 4, d. 4, ll. 119–24 (pay scales for 1921 Moscow tarif); on craft wages in Europe, see Eric Hobsbawm, *Labouring Men* (Garden City, N.Y., 1967), 407.

25. *Istoriia leningradskogo soiuza*, 29, 36–42; also Steinberg, *Moral Communities*, 74–88.

26. Steinberg, *Moral Communities*, 27.

tradictory, and divisive process of inventing a socialist economic system. It is essential to probe beneath the veneer of "systemic socialism" to explore how the new relations of production shaped everyday experience and high politics alike. Socialized industry differed in important ways from its capitalist predecessors, and understanding the socialization process in the printing industry is essential if we are to appreciate the challenges faced by workers and trade union alike.

The printing industry in prewar Russia served a variety of customers, from publishers of daily newspapers and books to government agencies to small job printers producing business cards, posters, and privately published collections of poetry. Most customers resided in St. Petersburg and Moscow, and two-thirds of the industry's enterprises and workers were located there. A huge variability in plant size characterized the industry as well. A few enterprises in Moscow and Petrograd employed as many as 1,500 workers; important medium-sized plants in both cities employed between 400 and 600 workers, but most enterprises employed fewer than 30 workers.[27] Small shops bred an intimacy that encouraged worker camaraderie, but this kind of spatial solidarity could also be replicated within individual work units of larger plants.

On the eve of the World War, most printing enterprises were privately owned, either by individuals or by incorporated firms. State and local governments operated their own enterprises: Petersburg, as the capital, led the way with the State Engraving Plant and numerous ministerial and military enterprises.[28] After the February 1917 revolution, the industrial playing field emerged as a capitalist one. Organized labor would pit its strength against organized capital, but the very process of revolutionary conflict combined with the already strong role of the state to raise expectations for some sort of social ownership of the economy.[29] This outcome was not foreordained by the events of the February revolution, but it did represent a logical evolution in the social relations among labor, capital, and the state. This evolution can be seen in the case of the Fedor Kibbel' shop in Petrograd, which exemplifies the complicated history of nationalization and state control in the early years of the revolution.

In the summer of 1917, the newly legal Petrograd Union of Workers in the Printing Trade (Soiuz rabochikh pechatnogo dela) labored to negotiate a collective contract with the industry that included uniform wage rates across enterprises and a series of benefits and rules changes, including an eight-hour

---

27. S. Arbuzov, *Polozhenie russkoi poligraficheskoi promyshlennosti* (Moscow, 1921), 8; *Fabriki i zavody vsei Rossii. Svedeniia o 31,523 fabrikakh i zavodakh* (Kiev, 1913), col. 1306–80. Moscow figures from *Spisok fabrik i zavodov g. Moskvy i moskovskoi gubernii* (Moscow, 1916).

28. A. Tikhanov, "Rabochie-pechatniki v 1917 g.," in *Materialy po istorii professional'nogo dvizheniia v Rossii*, vol. 4, 157–99 (Moscow, 1925); *Fabriki i zavody vsei Rossii*, col. 1306–80.

29. See, among other works, Koenker, *Moscow Workers*; Diane P. Koenker and William G. Rosenberg, *Strikes and Revolution in Russia, 1917* (Princeton, 1989); Ziva Galili, *The Menshevik Leaders in the Russian Revolution: Social Realities and Political Strategies* (Princeton, 1989); S. A. Smith, *Red Petrograd: Revolution in the Factories, 1917–1918* (Cambridge, 1983).

workday and "autonomy rules" that allowed workers' representatives to regulate hiring and firing. After long and fractious discussions, the owners' association and the union signed an agreement on 15 September 1917, but several owners refused to go along. When Kibbel' workers failed to receive their scheduled pay on 2 October 1917, they demanded a resumption of talks on the collective contract. Management refused, and the workers struck with the blessing of the trade union.

Any strike in Petrograd in October 1917, awash in rumors of Bolshevik coups and rightist countercoups, represented more than a conflict between individual owners and their workers. After a week of impasse, newspapers in the capital reported that workers had seized the print shop, a common accusation and rumor in these tense times. The Menshevik newspaper *Rabochaia gazeta* responded by emphasizing the reasonableness of the workers' demands: workers merely wanted to apply the new collective wage agreement retroactively to 1 August. The paper explained that the "seizure" was really the workers' militia protecting the property of the plant until they could go back to work. Eventually, the workers did take over the plant and resume operations; the shop was "liquidated" in March 1918, but started up again owing to workers' pressure on the Petrograd printers' union, which "requisitioned" the plant and renamed it the First State Lithographic Plant. But the lithography business, largely dependent on consumer advertising, did not find many customers, and the shop was closed in 1919, not to be reopened until 1924, as the Tomskii Lithographic Plant, named after the leader of the All-Union Council of Trade Unions (VTsSPS).[30] This story of socialism from below, of a local and individual response to a more widespread problem, would repeat itself throughout the years of the Civil War.

The chaotic nature of the emerging industrial organizational structure has been well documented, and the origin of state control over the printing industry reinforces this view.[31] A 1921 report on the industry asserted, "One cannot even speak about planned nationalization here: print shops were seized by whoever needed them, and the stronger the agency, the bigger the print shop they were able to grab."[32] This process had begun immediately after the October revolution, as print shops, both government and private, passed into the hands of central government institutions, soviets, commissariats, and military units. When the capital was moved to Moscow, new agencies and old ones rushed to

30. *Izvestiia petrogradskogo soveta rabochikh deputatov*, 5 October 1917; *Rabochaia gazeta*, 13 and 21 October 1917; *Pechatnoe delo* 19 (10 April 1918): 13; 21 (29 April 1918): 13; Tikhanov, "Rabochie-pechatniki v 1917 g.," 193; *Pechatnoe delo* 25 (26 August 1918): 12–13.

31. Among a number of studies of industrial organization in the early Soviet period, see Thomas F. Remington, *Building Socialism in Bolshevik Russia: Ideology and Industrial Organization, 1917–1921* (Pittsburgh, 1984); William B. Husband, *Revolution in the Factory: The Birth of the Soviet Textile Industry, 1917–1920* (New York, 1990); Chris Ward, *Russia's Cotton Workers and the New Economic Policy: Shop Floor Culture and State Policy, 1921–1929* (Cambridge, 1990).

32. Vysshii sovet narodnogo khoziaistva (hereafter cited as VSNKh), Poligraficheskii otdel, *Obzor deiatel'nosti za 1918–1920 gg. [K X-mu s"ezdu R.K.P.]* (Moscow, 1921), 1.

appropriate the best-equipped enterprises there.[33] In Petrograd, as the Kibbel' experience illustrates, socialization proceeded from the bottom up. Capitalist owners were shutting down their enterprises and laying off workers. Workers turned to "their" government to save their shops and their jobs.[34]

The history of the printing industry during the Civil War years reflects the countervailing pulls of central rationalizing authority and autonomous local control. To contain and coordinate the headlong grab of printing resources, the Supreme Economic Council (Vesenkha) created in April 1918 a central agency, the Printing Section (Poligraficheskii otdel). At the same time, the Moscow Economic Council created its own department to coordinate the print shop rush in Moscow. By the end of 1920, seventy-two provincial sections had been created to coordinate the respective local printing industries.[35] Rationalization, however, proved elusive, and continual conflicts arose among the Moscow, Petrograd, and central printing sections. In October 1920, Vesenkha formally redrew the boundaries and convened an all-Russian conference to better coordinate the affairs of the industry.[36] This solution lasted less than a year, when the inauguration of the New Economic Policy reduced the role of government enterprise and confronted the industry with new organizational challenges.

The nominally mixed economic system in the printing industry up to 1921, then, consisted of a range of "nationalized" enterprises belonging to government agencies, to political bodies, to military units, and to the printing sections of the state. Only a few small enterprises remained in private hands. In principle, the printing sections acted as central management: they decided which enterprises to nationalize and which to close, they assigned directors, they allocated funds for operations and repairs, and they received individual and collective requests from workers for pay, firewood, and other day-to-day requirements.[37] The trade unions were also vitally interested in these functions: they shared responsibilities with members of the printing sections, and union officials actually shuttled back and forth from their union posts to positions inside the printing sections, sometimes holding two positions at the same time.

Alongside this haphazard and chaotic system of competing managerial au-

---

33. *Pervyi vserossiiskii s"ezd soiuzov rabochikh poligraficheskogo proizvodstva (2–7 maia 1919). Protokoly i postanovleniia s"ezda (izvlechenie iz stenogramm)* (Moscow, 1919), 43; *Sbornik dekretov i postanovlenii po narodnomu khoziaistvu (25 oktiabria 1917 g.–25 oktiabria 1918 g.)* (Moscow, 1918), no. 254 (9 January 1918), 320; *Plenum Tsentral'nogo komiteta vserossiiskogo soiuza rabochikh poligraficheskogo proizvodstva (7–11 dekabria 1920 g.). Doklady i rezoliutsii* (Moscow, 1921), 15.

34. *Pechatnoe delo* 18 (1 April 1918): 13; see also *Pechatnoe delo* 16 (25 [12] February 1918): 11–12; 17 (11 March 1918): 10, 12; 18 (1 April 1918): 10, 12; 19 (10 April 1918): 13; 21 (29 April 1918): 5–6, 12–15; 26 (23 October 1918): 11, 12.

35. VSNKh, Poligraficheskii otdel, *Obzor deiatel'nosti za 1918–1920*, 1, 10; *Vserossiiskii pechatnik* 4–5 (20 March 1920): suppl., 1–8.

36. Gosudarstvennyi Arkhiv Rossiiskoi Federatsii (hereafter cited as GARF), f. R-5525, op. 2, d. 49 (meetings of collegium of Printing Section of Moscow Sovnarkhoz, 1920), l. 51.

37. Ibid., op. 1, d. 50 (meetings of Printing Section of Moscow Sovnarkhoz, 1919), ll. 2, 3, 5–8.

thority was the general perception shared by everybody in the industry that they were the "stepsons" of socialist industry: Vesenkha (and the Central Council of Trade Unions) had more important clients than the printers and devoted few organizational or economic resources to their operation or recovery.[38] Official centralized authority rarely translated into efficient and rational economic relations. Individual print shops, "like castles," hoarded their resources—labor and material—so that the printing sections would not be able to reallocate them. The lines of authority were unclear. "We have three masters," complained a delegate to the Second Moscow Guberniia Congress of the Printers' Union in May 1921: one distributed paper, ink, type, and labor; another generated orders; and a third state monopoly distributed the finished product.[39]

These messy local realities contradict the ideal of rational centralized order, and they help to shape a new picture of revolutionary transformations, limits, and possibilities. Local examples best illustrate the broader processes under way, and I have selected seven cases for close study, based on the richness of their archival records.

Before the revolution, Moscow's First Model Print Shop (Pervaia Obraztsovaia) belonged to the mass publisher I. D. Sytin. Founded in 1883, Sytin's empire specialized in producing inexpensive commodities for a growing mass market. By 1915, the Sytin firm was the largest printing firm in the empire, with several plants, including a modern new one on Piatnitskaia Street in southern Moscow. Some 1,500 printers worked here on the eve of the revolution. Nationalized in November 1919, the Piatnitskaia shop became Print Shop Number One, employing 1,170 workers in the hungry year of 1920. In 1921 it received the additional honor of being designated a "model" enterprise. First Model worked primarily for the state publishing house, Gosizdat, and although its immediate superior was the Printing Section of Vesenkha, representatives from both state agencies negotiated with angry workers when conflicts arose. In November 1921, the First Model plant was reassigned to the newly formed Mospechat' trust, whose board of directors included the Communist leader of the Moscow printers' union and I. D. Sytin himself, who had agreed to work for Soviet power.[40]

---

38. Ibid., op. 3, d. 41 (Petrograd Printers' Union guberniia conference, 25–26 January 1921), l. 122; TsGAMO, f. 699, op. 1, d. 74 (general meeting of workers at First Model, 18 May 1920), l. 32.

39. *Vtoraia moskovskaia gubernskaia konferentsiia rabochikh poligraficheskogo proizvodstva (stenograficheskii otchet) 12 maia 1921 g.* (Moscow, 1922), 66–67.

40. V. P. Orlov, *Poligraficheskaia promyshlennost' Moskvy: Ocherk razvitiia, do 1917 g.* (Moscow, 1953), 199, 250–52; N. M. Sikorskii, ed., *Knigovedenie: Entsiklopedicheskii slovar'* (Moscow, 1981), 523–24; Jeffrey Brooks, *When Russia Learned to Read: Literacy and Popular Literature, 1861–1917* (Princeton, 1985); Charles A. Ruud, *Russian Entrepreneur: Publisher Ivan Sytin of Moscow, 1851–1934* (Montreal, 1990), 158, 174–86; L. K. Zorev, *Pervaia obraztsovaia* (Moscow, 1967), 13; *Pervaia obraztsovaia tipografiia imeni A. A. Zhdanova za 40 let sovetskoi vlasti* (Moscow, 1957), 34; TsGAMO, f. 699, op. 1, d. 44 (factory committee meetings at Sytin [First Model], 1919), l. 85; d. 145 (factory committee and general meetings at First Model, 1921), ll. 52, 73; *Moskovskii pechatnik* 3 (1 March 1921): 9.

In the center of the city, A. A. Levenson had established in 1887 a modern speed press enterprise that employed 670 workers by the turn of the century, when Levenson commissioned the architect Franz Shekhtel' to design a new building. By 1900, Levenson operated six of the city's eighteen high-speed rotary presses, producing prize-winning illustrated books, posters, and plates. During the war, the shop was acquired by a patriotic public organization, the Union of Cities and Towns, and after the October revolution, the firm passed under state control. With 900 workers at the start of 1919, the "formerly Levenson" shop printed a variety of materials for government agencies, including announcements and journals. During 1920, the shop was transferred to the jurisdiction of the Moscow Economic Council; as State Print Shop Number Sixteen, it passed into the hands of the Mospechat' trust at the beginning of 1922.[41]

Publisher of newspapers and books, the Ivan Kushnerev firm was founded in 1869, and in 1903 it became the first Moscow firm to acquire a Linotype machine, to be quickly followed by Levenson and Sytin. In January 1918 its workers petitioned to be accepted as a state enterprise, but it was not formally nationalized until 1919, when the shop and its reduced workforce of 300 were assigned to the Printing Section of the Moscow Economic Council. In January 1922, now 540 strong, the shop entered the Mospechat' trust, and in another industrial reorganization in October 1922, the former Kushnerev plant became Print Shop Number Twenty of the Mospoligraf trust, with the additional name Red Proletarian, Krasnyi Proletarii. Less than a year later, Mospoligraf leased Krasnyi Proletarii to the publisher Red Virgin Soil for a three-year period, and when the publisher merged with Gosizdat in October 1924, Krasnyi Proletarii became part of Gosizdat's publishing empire. By then it employed 1,210 workers.[42]

While these Moscow enterprises grew along with Soviet power, the history of the Petrograd cases reflects a contrary trend, the erosion of their once high status within the printing industry. Petrograd's leading print shop, Pechatnyi Dvor, the Court of Printing, was founded in 1827 to serve the state chancellery of Nicholas I; it was renamed the State Print Shop (Gosudarstvennaia tipografiia) in 1882, and in 1910 it moved to a grandiose building on the Petersburg side of the city, where it employed over 1,000 workers on the eve of the World War. After the 1917 revolution, the enterprise adopted the name First State Print Shop and remained under government control. This shop had thus

---

41. William Craft Brumfield, *The Origins of Modernism in Russian Architecture* (Berkeley, 1991), 131–32; A. A. Levenson T-vo skoropechatni, *T-vo skoropechatni A. A. Levenson na vystavke pechatnogo dela i grafiki v Leipzige 1914 g.* (Moscow, 1914), 9–13; Orlov, *Poligraficheskaia promyshlennost'*, 189, 260; TsGAMO, f. 699, op. 1, d. 266 (factory committee and general meetings at Sixteenth, 1922), l. 66; *Pravda*, 10 January 1919, 22 August 1922.

42. Orlov, *Poligraficheskaia promyshlennost'*, 185, 198, 228; Sikorskii, *Knigovedeniie*, 301–2; *Pechatnoe delo* 16 (25 [12] February 1918): 11; *Fabrika knigi Krasnyi Proletarii. Istoriia tipografii byvsh. "T-va I. N. Kushnerev i K."* (Moscow, 1932), 124–29.

always been a public enterprise. Managed by the Petrograd Printing Section before the New Economic Policy, the shop passed to Gosizdat in October 1922 and received the name Pechatnyi Dvor. By the end of 1923, its labor force numbered nearly 700 workers.[43]

The A. F. Marks shop in St. Petersburg had been founded in 1881, and published the popular weekly journal *Niva* and a wide range of literature and atlases. In 1916 I.D. Sytin purchased a controlling interest in the company, adding Marks to his publishing empire. After the revolution, the enterprise languished until 1920 or 1921, when it became the Twenty-sixth State Print Shop and on 1 January 1922 a founding member of the Petropechat' trust. Later it was renamed after Evgeniia Sokolova, a young brochurist and Communist Party activist who had worked briefly at the plant in the autumn of 1918 before perishing in an espionage mission during the Civil War. One of the leading customers of the shop was the Communist International, which in late 1920 began to publish its multilingual journal there.[44]

The Fourteenth State Print Shop, another all-purpose press, had been seized from its private owner by the Petrograd Military Revolutionary Committee during the October revolution in order to print the Bolshevik newspaper, *Pravda*, and it continued to print *Petrogradskaia pravda* after the transfer of the capital to Moscow. Like the other Petrograd enterprises, it was managed during the Civil War by the Printing Section of the Petrograd Economic Council. In late 1921, the shop was threatened with closure, a victim of the precipitous collapse of printing activity in the former capital, but a subsidy from the Petrograd Committee of the Communist Party bailed it out. Another threat in 1922 was staved off by the energetic efforts of its red director, Dmitrii Dudarev, a Linotypist who had risen from the chairmanship of the factory committee to head the enterprise earlier that year. In 1922 the shop was given the additional honor of carrying the name of the party chief of Petrograd, Grigorii Zinov'ev.[45]

The Voronezh printing industry will serve as a proxy for the 43 percent of printing union members who in 1917 worked in smaller cities and towns.[46] Voronezh, located 224 miles southeast of Moscow, was a provincial capital with 122,000 inhabitants by the mid-1920s. On the eve of the World War, the

---

43. *Pechatnyi dvor*, 14 January 1923; *Pechatnyi dvor. Piatiletniaia rabota dlia knigi* (Moscow and Petrograd, 1923), 5–10; Tsentral'nyi Gosudarstvennyi Arkhiv Istoriko-Politicheskikh Dokumentov Sankt Peterburga (hereafter TsGAIPD SPb), f. 457, op. 1, d. 65 (reports on political mood, 1922), l. 284; f. 435, op. 1, d. 78 (meetings of party bureau of Petrograd Printers' Union, 1921–23), l. 47.

44. Sikorskii, *Knigovedenie*, 334; Orlov, *Poligraficheskaia promyshlennost'*, 253–54; TsGAIPD SPb, f. 435, op. 1, d. 86 (party collective at Twenty-sixth, 1922), l. 4; I. P. Viduetskaia, *A. P. Chekhov i ego izdatel' A. F. Marks* (Moscow, 1977); *Iskry*, October 1925; Tsentral'nyi Gosudarstvennyi Arkhiv Sankt Peterburga (hereafter cited as TsGA SPb), f. 4804, op. 4, d. 19 (meetings in Petrograd print shops, 1920), l. 281; *Petrogradskaia pravda*, 22 June 1921.

45. TsGAIPD SPb, f. 435 op. 1 d. 29 (party collective meetings in Petrograd print shops, 1921), l. 211ob.; TsGA SPb, f. 4804, op. 6, d. 34 (meetings in Petrograd print shops, 1922), l. 103ob.; Vechtomova, *Zdes' pechatalas'*, 9, 80, 120, 145.

46. *Vtoraia vserossiiskaia konferentsiia soiuzov rabochikh pechatnogo dela*, 1917, 10–11.

province of Voronezh listed twenty-two print shops, fourteen of them in the city itself. During the Civil War, Voronezh was overrun several times by armies of the Whites and the Reds, with devastating results for its small manufacturing economy. Printers' union membership dropped to 667 by January 1920. The beleaguered industry administrators—a coalition of trade union and state officials—closed enterprises and concentrated their workers and equipment in a few large plants. By 1921, only four operating print shops remained in the city of Voronezh, all of them under state management. In this respect, Voronezh was quite typical of the provincial printing industry.[47]

## THE FATE OF THE PRINTING INDUSTRY IN THE CIVIL WAR

Although shreds of utopianism may have been responsible for some of the Communist Party's vision of industrial organization at this time, the structure of industry was shaped as well by the pressure of economic realities and by politics. The Voronezh example illustrates the inescapable fact that the Russian economy was in a state of ruin (*razrukha*) by the end of 1920. Assigning blame for the disaster and arguing over solutions for recovery became a primary occupation of the leaders both of industry and of the printers' trade union. Identifying the contours of the collapse of the printing industry in relation to broader economic trends will here provide some context for subsequent discussions of the political debates that took place on the shop floor, in the halls of union meetings, and in the closed offices of union and party leaders.

Printers had enjoyed a brief moment of economic expansion in 1917, as the February revolution opened new publishing opportunities and increased the demand for skilled typesetters and press operators.[48] The October revolution, however, brought new unemployment to the industry. The Bolsheviks' monopoly on the press reduced the number of newspapers, pamphlets, and advertisements that were printed. Meanwhile, demobilized soldiers began to return to the cities, demanding their old jobs back. The high wages won by printers through collective bargaining now convinced some wary entrepreneurs that they could no longer operate profitably under the new regime, and they began to close their shops. By January 1918, the national printers' union reported that of its 81,318 members, 3,341 (4.1 percent) were unemployed. Expecting a flood of job seekers because employment outside the capitals was drying up, the Moscow union publicly warned printers in the provinces that there was no work in

47. *Goroda Rossii. Entsiklopediia* (Moscow, 1994), 92; *Fabriki i zavody vsei Rossii*, col. 1318; GARF, f. R-5525, op. 1, d. 22, ll. 17–20, 24 (report on the work of the board of the Voronezh union, 1919); *Otchet pravleniia voronezhskogo gubernskogo otdela soiuza rabochikh poligraficheskogo proizvodstva za 1920 god* (Voronezh, 1921), 26; GARF, f. R-5525, op. 2, d. 29 (presidium of Voronezh Printers' Union board, 1920), l. 42; VSNKh, Glavnoe upravlenie poligraficheskoi promyshlennosti, *Vtoroi vserossiiskii s"ezd oblastnykh i gubernskikh poligraficheskikh otdelov (3–8 iiunia 1921 g.) Stenograficheskii otchet* (Moscow, 1922), 53.

48. TsSU, *Trudy*, vol. 7, 10–11; vol. 26, vyp. 2, 1; *Pechatnik* 1–2 (25 January 1919): 7; *Pechatnoe delo* 15 (31 January [13 February] 1918): 2.

Moscow either. The transfer of the capital from Petrograd to Moscow inflicted an especially huge blow on the printers of Peter's city on the Neva, who had become accustomed to thinking of themselves as the crème de la crème of the printing industry. By May 1918, the union reported 4,000 unemployed printers in Petrograd, as opposed to 1,600 unemployed in Moscow.[49]

By the end of 1918, the level of employment in printing had fallen substantially. And even a secure job did not necessarily mean a secure living: productivity in the industry fell even more dramatically than employment, as printers coped with shortages of food supplies, with the lack of electricity, ink, and paper, and with the disappearance of paying customers, especially in Petrograd. Absenteeism rose as workers took unauthorized and illegal leaves of absence to seek food outside their cities.[50]

Of course, all industrial workers faced similar circumstances in these years. Printers complained that no one suffered as much as they did, but comparative figures on wage levels do not bear out this claim. Workers in the printing industry consistently received among the highest average wages in all Russian industry: in 1913 their wage levels were second only to those of workers engaged in the production of artistic goods, and in 1917 they again occupied second place, behind chemical workers, on the scale of average wage levels. Following the trend into the Civil War years is more difficult, and wages of course became a less useful indicator of overall well-being, but even in hungry Petrograd, the average wages of printers had moved from fourth place (among ten groups) in the second half of 1918 to first place in 1919 and 1920.[51] The expectation of relatively high wages would lead to a sense of entitlement that shaped the politics of production for the remainder of the decade.

The collapse of living conditions by the end of 1920 and the beginning of 1921 spurred a wave of worker unrest in Petrograd, Moscow, and elsewhere, and the regime responded by relaxing its restrictions on the importation of food into the cities and by restoring market principles to the administration of industry. Dependent as it was on state orders and state subsidies, the printing industry responded slowly to the new commercial climate permitted by the New Economic Policy. Privatization was not an option, but even in state-owned industry, the official ideology was now *khozraschet,* or cost accounting, and public enterprises faced pressure to cut costs and reduce the need for subsidies.[52] Invariably this meant laying off workers for whom there was no work. By the

---

49. *Pechatnik* 3–4 (1918): 2, 6, 8, 17; *Vestnik vserossiiskogo soiuza rabochikh pechatnogo dela* (hereafter cited as *Vestnik vsrpd*) 1 (25 January 1918): 16.

50. *Pechatnoe delo* 20 (18 April 1918): 7; 22 (18 May 1918): 4; *Vestnik vsrpd* 4 (20 October 1918): 2; *Pechatnik* 9–10 (10 October [27 September] 1918): 16. For Moscow, *Krasnaia Moskva, 1917–1920 gg.* (Moscow, 1920), appendix 1; *Revoliutsionnyi pechatnik* (Moscow) 8 (27 July 1919): 9.

51. TsSU, *Trudy,* vol. 26, vyp. 1, table 14; *Istoriia rabochikh Leningrada,* vol. 2 (Leningrad, 1972), 97.

52. *Vserossiiskii pechatnik* 9 (15 January 1921): 10–11.

autumn of 1921, production was beginning to increase under the influence of new rules of compensation and discipline, but unemployment also began to rise as veteran printers began to trickle back to their native cities.[53]

The specter of unemployment as reality and danger would remain central to printers' discussions of their position in the Soviet economy, reinforcing the primacy of material considerations that would remain a hallmark of printers' socialist expectations. This materialism would be variously interpreted at different times and by different political actors, but as far as printers were concerned, satisfaction of their material needs would remain one of their most consistent demands of the socialist regime. The sites in which these demands were articulated were the new socialist system of labor-management relations, on the one hand, and the new political institutions of socialist democracy—the trade union, soviets, and Communist Party—on the other. Let us concentrate here on the system of socialist labor relations.

## THE CONSTRUCTION OF A SOCIALIST SYSTEM OF INDUSTRIAL RELATIONS

No consensus existed in November 1917 on the nature of a socialist system of labor relations. The socialization of the printing industry emerged in large part through the ad hoc responses of individual union, party, and industry leaders to the exigencies of production, consumption, and war. Debates over labor relations and the related role of trade unions focused on five major areas, and underlying the specific choices available to these leaders was a broader philosophical conflict about the organization of the state and its economic structures. In the area of workplace authority, discussion and solutions revolved around the nature of ownership, whether private or public; around administrative autonomy, whether centrally directed or locally independent; and around the extent of rank-and-file workers' involvement in industrial management and decision making.[54] In the area of productivity and incentives, policy makers and union leaders worried about the desirability of monetary incentives versus moral ones. In addition, the role of discipline in the socialist workplace as a corollary to incentive systems remained to be defined. A third area of contention was the problem of conflicts. How should disputes between workers and management be resolved? The classic form of conflict, the strike, was widely considered to be inappropriate under socialism, and union and state leaders preferred arbitration, conciliation, and labor tribunals as socialist alternatives to strikes.

Linking these three areas of labor relations was a crucial fourth one, the role of the trade unions, both their relation to the state and its economic organs and

---

53. TsGA SPb, f. 4804, op. 6, d. 24 (transcript of 8 September 1922 Petrograd guberniia conference of Printers' Union), l. 13.

54. See the discussion in Diane P. Koenker, "Labor Relations in Socialist Russia: Class Values and Production Values in the Printers' Union," in Siegelbaum and Suny, *Making Workers Soviet*, 161–64, for a fuller elaboration of these areas.

their relation to workers on the shop floor. Would socialist trade unions exist outside the state's economic apparatus or within it? Was it possible for unions to disagree among themselves, and if so, could individual unions follow their own policy or were they bound by the union movement as a whole? Were workers' interests identical to those of the state and its organs or somehow different? It was precisely on the question of union independence that Communists and Mensheviks were most sharply divided, but the Communists themselves were split over this issue. The "trade union debate" dominated Communist political discussion in 1920.[55]

Equally central to the problem of labor relations under socialism was the nature of the state. Would the socialist state subsume all sectors of society, or would the state function as superarbiter, balancing conflicting demands on its resources, resolving inevitable conflicts among different elements of society? In the economy, would the state function as regulator or manager? And who would regulate state policy—was a dictatorship of the proletariat incompatible with socialist democracy? The emergency of the Civil War reinforced the coercive tendencies of the new Soviet regime, but in practice the state also served as arbiter between factions within industry and within trade unions.

The reorganization of industry after the revolution proceeded in a close relationship with national and local politics. Trade unions played a novel and still evolving role in the socialist industrial landscape after the revolution, and their relation to the economy and to the politics of production was a crucial one for this story, as the next chapter will show. Enterprise-level concerns and preferences also modified the decisions taken by the center concerning the structure of industry. The *relationship* between workers and their superiors, what we can call industrial relations, remained to be determined through practice as well as policy. The experience of the first four years of the revolution thus helped to establish the rules of the new game of socialist industrial relations.

The role of workplace authority and the distinction between "workers" and "bosses" is central. As far as identity was concerned, there was to be no difference between workers and bosses under socialism: the socialist state privileged persons of proletarian pedigree, and its officials, whatever their particular social background, were obligated to administer the state in the interests of the workers. Functionally, of course, there would be a wide variety of jobs to fill in the socialist economy, and some "workers" would give orders while others would take them. Two types of linkages would ensure that the "worker-bosses" acted in the best interests of the "workers" and fulfilled the promise of the revolution. One was the incorporation of workers from production into positions of administration and leadership, a practice that led to an obsession with social

---

55. E. H. Carr, *The Bolshevik Revolution, 1917–1923*, vol. 2 (London, 1952), 220–22; see also William G. Rosenberg, "The Social Background to Tsektran," in *Party, State, and Society in the Russian Civil War*, ed. Diane P. Koenker, William G. Rosenberg, and Ronald Grigor Suny (Bloomington, 1989), 349–73.

origin and social identity.[56] The other was the practice of democracy at the shop floor level, which provided a series of mechanisms by which "bosses" could hear what was on the workers' minds and act accordingly. "Workplace democracy" became a focus of the conflict between Mensheviks and Communists in the printers' union, and found its first expression in the structure of workplace management in the years of the Civil War.

Who ran the print shops from day to day? The term "factory troika" describes the formal definitions of enterprise structures: the manager represented the administrative side of factory life, the factory committee defended the interests of workers, and the Communist Party committee looked after the overall interests of state policy. In practice, there was much overlap among these functions and individuals. Communist Party theorists disagreed on the proper form of socialist management: the Workers' Opposition favored collegial management as the appropriate socialist form of industrial organization, whereas Lenin and others favored one-person management (*edinonachalie*).[57] By 1920, the Moscow Printing Section had decided to terminate all collegial management in enterprises under its jurisdiction and to appoint individual managers.[58]

Successful managers frequently emerged from the enterprise itself. While the Communist Party approved all appointments through its representatives in the trade union, the scarcity of qualified leaders and the preferences of the shops' workers limited the party's freedom to impose its choices. The Twentieth print shop's P. M. Bokov had served his political apprenticeship as an activist in the Menshevik Party and the printers' union; he was elected as the plant's factory committee chair in 1917, and by 1919 (in the meantime having discarded his Menshevik affiliation) he had assumed the duties of director. Even after he became director, he remained active in the factory committee, and he dominated its written record. Bokov regularly reported to the factory committee and to general meetings on the status of the enterprise, and he reported on the plant in the press. This director emerges in these accounts as a paternal protector of the welfare of his workers, and he believed that the factory committee should be the valued right-hand assistant of the factory administration.[59] At Pechatnyi Dvor, the factory committee chairman, Ivanov, first became assistant man-

56. Sheila Fitzpatrick, "The Problem of Class Identity in NEP Society," and Diane P. Koenker, "Class and Consciousness in a Socialist Society: Workers in the Printing Trades during NEP," both in *Russia in the Era of NEP: Explorations in Soviet Society and Culture*, ed. Sheila Fitzpatrick, Alexander Rabinowitch, and Richard Stites (Bloomington, 1991), 12–33, 34–57; Haimson, "Problem of Social Identities," 1–20.

57. E. G. Gimpel'son, *Rabochii klass v upravlenii sovetskim gosudarstvom: Noiabr' 1917–1920 gg.* (Moscow, 1982), 281; see also Remington, *Building Socialism*, 86–87; Carmen Sirianni, *Workers Control and Socialist Democracy: The Soviet Experience* (London, 1982), 209–22; Silvana Malle, *The Economic Organization of War Communism, 1918–1921* (Cambridge, 1985), 128–42.

58. Print shop managers were called *zaveduiushchie*; the term *direktor* was seldom used in the industry. GARF, f. R-5525, op. 2, d. 49, l. 40.

59. TsGAMO, f. 699, op. 1, d. 136 (general and factory committee meetings at Twentieth, 1921), d. 266 (general and factory committee meetings at Sixteenth, 1922); *Moskovskii pechatnik* 7 (1 August 1921): 6; 10 (1 November 1921): 7; *Rabochaia Moskva*, 23 February 1923.

ager in March 1921, and within a few months he was named the manager. When the Petrograd printers' union tried to replace Ivanov with someone more sympathetic to their political line in December 1921, the plant's workers objected and persuaded the union's leader to leave him in place.[60] Only when Pechatnyi Dvor became directly subordinate to Gosizdat in 1922 was the workers' choice replaced with a "professional" manager, Ivan Galaktionov, another veteran printer who had been managing shops since 1905.[61]

The factory committee stood at the apex of workers' shop organizations. Officially the committee was the local agent of the trade union, which closely monitored its activities. In practice, especially before 1922, factory committees enjoyed substantial autonomy and they often shared managerial functions with the plant directors. At the First Model Print Shop, the factory committee and plant administration occasionally met in joint session and agreed to coordinate their work by exchanging minutes of their meetings.[62] With the departure of private owners or, as in so many cases, of the former institutional owner of government shops, the factory committee assumed primary responsibility for the day-to-day operations of the enterprise, reporting variously and sometimes simultaneously to the local printing section, the trade union, and the state agency that had appropriated the shop for its use. Each factory committee also appointed commissions to oversee various aspects of workers' interests in the shop. At the First Model Print Shop, for example, the newly elected factory committee in May 1921 appointed commissions for housing, labor safety, improving workers' daily life, combating labor desertion, rations, culture, firewood, productivity, and conflicts.[63] One of the most active and important of the commissions, certainly in terms of labor relations, was the conflict commission. This body consisted of representatives chosen by the workers and by management, and it heard appeals from workers about individual disagreements, whether over the assignment of a pay grade, granting of vacation time or sick leave, or personal insults. The commission also functioned as a disciplinary body.[64]

During the years 1918 to 1920, another workers' institution functioned at the factory level, often in parallel with the factory committee: the council of representatives (*sovet upolnomochennykh*). The name itself reflected the printers' distinctive self-image: elsewhere, these individuals would be called delegates (*delegaty*), but printers preferred their own terminology. Dating from the 1905 revolution, these bodies revived after the February 1917 revolution, and

---

60. TsGAIPD SPb, f. 435, op. 1, d. 27 (Petrograd Printers' Union party bureau, 1921), l. 56; TsGA SPb, f. 4804, op. 5, d. 76 (factory committee meetings in Petrograd print shops, 1921), l. 46; *Petrogradskaia pravda*, 2 March 1923.

61. See Steinberg, *Moral Communities*, on Galaktionov, 98, 106–7, 239.

62. TsGAMO, f. 699, op. 1, d. 44, l. 97; d. 74, ll. 6, 67; joint meetings continued into 1922 (d. 270, l. 26).

63. Ibid., d. 145, l. 7.

64. Ibid., l. 23.

in the largest print shops they played a significant role in factory politics. Indeed, as the factory committees assumed greater managerial responsibility in 1918 and 1919, it was the councils of representatives that asserted themselves as the representatives of *workers'* interests.[65]

The Communist Party's role as the third leg of the factory troika remained problematic in the printing industry until at least 1922, as the next chapter will show. The Communists faced sharp opposition within the industry from so-called independent workers and activists, who rallied around the increasingly persecuted Menshevik Party. This independent opposition was more successful in Moscow, where the Communist Party leadership was more tolerant of difference. In Petrograd, Grigorii Zinov'ev ruled the party with an iron hand, and his protégé, Nikolai Gordon, did the same for the printing industry. The Communist presence inside print shops here was more palpable.[66] Communist Party members in each print shop formed collectives or cells, which selected a bureau—normally those Communists already active in factory politics. These bureaus reported regularly to the district committee of the party, and almost always met in advance of factory committee meetings to determine policy, to set candidates' lists for elections to factory committees, and generally to anticipate and forestall any opposition from the shop floor. It was in this arena of the party that the divisions between "workers" and "bosses" were most hopelessly obscured, because both factory committee leaders and management came from party ranks. In Pechatnyi Dvor, for example, the manager, Ivanov, formerly the factory committee chair, also chaired the party bureau.[67] Frequently all three legs of the troika met together.

The structure of workplace organization in this early period thus lacked rigid distinctions between workers and bosses. Individuals moved back and forth from one portfolio to another. Pragmatics rather than theory dictated the form of socialist industrial organization. But this structure of interlocking authority gave symbolic reinforcement to a socialist vision in which workers and bosses were equal partners in the protection of the society's economic interests.

## THE WAGE FORM IN SOCIALIST INDUSTRY

Even if the lines of authority and identity between workers and managers remained fluid and blurred, there existed an important axis of conflict: remuneration for work performed. The wage form—the way in which workers were compensated—and the politics of wages constituted two very important themes of labor relations in this period, and practices developed during the Civil War

---

65. Steinberg, *Moral Communities*, 197–98; GARF, f. R-5461, op. 1, d. 29 (meetings of the board of the Moscow Union of Workers in the Printing Trade, 1919), ll. 56–590b.

66. TsGAIPD SPb, f. 435, contains the records of the Petrograd/Leningrad Printing Industry Workers' Union party fraction from 1918 to 1929.

67. Ibid., op. 1, d. 29 (meeting of bureau of collective of the First State print shop, 18 April 1921), l. 103.

would affect relations for years to come. Negotiations about wages easily spilled over into the sharper issues of union and national politics, and as we will see, the material position of printers—of all workers—in this period was a hugely important catalyst for political challenges to the regime as well as to the development of workers' identities. A careful look at the structures of remuneration will help put these political issues into context.

Two parallel systems of remuneration emerged in the course of the first revolutionary years. The principle of work-based remuneration remained the norm: workers would be paid for the work they performed, and discussion centered on whether the unit of work should be the unit of output (piece rates) or unit of time spent at work. This principle was the centerpiece of continuing trade union efforts from 1917 to 1922 to negotiate terms of employment with the industry's management. At the same time, deteriorating economic conditions led to a second system of remuneration based on the right to subsist. These existence-based "wages" grew out of the rationing climate of 1917 and came to supply the bulk of workers' compensation during the economic chaos of the Civil War. All citizens became entitled to a level of rations of food and other goods, graded according to their social position. Workers were generally placed on the highest level of rations, the "bourgeoisie" on the lowest.[68]

The printers' trade union believed in work-based remuneration, and the principles that underlay their efforts to negotiate wage contracts remained constant: printers' relative wages within the industry should be based on skill and on equality in comparison with skilled workers in other industries and across all regions. An unskilled worker in the printing trade should receive the same wage as an unskilled worker in the metal industry, for example, and, allowing for differences in the cost of living, the same as an unskilled worker in Tomsk or Erevan. Beyond wages, the trade unions also bargained for an entire package of rules and benefits. The contract, or *tarif,* included general work conditions, rules for workplace safety and hygiene, sick pay, shop rules that gave factory committees authority over hiring and firing, and finally, a schedule of monthly wages, in rubles (the pay grid, or *stavka*), for workers in various occupations in the industry.[69]

Pay scales constructed after the revolution generally tended toward more egalitarian wages, but they still preserved distinctions of skill. In the ethos of the union, skill was a valuable quality that needed to be rewarded, whether under capitalist conditions or under socialism. Generally, the highest paid workers were proofreaders and hand newspaper compositors, followed by machine compositors (both text and newspaper). At the other end of the scale, the least well-paid compositors and lithographers earned more than the least-skilled

---

68. Mary McAuley, *Bread and Justice: State and Society in Petrograd, 1917–1922* (Oxford, 1991), 286–94, offers an especially clear and detailed discussion of this system.

69. The tarif talks dominated the discussions in the trade union's periodical publications (*Pechatnik,* 1917; *Pechatnoe delo,* 1918).

press workers and binders.[70] The inflation of 1918, however, nullified the achievements of the printers' union contracts, often even before the ink was dry on the collective agreements. Depreciated wages no longer measured skill and status; they could no longer even provide a living. By the summer of 1918, the cost of an average market basket of the food consumed by a Petrograd worker had risen to more than double a skilled worker's salary. Attempts to renegotiate the contract continued throughout 1918, even as prices soared and productivity plummeted. At the same time, existence-based wages—rations issued by the municipalities—began to constitute an important component of workers' income. Initially, printers had been excluded from the highest ration category, but by October 1918 had managed to win the right to first-category rations.[71]

With productivity falling, print shops closing, and food supplies shrinking, the printers' union persisted in its commitment to a parity-based, single tarif for the entire industry.[72] The new tarif worked out with state agencies and the Central Council of Trade Unions preserved pay differentials by level of skill, introducing twelve grades, *razriady*, for production workers. Printers debated whether such inequality was appropriate in a socialist system at their August 1919 congress: under communism, skill differences would eventually not matter, argued one, but for the moment, pay differentials were essential to retain a skilled labor force. A tarif that was *too* egalitarian would drive away skilled workers who might sell their skills elsewhere. The industry had lost a "colossal number of typesetters" because of the "spontaneous unconscious drift to socialism on the part of the uncultured elements" in the industry; in other words, zealous socialists who ignored the culture of the skilled workers and insisted on reducing all wages to the level of the unskilled.[73] Such discussions confirmed a fundamental tension between socialist values of equality and the skilled workers' pride in skill and difference.

The work culture of socialism would become an important theme in printers' politics: once the economy had achieved a socialist equilibrium, activists would argue, *cultured* workers would not need to be lured to work for pay, they would work out of devotion to craft, to class, and to revolutionary nation. The same argument predominated in discussions about abandoning time pay in favor of piece rates. Management preferred piece rates as an efficient way to enforce output norms and to maintain productivity. Printers argued that the episodic and varied nature of the work process made piece rates impossible to

70. TsGAMO, f. 699, op. 1, d. 4, ll. 37–44 (1918 Moscow tarif).

71. Ibid., ll. 41–42; E. G. Gimpel'son, *Sovetskii rabochii klass, 1918–1920 gg.* (Moscow, 1974), 256; *Pechatnik* 5 (1918): 11; *Pechatnoe delo* 24 (13 July 1918): 11. See also the review of the negotiations in *Pechatnik* 9–10 (10 October [27 September] 1918): 8–9; *Pechatnik* 11 (10 November [28 October] 1918): 10.

72. *Pechatnik* 12 (10 December [27 November] 1918): 9; 1–2 (25 January 1919): 11–12; 3–4 (1 April 1919): 18.

73. GARF, f. R-5525, op. 1, d. 10 (transcript of all-Russian extraordinary congress of Printers' Union, 18–23 August 1919), l. 121.

apply fairly.[74] Nonetheless, a return to piece rates, in the form of a bonus (*premiia*) for extra output above and beyond the tarif stavka, appeared in union discussions by January 1919. This bonus system appealed to many workers ("Our life is so hard, we can't speak about a contract, we live from day to day").[75] It also appealed to a union leadership increasingly responsible for raising productivity among its members, even though workers soon figured out how to lower their normal output in order to earn higher bonuses, with a net fall in productivity.[76]

By 1920, printers, like all workers, received compensation on a two-tiered system. The tarif, with its twelve pay grades, remained the basic form of work-based remuneration. At the same time, the fixed ration, payable in kind, provided workers with the basic necessities of life. But the resources to provide this ration were far from secure, and new "special categories" had to be created to reward the most critical contributors to the economy and the Civil War effort. Even a ration system, in other words, had to mimic the gradations of the pay system in order to persuade key workers to continue to perform their jobs. Printers lobbied hard to be included first in the highest ration category, reserved originally for Red Army soldiers, and then in 1920 in the so-called reserved (*zabronirovannyi*) ration category.[77]

The ration system was meant to provide a bare minimum of subsistence, and the gap between rations and survival had to be filled through wages or other types of economic activity. Printers in Viatka, for example, received the same ration as every citizen of the town, including a pound of rye bread a day, a half-pound of salt per month, three boxes of matches a month, 325 cigarettes every five months, and a third of a pair of shoes. Everything else for survival had to be purchased on the market with money earned as wages. In Viatka the average skilled worker at this time earned 2,000 rubles a month, the amount of money required to purchase a quart of milk, ten eggs, and three pounds of meat.[78]

Money itself became increasingly worthless in this economy of shortages and inflation, and by the end of 1920, workers were clamoring for their bonuses—the wage they received for extra work—to be paid in kind rather than in cash. "Kind" included food products and manufactured goods, especially clothing, whose market prices were out of the reach of workers.[79] Factory committees were now allocating compensation to their workers in the form of clothing, footwear, and food products. Potatoes and coffee could perhaps be distributed

74. *Pechatnoe delo* 23 (10 June 1918): 11; GARF, f. R-5525, op. 1, d. 10, ll. 132–33; see also the 1921 discussion in TsGA SPb, f. 4804, op. 5, d. 72 (transcripts of conferences, 1921).
75. TsGA SPb, f. 4804, op. 3, d. 18, l. 62 (delegates' conference, May 1919).
76. GARF, f. R-5525, op. 2, d. 17, l. 53 (Petrograd factory committee conference, 9 May 1920).
77. Ibid., f. R-5461, op. 1, d. 30 (Moscow representatives' meeting, 30 December 1919); f. R-5525, op. 2, d. 5 (presidium of union central committee, 2 March 1920), l. 9.
78. Ibid., f. R-5525, op. 2, d. 48 (all-Russian tarif conference, 17–20 June 1920), ll. 14–15.
79. Ibid., d. 34, l. 19 (meeting of the Petrograd guberniia board). The document is misdated 26 October 1926.

equitably among workers, but how should one distribute five pairs of boots (at 20,000 rubles a pair) to a shop with hundreds of workers? By 1921, in fact, the bulk of work-based compensation as well as all existence-based rewards (rations) came in the form of goods: with the March 1921 decision to allow free trade, workers were expected to turn to the market to convert their galoshes (or 20,000 ruble boots) into whatever they really needed.[80]

The link between compensation and productivity was reaffirmed as a national principle in mid-1921, when the regime adopted a new policy on labor remuneration. Rather than reward workers as individuals, the new system would reward them collectively, through the program known as collective supply—*kollektivnoe snabzhenie*.[81] Enterprises enrolled in this program would receive a lump sum of goods and cash, based on the size of the enterprise at the time it entered into the program. The enterprise could decide itself how to reward productivity, but the intention was to provide substantial incentives for hard work and for efficiency. Workers on one shop floor in Petrograd remained confused about this new policy, but they were assured that in money terms, highly skilled workers on collective supply would receive no less than 1.2 million rubles a month, at a time when the average Petrograd typesetter was earning about 450,000 rubles a month. Workers in Moscow demanded that the traditional 2-to-1 pay differential between skilled and unskilled workers be preserved, and that bosses would not receive more food than a skilled worker.[82]

As late as September 1922, a year and a half after the inauguration of the New Economic Policy, wage policy for printers remained problematic and highly negotiable. As shall be seen in Chapter 4, wages continued to be paid in kind into 1922, and the reintroduction of money wages by the end of that year frequently led to situations in which firms did not have enough cash to pay workers what they had earned. The material insecurity of the Civil War years abated very slowly for workers in the printing trades. Significantly, even under socialism, the wage form and wage differentials remained central elements of labor policy and of printers' own efforts to defend their position within the new economy. "Fairness" included equality but it also embraced traditional recognitions of skill and status differentials. Printers' consciousness of the precariousness of their material situation and of their entitlement to skilled workers' status would continue to structure their relations to authority, whether the factory administration, the trade union, the party, or the state.

---

80. Ibid., d. 17, l. 71; TsGAMO, f. 699, op. 1, d. 134, l. 50 (general meeting at Sixteenth, 8 November 1921); *Tretii vserossiiskii s"ezd soiuza rabochikh poligraficheskogo proizvodstva (2–6 iiunia 1921 g.). Protokoly i postanovleniia s"ezda (izvlechenie iz stenogramm)* (Moscow, 1921), 61, 82; TsGA SPb, f. 4804, op. 5, d. 76, ll. 27–27ob.; d. 78 (delegates' meetings at Petrograd print shops, 1921), l. 46.

81. See Paul Ashin, "Wage Policy in the Transition to NEP," *Russian Review* 47, no. 3 (1988): 293–313.

82. *Moskovskii pechatnik* 9 (1 October 1921): 4–5; TsGA SPb, f. 4804, op. 5, d. 78, l. 46; *Krasnyi pechatnik* 1 (26 November 1921): 7; TsGAMO, f. 699, op. 1, d. 145, ll. 22, 24 (general and factory committee meetings at First Model, 21 July 1921 and 27 July 1921).

The economic catastrophe of the Civil War years, the disappearance of orders, supplies, jobs, and wages, affected printers equally, regardless of skill level or prerevolutionary sense of status. Subsistence wages borne of scarcity compressed the differentials between traditional high-skill positions and low-skill ones. In bargaining with the new regime, printers and their union tried to preserve customary differentials, but this trade had always balanced a sense of community with a recognition of individual distinction within it. Printers' commitment to the common trade of printing combined with a celebration of the particularities of their place in the work process. Now under socialism, the common features of the trade grew stronger: printers worked for the state, and they looked to the state to guarantee their livelihoods, work conditions, and status.

Social ownership, however, did not bring an end to the inherently conflictual relationship between socialist workers and socialist management. The economic conditions of the war years and the claims of many workers on the scarce resources of the state meant that printers needed to continue to bargain to defend their economic positions, the foundation of their identity as workers. The socialist enterprise became the laboratory for the development of a new kind of industrial relations, one that could balance the conflicting interests of workers and bosses with the overall interests of society. Within the enterprise, workers occupied all the positions, but they served sometimes as managers, sometimes as judges, sometimes as producers. All had a stake in the success of the enterprise. This legacy of workplace survivalism became the birthright of the Soviet printers' union, regardless of the fierce political struggles that would shape trade union politics in the years to come. Living from day to day, printers developed an activism that centered on their material needs first and foremost. But their values of collectivism and pride in craft would provide the bedrock on which this activism was articulated. They would demand from their trade union leaders a responsiveness to their specific needs that I will label "workerism": a demand that grew equally out of the attributes they brought with them to the socialist experiment and from the economic hardships they endured in the experiment's founding years.

# CHAPTER 2

## THE STRUGGLE FOR A COMMUNIST PRINTERS' UNION, 1918–1922

*We have to lead the workers' struggle on our own.... We must demand that policies be set not by those above, but from below, so that the voice of true workers will be heard. Down with the Civil War!*

MOSCOW PRINTER,
11 JULY 1919

The radicalization of social and political life during 1917 had eroded the moderate Menshevik Party's hold over Russia's fledgling trade union movement. By the beginning of 1918, Communists were firmly in the majority in most trade union organizations, and their delegates dominated the First All-Russian Congress of Trade Unions in January 1918. The printers' union, however, famously resisted Communist pressures. From 1918 to 1920, Menshevik printers led the union's central council and many of its local branches, and their primacy provoked repeated and forceful attempts by Communist printers to win the union over to their vision of a trade union subordinated to state interests. By the middle of 1920, the Communists had won, but their takeover was not part of a concerted and general assault by the party center. The struggle for the union took place within the union and among printers themselves: the catastrophic material conditions of the Civil War years provided the terrain of battle, and debates over the role of trade unions under socialism furnished the discursive weapons for the contest.

In the course of the attempts to manage and revive the revolutionary economy, alternative approaches and philosophies in respect to labor relations and trade unions had crystallized into two basic variants. One was productivist and statist, the other "workerist" and independent. One subsumed all social life into state institutions, the other insisted that trade unions should play an autonomous role in civil society. The Communist-dominated trade union congresses in 1918 and 1919 codified the primacy of production and the centrality of the state, and Communist printers carried this message to their supporters: "Trade unions, as the class organization of the proletariat, should undertake the primary task of organizing production and renewing the shattered productive forces of the country."[1] Productivist interests could be served only by state regulation of all printing enterprises and by centralized economic administration, with orders and policies transmitted from state economic organs through trade unions to the factory committees. In any conflict between workers' welfare and production, production came first: only higher productivity could produce a higher standard of living. Factory committees served as agents of the state. Conflicts in this productivist system, where the unions and managers represented workers' collective best interests, could only be individual, not collective.[2]

Trade union independence became the keystone of an alternative model of labor relations embraced by the Menshevik Party. Regardless of the economic system under which workers were employed, they argued, the interests of workers as sellers of labor conflicted with the interests of those who purchased their labor. Only trade unions independent of their employers could properly represent workers' interests. For proponents of this model, which could be labeled "workerist," the nature of plant ownership was irrelevant for the tasks of trade unions. Whether workers confronted socialist or capitalist managers, they needed to defend their immediate interests first. Unions could do this through organized collective bargaining: gathering information, preparing proposals, and negotiating on behalf of the sellers of labor as equals of the buyers of labor. The rules of their interaction would be defined through the democratic process, not by arbitrary use of state force.

In the independent model of labor relations, as in the statist model, production was in workers' best interests. Within this system of bargaining, workers were prepared to accept output norms and negotiated wage scales. Menshevik union leaders therefore agreed to participate in the economic agencies that directed their industry, the better to represent the interests of workers. Strikes that halted production were to be discouraged, but the right to strike had to be retained as the final weapon of workers in defense of their interests.[3]

1. *Pervyi vserossiiskii s"ezd professional'nykh soiuzov, 7–14 ianvaria 1918. Polnyi stenograficheskii otchet s predisloviem M. Tomskogo* (Moscow, 1918), 119.
2 Discussion of this model in the printing industry can be found in *Vserossiiskii pechatnik* 10 (15 February 1921): 2–9 and 11 (15 March 1921): 7; and in *Moskovskii pechatnik* 2 (15 February 1921): 3–4.
3. *Pechatnik* 12 (10 December [27 November] 1918): 2, 8; 5 (30 May 1919): 15. The Men-

Two additional models of labor relations can be constructed from the practical experience of the Civil War economy. Both Communists and Mensheviks warned against implementation of an anarchist model, whose key feature was ownership and management of an enterprise by the workers themselves. Independent factories, operating as "federated republics," would never subordinate their immediate interests to the collective good.[4] Without markets (which were capitalist) and without central authority, there would be no way to allocate resources to these plants or to distribute their output. Furthermore, neither party's leaders had much confidence in the ability of Russia's "backward" labor force to master the complicated science of factory management. They feared that under worker self-management, in Russian conditions, workers would sell off the capital stock of their plant and go to the countryside on the proceeds. Self-management was therefore a recipe for the rapid collapse of Russia's remaining industrial capacity. Such a model received little theoretical support from printing workers, but practical experience pushed workers toward such a system, as we will see.[5]

Mensheviks and Communists alike also denounced what they labeled the "narrow-minded" or "selfish" (*obyvatel'skii*) worker's model of labor relations. As Lev Trotskii had argued, too many workers, left to their own devices, would choose a system that guaranteed a maximum of compensation for a minimum of work. Capitalism or socialism, dictatorship or democracy, dependent or independent trade unions, the "broad interests" of class or society—all were equally irrelevant to narrow-minded workers, who chose whichever alternative provided for their immediate material interests.[6] Printers "live their own lives, live only for what today's need prompts them to do."[7] If one system did not deliver, they would choose another. The narrow-minded printer was indifferent to which party promised bread, clothing, and freedom to travel in search of food, complained the Communist union journal. "He wants to have all of this—and that's sufficient."[8] For socialists, this attitude was dangerously shortsighted. Trotskii proposed to combat it by force and the Mensheviks by orga-

---

shevik Nikolai Chistov joined the collegium of the Moscow Printing Section in February 1920: TsGAMO, f. 699, op. 1, d. 60 (meetings of the Moscow Printers' Union presidium, 1920), l. 17; *Pechatnik* 5 (30 [17] April 1918): 8–9.

4. *Vtoraia vserossiiskaia konferentsiia soiuzov rabochikh pechatnogo dela, 1917*, 63.

5. Indeed, in the post–Civil War narrative of this industrial collapse, as recounted in a 1922–23 contest for best "red director," the good directors were those who kept their factories running, even as federated republics, in the face of orders to shut down by the rational central administration. See Diane P. Koenker, "Factory Tales: Narratives of Industrial Relations in the Transition to NEP," *Russian Review* 55, no. 3 (1996): 384–411.

6. A study of workers under socialist governments in France and Spain argues that workers were just as resistant to work under these regimes, much to the displeasure of the socialist governments. See Michael Seidman, *Workers against Work: Labor in Paris and Barcelona during the Popular Fronts* (Berkeley, 1991).

7. GARF, f. R-5525, op. 1, d. 10 (transcript of All-Russian Special Congress of Printers' Union, 18–23 August 1919), l. 14.

8. *Vserossiiskii pechatnik* 6 (10 June 1920): p. 3.

nization. On the shop floor, however, workers practiced a tenacious resistance to the politics of sacrifice advocated by their leaders, using any means practicable to defend their own interests.

These four models of labor relations—productivist, workerist, anarchist, and narrow-minded—describe a range of choices available to Russian workers in building the socialist economy and state. If we were to position these models on a continuum, the productivist, statist model would be located at one extreme and the anarchist model at the opposite end. In practice, as we shall see, workerism and narrow-mindedness were often positioned very close together in the center of the spectrum. This position, which would be labeled philistinism (*obyvatel'shchina*), petty-bourgeois (*meshchanstvo*), selfishness (*shkurnichestvo*), Menshevism, opportunism, rightism, and tailism, is one of the elements most crucial to grasp if we are to understand the Russian revolution. A comfortable material life for all citizens was the goal; socialism was the means by which to increase the economic capacity of society and to distribute its product most equitably. The real difference between the so-called narrow-minded workers and the far-seeing socialists was where they drew the limit to "self": at themselves, their family, their workshop, their industry, their class, their country, or the world. This struggle over socialism and the meaning of socialist labor relations constituted the central theme of trade union history during the years of the Civil War, and it reached a particularly shrill level in the Trade Union of Printers.

## MODELS IN CONFLICT: TWO MODELS, TWO UNIONS, 1918–1920

The struggle for the printers' union pitted the productivist model against a workerist one, Communists against nonparty printers and Mensheviks, the center against the localities, and Moscow against Petrograd. The conflict employed a full range of organizational tools: oratory, shop floor democracy, dual unionism, material incentives, and repression. The turning point came in the summer of 1919, when the minority Communist faction in the union broke away and organized its own red union. Dual unionism was anathema to the Russian practitioners of organized labor (as it was elsewhere in the international labor movement), and the renegade Communists initially fought both their own leaders and rival supporters of the independent printers' union. A special national congress in August 1919 resulted in the rout of the Menshevik-led central leadership of the printers' union and of its independent trade union line as radical Communist printers forced the hand of the more moderate Communist trade union leadership.

The association of the Printers' Union with the Menshevik Party had begun in the heady organizational days of the 1917 revolution. By October of that year, when most trade union organizations had swung over to the Bolshevik camp, printers' unions across Russia continued to select Mensheviks as their leaders: Mensheviks outnumbered Bolsheviks at the December 1917 All-Russian Printers' Union Conference by 50 delegates to 17. In Moscow and elsewhere, printers elected Menshevik majorities to their boards (*pravlenie*) and Mensheviks as their union delegates. Moscow printers were nearly alone among the city's unions in opposing the "premature" seizure of power in October. Petrograd printers were more radical, and replaced their Menshevik board with a Bolshevik one in November 1917.[9]

Russian trade union activists had learned their organizational skills in a universe in which unions had to defend workers' interests against state and capitalist opponents. With socialists in power, however, the "workers' interest" was no longer a simple calculation, and these interests were challenged on two fronts in the weeks after the October revolution. On one hand, printers were engaged in protracted economic struggles with their employers, who resisted implementing citywide collective agreements. Continuing inflation provoked rank-and-file demands for raises outside the collective agreement.[10] This was familiar territory for the adherents of the independent model of labor relations.

On the other hand, workers also faced conflict with the new proletarian regime. One of the first moves of the government, on 28 October 1917 (old style), was to close down newspapers that openly opposed Soviet power.[11] This move violated the right of press freedom, which the Mensheviks as well as many Communists supported, and it also put many printers out of work. If printers opposed communism because they felt not enough of them would be able to make a living under a proletarian dictatorship, such a sentiment was rarely raised in these crassly materialistic terms. Freedom of the press was couched instead as a matter of principle. The Petrograd union organization was sharply divided: when the union's Council of Representatives threatened to call for a general strike unless press freedom was restored, the majority of Petrograd printers reacted by reelecting a new union board with a Bolshevik majority. But the Representatives' Council continued to represent the voice of independent printers. The balance of political power in Petrograd was so equal that the coun-

9. *Vtoraia vserossiiskaia konferentsiia soiuzov rabochikh pechatnogo dela*, 1917, 10; the degree of support among printers for the Socialist Revolutionaries (SRs) is hard to determine. The Menshevik Party had the more dynamic leaders and dominated the political discourse, especially after 1917. An indeterminate number of printers claimed membership in the SRs, but their voices are indistinct and blurred in the historical record. To the Bolsheviks who used this record to label their enemies, everyone who opposed them after 1917 became a "Menshevik." A case in point is the Petrograd printer Dmitrii Dudarev, who shows up in documents with both Menshevik and SR labels.

10. Collective agreements can be found in TsGAMO, f. 699, op. 1, d. 4. Other individual cases are reported ibid., d. 5 (correspondence between Moscow union officials and print shop administrators), l. 7; *Pechatnik* 5 (30 [17] April 1918): 13; for Petrograd, *Pechatnoe delo* 15 (13 February [31 January] 1918): 10; TsGAMO, f. 699, op. 1, d. 34 (protocols of workers' and employees' meetings on settling conflicts in enterprises, 1918–22); *Pechatnik* 1–2 (13 February [31 January] 1918): 19; 3–4 (31 [18] March 1918): 17; 9–10 (10 October [27 September] 1918): 7–8; 11 (10 November [28 October] 1918): 12; *Pechatnik* 9–10 (10 October [27 September] 1918): 5; 12 (10 December [27 November]1918): 2.

11. Leonard Schapiro, *The Origin of the Communist Autocracy: Political Opposition in the Soviet State, First Phase, 1917–1922*, 2nd ed. (Cambridge, Mass., 1977), 76.

cil forced the board to send two Mensheviks and two Communists as the Petrograd delegation to the First All-Russian Congress of Trade Unions in January 1918.[12]

The impending schism within the printers' union received further impetus when workers at the print shop of the Moscow newspaper *Russkoe slovo* declared a strike against their new administrators, the Moscow Soviet of Workers' Deputies. This conflict exemplifies the changing character of labor relations, the erasure of the distinction between economics and politics, and the shifting ground rules of strikes. *Russkoe slovo* had remained a tribune of liberalism after the February revolution, and it continued to defend the Provisional Government after the Communist takeover in October. In response to the newspaper's inflammatory opposition to Soviet power, the Moscow Soviet closed the paper on 28 November 1917. An armed guard occupied the shop and ordered its workers home. The next day the workers met and declared a strike against the government, but the Menshevik leaders of the Moscow Printers' Union intervened and persuaded the Moscow Soviet to retain the workers to print the soviet's newspaper, *Izvestiia*, on the same terms as before. Workers became employees of the soviet, and they duly signed a collective agreement with their new "owners." Two weeks later, when the soviet failed to pay these workers, they struck again, charging breach of contract. The soviet and its local labor commissar immediately labeled this a political strike and refused to negotiate. Red Guards occupied the print shop, and its 1,500 workers were dismissed. The unemployed printers refused to accept their discharge and continued to "strike." Was this a political strike now, or an economic one? The union and the *Russkoe slovo* workers claimed they wished only to be paid their rightful wages from their ordinary employer, which happened to be a state agency. The soviet replied it did not see itself as an ordinary employer: in a socialist state the labor commissar was the supreme authority in matters of labor disputes.[13]

When word leaked that the shop's former owner had given the workers money to tide them over the Christmas holidays, the *Russkoe slovo* strikers now genuinely seemed to be colluding with the class enemy. Even the Moscow Printers' Union Council of Representatives ruled that the strike had been political from the start, and that there was no difference now between economic and political action. In the new republic, all strikes harmed production, harmed the regime, and harmed the revolution: they were therefore all political. To challenge one's economic superior was now to challenge the revolution.[14]

The language in this conflict reveals the ambiguities that socialist power had brought to the discourse of class. Workers demanded that their employer, the Moscow Soviet, honor its commitments to workers as would any other em-

---

12. *Materialy*, 90–91; *Rabochaia gazeta*, 7 November 1917; *Pechatnoe delo* (8 December 1917): 5; *Pechatnik* 1–2 (13 February [31 January] 1918): 15.

13. *Materialy*, 142–56; *Pechatnik* 1–2 (13 February [31 January] 1918): 19; see also Ruud, *Russian Entrepreneur*, 175–76.

14. *Pechatnik* 1–2 (13 February [31 January] 1918): 21.

ployer; the soviet countered that to strike against a socialist institution was counterrevolutionary. The Moscow Menshevik union charged that the Moscow Soviet was acting as a "strikebreaker," "locking out" workers, behaving more like a tsarist governor than a "class-proletarian" government. In the debate over this conflict, class identities gave way to more localized ones. The *Russkoe slovo* workers claimed that the "workers' government" had chased them out of the factory "that we created with our own sweat and blood."[15] Their identity, in other words, came not from their relation to the society at large but from their role at the point of production. Such a sentiment could be seen to lead dangerously toward the anarchist model of labor relations, in which the factory became the workers' own federated republic.

The *Russkoe slovo* affair polarized the Moscow Printers' Union. Communist printers strengthened their party organization and began to publish their own journal, called *Revoliutsionnyi pechatnik* (Revolutionary printer) to rival the union's official *Pechatnik*.[16] A month later, the Moscow representatives again supported the Communist position. Printers' radicalism at this moment seemed genuine. The events of October, the resistance of the old ruling classes to the decrees implementing socialism, the promise of a socialist order, the peace negotiations to end the war, these had legitimately pushed the sentiment among printers—some of the most moderate workers in Russia—toward identification of their local interests with those of the Soviet state.[17]

But as economic conditions continued to deteriorate, printers lost confidence in the statist solution. The Communist-led union in Petrograd presided over the collapse of that city's printing industry, and the rank and file blamed their leaders. A March 1918 meeting attracted some five thousand Petrograd printers, who turned the Communist board's report into a trial of economic mismanagement. Communist labor policy, they argued, contributed only to growing unemployment, the opposite of what workers expected from socialism. In a tumultuous conclusion, the meeting adopted a resolution denouncing the union's failure to defend workers' interests in the four months that it had been led by Communists, and they demanded immediate new leadership elections. The Moscow and Petrograd unions both reelected their boards in April 1918, and in each city the independent Menshevik candidates won handily, with about two-thirds of the votes.[18]

Armed with this mandate, the Moscow union leaders attempted to prove that theirs was a union that defended its members' interests. This stance required them to bargain collectively not only with private and state owners but

15. Ibid., 19–20; *Materialy*, 154–55.
16. *Pechatnik* 1–2 (13 February [31 January] 1918): 4.
17. Ibid. 3–4 (31 [18] March 1918): 14; *Vestnik vsrpd* 2 (20 March 1918): 6; 3 (18 April 1918): 4.
18. *Pechatnik* 3–4 (31 [18] March 1918): 11; *Pechatnoe delo* 19 (10 April 1918): 11; 21 (29 April 1918): 11; *Vestnik vsrpd* 3 (20 April 1918): 14; *Gazeta pechatnika*, 16 December 1918; *Pechatnik* 5 (30 [17] April 1918): 6–8.

also with the regime's commissar of labor and the Central Trade Union Council. All of these institutions claimed a role in determining economic relations within the industry, but even the various Soviet agencies did not always agree on their approach to the independent printers. The makers of Communist labor policy appeared to be divided over whether to punish the printers for their Menshevism (the Council of Trade Unions) or to wean them away from opposition by acceding to their special demands (the labor commissar). Persistent conflicts over the tarif and its modifications, the refusal of Communist board members to engage in day-to-day organizational work, and increasing divisions among printers themselves continued to tax union resources.[19] The independent trade union found itself hard pressed to service its members in the realm of "ordinary" class struggle.

As proponents of the productivist model of labor relations, the Communist government sought to insert itself at all levels of activity, from trade union boards and councils to labor commissars to economic management. Communist printers ousted or alienated from Printers' Union activities found refuge in the Printing Section of the Supreme Economic Council or in one of its fifteen provincial affiliates. These activists, such as Nikolai Gordon and Nikolai Derbyshev in Petrograd and Aleksandr Borshchevskii in Moscow, used their new managerial positions on behalf of the productivist model of labor relations. In the process, they found themselves coming into increasing conflict with the printers they wished both to represent and to manage. Institutions of worker control and worker self-management did little to alleviate the inherent conflicts between managers and workers. At Girshfeld's book bindery in Moscow, the factory committee chairman behaved as "Tsar and God" toward workers, promising Christmas bonuses only to workers who refrained from criticism. In shops where one-man management replaced collegial administration, workers faced the same kinds of authoritarian management that they thought existed only under capitalism. Increasingly, embattled commissars and committees called on the forces of state power to discipline their unruly workers. When workers at the nationalized print shop of Ostrogozhsk (Voronezh guberniia) complained in 1919 of excessive layoffs and loss of back pay, the chairman of the town's revolutionary committee gave the order (in the manner of Trotskii, the Red Army commander in chief): "Shoot every tenth man—and the rest will be silent."[20]

As the printing industry plunged ever further into ruin, Mensheviks and Communists consolidated their diametrically opposed positions on the causes of and remedies for the economic disaster. The Menshevik union leaders reiterated that the interests of employers, whether socialist or capitalist, were in-

19. *Biulleten' moskovskogo obshchestva tipo-litografov*, 1918; *Pechatnik* 5 (30 [17] April 1918): 15–16; 12 (10 December [27 November] 1918): 1–2; TsGAMO, f. 699, op. 1, d. 34, ll. 178–79.
20. *Pechatnik* 9–10 (10 October [27 September] 1918): 16, 20–21; 1–2 (25 January 1919): 4, 15; 12 (10 December [27 November] 1918): 12, 13; 11 (10 November [28 October] 1918): 14; GARF, f. R-5525, op. 1, d. 22 (materials on guberniia branch activities, A–O, 1919), l. 19.

evitably in conflict with those of workers. They argued also that arbitrary and thoughtless administration had further damaged the productive capacity of the industry. Communists claimed, on the contrary, that industry would recover only if union officials devoted all their activism to organizing production, not defending workers' rights. "Whoever is against the organization of production," editorialized Moscow's *Revoliutsionnyi pechatnik* in June 1918, "whoever is against the organization of strict accounting and distribution procedures—here is the direct enemy of the working class."[21]

Similar fissures split apart the entire Russian working class in these months, shattering the class-based sense of purpose that had contributed to the Communist victory in October 1917.[22] Among printers, political party divisions now assumed an even more prominent role as Communists and Mensheviks tried to rally support for their respective visions of labor relations and the socialist revolution. Workers' dissatisfaction with Communist policies reached a peak in May and June 1918. A growing opposition movement in Petrograd called for new elections to the soviet and the convocation of an independent workers' congress, and printers there added their voices to the chorus of opposition.[23] Communist influence among workers seemed weaker in mid-1918 than ever. And at the same time, the erupting Civil War now threatened the regime's survival. The task of building socialism in a wrecked economy was compounded by a renewed military emergency, and the Communist regime responded with emergency measures against all who would oppose its policies.

In Petrograd, Communist printers found their minority position intolerable, and they began an intensive campaign to win back control of their union by whatever means necessary. Electoral methods had failed to produce a Communist majority among rank-and-file printers, but frustrated Communists disagreed on how to respond. Leaders at the center continued to uphold traditions of trade union democracy: local boards must be elected by the rank and file, and national leaders must be chosen by the union's elected representatives at a legitimate national congress. Moscow's Communist printers shared this vision of trade union rules, and they continued to attempt to win control of the union as they had done in 1917, through shop-level agitation and local elections. Petrograd Communist printers, however, led by Nikolai Gordon, argued that the situation was much too serious for the niceties of trade union solidarity. They saw the independent trade union as a Menshevik platform for counterrevolu-

---

21. *Revoliutsionnyi pechatnik* (Petrograd) 3 (6 June 1918): 6; *Revoliutsionnyi pechatnik* (Moscow) 2 (12 June 1918): 2.

22. See, among others, Smith, *Red Petrograd*, chap. 10; William G. Rosenberg, "Russian Labor and Bolshevik Power after October," *Slavic Review* 44, no. 2 (1985): 213–39; Vladimir N. Brovkin, *The Mensheviks after October: Socialist Opposition and the Rise of the Bolshevik Dictatorship* (Ithaca, 1987); Donald J. Raleigh, "Languages of Power: How the Saratov Bolsheviks Imagined Their Enemies," *Slavic Review* 57 (1998): 320–49.

23. M. S. Bernshtam, "Nezavisimoe rabochee dvizhenie v 1918 g. Dokumenty i materialy," in *Narodnoe soprotivlenie kommunizmu v Rossii* (Paris, 1981); *Pechatnik* 6 (23 [10] June 1918): 9–10.

tion, and if it could not be defeated democratically, then Gordon was willing to employ the coercive force of the state on the Communists' behalf. And if repression did not intimidate printers into voting for Communist leaders and the productivist line, then Gordon insisted that printers should organize "our own proletarian union," a red printers' union to compete with the official union for members and for state recognition.[24]

The growing protests by independent workers in Petrograd in the summer of 1918 provided the justification for the strategy of repression. The national Printers' Union leader, M. S. Kefali, was arrested in June for his part in mobilizing the opposition, and on the eve of a citywide political protest strike on 1 July the entire Petrograd union board was temporarily arrested. Gordon, who was present at the time of the arrests, denied any responsibility. Nonetheless, the account of this denial added that "during this speech, Gordon continually resorted to sharp and insulting expressions toward individual members of the board and toward the Council of Representatives as a whole." When interrupted from the floor with the claim that Soviet power shot anyone who disagreed with it, Gordon allegedly replied, "And it will continue to shoot them."[25]

Repression might be justified under the gathering threat of Civil War, but the specter of a schism within the trade union movement horrified Communist leaders. Responding to Gordon's accusations that the Petrograd Printers' Union was counterrevolutionary, the Communist-dominated Petrograd Council of Trade Unions refused to dissolve the Menshevik board or to sanction the creation of a second, Communist printers' union. Communist printers themselves were divided about the dual-union strategy: should they push for new union elections or should they forge ahead with plans for the schismatic red printers' union? A party meeting on 17 September hotly debated the issue. One supporter of the electoral strategy insisted, "We need to exhaust every method that can allow us to seize [*zakhvatit'*] the union without a split." Gordon rejected any further compromise with independent printers, and the majority of the meeting supported his plan to launch a separate union. The old union had lost the right, said the Communists, to belong to the "family of revolutionary worker unions, and they ought to be excluded from this family." They agreed, moreover, to punish anyone who agitated against the new union with dismissal from the job.[26]

The Petrograd Mensheviks could not resist this pressure. The lawful union agreed to call new board elections to settle the issue democratically, but before a vote could be organized, the conflict came to a head. On the eve of the first anniversary of the October revolution, in November 1918, a "claque" (*kuchka*)]

---

24. *Petrogradskaia pravda*, 13 June 1918.
25. *Pechatnoe delo* 25 (26 August 1918): 12.
26. TsGAIPD SPb, f. 435, op. 1, d. 3 (protocols of the Petrograd Printers' Union party fraction, 1918), ll. 20b., 6aob., 9ob.

of red printers rushed from a Communist rally to the union's office, expelled officials working there, and demanded they hand over all documents and keys. Threatened by overpowering force, the old officials agreed to capitulate to the Petrograd Trade Union Council, which accepted their "resignation."[27] Three weeks later, on 24 November, a mass meeting convened to elect a new board. Menshevik reports estimated no more than 1,500 printers (of a maximum of 18,000 members) attended. After noncommunist speakers were denied the floor, only about 900 remained to elect by a show of hands a new all-Communist board of directors.[28] Yet the Petrograd Communists stood nearly alone in their revolutionary audacity. When 176 Moscow printers attempted to constitute themselves as a new red union, the Moscow Communist Party City Committee approved, but the Communist-dominated Moscow Trade Union Council continued to oppose the existence of separate unions. The printers of the Moscow red union remained officially "schismatics."[29]

At this point, the Petrograd and Moscow red unions turned their attention to the creation of a second national printers' union, calling their own nationwide congress of red printers to rival the planned congress organized by the existing union's central council. Once again, the red separatists were thwarted by their Communist comrades, this time in the national union center, the All-Russian Council of Trade Unions, whose organizational department insisted that the red congress was unauthorized. The reds appealed to the VTsSPS presidium, and meanwhile toured the country to rally support for their congress. In Voronezh, however, to take one provincial example, when the Communist-dominated union board proposed to a provincewide conference to send delegates to the red congress, they were voted down overwhelmingly, with 362 of 391 printers voting for the existing union and against the Communists. When the renegade congress opened at the beginning of May 1919, some ninety delegates had arrived, claiming to represent 56,000 printers from across Russia. The independent union later questioned this figure, conceding that the red congress may have represented 14,000 or 15,000 printers at most.[30] Two years into the revolution, Communists could still claim the support of perhaps one-third of the country's printers, but no more. The VTsSPS therefore refused to recog-

---

27. *Vestnik vsrpd* 5 (16 November 1918): 3; 6–7 (1 December 1918): 19; *Pechatnik* 9–10 (10 October [27 September] 1918): 16; 11 (10 November [28 October] 1918): 2; 12 (December 10 [November 27] 1918): 10; *Materialy*, 104–15 (recollection by Nikolai Gordon).

28. *Gazeta pechatnika*, 16 December 1918; *Vestnik vsrpd* 6–7 (1 December 1918): 1, 21; *Pechatnik* 12 (10 December [27 November] 1918): 10; TsGA SPb, f. 4804, op. 2, d. 4 (Petrograd Printers' Union board, 1918), ll. 3–30b.

29. *Gazeta pechatnika*, 19 and 23 January 1919; *Materialy*, 189; GARF, f. R-5525, op. 1, d. 34 (general and delegates' meetings of workers in the printing industry, 1919, M–P), ll. 3, 5; *Moskovskii pechatnik* 1 (15 January 1921): 6.

30. *Professional'noe dvizhenie*, 4 April 1919, 10; 9 May 1919, 3; *Vestnik vsrpd* 4 (20 April 1919): 16; *Pervyi vserossiiskii s"ezd soiuza rabochikh poligraficheskogo proizvodstva*; GARF, f. R-5525, op. 1, d. 8 (mandate commission report for Special Congress, 1919); *Vserossiiskii pechatnik* 1 (May 1919): 11–18; *Vestnik vsrpd* 6–7 (15 July 1919): 5.

nize this congress as legitimate, and called on both reds and independents to organize a new special congress that would end the schism and determine the union line and leadership. Accepted trade union rules still depended nominally on democratic procedure and majority rule, even if Nikolai Gordon cared little for either.[31]

There would be no dual unionism in revolutionary Russia, but the radical Communists had other weapons with which to seize control of the printers' union. Organizers from both Menshevik and Communist factions traversed the country, seeking to win the majority of the printing delegates to the new congress, scheduled for August 1919. The Communists enjoyed a decided advantage thanks to their role in state industry, and they used their managerial positions to silence dissenters with firing and arrests. A compositor, Bogomozov, was arrested on authority of his factory committee chairman after he complained about a meeting at which only Communists were allowed to speak. Distribution of the central union's *Vestnik,* which publicized such cases, was banned in Petrograd. Attendance at factory meetings was enforced at times by armed guards; workers were expected to endorse Communist resolutions unanimously and to elect Communist delegates to conferences by acclamation.[32]

Communists also employed a repertoire of "democratic procedures" to ensure their victories, alleged the Mensheviks. If a lawful council of representatives voted against a Communist proposal, the Communists would call a conference of factory committee representatives and claim that this body was more authoritative. Mensheviks argued that such groups were merely easier to manipulate. When a general meeting of 210 printers in Voronezh elected two independents to the congress, the provincial trade union council canceled the election and organized a new ballot in each print shop. In one shop, the red candidate warned the printers that if he were not elected, he would use his authority in the local printing section to have them all drafted into the Red Army. In the end, the independents outpolled the reds, 279–139, and the guberniia council of trade unions decided to send one delegate from each side to the congress. In Petrograd, a conference of factory committees elected fourteen independents to the fifty-person delegation, but the Petrograd Trade Union Council refused to confirm even this result and called a new election. The reds, for their part, charged the independents with similar tricks.[33]

31. GARF, f. R-5525, op. 1, d. 20, l. 7 (Printers' Union Central Committee "presidium" meeting, 8 May 1919, even though the Central Committee had not formed yet).
32. *Pechatnik* 11 (10 November [28 October] 1918): 1; 9–10 (10 October [27 September] 1918): 20; 3–4 (1 April 1919): 15, 22–23; GARF, f. R-5461, op. 1, d. 30 (meetings of Moscow union representatives, 1919), l. 26; GARF, f. R-5525, op. 1, d. 22, l. 19; *Vestnik vsrpd* 6–7 (1 December 1918): 20; 5 (30 May 1919): 13; 6–7 (15 July 1919): 13 (the original of this item, a letter from A. Dikhter, is in GARF, f. R-5525, op. 1, d. 24, l. 17).
33. GARF, f. R-5461, op. 1, d. 30 (meetings of Moscow representatives, 1919), l. 50b.; *Pechatnik* 1–2 (25 January 1919): 14; *Vserossiiskii pechatnik* 1 (28 October 1919): 8; *Pechatnik* 3–4 (1 April 1919): 2; GARF, f. R-5525, op. 1, d. 22, l. 18; *Vestnik vsrpd* 8 (15 August 1919): 5–6, 8;

When the Special Congress of Workers in the Printing Industry opened on 18 August 1919, the red organizers claimed to represent 48,600 union members. The 127 delegates in attendance included 104 Communists or Communist sympathizers, 4 Social Democratic Internationalists, 1 Zionist, 1 anarchist, 2 Mensheviks, and 15 without party affiliation. Meanwhile, the Menshevik leaders of the independent union had decided to meet separately with their own 97 delegates, and they refused to legitimate the Special Congress by giving the standard account of their activities during their term of office. The VTsSPS chairman, Mikhail Tomskii (himself a former printer), gave a conciliatory address at the congress's opening, but he concluded that the existing independent union had refused all efforts to end the divisions between the two groups. The schism engineered by the Communist Gordon now became the crime for which the Mensheviks were to hang. Before the congress had concluded its business, the VTsSPS ruled that the old central council was dissolved, and that the central committee elected at this congress would henceforth represent the new All-Russian Union of Workers in Printing Production—a name chosen deliberately to include the widest possible range of workers and to distinguish itself from the old Union of Workers in the Printing Trade.[34] There would be no dual unions.

Communist printers now ruled the national union, its Petrograd branch, and many locals, but Moscow printers remained loyal to their independent line and their Menshevik leaders. Even in the aftermath of the Special Congress, Moscow printers voted by secret ballot in December 1919 to preserve the Menshevik majority, giving eighteen of twenty-five seats on the board to supporters of trade union independence.[35] Conflict between the Communist center and the Menshevik majority in Moscow continued to boil, and Communists themselves remained divided. Nikolai Gordon repeatedly called on Aleksandr Tikhanov, chairman of the union central committee, to dissolve the Moscow board. Tikhanov refused, replying that to dissolve the Moscow board by force was a confession of weakness, not a show of strength. Other Communists agreed. Gordon's man on the union central committee in Moscow, Gegel', sent a discouraged letter back to Petrograd on 24 April 1920. Their proposal to dissolve the Moscow union had suffered utter defeat in the Moscow Trade Union Council, for which Gegel' blamed its Communist chairman, Grigorii Mel'nichanskii. Nor could Gegel' find much support among former Moscow Communist printers, now ensconced in the party and industrial bureaucracy: none of them wanted to return to their shops or to their union responsibilities. We found them

---

GARF, f. R-5525, op. 1, d. 6 (materials on the First All-Russian Congress of the Printers' Union, 1919), l. 6; *Vserossiiskii pechatnik* 1 (28 October 1919): 6.

34. GARF, f. R-5525, op. 1, d. 12 (report on the Special Congress of the Printers' Union, 1919), ll. 2-3; *Vserossiiskii pechatnik* 1 (28 October 1919): 6; GARF, f. R-5525, op. 1, d. 10, ll. 9-10, 198; *Professional'noe dvizhenie* (22 August 1919): 4.

35. *Professional'noe dvizhenie* (19 December 1919). The victory was not widely reported.

these posts with great difficulty, complained Gegel', and now they've become careerists and scoundrels and don't give a fig for the union. He tried to appeal to the Cheka to repress the Moscow Mensheviks, but came up against the unexpected resistance of Tomskii and Mel'nichanskii. "Moscow is a genuine swamp, in which you can be drowned any minute ... ," he wrote. The Moscow leader Kefali was going around the city denouncing Lenin and the Communists, but he had such powerful defenders that he remained immune to prosecution. "I need as much evidence as possible against him, so Mel'nichanskii and Tomskii can't save him."[36]

Moscow leaders perhaps played into Gordon's and Gegel''s hands, or perhaps they felt that political momentum was shifting in their favor. The Moscow board took advantage of a visit by an English trade union delegation to call a general meeting of printers on 23 May 1920, an episode that propelled the Printers' Union into the historical limelight for a brief moment.[37] A thunderous attack on Soviet power by the union leader Kefali, followed by an appearance by the fugitive leader of the Socialist Revolutionary Party, Viktor Chernov, led to the arrest of several Moscow board members.[38] Gordon, meanwhile, feared the union central committee was still dragging its feet. He urged that the Moscow board be dissolved without further delay: to this effect, he was sending a "shock group" of printer-agitators to Moscow and organizing a big mass rally in Petrograd to denounce the "Moscow yellow sons of bitches."[39] On 17 June a printers' conference negotiating a new industry tarif voted 30–5 to demand the dissolution of the Moscow union as a band of "saboteurs and Pilsudski supporters." The following day, at long last, the Moscow Trade Union Council capitulated to the party radicals and agreed to dissolve the "counterrevolutionary" board. Eleven members of the old board and twenty-nine elected representatives, factory committee members, and union members were arrested by the Moscow Cheka and held without charge for three months; some of them were then sentenced to concentration camp terms of from six months to two years.[40] The union apparatus was now and henceforth permanently in the hands of the Communists.

The Menshevik losers argued with much justification that the Communists had won the printing workers over to the principles of productivism by illegitimate methods, by the methods of "Cheka, prison, and bullets." Writing in de-

---

36. Gordon to Tikhanov, 2 March 1920, and Tikhanov to Gordon, 16 March 1920, in GARF, f. R-5525, op. 2, d. 11 (correspondence with guberniia branches on liquidation of Menshevik leadership), ll. 75–76; Gegel' to Gordon, 24 April 1920, in TsGAIPD SPb, f. 435, op. 1, d. 41 (correspondence with Gordon), ll. 85–85ob.

37. Vladimir N. Brovkin, *Behind the Front Lines of the Civil War: Political Parties and Social Movements in Russia, 1918–1922* (Princeton, 1994), 254–56; Jonathan Aves, *Workers against Lenin: Labour Protest and the Bolshevik Dictatorship* (London, 1996), 65–69.

38. *British Labour Delegation to Russia, 1920. Report* (London, 1920).

39. Gordon to Tikhanov, 5 June 1920, in GARF, f. R-5525, op. 2, d. 11, l. 74.

40. GARF, f. R-5525, op. 2, d. 48 (materials on the all-Russian tarif conference, 1920), l. 5; *Professional'noe dvizhenie*, 26 June 1920: 3; *Sotsialisticheskii vestnik* 1 (1 February 1921): 15–16.

spair from his hospital bed in Petrograd in May 1919, a Menshevik printer named Rubin had told his Moscow comrades that resistance to the reds' tactics seemed impossible: the Communists packed meetings with their supporters and threatened any dissidents with arrest. Even if the Mensheviks could gain a majority at a meeting, he wrote, "the same old song would begin again." The Communists would "rail from the podium about breaking up the union and arresting our leaders." This was a crucial difference between the two parties. The Mensheviks proudly insisted they would never use the Communist methods of "lies, slander, demagogy, and bayonets," only "speech, the pen, and the ballot." We criticize in words but obey in our actions, the union leader Kefali editorialized in April 1919.[41]

The Communists seemed not to share the Mensheviks' commitment to democracy and democratic methods. At the February 1919 meeting that gave birth to the red splinter union in Moscow, the Communist Perepechko reportedly said that the idea of popular rule (*narodopravstvo*) should be consigned to the archive, that it was time for the dictatorship of the proletariat to be established throughout the world through means of "blood and iron."[42] But was this rejection of democratic procedure an inherent attribute of the Communists' ideology or only the position of a militant faction within it? Is it possible to see the Communist takeover of the printers' union as part of a concerted and general assault by the party center, a coordinated effort to implement its monopoly of power wherever and however it could? The history of this particular Communist victory suggests otherwise, and thus offers important insight into the process of the Communists' consolidation of power.

Trade unionists, Communists and independents alike, believed in trade union unity, even if for Communists unity meant tolerating elements that opposed their cardinal principles of socialist labor relations. The idea of two or more unions representing the same workers was anathema to most Communist union leaders. But to other Communists less imbued with the principles of the historic trade union movement, the existence of a so-called proletarian union that opposed the tasks of socialist construction was an even greater insult to proletarian values. Communists, consequently, were divided in their attitudes toward the independent printers' union. The leading Moscow Communist printer, Aleksandr Borshchevskii, and leaders of the VTsSPS such as Tomskii and S. A. Lozovskii placed greater value on unity than on ideological purity.[43] For Nikolai Gordon, the correct ideological line was more important than outmoded trade union solidarity, and power was more important even than the correct ideological line. In the battle over the Printers' Union, Gordon and his supporters

---

41. *Pervyi vserossiiskii s"ezd soiuza rabochikh poligraficheskogo proizvodstva*, 59; *Pechatnik* 1–2 (25 January 1919): 2; 12 (10 December [27 November] 1918): 3; 3–4 (1 April 1919): 7; GARF, f. R-5461, op. 3, d. 12 (correspondence of the Central Council of the Union of Workers in the Printing Trade on the struggle between noncommunist and communist printers, 1919), l. 790b.
42. *Pechatnik* 3–4 (1 April 1919): 20.
43. GARF, f. R-5525, op. 1, d. 10, ll. 9–10.

were directly responsible for the manipulative and coercive way in which the independent printers' union was defeated.

The assault on the Petrograd union in 1918 had begun on the personal initiative of Gordon, who had been agitating against the Menshevik majority since being outvoted in April 1918. But he met with opposition within his own party and among workers. When Gordon was agitating for the dissolution of the Menshevik union majority in September 1918, his party fraction proposed to send him off to the Red Army, causing him to storm out of the party meeting in a fury. A year later, in the midst of the campaign to organize the Special Congress, a printer at the First State Print Shop protested when Gordon showed up at a meeting there armed with a revolver: "Our union chairman has to come to our meeting armed like a gendarme, and the union is now acting like the [tsarist] 'State Council.'" Several times Gordon's calls to dissolve the Petrograd board of directors had been rejected by the city's trade union council and by the VTsSPS. Even in planning their coup against the union in November 1918, Gordon's Communists feared a reaction to their highhanded methods, and were relieved and surprised when none materialized. The fait accompli of 6 November was successful but unpopular with party union bosses; Moscow Communist printers applauded the victory but condemned the tactics Gordon had employed. The Petrograd Trade Union Council also acceded to the coup only after the fact.[44]

Radical pressures acted in Moscow, too, although not directly from printers. The soviet of the district in which the union office was located tried twice late in 1918 and again in 1919 to evict the union, only to be overruled by the Moscow Soviet and the Moscow Trade Union Council. The union journal, *Pechatnik,* was closed "forever" for anti-Soviet propaganda in September 1918 by order of the Press Department of the Moscow Soviet, but this order was overruled on pressure from VTsSPS. The initiative to follow Petrograd's lead came from Petrograd, not from the Moscow party. The final decision to walk out of the union board of directors was made in Moscow by a small group of Communist printers. On the day after the walkout, the Communist fraction of the Moscow Trade Union Council unanimously objected, and the Moscow City Party Committee also condemned the Communist printers' action. Radical Communist printers thus found themselves estranged from the party mainstream.[45]

It is difficult to assess the extent of genuine rank-and-file support for these tactics or for this outcome. Communists like Gordon had their supporters; 400 printers joined in the assault on the Petrograd union in November 1918. Three

---

44. TsGAIPD SPb, f. 435, op. 1, d. 3, l. 3; TsGA SPb, f. 4804, op. 3, d. 22 (general meetings in Petrograd print shops, 1919), l. 62; *Materialy,* 104–5; *Pechatnik* 9–10 (10 October [27 September] 1918): 16; 12 (10 December [27 November] 1918): 10.

45. *Pechatnik* 12 (10 December [27 November] 1918): 8; 1–2 (25 January 1919): 12; 3–4 (1 April 1919): 18; 9–10 (10 October [27 September] 1918): 2; 11 (10 November [28 October] 1918): 9; *Materialy,* 185–86 (memoirs of Borshchevskii).

thousand Petrograd printers voted for Communist board members in that union's last open election in April 1918; 4,000 voted for Moscow's Communists in April 1918 and some 2,000 would vote for them in the next official election in late 1919.[46] But the majority of printers in both capitals supported the Menshevik position. The situation in the provinces was more complex and unsettled. Workers in many localities had little knowledge of the split between Mensheviks and Communists, or tended to attribute it to personality conflicts and local squabbles. In the provinces, and perhaps in the capitals as well, material life—"bread and sugar"—interested workers much more than ideology.[47] Yet Mensheviks enjoyed strong support in areas such as Kiev and along the Volga. How then did the minority faction manage to triumph?

First, the Communist position enjoyed some legitimate appeal. A majority of the trade union movement, after all, had adopted the productivist principle of labor relations, and this issue remained central in the campaign to oust the Mensheviks from union leadership. The Communist union journal argued that the Menshevik board had opportunistically appealed to the greed of workers, and by negotiating high wages instead of supporting the drive for labor discipline, they had contributed to the decline of production. Moreover, high wages only led to more unemployment. Communists also sought to win votes by criticizing the inactivity of the Menshevik center: it had failed to call a national congress, it had failed to organize provincial unions.[48] Communists also appealed to patriotism and to the good "instincts" of printers, claiming they had been manipulated and led astray by the "yellow generals," moderate socialists who used the printers' union as their last legal bastion in the opposition to Soviet power.

But there is no question that Communists also willingly and readily embraced tactics of manipulation, coercion, and repression. Nikolai Gordon may have been more ruthless and less principled in his crusade to drive out the Mensheviks than other Communists, but all Communist printers welcomed the final outcome of a Communist, productivist union of printers and few tears were shed in public for the vanquished Mensheviks. Although both sides strove to place a democratic veneer on their claims for legitimacy, the times were not favorable for democratic procedure. A White army had come near to capturing Petrograd in the summer of 1919, and another would strike only 250 miles from Moscow in October. Shortly after the Voronezh election, the city was raided by an advance party of anti-Soviet cavalry, and the union board had to go into hiding for twenty-five days.[49] The rank and file remained hostage to the suppliers

---

46. *Gazeta pechatnika*, 16 December 1918; *Pechatnik* 5 (30 [18] April 1918) 6; *Professional'noe dvizhenie* (19 December 1919).

47. GARF, f. R-5525, op. 1, d. 10, l. 6; *Pervyi vserossiisskii s"ezd soiuza rabochikh poligraficheskogo proizvodstva*, 14–26.

48. *Vserossiiskii pechatnik* 2 (July 1919): 2; *Vestnik vsrpd* 8 (15 August 1919): 4; *Pervyi vserossiiskii s"ezd soiuza rabochikh poligraficheskogo proizvodstva*, 31.; GARF, f. R-5525, op. 1, d. 6, l. 8; *Vserossiiskii pechatnik* 1 (May 1919): 4, 21–23, 30; GARF, f. R-5525, op. 1, d. 10, ll. 14–15.

49. GARF, f. R-5525, op. 1, d. 22, l. 9.

of food, fuel, and shelter. Communists in the rear argued that they were facing a life-or-death struggle for the survival of the revolution. Since mid-1918, the Menshevik leaders of the printers' union had been branded as heinous betrayers of that revolution. At such times, the relatively democratic impulses of such Communists as Mikhail Tomskii gave way to the coercive and authoritarian doctrine of such Communists as Nikolai Gordon.

The battle for productivist trade unionism, however, had not yet been won. The Communist union leaders now had to demonstrate that their approach could bring benefits to their members. Menshevik voices would remain to offer principled critiques of the Communist union's practices and policies. But the history of the struggle for Communist hegemony here, so much more belligerent in this union than anywhere else, would remain part of the troubled legacy of the Printers' Union. The memories evoked by this struggle would shape a language of mutual recriminations that would embitter relations within the union and would be used again and again to ostracize dissidents and suppress discussion.

## COMMUNIST LABOR RELATIONS IN PRACTICE

Although the Communists used repression and brute force to defeat their Menshevik opponents, they also needed to win rank-and-file support through the positive appeal of their model of labor relations. Apathy was as dangerous an enemy as Kefali, and even Petrograd Communists were concerned about the lack of enthusiasm for their cause.[50] The Communists in power had to prove that their regime could best address the most pressing concerns of their worker supporters. Productivism remained the method, but consumption was the goal: "Produce more and you will eat better" was the message of the union leaders. But the years of partisan struggle had taken their toll. The rank and file seemed thoroughly disaffected from the union and its policies. A few large shops in Moscow struck in defense of the disbanded Moscow union board in 1920, but they saw their factory committee representatives arrested and replaced with more compliant ones.[51] The union and regime were now free to implement their model of labor relations, to demonstrate how centralized and coordinated economic leadership would raise production and improve the well-being of the working class.

Even fully in power, Communists continued to clash with one another over policy and practice. Symbolizing the victory of the productivist line, the union's permanent secretary, Aleksandr Tikhanov, also headed the economic organ that administered the industry, the Printing Section of the Supreme Economic Coun-

50. TsGAIPD SPb, f. 435, op. 1, d. 14 (meetings of party fraction of Petrograd Printers' Union, 1919), ll. 4–5; d. 23 (meetings of party fraction of Petrograd Printers' Union, 1920), ll. 9–100b.
51. For example, at the First Model State Print Shop: TsGAMO, f. 699, op. 1, d. 74 (First Model factory committee meetings, 1920), ll. 39, 40; GARF, f. R-5525, op. 2, d. 5 (meetings of presidium of Printers' Union Central Committee, 1920), l. 29.

cil. But he faced competition from the Moscow Printing Section, led by another Communist, Aleksandr Borshchevskii. Only late in 1920 was the situation resolved by subordinating the central section to the Moscow section: perhaps this was a reward to Moscow for finally cleaning its house of Mensheviks. Worse was the status of production in the industry: there were insufficient supplies of ink, grease, kerosene, spare parts and type, and fuel. Management conducted its work unsystematically; it failed to account for materials. Poor food supply forced workers to leave their jobs to search for bread for themselves and their families.[52]

The printing sections had little power to solve these problems. The issue of food supply had remained utterly central to Russian revolutionary politics since the first salvos of the February revolution.[53] Within the industry, managers and the productivist union tried to optimize remaining scarce resources by drastically concentrating enterprises. But most pressing was the need to stimulate individual and collective productivity with material rewards. Workers on the shop floor remained resistant to working for nothing, and together the union and industry administration attempted to implement one wage system after another in efforts to lure workers back to work. As we have seen, promised supplies of food were insufficient to reward individuals for higher productivity; what supplies reached the union ended up being divided equally among all workers, and even then, workers complained that the amount was too little to live on.[54]

Union officials blamed the poor conditions on the undervaluing of printers by the higher economic and trade union organizations. But V. V. Shmidt, the Communist labor commissar, said this was nonsense: printing was recognized as an important industry, but no union had defended its members as poorly as this one. If the union would only gather the facts and defend its requests properly, he promised to listen.[55] Was this the legacy of the Communist printers' obsession with seizing control of their union from the Mensheviks, which left them no time or energy to conduct the trade union business that their members required? Or were these Communists (like others in industry, and as the Mensheviks had long warned) simply incompetent to manage complicated economic enterprises? To preserve what levels of production they could, union officials sought to appease workers in piecemeal fashion, here managing to put a shop on the higher Red Army ration, there responding to individual requests for

52. GARF, f. R-5525, op. 2, d. 49 (collegium of Printing Section of Moscow Sovnarkhoz, 1920), ll. 30, 51.
53. See Lars T. Lih, *Bread and Authority in Russia, 1914–1921* (Berkeley, 1990); McAuley, *Bread and Justice*; Aves, *Workers against Lenin*; Paul Avrich, *Kronstadt 1921* (New York, 1970).
54. *Plenum tsentral'nogo komiteta vserossiiskogo soiuza rabochikh poligraficheskogo proizvodstva, 1920*, 19; *Vserossiiskii pechatnik* 4–5 (20 March 1920): suppl., 4; *Moskovskii pechatnik* 5 (15 April 1921): 4–5; *Vserossiiskii pechatnik* 11 (15 March 1921): 8.
55. *Plenum tsentral'nogo komiteta vserossiiskogo soiuza rabochikh poligraficheskogo proizvodstva, 1920*, 40–41.

boots or overcoats.[56] This practice helped to keep individual shops in competition with one another and to strengthen the primacy of the workplace as a unit. Internal divisions by political party, skill, gender, or age mattered less now than the survival of the workshop unit.

The struggle for resources was similarly chaotic. The Moscow Printing Section calculated that it employed 300 individuals full-time in the effort to gain supplies for the industry. Their system of allocating these supplies was in turn laden with bureaucracy and red tape. Other complaints came about the Printing Section's inability to administer the industry. Presses taken for repair disappeared for months at a time. The Printing Section was too ignorant of local conditions to allocate labor and materials rationally.[57]

Workers on the shop floor expected more from their union and more from socialism. Anger over economic conditions and the Communists' inability to feed their supporters had already fueled serious unrest in the summer of 1918, leading to political strikes and repression in that pivotal summer. Moscow printers, through their council of representatives, began to press hard in the spring of 1919 for a full month's annual vacation, in view of the special hardships of their industry and to allow more time to scour the countryside for food for their families. By the summer of 1919, the food-supply crisis was even worse, its politics now exacerbated by the simultaneous assault by the Communists on the Menshevik-led unions and the impending Special Congress. "In the name of all the freedoms we wrested from the hands of tsarism, we are prepared to march shoulder to shoulder and to repulse those who stand in the way of our achieving our demands," said a representative in July. "The consciousness of print shop workers is such that we will defend our right to a crust of bread with all our strength, that's our position." Insofar as the Communists blamed the Civil War for the shortages and crisis, Moscow printers now demanded an end to the war: "We have to lead the workers' struggle on our own.... We must demand that policies be set not by those above, but from below, so that the voice of true workers will be heard. Down with the Civil War!"[58]

A series of turbulent meetings of Moscow printers' representatives in 1919 demanded a change in food-supply policy: workers cannot work a whole day on only a half pound of bread, said one printer at an 11 July meeting: "bread and peace—that is the essence of our mood." Even after the Communists took over the national union, the confrontational mood continued into the autumn and winter of 1919. Workers at the Sixteenth and First Model print shops had

56. GARF, f. R-5525, op. 2, d. 5, l. 9; d. 33 (meetings of the Moscow union board and presidium, 1920); op. 3, d. 64 (meetings of the Petrograd union board and presidium, 1921), ll. 11, 32; TsGAMO, f. 699, op. 1, d. 63 (meetings of Moscow union presidium, 1920), l. 21.

57. *Vserossiiskii pechatnik* 4–5 (20 March 1920): suppl., 7; *Moskovskii pechatnik* 2 (15 February 1921): 8; GARF, f. R-5525, op. 3, d. 103 (Printers' Union materials on the struggle with labor desertion and theft, 1921); *Vtoraia moskovskaia gubernskaia konferentsiia 1921*, 69.

58. GARF, f. R-5461, op. 1, d. 30, ll. 17, 18ob., 30–36.

already struck on their own to demand changes in the food-supply policy; at the First Model shop, striking workers demanded the presence of Soviet officials, including the trade union chief, Tomskii, who urged restraint and promised to equalize the food-supply status of printers with that of workers in other industries. A week later, these shops had stopped work again, and angrily demanded higher wages and changes in food policy. The political content of the unrest was obvious: responding to the Menshevik union leader's suggestion that wages be tripled, a voice from the floor cried out, "He speaks correctly, and he speaks like that because he doesn't wear a leather jacket" (the standard uniform of Communist officials). The spokesperson for the Eighth State Print Shop read a resolution from fellow workers: "We workers, employees, and our families cannot live by the current regime's promises alone, we and our families are dying of starvation and cold, and we cannot live on the wages that workers in the printing trades receive." The resolution went on to demand an increase in the wage rate, a daily bread ration of one and a half pounds, freedom of the opposition press, and workers' control over the local food-supply agency. Six months later, First Model printers raised the same issues, demanding to be treated equally with workers in other industries.[59]

The Communists answered by dissolving the Menshevik union center, as we have seen, and shifting blame to the general situation, the Civil War, and the "yellow self-seekers" still left in the union movement. Printers in Petrograd, perhaps because the growing unemployment there left them especially vulnerable to retaliatory measures by the Communist leadership, endured these new tribulations silently and privately. It was during this period that Gordon came to local factory meetings armed with his revolver. Individual factory committees there prepared their own garden plots and queued at union headquarters to receive whatever cabbages, dried fish, and bread were being supplied to the city. But even in "red Petrograd," party officials admitted that "workers curse the union because of food supply; they pay their dues, but get nothing in return."[60]

Moscow printers, with a Menshevik board still in control, spoke out more forcefully. Gathering to express their anger in March 1920, Moscow printers denounced the union's failure to secure food for its members. "Our impoverished conditions, our starving families have forced us to gather here," cried one worker. "We are branded as saboteurs by the workers' and peasants' regime only because we ask for bread for our children." "The faces of starving children create the mood the regime calls 'sabotage,'" said another. The regime recommended that printers abandon their support for the Menshevik union, whose leaders cared more about political opposition than about the welfare of their members.[61]

---

59. Ibid., ll. 32, 119–119ob., 120–21; TsGAMO, f. 699, op. 1, d. 74, l. 32 (general meeting at First Model, 18 May 1920).
60. See, for example, TsGA SPb, f. 4804, op. 3, d. 22; TsGAIPD SPb, f. 435, op. 1, d. 23, l. 90ob.
61. TsGAMO, f. 699, op. 1, d. 12 (general meeting of Moscow printers, 28 March 1920), ll. 4–5; *Vserossiiskii pechatnik* 7 (29 June 1920): 1–2.

But a year later, in May 1921, after ten months under the new productivist Moscow union, a conference of the guberniia's printers remained unsatisfied. "We were urged to elect a new board to replace the yellow one, and this would place us at the forefront of the Red Army," said one delegate. "But there have been no improvements, we don't even get the bare minimum living standard. How can we work calmly?" Another agreed: "A year of the red board, from which we dreamed we'd get relief, and what do we have? A statement that they've organized 610 meetings."[62]

Printers at the Sixteenth State Print Shop were especially enraged. A month before this conference, they met to complain about the irregular distribution of pay in kind, demanding that all printers in Moscow receive the same high level of rations as certain shops designated "exemplary," demanding cash payments, clothing, and the right to move freely. These were the claims that had animated serious unrest in Petrograd in February and March 1921, the background to the revolt against Soviet power at the Kronstadt naval base.[63] The demands at the Sixteenth remained unsatisfied, and workers there stopped work on the morning of 8 June 1921 over the lack of food rations, which had not been issued since January. The political message was clear: Since the Communist Party had taken power, said the workers' resolution, "we printers have been in the most abnormal circumstances and a position of poverty. We will not work until our demands are met." Two months later, food supplies were again promised with no result. Once again the workers here stopped work, "because they have deceived us many times."[64]

The stoppage at the Sixteenth shop was never labeled a "strike," although the workers had clearly downed their tools, an action that is not always obvious from the historical record. The wide array of euphemisms for strike actions testifies to the symbolic import of this most extreme weapon in the workers' arsenal. Rather than report a strike (*stachka* or *zabastovka*), trade union and factory committee minutes recount episodes of "work stoppages" (*ostanovka raboty*), "ferment" (*brozhenie*), and "slowdowns" (*volynki*).[65] Strikes were not publicized. For example, although the Moscow union published the normally complete minutes of its presidium meetings in the union journal, in at least one case a discussion of a strike was omitted from the published version. All the same, the secret police seemed keenly aware of strike episodes, and reported them as such. The term "strike" occurred in public discourse perhaps more as

---

62. *Vtoraia moskovskaia gubernskaia konferentsiia*, 1921, 15–17.
63. TsGAMO, f. 699, op. 1, d. 134, l. 1; Aves, *Workers against Lenin*. Petrograd printers remained relatively quiet during these disturbances, a fact proudly noted by the union leadership there, and they were rewarded with special bonuses of shoes and clothing. TsGAIPD SPb, f. 435, op. 1, d. 27 (meetings of party fractions at Petrograd print shops, 1921), l. 11.
64. TsGAMO, f. 699, op. 1, d. 134 (general and factory committee meetings at Sixteenth, 1921), ll. 3, 9–13, 20.
65. See also the discussion in Aves, *Workers against Lenin*, 111–12, and Fedor Dan, *Dva goda skitanii (1919–1921)* (Berlin, 1922), 105.

a threat than as a reality. To indicate the depth of workers' opposition in October 1919, one speaker noted that the word "strike" had come from the lips of a "worker from the bench," that is, from a real worker and not a party leader. Others were congratulated by union leaders for refraining from "strikes," thus demonstrating their political maturity.[66]

The record on strikes is so incomplete that questions concerning the extent of unrest and the role that strikes played in the formation of workers' political attitudes cannot be conclusively answered. Nonetheless, the evidence at hand does illustrate some important differences within the Communist union leadership. Moscow Communists reacted to strikes as a normal if unfortunate element of labor relations. The day-to-day discussions of shop floor conflicts in the union record reflect acceptance of the notion that most conflicts had reasonable, if unfortunate, causes, and that the solution of the conflict required removing the causes, if possible, or appealing to workers' patriotism, if wages or food could not be procured immediately. A pragmatic workerism prevailed among trade union leaders in Moscow and would continue to characterize the movement there even into the 1930s.

The record in Petrograd suggests a different, more politicized understanding of labor conflict. Here Gordon's militancy gave little credit to workers' expressed needs. The Petrograd leadership interpreted strikes as something quite alien to a consciously socialist proletariat. Instead of reporting the specific circumstances of a given labor stoppage, the Petrograd union leaders were more likely to blame some "enemy" or "outside agitator" for the event, as though workers themselves could not possibly wish to use "extreme measures" to defend their interests. Discussing unrest in enterprises in May 1920, the union board suggested "black hundreds" elements might be responsible in one shop. In another case small groups of workers hostile to communism were blamed for infecting the rest of their shop: here the union appointed special factory guards to inform the factory committee immediately about conversations on the shop floor. The Petrograd party believed that factory committee leaders encouraged strikes in order to ingratiate themselves with their workers. A February 1922 strike at the Fourteenth State Print Shop was blamed on the plant's own red director, the Communist Dudarev, who should have tried harder to wrest extra pay from his trust. The same police report that described the strike recounted Dudarev's entire political past: he was allegedly a Menshevik who had reported on his party application that he had formerly been a Socialist Revolutionary. Dudarev was thus ascribed with guilt by association and for masking his true past. A wave of strikes in August 1922 was blamed not on the market or economic circumstances but on the "criminal behavior" of

66. The strike is discussed in the minutes of the Moscow union presidium meeting, 22 May 1920, in GARF, f. R-5525, op. 2, d. 5, l. 19; the corresponding journal report is *Vserossiiskii pechatnik* 7 (29 June 1920). Cheka reports were available only for Petrograd: TsGAIPD SPb, f. 457, op. 1, d. 53 (political reports on Petrograd industry, 1921), ll. 472–75; GARF, f. R-5461, op. 1, d. 30, l. 35; TsGAIPD SPb, f. 435, op. 1, d. 27, l. 11.

the local printing trust.[67] Conscious workers did not strike against socialist industry.

Strikes were symbolically dangerous to the regime and hence provoked special attention. Other forms of everyday resistance were less risky and more widespread. Absenteeism (*progul*) was epidemic: workers left work for days at a time, even in the face of strict punishment (including arrest) for such "indiscipline." The problem of absenteeism was solved only by improvement in the regularity and amount of pay. Theft of factory property also increased, as workers took paper, light bulbs, and anything they could steal that could be exchanged for food on the black market.[68] Such behavior indicated to both Communists and Mensheviks the "immaturity" of Russia's working class, its "narrow-mindedness," its lack of a proper "socialist consciousness." For Mensheviks, the low cultural level of the "masses," even in the highly skilled printing industry, was one reason why Russia was not ready for socialism and why the Communist experiments in socialist labor relations were doomed to fail. Communists preferred to blame short-term factors for the behavior of this mass: the "best workers" had volunteered for the Red Army or were posted to Soviet commissariats. What remained even in the printing industry, they claimed, were women, youths, and semipeasants whose exposure to a proletarian ethos was too brief to generate the proper consciousness.[69]

Both parties were wrong to characterize the printers, with their traditions of intellectualism and independence, as a "mass" driven only by their stomachs, not their heads. Activists were blinded by old dichotomies between "economic" and "political" consciousness, and their political rhetoric failed to acknowledge the fundamental symbiosis between welfare and politics. The issue of food had been an important political catalyst in revolutionary Russia. It was the failure of the Provisional Government to improve the supply of bread and foodstuffs that contributed to its loss of popular support in October 1917. Subsistence was seen as a basic human right. The Communists in power blamed their failure to improve the food supply on many obstacles beyond their control—loss of territory, blockade, and war—but workers' protests over the regime's continuing failure to supply food signaled not only that workers were starving but also that the socialist government had broken the social contract. It was illegal and dangerous to couch these protests in terms of rights and of the social contract

---

67. TsGAIPD SPb, f. 435, op. 1, d. 23, l. 90b.; d. 29 (meetings of party collectives of Petrograd print shops, 1921), l. 157; d. 78 (meetings of the party bureau of the Petrograd union, 1921), ll. 1, 35; f. 457, op. 1, d. 65 (Petrograd political reports, 1922), l. 91.

68. GARF, f. R-5525, op. 3, d. 103, ll. 3-8; TsGAMO, f. 699, op. 1, d. 136 (general and factory committee meetings at Twentieth, 1921), ll. 5, 36; d. 145 (general and factory committee meetings at First Model, 1921), ll. 20, 23, 24; GARF, f. R-5525, op. 3, d. 106 (Petrograd union comrades disciplinary courts, 1921), ll. 175-209; TsGA SPb, f. 4804, op. 4, d. 19 (meetings at Petrograd print shops, 1920), l. 162.

69. *Vestnik vsrpd* 2 (20 March 1918): 12; 3 (18 April 1918): 7; *Pechatnik* 5 (30 [17] April 1918): 7-8; *Vserossiiskii pechatnik* 2 (July 1919): 11; 6 (10 June 1920): 1; 10 (15 February 1921): 9; *Materialy*, 93.

in 1920. In 1920, as in 1916, the cry "We're starving!" was morally indisputable and therefore safer than the claim "The government doesn't protect our welfare."

And workers *were* starving. Early in 1918 the regime enacted measures intended to make urban food supply totally dependent on the state, including curbs on workers' right to travel beyond the city limits to purchase grain and severe punishment for "speculation." But the state struggled in vain to satisfy the subsistence needs of its dependents. By January 1919, for example, only five or six days' reserve of flour remained in the capital. In Moscow printers were entitled to one pound of bread a day in 1920, but there, as elsewhere, delivery was not guaranteed. Production plummeted as workers devoted all their time and resources to foraging for food, and many died. At the First Model State Print Shop in Moscow, 174 printers—9.5 percent of the plant's workforce—died in eleven months from mid-1919 to May 1920. The average death rate for all government print shops in this period was the same.[70]

Even at this margin of subsistence, however, supposedly "narrow-minded" printers remained conscious of more than their stomachs. They were especially incensed that workers in the tobacco, leather, chemical, and metal industries, whose products had immediate value in exchange for food, lived better than printers, whose printed word had been as valuable for the revolution as bayonets and bullets. We don't want privileges, argued the delegate Kazatskii in 1921, "we speak only of equalization. . . . It's not a misfortune when everyone suffers, but if I suffer and my neighbor finds a way not to suffer, then this causes unrest." The failure of the regime to feed its citizens was a political failure: it was not Lloyd George who blocked Russia's food supply but the regime's policy of seizing grain by force, they had argued in December 1919. "The workers' power does not support workers' interests!"[71]

Communists and Mensheviks accused each other of exploiting the workers' subsistence demands, a practice they labeled demagoguery. One unionist argued that the 80 percent of Printers' Union members who belonged to no party cared only about food. But in the town of Penza, when local Communists promised cheese and butter to workers who joined the red union, just like those who had earlier left the independent union, printers said no. "We're workers, not sandwich makers." How were workers and union leaders to translate this anger into programmatic terms when both sides claimed to represent "class" interests? Opponents could be called foul names. Communists charged that the "leaden army" under the Mensheviks "smelled like decay and mold, as from a swamp"; the independent union was a "yellow sore," a "yellow depravity." The Men-

70. TsGAMO, f. 699, op. 1, d. 60, ll. 25, 38; *Gazeta pechatnika,* 19 January 1919; TsGAMO, f. 699, op. 1, d. 12, ll. 2, 5; d. 74, ll. 8, 32; GARF, f. R-5525, op. 1, d. 34, l. 6; VSNKh, Poligraficheskii otdel, *Obzor deiatel'nosti za 1918–1920,* 34.

71. TsGAMO, f. 699, op. 1, d. 74, l. 32; GARF, f. R-5525, op. 1, d. 34; TsGAMO, f. 699, op. 1, d. 12; *Vtoraia moskovskaia gubernskaia konferentsiia, 1921,* 18; GARF, f. R-5525, op. 1, d. 34, ll. 10, 17.

sheviks countered by attacking the Communists' bureaucratization of the union: You've taken away the workers' soul and instilled in the union the soul of pencil pushers and typists, one of them claimed at their national congress in 1921.[72]

How did such class identities emerge from and structure the politics of this period? In political terms, this core of pride in their status as workers, their proletarian collectivism and egalitarianism found greatest scope for expression at the level of individual print shops. The failure of the centralized economic apparatus to support workers and their families reinforced the centrality of the workshop, which assumed more and more welfare functions. To some extent, the factories did become the "federated republics" denounced by the activists as unacceptable anarchism. Indeed, the more the central union arena focused on the struggles between the Communists and the Mensheviks, the productivists and the independents, the more important and autonomous became the individual units of production. The individual print shop emerged in the course of this political and economic contest as a site of politics, production, and welfare.

## SOCIAL DEMOCRACY ON THE SHOP FLOOR

Continuing a practice begun in the course of the 1917 revolution, the factory meeting remained the foundation for direct socialist democracy. The general meeting elected factory committees, soviet deputies, and delegates to conferences. The general meeting expressed the will of the workers when they wanted to convey their views to their superiors and their representatives, as we have seen. Workers at meetings listened to reports from delegates, factory management, and union officials on current problems and progress.

It is clear that in the first years of the revolution, regular meetings took place at frequent intervals, often for an hour or more after the end of work. At the First Model Print Shop, for which records go back as far as 1919, workers met together two or three times a month, and in 1920 often weekly, although there appears to be no set pattern for the meeting intervals. General meetings were especially frequent during times of crisis: at the Sixteenth Print Shop, for example, workers' grievances over pay led to a series of work stoppages in the spring of 1921, all of them accompanied by meetings at which workers raised their demands and officials tried to respond to them. Emergency meetings sometimes went on for hours.[73] The bureaucratization of factory democracy ob-

---

72. GARF, f. R-5525, op. 1, d. 34, ll. 7, 18; *Tretii vserossiiskii s"ezd soiuza rabochikh poligraficheskogo proizvodstva, 1921*, 9, 15, 14; *Vtoraia moskovskaia gubernskaia konferentsiia, 1921*, 15; *Vestnik vsrpd* 8 (15 August 1919): 7; *Revoliutsionnyi pechatnik* (Petrograd), 1 January 1919, 9.

73. TsGAMO, f. 699, op. 1, d. 44 (general and factory committee meetings at First Model, 1919), d. 74, d. 145, d. 269 (general and factory committee meetings at First Model, 1922). The minutes of meetings at the Sixteenth shop were the only ones to record the time of the meetings: ibid., d. 134 for 1921 and d. 266 for 1922.

served by Marc Ferro as part of the breakdown of the revolutionary enthusiasm of 1917 was reversed in this period when the factory had become the focus of production and subsistence for Russian printers.[74] In fact, this level of participation would never again be attained, but the ideal of total mobilization through participatory print shop life would remain a permanent aspiration of the trade union.

Empowered by the general meeting, the factory committees constituted another key unit of democratic practice in Soviet Russia. Communist political culture prized democratic legitimacy, however symbolic and forced, at least during this early period of Soviet rule. According to standard procedure, committees were to be elected, evaluated, and reelected at regular intervals at general meetings. In practice, the productivist trade union sought to subordinate factory committees to trade unions and to standardize their operations and behaviors.[75] Local Communist Party cells ensured political reliability by discussing and approving candidates for the factory committees in advance. In shops where Communist influence was weak, however, as at the First Model Print Shop, elections proceeded differently. Here in May 1920, an election commission supervised the preparation of "party lists" of factory committee candidates. To be eligible for election, a list had to be endorsed by the signatures of at least fifty plant workers. Elections to the committee were conducted by list, with the elected committee to represent the proportional support for each of these lists. In the end, representatives of three lists secured seats on the new committee: the "nonparty trade union independence list" (a euphemism for the politically endangered Mensheviks) elected six members; the "nonparty" list (representing a halfway house to Communism) elected two members; and the Communists elected one.[76]

The party and party-dominated trade union could monitor these deviations from proletarian unity, but could not or did not yet dare to prevent them altogether. Nonetheless, all actions of local enterprises were ultimately subject to approval by the superior trade union body. Factory committees could be recalled by their own constituents, and their election also needed to be ratified by the trade union's guberniia board, a requirement that gave the boards substantial power to intervene in local affairs. It should be clear by now that the workers at Moscow's First Model plant demonstrated a fiercely independent political line, protected perhaps by their large numbers. They were much more willing than workers in other enterprises to link their economic discontent, which everybody shared, to political support for the Menshevik opposition. The Mensheviks' leader, Fedor Dan, represented First Model in the Moscow Soviet un-

74. Marc Ferro, "La Naissance du système bureaucratique en URSS," *Annales: Economies, Sociétés, Civilisations* 1976: 243–60; see also Ferro, *La Révolution de 1917: Octobre, naissance d'une société* (Paris, 1976).

75. See Husband, *Revolution in the Factory*; Sirianni, *Workers Control and Socialist Democracy*, chap. 2.

76. TsGAMO, f. 699, op. 1, d. 74, ll. 34–36.

til the summer of 1920, when he was forced to flee Moscow.[77] Even as late as March 1922, Mensheviks joined Communists in the factory committee leadership. The union tried to oust this committee and other Mensheviks by fixing election rules to ensure the victory of Communists only, but the workers and the committee would have none of this, using a secret ballot to elect Mensheviks, including the veteran V. Fedotov.[78]

At this point, the regime decided to break the Menshevik hold at First Model once and for all, but still the printers fought back. Using the excuse of a decline in orders, the plant administration announced that it would have to lay off workers. On 7 March 1922, Fedotov announced to the factory committee that he had seen the lists of those designated to be dismissed: "It's clear that what's happening is a fundamental purge of the enterprise of elements that are politically undesirable." Outraged printers here agreed to seek mediation, but they also threatened a one-day strike to protest the firings, "a flagrant reprisal against workers who dared to oppose their opinion to the will of the entrepreneurs [*predprinimatelei*]." The dismissals proceeded anyway, and the people fired were unable to find work elsewhere: they had been blacklisted by the union. A new general meeting on 24 March 1922 denounced this action (by a vote of 800 to 10, with 15 abstentions), but to no avail. By the end of March, the union leadership had annulled the earlier factory committee election and the local Communist cell selected a more compliant group of local leaders. Echoes of the opposition lingered into the summer, when workers attempted to elect Fedotov as their delegate to the union's guberniia congress, even though he had been expelled from the union.[79] Unanimity had given printers at the First Model shop the resources to resist the union's political manipulations, but Communist control of work and employment ultimately proved an insurmountable obstacle to these printers' political self-expression.

While the political struggle was more sharply articulated at First Model than elsewhere, the relationship of factory committees with their worker constituents rested everywhere on a mutuality of interests. The factory was both the point of production and the point of survival, and the factory committee played a vital role in defending its workers' ability both to produce and to survive. As Chapter 1 has shown, the boundaries between workers and management were porous indeed, since so many plant directors had risen through the factory committee ranks. The distinction between bosses and bossed was further diminished because the factory committee assumed so many production and disciplinary functions. This was part of the productivist program of the Communist Party trade unionists, but life itself taught that print shops would

77. Ibid., l. 56; Dan, *Dva goda skitanii*, 22–24.
78. TsGAMO, f. 699, op. 1, d. 269, ll. 55, 71–72; *Pechatnik* 20 (8 October 1925): 11.
79. TsGAMO, f. 699, op. 1, d. 269, ll. 78, 125; d. 270 (general and factory committee meetings at First Model, 1922), ll. 59, 63–66, 82, 125, 95; see also Simon Pirani, "The Moscow Workers' Movement in 1921 and the Role of Non-Partyism," *Europe-Asia Studies* 56, no. 1 (2004): 143–60.

not provide livelihoods for their workers unless they continued to produce and to produce efficiently.

Factory committees, consequently, were intimately involved with questions of productivity, rates of pay, work rules and hours, and discipline. In each of these areas they earned the support of their constituents only insofar as they mediated between what the economic circumstances demanded and what the workers thought was possible. Theft constituted a serious drain on enterprise resources, and factory committees themselves would punish culprits with dismissal if necessary. The First Model factory committee repeatedly took up the question of mass pilferage. Slacking on the job also drew reprimands from the factory committees, who organized conflict committees and comrades' courts to adjudicate complaints and mete out penalties. By 1920, the factory committee at First Model, that citadel of Menshevik independence, had become productivists despite themselves. At the same meeting in November 1920 in which they rejected attendance at their meetings by a Communist union official, the factory committee adopted strict new rules to discourage tardiness, with penalties ranging from loss of pay and bonuses to trial by factory committee and ultimately by a disciplinary court.[80]

Factory committees assumed these functions because no other authority was capable of carrying them out in the chaotic economy of the Civil War period. The Cheka had its hands full monitoring political dissent, and limited its coercive powers to arresting workers for overt political deviations, not for crimes of production. The factory committee's powers of coercion were much more immediate, and its authority was much more legitimated by its intimate involvement in administering positive rewards for production and compliance: the all-important food and commodity rations. While democratic processes and production needs occupied an important place on the agendas of factory-level representative bodies, distribution and welfare functions occupied the overwhelming majority of the factory committee's time and activities. Success in this realm (which was aided by maintaining a minimum level of production) furnished these committees with their legitimacy before their constituents.

Food supply, an essential component of wages in most of this period, absorbed a huge amount of energy. A general meeting at First Model in January 1920 voted on how to distribute a newly arrived delivery of meat. Sausage, flour, millet, horsemeat, potatoes, cabbage, beets, and apples—all passed through the hands of the factory committees, to be distributed by elaborate systems of priority and entitlement. Larger enterprises, such as First Model, ran their own public canteens and shops, whose boards were elected by workers and monitored by the factory committees. Enterprises set up produce gardens, devoting many hours to the problems of locating labor, draft horses, and seed.[81]

---

80. *Moskovskii pechatnik* 5 (15 April 1921): 14; TsGAMO, f. 699, op. 1, d. 44, l. 32; d. 74, ll. 11, 66, 72, 73; d. 145, ll. 20, 23; d. 136, l. 5.
81. TsGAMO, f. 699, op. 1, d. 74, ll. 2, 12, 17, 29.

They administered communal housing for their employees, organized dentists, medics, barbershops, shoemakers, laundries, and nurseries to serve workers and their families. Even in 1922, a year after the inauguration of NEP and new money-based wage systems, factory committees remained active in distribution of basic necessities.

Many other influences and loyalties competed with the enterprise, but the intensity of the effort to keep production alive and the centrality of the elected workers' committees in this process indicate how central the enterprise unit had become as the source of identification and solidarity. To a great extent, the relation of workers to the means of production was direct and all-encompassing. The factory was life: it was their livelihood, the foundation of their politics, and the very means of subsistence.

Politics at the level of the shop and the trade union pitted Mensheviks against Communists, but also revealed significant disagreements among Communists themselves, officials who occupied contradictory class positions as managers, union leaders, and state bureaucrats. By the end of 1920, serious conflicts at the top of the Communist Party had also emerged over the interpretation of workers' protests and the direction of party policy. As William Rosenberg has shown, the discontent and anger at the shop floor level provided the raw material that fueled the so-called Trade Union Debate and the controversy over the militarization of the transport industry, as party leaders sought to use workers' anger to support their own visions of the socialist path. On one side, Trotskii demanded the subordination of trade unions to the discipline of the central state. On another, the Workers' Opposition called for a syndicalist system in which trade union democracy would constitute the foundation of the state.[82] At this moment, when the Communist leadership of the Printers' Union appeared on the national stage, it unanimously supported the Platform of the Ten, a compromise position endorsed in early 1921 by Lenin, Zinov'ev, and, most important, the national trade union leadership. Although personality conflicts produced serious splits and continual bickering within the Printers' Union, the great philosophical and political gulf between Mensheviks and Communists in the union perhaps compelled all of the Communists to rally around the trade union leadership in matters of national importance, such as the Trade Union Debate of 1920–21. The most ardent defender of the Platform of the Ten in the Printers' Union press was Aleksandr Tikhanov, at one time a Menshevik but now member of the union's central committee.[83] He and Gordon had quarreled on numerous occasions; the fact that they were now on the same side reinforces the sense that the Printers' Union feared much tougher political alternatives than the transport workers' union's central committee (Tsektran) versus the

---

82. Rosenberg, "Social Background to Tsektran"; see also Schapiro, *Origin of the Communist Autocracy*, 253–95.

83. *Vserossiiskii pechatnik* 10 (15 February 1921): 2–9. Tikhanov's editorial on the Brest peace in March 1918 was fiercely anti-Bolshevik: *Vestnik vsrpd* 2 (20 March 1918): 2.

VTsSPS. Gordon's authoritarian style might have made him more sympathetic to Trotskii's disciplinarity, but Gordon was above all a creature of Zinov'ev, and he did not speak publicly against him in the trade union discussion. Victory over the Menshevik heresy among the rank and file was too precious, too fragile, and too costly to risk inviting a new division within the union.

This first phase of the Russian revolution, from the October revolution to the Communist victory in the Civil War, helped to determine the political contours of the socialist regime. Party ideology combined with material exigencies and competing socialist visions to produce a centralist, coercive, and militant political culture, yet the political and organizational experience of the Printers' Union during the Civil War suggests that this political culture did not go unchallenged. The straitened economic circumstances accompanying the socialist revolution and the Communists' own preferences had shaped a trade union politics that emphasized the statist, productivist model of labor relations, but the Menshevik alternative of a trade union apparatus independent of the state found special resonance among the printers. Quite independently of either of these social democratic viewpoints, printers on the shop floor often implemented their own more autonomous models of labor relations: a "narrow-minded" approach that demanded satisfaction of workers' material needs and occasionally an anarchist approach that pitted shop against shop or city against city for access to scarce resources. Communist trade union procedure in principle subordinated local units to central authority and control; trade union practice, whether Communist or Menshevik, revealed that local factory committees and managers assumed many of the economic and distributive functions that a productivist model would have reserved for the state.

The trade union experience during the Civil War was a fundamentally conflictual one, but it was especially so among printers. Communists themselves disagreed about policy and practice, whether in the realm of labor relations or democratic procedure. Most of the principals in the struggle to subdue the independent Menshevik-dominated Printers' Union were Communists, yet they hardly spoke with a single voice: the Moscow party organization supported a dual union strategy if it would help to oust the Mensheviks, but the Moscow trade union leadership opposed this policy. Local Communists disagreed on tactics for winning elections and governing their enterprises. Political conflict in the Printers' Union may have been more visible than elsewhere because the conflict here pitted Communists against Mensheviks as well as Communists against one another, and the parties in the conflict were more ready to invoke their alternative visions of the revolution in support of their cause. But the printers' experience demonstrates that the kind of political ferment that erupted in late 1920 and early 1921 with a series of oppositions to the Leninist leadership had roots that went deep into the working class and socialist party organizations. The printers' experience also reveals the variety of political styles that shaped the course of the revolution and the building of socialism in Soviet Russia. Petrograd and Moscow differed on many levels, and also in the political culture of their Printers' Union branches: Petrograd's Nikolai Gordon led his union with an authority that bordered on ruthlessness. He would not be deterred by democratic principles when it came to establishing Communist power within the Printers' Union. The Moscow Communists seemed more easygoing, more tolerant, and more pragmatic. For them, trade unionism required mass unity and solidarity, even at the expense of ideological purity. These differences would continue to affect the practices of the Printers' Union in the years to come.

Finally, although printers themselves would choose among four visions of labor relations, or practice any of them at different times and for different reasons, their political responses remained predicated on a fundamental and unshaken identity as workers and as members of the working class. "We're workers, not sandwich makers." The importance of this class identity and how it helped to structure the way printers made sense of their role in the new socialist society are the subjects of the next chapter.

## CHAPTER 3

## THE CIVIL WAR AND WORKING-CLASS CULTURE

*Not one class has starved like the printers.*
—Delegate from Sixteenth Print Shop, May 1921

The experiences produced by the Russian Civil War left a lasting impact on Soviet political culture. The values and identities of socialist Russia's citizens were shaped in conflict: in economic struggle between those with wealth and those without, in internecine conflicts between city and country, among socialist parties, between metropole and mobilized ethnic separatists, and in a national struggle pitting Russian revolutionaries against the forces of foreign armies and capital. Soviet identities were also forged in conditions of desperate scarcity, as has been seen. The war experience itself contributed to a culture of militarism and masculinity; its heroes—the Red Army commanders Lev Trotskii, Vasilii Chapaev, and Semen Budennyi—were men of action and will who became celebrated for their individual exploits.[1]

In their native print shops, at home in the cities, Russia's printers struggled to preserve their political organizations, their workshops, their families, and themselves. For workers such as these, the Civil War experience of conflict and scarcity also helped to shape and reshape their identities as workers, as men and women, and as revolutionary citizens. In this process, Russia's printers engaged these challenging circumstances in terms of class, a familiar and historically rooted source of identity and recipe for action. But the specific experience of printers in this period demonstrates the multiplicity of class positions, as well as the appeal of identities based on smaller aggregates than class: city, workshop, and family. If the Soviet regime and its local plenipotentiaries, the red trade unions, sought to impart a uniform, single working-class culture, workers on the shop floors and in the communities resisted this pressure to create a monolithic culture and to subscribe to a single overarching class-based collective identity.

## THE PROLETARIAN MYTH IN RUSSIAN HISTORY

The centrality of the proletarian myth in Russian revolutionary history—the idea that the proletariat is the one true revolutionary class—relates to the well-known narrative of Russian backwardness. Unlike Western European societies, whose capitalist structures developed gradually, Russian society advanced suddenly and dramatically into the industrial world. Village peasants, with little experience of markets, cities, or industrial work habits, tumbled into the alien world of the factory with no mediating experience to soften the impact of this transition on their mental worlds. The resulting paradigm of a peasant/proletarian dichotomy has dominated the historiography of Russian labor since the 1870s, when G. V. Plekhanov first noted the difference between urban and rural workers, the city *zavodskii* and the peasant *fabrichnyi,* yet the significance of this difference has remained open to debate.[2] Some scholars have argued that the rural ties of urban workers facilitated revolutionary activism; others followed Plekhanov's argument, the predominant Soviet historiography, and comparative studies of Western European labor to assert that political consciousness and activism were most pronounced and sophisticated among the urbanized, hereditary proletariat, which was thus destined to become the vanguard of the revolutionary movement.[3] Other scholars have tried to soften the

---

1. Sheila Fitzpatrick, "The Civil War as a Formative Experience," in *Bolshevik Culture: Experiment and Order in the Russian Revolution,* ed. Abbott Gleason, Peter Kenez, and Richard Stites, 57–76 (Bloomington, 1985); James von Geldern and Richard Stites, eds., *Mass Culture in Soviet Russia: Tales, Poems, Songs, Movies, Plays and Folklore, 1917–1953* (Bloomington, 1995); Barbara Clements, *Bolshevik Women* (Cambridge, 1997).

2. G. V. Plekhanov, *Russkii rabochii v revoliutsionnom dvizhenii,* in his *Sochenenii,* vol. 3 (Moscow and Leningrad, 1928). See also Reginald E. Zelnik, "On the Eve: Life Histories and Identities of Some Revolutionary Workers, 1870–1905," in Siegelbaum and Suny, *Making Workers Soviet,* 27–65.

3. Leopold H. Haimson, "The Problem of Social Stability in Urban Russia, 1905–1914," *Slavic Review* 23, no. 4 (1964): 619–42 and 24, no. 1 (1965): 1–22; a position revised in Leopold H. Haimson with Eric Brian, "Changements démographiques et grèves ouvrières à St. Petersbourg, 1905–1914," *Annales: Economies, Sociétés, Civilisations* 4 (July–August 1985): 781–803. See also Robert Eugene Johnson, *Peasant and Proletarian: The Working Classes of Moscow in the Late Nineteenth Century* (New Brunswick, 1979); Koenker, *Moscow Workers;* Engelstein, *Moscow,*

starkness of the urban/rural dichotomy by emphasizing process and evolution.[4] Nonetheless, the two poles of Russian worker experience remain embedded in many approaches to the study of workers, as titles of representative works suggest: *Peasant and Proletarian, Muzhik and Muscovite, Peasant Metropolis, From Peasant to Petersburger.*[5]

The polarity of the peasant/proletarian dichotomy has conditioned the way historians understand the meanings of these social categories for individual identities and collective mentalities. Peasantness provides one set of identities, urbanness another. The peasant worker is depicted as "gray" and unconscious; if the peasant is radical, it is an unconscious radicalism. Consciousness belongs to urban workers, and especially to the rarified stratum of urban workers who set themselves apart even from ordinary workers, who are still seen to be too much under the influence of the Russian village. "Worker-aristocrats," although labeled pejoratively by V. I. Lenin, saw themselves as the most highly evolved of Russian proletarians.[6] Approaching the peasant/proletarian paradigm in terms of class formation reinforces the primacy of the urban worker, the labor aristocrat, the conscious worker as the agent of activism. The problem with the paradigm is the danger of oversimplification and the hazardous assumption that social traits and identities cluster in predictable and uniform ways around the polar labels. The peasant becomes the repository of everything that is spontaneous, irrational, and uncontrollable.[7]

At the other end of the peasant/proletarian dichotomy is the idealized proletarian, a construct that exerted strong normative hegemony even at the time of Soviet working-class formation and whose conceptual pull has influenced subsequent studies of Soviet workers. This ideal, which I will label the total proletarian, emerged as an element of the totalizing project of Soviet society. Total unity (*vseedinstvo* in the philosopher Vladimir Solov'ev's terminology) was the key to the social future of the postrevolutionary communist utopia, a future in which classes, the fundamental source of all difference, would be eliminated,

---

*1905*; Bonnell, *Roots of Rebellion*; Smith, *Red Petrograd*; M. David Mandel, *The Petrograd Workers and the Fall of the Old Regime* (London, 1983) and *The Petrograd Workers and the Soviet Seizure of Power* (London, 1984); Koenker and Rosenberg, *Strikes and Revolution in Russia.*

4. Diane Koenker, "Urban Families, Working-Class Youth Groups, and the 1917 Revolution in Moscow," in *The Family in Imperial Russia: New Lines of Historical Research,* ed. David L. Ransel, 280–304 (Urbana, 1978); Reginald E. Zelnik, *Law and Disorder on the Narova River: The Kreenholm Strike of 1872* (Berkeley, 1995).

5. Johnson, *Peasant and Proletarian;* Joseph Bradley, *Muzhik and Muscovite: Urbanization in Late Imperial History* (Berkeley, 1985); David L. Hoffmann, *Peasant Metropolis: Social Identities in Moscow, 1929–1941* (Ithaca, 1994); Evel G. Ekonomakis, *From Peasant to Petersburger* (New York, 1998).

6. V. I. Lenin, *Imperialism: The Highest Stage of Capitalism* (New York, 1939), 105–7.

7. This is a familiar theme in studies of urbanization: Oscar Lewis, "Urbanization without Breakdown: A Case Study," *Scientific Monthly* 75 (1952): 31–41; Joan Nelson, "The Urban Poor: Disruption or Political Integration in Third World Cities?" *World Politics* 22 (1970): 393–414; Hoffmann, *Peasant Metropolis;* Moshe Lewin, *The Making of the Soviet System: Essays in the Social History of Interwar Russia* (New York, 1985).

and hence difference itself would disappear as a constitutive factor of social and political life.[8] The total proletarian, as he emerged in the discourse of Soviet state-building in the first decade or so after the revolution, was defined by prescriptive literature published by a variety of Communist theorists from Lev Trotskii to Aleksandra Kollontai to propaganda poster artists.[9] But this theoretical image of the total proletarian found reinforcement in the earnest discussions of the negative, unproletarian behaviors and attitudes that emerged in everyday public conversations in the trade union press.

The total proletarian was skilled and politically conscious. He—it was always a he—was a prerevolutionary Bolshevik or a Civil War Communist. If he was not a member of the party, then he was an aspiring member, a "nonparty" sympathizer. He was mature, at least twenty-four: too old to be a member of the Communist Youth (Komsomol), whose immaturity invited undisciplined and disruptive behaviors. The total proletarian was devoted to production, to its improvement, and to work. He participated in shop floor production conferences, he made suggestions to management to improve the work process, and he invented new work processes in his spare time. He had no family: perhaps he had no sex, but the neutered proletarian was at the same time male. He loved to study, but he was interested only in practical subjects, such as technology and science. He was a principled atheist. A city dweller, he was totally at home in the modern clamor of urban transport, elevators, and complex machinery. Nature provided an antidote to the rigors of production life, used only to cast his urbanism in more positive relief. He took good care of his body, because he had to be strong as well as intelligent to do his job. Therefore he did not drink and carouse, but engaged in healthy and intelligent leisure in the reading room or in the out-of-doors. His preferred form of social life was shop floor conferences, party meetings, or an evening at the worker club devoted to remembering revolutionary heroes of past times. You can see his beaming face in countless posters from the 1920s and 1930s and in issue after issue of the daily press.

It might be tempting, in emphasizing the artificiality of this ideal proletarian, to dismiss as well the tropes of class structure and consciousness that the concept employs. Does class as a unifying heuristic device inevitably lead to the total proletarian distortion and to the "virtual class" society that becomes impervious to class analysis? Recent scholars have importantly stressed the adaptation of social traits and identities in new settings, breaking down the rigidity of the clusters of peasant and urban identity. Chris Ward details how particular relationships between work, farms, wages, and the journey to work helped to shape a particular worker culture in the textile towns of Ivanovo-Voznesensk

---

8. See Edith W. Clowes, "The Limits of Discourse: Solov'ev's Language of Syzygy and the Project of Thinking Total-Writing," *Slavic Review* 55, no. 3 (1996): 561.

9. Leon Trotsky, *Problems of Everyday Life and Other Writings on Culture and Science* (New York, 1973); Alexandra Kollontai, *Selected Writings of Alexandra Kollontai*, ed. and trans. Alix Holt (London, 1977); Victoria E. Bonnell, "The Iconography of the Worker in Soviet Political Art," in Siegelbaum and Suny, *Making Workers Soviet*, 341–75.

in the 1920s. Nikolai Mikhailov emphasizes how the collectivist mentalities of peasant workers could synchretize with urban factory-based solidarities, eliding the traditionally understood differences between urban and rural. Mark Steinberg's study of worker writers stresses the uniqueness of this cohort of workers even within the urban pole.[10] Russian printers as much as any occupational group qualified as "urban proletarians," and yet few of them, if any, conformed to the ideal of the total proletarian. For them, the more elastic term "worker" might better encapsulate their varied experience and the expectations they placed on themselves than the normative "proletarian." As we will see, sources of identity even for this relatively socially homogeneous and quintessentially urban group of workers were complex and contradictory.

Nonetheless, "class" was indeed present in the language of the time and therefore in the ways in which Russians understood their place in society.[11] Class, in other words, was one of the *available* identities for Russian workers and their families. I would argue that it was a particularly powerful identity because of the history of the labor movement in Russia, in which the most important rituals and symbols evoked the strong social collectivities of class. After the revolution, work and production came to occupy a central place in the myth of the socialist state, deriving from and reinforcing the primacy of class in the regime's vocabulary. It is true, of course, as Sheila Fitzpatrick argues, that class labels were also ascribed, and that individuals were encouraged through positive and negative mechanisms of incentives to identify themselves as members of the proletariat. In this respect, one might argue that class had become an artificial construct, that "true" working-class consciousness, deriving from the experiences of production, exploitation, and conflict, did not exist and could not exist in the Soviet Union. Under such circumstances, "class" could become an empty shell, the premises of class solidarity a mockery as the regime labeled any protesting worker an "enemy of the working class."[12]

With such obvious challenges to the ideal of class solidarity, as well as because of factors of culture, politics, and materiality shaped by the socialist economy and political structure, class identity competed with other identities, other solidarities, formed through work, politics, kinship, and daily life. The particular circumstances of the formation of a Soviet working class demand our constant attention: as the first two chapters have made clear, the "class-proletarian" government had to establish its power and its symbols on the harsh terrain of perpetual emergency.

---

10. Ward, *Russia's Cotton Workers*; N. V. Mikhailov, "Samoorganizatsiia trudovykh kollektivov i psikhologiia rossiiskikh rabochikh v nachale XX v.," in *Rabochie i intelligentsiia Rossii v epokhu reform i revoliutsii 1861–fevral' 1917*, ed. S. I. Potolov et al. (St. Petersburg, 1997), 149–65; Steinberg, *Proletarian Imagination*, chaps. 1–3.
11. See Koenker, *Moscow Workers*, 8–10 and throughout, on the language of class.
12. *Revoliutsionnyi pechatnik* (Moscow) 2 (12 June 1918): 2; *Pechatnik* 1–2 (13 February [31 January] 1918): 19–20; Fitzpatrick, "Ascribing Class."

## THE MYTH OF THE MENSHEVIK PRINTERS

Understanding class identity among printers is further complicated by the Menshevik factor. Printers have been celebrated for their identification with the Menshevik Party, in distinction to all other groups of industrial or craft workers. In relatively open voting between 1918 and 1920, two-thirds of Petrograd and Moscow printers indeed cast their ballots for the Menshevik, independent leadership of their trade unions, and the Mensheviks were driven out of the union leadership and from factory committee positions only by force, not by democratic choice. What explains this consistent support for the anti-Bolshevik socialist position during the Russian revolution, and what did it mean?

One set of explanations centers on the relationship between the socioeconomic position of printers and their political moderation. In particular, printers themselves cultivated an image as "labor aristocrats," whose high wages encouraged the adoption of a lifestyle that could separate them from the mass of other workers. In Marxist theory, such a labor aristocracy has been blamed for dampening the revolutionary potential of working classes in Europe, but this argument has turned out to be controversial. Historians of the labor movement have identified four elements of the labor aristocracy that set them apart from ordinary "proletarians," whose class position theoretically better suited them to wage class struggle. Labor aristocrats could be identified by their high wages, their control over the work process, "respectability" (they eschewed drink and sought to preserve a good moral tone, much like the ideal total proletarian of Communist mythology), and a self-conscious aloofness from workers in other strata.[13] Yet the link between these traits and conservative politics has proved to be difficult to establish. Robert Q. Gray has argued that occupational subcultures in Britain were not usually divisive, that many labor leaders emerged from these well-paid and autonomous strata of the working class, and that context mattered more than sociology in explaining workers' politics.[14] Russian printers indeed wrote about themselves as "aristocrats of labor," they defended their high-wage position, and they stressed the uniqueness of their trade. This predilection for independence may have predisposed them to support minority political positions such as Menshevism (and later, perhaps, Trotskyism), but they remained squarely within the socialist political camp. Bourgeois and liberal parties found no supporters in Russian print shops.

Working-class radicalism, for its part, has been attributed to the effects of

---

13. Hobsbawm, *Labouring Men*, 321–70; Eric Hobsbawm, *Workers: Worlds of Labor* (New York, 1984), 227–51; Iu. N. Netesin, "K voprosu o sotsial'no-demokraticheskikh korniakh i osobennostiakh rabochei aristokratii v Rossii," in *Bol'shevistskaia pechat' i rabochii klass Rossii v gody revoliutsionnogo pod"ema (1910–1914 gg.)* (Moscow, 1965), 192–211; Robert Q. Gray, *The Labour Aristocracy in Victorian Edinburgh* (Oxford, 1976); H. F. Moorhouse, "The Marxist Theory of the Labour Aristocracy," *Social History* 3 (1978): 61–82. More recently, Kenneth M. Straus has applied the label "labor aristocrat" to all urban male workers in Soviet-era factories: *Factory and Community in Stalin's Russia: The Making of an Industrial Working Class* (Pittsburgh, 1997).

14. Gray, *Labour Aristocracy*, 190.

technological change on hierarchies of status within the working class: historians have argued that metalworkers dominated the radical labor movements in Britain, the United States, and Russia at the start of the twentieth century because scientific management methods had begun to erode their accustomed privileges and threatened to "deskill" the skilled workman.[15] Within the printing industry in Russia, technological change had proceeded unevenly. Composing work was still done mainly by hand, and in Russia, as elsewhere, compositors had been able to control the terms of the transition to the Linotype and preserve their high wages. Presswork and binding, by contrast, had become increasingly mechanized, so one might predict that press operators might tend more than compositors toward the radical Bolsheviks. Using evidence of occupation and party affiliation of printers who ran for office in 1917, however, one can discern no sociological explanations. Highly skilled and highly paid compositors were disproportionately active as political figures, but some supported the Bolsheviks and others the Mensheviks.[16]

Yet even Communist printers wondered if there was something about their craft that made them innately conservative and unsuited for the rough world of revolutionary class struggle. Speakers at the Communist-dominated 1919 congress, including the trade union leader Tomskii, suggested that perhaps there were material reasons for this seeming difference in political preferences: typesetters, unlike machinists or turners, depended not on tools but only on their hands, and this "created a well-known confusion on the part of the very best typesetters," who dressed more like bank clerks than workers. They worked in an innately "petty-bourgeois" industry, whose small scale and close relations to their employers fooled them into thinking that class struggle might be overcome by cooperation. And because in the past they tended to read bourgeois books and newspapers as they set them in type, these printers feared they might have unconsciously absorbed the values and worldview of these bourgeois authors.[17] This argument does not explain why typesetters did not uniformly support the more conservative Menshevik trade union, or why many pressmen, who presumably did not imbibe the bourgeois content of their printed works, also supported the Menshevik position.

Significantly, compositors in the United States also stood out for their vibrant two-party trade union system. During the years 1912 to 1928 in particular, the members of the International Typographical Union were quite evenly divided between progressives and moderates, and they contested union elections in lan-

---

15. James Hinton, *The First Shop Stewards' Movement* (London, 1973); David Montgomery, *Workers' Control in America* (Cambridge, 1979); Heather Hogan, *Forging Revolution: Metalworkers, Managers, and the State in St. Petersburg, 1890–1914* (Bloomington, 1993).

16. See Diane P. Koenker, "Rabochii klass v 1917 g.: Sotsial'naia i politicheskaia samoidentifikatsiia," in *Anatomiia revoliutsii: 1917 god v Rossii: Massy, partii, vlast'*, ed. V. Iu. Cherniaev (St. Petersburg, 1994), 214–17.

17. GARF, f. R-5525, op. 1, d. 10 (transcript of the Special All-Russian Congress of Printers, 18–23 August 1919), ll. 38–42.

guage very similar to that used by Mensheviks and Communists in Russia. What distinguished printers in both Russia and the United States was not just the moderate politics of some but the fact that they embraced political diversity. In Russia the Mensheviks alone defended the principle of union democracy, whereas in the United States both parties followed democratic rules. Seymour Martin Lipset, Martin Trow, and James Coleman attribute this unique form of union politics to the economic organization of the industry: all members shared roughly the same incomes and status, which led to socializing outside of work and the creation of voluntary organizations that reinforced habits of pluralism. It is harder to explain why some U.S. typesetters became liberals and others conservatives: the positions they took on union matters reflected "the different values the men brought with them to the union," shaped by such nonwork factors as religion, education, age, and immigration status.[18] The structure of the industry and the commonalities of highly skilled work may have predisposed Russian printers to support democracy and a politics of pluralism. Menshevism stood explicitly for democratic principles, and moderate Communists in the union also defended trade union democracy.

The intensity of the political contest in Civil War Russia rigidified the boundaries between "Menshevik printers" and "Communist proletarians" for participants (and historians) and has obscured more contextual and conditional explanations for political choices. I would argue that choices of partisan political positions were determined far less by ideology or sociology than by context and by the chance of personality. Printers, like other Russian workers (and many intellectuals), harbored a deep-seated hostility to capitalism, but their commitment to partisan political positions was more fluid. Some printers— the 1918 union chair, Mark S. Kefali, and Aleksandr F. Deviatkin—had become ardent and ideological right-wing Mensheviks by 1918; others, such as Mikhail Tomskii, Nikolai Gordon, and Aleksandr Borshchevskii, had adopted an equally strong commitment to Bolshevism. But for better or for worse (and both parties thought it was for the worse), many printers had little interest in partisan politics. Some of the delegates to the May 1919 congress, whose purpose was to establish a separate Communist union, had arrived with instructions to bring the two factions together.[19] Some local leaders of the printers' unions had easily switched political allegiances in the course of the Civil War: the first secretary of the Communist-led union in 1919, Aleksandr Tikhanov, had earlier been a Menshevik; the popular director of the Zinov'ev print shop in Petrograd, Dmitrii Dudarev, had also made the transition from Menshevism to Communism. His authority within the shop derived not from his political ideology but from his willingness to stand up for the interests of his fellow workers.

Much depended on the authority and popularity of local leaders. Where ac-

---

18. Lipset et al., *Union Democracy,* 45, 313–30.

19. GARF, f. R-5525, op. 1, d. 10, l. 14; *Pervyi vserossiiskii s"ezd soiuza rabochikh poligraficheskogo proizvodstva,* 1919, 10, 25; *Vestnik vsrpd,* 6–7 (15 July 1919): 4, 14; 5 (30 May 1919): 6.

tivists belonged to the Menshevik Party, as at the First Model Print Shop in Moscow, the workers as a whole supported the Menshevik line of the union until their leaders were forcibly removed from the factory committee. The Communism of other shops, such as Pechatnyi Dvor in Petrograd, may similarly have resulted from personal loyalties to local leaders who had opted for Bolshevism. Did workers choose these leaders because of prior partisan positions, or did they absorb the partisan attitudes of the men they trusted to represent them? The consistent support for such local leaders as Dudarev and Bokov in Moscow, regardless of their political shifts, suggests that personal qualities played an important role.

The leaders of the Menshevik Party, for their part, paid little attention to the needs or particular situations of "their" printers. The Printers' Union offered the party a symbolic bridgehead to the labor movement, proof positive that workers did not unanimously support Communist policies and tactics. Newly published collections of Menshevik Party documents indicate little day-to-day attention to the problems of the Printers' Union or to labor organization.[20] The issues that divided the Menshevik Party at the top, between internationalism and revolutionary defensism in 1917, between work within the Soviet system and illegal resistance thereafter, had little to do with the crisis of labor relations and the challenges faced by the trade union movement. In fact, party leaders acknowledged in 1918 that their position on trade union politics had become embroiled in their other "deep disagreements of principle."[21] The refusal of the Printers' Union's Menshevik leaders to participate in the founding congress of the new union in August 1919 can be seen as part of the Menshevik Party's principled stance in opposition to Communism, but this decision also abandoned its less ideological supporters to the appeal and blandishments of the Communist union.

Some printers would continue to follow the Menshevik line, even when their belief led to arrest and exile.[22] Communist repression surely discouraged others from placing principle above personal survival. Communists would henceforth quickly label any expression of heterodoxy as a "Menshevik residue," and the memory of the contest between the two Social Democratic factions would continue to structure the trade union's political discourse, as we will see. But the assumption of a tight correspondence between printers' self-identification and the Menshevik Party cannot be sustained. The myth of the Menshevik printers served both the Mensheviks and the Bolsheviks in their efforts to de-

---

20. *Men'sheviki v 1918 godu*, ed. Z. Galili and A. Nenarokov (Moscow, 1999); *Men'sheviki v 1919–1920 gg.*, ed. Z. Galili and A. Nenarokov (Moscow, 2000); *Men'sheviki v 1921–1922 gg.*, ed. Z. Galili, A. Nenarokov, and D. Pavlov (Moscow, 2002).

21. Galili and Nenarokov, *Men'sheviki v 1918*, 263.

22. The GPU chief, Feliks Dzerzhinskii, indicated that underground Mensheviks retained strong connections with printers even in February/March 1924 (RGASPI, f. 76, op. 3, d. 150, l. 27, reproduced in *Men'sheviki v 1922–24*, ed. Z. Galili et al., forthcoming. I am grateful to Ziva Galili for sharing the manuscript with me.)

fine social identities and establish claims to legitimacy, but it ignores the far more complex relationships among printers' sense of class identity, occupational positions, and political choices. To understand these relationships, we need to look more closely at the craft and class-based sources of printers' identities.

## CRAFT AND CLASS AMONG RUSSIAN PRINTERS

The workplace and relations at work played a major, if not always dominant, role in structuring identities and solidarities, even when the workplace provided such a tenuous link to survival as it did during the Civil War. These identities, however, were not always or necessarily conditioned by the relation to the means of production common to all workers, whether alienated under capitalism or as owners, officially, under socialism. The workplace in fact structured identities in far more varied and particular ways: differently for steelworkers and bread bakers, differently even for typesetters in the relative quiet of dusty composing rooms, press operators amid the constant clamor of complicated machinery, and the workers who operated folding and binding machines that stitched up the printed product.

The importance of craft identities has been well documented by labor historians, whether as a constituent element of class identity or as a competing one.[23] In Erik Olin Wright's terms, craft provides a fundamental example of a competitive class location, one that is defined by the asset of skill. The craft pride of Russian printers was based on the centrality of their products—printed books and periodicals—for the modern world. (It is noteworthy, however, that they claimed no public pride in their contributions to capitalist marketing, such as advertisements, account books, and product labels. These jobs accounted for a large share of the printing business before the revolution.) They stressed the complexities of their work, the literacy and level of culture required to perform their jobs well, and the hazards of the job that produced tragically short life expectancies. Printers also drew pride from the political history of their craft, which had stood in the forefront of the trade union movement before 1917, and one of whose members, Mikhail Tomskii, served the Communist regime as the leader of the Soviet trade union apparatus.[24]

This pride in craft was the product of long years of traditions honed in workplaces, passed down from masters to apprentices, and reinforced in myriad workplace rituals from drinking ceremonies to funerals.[25] Craft and skill were inextricably linked to masculinity. Women's work in the industry had been

---

23. An important discussion of the Russian case is S. A. Smith, "Craft Consciousness, Class Consciousness: Petrograd, 1917," *History Workshop* 11 (1981): 33–56; see also Chris Ward, "Languages of Trade or a Language of Class? Work Culture in Russian Cotton Mills in the 1920s," in Siegelbaum and Suny, *Making Workers Soviet*, 194–219.

24. *Pechatnik* 3–4 (1 April 1919): 5; Wright, *Debate on Classes*.

25. Steinberg, *Moral Communities*.

strictly limited to auxiliary, supportive positions, and the rituals of work—drinking, swearing, bawdiness—emphasized the separation of the sexes and carved out the workplace as a site of male camaraderie. Many male workers refused to believe that women could ever acquire skills comparable to those of men, as will become clear.[26]

Socialism would add new elements to workplace traditions, including the expectation that women and men could be equal participants in production and public life. Above all, socialism would rest on the centrality of the printed word for the transmission of socialist ideas and the building of a new society.[27] Socialism also facilitated an insistence that the innate attributes of the craft, rather than issues of supply and demand, determined the level of compensation for printers' work. In other words, it did not matter whether there was work for skilled typesetters: their craft identity entitled them to twice as much food as an unskilled worker, and the same food as an administrator.[28]

The particular conditions of the Civil War—the economy of extreme shortages and the schism between the two printers' unions—reinforced sensitivities of craft separatism and craft pride, as each side in the political contest sought to prove that they were the "real" printers, the real workers. Printers of all political allegiances adopted a class rhetoric to justify their complaints about unequal treatment. In the moneyless economy, workers were being paid with the products of their labor, and tobacco, leather, and chemical workers were all earning goods that they could barter for grain. Printers had nothing to trade. "If you believe that the printed word has as much importance in the struggle with the enemies of workers and peasants as bayonets and bullets, then there ought not to be such stepsons as we printers."[29] The response of the independent Menshevik union to attacks by the reds also summoned up images of the special role of printers: How could we be "yellow," a company union? Didn't we fight capital? We *printers* were the first to form a class union, we stood for socialism under tsarism.[30]

Socialist values would reconcile craft identities with those of class, and press

---

26. In this respect Russian print worker culture was not unique. See Ava Baron, "Questions of Gender: Deskilling and Demasculinization in the U.S. Printing Trade, 1830–1915," *Gender and History* 1 (Summer 1989): 178–99; Baron, "An 'Other' Side of Gender Antagonism at Work"; Cockburn, *Brothers;* Reynolds, *Britannica's Typesetters.*

27. TsGA SPb, f. 4804, op. 6, d. 24 (Fourth Petrograd Guberniia Printers' Congress, 8 September 1922), ll. 20–22; GARF, f. R-5525, op. 2, d. 17 (guberniia meetings and conferences, 1920), l. 8 (Voronezh city printers' conference, 30 January 1920).

28. *Vestnik vsrpd* 2–3 (20 February 1919): 5–6; 3 (20 April 1919): 6; *Moskovskii pechatnik* 5 (15 April 1921): 12; GARF, f. R-5525, op. 1, d. 10, ll. 120–21; f. R-5461, op. 1, d. 30 (meetings of Moscow union representatives, 1919), l. 118; TsGAMO, f. 699, op. 1, d. 145 (general and factory committee meetings at First Model, 1921), l. 22. The 2-to-1 pay differential between skilled and unskilled workers was canonic throughout Europe; see Hobsbawm, *Labouring Men*, 407. See also More, *Skill and the English Working Class*, chap. 1.

29. TsGAMO, f. 699, op. 1, d. 74 (general and factory committee meetings at First Model, 1920), l. 32; GARF, f. R-5525, op. 2, d. 17, ll. 5, 8.

30. *Pechatnik* 11 (10 November [28 October] 1918): 4.

campaigns elaborated the positive values that could help shape the identities of workers in socialist Russia. Beginning in 1921, at the same time that market-based wages returned to the industry, the Printers' Union press began to celebrate "heroes of labor." Descriptions of these heroes offer a point of entry into the values that the regime hoped the workers would absorb, values rooted in the prerevolutionary culture of the craft.[31] All of these heroes were veterans of labor, with thirty or more years in the profession. They were honored for the personal diligence that had allowed them to work their way through the ranks: many of their biographies related their trajectories from apprentice to skilled worker to foreman. Some had begun their lives in nonfactory occupations, as peasants or children of yard sweepers: they had transformed themselves into hero workers by their own diligence. These heroes were hard workers: twenty years on the night shift, they worked even when ill, they worked overtime for no extra pay. They did not skip work and they came to work on time. They perfected new methods of working, and they passed on their skills to the apprentices they trained. These were not just craft-specific values: the identity of hard and disciplined worker was one to which all should aspire.

At the other end of the work-based spectrum, craft identities could also be subdivided. The print shop employed workers with diverse specializations, representing different levels of skill and experience, and conflicts over the variable levels of compensation assigned to these subgroups produced new expressions of identity. When the rates bureau of the VTsSPS proposed to exclude binders and lithographers from the supplemental vacations allocated to other printers, one Moscow printers' delegate protested: "Printers—they are children of one family. Solving the issue of vacations shouldn't introduce dissension by privileging one group of workers over another." The issue of differential pay for different levels of skill provoked serious divisions throughout this early period. For unskilled workers, the revolution meant a leveling of pay: as "workers" they were just as worthy as "skilled workers." But union leaders recognized that a wage scale that was too egalitarian drove skilled workers away from the workplace and created havoc in industry. Others argued that differential pay was an essential element of socialist justice when it took years for a skilled worker to learn a job and an unskilled worker learned a job in a week.[32]

Other divisions persisted as well. Despite the tarif in force in Moscow, newspaper typesetters in state enterprises received 50 percent more than those employed under the collective contract. New tarif proposals pitted skilled workers against unskilled, fanning a perpetual source of discord. The Printers' Union actually proposed a smaller differential between the highest and lowest pay categories than the government's economic organs did. Urban workers chastised their colleagues with rural ties, who now walked away from the city with two

---

31. This discussion is based on some thirty heroes celebrated in the union journal *Moskovskii pechatnik* 8 (15 September 1921): 8–9; 10 (1 November 1921): 13; 3 (1 May 1922): 2, 15–16.
32. GARF, f. R-5461, op. 1, d. 30, l. 23.

months' severance pay instead of staying on to help restore industrial production. Workers were also divided by disputes over which branches of printing were hazardous enough to warrant extra summer leave or special rations.[33]

The role of gender in the formation of class identity was particularly vexing. Socialist egalitarianism preached that women and men would become equal citizens in a world without capitalism, but as long as worker identity remained so strongly linked to skill and skill to masculinity, the meaning of "worker" in the printing industry remained fundamentally male. Women were incapable of acquiring skills, believed most trade unionists, and therefore they were incapable of becoming "workers" in the complete sense of the term. Women bore the brunt of industrial demobilization policies that allowed only one member per family to be employed in a given print shop, even though they tried to assert their own claim to socialist citizenship through work. When socialist labor commissars decided in 1918 that women should be the first to be laid off to fight the growing problem of unemployment, two hundred women workers at Kushnerev gathered to protest. They had heard that women would be fired because they were less skillful (*iskusstnyi*) and because their husbands worked. The women had worked hard in the men's place during the war, they complained, but now "they want to take away our right to a share of bread, a right of every citizen. They want to deprive us of that right and throw us in the street."[34]

As conditions of existence became ever more fraught in 1919 and 1920, printers increasingly drew the limits of their loyalty around the narrowly defined walls of their own workplaces. Within the workplace, the primary source of affiliation was usually the shop (*tsekh*) or department (*otdel*). Most large print shops organized their operations into three main shops: typesetting, press, and binding. Not only work but political life revolved around the departments. Shops elected delegates to representatives' assemblies for the entire print shop, the Communist Party organized its fractions by shop, and elections to the factory committee and to local soviets were also often conducted at the shop level. Loyalty to one's enterprise was a crucial element of economic survival in the Civil War years and those that immediately followed. When the economic rationalizers proposed reorganizing Moscow's printing industry by closing down some shops and moving workers to better outfitted enterprises, workers resisted at the shops targeted for closure. They resented any hint of favoring one enterprise over another.[35]

At the same time, the structures of trade union organization, in practice as well as in theory, offered revolutionary Russia's printers a framework for forg-

---

33. *Pechatnoe delo* 17 (11 March 1918): 2; *Vestnik vsrpd* 3 (20 April 1918): 7; GARF, f. R-5525, op. 1, d. 10, ll. 120–21; *Moskovskii pechatnik* 5 (15 April 1921): 12; *Pechatnik* 11 (10 November [28 October] 1918): 9; 9–10 (10 October [27 September] 1918): 3–4, 9, 10; 1–2 (13 February [31 January] 1918): 19.

34. *Pechatnik* 5 (30 [17] April 1918): 11; 1–2 (13 February [31 January] 1918): 19.

35. *Vtoraia moskovskaia gubernskaia konferentsiia*, 1921, 26, 77–78. Enterprise loyalty emerges strongly in the praises of the best red directors in 1922. Koenker, "Factory Tales."

ing solidarities. Despite the troubled recent history of the Printers' Union, trade unionism more generally had acquired a legitimacy forged in the long prerevolutionary history of organization in the printers' trades. In the years immediately after the revolution, as was shown in Chapter 2, the Printers' Union erected increasingly bureaucratic structures for uniting workers and adjudicating their disputes. The trade union, however, also served as a partner in the economic administration of industry, so the union was both a source of solidarity and a representative of the bosses, a conflict of interest that workers frequently pointed out.[36] The particular history of the Printers' Union complicated materially based sources of solidarity. As the upstart red union fought in 1918 and 1919 to win over the majority of printers to its cause, it employed, among other means, the tactic of branding its opponents as class enemies, saboteurs, and lackeys of capitalism.[37] Only a Communist was a real proletarian, only false proletarians would support the Mensheviks. In the struggle over the union in the print shops, unlike elsewhere in Soviet industry, parallel sources of loyalty were raised to high principles of class identity, with membership in the right union signifying class position.

Even in the proletarian dictatorship, union membership represented a crucial marker of worker identity, but the attempt to define union members also revealed the complexities of class and class identity. Who should join the union? Who was a worker? The official principle of Soviet union organization insisted that industry, not craft, was the source of solidarity: all workers in a given industry should belong to that industrial union.[38] Yet the Printers' Union was loathe to allow printers in small private or cooperative shops to join the proletarian union; for them, class was located in large-scale enterprises, where workers sold their labor, not their product.[39] Equally problematic was the position of administrators in the industrial union: many managers and plant directors in the early years after the revolution were workers promoted from the shop floor, men experienced in trade union and factory committee affairs. They were union members once: keeping them in the union would reduce the chances that these red directors would exploit their workers, argued one delegate at the August 1919 union congress. White-collar employees constituted another complicated category of workers: industrial union principles suggested that they be included in the union along with the managers; but inasmuch as they provided services and not a product, engaged in mental labor and not physical, Com-

36. *Pechatnoe delo* 22 (18 May 1918): 2.
37. *Revoliutsionnyi pechatnik* (Moscow) 2 (12 June 1918): 2; *Materialy,* 154–55, 159; *Pechatnik* 12 (10 December [27 November] 1918): 12.
38. *Pervyi vserossiiskii s"ezd professional'nykh soiuzov,* 375. Also Carr, *Bolshevik Revolution,* 2:104–8, 204.
39. *Vserossiiskii pechatnik* 14 (September–October 1921): 9; *Moskovskii pechatnik* 6 (30 August 1922): 4; GARF, f. R-5525, op. 1, d. 10, ll. 102–3. But highly specialized master technicians were allowed to join the union: *Pechatnik* 1–2 (25 January 1919): 12; *Revoliutsionnyi pechatnik* (Petrograd) 6 (25 February 1919): 8.

munist printers argued there was no place for employees in a "purely proletarian union." "Cultural workers," too, such as journalists and writers, although they participated in the production of the printed word, belonged in their own cultural union, not a production union like the printers'.[40]

The issue of voluntary union membership also raised questions of identity. Should the union consider as members all workers in the industry (class in itself), or only those workers who paid their dues and participated in the life of the union (class for itself)? Some argued that workers who were automatically enrolled in the union by virtue of their employment risked losing their class identity and commitment to class solidarity because solidarity came so cheaply.[41] And workers were regularly expelled from the union for violating proletarian discipline: coming to work late or drunk or both.[42] Consciousness mattered as well as the fact of employment in production.

It is important to separate identity-based *behavior* from the language of identity. In work-based practice, workers engaged in acts of solidarity, but not always necessarily at the level of class or proletariat. "Class" was certainly an important word in printers' vocabulary, but it could signify division as well as solidarity: "Workers shouldn't be divided by classes and privileges"; "Not one class has starved like the printers." But "class" also structured a fundamental unity based on the primacy of labor. Printers insisted in 1918 and again in 1922 that they needed a "class union," whose job was to defend not narrow shop interests but the interests of the working class as a whole. "Class struggle" existed, representing a contradiction between the interests of workers and work givers. Giving special privileges to some workers (cigarette rollers) and not others was "plundering the working class."[43]

What did it mean now, in 1919 and 1920, to be a member of the "working class"? Printers observed the desperate struggle among workers for extra hazard pay, for special rations, for access to vacation rest homes, and lamented "the atmosphere that now prevails in the working class." When printers complained that "not one class has starved like the printers," they meant the class of tobacco workers, the class of textile workers, what other critics had labeled

---

40. GARF, f. R-5525, op. 1, d. 10, ll. 71, 74; op. 3, d. 9 (transcript of union central committee plenum, 3–5 October 1921), l. 41. Other discussions in *Tretii vserossiiskii s"ezd soiuza rabochikh poligraficheskogo proizvodstva, 1921*, 55–58, 74–75. See also, from the employees' perspective, Daniel Orlovsky, "The Hidden Class: White-Collar Workers in the Soviet 1920s," in Siegelbaum and Suny, *Making Workers Soviet*, 220–52.

41. GARF, f. R-5461, op. 1, d. 29 (board and presidium of Moscow Union of Workers in the Printing Trade, 1919); TsGAMO, f. 699, op. 1, d. 266 (general and factory committee meetings at Sixteenth, 1922), l. 111. See also GARF, f. R-5525, op. 4, d. 1 (transcript of Fourth All-Russian Congress of Printers' Union, 18–21 October 1922), l. 111.

42. GARF, f. R-5525, op. 4, d. 62 (board and presidium meetings of Moscow guberniia union, 1922), l. 53, provides one example of many.

43. TsGAMO, f. 699, op. 1, d. 44 (general and factory committee meetings at First Model, 1919), l. 370b.; *Vtoraia moskovskaia gubernskaia konferentsiia, 1921*, 18, 31; TsGAMO, f. 699, op. 1, d. 270 (general and factory committee meetings at First Model, 1922), l. 63; *Pechatnoe delo* 26 (16 October 1918): 11; *Krasnyi pechatnik* 2 (April 1, 1922): 7; *Pechatnoe delo* 22 (18 May 1918): 2.

"closed corporations." Internal class divisions structured printers' conversations about themselves as often as did class solidarity. Printers often invoked difference and commonality in the same breath. At the militantly independent First Model Print Shop, for example, workers expressed their political distinctiveness in class terms. Rejecting productivist Communist slogans for the May Day banners in 1920, they nonetheless appealed to class solidarity: "Freedom and Independence of Class Organization" and "Unite the Proletarian Front."[44]

The challenge of socialism for the Russian working class was to reconcile these competing forces of sectional loyalties and class unity. "Working class" in socialist Russia, whether for militant or moderate printers, still excluded readily identifiable "others." Printers did not seek alliances or claim to share interests with anyone construed to be a nonworker. Peasants were anathema; peasant workers were not real proletarians, they subverted work discipline with their casual country ways, or they sought urban jobs only as a way to avoid military service.[45] Printers also rejected any common identity with white-collar workers—factory employees who would not dirty their hands and did no "real" production work. Thus "class" and its synonyms—"red," "proletarian," "production," "laboring mass"—offered an important source of identity, defining a set of locations, in Wright's terms, in which members of a working class, and only they, could be found.

As many historians have argued, however, class is equally constituted outside the walls of the workplace, in the family and in the community.[46] In a search for patterns of identity and affiliation, it can be useful to reframe these questions of multiple and conflicting identities in terms of two parallel hierarchies of loyalties, or solidarity, arranged from the particular to the general. It is important to differentiate between workplace hierarchies, which privilege the male skilled worker, and community-based hierarchies, in which other relations might be privileged. At every stage of these hierarchies, printers (and all workers) formed strong bonds and developed powerful loyalties, each with different characteristics but all with their own logic.

A basic building block of community was the family. The private lives of Russian workers are difficult to reconstruct, but these urban workers frequently invoked the language of family to locate themselves in the broader social fabric.

---

44. *Vtoraia moskovskaia gubernskaia konferentsiia, 1921*, 17, 31; TsGAMO, f. 699, op. 1, d. 74, ll. 32, 26.

45. *Pechatnik* 1–2 (13 February [31 January] 1918): 19; 1–2 (25 January 1919): 16; *Pravda*, 1 April 1922.

46. Examples include Temma Kaplan, "Female Consciousness and Collective Action: The Case of Barcelona, 1910–1918," *Signs* 7 (Spring 1982): 545–66; Sonya Rose, *Limited Livelihoods: Gender and Class in Nineteenth-Century England* (Berkeley, 1991); Alice Kessler-Harris, "Treating the Male as 'Other': Re-defining the Parameters of Labor History," *Labor History* 34, no. 2–3 (1993): 190–204; Ellen Ross, *Love and Toil: Motherhood in Outcast London, 1870–1918* (New York, 1993); Alf Lüdtke, "Cash, Coffee-Breaks, Horseplay: *Eigensinn* and Politics among Factory Workers in Germany circa 1900," in *Confrontation, Class Consciousness, and the Labor Process*, ed. Michael Hanagan and Charles Stephenson, 65–95 (New York, 1986).

The Menshevik union had no place in the "family of revolutionary worker unions, they ought to be excluded from this family." "Children of the same stepmother" should be rebaptized, after the revolution, with new revolutionary names. The red union would coalesce "as one worker family unified around [Communist] leadership."[47]

While the family metaphor might have indicated patriarchal relationships between owners and workers before the revolution, after 1917 the family of printers appeared to be an egalitarian family.[48] Printers were "children of one family," who were entitled to equal treatment with other family members. There should be no "sons and stepsons" in the union movement. Printers could bear equal hardships if they were treated like one common family. In the "friendly family of printers" there should be no internal conflicts.[49]

Dissent and opposition could also be understood in family terms. "There's no family without its freak" was a folk saying that appeared regularly in the columns of the worker press. Denouncing the Menshevik printers, for example, Grigorii Zinov'ev proclaimed to a general meeting of Petrograd printers in 1920, "There's no family without its freak—but do you want this freak in your family? [Cries: No! No!]" And in time the family metaphor was perhaps better able than class to reinscribe hierarchy into Soviet social life, by reinvoking patriarchal principles. In response to criticism of the union leadership for having failed to secure decent wages and benefits for its members, the union boss Derbyshev responded calmly: In a family, the oldest son criticized Papa, the younger son would then praise him. Moscow and Petrograd printers here played the role of the older son, the provincial unions the younger. But, he added, Papa is necessary all the same. And likewise, we printers are like sons to the Central Trade Union Council, and must accept their leadership as well.[50]

The family thus played an important metaphorical role in workers' self-expressions. It also played a crucial social role in Russia, as in many other industrial settings.[51] Evidence for Russian working-class family life is often indirect

---

47. TsGAIPD SPb, f. 435, op. 1, d. 3 (Leningrad union Communist fraction protocols, 1918), l. 6a ob.; *Revoliutsionnyi pechatnik* (Moscow) 2 (2 June 1918): 6; TsGA SPb, f. 4804, op. 2, d. 6 (general and delegates' meetings in Petrograd print shops, 1918), l. 17; *Pechatnoe delo* 15 (13 February [31 January] 1918): 9.

48. See Steinberg, *Moral Communities,* 56–61, and Jacqueline Dowd Hall, James Leloudis, Robert Korstad, Mary Murphy, Lu Ann Jones, and Christopher B. Daly, *Like a Family: The Making of a Southern Cotton Mill World* (Chapel Hill, 1987), xvii.

49. GARF, f. R-5461, op. 1, d. 30, l. 23; *Moskovskii pechatnik* 1 (January 1922): 15; TsGA SPb, f. 4804, op. 5, d. 73 (conferences of Petrograd factory committees, 1921), l. 10; *Vtoraia moskovskaia gubernskaia konferentsiia, 1921,* 21; *Tretii gubernskii s"ezd moskovskogo gubernskogo soiuza rabochikh poligraficheskogo proizvodstva 16–20 fevralia 1922 g.* (Moscow, 1922), 12; TsGA SPb, f. 4804, op. 5, d. 10 (conference of Petrograd printing industry officials, 5 February 1921), l. 70.

50. TsGA SPb, f. 4804, op. 4, d. 19 (general meetings at Petrograd print shops, 1920), ll. 246–246a.; GARF, f. R-5525, op. 4, d. 1, l. 134.

51. Among others, see Tamara K. Hareven, *Family Time and Industrial Time: The Relationship between Family and Work in a New England Industrial Community* (New York, 1982), James R.

but pervasive, although the extent to which the family was an affective social unit remains unclear. It was certainly a crucial economic unit. Families used employment, education, and child-rearing strategies to maximize what has been called the family wage, the collective income of a household leveraged among all its members.[52] The largest print shops responded to the intense pressure for housing by rehabilitating old structures or building new ones to serve as homes for their workers, with families receiving priority in assignments.[53] Whether voluntarily or not, the worker family constituted an essential unit of social life.

Both families and enterprises existed in real space, and the importance of regional loyalties stands out in the historical record. Moscow and Petrograd printers both strongly identified with their native cities. At the same time that the union was bitterly rent by the division between the Communists and Mensheviks during the Civil War, the urban rivalries between the two cities' Communist fractions sometimes seemed to overshadow the interparty rivalry. Nikolai Gordon spoke with pride about how old printers were returning to Petrograd at the end of the Civil War even though no jobs were to be had. "They were pulled back to their native Petrograd; the old fellows want to die in Red Petrograd." Toward 1922, the industry recovered much faster in Moscow than in Petrograd, and to ease the unemployment crisis, hundreds of Petrograd printers were transferred to Moscow. They did not assimilate, and retained with competitive pride their Petrograd identities. Moscow workers, for their part, complained that the Petrograd printers were better dressed and lived better than they did.[54] Beyond these attachments to a particular place was an identity of urbanism, most pronounced in the two largest cities of Petrograd and Moscow. "Piter is not the provinces," argued the union leader there on behalf of more subsidies for Petrograd printers.[55] The city and its workers were superior to those provincial towns with their unsophisticated workers.

---

Barrett, *Work and Community in the Jungle: Chicago's Packinghouse Workers, 1894–1922* (Urbana, 1987), 64–117; Tessie Liu, *The Weavers' Knot: The Contradictions of Class Struggle and Family Solidarity in Western France, 1750–1914* (Ithaca, 1994); Kathleen Canning, *Languages of Labor and Gender: Female Factory Work in Germany, 1850–1914* (Ithaca, 1996); Ward, *Russia's Cotton Workers*.

52. On the family wage in general, see Louise A. Tilly and Joan W. Scott, *Women, Work, and Family* (New York, 1978); Jane Humphries, "Class Struggle and the Persistence of the Working-Class Family," *Cambridge Journal of Economics* 1 (1977): 241–58; for Russian examples, see Koenker, "Men against Women," and E. O. Kabo, *Ocherki rabochego byta: Opyt monograficheskogo issledovaniia domashnego rabochego byta* (Moscow, 1928).

53. TsGAMO, f. 699, op. 1, d. 145, l. 82, 64; d. 266, l. 72; d. 269 (general and factory committee meetings at First Model, 1922), ll. 88, 24, 115, 112; d. 270, l. 76.

54. Even a British visitor in 1920 was quickly made aware of the rivalry between the two cities: Mrs. Philip Snowden, *Through Bolshevik Russia* (London, 1920), 61–62; GARF, f. R-5525, op. 4, d. 7 (union Central Committee presidium meetings, 1922), l. 11; op. 2, d. 11 (correspondence with guberniia branches on liquidation of Menshevik leadership), l. 75; TsGA SPb, f. 4804, op. 6, d. 24, l. 12; op. 7, d. 77 (Petrograd guberniia union conferences, 1923), l. 33; *Zhizn' pechatnika*, 1 January 1923; *Vtoraia moskovskaia gubernskaia konferentsiia, 1921*, 39.

55. TsGA SPb, f. 4804, op. 5, d. 73, l. 90b.

Comrade Borshchevskii, chairman of the Moscow printers' union and a "patriot of his country." Holding a banner that reads "Long live the printers," Borshchevskii towers above a map on which Moscow print shops constitute the federated territories of his "country." (*Moskovskii pechatnik* 12 [29 October 1923]: 9.)

Work and the workplace as a source of identity and solidarity would remain a central tenet of printers' self-understanding in the years to come. It was an identity that privileged skill and maleness and thus readily excluded young people, women, and common laborers. The language of craft and work permeated printers' conversations about their politics and their role in the new socialist society. Sometimes this language generalized to a more universal concept of class, marking an identity that drew its essence from the work experience. The metaphor of family, however, was both more restrictive than class and more expansive, and its interchangeability with terms invoking class identity confirms the contingency and malleability of the identity of skilled workers in the years in which the Soviet system was established.

## FINDING IDENTITY THROUGH CULTURE

Identities and class position for Russian workers reflected perceptions of material reality, social positions within industry, political conflict, a sense of others, and prevailing modes of discourse characterizing production relations and the production process. Work in its many forms and relationships therefore played a key role in class formation in the Soviet Union, as elsewhere. But the production and reproduction of everyday life occurs through culture, and in the process becomes just as constitutive of identities as the production of the material means for life. The reproduction of everyday life reflects the consciousness of social identities and boundaries shaped by occupational, shop, trade, and neighborhood identities, and also helps to shape that consciousness. Examining the relationship between identities and culture requires us to recognize that formal distinctions between "old culture" and "new" are arbitrary and themselves the products of negotiation, and that the relationship between culture and identity is a reciprocal one. Identities shaped cultural forms and choices; cultural practices produced new identities.

The concept of "proletarian culture" in the history of the Soviet Union has come to connote forms of high and formal culture—literature, the visual arts, drama, education—created for or by the proletariat as symbolic of a new social system predicated on the social ownership of the means of production. It connotes a culture of egalitarianism, functionalism, and industrialism. "Working-class culture," on the other hand, tends to refer to the practices of everyday life that construct meaning for wage laborers and their families, whether under capitalist or socialist systems. Such working-class culture partakes of elements of formal culture, and in some cases absorbs the results of socialist efforts to construct new cultural forms from without, but it remains a broader terrain on which identities are constructed as well as expressed. Culture in this sense, as Wolfgang Kaschuba has suggested, "tries to shed light on the large-scale, encompassing symbolic orders of such life-world systems—modes of experiencing, rules for behavior, meanings and values." Régine Robin has similarly suggested that the search for a new cultural base in socialist Russia included new social codes and new behaviors, "in what characterised the attitudes towards sexuality, dietary codes, forms of sociability, the different ways of being together in society, of drinking *samogon* and rolling under the table, for example."[56] Given the penurious conditions of the Civil War years, workers had little opportunity to choose dietary codes or much surplus to divert to purchasing home brew and rolling under the table, but survival in the Civil War years was not merely about industrial, military, or political combat. In their everyday lives

---

56. Wolfgang Kaschuba, "Popular Culture and Workers' Culture as Symbolic Orders: Comments on the Debate about the History of Culture and Everyday Life," in *The History of Everyday Life: Reconstructing Historical Experiences and Ways of Life*, ed. Alf Lüdtke, trans. William Templer (Princeton, 1995), 172; Régine Robin, "Stalinism and Popular Culture," in *The Culture of the Stalin Period*, ed. Hans Günther (New York, 1990), 22.

too, in their pursuit of food, shelter, and recreation, Russian printers were working out new social practices and new social codes that would shape a new kind of socialist culture.

On 15 November 1920, as the Civil War neared its close and Communist leaders debated the future structure of the socialist society, Petrograd union leaders summarized the mood of printers in the local shops: workers could not live on the union's allocations of rotten apples, spoiled cod, and overroasted tea. "The war, they say, is over, and now it's time to think more about us."[57] We have already seen how the politics of food supply constituted a fundamental source of political division in the union, between Mensheviks and Communists, between rank and file and union leadership. "Questions of the stomach" occupied workers much more than organizational questions even in 1919, when the red union was mounting its campaign to win printers over from the Mensheviks. The procurement and distribution of food had become an all-consuming task of local enterprises and trade unions. Another solution to the food-supply problem was for workers to produce their own agricultural products: trade unions and enterprises were offered the use of confiscated farms adjacent to their cities so that they could set up their own market gardens. As it turned out, however, urban workers, printers among them, expressed little interest in the production of food or in its preparation. The Petrograd Printers' Union's efforts to run its own farm only drew criticism from the workers. A couple of years later, workers at the First Model Print Shop in Moscow reviewed the question of taking out a lease on a one-desiatina plot to make a garden, and decided against the plan. Without a supply of labor or draft horses, workers could not farm effectively: they had tried before, they recalled, harvesting 70 poods of grain from the 500 they had sown![58] In the end, printers were unable to produce for their own consumption. As they had claimed in Penza, "We're workers, not sandwich makers"; neither were they agriculturalists.

Food ways during the Civil War offered little scope for cultural construction. Workers subsisted on the rations their factory committees or unions could provide and on the supplies they could bring back through individual foraging and bartering with peasants. The city governments of Petrograd and Moscow continually adjusted and readjusted their ration categories and eligibilities to respond to protests from below as well as to the availability of food for distribution.[59] Workers made access to food and the highest level of rations the center of their political and economic protests, and they couched their demands in terms of their identity as workers, as members of the working class.

Both Moscow and Petrograd city governments organized networks of public canteens to utilize their meager food supplies in the most efficient ways as

---

57. TsGA SPb, f. 4804, op. 5, d. 72 (Petrograd union conferences, 1921), l. 275 (typewritten minutes of Petrograd conference, 14–16 November 1920, misfiled with materials from 1921).
58. Ibid., ll. 275–76; TsGAMO, f. 699, op. 1, d. 270, l. 50.
59. See McAuley, *Bread and Justice*, 286–99.

well as to instill a sense of communalism through the culture of food. Mary McAuley indicates that in 1920, between 60 and 70 percent of the adult population of Petrograd obtained some of their meals from the canteens. By September 1921, however, attendance at the canteens had dropped to 20 percent of the population, but McAuley confesses that whether this change reflected a decline in the number of canteens or individuals' preference to eat at home is impossible to tell.[60] In 1921 women printers were already complaining that their children were being short-changed in one of the free canteens run especially for youngsters under age fourteen: the fat reserved for the children's soup was being diverted to canteens for "those above." When they protested, the management simply reassigned the canteen to serve adults only.[61] Thus the public canteens failed to draw support from their worker clientele.

In the printing industry, factory-based canteens perhaps took up the slack left by the dwindling number of centralized dining rooms. Canteens attached to specific enterprises, whose managers were responsible to the factory committees, were presumably more likely to respect the workers' preferences for norms of distribution. In March 1921, the Fourteenth State Print Shop in Petrograd announced that its canteen would be open only to workers and their families, defined as husband, wife, children, mother, and father. In Moscow by the end of 1921, the biggest enterprises, including the First Model Print Shop, had opened canteens. Forty enterprises still lacked such facilities, forcing workers there to bring their noon meals with them to consume where they worked, and prompting union sanitary experts to warn against cooking potatoes in the print shop's glue boilers.[62] How many printers in fact took their noon meals with their comrades is not known. The enterprise canteen would remain an important ideal in the 1920s, another mechanism that helped to foster factory solidarity and factory patriotism, and we will return to this setting in Chapter 6.

The alternative to dry rations consumed at the workbench or a hot meal shared in the factory canteen was to return home for a hot and nourishing meal prepared by one's landlady, mother, or wife. This scenario presumes a lodging with a kitchen that one could return to. In Petrograd, the municipality could not cope with the maintenance of its deteriorating housing stock, and adopted a policy of resettling worker families in bourgeois apartments in the center. Mary McAuley estimates that perhaps 65,000 families were resettled in the peak years of this transition, 1918 and 1919. In Moscow, too, the city's already dismal housing stock for workers deteriorated during the Civil War, as dilapidated buildings were scavenged for their firewood or otherwise damaged be-

---

60. Mauricio Borrero, "Communal Dining and State Cafeterias in Moscow and Petrograd, 1917–1921," in *Food in Russian History and Culture*, ed. Musya Glants and Joyce Toomre (Bloomington, 1997), 167; McAuley, *Bread and Justice*, 285–86.

61. TsGA SPb, f. 4804, op. 5, d. 73, l. 4.

62. Ibid., d. 76 (Petrograd factory committee meetings, 1921), ll. 11, 32; TsGAMO, f. 699, op. 1, d. 145, ll. 31, 57; *Otchet gubernskogo otdela vserossiiskogo soiuza rabochikh poligraficheskogo proizvodstva s sentiabria 1920 g. po mart 1921 g.* (Moscow, 1921), 20.

yond repair. Resettlement in Moscow also produced significant mobility, with an estimated 500,000 people changing their lodgings by 1921.[63]

By the end of the Civil War, with the municipal authorities unable to cope with the horrendous state of workers' accommodations, trade unions and individual factories stepped in to manage yet another aspect of their workers' everyday lives. The biggest enterprises, such as the First Model printing plant, were best positioned to commandeer housing for their workers. In December 1920, the enterprise controlled six public housing units, "house communes," although only two of them were really fit for human habitation. With financial subsidies from the printing industry trust, the enterprise managed the housing units, hiring cleaners, stove men, and yard sweepers and monitoring the social composition of the residents. Clearly not all the residents in these units earned their living as printers, and complaints over the presence of "nonworking" elements became a regular item of factory committee and union business in 1921 and 1922. On 28 June 1921, the union's central committee appealed to the Moscow city government to evict nonworkers from bourgeois apartment buildings and to resettle printers there. But the city soviet resisted, claiming that these so-called nonworkers were in fact soviet employees, white-collar workers whose jobs were just as important for the socialist regime as were those of production workers.[64] Access to food and entitlement to housing were thus expressed in class terms. In this way, daily life reinforced class identities shaped on the shop floor and at the same time implicated nonworking family members in the game of class identity.

In this early period workers' expectations were quite minimal. A heated and dry apartment was a luxury; enough calories per day to keep working constituted a decent standard of living. Whether this ascetic minimal everyday life was a value to be preserved or an accommodation to temporary hardship would continue to be contested in workers' discussions and in their cultural productions. In August 1921, Nikolai Gordon acknowledged that workers demanded material compensation for their labors, and he described his vision of the good life: "When [the worker] receives a decent wage, he can buy a pound of potatoes at the market, a pound of butter, and on Sunday a bottle of wine, and he can earn this from honest work; but if he wants to buy this wine in a café on Nevskii Prospekt, where music is playing, and he can't afford this because his wages are too low, then he'll stop working." A year later, Gordon again posed the question of material incentives and the fact of disagreements about what was sufficient. Petrograd printers' demands were simple, he said: "Breakfast, dinner, supper, some books, the theater, and pastry at the theater. But some comrades say trousers are necessary, too."[65]

63. McAuley, *Bread and Justice*, 267–75; William J. Chase, *Workers, Society, and the Soviet State: Labor and Life in Moscow, 1918–1929* (Urbana, 1987), 27–31.

64. TsGAMO, f. 699, op. 1, d. 145, l. 82; GARF, f. R-5525, op. 3, d. 10, l. 31 (Printers' Union central committee presidium meetings, 1921); TsGAMO, f. 699, op. 1, d. 270, l. 76; d. 269, l. 90.

65. TsGA SPb, f. 4804, op. 5, d. 71 (Petrograd Guberniia Union Conference, 15–16 August 1921), l. 7; op. 6, d. 24, l. 11.

The possibilities of material prosperity thus would alter what workers considered to be their "living minimum," and introduce the element of consumption and commodities into the set of factors that shaped workers' identities. Anthropologists discuss the ways in which commodities and consumption rituals are integral elements of social life, "mustering solidarity, attracting support, requiting kindnesses." Commodities function to send and receive social messages.[66] Communist social theorists also recognized the power of commodities to signify negative bourgeois values. Insofar as the commodities one possessed reflected individual preferences and private values, they reinforced private and family identities. A culture of consumption thus presented clear dangers for the project of socialist class formation. It is not so surprising, then, that the ideological focus of Soviet socialism remained production, a social process, rather than consumption, which could too easily become private and class-dissolving. The total proletarian should have no desire for things.

Nikolai Gordon's concern for the consumer needs of printers underscores an essential element in the socialist project, the possibility that socialism would transform not only production life but everyday life. It was the responsibility of the socialist movement to provide the means for this transformation. The socialist cultural project would reduce the private space of the individual worker and worker family in favor of expanding the public space in which culture could be transformed. In this process, class as a primary source of identity could exercise its dominance over competing forms of allegiance and sociability. The young Soviet trade union movement in particular assumed the responsibility for providing the menu and program of cultural and leisure activities for its workers. "Cultural work," a hallowed trade union function that had already been well developed by German Social Democratic forebears, included the fostering of a distinctly proletarian culture, the raising of the level of culture more generally, and the provision of proper socialist leisure activities for workers in their off-work hours.[67] Cultural work was synergistic: each of the three elements of this program reinforced the other. All three together would combine to shape, over the years and generations, a new socialist personality. As we shall see, however, the dreams of trade union culturalists would be derailed by two fundamental obstacles. Despite lofty ambitions, when it came to allocating scarce trade union resources, cultural work always came last. And the consumers of trade union culturalism, the workers themselves, often harbored their own ideas about how they wanted to spend their leisure hours and their cultural rubles.

---

66. Mary Douglas and Baron Isherwood, *The World of Goods: Towards an Anthropology of Consumption* (London, 1996), introduction to 1996 ed., xxi; Arjun Appadurai, "Introduction: Commodities and the Politics of Value," in *The Social Life of Things: Commodities in Cultural Perspective*, ed. Arjun Appadurai (Cambridge, 1986), 31.

67. Vernon Lidtke, *The Alternative Culture: Socialist Labor in Imperial Germany* (New York, 1985); Kaschuba, "Popular Culture and Workers' Culture"; Mary Nolan, *Social Democracy and Society: Working-Class Radicalism in Düsseldorf, 1890–1920* (Cambridge, 1981).

Cultural work had been a practical element in trade union activity in Russia when open political activity and strike organizing remained illegal. On the eve of the February revolution, for example, the Moscow Professional Society of Workers in Printing Work sponsored a library, distributed theater tickets, and organized museum excursions. And when the fall of the autocracy permitted trade unions to organize legally and fully, some of the first items on the agenda of the newly liberated Moscow Union of Workers in the Printing Trade were the creation of a library, formation of a political club, and cultural-educational work. With the victory of socialism, trade union activists insisted that cultural work would be as important as economic work.[68]

During these first years of Soviet power, when socialists sought to define their mission, the particular struggle between Communists and Mensheviks for the allegiance of printers saw extensive action along the "cultural front." In the contest for the union leadership, each side tried to claim superiority in providing cultural fare for the industry's workers. Each faction made young printers the focus of their cultural offensive: the Mensheviks' Society of Young Printers competed in Moscow with a Communist club organized to woo the younger generation away from the Mensheviks, featuring food as the lure toward Communist culture. And young printers did go to the Communist club for its *bufet*, admitted Menshevik union activists. But when the youth discovered that the cultural work there was unsatisfactory, they returned to the Menshevik club and the Society of Young Printers. The Menshevik youth society offered a range of activities each evening: on Mondays, drama and music circles and woodwork shop; Tuesdays were devoted to the art circle, woodwork, and the reading room; on Wednesdays the drama and music circles returned; Thursdays featured storytelling; and Fridays were given over to the meeting of the club board as well as the art and woodwork groups. Individual enterprises scheduled their own activities, or so said the Menshevik press. *Pechatnik* reported on a concert at the First Model Print Shop, with artists from the state theaters, but the Communist daily *Pravda* printed a letter from a woman worker at the same enterprise who denounced the shop's cultural work for existing only on paper, for an array of activities that was all propped up like a Potemkin village.[69] Given that the war between the Mensheviks and Communists raged along this cultural front as well as elsewhere, all reports from the front must be read with great care and skepticism. But the list of activities is nonetheless remarkable under the circumstances of scarce food, nonexistent heat, and uncertain future.

68. *Istoriia leningradskogo soiuza*, 78, 91, 100, 305; *Trudovaia kopeika*, 11 and 26 January 1917 (old style); *Vpered!* 10 March 1917 (old style); *Pechatnik* 3–4 (31 [18] March 1918): 15.
69. *Pechatnoe delo* 21 (29 April 1918): 7; *Pechatnik* 12 (10 December [27 November] 1918): 1. See also TsGA SPb, f. 4804, op. 3, d. 7 (meetings of the Petrograd guberniia union board, 1919), l. 4a; *Revoliutsionnyi pechatnik* (Moscow) 2–3 (23 February 1919): 20; *Revoliutsionnyi pechatnik* (Petrograd) 6 (25 February 1919): 6; *Moskovskii pechatnik* 5 (15 April 1921): 8; 7 (1 August 1921): 7; GARF, f. R-5461, op. 1, d. 29, ll. 27–27ob.; *Pechatnik* 3–4 (1 April 1919): 20, 21; *Pravda*, 6 April 1919.

This war confirms that culture mattered. At nearly every union conference and congress, whether Communist or Menshevik, "cultural-educational work" found a place on the agenda.[70] While central trade unionists would continue to debate the proper role of culture and the identity of "proletarian culture," many local trade union organizations and factory committees plunged ahead to organize cultural activities for their members. Ambitious plans called for clubs in every large enterprise and district and central clubs to link printers in smaller shops. Every club would have a library and reading room, and a mobile library would serve enterprises without their own clubs. Clubs would sponsor amateur circles for drama and music, drawing classes, Marxist study circles, sports groups, and handicraft circles appealing to men (woodworking, drafting, bootmaking) and women (sewing and knitting). Additionally, clubs and related cultural commissions would sponsor lectures, excursions to museums in the winter and out of town in the summer, performances by local amateurs and visiting guest artists, and children's parties.[71]

Culture mattered, but some Printers' Trade Union organizations paid more attention to cultural projects than others. Both the Moscow central organization and numerous enterprises sponsored a number of cultural activities in the Civil War years. The First Model Print Shop, as employer of the largest number of workers (but also a center of Menshevism), launched its cultural program early in 1918 with a survey of workers' family status, their preferences in lectures, and what musical instruments they could play. For Christmas in January 1918, the musical section sponsored a party for 600 children and a concert for adults. By the end of 1921, the club at the First Model Print Shop supported two drama groups, preparatory courses for advanced educational institutions, and a library. By 1922, the Moscow union reported a long list of performances and lectures mounted in its central club, including lectures on science, productions by Moscow theater companies, and readings of literary works that drew up to 350 auditors.[72]

Other localities also took their cultural mission seriously. "We don't lag behind the capitals," boasted a union representative from Smolensk at the May

---

70. *Tret'ya Vserossiiskaya Konferentsiya Professional'nykh Soyuzov, 1917* (reprint ed., ed. Diane Koenker, London, 1982), 502; *Vtoraia vserossiiskaia konferentsiia soiuzov rabochikh pechatnogo dela, 1917; Pervyi vserossiiskogo s"ezda soiuza rabochikh poligraficheskogo proizvodstva, 1919,* 42; *Tretii vserossiiskii s"ezd soiuza rabochikh poligraficheskogo proizvodstva, 1921,* 6.

71. GARF, f. R-5461, op. 1, d. 29, l. 27; TsGAMO, f. 699, op. 2, d. 21 (Moscow union factory committee conference, 9 July 1920), ll. 151–52; d. 145, ll. 66, 83; d. 269, l. 26; TsGAIPD SPb, f. 435, op. 1, d. 29 (general meetings of party collectives in Petrograd print shops, 1921), l. 119; GARF, f. R-5525, op. 4, d. 19 (report of Central Committee representatives on visit to Voronezh, 1922), ll. 2–3; *Otchet moskovskogo gubernskogo otdela vserossiiskogo soiuza rabochikh poligraficheskogo proizvodstva s ianvaria 1922 g. po avgust 1922 g.* (Moscow, 1922), 43–66; and the journals *Pechatnik, Pechatnoe delo, Revoliutsionnyi pechatnik, Moskovskii pechatnik,* and *Vserossiiskii pechatnik* for 1918–22.

72. *Pechatnik* 3–4 (31 [18] March 1918): 18; TsGAMO, f. 699, op. 1, d. 145, l. 83; *Otchet moskovskogo gubernskogo otdela,* 1922, 45–47.

1919 congress. The red union here sponsored theater and music studios, a library, excursions, lectures, and variety shows.[73] In Petrograd, by contrast, very little activity had taken place on the cultural front; in 1920, a visitor reported that cultural work here consisted entirely of distributing free tickets to city theatrical performances, and the central union club in fact shut down entirely between mid-1921 and mid-1922. The critical economic situation in Petrograd hampered the work of clubs and cultural organizers: in the winter, workers stayed away from the unheated club premises, and in the summer they were too busy working outside of town growing vegetables for themselves. The general impoverishment of Petrograd's economy and of the printing industry in particular kept the Petrograd union woefully short of funds.[74] But leadership styles and political differences also played a role: Nikolai Gordon seemed willing to pay lip service to the cultural front in support of the struggle against Menshevism, but at other times he expressed impatience with cultural matters.[75]

Ambivalence or outright disagreements about the role of culture in the life of workers and the proper form culture should take also may have worked to dissipate energies available for struggle on the cultural front. The history of the proletarian culture organization, Proletkul't, richly illustrates the dilemmas in regard to leadership, content, and mass tastes.[76] The trade unions themselves represented this mass taste, fostering a trade union consciousness that needed to be raised by the victors of the revolution into an activist revolutionary consciousness. But the trade union cultural activists in their turn resented the hegemonic assumptions of intellectuals' cultural organizations in the center. Workers needed culture, argued one Kositskii at the May 1919 red union congress, but the state's purveyors of culture, who spoke in the name of the workers but were not workers themselves, should stand aside, "because pettybourgeois elements have entered into all of these proletkul'ts and even into the Commissariat of People's Enlightenment." Mirroring the ongoing discussion about whether revolutionary culture should invent its own new forms or assimilate the best of bourgeois culture, some union culturalists insisted that workers needed to master classic methods and repertoires; an amateur actor who would soon move on to other pursuits did not need to invent radical new forms of art. "And as for Isadora Duncan's revolutionary dances," commented a worker correspondent in 1922, "I'm a poor expert and an even worse

---

73. *Pervyi vserossiiskii s"ezd soiuzov rabochikh poligraficheskogo proizvodstva, 1919*, 21; GARF, f. R-5461, op. 3, d. 7 (materials on guberniia conferences of Union of Workers in the Printing Trade, 1919), l. 2.

74. GARF, f. R-5525, op. 2, d. 7a (report of instructors on trips to Petrograd, Rybinsk, and Tver'), l. 3; *Vserossiiskii pechatnik* 8 (23) (August 1922): 6; *Krasnyi pechatnik* 3 (September 1922): 19; TsGAIPD SPb, f. 435, op. 1, d. 29, l. 119; TsGA SPb, f. 4804, op. 5, d. 71, l. 14; op. 6, d. 24, l. 6; op. 7, d. 90 (general meetings at Petrograd print shops, 1922–23), l. 120; *Vserossiiskii pechatnik* 8(23) (August 1922): 5–6; *Otchet tsentral'nogo komiteta vserossiiskogo soiuza rabochikh poligraficheskogo proizvodstva s 1 iiunia po 1 sentiabria 1922 g.* (Moscow, 1922), 143.

75. GARF, f. R-5525, op. 1, d. 10, l. 195.

76. This is the subject of Mally, *Culture of the Future*; see esp. chap. 6.

judge ... but is this art? ... Did we need any revolution for this, let alone October?"[77]

Finally, cultural activists had to confront union members' demand for pure entertainment instead of proletarian enlightenment. Dancing came to symbolize the philistine and frivolous preferences of rank-and-file workers. The Civil War was a time of emergency, lamented the leading union cultural organizer, Ivan Lomskii, "when we needed to intensely inculcate a class spirit among our printing masses," but local cultural commissions went ahead and organized extravagant dances. Local clubs organized dances even during the week-long campaign to aid the famine victims in 1921, "when no dancing should have been done." The Voronezh union organization admitted with consternation that once they prohibited dancing after their club events, attendance fell precipitously.[78] Such arguments foreshadowed the continuing concern over proletarian culture and values that would occupy cultural activists throughout the 1920s: should workers' clubs prohibit dancing, films, and beer as inappropriate forms of leisure, ensuring in the bargain that the majority of their members would stay away? Others would argue that cultural purists needed to make concessions to workers' unproletarian tastes in order to gain the opportunity to launch their projects of cultural transformation.

As long as discussions of workers' cultural needs and preferences were filtered through the voices of the activists, it remains difficult to distinguish an "authentic" cultural and leisure aspiration for the rank and file, let alone to identify subcultures among Russian printers or workers as a whole.[79] The normative prescriptions found in the union journals and voiced at local and national congresses, however, expressed reactions to what activists perceived to be the real subculture. What the activists called "bad" the historian can reasonably conclude was something workers did. Young workers liked to dance, even in the hungriest days of the Civil War, and even if women were most frequently denounced for the dancing deviation, they must have found partners at the dances. Workers enjoyed the cinema, even if the content was not proletarian. One Petrograd organizer admitted that workers stopped coming to his lectures until he arranged to follow each lecture with a film, whereupon he spoke to full houses.[80]

Above all, ordinary workers seemed to reject the enforced collectivism of the new proletarian cultural project. Despite an ambitious program of summer ex-

---

77. *Pervyi vserossiiskii s"ezd soiuzov rabochikh poligraficheskogo proizvodstva*, 1919, 37; *Moskovskii pechatnik* 4 (1 July 1922): 6–7.
78. *Moskovskii pechatnik* 1 (1 January 1921): 11; GARF, f. R-5525, op. 4, d. 19, l. 2.
79. Helmut Gruber discusses this problem in regard to the Viennese socialist movement and working class in *Red Vienna: Experiment in Working-Class Culture, 1919–1934* (Ithaca, 1991), esp. 7–9.
80. *Pervyi vserossiiskii s"ezd soiuzov rabochikh poligraficheskogo proizvodstva*, 1919, 38, 40. See also Richard Stites, *Russian Popular Culture: Entertainment and Society since 1900* (Cambridge, 1992), and Denise J. Youngblood, *Movies for the Masses: Popular Cinema and Soviet Society in the 1920s* (Cambridge, 1992).

cursions in 1922, the Moscow union cultural specialists admitted that most workers preferred to travel on their own. And the most successful element of the cultural program throughout this period remained the issuance of free or discounted theater tickets, tens of thousands of them in Moscow and Petrograd. Workers could attend the theater as individuals and engage in a personal relationship with the play, the actors, and the message. Uncounted workers, especially adults with or without families, preferred to spend their free time at home or drinking with their friends in neighborhood taverns.[81]

Activists called such individualism a "yellow infection" or inertia: "Culture is possessing the tools of knowledge. Everything else is petty bourgeois."[82] If only they had more money and more cultural activists (cadres could decide everything), they could accomplish their cultural goals, and turn every worker into a total proletarian. Their notion of a worker identity was uniform, monochromatic, and often rigidly puritanical. Any "worker culture" or "worker identity" that fell outside the parameters defined by these activists was treated as an illness to be cured through hard work and culture; many workers themselves, however, were perfectly comfortable with more flexible patterns of cultural consumption.

Class as a concept and presumed basis of solidarity played a central role in the articulation of printers' experiences during the Civil War, but it remained a complicated and changeable attribute and identity. Class solidarity smoothed over and potentially healed numerous sources of divisions, but such divisions could also survive subterraneously as craft identities and alternative socialist imaginaries. The dream of a total class would remain a goal of those who imagined that communism would create a new personality, the total proletarian, but real workers in real places retained their own aspirations and understandings about what socialism meant for them. Political will, economic circumstances, and ideas of class and identity would continue strongly to affect printers' identities and affinities as the country struggled to put its socialist experiment on the road to a new model society.

---

81. *Otchet moskovskogo gubernskogo otdela, 1922*, 45; *Pechatnik* 11 (10 November [28 October] 1918); *Vserossiiskii pechatnik* 8 (23) (August 1922): 5; GARF, f. R-5525, op. 2, d. 7a, l. 3; TsGA SPb, f. 4804, op. 4, d. 19, l. 224a; *Moskovskii pechatnik* 6 (1 May 1921): 6; *Otchet gubernskogo otdela (Moscow) 1920/21*, 56; *Otchet moskovskogo gubernskogo otdela 1922*, 60. On drink, see Laura L. Phillips, *Bolsheviks and the Bottle: Drink and Worker Culture in St. Petersburg, 1900–1929* (DeKalb, 2000), 88–90.

82. GARF, f. R-5525, op. 1, d. 10, l. 190; *Moskovskii pechatnik*, 2 (15 February 1921): 15; *Otchet o deiatel'nosti pravleniia moskovskogo gubernskogo otdela soiuza rabochikh poligraficheskogo proizvodstva (s maia 1921 g. po fevral' 1922 g.)* (Moscow, 1922), 52.

# PART II

## THE "GOLDEN YEARS" OF THE NEW ECONOMIC POLICY, 1922–1927

## CHAPTER 4

## A NEW FORM OF LABOR RELATIONS

*"Can it really be true that as soon as [a printer] leaves your ranks and sits in the manager's soft chair, he becomes a parasite and a serpent?"*

*"It happens."*

EXCHANGE AT LENINGRAD GUBERNIIA UNION CONGRESS, 1926

The years of the New Economic Policy brought economic recovery to urban Russia, at the same time providing space to elaborate new economic, political, and social schemes that would befit the first socialist country in the world. Traditional economic periodization notes a slow recovery from seven destructive years of war, climaxed by the "scissors crisis" at the end of 1923, when high prices diminished demand and stalled the economic recovery. Once the government had closed the scissors, forcing prices down through a combination of higher productivity and looser credits, the Soviet economy grew steadily for several years. In the golden years of "high NEP," 1924 and 1925, industry returned to its prewar levels of output, old plants finally produced at full capacity, and harvests were relatively abundant.[1] Thereafter, the story told

1. Alec Nove, *An Economic History of the U.S.S.R.* (Harmondsworth, 1969), 87–96, 113–18; E. H. Carr, *The Interregnum, 1923–1924* (London, 1954), 3–149, and *Socialism in One Country, 1924–1926* (London, 1958), vol. 1; see also Lewis H. Siegelbaum, *Soviet State and Society between Revolutions, 1918–1929* (Cambridge, 1992), 100–113, 165–80.

by economic historians begins to focus on the debate over planning, which would culminate in the adoption and implementation of the First Five-Year Plan in 1927 and 1928.

The standard story of the NEP economy is one of industrial policy willed from the top down. Small executive bodies in the Moscow center—Vesenkha, the Politburo, the Council for Labor and Defense—adopted decisions about productivity, quality, rationalization, and industrial organization, and transmitted directives to their lieutenants in industry. Trade unions were ordered to leave economic management to the managers, and they did. Workers were ordered to work by the piece in order to raise their productivity, and they did. Centralization and standardization were meant to be the order of the day.

Exploring the economic experience of the printing industry complicates the standard picture of the NEP economy. The Printers' Union and local workers indeed received the commands about productivity, quality, and acceptance of managerial authority, but a look at the NEP economy from below reveals multiple points of dissonance, incompetence, and contradiction that help to explain the precarious nature of the golden breathing space of NEP. State-owned enterprises were asked to operate according to market principles. The trade union represented both the interests of workers and the needs of the state as though they were in complete accord. New socialist managers, with little experience in industrial management, juggled the requirements of industrial revitalization with workers' expectations for their own welfare. The printing industry as a whole found itself ignored and increasingly powerless in competition for scarce state resources. Workers and managers all responded to these challenges with demands for more central regulation and less free market. The union leaders envisioned, however, that regulation would provide them with a central and collaborative role in the running of socialist industry.

## THE PRINTERS' NEP

The New Economic Policy adopted by the Tenth Communist Party Congress in March 1921 envisioned a mixed economy of socialized industry amidst a sea of private agricultural producers, services, artisans, and distributors. Eyewitnesses such as Emma Goldman noted the instantaneous effect of the new policy on urban economies: "Trade became the new religion. Shops and stores sprang up overnight, mysteriously stacked with delicacies Russia had not seen for years. Large quantities of butter, cheese, and meat were displayed for sale; pastry, rare fruit, and sweets of every variety were to be purchased."[2] The industrial sector took longer to recover, and the printing industry experienced NEP as a period of general economic crisis superseded only briefly by moments of relative prosperity. For printers, the years 1921 and 1922 remained difficult

---

2. Emma Goldman, *My Disillusionment in Russia* (New York, 1970), 201.

ones, and overall, the printing industry began to emerge from the collapse of the Civil War years only by the beginning of 1923.[3]

The growing pains of the new socialist organization of industry further complicated the recovery of printing. The state had decided in August 1921 to streamline and rationalize industry by consolidating the biggest and most successful enterprises into state-owned trusts, to be organized on principles of cost accounting and financial autonomy. Other plants would be available for leasing to government agencies or private entrepreneurs. The printing industry accounted for 24 trusts by August 1922, with a total of 15,400 workers in 198 enterprises, but these trusts represented only a fraction of the socialized printing industry. The military claimed a number of printing plants for its own use, and other enterprises passed under the control of individual government agencies or cooperatives. One of the biggest agencies was the State Publishing House, Gosizdat, which exercised suzerainty over some of the biggest and best-equipped shops in the country. Private entrepreneurs took up few leases in the printing industry and only among the very smallest of firms.[4]

The two largest trusts, Petropechat' in Petrograd and Mospechat' in Moscow, began to consolidate their operations in November 1921, Petropechat' operating nine enterprises and Mospechat' six. Other enterprises that had been managed by the local printing sections were slated for closing, their equipment to be cannibalized by the enterprises still operating. Sometime in early 1922, a second Moscow trust emerged, called Mospoligraf, and by the middle of the year it had acquired nine print shops and four wallpaper factories, with 2,523 workers. Arguing that the existence of two competing trusts was inefficient, the Moscow Printers' Union recommended that the two be merged, but it was overruled by the Supreme Economic Council, Vesenkha. Gosizdat also became a major player in the printing industry, convincing Vesenkha to transfer to its jurisdiction some of the best shops still outside any trust. Later as well, the Transportation Commissariat formed a trust, Transpechat', to link the numerous shops under its control.[5] State ownership dominated the industry, but it remained decentralized and fragmented.

3. *Pechatnik* 1 (34) (20 December 1922): 4; TsGA SPb, f. 4804, op. 6, d. 24 (Fourth Petrograd Guberniia Printers' Union Congress, 8 September 1922), d. 27 (Leningrad factory committee conferences, 1922); *Pechatnik* 5 (23 April 1923): 3; *Otchet pravleniia moskovskogo gub'otdela vserossiiskogo soiuza rabochikh poligraficheskogo proizvodstva ot 1 sentiabria 1922 g. po 1 sentiabria 1923 g.* (Moscow, 1923), 3; TsGAIPD SPb, f. 435, op. 1, d. 78 (meetings of the bureau of the Communist Party fraction, 1921–23), l. 81; *Ekonomicheskaia zhizn'*, 9 October 1924; *Stenograficheskii otchet piatogo s"ezda soiuza rabochikh poligraficheskogo proizvodstva SSSR 20–24 dekabria 1924 g.* (Moscow, 1925), 65–68, 113–48.

4. Carr, *Bolshevik Revolution*, 2:303–4, 307; V. Z. Drobizhev, *Glavnyi shtab sotsialisticheskoi promyshlennosti: Ocherki istorii VSNKh, 1917–1932 gg.* (Moscow, 1966), 144; *Na novykh putiakh: Itogi novoi ekonomicheskoi politiki 1921–1922 gg.* (Moscow, 1923), 3:1, 71, 80–81; *Otchet pravleniia moskovskogo gub'otdela 1922/1923*, 10. See also Ia. S. Rozenfel'd, *Promyshlennaia politika SSSR (1917–1925 gg.)* (Moscow, 1926), 216–18.

5. *Krasnyi pechatnik* 1 (26 November 1921): 7; *Otchet pravleniia moskovskogo gub'otdela*

Every trust and individual state-run plant agreed to adopt the principle of cost accounting (*khozraschet*), but the transition from an industry heavily subsidized by the state to one expected to pay its own way would create havoc in both industrial organization and the lives of the workers. Petropechat', for example, was awarded the largest enterprises in Petrograd and controlled two-thirds of the city's newspaper presses, but the firm lacked capital, and its state customers were unaccustomed to paying for its orders on time or at all. Lack of payment for orders meant that workers were not paid on time, either. The trust's officials saw no alternative but to beg Vesenkha in Moscow for subsidies (a trillion rubles would save the day, they reported in early 1923) and orders. But whatever subsidies they managed to obtain mysteriously disappeared; by April the trust announced that it had no money to pay the April wage bill. Meanwhile, individual firms were escaping from the trust and seeking their own arrangements for affiliation. By June 1923, Petropechat' had been dissolved.[6] Moscow profited at Petrograd's expense. Mospechat' also disappeared, its directors jailed for a kickback scheme, but by December 1923 Mospoligraf could boast it was the biggest printing trust in the republic, with fourteen typographical firms and auxiliary enterprises. On the commercial side, Mospoligraf operated four wallpaper stores and five stationery outlets, with shops in seven cities across the country. By 1925–26, Mospoligraf's empire had grown to twenty-four enterprises, including eleven print shops.[7]

Historians of NEP point out that individual enterprises were subordinated to their trusts and to Vesenkha even during NEP, that they lacked rights in law, and that their managers possessed no autonomy.[8] The printing industry, as always, claimed to be exceptional, and Mospoligraf insisted that it gave great leeway to local management.[9] Whether exceptional or rather emblematic of the complicated local reality of the NEP economy, the experience with industrial reorganization of my seven case studies depicts an industry suffering from too much local autonomy and desperately seeking authority and central structure.

As three of the biggest and best enterprises in Moscow, the First Model Print Shop, the Twentieth (Krasnyi Proletarii) Print Shop, and the Sixteenth (formerly Levenson) Print Shop, all entered first into the Mospechat' trust, and then with its demise they became units of Mospoligraf. In June 1923, however, Mospoligraf underwent reorganization in order to increase efficiency, and it handed

---

*1922/1923*, 10; *Moskovskii pechatnik* 5 (5 August 1922): 5; GARF, f. R-5525, op. 4, d. 1 (transcript of Fourth All-Russian Congress of Printers' Unions, 18–21 October 1922), l. 115; *Pechatnik* 1 (34) (20 December 1922): 24.

6. *Trud*, 10 February 1922, 19 June 1923; *Krasnyi pechatnik* 2 (1 April 1922): 13; GARF, f. R-5525, op. 4, d. 7 (meetings of presidium of Printers' Union Central Committee, 1922), l. 17; op. 5, d. 70 (meetings of board and presidium of Petrograd union, 1923), ll. 110b., 14, 170b., 67; *Pechatnik* 9 (August 1923): 9 and 5 (15 March 1924): 12.

7. *Pechatnik* 1 (34) (20 December 1922): 24; 14 (15 December 1923): 7; 19 (1 October 1925): 4–5.

8. Nove, *Economic History*, 97; E. H. Carr and R. W. Davies, *Foundations of a Planned Economy, 1926–1929* (London, 1969), 1, pt. 1: 372.

its largest firms over to outside operators on three-year leases. The First Model Print Shop and Krasnyi Proletarii were leased to Gosizdat, but the state publishing firm in turned awarded Krasnyi Proletarii to the journal *Krasnaia Nov'* (Red virgin soil) for its exclusive use. The Sixteenth Print Shop continued to work directly under Mospoligraf, producing a wide variety of printed products, including journals, books, and newspapers. The First Model Print Shop, meanwhile, continued to report to two masters: it was "owned" by Mospoligraf but operated by Gosizdat, which paid Mospoligraf 10 percent of its fees for the right to control the enterprise.[10] Other Mospoligraf enterprises also served the large public sector. The Seventh Mospoligraf shop, for example, reported that in 1923, 26 percent of its orders came from state organizations, 10 percent from trusts, enterprises, and cooperatives, 60 percent from the Communist Party, and only 4 percent from private customers.[11]

Without a strong trust to organize production and negotiate orders, Petrograd enterprises found themselves more vulnerable to the changing vicissitudes of the industry. Vesenkha had slated both Pechatnyi Dvor and the Fourteenth State Print Shop for closure in 1922, a decision "illegally" resisted by its activist managers. With the demise of Petropechat', Vesenkha leased Pechatnyi Dvor to Gosizdat, which invested heavily in new equipment, motors, and staff. By the end of 1923, Pechatnyi Dvor under its new management had returned to producing at 100 percent of its capacity, and its workforce had grown from 600 to 900 workers. The Fourteenth Print Shop was not so fortunate: by the beginning of 1923, its financial situation was so bleak that no trust wanted to inherit its huge deficits, but politics saved the day. The Petrograd Communist Party decided to lease the Fourteenth shop as a backup printer for its *Petrogradskaia pravda*. The Twenty-sixth (Sokolova) Print Shop faced similar uncertainties. With the liquidation of the Petropechat' trust, Sokolova remained unleased, and worked directly under the authority of Vesenkha until mid-1924, when it signed an agreement to print for the Priboi publishing house.[12]

The situation in Voronezh can hardly be compared with the experience in Moscow and Petrograd, but it exemplifies the experience of the small-scale provincial printing industry. The entire labor force of the Voronezh printing industry came to less than that of any one of the six enterprises mentioned above in the capital cities. Here the guberniia's economic council continued to play

---

9. *Moskovskii pechatnik* 13 (12 November 1923): 15–16.

10. *Pechatnik* 26 (18 September 1927): 9–10; 6 (16 May 1923): 8; TsGAMO, f. 699, op. 1, d. 396 (meetings in print shops in Zamoskvorech'e district, 1923), l. 44.

11. *Moskovskii pechatnik* 8 (16 June 1923): 18.

12. TsGA SPb, f. 4804, op. 6, d. 27, l. 13; op. 7, d. 90 (general meetings at Petrograd print shops, 1922–1923), l. 73; TsGAIPD SPb, f. 435, op. 1, d. 78, l. 50; d. 49 (meetings of party fraction of Leningrad union, October 1923–December 1924), l. 24; *Petrogradskaia pravda*, 1 April 1923; 9 September 1923; *Pechatnyi dvor*, 2 June 1923; GARF, f. R-5525, op. 5, d. 70, ll. 8, 75; *Zorkii glaz*, 1 May 1926; *Pechatnik* 18 (1 October 1924): 13; *Otchet leningradskogo gubotdela professional'nogo soiuza rabochikh poligraficheskogo proizvodstva S.S.S.R. za 1926–1927 gg.* (Leningrad, 1928), 42.

the leading managerial role in Voronezh's printing industry. One of the best shops in the city, the Southeastern Railway Print Shop, was transferred to a regional trust, and then in 1923 the remaining enterprises passed to individual agencies. By 1924, most of Voronezh's 580 printers worked in three large shops: the Railway Print Shop; the shop that printed the party newspaper, *Voronezhskaia kommuna;* and a shop that worked directly for Vesenkha. Outside provincial capitals, uezd soviet executive committees "owned" the local shops in their central towns. "Private" enterprise did not exist, but the print shops in Voronezh, each independently controlled, competed with one another for orders, driving down prices and wages and leading the union to demand a trust in order to escape the "exploitation" of their government bosses.[13]

For socialists, the key remained organization and integration, not fragmentation and competition. Printers' Union officials recognized that other problems besides organization contributed to the industry's slow recovery. The poor quality of paper contributed to ruined jobs and excess waste; insufficient paper supplies caused delays in fulfillment of orders. The low quality of domestically produced printers' ink and lack of type also contributed to the high expense of printing jobs and helped stall the industry. Publishers who failed to understand their markets also came in for their share of blame. On the eve of the textbook season in 1924, for example, Gosizdat was still publishing fiction, which was not selling, and failed to produce textbooks, for which the union presumed there was an unlimited demand. Excessive numbers of white-collar staff in print shops, at publishers, and in economic agencies also reportedly contributed to huge waste and high overhead. In addition, technological stagnation contributed to the erosion of the industry's productive capacity. By 1926, only two enterprises in Moscow could be considered technologically adequate, reported a special commission investigating quality problems in the industry. The rest of them could be considered "museums of printing."[14]

Despite all these factors, however, the chief cause of the crisis was seen to be the lack of sufficient regulation and oversight. Officials in the trade union never

---

13. GARF, f. R-5525, op. 4, d. 19 (report of Central Committee representatives on visit to Voronezh, 1922), ll. 3–4; d. 53 (meetings of Voronezh board, 1922), ll. 125–26; op. 5, d. 32 (Third Voronezh Guberniia Congress, 21 June 1923), l. 63ob.; *Otchet o deiatel'nosti pravleniia gubotdela soiuza rabochikh poligraficheskogo proizvodstva s 1 iiulia 1922 g. po 31 maia 1923 g.* (Voronezh, 1923), 11–12; *Otchet o deiatel'nosti pravleniia voronezhskogo gubotdela soiuza rabochikh poligraficheskogo proizvodstva s 1/VI 1923 g. po 1/X 1924 g.* (Voronezh, 1924), 22–23; *Protokol zasedaniia IV-go gubernskogo s"ezda rabochikh i sluzhashchikh poligraficheskogo proizvodstva 21–23 oktiabria 1924 goda* (Voronezh, 1924), 10–11, 19–22, 25–26; *Pechatnik* 23–24 (15 December 1924), 24; *Protokoly zasedaniia V-go gubernskogo s"ezda rabochikh i sluzhashchikh poligraficheskogo proizvodstva 24–25 oktiabria 1925 g.* (Voronezh, 1925), 20; *Pechatnik* 44 (30 October 1926): 9; *Otchet o rabote pravleniia gubotdela VI sozyva s 15/XI 1926 g. po 15/XI 1927, VII-mu Gubs"ezdu SRPP* (Voronezh, 1927), 1–2, 10–17.

14. The sad state of the paper industry was a running theme in the pages of *Ekonomicheskaia zhizn'* throughout the 1920s; *Moskovskii pechatnik* 23 (15 June 1925): 15; *Shestoi moskovskii gubernskii s"ezd rabochikh poligraficheskogo proizvodstva 23–26 oktiabria 1924 g.* (Moscow, 1924), 72; *Pechatnik* 28 (10 July 1926): 8.

accepted the decentralization of NEP, and they fought a losing battle with Vesenkha to keep the old unified structure that had prevailed during the years of the Civil War. They blamed the repeated crises in the industry on "unhealthy," "Bacchanalian," "predatory," "savage," and "destructive" competition for orders and jobs, and they persistently demanded an overarching regulatory body.[15] In their repeated requests for system, authority, and centralization, union officials appealed often to the tradition of the Civil War, endorsing the integration of trade union and managerial apparatuses. Programmatic articles by the union veterans Derbyshev, Davydov, and Tikhanov called for a "state organ with full power [*vlast'*]" that would set uniform prices, allocate supplies, and lobby for state subsidies. Government agencies responded favorably to the union's plea for a central authority that would facilitate the productive collaboration of workers, management, and the party.[16]

Symptomatic of the Printers' Union's weakness in the trade union and political hierarchy, the all-powerful organ only slowly came to life. In the middle of August 1925, *Izvestiia* reported that Gosplan was organizing a "Main Committee on the Affairs of the Printing Industry," with responsibility to organize accounting, expansion, and liquidation of enterprises, work out methods of cost calculations, and negotiate foreign orders. Yet by the end of the year, *Pechatnik* would complain that such committees were not effective, and the industry needed an overarching "Bureau of Congresses of the Printing Industry." Officially, trade unions were supposed to stay out of the administration of the economy, but the productivist strain in the Printers' Union exerted a powerful pull. Finally, in the middle of 1926, as the industry continued to rock through crises of overproduction and underemployment, an All-Union Congress of Representatives of the Managerial Organs of the Printing Industry met to decide the question of the "all-powerful" center. The congress's final session on 20 June elected a nineteen-person Council of Printing Congresses, known as the Council of Congresses (Sovet s"ezdov). Its members included representatives from the main printing trusts around the country, and its general secretary was G. Kagarlitskii, head of the Printing Committee under Vesenkha and a longtime union official as well.[17]

Yet the Council of Congresses, representing a fusion of economic and trade union interests, disappointed its backers. Instead of promoting industrial expansion, it recommended the closing of enterprises and the shrinkage of the in-

---

15. GARF, f. R-5525, op. 4, d. 1, l. 114; dissolution discussions in *Ekonomicheskaia zhizn'*, 21 April and 21 July 1922. Competition adjectives in *Trud*, 14 December 1923; *Pechatnik* 8 (July 1923): 3; 2 (1 February 1924): 7; 12 (1 July 1924): 4; *Ekonomicheskaia zhizn'*, 9 October 1924; *Stenograficheskii otchet piatogo s"ezda soiuza*, 1924, 118, 213, 221, 237.

16. *Pechatnik* 2 (1 February 1924): 6–7; 5 (15 March 1924): 8; 19 (15 October 1924): 3; 20–21 (15 November 1924): 3–4; *Stenograficheskii otchet piatogo s"ezda soiuza*, 1924, 86, 122, 134, 162, 213, 227, 232, 335; *Ekonomicheskaia zhizn'*, 7 June 1924.

17. *Izvestiia*, 23 August 1925; *Pechatnik* 28 (8 December 1925): 2–3; *Ekonomicheskaia zhizn'*, 20 June 1926.

dustry. At the Printers' Union's Seventh All-Russian Congress, Nikolai Gordon, now representing the Khar'kov printers, denounced the council: "Let the regulatory organ regulate but not hinder our work." Union officials continued to complain about the lack of system in the industry, fragmentation, and unhealthy competition: grandiose new enterprises, such as a new *Izvestiia* printing plant and office, had been erected at the same time that perfectly fine print shops were forced to close. By the end of 1927, with the Five-Year Plan already in preparation, the industrial managers in the Council of Congresses voted to disband the council, but the trade union's central committee continued to demand "authoritative coordination" that could decide on the priorities of refitting, concentration, rationalization, regulating unhealthy competition, and providing the correct cost calculations.[18]

After seven years of the New Economic Policy, the trade union had never abandoned its belief that a command-administrative economy could best protect the interests of its members as well as manage the economy. They failed to recognize, however, that throughout the seven years of the New Economic Policy, the industry had been operated under one form or another of a command-administrative system, based on subsidies, soft budget constraints, and an absence of accountability. The much-vaunted quasi-market relations of NEP had never gained much of a foothold in the printing industry, in large part because there was no one representing the industry, either in the trade union or in the economic organs, who cared much for the economic principles of the market. Neither plan nor market appeared to solve the chronic problems of industrial organization in the printing industry, but perhaps the problem lay in the relations of production rather than in its organization. The conditions of relative prosperity thus provided a crucial testing ground for working out a new system of labor relations based on the community of interests between worker and boss.

## LABOR-MANAGEMENT RELATIONS IN A SOCIALIST KEY

The introduction of NEP, with its emphasis on sound management principles and the coexistence of capitalist and socialist economic forms, had changed the role of trade unions with respect to production. If during the early years of the revolution the trade unions had claimed a syndicalist role, sharing responsibility for production with the state, now under NEP the trade unions retreated to a more traditional role of defender of workers' interests. Nonetheless, the position of trade unions remained contradictory in this socialist state, a contradiction acknowledged by a Communist Party Central Committee resolution in early 1922. The party recognized the paradoxes in socialist trade union practice. Trade unions' defense of workers' interests was countered by the pressure

---

18. *Izvestiia,* 28 November 1926; *Pechatnik* 15–16 (1 June 1927): 2–3, 14; 17 (15 June 1927): 1–2; 36 (25 December 1927): 3; *Ekonomicheskaia zhizn',* 9 August 1927.

they could exert on workers because unions shared responsibility for the construction of the economy. The requirements of class struggle preached hostility toward management, but under socialism, labor and management required collaboration in order for both to prosper.[19]

The Communist Printers' Union had defeated its Menshevik opponents in the name of productivism and integration with state administrative and economic structures, but it now found itself defending the principles of independence and autonomy that had been the basis for the Menshevik challenge all along. The awkwardness of this new role found frequent expression in the statements of trade union leaders. Once the trade union activists had occupied positions in the committees and sections that ran the industry. Now after 1922, they acknowledged (and regretted) their distance from the seat of economic decision making.[20] The relations between labor and management at every level of the production process continued to reflect the fundamental contradiction between the union's productivist and workerist responsibilities: was the trade union a collaborator with management or an adversary? Collaboration should not be entirely surprising in the case of the printers, given the history of the industry.[21] The socialist workplace also reflected this tradition of collaboration. The Printers' Union had favored collegial administration throughout the Civil War, opposing the party's growing preference for one-man management. Even as the union lamented its enforced separation from economic decision making, the union's central committee and its local boards helped to make personnel decisions about staffing the boards of the printing trusts.[22]

Local direction of enterprises represented a prime example of the porosity of the line between labor and management. During the Civil War, the regime and the trade union had recruited red directors from among good workers and Communists, but the shift at the start of NEP toward a more businesslike approach to economic management often meant that competence triumphed over political hue in the appointment of factory directors. At the same time, directors were supposed to lose much of their autonomy to the overarching trusts. Yet the Printers' Union continued to play a key role in the appointment of bosses even after the transition to the New Economic Policy and the reorganization of the industry into trusts. The minutes of the Moscow union board for 1922 are peppered with approvals of the names of managers appointed to administer various shops. The board's concern was economic as well as partisan: in 1922, when the Petrograd union presidium discussed appointments of print shop di-

---

19. *Pravda*, 17 January 1922. See the discussion of decisions on the role of trade unions in Carr, *Bolshevik Revolution*, 2:323–30.

20. GARF, f. R-5525, op. 4, d. 1, l. 84; *Krasnyi pechatnik* 2 (1 April 1922): 3. Other comments on the union's new status outside production can be found in *Pechatnik* 8 (July 1922): 4; 6 (16 May 1923): 27; 15 (30 December 1923): 1–2, 4; 2 (1 February 1924): 3; *Otchet pravleniia moskovskogo gub'otdela 1922/1923 g.*, 31.

21. Steinberg, *Moral Communities*.

22. TsGAIPD SPb, f. 435, op. 1, d. 78, ll. 46, 55ob.; GARF, f. R-5525, op. 4, d. 1, l. 123.

rectors, they pointed out that "we don't have to consider the candidacy of a manager from the political point of view; the trust wants people with managerial expertise [*khoziaistvennye liudi*]." Given such concerns, qualified managers were hard to find, and turnover among directors was notably frequent. At the Motor print shop, four managers had come and gone in the first five months of the enterprise's existence, changing "like European governments."[23]

Workers and the union looked to the promotion of a new generation of experienced workers who could run their industry, since the holdovers from the old regime could not be trusted to manage the new labor relations. Capitalists who ran private enterprises would naturally flout the regime's labor laws, refuse to forward dues to the union, and cheat on overtime pay, argued *Moskovskii pechatnik* in 1923.[24] Good managers looked out for their workers' interests as well as the state's. And who better to understand workers' interests than those with work experience themselves? Such red directors knew that workers valued clear and honest reports, and they concealed nothing, sharing the enterprise's problems with everyone. Work could go well with such red directors who threw their proletarian work ethic into the job: the new manager of the Trud i Kniga shop in Moscow, Chusov, was forty-three years old and still did the work of three men, expanding production throughout the shop. "It was no coincidence that he himself had come from the ranks of the workers."[25] Workers, if not the party, believed that proper class credentials would lead to competent economic performance.

Nonetheless, political reliability was seen to be a necessary but not sufficient requirement for a successful manager. The union journal also reported many cases of well-meaning proletarians who did not understand the technology of the shops they directed, such as the metalworker who first set foot in a print shop the day he became its manager.[26] Power would sometimes go to their heads. Once promoted to management, even workers would become "Taylorists, Americanists, cost-cutters, and road hogs." The worker-director of the Sixteenth State Print Shop in Moscow, F. A. Miakin, ran his shop fairly successfully but without any real contribution of his own, and the power and money associated with the position soon went to his head. His passion for "alcohol, ladies, and the high life" led to his conviction for embezzlement in early 1924.[27]

---

23. Carr, *Interregnum*, 40; GARF, f. R-5525, op. 4, d. 62 (board and presidium meetings of Moscow Guberniia Printers' Union, 1922), ll. 48, 74, 78, 79; d. 67 (board and presidium meetings of Petrograd Guberniia Printers' Union, 1922), l. 1; *Pechatnik* 14 (15 May 1927): 8; 28 (10 October 1927): 2; *Moskovskii pechatnik* 4 (28 January 1925): 11.

24. *Moskovskii pechatnik* 10 (12 August 1923): 18; other vilifications of private owners appear ibid. 11 (22 September 1923): 12–13; *Pechatnik* 12 (1 July 1924): 15.

25. *Protokol zasedanii IV-go gubernskogo s"ezda, 1924* (Voronezh), 24; *Pechatnik* 4 (March 1923): 22; *Moskovskii pechatnik* 15 (23 April 1925): 9.

26. *Moskovskii pechatnik* 7 (22 February 1925): 10; also ibid. 8 (16 June 1923): 18; 33 (7 November 1924): 8; 30–31 (12 August 1925): 15.

27. Ibid. 6 (February 1926): 17; *Pravda*, 19 November 1925; 6 March and 10 June 1924;

The duty of managers to promote production but also to look after their workers led inevitably to conflict. The socialist manager under NEP was responsible to the economic agency that supervised his shop, transmitted orders, and provided working capital, but also to the trade union, which approved his appointment. The political role of the manager was therefore a delicate one, for in fact he had many masters. The case of another manager named Chusov illustrates the contradictions inherent in the position of the red director.

The case arose in March 1922, during the transition to the new era of cost accounting and one-man management. The factory committee chairman at the Third State Print Shop complained to the Moscow union board that the shop's manager, Chusov, had ignored the factory committee and the union's directives, did not pay workers accurately, fired and hired workers unilaterally, arbitrarily assigned pay rates to particular workers, and regularly insulted workers, especially women.[28] At a public hearing the factory committee chairman spoke in defense of workers' interests, citing conflicts that had arisen when Chusov determined who would be laid off without allowing the factory committee to advise, when workers failed to receive promised benefits, and when Chusov refused to report to the factory committee on the state of the enterprise. He had denied the workers' committee any role in decision making or even consultation. Those who opposed Chusov quickly found themselves unemployed. Other workers testified to Chusov's rudeness, his favoritism, and his contempt for the factory committee.[29] While Chusov's personal style had certainly aggravated relations, the case drew its significance from the way Chusov had violated the spirit of participatory labor relations that had developed during the first years of socialism. Chusov, in his rebuttal, admitted his disdain for the factory committee: they were incompetent, and if he insulted his workers, it was because they deserved it, they were slackers and pilferers. The investigating commission found Chusov guilty on all counts, and the union board, siding with the workers' committee, transferred Chusov to another post. Thus even one-man management did not mean that managers could exercise their authority with impunity.[30]

Directors, especially red directors, found themselves in a delicate position in the new labor relations of socialism. They had an obligation—both in law and in custom—to include workers' interests in their calculations. In the portrayals of managers in the Printers' Union press, the quality of accessibility and equality stands out as a key feature of proper labor relations in the new regime. Being "one of us" meant that the red manager treated workers with respect, reported regularly, and shared the problems of the enterprise with his workers.

---

TsGAMO, f. 699, op. 1, d. 438 (general and factory committee meetings at Krasnyi Proletarii, 1923), l. 31.

28. GARF, f. R-5525, op. 4, d. 62, l. 24. Indeed, Chusov had earlier been named in the press for his hostile attitude toward women workers: *Pravda*, 24 October 1920.

29. TsGAMO, f. 699, op. 1, d 185 (factory committee, tarif-norm commission, and investigatory meetings at Sixteenth, 1921–22), ll. 49–490b.

30. GARF, f. R-5525, op. 4, d. 62, l. 24; TsGAMO, f. 699, op. 1, d. 185, ll. 49–66.

At the same time, workers expected their directors to be able to overcome those problems. Here is where the innate contradictions between workers' immediate interests and the long-term interests of the workers' state could arise. As one worker-manager, Trauberg, explained at the congress of the Leningrad union in 1926, managers were by and large workers promoted from the bench, and often they were party members as well. "Can it really be true that as soon as he leaves your ranks and sits in the manager's soft chair, he becomes a parasite and a serpent?" ("It happens," came a voice from the floor). No, said Trauberg: the manager has to balance the workers' interests with those of the state, and this meant cost-cutting, layoffs, and a sharp eye for the bottom line.[31] These contradictory interests continued to generate tension in the workplace even as the number of worker-administrators rose: by 1927, satiric barbs at incompetent, arrogant, and superfluous administrators had become a standard feature in the union's journal.[32]

Similar conflicts of culture and interest prevailed at lower levels in the printing industry. The managers (*zaveduiushchie*) of departments in large plants reflected the same social profile as the plant managers: some were former specialists promoted to positions of authority, many were workers promoted from the bench. Technical specialists in the printing industry, unlike those elsewhere, shared this characteristic working-class origin.[33] Foremen, masters, and instructors, too, had almost always emerged from among rank-and-file workers, both before and after the revolution. The best of them spoke the workers' language, but others had had their worker identities corrupted by the prerogatives of authority.[34]

Additional contentious issues helped to structure labor relations in the new socialist state. Key among these, of course, were questions of compensation and incentives, the very heart of the wage labor bargain in any wage-driven economy. And a key challenge to the new workerist labor relations would be to balance the need for equality and fairness in compensation with the demand for efficiency and output.

Starting in 1922, bargaining over wages, fairness, and efficiency took place within the institution of the collective agreement negotiated between trade unions and individual enterprises or trusts. The abandonment of the Civil War's command-economy system required a return to the principles of contracts and

---

31. TsGA SPb, f. 4804, op. 10, d. 4 (stenographic report of Leningrad Union Seventh Congress, 14 March 1926), ll. 531–33.
32. *Pechatnik* 20 (10 July 1927): 25–26; 28 (10 October 1927): 2, 26.
33. "They are almost all 'workers from the bench,'" wrote a union official in 1924: *Pechatnik* 6 (1 April 1924): 3; see also *Moskovskii pechatnik* 18 (27 February 1924): 6.
34. *Iskry*, May 1926; *Zorkii glaz*, 21 January and 9 April 1926. See also S. A. Smith, "Workers against Foremen in St. Petersburg, 1905–1917," in Siegelbaum and Suny, *Making Workers Soviet*, 113–37; Lewis H. Siegelbaum, "Masters of the Shop Floor: Foremen and Soviet Industrialization," in Rosenberg and Siegelbaum, *Social Dimensions of Soviet Industrialization*, 113–37; J. Melling, "'Non-Commissioned Officers': British Employers and Their Supervisory Workers, 1880–1920," *Social History* 5 (1980): 183–222.

bargaining, familiar terrain for veterans of the trade union movement. Trade unions were directed to conclude comprehensive agreements with representatives of their industries, and most important, to secure the participation of their members in the agreement. The process of consultation among factory committees, unions, shop floor delegates, and economic organs would demonstrate that the old command (*prikaz*) methods had been left behind, and that workers were now full participants in the labor relations process.[35] The process of ratifying these contracts in the printing industry mirrored standard Soviet industrial practice: with more or less input from workers' representatives and a great deal of direction from the Labor Code, Vesenkha, and the Central Council of Trade Unions, individual trade unions prepared draft agreements that then had to be ratified by the rank and file in highly publicized rounds of meetings.[36] These ratification campaigns, which occurred every time the contract expired, educated local workers about the terms of their employment, their rights, and their responsibilities.

Since the Labor Code stipulated most of the nonpecuniary rights of workers (vacations, hours, and insurance, for example), the most contentious issues of the agreements always concerned wages, both their level and their form.[37] Initially, collective agreements were negotiated for brief terms, and the process of arriving at an agreement sometimes took longer than the actual period of its duration. Contracts valid for only three months were common in 1922 and 1923, when rapidly changing economic conditions required continual adjustment of wages. Gradually the terms of the contracts (themselves part of the negotiations) lengthened to six months, then to a year. Meanwhile, the period of time designated for public discussion of the contract was reduced. By 1927, the union had streamlined the ratification process so that it should take only one month for all enterprises to discuss and approve their new contracts.[38] The more the process was routinized, the more formalistic it became.

The collective agreement ratification process revealed further tensions in the socialist workplace among workers, unions, and employers. Newspaper compositors, citing their unusually difficult working conditions, continued to insist that their compensation should be up to 50 percent higher than ordinary workers'. One enterprise proposed a resolution (with "familiar Menshevik phrases,"

---

35. See, for example, *Moskovskii pechatnik* 3 (1 May 1922): 2.

36. For the textile industry, see Ward, *Russia's Cotton Workers*; Donald Filtzer, *Soviet Workers and Stalinist Industrialization: The Formation of Modern Soviet Production Relations, 1928–1941* (Armonk, N.Y., 1986), 22–23.

37. *Moskovskii pechatnik* 9 (12 July 1923): 6; 10 (12 August 1923): 15; 18 (27 February 1924): 17; *Pechatnik* 9 (August 1923): 8; 1 (34) (20 December 1922): 6; *Trud*, 8 July 1922; TsGAMO, f. 699, op. 1, d. 440 (general and factory committee meetings at Sixteenth, 1923), l. 9.

38. *Trud*, 6 September, 8 July, and 17 August 1922; *Pechatnik* 9 (August 1923): 8; 16 (15 August 1925): 2; 28 (8 December 1925): 1; 25 (19 June 1926): 1–2; 32–33 (28 November 1927): 4; *Moskovskii pechatnik* 18 (27 February 1924): 18; *Leningradskaia pravda*, 22 November 1925; *Ekonomicheskaia zhizn'*, 30 September 1927; TsGAIPD SPb, f. 435, op. 1, d. 68 (meetings of bureau of fraction of Leningrad union party, 1927), l. 75.

said the report of the meeting) denouncing the union for retreating from its position of 1905 in defense of the workers. Elsewhere, after a polite round of questions and answers at a delegates' meeting, a frustrated worker burst out, "Speaking out here makes no difference. Whatever they write down—that's what will happen." The process was carefully monitored by the party watchdogs, of course. In Leningrad in 1925, discussion of the new agreement at the Volodarskii Print Shop took on a "flagrantly demagogic" (i.e., oppositional) tone, and the agreement was voted down by the general meeting.[39]

Much of this discussion reflected easily recognized material self-interest: "Charity begins at home," more than one worker said in the course of these campaigns.[40] We need to consider quite carefully, however, the ways in which the wage bargain and its negotiation reflected fundamental worker identities and values, as well as how these values evolved in the effort to build a socialist system of labor relations. Examining conflicts over the wage form and the actual implementation of these wage agreements on the shop floor provides just such an opportunity. This examination also reveals the limits of central direction and illustrates the ways in which workers may have consented to agreements nationally but in fact bargained locally.

From the regime's point of view, the function of the wage form was to "interest" workers in their work; in other words, to provide sufficient material incentives to keep workers from seeking alternative employment (as during the Civil War) and to encourage them to produce as efficiently and effectively as possible. In this endeavor the socialist economic managers were no different from their capitalist counterparts. The wage was also important, however, as a means to signify the equality and dignity of labor, and the regime sought forms that would make it clear to workers that parity and equality were the order of the day: thus the trade union hierarchy promoted simple wage schemes, in which earnings were pegged to consistently labeled skill differentials.

Productivity and parity served as twin motors of Soviet wage policy in the early years of the socialist experiment. Parity had prevailed during the Civil War, in the form of pay in kind and collective supply. But economic recovery required more rigorous mechanisms to promote productivity, and by 1922, official wage policy promoted payment by results—piece rates—in all appropriate industrial sectors. Like workers elsewhere in industrial economies, printers resisted this wage form, as will be seen, but it gradually came to apply to the majority of the industry's labor force by 1926.[41] Then in 1927 the pendulum

---

39. *Moskovskii pechatnik* 10 (12 August 1923): 15–16; TsGA SPb, f. 4804, op. 9, d. 44 (general and factory committee meetings at Sokolova, 1924–25), l. 42; TsGAIPD SPb, f. 435, op. 1, d. 60 (meetings of bureau of fraction of Leningrad union party, 1925), l. 7.

40. *Moskovskii pechatnik* 10 (12 August 1923): 15.

41. John Child, *Industrial Relations in the British Printing Industry: The Quest for Security* (London, 1967), 71, 141; Peter Stearns, *Lives of Labor* (London, 1975), 209–15; David Montgomery, *The Fall of the House of Labor* (Cambridge, 1987), 148–54; Hinton, *First Shop Stewards' Movement*, 56–100.

swung the other way, and wage planners, still in the name of efficiency and productivity, began to implement pay systems based on time rather than results. Why? Scholars have normally paid attention to macroeconomic or political factors in explaining industrial policies: the scissors crisis or the bad harvest of 1927 forced industry to tighten its belt; industrial growth in 1926 and 1927 allowed the regime to relax the pressure on productivity. The threat of opposition from Trotskii on the left and Tomskii on the right may have encouraged the regime to loosen the industrial screws. And planners, whose power was more formidable in the second half of the 1920s, found that they could much more easily account for wage costs if workers were paid by standard time rather than by the piece.[42] What has been missing from this discussion has been the power of workers at the point of production to resist schemes of intensification and to modify the regime's wage policies to their own advantage.

The fundamental point of contention between workers and employers, in the socialist system as in any other, was the level of remuneration for a given quantity of work. That level was influenced by the market (the relative scarcity of work or workers) but also by custom (a "fair day's pay for a fair day's work") and by politics (labor laws, trade union power, and police enforcement of managerial prerogatives). At this fundamental level, management wanted to maximize the level of usable output (hence a concern for quality as well as quantity); workers wanted to maximize their income. In systems of pay based on the amount of time worked, management ensured output by establishing daily or monthly norms and by closely supervising the workforce. Under piece rates, the incentives were more purely pecuniary: the more a worker produced, the more could be earned. Management saved on supervision costs what it spent in extra wages. And by carefully limiting the amount paid for each piece, management could keep output high while still minimizing costs. Experienced workers, in turn, learned that if they cooperated in limiting their own production, they could bargain that piece rate upward.[43]

The standard in the printing industry was mixed, but pressmen, bookbinders, and many compositors had always been paid by time.[44] Thus the decision by the Fifth All-Russian Trade Union Congress in 1922 to countenance piece rates in order to raise productivity provoked immediate resistance from most Printers' Union members. Many admitted that workers' incomes could rise if they worked by the piece, and the method was said to be favored by those who "chased after the big ruble" and did not mind the intensification of work. "Imagine: a gang of suicide piece workers work day and night, completing this 'extra work' week after week." Union officials admitted as well that piece rates stimulated workers to work more productively, increasing output, reducing

---

42. See Carr and Davies, *Foundations of a Planned Economy*, esp. 1 (2): 282, 535.
43. See Eduard M. Dune, *Notes of a Red Guard*, ed. Diane P. Koenker and S. A. Smith (Urbana, 1993), chap. 1; Montgomery, *Workers' Control in America*, chap. 1, on the "stint."
44. Svavitskii and Sher, *Ocherk polozheniia; Istoriia leningradskogo soiuza*.

costs, and thus improving the economic health of the industry and of the country.[45] But nonetheless, the Printers Union, led by the Moscow branch, dragged its feet in implementing the new wage form and continued to defend remuneration by time.

For one thing, they argued, the intensification of labor that resulted from workers' running after higher wages led to a decline in the quality of their output. Printing demanded "thoroughness and artistry of execution." Proper typesetting meant paying attention to careful spacing of letters and watchful corrections; pressmen needed to keep their machines cleaned and well aligned. All of these things suffered when the only thing that mattered was the quantity of production. And not only was quality at risk, but so were the health and safety of workers when the lure of the big ruble tempted the "suicide piece workers" to "step on the pedal." Printers on piece rates not only worked more intensively but tended to work longer hours in order to complete even more pieces. This only wore them out and prevented them from engaging in socially healthy public work. Moreover, when printers' ability to complete their tasks was compromised by late copy, faulty paper, and other circumstances beyond their control, their wages would also vary, causing stress and anxiety.[46]

With these arguments, workers were pursuing the same goals as the regime. But workers had other reasons to favor time pay over piece rates that did not necessarily coincide with the party line. They were ready to trade the efficiency and productivity incentives of piece rates for a slower pace of work, for sharing the work so that unemployment could be reduced, and for the power to negotiate the wage bargain individually. The factory newspaper at the Pechatnyi Dvor shop in Petrograd featured a regular column, "Not Anecdote but Fact," which chastised workers for unsocial behavior but also revealed the existence of a "well-ingrained habit not to hurry." In April 1923 the column noted a number of instances of slacking by time workers. In one of them, the supervisor called three loafing typesetters to pick up their rulers and get back to work, only to be told, "Talk to someone else. We fulfilled our monthly norm on the sixteenth, and now we have a right to rest until the end of the month. We know the law."[47] Other printers invoked the egalitarianism of time pay, under which workers were not divided into "good" and "bad" categories, and in

---

45. *Krasnyi pechatnik* 3 (September 1922): 7; *Nasha zhizn'*, 28 March 1924, 19 December 1925; TsGA SPb, f. 4804, op. 6, d. 24; *Moskovskii pechatnik* 11 (22 September 1923): 6–7; 10 (12 August 1923): 16; 7 (1 April 1925): 1.

46. TsGA SPb, f. 4804, op. 8, d. 56 (stenographic report of Petrograd Guberniia Fourth Congress, 15–17 December 1924), l. 12; *Moskovskii pechatnik* 7 (February 1926): 1–2; 32 (20 August 1925): 1–2; 23–24 (June 1926): 10; 10 (12 August 1923): 16; 8 (16 June 1923): 8; 36 (22 September 1925): 3; *Trud*, 21 October 1922; *Nasha zhizn'*, 19 December 1925, 28 March 1924; TsGA SPb, f. 4804, op. 8, d. 56, l. 12; *Stenograficheskii otchet piatogo s"ezda soiuza 1924*, 316; *Pechatnik* 15 (1 August 1925): 5.

47. *Pechatnyi dvor*, 2 June and 25 April 1923, 18 August 1926; *Pechatnik* 6 (15 March 1925): 7; TsGAMO, f. 699, op. 1, d. 849 (general, factory committee, and conflict commission meetings at Sixteenth, 1926), l. 116. See Chapter 6 on the ethics of job sharing in the face of unemployment.

which workers did not hide materials from one another to increase their own output.[48]

Money figured importantly in these conversations, but in contradictory ways that suggest added layers of meaning were embedded in the wage form. Workers sometimes acknowledged that they could earn more on piece rates—this was how the regime was going to interest them in their work, after all. But they also worried that clever managers would set the piece rates to result in lower earnings for workers, not higher. And they criticized their comrades who rushed headlong in the chase for the big ruble, putting personal earnings and interests above those of the collective. At the same time, printers indicated that under time pay, they had more control over both the pace of their work and their earnings. With time pay, workers' earnings were pegged to their skill grade, the razriad, and it was easier to bargain with the local rates commission about a higher razriad than about higher rates or lower norms.[49]

In fact, bargaining over job rates and norms was an everyday part of the work process. Work in the printing industry was too idiosyncratic and the machinery too various to permit easy application of standard norms and rates. Even two identical presses could not be expected to produce at the same rate if one was more worn than the other, lubricated with dirty grease, or fed with inferior paper. Differences in economies of scale from enterprise to enterprise also affected workers' ability to produce at standard levels. Thus workers insisted that rates and norms had to be set locally.[50] Who knew the peculiarities of the job and the machines better than the workers themselves? Local knowledge was essential in determining the feasible set of production possibilities, and printers clearly made use of their "manager's brain under the workman's cap."[51]

Given their local knowledge of the shop floor, workers engaged in a continual effort to shift the terms of employment in their favor, whether on piece rates or time pay. More important, this effort was frequently collective. Reviving a prerevolutionary tradition, printers organized themselves into "companies" and "kettles," which bargained as a unit for each job, whether for a certain piece rate or for a lump sum. Such negotiations typically bypassed the local

---

48. *Pechatnik* 12 (15 June 1925): 11; *Nasha zhizn'*, 31 October 1924.

49. TsGA SPb, f. 4804, op. 8, d. 56, l. 12; TsGAMO, f. 699, op. 1, d. 728 (meetings of rates and conflict commission at Sixteenth, 1925), l. 86; TsGA SPb, f. 4804, op. 7, d. 77 (Petrograd guberniia union conferences, 1923), l. 36.

50. *Moskovskii pechatnik* 29–30 (September 1924): 4; 22 (7 June 1925): 5; 4–5 (January 1926): 15; 36 (22 September 1925): 3; 11 (22 September 1923): 6; *Pechatnik* 19 (15 October 1924): 4; 7 (1 April 1925): 2; 15 (1 August 1925): 4–5; 21 (15 October 1925): 1; 17 (24 April 1926): 8; 5 (30 January 1926): 6–7; *Pechatnyi dvor*, 30 July 1923; *Zorkii glaz*, 22 December 1924; TsGA SPb, f. 4804, op. 11, d. 99 (general and factory committee meetings at Pechatnyi Dvor, 1926–27), l. 261ob.; TsGAMO, f. 699, op. 1, d. 849, ll. 54, 56, 58–59; see also Lewis H. Siegelbaum, "Soviet Norm Determination in Theory and Practice, 1917–1941," *Soviet Studies* 36, no. 1 (1984): 45–68.

51. The phrase is from Montgomery, *Fall of the House of Labor*, chap. 1, describing precisely the way workers' collectives organized the labor process.

trade union structures. Within the company, the wages paid to the unit were reallocated in accordance with an internally determined hierarchy. These companies also functioned as cohesive and restrictive social units, as in the old days: one entered only on invitation, and membership included the *Bruderschaft* of regular drinking parties. Women, regardless of their skills, tended to be excluded, and the trade union condemned the persistence of the restrictive "companies." On the other hand, collective piece rates pooled in a group called the *kotel,* or kettle, remained within the boundaries of acceptable shop floor organization, especially since they tended to raise productivity levels. Typically, a kotel would consist of a highly paid elder (*starosta*) and a team of variously skilled workers. As with the company, the kettle's earnings were divided within the group in accordance with their place in the skill hierarchy. And here too the collective could often manipulate the rates and payments to their own advantage. They would bid for the most profitable jobs, leaving cleanup duties, for example, to other workers.[52] In the most extreme cases, the collectives encompassed twenty to thirty workers or even an entire shop, monopolizing the negotiation of rates, effectively setting their own work tempos, and allegedly lowering productivity.[53]

The results of printers' ability to negotiate the terms of their employment can be seen in the overall levels of real wages by industry. Despite the repeated hand-wringing about the crisis of the printing industry, the glut of unsold books, and the significant unemployment in the trade, printers' wages remained among the highest of Soviet industrial workers. Figure 1 indicates that, although the gap between printers and other workers began to narrow in mid-1925, printers were among the highest paid industrial workers throughout most of the 1920s. In adjusted Moscow rubles, printers maintained their position as the highest paid group of workers until the beginning of 1926, when they fell to second place (behind leather workers), and then briefly to third (behind metalworkers) in the third quarter of 1926.

Here, then, lay the reasons for the industry's return to payment by time in 1926. Piece rates simply did not work to raise productivity or slow wage inflation. Wages in the industry continued to remain high even while overall output

---

52. *Moskovskii pechatnik* 9 (12 July 1923): 17; 41 (27 October 1925): 12; *Pechatnik* 19 (15 October 1924): 4–5; 50–51 (20 December 1926): 24; 15 (10 April 1926): 1–3; 23–24 (15 December 1924): 19; *Otchet pravleniia moskovskogo gubernskogo otdela vsesoiuznogo soiuza rabochikh poligraficheskogo proizvodstva oktiabr' 1923–oktiabr' 1924 gg.* (Moscow, 1924), 98; *Iskry,* 25 December 1925.

53. *Pechatnik* 15 (10 April 1926): 1–3; 23–24 (15 December 1924): 32. On the artel tradition in Russia, see Hiroaki Kuromiya, "Workers' Artels and Soviet Production Relations," in *Workers in the Era of NEP: Explorations in Soviet Society and Culture,* ed. Sheila Fitzpatrick, Alexander Rabinowitch, and Richard Stites (Bloomington, 1991), 72–88. Teams or companies could be found in other industrial settings; see Carter L. Goodrich, *The Frontier of Control: A Study in British Workshop Politics* (New York, 1920), 155; Joan Wallach Scott, *The Glassworkers of Carmaux: French Craftsmen and Political Action in a Nineteenth-Century City* (Cambridge, Mass., 1974), 99.

Dynamics of Wages by Industry, 1922–1927

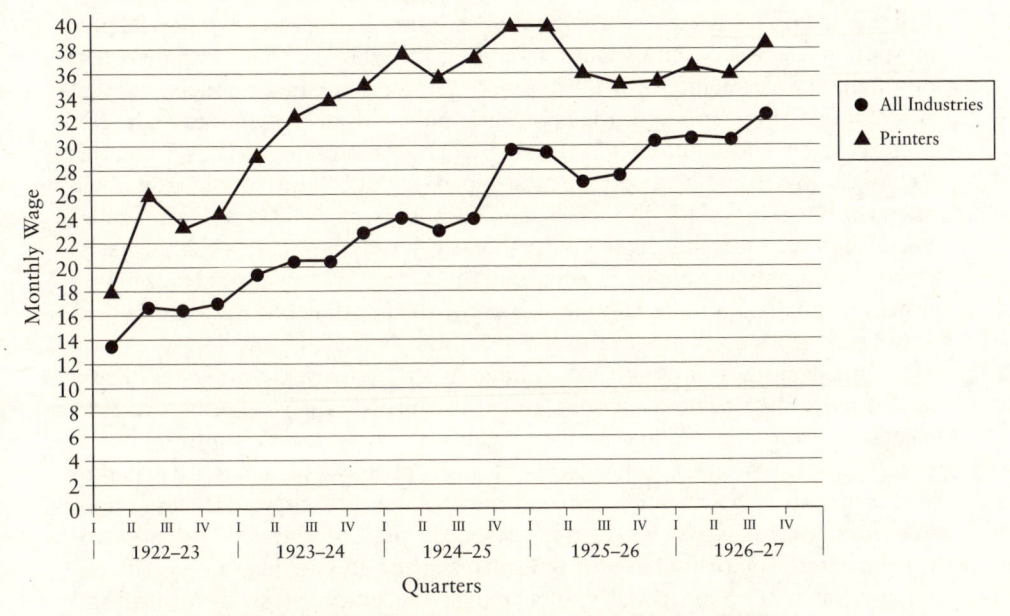

Source: A. G. Rashin, *Zarabotnaia plata za vosstanovitel'nyi period khoziaistva SSSR 1922/23-1926-27 gg.* (Moscow, 1928), 6, 11.

Figure 1. Monthly wages in the printing industry and in all industries, 1922–1927, by quarter. Source: A. G. Rashin, *Zarabotnaia plata za vosstanovitel'nyi period khoziaistva SSSR, 1922/23– 1926/27 gg.* (Moscow, 1928), 6, 11.

was low. Workers were able to subvert the productivity incentives of piece rates by their control of the labor process, their ability to combine into work-reducing collectives, and their proficiency in bargaining wage rates at the point of production. The concepts of a craftsman's fair day's work for a fair day's pay and a differential "fairness" remained remarkably resilient even in this socialist society in which the regime itself was pledged to fairness for all.

With respect to pay incentives, socialist labor relations looked quite similar to relations in capitalist societies. Skilled workers exploited their unique knowledge of the job to win privileges in both systems. The Soviet system differed from capitalism, however, in its extensive exhortatory and participatory mechanisms designed to promote productivity and to instill a new voluntarist work ethic. In fact, throughout the 1920s, the union and economic leadership appeared to throw one scheme after another into industrial practice, each with the aim of extending responsibility for socialist production to the workers on the shop floor.

In the early days of NEP, trade union publicists employed propaganda and publicity campaigns to educate workers about the importance of productivity.

Workers needed to learn, insisted the factory newspaper at Pechatnyi Dvor in early 1923, that they did not come to the enterprise for eight hours merely to earn their pay: they needed to ask themselves if they had *earned* that pay. "There are quite a few unconscious workers among us, who are so shortsighted that although they are members of a firm [*khoziaistvo*], they cannot understand that the welfare of that firm depends upon their personal level of energy." The column "Not Anecdote but Fact" reproved workers for poor work habits in this exchange: "Svistkov: Your press has stopped again." "How can it stop again when I haven't started it?"[54] All factory newspapers, as well as the central union journals, carried out this productivity theme not only in 1923, when the newspapers began publication, but throughout the 1920s. Wall newspapers, whether printed or posted on bulletin boards, became the first line of assault in the battle to teach workers their socialist work responsibilities.[55]

As much as they honored the printed word, however, printers evidently needed more than printed encouragement to cultivate their newfound roles as masters of production. While the theme of productivity never disappeared from reports of shop floor life, other mechanisms to promote productivity began to appear in early 1924. One of them was the production contest. Articles in both *Pechatnik* and *Moskovskii pechatnik* called on printers to revive the prerevolutionary tradition of contests for typesetting speed and quality: with each contest, output rose. Soon articles appeared in the union press reporting local contests in both journalistic and fictional form; in late 1926, the practice was revived at the apparent instigation of young workers who had noticed their comrades' indifference to work.[56]

The production contest drew much of its propaganda and productivity effectiveness from its extraordinary quality: workers would pay extra attention to the elements of good work precisely because the contest took them out of their everyday habits. Once the new scheme became routine, though, printers would regress to their previous levels of effort, and new measures were required to stimulate their enthusiasm. Contests alone, therefore, were not sufficient to change printers' permanent work habits. The new response to workers' indifference would be the production circle or conference, an institution designed to raise productivity by bringing workers' and managers' minds together to solve problems. Such councils had been a widespread feature of labor-management collaboration in Europe during and after the World War, but they had disappeared under new capitalist offensives by 1922. Production councils appeared on the Soviet trade union agenda beginning in late 1923. Variously called production circles, production conferences, and production meetings, these institutions spread to most printing enterprises, at least formally, in the course of

---

54. *Pechatnyi dvor*, 14 January, 15 March, 25 April, and 2 June 1923.
55. *Nasha zhizn'*, 11 October 1923; *Zorkii glaz*, 13 October 1925.
56. *Moskovskii pechatnik* 33 (7 November 1924): 9; 5 (8 February 1925): 5; *Pechatnik* 20–21 (15 November 1924): 20; 3 (1 February 1925): 12–13; *Pravda*, 26 November 1926.

"For the next contest, I am learning how to set type with both hands," a response to the new emphasis on contests. Such efficiency is rendered here as subhuman; only an ape with prehensile toes could achieve such a feat. (*Pechatnik* 3 [1 February 1925]: 13.)

1924 and 1925.⁵⁷ For example, the factory newspaper at the Sixteenth Print Shop picked up the theme in an issue in June 1924, announcing that conferences would begin "soon" to educate workers and involve them in the production process. The conferences would include selected representatives from

57. A. E. Musson, *The Typographical Association: Origins and History up to 1949* (London, 1954), 373; Bernard Bellon, *Mercedes in Peace and War: German Automobile Workers, 1903–1945* (New York, 1990), 172–207; Chase, *Workers, Society, and the Soviet State*, 264–89; E. B. Genkina, "Vozniknovenie proizvodstvennykh soveshchanii v gody vosstanovitel′nogo perioda (1921–1925)," *Istoriia SSSR*, 1958, no. 3: 63–89.

around the enterprise, and would be open to all workers who wished to attend. To complement this new activity, the newspaper promised to expand its "Improving Production" column and to rename it "Khoziaiskoe oko" ("The careful [or manager's] eye"). On 29 January 1925, 200 production circle delegates at the First Model shop assembled to hear reports on three departments in the lithography shop, focusing on the supply of labor, materials, and orders. Subsequent discussions focused on specific problems and suggestions for their remedies.[58]

Such a format looked very similar to the pattern of semi-annual general factory meetings, at which the factory administration would be called to report on the state of the enterprise and workers would be able to ask questions. The production conferences may have been intended to increase and energize the circle of workers who took an interest in production, but they too quickly lost the appeal of novelty, and complaints about their utility began to appear within a year of their introduction in the industry. In November 1924 a Leningrad correspondent lamented workers' indifference to the conferences; as a remedy, he proposed a contest for best and worst production circles! Workers quickly tired of the futility of proposing production improvements that management failed to implement. "It's not very interesting to sit still at our Monday meetings for three hours, knowing almost for sure that it's all for nothing and that everything will happen the way the director wants."[59] The report of a meeting at one Moscow shop was typical: 65 of the shop's 192 workers signed up to come to the production meeting, but by the end of the discussion, the conference consisted of five local officials and five workers. An exception, the *Krasnaia gazeta* shop in Leningrad, boasted that its conferences had implemented many good suggestions, that 25 percent of its 1,000 workers participated, and that as a result, relations with the plant administration were "almost normal."[60] The exception too indicates that even if it were possible to involve workers more actively in the production decision-making process, the interests of workers were not those of their bosses. Issues of remuneration and the wage form drew much more interest from workers than these production meetings.

Production conferences and circles remained on the official roster of worker activist projects, but new schemes to incorporate workers into the production process continued to parachute down from the trade union and economic leadership. Workers were promised prizes for innovations in materials and pro-

---

58. TsGAMO, f. 699, op. 1, d. 570 (general, factory committee, and conflict commission meetings at Sixteenth, 1924), ll. 82–83, 840b.; d. 725 (production conferences at First Model, 1925), ll. 21–23; *Nasha zhizn'*, 21 June and 31 October 1924.

59. *Pechatnik* 20–21 (15 November 1924): 14; 7 (13 February 1926): 6; 22 (23 October 1925): 2; 22 (29 March 1926): 8; 30 (24 July 1926): 6; *Pravda*, 31 January 1925, 23 March 1926; *Moskovskii pechatnik* 10 (15 March 1925): 9; TsGAMO, f. 699, op. 1, d. 787 (protocols of the Third Moscow Guberniia Union Conference, October 1926), l. 51.

60. *Pechatnik* 3 (1 February 1925): 3; 43 (23 October 1926): 7; *Moskovskii pechatnik* 12 (29 March 1925): 10.

cesses.[61] At the end of 1925, a broadside from Lev Trotskii in *Moskovskii pechatnik* announced a new campaign to improve the quality of production. We need more literate compositors, proofreaders, and supervisors, he wrote. We must have paper that doesn't tear, ink that doesn't smear. The Vesenkha presidium called a special conference, to be chaired by Trotskii, to address quality issues. Letters appeared in the union journals attesting to problems of quality with suggestions for improvements, and commissions were assembled to investigate the causes of low-quality work.[62]

By mid-1926 the quality campaign had all but disappeared, replaced by a new method to build socialism, the "regime of economy," an aggressive belt-tightening and cost-saving campaign that swept through Soviet industry. Justified by the need to accumulate capital through self-financing, the regime of economy required officials and workers to expose cases of bad management, eliminate unnecessary expenses, continue to raise labor productivity, and publicize the results of this campaign in the press. Naturally enough, a new column appeared in Printers' Union periodicals and factory newspapers, "For the Regime of Economy," and the verb "to regimize" (*rezhimit'*) entered the industrial lexicon in laudatory and subversive ways. Worker correspondents emphasized how workers often came up with better cost-saving recommendations than management, whose excessive paperwork did not promote a "regime of economy" (*rezhim ekonomii*) but rather "butchered" the economy (*rezhem ekonomii*). In Tashkent and Leningrad, the coercive elements of the new campaign were captured in the usage "clamping down of the economy" (*prizhim ekonomii*). Elsewhere, correspondents reported the appearance of "mutant" forms of the regime: some enterprises created completely superfluous "regime commissions" to add to the production-monitoring burdens of factory committees and production commissions. The manager of one shop turned off the heat over the weekend to save money, and by Monday morning the place was so cold that the typesetters could not work at all. The regime of economy, like the cost-accounting campaigns earlier, seemed to be carried out at the expense of the workers, they grumbled.[63]

Nor did the regime of economy provide sufficient worker involvement. A year later came the leadership's introduction of a rationalization campaign, on top of production conferences and the regime of economy. Now workers were

---

61. *Pechatnik* 27 (1 December 1925): 7; *Otchet moskovskogo gubotdela professional'nogo soiuza rabochikh poligraficheskogo proizvodstva SSSR. VIII gubernskomu s'ezdu. Ianvar' 1926 g.—iiun' 1927 g.* (Moscow, 1927), 50.

62. *Moskovskii pechatnik* 49 (12 December 1925): 1–3; *Pravda*, 4 April 1926; *Ekonomicheskaia zhizn'*, 6 January 1926; *Izvestiia*, 28 January, 3 February, and 2 June 1926; *Pechatnik* 6 (6 February 1926): 5; 26 (26 June 1926): 10.

63. *Direktivy KPSS i sovetskogo pravitel'stva po khoziaistvennym voprosam* (Moscow, 1957), 1:578–83; *Pechatnik* 24 (12 June 1926): 5; 25 (19 June 1926): 4; 27 (3 July 1926): 5; 48 (27 November 1926): 12; 28 (10 July 1926): 11; 39 (25 September 1926): 11; 36 (4 September 1926): 6; 2 (22 January 1927): 16; *Zorkii glaz*, 1 May 1926; *Moskovskii pechatnik* 23–24 (June 1926): 2, 6; TsGA SPb, f. 4804, op. 11, d. 158 (meetings of Leningrad unemployed, 1926–29), l. 212.

invited to organize control commissions, to "deepen" the good work of production conferences in "engaging the broad worker mass in the business of the practical construction of the Soviet economy." Although they seemed to duplicate the functions of the production commissions and the factory committees, control commissions attracted an initial burst of enthusiasm at the Pechatnyi Dvor shop, where the commissions proposed sweeping reorganizations of the major departments in order to produce greater efficiencies. But local union organs and factory committees elsewhere proved less welcoming to this latest productivity scheme, and they failed to link the new institutions with the old ones to any positive effect.[64] The tempo of introducing new nonpecuniary production incentives would continue to accelerate as the Five-Year Plan swung into high gear in 1928 and 1929, as we shall see. The frequency and shrillness of these campaigns may suggest the growing urgency of the industrialization effort, but given the response of workers in the printing industry to each new program, it would appear that the rapidity of new schemes served as much to numb workers' interest in production issues as to spur them on to greater and more glorious production feats.

The efforts of Soviet planners to rationalize the work process and to increase labor productivity echoed similar campaigns in the capitalist economies of Western Europe and the United States. The shocks of war and the "red years" of 1917–19 had propelled many industrialists to turn to schemes of welfare capitalism, under which class collaboration would replace costly class conflict. Lizabeth Cohen has documented how progressive Chicago manufacturers endeavored in the 1920s to reconstruct interpersonal relationships in their plants, experiment with works councils and conference boards, institute welfare programs, and implement wage and promotion mechanisms. German industrialists joined with the ruling Social Democratic Party in translating American methods to German factories. They sought the application of Fordism—high wages and low prices—to win workers over to a common commitment to rationalize the workplace and increase productivity.[65] These methods provoked resentment and resistance in workers under both capitalism and socialism: Soviet printers did not like "Taylorist" and "Americanist" managers. Production conferences, whether in Moscow or Chicago, failed to convince workers that they were truly partners in production. Class conflict on a broad scale had been ameliorated, but the shop floor remained contested terrain under welfare capitalism. Socialist industry also faced continuing antagonisms between work givers and work doers.

---

64. *Direktivy KPSS*, 1:666–72; *Profsoiuzy SSSR. Dokumenty i materialy v chetyrekh tomakh (1905–1963 gg.)* (Moscow, 1963), 2:451–53; *Pechatnik* 23 (15 August 1927): 7; 24 (25 August 1927): 4.

65. Lizabeth Cohen, *Making a New Deal: Industrial Workers in Chicago, 1919–1939* (Cambridge, 1990), 159–83; Mary Nolan, *Visions of Modernity: American Business and the Modernization of Germany* (New York, 1994).

## ONE THOUSAND POINTS OF CONFLICT

The participatory production schemes aimed to promote positive attitudes toward production and to incorporate workers in the processes of economic construction. In theory, this would remove any discursive foundation for the articulation of conflict between the interests of workers and those of management. The new socialist factory order erected multiple mechanisms for the individualization and defusing of conflicts, as we have seen. In addition, labor-management conflicts early in the Soviet period were relabeled as the political opposition of Menshevik renegades, with resultant political costs attached to workplace dissent. Still, conflicts continued to arise in the industry, and the ways they were managed and articulated contributed to definitions of new socialist labor relations.

Strikes and other forms of labor protest provide evidence of mobilization and resistance; they also serve as catalysts that shape attitudes of rebellion. From a rich body of scholarship, three key sets of interpretive frameworks have emerged that help to analyze the role of conflict in a socialist system of labor relations.[66]

The first set of frameworks presents strikes and conflicts as normal elements of modern industrial life. Strikes function as a safety valve, as an adjustment mechanism for the allocation of resources in society. They serve as a barometer of the key deficiencies of the industrial system: strikes over late pay in the Soviet Union thus signaled to the economic planners the need to adjust the rules and incentives for management in operating their firms. Strikes can also be seen in this framework as mistakes, as breakdowns in preferred forms of bargaining and negotiation. Types of strikes matter a great deal in this framework: local strikes over bread-and-butter issues (issues of the stomach) most comfortably fit inside an interpretation of strikes as ways to adjust the smooth running of production. In this vein, too, strikes could be attributed to cultural backwardness, a practice employed by workers who had not yet learned the rules of the game.[67]

A second set of frameworks privileges power relations: strikes and labor conflicts may or may not be normal, but at their heart lies struggle over the distribution of power. Workers shut down production in order to assert their collective right to a share of economic benefits, decision-making authority, and

---

66. See Koenker and Rosenberg, *Strikes and Revolution in Russia*, chap. 1, for a discussion of theoretical approaches to strikes. See also Leopold H. Haimson's articles in *War, Strikes, and Revolution: Patterns in the Evolution of Industrial Labor Conflicts in the Late Nineteenth and Early Twentieth Centuries*, ed. Haimson and Charles Tilly (Cambridge, 1988), and in *Strikes, Social Conflict, and the First World War: An International Perspective*, ed. Haimson and Giulio Sapelli (Milan, 1992); Zelnik, *Law and Disorder*. Beyond Russia, see Edward Shorter and Charles Tilly, *Strikes in France, 1830–1968* (Cambridge, 1974), and James E. Cronin, *Industrial Conflict in Modern Britain* (London, 1979), for statistical approaches to strike analysis; and Michelle Perrot, *Les Ouvriers en grève: France, 1871–1890*, 2 vols. (Paris, 1974), and Elizabeth J. Perry, *Shanghai on Strike: The Politics of Chinese Labor* (Stanford, 1993), for more qualitative discussions.

67. See Mary McAuley, *Labour Disputes in Soviet Russia, 1957–1965* (Oxford, 1969), 30.

status. In this framework strikes are seen not only as barometers of economic or political relations but as actions that can change these relations. Strikes thus constitute a key element in class formation, and the suppression of strikes serves also to shape attitudes and expectations about the balance of power in society. Menshevik critics of the Communist regime regularly cited strikes as indicative of political dissent in Soviet society, and the state's extensive surveillance apparatus also suggested the regime's concern for the mobilizing potential of labor stoppages. Types of strikes matter here, too: strikes over authority within the workplace are seen as more politically potent than those concerning issues of the stomach. And the timing of strikes could also be crucial if they turned out to be correlated with moments of economic or political crisis.[68]

A final set of frameworks situates strikes and conflicts in the everyday: strikes or other forms of labor conflict represent "weapons of the weak" and "everyday resistance," along with a host of other behaviors that can be subsumed under the heading of infrapolitics, from working to rule (the "Italian" strike) to gossip to body language to sneaking out the back door in the middle of factory meetings. In such a framework, any action can properly be laden with political meaning. Related to the everydayness of strikes, moreover, is the strike as what Michelle Perrot called a festival, a fête of liberation: a strike represented a break from the everyday, from routine.[69] An occasional strike could also represent a ritual of the work experience as meaningful in defining the culture of work as the apprentice's initiation rites or the honoring of heroes of labor.[70] Underlying all three frameworks remains the fundamental ambiguity of strikes and protests: they could serve to disrupt the status quo by mobilizing workers to overturn the very structure of power, as they did in 1917, and they could serve to cement the status quo, creating solidarities among workers that could be used in more reformist ways, or to release sufficient pressure to allow the system to continue to survive.

The socialist revolution had eliminated the need for workers to strike to change power relations. Symbolically important as a signpost on the path to revolution, strikes about power and control could now be consigned to memory projects and museums. The Soviet regime, particularly the trade union and economic leadership, therefore took the position that strikes measured the normal running of the industrial machine. Soviet registrars of labor relations consequently paid attention to and collected statistics on "strikes and other forms of conflict," which had consequences just as detrimental to the economy as accidents, illness, and absenteeism: they took workers away from production. Strikes were thus part of the public record, the public transcript of socialist labor relations, and strike reports helped to fix a notion of conflict as a manage-

68. Shorter and Tilly, *Strikes in France;* see also Haimson and Tilly, *War, Strikes, and Revolution.*
69. Perrot, *Ouvriers en grève,* 2:548–84, and Koenker and Rosenberg, *Strikes and Revolution,* 110.
70. Scott, *Weapons of the Weak;* Kelley, "'We Are Not What We Seem'"; Hunter, *To 'Joy My Freedom,* 74–97.

able part of these relations. Finally, strikes in the USSR were represented as mistakes in judgment, caused primarily by backward peasant workers, and once this mass of new workers was properly socialized, strikes could be expected to disappear.[71] The private transcript of labor relations, as we shall see, privileged a different framework: Communist and trade union officials knew that strikes and related forms of infrapolitics always concerned power, and Soviet surveillance of workers' attitudes can be understood as an effort to anticipate and defuse conflict that could spill beyond the bounds of normal labor relations and the everyday.

There is no single uniform compilation of strikes for the Soviet period, and it is virtually impossible to construct meaningful time series or aggregate analyses of strikes in the socialist period.[72] Yet we can still assess the significance of strikes in socialist labor relations in a more qualitative way. Strikes in the printing industry were relatively rare, according to the available compilations, but conflicts erupted all the same. In 1922, compositors at the Fifth State Print Shop in Moscow, objecting to the "uncomradely" way their boss related to the workers, carried out a strike without informing the trade union and rejected the union's mediation. A large proportion of conflicts in 1922 concerned late pay: on 25 February 1922, nine Petrograd print shops stopped work to demand their delayed wages. The Menshevik émigré publication *Sotsialisticheskii vestnik*, relying on reports smuggled abroad, described a rise in "Italian" strikes, or slowdowns, in 1925 and 1926 over lowered pay and other grievances. Such strikers were fired, but it was easy to mask protest: when *Izvestiia* appeared late, was the delay due to a breakdown in machinery or a deliberate slowdown by workers? The risk in daring to strike lay in not knowing when the boundary between normal protest and antisocialist agitation would be crossed. Workers who struck in June 1926 because of their low pay rates and the absence of a collective agreement were told by union organizers that if they were unhappy, they could return to the unemployment lines and let someone else take their place.[73]

By and large, union and party officials managed to contain worker unrest within the institutional boundaries of labor mediation. But if "strikes" occurred infrequently, "conflicts" were endemic, and they provide a valuable sense of workers' grievances and the points of contention in the system of socialist labor relations. The union admitted that dozens of conflicts occurred every day. "Union representatives spend 75 percent of their time resolving conflicts," complained one harried activist. Only the most intractable found their way into the

---

71. P. N. Avdeev, *Trudovye konflikty v SSSR* (Moscow, 1928), 7.

72. McAuley, *Labour Disputes*, 15n, and Avdeev, *Trudovye konflikty*, 10, 15, chap. 3; see also Iu. I. Kir'ianov, V. Rozenberg, and A. N. Sakharov, eds., *Trudovye konflikty v sovetskoi Rossii, 1918–1929 gg.* (Moscow, 1998).

73. Kir'ianov et al., *Trudovye konflikty*, 90–97, 308–9; GARF, f. R-5525, op. 4, d. 62, l. 63; TsGAIPD SPb, f. 457, op. 1, d. 65 (Petrograd political reports, 1922), l. 86; f. 435, op. 1, d. 64 (meetings of bureau of party fraction of Leningrad union, 1926), ll. 34, 257; *Sotsialisticheskii vestnik* 7–8 (101–2) (25 April 1925): 17.

records of labor arbitration, but even these were numerous: *Trud* reported thirty-four conflicts in the Moscow printing industry involving pay, dismissals, collective agreements, work time, and labor safety in September 1922 alone. In order to keep from being overwhelmed by the arbitration workload, by 1925 the union leaders withdrew from the line of appeal. The key to managing conflict in socialist society, they reiterated, would be found in the local conflict commissions in the enterprise.[74]

The records of these local commissions provide a rich source for understanding the extent of workers' grievances and the methods they chose for resolving them. The unions provided aggregate figures for conflicts and the degree to which the workers' side won. Their records also indicate the range of complaints that would be raised in the conflict commissions. Both management and labor could bring cases to the commissions, and both individual workers and groups could file appeals. The most frequent source of complaint throughout the period remained wages, expressed in petitions to be assigned to a higher rank on the pay scale (razriad). This was always a highly individualized request. Once negotiated in the periodic collective agreements, the wage scale itself—the tarif—retained its canonic legitimacy. Workers needed to claim special personal worth—skill meriting a different placement on the pay grid—in order to climb the ladder to the big ruble. In Moscow and Leningrad, these formal appeals represented between half and two-thirds of all cases to come before the conflict commissions.[75]

Complaints and appeals about improper dismissals constituted a second major source of conflict. In the fall of 1923, when the Petrograd industry contracted so severely, fully 91 percent of conflict commission cases involved firings; in Moscow, by contrast, only 19 percent of cases in the 1922–23 fiscal year involved dismissals. In Leningrad by 1926–27, between 13 and 17 percent of conflicts involved appeals of improper dismissals. Like appeals for pay grid adjustments, these cases about firings had a predominantly personal, individual character. Other kinds of cases filed by workers included appeals about vacation rights, appeals to change jobs, complaints about fines or deductions from wages, output norms, sick pay, and disputes between workers, particularly over personal insults.[76] Management used these commissions to discipline their workers for lateness, absenteeism, and drinking on the job. In June 1924, for example, the rates-conflict commission at the Sixteenth State Print Shop fired

---

74. *Moskovskii pechatnik* 4–5 (January 1926): 14; *Trud*, 28 October 1922; *Otchet pravleniia moskovskogo gub'otdela 1922/1923 g.*, 29–30; see also the figures for conflicts by industry from official trade union sources in Kir'ianov et al., *Trudovye konflikty*, 33; *Otchet leningradskogo gubotdela, 1926–1927*, 38; *Otchet moskovskogo gubotdela, 1926–1927*, 35–36.

75. *Otchet pravleniia moskovskogo gub'otdela 1922/1923 g.*, 30; *Otchet pravleniia moskovskogo gubernskogo otdela vsesoiuznogo soiuza rabochikh poligraficheskogo proizvodstva s 1 oktiabria 1924 g. po 1 oktiabria 1925 g.* (Moscow, 1925), 17; *Otchet moskovskogo gubotdela 1926–1927*, 36.

76. *Otchet leningradskogo gubotdela 1926–1927*; *Otchet pravleniia moskovskogo gub'otdela 1922/1923 g.*; GARF f. R-5525, op. 4, d. 67, l. 100; TsGAMO, f. 699, op. 1, d. 570, l. 61.

two workers for systematic drunkenness, and it issued warnings to nine others. The commission also decided to combat tardiness by shutting the plant's control gate fifteen minutes after the start of the workday: a worker who appeared later than that could not work that day.[77]

The Sixteenth shop's rates and conflict commission kept particularly careful records of its weekly meetings, and these records provide an excellent picture of the everyday contentiousness and bargaining that occurred in the workplace. For the most part, the commission handled petitions and disagreements about workers' positions in the pay scale and about rates for particular jobs. Bargaining over rates had become especially important in the campaign to switch over to piece rates. For example, workers in the lithographic department claimed that their pay for producing Ira cigarette packets, in which the letters appeared in relief, should be calculated at the higher rate for complex work. Workers' behavior also provided a steady stream of cases for the rates and conflict commission. For absenteeism and coming to work drunk, an official warning was the frequent penalty. Repeat offenses, though, merited dismissal. Theft of materials was another crime that could result in the sack, but such cases received careful hearings and discussions. When the smelter Murashov was accused of stealing a piece of metal, he claimed he had permission to take it to be melted down, but his real problem, the testimony revealed, was his bad manners, his drinking, and his disrespect toward his shop supervisor. After hearing from all sides, the commission fired Murashov.[78]

One particular case illuminates the complicated terrain of socialist labor-management conflict. Six newspaper Linotype operators objected to their low rates, lower even than those for book compositors, who historically had earned less than newspaper compositors. Moreover, the newspaper compositors struggled daily with the poor penmanship of newspaper reporters. Finally they embarked on a systematic slowdown, an Italian strike, and for this they were hauled before the rates and conflict commission. We could have worked this out in negotiation, said the workers. But "nowhere in our laws does it say that workers don't have the right to improve their position. These rates are abnormal." We could have negotiated this in the union, said the enterprise director. "But you've behaved in a way that doesn't accord [*ne garmoniruet*] with the existence of Soviet power." Their slowdown had stalled the work of the stereotype and rotation departments, forcing them to work overtime. Six typesetters had delayed the work of fifty others: for such "unconscious" behavior, the six—including one member of the Communist Party—were fired.[79]

On the one hand, the episode illustrates what has been termed the strict labor law of Soviet industry: strikes were punishable by firing, just as under cap-

---

77. About 5 percent of cases in Leningrad in 1926/27 concerned issues of discipline. *Otchet leningradskogo gubotdela 1926–1927*, 38; TsGAMO, f. 699, op. 1, d. 570, l. 96 ob.
78. TsGAMO, f. 699, op. 1, d. 728, ll. 86–87, 103, 56, 105, 139, 92.
79. Ibid., ll. 53–56.

italism. But the record also shows that this impasse had been reached only after efforts to compromise had failed. "We've been patient a long time," said the director. It also reflects the complicated relationship of economics, tradition, and Soviet patriotism. The newspaper compositors expected high wages as compensation for the demands of their job: rush work, daily deadlines, unreadable copy. If you're going to lower the rates, said the Linotype operators' spokesman, we'd rather work on something else and be satisfied with our three rubles. Their complaint also reflected an implicit socialist bargain: they had willingly worked hard and for little when the industry was in trouble; they stayed at their posts. But now that industry had revived, "when we could see the big ruble," management responded to their dreams of economic comfort by lowering the rates. The uniqueness of this case in the rates and conflict commission records for this period speaks to an important conclusion about socialist labor relations. Such breakdowns were indeed rare events. Both the institutionalized systems of bargaining and negotiation and the more informal day-to-day bargaining on the shop floor gave workers many outlets to seek redress of their grievances. Both helped to smooth over potential conflicts, and they gave workers considerable power to shape the terms of their wage and work bargains. But the system encouraged workers to seek redress and compensation as individuals, forestalling the need for collective action that might have furnished a basis for subsequent and more wide-scale political mobilization.

## WORKERS WITHOUT WORK

In turning to a discussion of unemployment in the printing industry, we come full circle from the initial consideration of the economic status of the industry. Unemployment levels among printers mirrored the dynamics of the economy as a whole, but the individual experience of unemployment and the union's and workers' responses to it bring together the issues of material scarcity, culture, and political responses in crucial ways. Most important, the experience of unemployment brings key issues of the economy back to the level of the individual.

Unemployment in general was one of the scourges of NEP. The initial economic boost from the loosening up of trade stimulated industrial growth in early to mid-1921, but by the end of 1921, joblessness returned. Between January 1922 and January 1923, the level of unemployed Soviet workers registering with labor exchanges increased fourfold, and the absolute numbers of unemployed continued to climb. Although trade union statistics differ from those reported by labor exchanges, the magnitude of the employment crisis was striking. In 1923, the unemployed constituted 8 percent of all union members; in 1924, 11 percent; and in 1925, 13.8 percent of union members were out of work. Although the number of industrial workers increased in this period, the number of those seeking work increased even faster, and industrial unemployment continued to grow, from 950,000 in January 1926 to 1.3 million by January 1928.[80]

The trend in the printing industry rose similarly but not quite so inexorably as the national industrial figures on unemployment. Overall, unemployment continued to increase until 1924, when industrial recovery and extensive job sharing (shortened workweeks and workdays) combined to create jobs for most of the skilled workers in the trade. The Leningrad union reported in July 1924 that unemployment had been "liquidated." "Zero unemployment," however, still registered at 1,335 unemployed printers in August 1924, but most of these people—754—were unskilled laborers. The number of skilled printers registered at the Moscow labor exchange hovered between 1,000 and 1,300 during late 1924 and the autumn of 1925, dipping to 732 during the summer, when annual vacations created a seasonal demand for temporary workers.[81]

The downturn in industrial growth occasioned by the glut of unsold books on the market began to manifest itself in the labor market in the autumn of 1925. The number of unemployed skilled printers in Moscow shot up to 1,500 in October 1925, and by January 1926 the figure stood at 1,677. The Leningrad union reported 2,005 unemployed printers in the same month, and overall, in the entire Russian industry, 8,110 printers were counted as unemployed. These figures—indicating the growing mass of the reserved army of unemployed printers—are reflected in the leveling off of wage increases shown in Figure 1. A year later, these numbers had more than doubled. Nearly 4,200 skilled Moscow workers were out of work in January 1927; the number of Leningrad unemployed stood at over 6,500, a threefold increase; and the number of printers unemployed nationally approached 20,000—18 percent of the industry's workforce. Even more troubling, these workers were now approaching the status of hard-core unemployed. Of Leningrad's 6,566 unemployed printers in January 1927, for example, 56 percent had been out of work longer than one year. By July 1927, the Moscow union reported that 22.3 percent of its members were unemployed; in Leningrad, the unemployment rate hit 28 percent by October 1927.[82]

The number of unemployed reflected more than an influx to the big cities of provincial or rural printers looking for work, although this flow was consider-

---

80. L. S. Rogachevskaia, *Likvidatsiia bezrabotitsy v SSSR 1917–1930 gg.* (Moscow, 1973), 74–77, 81, 142.

81. *Moskovskii pechatnik* 18 (27 February 1924): 8–9; GARF, f. R-5525, op. 6, d. 71 (board and presidium meetings of Petrograd guberniia union, 1924), l. 154; *Pechatnik* 17 (15 September 1924): 10. Monthly statistics on labor exchange registrations in the printers' section (not the unskilled laborers' section of the union) at the Moscow labor exchange were published regularly in *Moskovskii pechatnik* (and after 1926 in *Pechatnik*) from late 1924 until early 1927.

82. *Pravda*, 31 March 1927; *Trud*, 8 September 1927; *Otchet leningradskogo oblastnogo otdela soiuza rabochikh poligraficheskogo proizvodstva SSSR s 1-go oktiabria 1927 g. po 1-e oktiabria 1929 g.* (Leningrad, 1929), 5; *Otchet moskovskogo gubotdela 1926–1927*, 5; *Otchet leningradskogo gubotdela 1926–1927*, 12.

able. It reflects also the various campaigns to increase productivity and efficiency, which prompted enterprises to lay off redundant workers. The total number of workers employed in the industry actually fell during this period, when the overall Soviet labor force was expanding. Women were often the first to be fired, and their share of the unemployed was disproportionately large. Young workers, too, found that when they finished their training, there was no work to be had in the printing industry; some enterprises tried to hold their trainees back at the low apprenticeship rates of pay, but eventually the young workers were turned out of the industry altogether.[83] The raw unemployment figures suggest major crises of justice and of identity among workers in the printing trades.

## CONCLUSION: THE FRONTIER OF CONTROL

In 1920 a young American economist, Carter L. Goodrich, analyzed the extraordinary militancy of British organized labor over the "frontier of control," the division between management and labor concerning workplace decision making and authority. During the World War, European and American workers had waged aggressive and often successful struggles against employers and wartime states to wrest significant concessions in wages, conditions, and authority. The British shop stewards' movement represented one example of this militancy, and in this respect, the Russian revolution of 1917 was part of a global phenomenon of labor insurgency.[84]

Goodrich identified a series of points over which labor and management had waged this battle during the war. Roughly speaking, the issues fell into the areas of wages, supervision and autonomy, hiring, technological change, and work standards. In some areas, British unionists had won substantial power to dictate the terms of work; elsewhere, concluded Goodrich, unions remained content to cede authority to management, for example in areas of disciplining workers or introducing new technology. Some of these new arrangements became codified in state-sponsored collaboration institutions, such as the Whitley Councils in Britain.

Yet everywhere by 1921 and 1922, managers and state authorities had managed to roll back the frontier of control, whether through the cooptation of welfare capitalist schemes, repression, economic conditions that shifted the balance

---

83. *Otchet moskovskogo gubotdela 1926–1927*, 5; *Otchet leningradskogo gubotdela professional'nogo soiuza 1926–1927 gg.*, 10, 22; *Otchet leningradskogo oblastnogo otdela 1927/1929*, 50. See also Koenker, "Men against Women"; Diane P. Koenker, "Fathers against Sons/Sons against Fathers: The Problem of Generations in the Early Soviet Workplace," *Journal of Modern History* 73, no. 4 (2001): 781–810; and below, Chapter 6; *Moskovskii pechatnik* 28–29 (July 1926): 3; 30 (August 1926): 7.

84. Goodrich, *Frontier of Control*; James E. Cronin, "Labor Insurgency and Class Formation: Comparative Perspectives on the Crisis of 1917–1920 in Europe," in *Work, Community, and Power: The Experience of Labor in Europe and America, 1900–1925*, ed. James E. Cronin and Carmen Sirianni (Philadelphia, 1983), 20–48.

of power toward the capitalists, unionists' own calculations of interests and possibilities, or divisions within the union movement. We can see the breadth of change that socialism had brought to industrial relations in the USSR by comparing the frontier of control in the Soviet printing industry in the mid-1920s with the achievements of British labor at the height of its power in 1919.

The distinction between symbolic power and actual control complicates the comparison. In principle, Soviet workers, through the Communist Party, state, and trade unions, enjoyed unlimited authority. In reality, the party and state could act in arbitrary and coercive ways to limit challenges to their political power. But we have seen that at the level of the workplace in the printing industry, the frontier of control shifted toward workers in four key areas: relations with supervisors, issues of discipline, methods of pay, and consultation over the work process. Whereas British unions rarely sought to influence the selection of foremen, Soviet printers often exercised their right (through their trade union) to approve the appointment of managerial personnel, and they could act energetically to remove or discipline managers and foremen who violated workers' sense of appropriate relations. Workers and their representative committees likewise shared the disciplinary functions of management, handing out their own penalties for lateness or drinking on the job. Moreover, particularly among compositors organized in companies, Soviet printers exercised control over the allocation of work and the measurement of results.

Soviet printers, as we have seen, managed to subvert the aims of piece-rate reforms. Whereas British engineering workers resorted to strikes to fight the imposition of piece-rate schemes, Soviet printers used argument and individual bargaining to shift the frontier of control over payment methods in their favor.[85] Through individual negotiations over rates, they made the piece-rate system too expensive for cost-conscious industrial directors and they influenced the return to the preferred method of pay by time. Finally, Soviet printers, through the opportunity to participate in factory committees, production councils, and shop floor meetings at all levels, acquired formal and informal power to intervene in the work process in ways that could protect their own interests and preferences.

We should not overly romanticize the achievements of Soviet printers in gaining some control over their working lives. Economic realities, reflected in rising levels of unemployment, constrained the power of workers as well as managers to contest the frontier of control. So did ongoing divisions within the family of workers in the printing trades. Union members hotly debated methods for distributing fairly the burdens of unemployment throughout this period. The unemployed constituted a vocal constituency at union meetings and congresses, fueling fears that they would fall prey to political opportunists and turn against the regime. Issues of equity in hiring also pitted men against women, the old against the young, urban against rural in the printing industry labor

---

85. Goodrich, *Frontier of Control*, 118-25, 155.

force. And issues of proletarian corruption as well as egalitarianism would also emerge from discussions of fairness in hiring, in criticisms of the labor exchange process, and in the ways the union was handling the problem of the unemployed. How these issues were handled in political and cultural terms are taken up in the next two chapters.

## CHAPTER 5

## THE WORKING PEOPLE'S DEMOCRACY

*The fact is, workers are tired of going to meetings and speaking to no purpose.*

— Delegate to Leningrad Printers' Union Congress, 1926

By the end of the Civil War, the Communist Party had defined in principle the role of the trade union in the new Soviet state. Neither a subservient cog in the state machine (the Trotskii position) nor an autonomous agent of worker authority (the syndicalist Workers' Opposition position), Soviet trade unions acquired the roles of "transmission belt" and "school for communism." Union officials would represent the interests of workers in the councils of state, and they would convey to workers the decisions made by the state on their behalf. Equally important, trade union organizations would provide workers with direct experience of democratic participation, teaching them the principles of organization, cooperation, and democratic decision making.[1] But was this school progressive or authoritarian? Did the official centralization of the trade union apparatus and its subservience to party

---

1. See Jean-Paul Depretto, *Les Ouvriers en U.R.S.S., 1928–1941* (Paris, 1997), 268; Carr, *Bolshevik Revolution*, 2:325; *Chetvertyi vserossiiskii s"ezd professional'nykh soiuzov (17–25 maia 1921 g.); Stenograficheskii otchet (raboty plenuma i sektsii)* (Moscow, 1922), 154.

and state economic policy require the unquestioning loyalty of its members, or did the transmission belt in fact operate in both directions, from the center and from below? The contradiction between these two requirements gave rise to a peculiar form of democratic practice within the Printers' Union under the Communist Party that I will label "participatory dictatorship." The trade union required the assent and loyalty of its members; it feared their dissent and alienation. Dissent could be punished, but loyalty needed to be cultivated. Central directives could not always produce the desired result in local organizations or local enterprises. These golden years of NEP fostered a workplace political culture that reflected both the power of the central authority to dictate the state's political goals and the ability of workers to challenge and occasionally resist the authority of the center.

## DEMOCRATIC CENTRALISM IN THE ALL-UNION TRADE UNION OF PRINTING WORKERS

Although the trade unions had officially been stripped of their managerial functions with the transition to the New Economic Policy, production remained the highest goal of the socialist state. Trade unions had to balance their responsibilities to ensure the economic health of the state and at the same time to protect the more immediate interests of their members. This dilemma existed both in principle and, even more important, in practice. Although centralized and highly coercive, socialist institutions in Soviet Russia depended on the consent of the governed not only for their legitimacy but in order to make the system work. Workers had learned in the course of the Civil War that outright protest carried huge risks, but they could withdraw support from the regime in other ways: by hidden resistance and slowdowns at work, and by declining to participate in public activities in favor of the personal and the private.

Trade unions had emerged from the Civil War in a significantly weakened state, and their leadership recognized their "insufficient ties between trade union organizations and the broad mass of their members."[2] In order to serve the cause of socialist construction and state-building, trade unions needed to win back the loyalty of their members by delivering tangible benefits. Obviously, the most important of these benefits were economic, and we have already seen the difficulties for the Printers' Union of navigating the impossible passage between the Charybdis of supporting cost-saving measures and the Scylla of defending workers' standards of living and job security. Consequently, unions had to demonstrate their concern for their members in many other ways: by proving that the union officials cared about the workers' interests, by incorporating workers in decision-making activities, by listening to their grievances, and by standing up for them against higher authorities. This need to achieve relevance in the lives of the worker rank and file was not purely rhetorical: the proof of

---

2. *Profsoiuzy SSSR*, 2:282; *Chetvertyi vserossiiskii s"ezd professional'nykh soiuzov*, 154–62.

the success of the socialist experiment would be the mobilization of proletarian society around the goals of the socialist dream. If repression had already served as a convenient shortcut to manufacturing consent, the Printers' Union in the 1920s recognized that it needed to earn the active support of its members, and the union devoted considerable energy to demonstrating its responsibility and responsiveness to its constituents. In their criticisms of the union's fulfillment of these goals, workers too demonstrated that they expected no less than accountability and responsibility.

Democratic centralism, then, combined a centralized organizational structure with concern for the union's members. In organizational terms, the highly centralized structure of the Printers' Union followed the design of the Soviet trade union movement. Local organizations sent delegates to guberniia and national congresses, which chose a central committee to conduct the union's business. At the head of the committee stood the union chair, a role that loomed large in the 1920s, personalizing the otherwise faceless structure of union bureaucracy. From 1921 until 1926, Nikolai Ivanovich Derbyshev, a Social Democratic and trade union veteran, served as chairman of the union's central committee. A native Siberian, he began work as an apprentice typesetter at the age of fourteen in 1893. He soon became active in illegal unions and suffered prison and exile before coming to St. Petersburg in 1907. During the 1917 revolution, Derbyshev joined Trotskii's independent Social Democratic group and became active in both the Petrograd Union of Workers in the Printing Trade and the city's factory committee movement. After the October revolution, he sided with Grigorii Zinov'ev and Lev Kamenev against a narrowly Communist government. In 1920 he was named the administrator of the printing industry, but with the separation of trade union and economic functions in 1921, Derbyshev moved full-time into the leadership of the trade union. He remained at the head of the Printers' Union until 1926, when he became a victim of the purge of the supporters of Zinov'ev's New Opposition. Always an organization man, Derbyshev later headed the Transpechat' trust. He retired on a pension in 1933, at the age of fifty-four, and he lived until 1955.[3]

Aleksandr Borshchevskii, who replaced Derbyshev in 1926, had earned his trade union spurs in the Moscow Printers' Union, entering the trade as an apprentice bookbinder at the Kushnerev shop. Like Derbyshev, Borshchevskii was an early supporter of the Social Democratic movement, gradually became aligned with the Bolsheviks, and endured a series of arrests and exile between 1907 and 1916. In 1917 he emerged as one of the leaders of the Moscow Union of Workers in the Printing Trade, and helped to organize the small core of Bolshevik opposition within the union, the so-called printers' district of the party.

---

3. Much of this information is from Derbyshev's autobiography in *Deiateli SSSR i oktiabr'skoi revoliutsii* (Moscow, 1927–29); also *Who Was Who in the USSR* (Metuchen, N.J., 1972), 125; *Bol'shaia sovetskaia entsiklopedicheskaia slovar'*, 3rd ed., vol. 8 (Moscow, 1972), 110; *Pechatnik* 37 (11 September 1926): 10.

He too held managerial positions during the Civil War, serving as director of the Moscow Printing Section as well as helping to coordinate the red union's attack on the independent printers' movement. A proud and independent man, Borshchevskii was reprimanded in 1921 for criticizing the party line, but nonetheless he was appointed chairman of the Moscow Printers' Union organization in 1922, and served there until he replaced Derbyshev at the center in 1926. Closely aligned with the moderate trade union leadership, Borshchevskii lost his position in October 1929 along with other adherents of the "right-wing deviation." His subsequent history is unknown, except for the ominous date of his death, 1938, at the age of fifty-two.[4]

The union central committee in Moscow, with the chairman at its head, oversaw a network of guberniia-level branches, *gubernskie otdeleniia*, or *gubotdely*, and local organizations. In 1923 the union listed eighty-eight of these units. The largest by far, representing one-third of all Soviet printing trade workers, was the Moscow branch, with 24,000 of the 73,000 national members. The Petrograd branch, once the country's largest, represented only 13,000 members in 1923, but by 1927 it would claim 22,700 members to Moscow's 26,000. The remaining union members were widely scattered: the largest of these branches was the Khar'kov organization, with 3,000 members in 1923. Voronezh in this period had 488 members.[5] Centralization was thus not just an arbitrary administrative style, but reflected the geographic distribution of members: Moscow was the political, economic, and demographic center of the industry and of the union.

Trade union democracy rested on the institution of the periodic All-Union congress, where officials reported on their accomplishments and delegates debated policy and evaluated the leaders' performances. The All-Union Printers' Congresses in 1922, 1924, and 1926 provide vivid snapshots of union practice in these years. The Fourth Congress, in October 1922, officially terminated the conflict between Communists and independent trade unionists. "Issues of principle" had been resolved, reported Derbyshev at the congress's opening session, and the printer unionists could henceforth concentrate on practical and organizational work. Local delegates called for more attention from the center, and the center promised to fulfill the slogan of the day, "Nearer to the masses." Having just ceded its managerial role to state economic agencies, the Printers' Union devoted little discussion in 1922 to questions of production and economic welfare. Echoes of the political conflict of the earlier years still resounded two years later, however, at the December 1924 congress. In his opening remarks, Derbyshev declared the term "red printers" obsolete: "printers" alone conveyed the correct political coloration of the union members. Organizational questions

---

4. GARF, f. R-5525, op. 18, d. 20 (meetings of bureau of party fraction of Moscow union, 1922); *Bol'shaia sovetskaia entsiklopedicheskaia slovar'*, vol. 7 (Moscow, 1927), 202; *Leninskii zakaz* (Moscow, 1969), 73–87.

5. *Pechatnik* 12 (7 November 1923): 15; 22 (5 August 1927): 5; *Otchet leningradskogo gubotdela 1926–1927*; *Otchet o deiatel'nosti pravleniia voronezhskogo gubotdela 1923–1924*, 6.

continued to vex the assembled delegates, but economic issues also received long and vigorous discussion, especially in light of the looming crisis of unemployment. By the time the next congress met, in November 1926, the brief upturn in the economic position of the industry had come and gone, and the unemployment crisis gripped the attention of the 279 assembled delegates. In several stormy sessions they railed at the Central Committee leadership, particularly Derbyshev, for failing to respond either to unemployment or to allegations of embezzlement. (A union official in Khar'kov had just been sentenced to ten years in prison for theft of 2,000 rubles of union money.) Derbyshev responded to much of the criticism contritely, but lashed out at the delegates from the unemployed as "counterrevolutionaries"; a voice replied, "If we're counterrevolutionaries, then you're all crooks!"[6]

The waves of political turmoil that engulfed the Communist Party in the 1920s and have attracted the attention of political historians of the period find little overt reflection in the record of this trade union. The role of the Communist Party in directing the course of the trade union was fundamental: the union leaders belonged to the party and all appointments were approved first by the party fractions whether in the Central Committee, guberniia branches, or factory committees. There was also substantial personal conflict among the leaders of the union, even after the defeat of the independent activists. Evidence of any kind of opposition within the trade union leadership is hard to come by, but we can assume that Nikolai Gordon lost his position as head of the Leningrad union in early 1926 and Derbyshev by the end of that year because they were political clients of Grigorii Zinov'ev, whose several efforts to challenge Stalin's leadership resulted in his own demotion and that of his supporters.[7] Aleksandr Borshchevskii had tangled with authorities in 1921 but remained in the leadership until the wholesale purge of the trade union movement in 1929. But even the union's internal party record is largely silent on these issues of high politics. Gordon said farewell to his party fraction on 23 January 1926, and they praised his capable and efficient leadership. The union rank and file would not be so kind or so concerned. Eavesdroppers sent by the political police (GPU) to record the mood of workers on the shop floor in response to the political defeat of Zinov'ev's Leningrad supporters in 1925 noticed only two cases of dissent among printers. One was reported to have complained, "Everyone wants to be the boss [*vozhd'*] of the proletariat, and they've made a

---

6. *Trud*, 19 October 1922; GARF, f. R-5525, op. 4, d. 1 (stenographic report of Fourth All-Russian Congress of Printers' Union, 18–21 October 1922); *Stenograficheskii otchet piatogo s"ezda soiuza, 1924*; GARF, f. R-5525, op. 8, d. 1 (stenographic report of Sixth All-Union Congress of Printers' Union, 27 November–4 December 1926), l. 85. An abbreviated transcript of the congress appeared in *Pechatnik* 50–51 (20 December 1926): 8–18; *Izvestiia*, 30 November 1926, also reported on the congress.

7. See Leonard Schapiro, *The Communist Party of the Soviet Union*, 2nd ed. (New York, 1971), 290–300; Carr, *Socialism in One Country*, vol. 2; Robert Vincent Daniels, *The Conscience of the Revolution: Communist Opposition in Soviet Russia* (New York, 1960), 253–72.

scapegoat of the Leningrad organization." Elsewhere, political agitation was dismissed as an affair of "the bosses" (*nachal'stvo*).[8] Whereas workers dared to speak openly about their political preferences in 1917 and even 1919, party politics at the local level during NEP were carried out subtly and behind the scenes. Workers found other ways to influence policy or to express their demands than through open or closed party discussions.

Evidence such as this and reports published in *Sotsialisticheskii vestnik* reinforce the notion that trade unions had become just another instrument for the subordination and mobilization of individual workers to suit the purposes of state and party. And in fact, mobilization was certainly the goal of the trade unions and all other public organizations: revolutionary socialism was a public, not private, affair, and the task of its institutions was to eradicate private and self-interested behavior in favor of the collective good. Organization was an end in itself.

The Printers' Union dutifully accepted the national trade union template for proper union organization: the central committees would engage the guberniia branches, and these branches would coordinate work in local enterprises. Information would flow back and forth, through circular letters, local visits, and reports in trade union journals.[9] Local organizations were requested to report regularly to the center: factory committees were expected to forward copies of their minutes and those of other factory-level organizations to the guberniia board; guberniia boards sent the minutes of their meetings and protocols of regular congresses to the Central Committee. The salaried union officials in the Central Committee then reviewed the evidence they received and advised local leaders on ways to improve their procedures and responsiveness to members. This flow of documentation from local units to the center reinforced the accountability of individual union organizations, and it also provided the central organs with the mechanisms to monitor local activism and deviation.

Like all institutions in the Soviet Union, this two-way transmission belt did not work as well in practice as in the resolutions on the "organization question" of the trade union movement. Guberniia organizations of printers remained extremely unhappy about the low level of leadership they received from the Central Committee. The delegate from Orel province complained to the 1922 congress of the regrettable absence of contact between his union and the center: not only were there no personal visits, but not even written correspondence came their way, and the Orel printers failed to receive crucial advice on preparing for their collective agreements. Responding to such complaints, Derbyshev reported to the 1924 congress that the Central Committee had changed the pattern of their visits to locals: fewer visits, but with a longer stay in each locality. Moreover, the center would respond to local reports only if they perceived problems

---

8. TsGAIPD SPb, f. 16, op. 6, d. 6932 (survey by GPU of workers' mood and discussions concerning the Fourteenth Party Congress, December 1925–January 1926), ll. 4, 7.

9. *Chetvertyi vserossiiskii s"ezd professional'nykh soiuzov*, 1921, 154–62.

in them: no news from Moscow was good news. Derbyshev must have anticipated the tenor of the discussion in his preliminary remarks, for a number of delegates responded to his report with criticism and questions. Even the Moscow delegate complained that the Central Committee lagged in providing the wage information necessary for concluding collective agreements. Two years later, Derbyshev returned to the Sixth Congress of the Printers' Union to report on the center's response to the previous directive to "widen and deepen" union work. Indeed, complaints about inattention from the center had largely disappeared, to be replaced by concerns about excessive embezzlement and the union's lack of leadership in resolving the high level of unemployment in the industry.[10]

At this 1926 congress, in what would be his final appearance as chairman of the union central committee, Derbyshev also boasted of the numbers of printers who had been mobilized into the so-called *aktiv*, the cadre of active trade union members, who now numbered 15,000, or 14 percent of the union.[11] Developing this core of activists had been one of the tasks of trade union democracy. Passive membership was not enough, and the union adopted a number of practices to increase workers' involvement in their union. The payment of dues constituted one of the early measures to promote members' interest. Members' dues supported the trade union apparatus, which had no other source of revenue: 25 percent of local dues were designated for the upkeep of the Central Committee and its staff. Factory committee members released from work also had their salaries paid by the union dues of the members. Members' dues were calculated as a percentage of their pay, and while 2 percent was considered to be the requirement for support of union activities, extra assessments were made for social and cultural activities, unemployment funds, and other campaigns and projects. By early 1923, workers in Moscow were paying an average of 6 to 9 percent of their wages to the trade union for these varied activities: too much, decided the central union, which insisted on maximum deductions of 4 percent of a worker's pay, including 0.5 percent to the unemployment fund.[12]

The role of the union treasury in providing aid to the unemployed remained ambiguous in these early years of NEP. As unemployment in Petrograd became exceptionally acute in 1922, the Moscow Printers' Union instructed its workers to contribute 2 percent of their wages to the "fund for the unemployed" in addition to their union dues. Others opted to make voluntary contributions of a day's or half-day's pay to help support their Petrograd comrades. Workers at Moscow's Fourteenth Print Shop rebelled when asked to contribute 2 percent of their wages for the unemployed: that was the responsibility of the state, they claimed.[13] Union funds for the unemployed supplemented those provided by

---

10. GARF, f. R-5525, op. 4, d. 1, l. 109; *Stenograficheskii otchet piatogo s"ezda soiuza, 1924*, 74–76, 108–30; GARF, f. R-5525, op. 8, d. 1.
11. GARF, f. R-5525, op. 8, d. 1, l. 16.
12. *Pechatnik* 6 (16 May 1923): 30; 4 (March 1923): 11.
13. *Trud*, 17 June 1922; GARF, f. R-5525, op. 5, d. 70 (meetings of board and presidium of Petrograd union, 1923), l. 3; *Pechatnik* 2 (35) (January 1923): 27; *Pravda*, 13 June 1922.

the Central Insurance Fund of the Labor Commissariat, and were channeled through a system of labor exchanges. Until 1925, unemployed printers needed to register with their local exchange in order to receive subsidies as well as access to jobs.[14] With the sharp rise in unemployment after 1926, the union increased its support for the unemployed, extending support to family members as well as unemployed breadwinners: the union central committee budgeted over half a million rubles for aid to the unemployed for the first half of 1927.[15]

Underlying the discussion of the plight of the unemployed lurked the subtext of the meaning of union membership. Membership entitled workers to unemployment benefits and to jobs as they became available, but the union worried about the corrupting effect of these material incentives. Neither employment nor union membership alone was a sufficient marker of proletarian identity. The perennial problem of free riding was no less acute in a socialist union than under capitalism, as the union journal reminded its members when it reprinted the "Ten Commandments of a Bad Union Member" from an unidentified American trade union paper: "Don't go to meetings; but if you go, go as late as possible"; "Pay your dues as late as possible, or not at all."[16]

The union also adopted real disciplinary measures to signal proper member behavior and eliminate the truly incorrigible. Judging by the records of factory committees and union boards, expulsion or suspension of members (and consideration of petitions for readmission) occupied a substantial portion of their time. Expulsions allowed union organizations, both central and local, to define what membership in the union ought to entail in practice. Failure to pay dues on time was common, and persistent culprits could be punished by loss of membership.[17] Expulsion from the union meant losing seniority and the right to the union's defense in case of conflicts. Discussions of such instances carried a clear didactic message about what it meant to be a good proletarian. Considering a list of Moscow printers expelled for nonpayment of dues, the union journal professed alarm at two characteristics of the list. Half of them were typesetters: "The most cultured part of the members of our union stand at the head of the 'fighting' squad of printers who relate indifferently [*naplevatel'ski otnosiashchikhsia*] to their union organization." Second, most of the nonpayers received wages at the highest levels of the wage structure: "Members of the union who receive the lowest pay relate more consciously to their obligations than comrades who earn at the highest rates."[18] The union itself did not interrogate

---

14. *Pechatnik* 5 (23 April 1923): 13; 4 (15 February 1925): 6; *Moskovskii pechatnik* 12 (29 October 1923): 10; 12 (29 March 1925): 1. On labor exchanges, see also Rogachevskaia, *Likvidatsiia bezrabotitsy,* 95–98.

15. *Pechatnik* 5 (23 February 1927): 5; *Izvestiia,* 5 December 1926; *Pravda,* 31 March 1927.

16. *Pechatnik* 3 (15 February 1924): 8.

17. Ibid. 6 (15 March 1925): 7; 24 (7 November 1925): 10; *Moskovskii pechatnik* 19 (16 May 1925): 2.

18. *Zorkii glaz,* 25 August 1926; *Moskovskii pechatnik* 28 (15 August 1924): 2; *Pechatnik* 1 (15 January 1924): 17.

this fact, which flew in the face of their assumptions about the relationship of skill, culture, and Communist political consciousness. But they could hardly discuss in public the question whether compositors predominated among the free riders because they wished to sponge off their more obedient comrades, or because their resistance to union obligations signified resistance to Soviet politics as well.

Other misbehavior unworthy of union members also merited suspensions or expulsion, and in the process of its deliberations, the union further elaborated on the proper traits of the total proletarian in a socialist democracy. Bad behavior included earning money on the side, whether moonlighting in private manufacturing or in a printers' cooperative or artel. Fraud in gaining access to union benefits—forging a membership book or collecting unemployment benefits while fully employed—and bribe taking were other sins punishable by expulsion. The "unproletarian" behavior of swearing, fighting, insulting one's comrades, drunkenness, and "hooliganism" resulted in temporary or permanent suspension. By 1926 and 1927, embezzlement of union funds had emerged as the most common cause for expulsion, followed by forgery of union documents and drunk and disorderly behavior. Neither published nor private records of union expulsions suggest that this disciplinary action targeted political dissidence: printers lost their union membership for lack of organizational discipline or for behavior unbecoming a proletarian. The political winnowing process was more likely carried out through job dismissals, decisions made by the Communist Party in connection with factory management, not by the union.[19]

The trade union remained the symbol of proletarian solidarity rather than discipline, and its activity in these years emphasized the organizational goals of corralling individuals into membership in the group. Challenged by evidence of member apathy and alienation, the union responded with new efforts to make membership meaningful, to bring the union closer to the workers, to meet the workers' most pressing economic needs, and to mobilize members into a permanent state of participation. Underlying all these strategies was the prevailing Communist assumption that in the ideal socialist society, all participants would be constantly in action, not at rest. An important step along the way was the generation and expansion of the union's "activist" core, the aktiv about which Derbyshev had boasted at the 1926 union congress. The aktiv included elected

---

19. GARF, f. R-5525, op. 4, d. 62 (board and presidium meetings of Moscow guberniia union, 1922), ll. 75, 76; TsGAIPD SPb, f. 435, op. 1, d. 60 (meetings of bureau of party fraction of Leningrad union, 1925); d. 59 (meetings of local and guberniia union party collectives in Leningrad, 1925), l. 56; TsGA SPb, f. 4804, op. 10, d. 5 (meetings of Leningrad union board, October 1925–December 1926); TsGAMO, f. 699, op. 1, d. 1141 (protocols of Eighth Moscow Guberniia Union Congress, September 1927), ll. 55–59; *Pechatnik* 1 (15 January 1924): 17; 5 (1 March 1925): 14; 25 (19 June 1926): 9; 37 (11 September 1926): 12; 5 (23 February 1927): 7; 6 (28 February 1927): 7; 9 (25 March 1927): 3, 13; 12–13 (1 May 1927): 28; *Moskovskii pechatnik* 20 (April 1924): 17; 25 (1 July 1924): 7; 24 (21 June 1925): 9; 17 (April 1926): 4; 20 (May 1926: 8.

members of factory committees, and one reason for the frequent reelection of committees in the early 1920s was to involve as many workers as possible in the experience of responsibility and participation. Other activists at the factory level included shop delegates, women's delegates (*delegatki*) elected to attend special women's meetings, dues collectors, and members of factory commissions, club boards, and cooperative organizations.

Much of the work of the trade unions took place locally, in the guberniia branches. These units implemented trade union policy on all questions, and they also negotiated collective agreements with local economic organizations. Guberniia branches sponsored their own regular congresses, at which the performance of the union was reported upon and debated. They sent their paid staff members to review and evaluate the work of local factory committees. Some of them published regular journals, which publicized union activities.[20] Their efforts, like those of the central organization, could also degenerate into numbing bureaucratic routine. Reports of the numbers of meetings the branches had organized came to serve as a proxy for organization itself.[21]

Through its own circulars, instructions, and the central union journals, the union's central committee endeavored to systematize and standardize the operations of all trade union organizations. In practice, however, local units exercised substantial autonomy and demonstrated a vexing degree of variability. A closer examination of the three representative branches, Moscow, Leningrad, and Voronezh, shows that when union officials actually interacted with their rank-and-file members, the members wanted more than the trappings of organization and the opportunity to become members of a larger whole. They wanted concrete services and defense of their economic interests.

The Moscow union, with one-third of the entire union's membership, could almost function as a separate organization itself, something of which the Central Committee and other union organizations were very much aware. Its membership had grown from 21,000 in 1923 to 30,000 in 1926, and the Moscow unit also possessed substantial financial resources, maintaining a paid staff of sixty-four in 1924.[22] The political history of Moscow's union gave a distinct tone to the functioning of the branch. While the red union had emerged victo-

---

20. *Moskovskii pechatnik*, published from 1921 until 1926, was the most successful of the journals. Petrograd's *Krasnyi pechatnik* appeared in 1921 and 1922, but could not afford to continue; instead, the union here sponsored a special page in the central journal, *Pechatnik*. Several other branches published journals for a short time, but financial difficulties usually forced them to cease publication. Among those that survive in Russian libraries are *Ekaterinoslavskii pechatnik* (1922–24); *Khar'kovskii pechatnik* (1922–27); *Kurskii pechatnik* (1918–25); *Nashe pechatnoe slovo* (Krasnoiarsk, 1921–24); *Pechatnik Altaia* (1923–24); *Poligraf* (Smolensk, 1922–24); *Poligrafist* (Tomsk, 1923–24); *Slovo pechatnika* (Riazan', 1918–23).
21. *Pechatnik* 5 (23 April 1923): 13. Petrograd's board reported a similar spate of meetings: TsGA SPb, f. 4804, op. 6, d. 24 (Fourth Petrograd Guberniia Printers' Congress, 8 September 1922), l. 8.
22. GARF, f. R-5525, op. 5, d. 19 (monthly and quarterly reports from guberniia branches, M–N, 1923), l. 4; *Otchet pravleniia moskovskogo gubernskogo otdela, 1923–1924*, 11; 1926 membership in *Moskovskii pechatnik* 4–5 (January 1926): 4.

rious in Moscow, Moscow's Communists had been more reluctant to battle the Mensheviks than their colleagues in Petrograd, and a spirit of trade unionism, as opposed to partisanship, continued to characterize activities in Moscow. To be sure, arrests and banishments of leading Menshevik trade unionists in 1922 and after discouraged open opposition by the politically alienated among printers still at liberty. On the other hand, efforts at rapprochement with erstwhile oppositionists can be seen in the case of Nikolai Chistov, the veteran Menshevik leader of the Moscow Printers' Union, who found a place in the union apparatus throughout the 1920s, assigned the task of preparing a history of the union.[23]

Nor did the memory of repression of the Mensheviks discourage Moscow printers from criticizing the union and talking back to the leadership. The growth of unemployment in 1926 provoked independent meetings of unemployed workers, who shouted down union officials when they came to smooth over the situation. To take the organizational initiative back again, the Moscow branch called a special conference of union delegates in October 1926, but although it was well packed with loyal union activists, many delegates heatedly criticized their leaders. Managers were taking advantage of the labor glut by hiring their friends off the street, bypassing the orderly procedures of the labor exchange, claimed the delegates, and the union did nothing to stop them. In conflicts rising from the regime of economy, the trade union had failed to defend the workers, who invariably lost their cases. Women's representatives also railed at the union's indifference to their conditions: Borshchevskii, one said, says we don't need nurseries or kindergartens; "It's fine for him to speak, perhaps he has someone at home to look after things, but I have no one." Borshchevskii responded from his seat, "It's time to stop having children at your advanced age," and general laughter erupted in the hall.[24] Such confident joking suggests that the union leaders both expected such criticism and knew they could survive it. Even in such an atmosphere of tension and discord, union leaders could rally their followers around the differences of gender. Women, as shall be seen, had become the all-purpose scapegoat for male workers' frustrations with the union and the party.

The belligerent unemployed at this conference were led by a printer named Geller. The regime of economy "permits exploitation at the expense of workers," said one of the unemployed. Unemployment "threatens to declass the working class," added Geller. The union does nothing to solve the unemployment problem, continued a third. Local shops wanted to organize shortened workweeks to spread the work, but the union refused to approve this solution.

23. *Sotsialisticheskii vestnik* 13/14 (35/36) (20 July 1922): 15; 17 (39) (8 September 1922): 11; 1 (71) (10 January 1924): 13; 18 (88) (20 September 1924): 14; *Otchet pravleniia moskovskogo gubernskogo otdela, 1923–1924*, 18; TsGAMO, f. 4660, op. 1, d. 42 (meetings of the commission on the purge of the union apparat, August–October 1928), l. 15.

24. TsGAMO, f. 699, op. 1, d. 787 (protocols of the Third Moscow Guberniia Union Conference, October 1926), l. 48.

A union official, Dudnik, took special offense at Geller's accusations, and replied with a threat: "The actions of the delegates from the unemployed are inviting repression." ("Not true!" came the shout from the unemployed.) "They're drunk and behaving like hooligans." ("Not true! Shame on you!") "And everything I say is amply confirmed by the outbursts of these comrade-unemployeds." (Noise, cries, "Not true! Lies! True!" Applause.) Others defended the union board against the accusations of Geller and the others, but also lodged their own complaints about the failure of union leaders to attend properly to local affairs.[25]

A year later, the regularly scheduled Eighth Moscow Guberniia Congress proceeded less stormily, but criticism from the floor continued. "We know that the trade union is a school of socialism, but this school is built wrong." The union had failed to implement piece rate agreements to the workers' advantage; the labor exchange was riddled with corruption; the board ignored mass layoffs; workers waited four years for a pass to a sanatorium, while their directors went annually; the union failed to limit the imposition of fines by management.[26] Printers in Moscow expected their union to defend their economic well-being and to defend the justice of the collective cause. While there were surely limits to the kind of criticism that could be leveled in public, the proceedings at these conferences and congresses confirm that printers were willing to articulate their discontent and to demand more responsiveness from their leaders.

The Leningrad branch offers a similar picture, although the style here differed from Moscow's. Nikolai Gordon ran the Leningrad union as his autocratic patrimony, although he was frequently absent from the local union, engaged in work for the union's central committee or for the party's Leningrad committee. Gordon was quick to invoke accusations of Menshevism whenever local printers expressed criticism of the union leadership's competence, but here too workers demanded responsiveness and action from their leaders. At the 1922 Guberniia Congress, a delegate from the Pechatnyi Dvor shop, Murzich, claimed that the masses had become alienated from the union because criticism had been forbidden. If a worker dared to cite his three years of membership in the union as authority to criticize, Gordon would outdo him with his own union pedigree: "I was born in the union, and I will die in it." Whenever the rank and file demonstrated any initiative, continued Murzich, they were "immediately rebuked from the podium or from somewhere, that he sounds like a political capitalist, or he's speaking only for the sake of talking, or they're sympathizers of Menshevism or counterrevolution [applause].... I didn't speak to get applause.... There's no point in criticizing because nothing has been done and nothing can be done, even by Gordon if he were three times a Communist [applause]."[27]

Three years later, the low level of respect accorded to the local union again

25. Ibid., ll. 19, 44–45, 48, 55, 56.
26. Ibid., d. 1141, ll. 23–24.
27. TsGA SPb, f. 4804, op. 6, d. 24, ll. 36–37.

became a topic of concern. Staff members at the Sokolova print shop organized a party to celebrate the birthday of the red director, Mikhail F. Lavrov. Such celebrations had been an important part of the workplace paternalism of the printing industry before the revolution, and the particular event at Sokolova was not an isolated occurrence.[28] In this instance, however, the weekend party was attended by the acting secretary of the Leningrad branch, Vasil'ev, who became flagrantly drunk and drove around town in one of the union's automobiles "on a day when automobiles ought not to be out, because it wasn't a workday." Union party activists recognized that this embarrassing behavior fitted a larger pattern. It's not only anniversaries, said the chairman of Pechatnyi Dvor's factory committee: when you go to the union, many of the officials there are under the influence. Here at the closed meeting of union Communists, the main concern was about the effect of this kind of behavior on the union rank and file. It was one thing for the factory committees to know about the widespread drinking among the leadership, but every rank-and-file worker, every unemployed member, was now talking about it. Vasil'ev and others like him had damaged the union's authority.[29]

The discussion of this incident by the union's party fraction took place as Zinov'ev's New Opposition began to prepare for the coming Fourteenth Communist Party Congress in December 1925. Given the divisions within the party, it was especially important at this time for the party to demonstrate the highest morality, and widespread drunkenness among its officials was surely cause for alarm. Regardless of the politics of the intraparty struggle, party activists recognized that the guberniia branch did not enjoy authority among local workers. Vasil'ev's well-known incompetence discredited the union organization.[30]

Gordon was out of town during this affair, and four months later, as a consequence of the defeat of the Zinov'ev opposition at the Fourteenth Party Congress, he lost his position as head of the Leningrad Printers' Union. His fellow board members were respectful and regretful when Gordon announced that he had been "called to work in the Central Committee," but soon afterward the rank and file's representatives at the Seventh Guberniia Congress sang a different tune. The intensity of anger and criticism leveled at all of the union leaders suggests that Gordon's departure had released the pressure valve he had once kept tightly closed. A delegate to the Leningrad congress in March 1926 recalled ruefully Gordon's speech back in 1924, calling protesting unemployed workers Mensheviks and threatening to export them to Warsaw. Ia. Gotlib, the delegate from the Godless print shop, dared to say, "Although it's not good to speak ill of the dead, I'll recall the late Gordon. In his job as union chairman,

28. On prerevolutionary culture, see Steinberg, *Moral Communities*, 56–66.
29. TsGAIPD SPb, f. 435, op. 1, d. 60, l. 26; GARF, f. R-5525, op. 18, d. 41 (meetings of bureau of party fraction of Printers' Union Central Committee, 1925–29), unpaginated: report of 19 September 1925; TsGAIPD SPb, f. 435, op. 1, d. 60, l. 29.
30. TsGAIPD SPb, f. 435, op. 1, d. 60, l. 29; GARF, f. R-5525, op. 7, d. 68 (board meetings of Leningrad guberniia union, 1925), l. 89.

he devoted one day a week to the union's business. Comrades, this work was bloody useless. Gordon admitted that no work at all was done. Gordon is no longer here, and you should thank the Lord that he has departed, and thank those who departed him."[31]

Personalities and political style aside, substantively the issues that agitated Leningrad's printers in early 1926 were similar to those raised by Moscow's printers later that same year. Printers worried fundamentally about their economic situation, that of both the employed workers and the unemployed, and they squarely blamed the union for failing to defend their material interests. Another speaker at the March 1926 congress, a representative of the Leningrad unemployed, remonstrated: "We're always strutting around claiming that Western Europe suffers from hunger and unemployment, that they sell children, but this happens here. There are prostitutes on Ligovka Street. We live in terrible conditions, and the union pays no attention. In 1907, with strict repression, when we had unemployment we agreed to work three days each. . . . We've starved for eight years, and we'll starve for another ten. . . . If only we had the solidarity we had in 1907, when we weren't oppressed by Soviet power." One speaker after another railed against the union's lack of authority. Why was it so low? In some places, said Sokolov from the Fedorov print shop, it was hard to know where the union began and management stopped. The branch officials paid attention only to the largest enterprises: at one small shop, a representative of the union visited only once in the past year, and then only a week before this congress. "He came, he sniffed about (in Gogol''s words), and he left." The new union chairman, Matikainen, answered his critics one by one, but the tension at the congress remained high when the delegation from the Zinov'ev print shop demonstratively walked out of the meeting to protest the cutting off of discussion.[32]

The agitation came to a head with the nomination of the new branch board. As always, the Communist fraction of the union proposed a slate of candidates. A new name on the list was that of M. N. Rozov, a veteran Communist printer and the Central Committee's handpicked candidate to restore discipline to the post-Gordon Leningrad union organization. When his name was announced, there were whistles and hisses, and cries of "Down with him! It's the same old gang." Gotlib, who had earlier rejoiced at Gordon's departure, sprang up to denounce this nomination: trade unions are supposed to be the broad organization of the nonparty mass, as confirmed by the recent Communist Party conference. "We are recommended Rozov. . . . I want to know, is Rozov at the conference or not? I'm against these appointments, we should elect our leaders and not accept appointments. [Applause.]" From the side of the Communists

---

31. TsGAIPD SPb, f. 435, op. 1, d. 64 (meetings of bureau of party fraction of Leningrad union, 1926), l. 3; TsGA SPb, f. 4804, op. 10, d. 4, l. 466, 444.

32. TsGA SPb, f. 4804, op. 10, d. 4 (stenographic report of Leningrad Union Seventh Congress, 14 March 1926), ll. 520–22, 428, 477, 707; *Leningradskaia pravda*, 17 March 1926.

and guberniia branch, Ugorov retorted, "Comrades, God save us from our friends, but from our enemies we'll deliver ourselves. Gotlib is not a party member. We ourselves know how to defend the resolutions of the party conference, we don't need Gotlib to tell us. . . . [More applause.] Comrades, it's shameful to hear these words. Printers are the most cultured of unions. Printers know Rozov, he was in the underground with us, he was secretary of our union. [Voice: Show him.] I can't pull him from my pocket, he works in the Central Committee. . . . I think you should vote for Rozov, a Leningrad printer, he knows trade union work. We want him to be—this is not a secret—chairman of the union, we think he's worthy of being chairman. [Noisy applause.]" Rozov was duly elected and became the new chairman of the Leningrad branch. The union journal *Pechatnik* commented later (without reporting any substance) that there had never in Leningrad been such a lively meeting.[33] And there would never be such a lively one again.

Did this opposition to Gordon and his successors reflect an outburst of Menshevism dressed up in nonparty clothes? If Menshevism represented an ideological field of independence and articulate opposition rather than an organized political program, then Menshevism retained a following among the independent-minded printers. But once dissidence acquired a label and a political platform (whether inside or outside the Communist Party), Communist disciplinarians swooped to contain it. Dissidents could speak forcefully against their leaders, but they could not give their opposition a name, and this handicap diminished their ability to challenge the premises of Communist trade union power.

Similar evidence of dissent and engagement exists in Voronezh, but on a much smaller scale. Well into 1923, the local union organization included a vocal minority of "independent" printers, and at the union's guberniia congress in June 1923, this group attempted to block the adoption of the Communist slate for the new union board. Significantly, the congress was run by a plenipotentiary from Moscow, I. Minchin, who forced through the election of the Communist nominees. He then engineered a resolution to censure by name the thirteen delegates who had opposed the party line, but the leader of the opposition boasted that "conscious printers" would not print such a list, and the resolution failed.[34]

Subsequently, the union in Voronezh learned to follow standard organizational procedure. Overall, the record for Voronezh speaks of a union organization with few resources, financial or in personnel, a unit very much dependent on the center for direction and supervision, and a unit in which formalism may have dominated over genuine trade union activity on the ground. The union ritually reported on its efforts to implement central union policy, whether on piece rates, the incorporation of women into the workforce, or cultural activities.

---

33. TsGA SPb, f. 4804, op. 10, d. 4, ll. 924, 926; *Pechatnik* 15 (10 April 1926): 15.
34. GARF, f. R-5525, op. 5, d. 32 (Third Voronezh Guberniia Congress, 21 June 1923), l. 74.

Regular congresses of delegates ritually criticized the union board for its failure to live up to its obligations. The board ritually blamed local committees for their indifference. Local committees blamed the indifference of the "mass," who ignored union meetings and union issues.[35] When the central union brought in an outside activist to take charge of the Voronezh organization in 1925, the candidacy of G. B. Melamed was greeted much like that of Rozov in Leningrad: Voronezh printers objected to the appointment of this party and trade union veteran, and Melamed squeaked onto the board with a bare majority. Melamed's backers, it turned out, had failed to consider his personal history, although it was well known to Voronezh printers. Once at his Moscow print shop, Melamed had agreed to complete a rush job at normal rates, when his co-workers—even party members—had demanded a bonus. For his proletarian zeal he had been labeled a strikebreaker, and even Communist printers in Voronezh wanted to have nothing to do with him.[36] This provincial experience was very typical. Small local organizations looked to the center for leadership and learned to accept the very narrow limits of autonomy and self-defense.

The journals published by the union center linked the center with individual units and provided a forum for wide-ranging discussions and reports on union activities. To the outside reader, these journals describe a rich cultural and activist life, and the journals of the Printers' Union stand out among other unions' journals in the 1920s for their liveliness and substance. Trade union publications had nurtured the fledgling and often illegal union movement before the revolution; the end of censorship in 1917 had allowed such publications to flourish, and under socialism the printed word became an especially meaningful element of organization for the Printers' Union. *Pechatnik* became the organ of the union's central committee in 1922, appearing biweekly or weekly throughout the 1920s. The Moscow branch published its own *Moskovskii pechatnik*, beginning in late 1921, and the journal continued to appear monthly or weekly until it merged with *Pechatnik* at the end of 1926. Ideally, these journals would inform workers about the purposes of union organization and about the organizational and economic issues of current concern, and they would also connect the Central Committee or guberniia branch with the local units. Every worker who read the journal would realize that he or she was "a link in the chain" of the All-Russian Union.[37]

Much of every journal, which usually ran between twelve and thirty-two

---

35. *Otchet o deiatel'nosti pravleniia gubotdela, 1922–1923* (Voronezh); GARF, f. R-5525, op. 5, d. 16 (monthly and quarterly reports from guberniia branches, B–V, 1923); d. 32; *Pechatnik* 9 (August 1923): 15; *Otchet o deiatel'nosti pravleniia voronezhskogo gubotdela, 1923–1924*; *Protokol zasedanii IV-go gubernskogo s"ezda, 1924* (Voronezh), 17.

36. GARF, f. R-5525, op. 18, d. 41 (bureau meeting, 30 November 1925); *Protokol zasedaniia V-go gub. s"ezda, 1925* (Voronezh), 23–24; biographical information on Melamed in *Otchet o rabote pravleniia gubotdela, 1926–1927* (Voronezh), 3.

37. *Pechatnik* 9 (August 1923): 1.

pages, consisted of discussions of trade union policies and issues: collective agreements, reports on upcoming conferences and accounts of their achievements, issues of unemployment and utilization of women's and young people's labor. Most issues included discussions of technological change. *Pechatnik* included regular pages that featured news of guberniia branches, and when the Leningrad organization could no longer afford to publish its own independent journal, *Pechatnik* devoted a page in each issue to Leningrad activities. *Moskovskii pechatnik* featured a section, "Around the Print Shops," which offered items submitted by local worker-correspondents. The "cultural" section of the journals included short stories, photographic montages, poems, plays, and feuilletons that often focused on life in the print shop. Anniversary issues featured collections of reminiscences about the 1903 printers' strike in Moscow, the 1905 revolution, and the October 1917 revolution. The summer season brought reports on vacations and rest homes, and as the physical culture movement developed in the USSR, the journals began to highlight the activities of the union's sports competitions. Many issues featured chess and checkers problems, and a humor page usually concluded each issue.

Yet despite this rich content, internal evidence suggests that the journals were not terribly popular among the union rank and file, who never subscribed at the levels desired by the leadership. Such reader response creates problems for historical analysis: to what extent were these journals Potemkin villages, describing an ideal but unrealistic world of trade union activism? The union itself agonized over the problem of readership, as measured by subscriptions. Only a minority of union members subscribed. The circulation of *Pechatnik* rose to 9,000 in 1923 and peaked at 15,500 in early 1925, at a time when the total union membership stood at approximately 85,000. More Leningrad printers subscribed to *Moskovskii pechatnik* in 1923 than to the national *Pechatnik*. Activists complained that printers would rather spend 2,000 rubles on cigarettes than 10 kopecks on a journal.[38] Subscriptions to *Pechatnik* began to fall precipitously in 1926, from 14,000 in the winter to 9,000 by the end of the summer, and in the autumn it merged with the Moscow journal.[39] *Moskovskii pechatnik* never attracted more than 8,700 subscribers from a union base of 30,000. At some small print shops, a majority of workers received the journal, but the share of subscribers was only 8 percent at the large First Model Print Shop (none at all subscribed to *Pechatnik*) and 28 percent at the Sixteenth. Readers complained that the journal appealed only to the trade union activists.

38. Ibid. 3 (15 February 1924): 10.
39. Union membership in *Stenograficheskii otchet piatogo s'ezda soiuza*, 1924, 72; circulation figures in GARF, f. R-5525, op. 4, d. 1, l. 264; op. 5, d. 21 (monthly and quarterly reports from guberniia branches, including Leningrad, 1923), l. 48; *Pechatnik* 8 (July 1923): 8; 4 (15 February 1925): 8; 7 (1 April 1925): 18; 37 (11 September 1926): 5; *Moskovskii pechatnik* 10 (12 August 1923): 1; GARF, f. R-5525, op. 5, d. 126 (meetings of worker-correspondents and correspondence of *Pechatnik* editors, 1923), l. 26; *Otchet pravleniia moskovskogo gubernskogo otdela*, 1924–1925, 5; TsGAMO, f. 699, op. 1, d. 1141, l. 68.

The masthead of a 1924 issue of *Pechatnik* features a typesetter's composing stick, with the letters as a mirror image. (*Pechatnik* 5 [15 March 1924]: 1.)

"Around Our Print Shops" reads the heading of a column in *Moskovskii pechatnik*. (*Moskovskii pechatnik* 2 [15 January 1925]: 10.)

"While members of boards and factory committees in local shops are interested in reading programmatic articles on issues of trade union work, the ordinary worker-printer finds little of interest in such matters." At the same time, 17,000 copies of factory newspapers rolled off local presses in Moscow.[40] Printers responded best, it seemed, to local publications: the closer to their everyday lives, the better.

What role, then, did these journals actually play in representing the world of the Soviet printer? The trade union leadership wanted every union member to be a conscious participant in the life of the organization and therefore to be a conscious consumer of the union's publication. Their ideal reader was the selfless activist who dedicated his or her life to production, organization, and culture: the total proletarian would read the journal from cover to cover. The actual reader, union officials recognized, needed to be sold on the value and utility of the union journal, and therefore the journal had to be made attractive to

---

40. *Moskovskii pechatnik* 15 (7 January 1924): 8; 6 (15 February 1925): 3; 24 (June 1924): 4; *Pechatnik* 9 (August 1923): 1.

the real rank and file, to become relevant to their lives and responsive to their concerns. There was danger in too much responsiveness, which could deviate into workerism, or "tailism," in which the petty concerns of the rank and file drove the agenda of the leadership. And there was danger too that these local organs might stray into politically incorrect waters. The journals, like all publications in the Soviet Union, therefore underwent preliminary review: each printing enterprise employed a resident censor.[41]

The line between political correctness and readability was indistinct, but the problem of readability remained central. Scratching their editorial heads about how to reach the nonsubscribing majority, writers admitted that workers rejected *Moskovskii pechatnik*'s one-sided, one-dimensional articles with dry and outdated facts, with its silence on important issues such as wages, with its irregular and unaesthetic appearance. Workers wanted local news, they wanted to read about themselves (but not about others just like them in other cities); they did not want to read about union meetings and the tribulations of management. Rather, speculated these same writers, they wanted to read more international news, editorials on current political themes, articles on the state of the printing industry, fiction, and criticism of union and managerial organizations. The link between the editors and their imagined readers would be the worker-correspondent: if readers complained there was no local news in the journal, then it was the responsibility of local writers to submit articles for publication. As part of a broader campaign to develop worker-correspondents, *Moskovskii pechatnik* encouraged these correspondents with regular meetings at which they would discuss appropriate content for the coming journals; later these agenda items would be codified and printed in advance.[42]

The organizing mission of the trade union required interactive journals that would be read and thereby maintain the lines of transmission between central organization and those who needed organizing. They needed to bridge the gap between the "trade union aristocracy," the activist 10 to 15 percent, and the ordinary majority. This interactive element provides the historian with some assurance that these publications represent, to some degree, union realities. Nonetheless, readers preferred to interact with their own local kind: provincial journals, when branches could afford them, enjoyed more success than *Pechatnik*. The competition between the center and the local may have ultimately ended in the defeat of the center's dream of transforming all readers into ideal readers and all workers into total proletarians, but the competition itself furnishes invaluably candid insight into the nature of Soviet trade unionism. Understanding the limits but also the aspirations of these controlled publications, we can carefully mine their pages for evidence of the goals and values of Soviet workers.

41. GARF, f. R-5525, op. 5, d. 126, l. 16.
42. *Moskovskii pechatnik* 6 (30 August 1922): 23–24; *Pechatnik* 15–16 (1 June 1927): 44.

## DEMOCRACY FROM BELOW? WORKER PARTICIPATION AT THE LOCAL LEVEL

In discussing the role and failures of the union journals, the union leadership acknowledged the power of localism. And it was in the local print shops, in everyday contacts between leaders and led, that the real work of the trade union was carried out, where the rank-and-file worker would be won or lost for the republic of labor. The world of the "federated print shop" had not been abandoned with the new emphasis on centralization and system: the semiprosperous years of NEP gave local workplaces even more opportunities to assert their individualism and autonomy.

The factory committee remained the most important link between the central trade union organizations and the rank and file of workers. The committees continued to play a role in production and in defending workers' interests in negotiation with management. But more important, the factory committee was now called upon to be the key agent of the organization of the working class in the Soviet Union.[43] The permanent task of the factory committee, like that of the central union, was to promote the participation of every worker and many of their dependents in the work of building socialism. Thus the factory committee organized commissions to deal with production, occupational safety, mutual aid funds, cultural affairs, housing, cafeterias, consumer cooperatives, women's issues, youth issues (particularly apprenticeship), schools, volunteer activities such as partnerships with military units and rural villages, and the implementation of myriad campaigns instituted by Soviet and trade union bodies.[44]

Defense of workers' economic interests vis-à-vis management and the organization of the working class constituted the official duties of the factory committees. Their role as agent of welfare functions was meant to diminish with the turn to NEP, but nonetheless, the primary functions of many factory committees remained the allocation of "emergency vouchers" (*bony*): advances on wages, permission for overtime work, issue of firewood, food supplements, housing, and spots in rest homes. The union calculated in 1924 that 50 to 60 percent of the factory committee's time was occupied in supplying these credits, a task better managed by the enterprise's business office.[45]

Factory committees served as the school of democracy most closely connected to workers' everyday work lives. To keep that democratic element fresh and alive and to minimize the danger that factory committee membership would become a bureaucratic sinecure, trade union rules stipulated that the

---

43. *Pechatnik* 2 (35) (January 1923): 22 discusses the new tasks of factory committees.
44. *Pechatnik* 3 (36) (February 1923): 26; 12 (7 November 1923): 11; *Moskovskii pechatnik* 10 (12 August 1923): 9; 12 (29 October 1923): 6; 18 (27 February 1924): 16; 33–34 (6 September 1925): 23. A representative sample of factory committee meetings in 1924 and 1926 at the Sixteenth Print Shop can be found in TsGAMO, f. 699, op. 1, d. 570, d. 849.
45. GARF, f. R-5525, op. 5, d. 19, l. 42; d. 64 (presidium meetings of Moscow union board, 1923), l. 34; *Moskovskii pechatnik* 9 (12 July 1923): 18; 32 (15 October 1924): 2; 22 (7 June 1925): 2; *Fabzavkom*, supplement to *Trud*, 6 March 1924: 10; *Pechatnik* 21 (15 October 1925): 3.

The factory committee reviews documents and vouchers at the Krasnyi Maiak Print Shop, Moscow, 1924. (Rossiiskii Gosudarstvennyi Arkhiv Kinofotodokumentov, 1-58101. Used with permission of the archive.)

committees would be reelected every six months, usually in fall and spring.[46] Elections normally took place at general meetings at the workplace. The outgoing factory committee would give an account of its work during its term, and workers would discuss the committee's accomplishments and performance. The new committee, whose candidates were almost invariably selected in advance by the local party organization, would then be elected and installed. The elections allowed workers to discuss the most important issues of their workplace and to speak their minds.

Union officials regularly investigated the work of local factory committees and often published the results in the union journal, providing examples for committees to emulate and behavior to avoid. Some committees had become too cozy with management: this had been the Mensheviks' rallying cry during the struggle between the two unions, and it continued to echo, if faintly, in the years after the Mensheviks' defeat. Some workers complained that they did not know where the union ended and management began, a familiar phrase in rank-and-file criticism. By contrast, other committees were criticized for being too confrontational with management, harming the workers' interests with their

46. *Trud*, 13 June 1923.

constant quarrels with the administration. The overbearing factory committee chairman emerged as a common type in these years. This chairman was cut off from the workers, too bureaucratic, too imperious, too careerist. "We sent you to the factory committee to work, not to elevate yourself," wrote the worker-correspondent in one case. The *predzavkom*, factory committee chairman, was defined in the union journal's humor page as a "mysterious individual who shows up once a year at the preelection meeting." Such abuse of authority was made all the more likely by the practice of concentrating all factory committee work in the hands of a few overworked activists.[47]

The most common factory committee type, however, was the incompetent one. Such committees had no plan of work, they failed to supervise the work of their subcommittees, they did not collect dues, they failed to account for union funds or sometimes misappropriated them. Their members drank too much. They lacked authority. In only one case was a factory committee criticized for being too responsive to workers: the Seventh State Print Shop in Moscow had flouted the principles of good management by permitting 25,489 hours of overtime without union permission. Overtime work added precious income to the worker's family budget but interfered with the orderly planning of the enterprise budget. This too could be labeled incompetence in the broad scheme of socialist labor relations.[48]

The regular reviews of factory committee performance revealed the chronic tension between democratic forms and tight control by party organizations. In each enterprise, the Communist Party group (labeled variously fraction, cell, or collective) assumed the leading role in enterprise affairs, gathering in advance of each meeting to decide on an agenda and strategies to pursue. In enterprises with large party organizations, the executive organ of the fraction, its bureau, met first to determine procedures and decisions. Large factory committees, in turn, also concentrated their executive functions in a smaller presidium. By the time an issue reached the factory committee, therefore, it had already been thoroughly vetted by at least one round of discussion, and sometimes as many as three: in the bureau, in the fraction, and in the presidium. Little was left to democratic chance, a fact that quickly and predictably alienated the rank-and-file workers.

---

47. GARF, f. R-5525, op. 5, d. 64, l. 87; d. 19, l. 42; review of several committees in Leningrad: TsGA SPb, f. 4804, op. 9, d. 20 (meetings of Leningrad union board, December 1924–December 1925); op. 6, d. 24, l. 36; op. 10, d. 4, l. 428; *Pechatnik* 20 (15 May 1926): 7; 5 (23 February 1927): 21; TsGAIPD SPb, f. 435, op. 1, d. 98 (Leningrad factory committee reelections, 1923), l. 100b.; d. 55 (Leningrad Printers' Union secret correspondence with state organs, 1924), l. 10; *Moskovskii pechatnik* 23–24 (June 1926): 13; 4–5 (January 1926): 8–15; 10 (12 August 1923): 10; 21 (1 May 1924): 18; 6 (February 1926): 16; 50 (19 December 1925): 9; 10–11 (March 1926): 18; 6 (15 February 1925): 9; 25 (June 1926): 8; 16 (17 April 1926): 2; *Pravda*, 18 September 1926.

48. *Moskovskii pechatnik* 12 (29 October 1923): 16; 33–34 (6 September 1925): 23; 22 (June 1926): 10; *Pechatnik* 30 (24 July 1926): 8; 32 (7 August 1926): 7; 20 (10 July 1927): 13; TsGA SPb, f. 4804, op. 9, d. 20, l. 72. On embezzlement: *Moskovskii pechatnik* 29–30 (September 1924): 8, 9; 30–31 (12 August 1925): 14; 28 (15 August 1924): 3; GARF, f. R-5525, op. 5, d. 64, l. 34; *Pechatnik* 9 (1 May 1925): 14; 3 (16 January 1926): 8; 3 (36) (February 1923): 26; TsGAIPD SPb, f. 435, op. 1, d. 98, l. 9; d. 49, ll. 8, 14; GARF, f. R-5525, op. 5, d. 64, l. 34.

The Communist Party's thorough control of the democratic process had emerged in response to the continuing threat to its leadership and ideology from the independent-minded former supporters of the Menshevik line. Independence retained a strong hold among printers, particularly in Moscow, and the continuing poor economic conditions after the Civil War gave the Mensheviks new life in 1923. The regular factory committee elections could provide them with an ideal platform for mobilizing opposition. The Communists in the union, therefore, mobilized their own forces to use these 1923 elections to break the back of the Menshevik alternative once and for all. A meeting of Communist cell secretaries in March 1923 revealed that the situation everywhere was threatening. The mood at Krasnyi Proletarii was poor, Communists could be elected to the factory committee only with difficulty. The Thirty-ninth State Print Shop's man reported a "general and quite serious deviation toward Menshevism." Things were a little better at the Sixteenth State Print Shop, where three Communists served on the factory committee, but here too victory would be difficult to attain. The bureau then began a round of personnel reassignments to place reliable and capable Communists at the enterprises where the Menshevik danger was greatest. Throughout the summer, the party bureau continued to send fresh activists to troubled enterprises in efforts to keep a lid on continuing unrest and opposition.[49]

Krasnyi Proletarii remained a problem for the Communist Party, but opposition to the party line reflected internal Communist divisions as well as challenges from outside. The party's designated troubleshooter there quarreled with the red director and other party members, and he had to be reassigned. The handpicked candidate for the factory committee chair, Vasil'ev, also proved to be uncooperative, but the party faced stiff opposition when it proposed a factory committee slate that omitted him. Rather than accept the party's nominees, several departments offered their own slates of factory committee candidates, including Vasil'ev and his supporters. Borshchevskii himself attended the electoral meeting at Krasnyi Proletarii, a sign of the seriousness of the democratic challenge to the Communist Party. Ultimately the Communist slate won, but only by a majority rather than the usual unanimous vote.[50] The experience at Krasnyi Proletarii, for which the records are especially detailed, reveals a continuity of Communist practice from the Civil War period into the NEP. The Communist organization managed to win these victories through a combination of agitation, surveillance, exhortation, and the ever-present threat of dismissal. Printers on the shop floor dared to express opposition by using the electoral means at their disposal, but once defeated, they appeared to submit quietly.

49. GARF, f. R-5525, op. 18, d. 29 (meetings of bureau of party fraction of Moscow union, 1923): unnumbered, meetings 6 March–27 August 1923.
50. Ibid., meetings 27 August and 9 November 1923; TsGAMO, f. 699, op. 1, d. 438 (general and factory committee meetings at Krasnyi Proletarii, 1923), ll. 13, 11, 15.

Petrograd rank-and-file printers also expressed their resistance to the dictates of the party in this early phase of NEP. Printers at the Zinov'ev Print Shop met on 20 March 1923 to consider the work of the old committee and to elect a new one. The union's Communist Party fraction had already determined the composition of the factory committee, naming a new leader imported from outside. Although a delegates' meeting had approved the slate in advance, the general meeting itself was stormy, as Vasilii Kuznetsov lashed out at Gordon's report on the state of the enterprise. He was angry that too little attention had been paid to issues of workers' health. "The nightingales sing in the springtime, and they sing here, but they don't provide us with antidotes [for hazardous conditions], and I want to know from Gordon if we will receive antidotes. You are our defender, we have this right." When the time came to elect the new factory committee, voices from the floor proposed their own list in opposition to the Communist-approved one. "The general meeting can elect who it wants; the list dealt us by the [party] collective and the union is not a decree," said one participant. When Gordon pointed out that the enterprise's own delegates had approved the list, another worker responded, "It's not the union that has foisted this list on us that the workers don't want; we want to elect whom we want, and we don't need the union." This printer blamed the Communist Party for the suppression of democracy, but if the union failed to protest, he would reject the union as well. In the end, the meeting elected three from the Communist list and two from the opposition.[51]

The First Model Print Shop in Moscow, once a hotbed of Menshevism, offered a strikingly docile contrast at its 1923 committee elections. They had already been punished in 1922. By 1923, with the Mensheviks purged and the rank and file intimidated, the Communists could consider the situation well in hand. "If we wanted to, we could elect all Communists to the factory committee." The election ritual remained the same. The factory committee reported, individual workers criticized one aspect or another of the work, and then they passed a resolution generally approving of the committee's work and instructing the new committee to pay attention to ten particular points, beginning with the international situation. "The international situation" would become code for the irrelevancy of local meetings, and its appearance in this document bears no link to any of the issues discussed earlier. The "instructions" to the new committee probably bore little relation to the issues that concerned the workers themselves. The meeting next endorsed the proposed candidates for the new

---

51. TsGAIPD SPb, f. 435, op. 1, d. 78 (meetings of bureau of party fraction of Petrograd Printers' Union, 1921–23), l. 64; TsGA SPb, f. 4804, op. 7, d. 90 (general meetings at Petrograd print shops, 1922–23), ll. 73–75ob. Evidence of similar resistance exists for Pechatnyi Dvor in April 1923 (TsGA SPb, f. 4804, op. 7, d. 90, ll. 120–21) and at the Sixteenth Print Shop in Moscow, also in April (*Nasha zhizn'*, 1 May 1923). Factory elections at Sokolova followed Gordon's script more closely: TsGA SPb, f. 4804, op. 7, d. 90, l. 69; op. 8, d. 86 (general and factory committee meetings at Sokolova, 1924), l. 8.

committee, without reported discussion.[52] The First Model Print Shop had become a model of working-class submission.

Such multiple voices begin to disappear from the record after 1923. The union's Communists had demonstrated their ability to promote their supporters and to punish dissent, and dissent receded. The union now congratulated itself on the routinization of local democracy. Workers at the Thirteenth State Print Shop in Moscow approved the Communist list "without superfluous discussions." New elections at Krasnyi Proletarii in May 1925 called forth criticism of prices in the municipal canteen and the level of fines for spoiled work, but indicated no organized opposition. Six months later, the canteen again came in for criticism for poor food, and women in the brochure department raised objections to the arbitrary reduction of their wage grades. A *Pravda* account of this meeting labeled it "a businesslike assembly" (but omitted mention of the women brochurists' complaint). Most notable was the impressive attendance at the meeting: 1,300 of 1,600 workers, instead of the usual 200, had turned out. (*Pechatnik* mentioned, unlike *Pravda*, that the business meeting was followed by a performance of the Moscow trade union Blue Blouse theater troupe.)[53]

Printers responded to the withdrawal of real democracy by withdrawing their engagement with the union, but union leaders diagnosed this behavior as apathy rather than Menshevism. The leadership blamed local factory committees for failing to call meetings, for allowing one or two activists to dominate union affairs. But even when meetings were held, workers tried hard not to attend or to participate. The lack of interest in the union organization had become a running joke in the union journal: *aktivnost'* (activism) was defined in the "Union Organizer's Dictionary" as "the ability to sit through a report on the international situation to the end." The "international situation" was defined as "the first point on the agenda. Systematically employed, it serves as a method for a catastrophic reduction in the attendance at general meetings." In a sketch labeled "Sleeping Stupor," a worker-correspondent recounted a general meeting: the factory committee chairman gave his report in a tedious monotone while "Stepan Bezrazlichnyi" (Stephen the Indifferent) dreamed of his home, of tea on the table, or better yet, of the cozy tavern far away from his mother-in-law. Meanwhile, the chairman droned on: "'For the period in question,' buzzed the chairman, 'the factory committee has conducted an innumerable multitude of all possible manner of meetings, assemblies, conferences, and so on and suchlike. . . .'" Finally someone nudged our Stepan, who saw a forest of raised hands in front of him, and his half-asleep hand automatically went up, too.[54]

52. GARF, f. R-5525, op. 18, d. 29, 15 March 1923; TsGAMO, f. 699, op. 1, d. 396 (meetings in print shops in Zamoskvorech'e district, 1923), ll. 32–320b.
53. *Moskovskii pechatnik* 18 (21 February 1924): 17; TsGAMO, f. 699, op. 1, d. 704 (general meetings at Krasnyi Proletarii, 1925), l. 6; *Pravda*, 27 October 1925; *Pechatnik* 24 (7 November 1925): 13.
54. *Moskovskii pechatnik* 15 (7 January 1924): 2; 33–34 (6 September 1924): 23; 23 (1 June

It was no state secret, then, that workers avoided meetings like the plague. But what was to be done? Proposed remedies were almost as common as reports on the phenomenon itself. Better logistics would improve attendance, argued some. Perhaps the meeting place was too small, and there was no place to sit. More nearby housing would let workers attend more readily. The timing was bad: instead of meeting right after work, workers should be allowed go home first to take care of their domestic responsibilities, and return for a meeting an hour later. Others suggested more coercive measures to ensure good attendance: locking the doors once the meeting had begun to prevent workers from slipping out; taking down and posting the names of those who left the meeting. Workers could be bribed to attend meetings with the promise of a concert, film, or theatrical performance after the business portion of the meeting.[55]

Even more frequently came the plea for more interesting content and for the meetings to consider issues that directly affected workers. "Why bother to go to meetings—nothing happens there." Speakers failed to show up, or came unprepared. Along with better meetings, there should be fewer. "Look at how many different kinds of meetings we have: meetings of delegates, of dues collectors, of production commissions, factory and shop commissions, production conferences, meetings of the Friends of the Air Fleet, of the Society to Eradicate Illiteracy, etc., and then there's the work of the cooperative, which needs to be expanded, meetings of the bureau of the cooperative, meetings of delegates. . . . Let's reduce the calendar of meetings."[56]

Workers resented the absence of true democracy in these meetings. Too often, they complained, questions were decided in advance: "The fact is, workers are tired of going to meetings and speaking to no purpose." At the Goznak plant, workers heard a report on the new regime of economy and peppered the speaker with questions. But after the discussion, workers were presented with a ready-made resolution on the issue, "already typed." "Our enterprise is one of those where a few comrades want to dictate their opinion, and don't know how to consider the opinion of the mass." Workers feared to speak frankly, for too often they were criticized for speaking out and labeled "Mensheviks."[57]

---

1924): 13; 25 (1 July 1924): 6; 5 (8 February 1925): 8; 16–17 (1 May 1925): 19; 22 (7 June 1925): 2, 3; 45 (15 November 1925): 2; 1 (January 1926): 4; 7 (February 1926): 12; 10–11 (March 1926): 11, 18; 23–24 (June 1926): 5; 36–37 (September 1926): 5; 21 (May 1926): 17; *Pechatnik* 35 (18 December 1927): 4; 4 (1 March 1924): 2–3; 5 (30 January 1926): 6; 20 (15 May 1926): 7; 33 (14 August 1926): 3; 40 (2 October 1926): 4; 6 (28 February 1927): 4; 35 (18 December 1927): 4; 3 (31 January 1927): 17; TsGA SPb, f. 4804, op. 9, d. 20, l. 70; op. 10, d. 4, l. 481.

55. *Moskovskii pechatnik* 16–17 (1 May 1925): 19; 4–5 (January 1926): 10, 17; 36–37 (September 1926): 5; 22 (7 June 1925): 3; *Pechatnik* 38 (18 September 1926): 4.

56. *Pechatnik* 1 (15 January 1924): 3; 22 (1 December 1924): 7; 38 (18 September 1926): 4; 6 (28 February 1927): 3; 35 (18 December 1927): 5; *Moskovskii pechatnik* 16–17 (1 May 1925): 19; 22 (7 June 1925): 3; 37 (29 September 1925): 2; 36–37 (September 1926): 5; 22 (June 1926): 5, 10; 23–24 (June 1926): 5; 41 (27 October 1925): 12; 4–5 (January 1926): 13; 15 (April 1926): 9–10; GARF, f. R-5525, op. 8, d. 1, l. 46; TsGA SPb, f. 4804, op. 10, d. 4, l. 481.

57. *Pechatnik* 4 (1 March 1924): 3; *Moskovskii pechatnik* 1 (January 1926): 4; 4–5 (January

The decline in attendance at such meetings worried the union. They wanted the active support of their rank and file, not mute compliance, and in 1925 the union tried to revive democratic practices by limiting the role of the Communist Party. The masses had become alienated by the practice of nominating candidates from above, reasoned the party, and they were now sufficiently mature to be given more autonomy in running local affairs. The Moscow union provided results for the 1925 round of factory committee elections that confirmed the new reliability of the nonparty rank and file. In 1924, 73 percent of factory committee members had been Communists; in 1925, this proportion had fallen to 59 percent. This was a positive sign, implied the union, that the rank and file of the Printers' Union were now becoming interested in union activism. Henceforth, factory committees could dispense with party nomination of factory committee members. For the fall 1925 round of elections, the Moscow province branch instructed locals to nominate the best-qualified leaders and to encourage nominations from the floor, with ample time and opportunity for full and frank discussions. The Leningrad Comintern print shop duly complied with the new policy and reported that its election meeting had nominated twenty candidates for office, and after a full and serious discussion of each had elected the best seven.[58]

Significantly, however, archival records from the six Moscow and Leningrad print shops reflect little sign of this democracy campaign in 1925. The Krasnyi Proletarii shop held the large meeting noted above to elect its new factory committee in October, but the large attendance was probably manufactured by the promise of a theater performance, not by a greater chance for participation in the life of the enterprise. A large crowd also turned out for the committee elections at the Sixteenth Print Shop in Moscow, but there was no sign of any discussion or participatory democracy. And in Leningrad, the Sokolova Print Shop turned away from electing its factory committee at the customary general meeting in favor of a more selective delegates' meeting, which the party often favored because of the ease of controlling the outcome.[59] Indeed, the timing of the democracy campaign, carried out during the run-up to the Fourteenth Party Congress and the peak of the Zinov'ev opposition, suggests that the campaign may have been less a response to workplace apathy than a device to provide the party leaders with leverage to release the Leningrad rank and file from their obligations to their party chief, Zinov'ev.

Publicly, the union and its party core called for more openness and more

---

1926): 13; 36–37 (September 1926): 5; 23–24 (June 1926): 5; TsGA SPb, f. 4804, op. 10, d. 4, l. 428; op. 6, d. 24, l. 36.

58. *Moskovskii pechatnik* 22 (7 June 1925): 2; 37 (27 September 1925): 2; *Pechatnik* 14 (15 July 1925): 6; 17 (1 September 1925): 16; 22 (23 October 1925): 7.

59. At Krasnyi Proletarii, the factory committee's own minutes of this meeting merely listed the points of criticism of the committee's report. TsGAMO, f. 699, op. 1, d. 704, l. 15; *Pravda*, 27 October 1925; *Pechatnik* 24 (7 November 1925): 13; 4 (23 January 1926): 9; TsGAMO, f. 699, op. 1, d. 849, ll. 35–36.

democracy. This goal lay behind the shift to more open factory elections in 1925, and would be used to justify the campaign for self-criticism three years later. The union's journal wrote in 1927, "The Central Committee of the union considers it completely impermissible for the Communist Party cells or fractions of any organization to thrust their suggestions onto a workers' meeting, the Central Committee emphasizes the necessity for Communists to speak out before the nonparty mass in an organized manner, cohesively and openly defending the party directives."[60] But this would be organized democracy, prepared democracy.

Privately, union leaders responded anxiously to outbreaks of spontaneity and criticism. The party fraction of the Leningrad union worriedly proposed in early 1925 that inflammatory issues such as the tarif should not be brought up in a general meeting unless the local collective had thoroughly discussed the issue and prepared a unified response.[61] Eventually the union opted for better stage management rather than more genuine democracy. If general meetings were not putting union members to sleep or sending them out to drink, they were encouraging too much uncontrolled criticism. It was better, then, to forgo the inexpedient general factory meetings in favor of smaller shop meetings and delegates' meetings. Such a plan would "improve ties with the masses" by involving them more intimately in union discussion.[62] It would resolve the question of insufficient space for large meetings. And it would also permit the union to more easily manipulate the agenda and more effectively employ its scarce cadres of activists.[63] The "Stalinist" model of an authoritarian and tightly controlled relationship with the rank and file emerged in the Printers' Trade Union well before the Great Turn of 1929. If they had to choose between control and democracy, even the moderate and workerist leaders of the Printers' Union chose control.

## PARTICIPATORY DICTATORSHIP

The political culture of Soviet socialism began to mature in the mid-1920s, producing a peculiar form of democratic practice, a practice shaped not only by party intentions but by the interaction of party goals with the preferences and resistance of the rank and file. Open democracy, free and frank discussion of any and all issues, freedom to dissent, and freedom to organize were strictly limited, beginning, as we know, from the very assumption of Soviet power in October 1917. The party and trade union institutions offered democratic concessions from time to time in order to achieve their broader goals of mobilization and economic development, but such concessions were always accom-

60. *Pechatnik* 6 (28 February 1927): 3–4.
61. TsGAIPD SPb, f. 435, op. 1, d. 60, l. 7.
62. *Pechatnik* 27 (30 September 1927): 7.
63. Ibid. 35 (18 December 1927): 5; TsGAIPD SPb, f. 435, op. 1, d. 68 (meetings of bureau of party fraction of Leningrad union, 1927), l. 18.

panied by control. Control was imperfect because the union cadres themselves were imperfect: the goal was a system in which the individual melded into the collective, where all volunteered for the society of total mobilization. The system in place, the "dictatorship of the proletariat," can be better described as participatory dictatorship. The participatory element is important here. The experience of workers in the Printers' Union reveals that workers did talk back to their union leaders, whether vocally, through satire, or in their behavior. The balance of power, of course, was unequal: the regime controlled jobs and therefore welfare and security. Based on this unequal dialogue between the center and the rank and file, several hypotheses about this participatory dictatorship can be explored.

One hypothesis argues that the dominant form of political relations under Communism was repression. This was the critique of the Mensheviks, whose émigré journal *Sotsialisticheskii vestnik* publicized evidence of the dictatorship over the proletariat. Filling in the gaps of the official record, *Sotsialisticheskii vestnik* offered its own evaluation of the Moscow union: The union had been smothered, wrote a correspondent to the journal in September 1924. Its former leaders were all in exile, prison, or concentration camps. Communist cells and even factory committees had become junior partners of the GPU; Communist spies were everywhere, listening and reporting on conversations between politically suspicious individuals. Workers who had not learned how to keep their opinions to themselves had been the first to be laid off; those who exposed the heretical views of others were rewarded with apartments and good school placements for their children. The leadership, from the "drunkard Derbyshev" to the "Chekist Gordon," had long ago forgotten the interests of the workers. Elections and resolutions were manipulated in order to support the intrigues of the party ruling circles. "Prison is a bad thing, and the workers keep silent," wrote the Menshevik journal's informant. Printers, who once prided themselves on the opportunity to speak freely while working, now worked silently, and even during the dinner break were forced to endure the reading of some illiterate report from the "*komsy,*" the Communists. The central club was similarly monitored; printers could speak their minds openly only on the street.[64] Scattered but significant evidence in the union record confirms the presence of the heavy hand of repression, from the bold remarks denouncing Gordon's authoritarianism to occasional reports about politically motivated firing.[65]

At the same time, some workers, perhaps many workers, dared to resist the regime both in vocal protests at factory meetings and in more hidden forms, through the infrapolitics of gossip, jokes, and foot dragging. At a Communist cell meeting in Leningrad that approved the political firing of eight "anti-Soviet printers," the enterprise director requested permission to fire an additional

---

64. *Sotsialisticheskii vestnik* 18 (88) (20 September 1924): 14–15; 11/12 (105/106) (20 June 1925): 22.
65. TsGAIPD SPb, f. 435, op. 1, d. 59, l. 56.

complement of typesetters who were worthless to the enterprise "from the production point of view"; they had a poor attitude toward work, they were frequently absent, and they made careless mistakes.[66] Were these mistakes everyday acts of resistance, or were these simply bad workers? But how can we tell the difference? Similarly, were the 60 to 70 percent of workers who stayed away from factory meetings making a conscious political statement, reflecting a personal calculation that they had better things to do with their time, or, as the union officials alleged, were they insufficiently imbued with the trade union ethic? The complicated balance between participation and dictatorship in Communist trade union policy guaranteed that dissent and resistance would have to manifest themselves in subtle and indirect forms. The independent political history of the Printers' Union suggests that some of this behavior, although we can never know how much, surely conveyed a carefully chosen oppositional political message.

This suggestion supports, therefore, the validity of another hypothesis that argues that workers did enjoy certain limited individual rights in this society.[67] The rates and conflicts commissions gave them an opportunity for personal if not collective redress, and through their spoken and unspoken behavior they managed to convey to their leadership the range of their concerns and the degree of their grievances. The record amply indicates plentiful opportunities for discussion: criticizing the factory committee was a sport that all engaged in. Criticizing the higher bodies as well may have acquired a ritual flavor at the regular conferences and congresses, but as long as workers stayed within the limits of "businesslike" exchange of views, dissent was permitted and presumably noticed. The avalanche of campaigns and schemes to mobilize workers and to encourage their enthusiasm must be seen in part as a response to the grievances expressed up and down the line of the trade union's "democratic" institutions.

We must also recognize that some of the rank and file actually approved of and supported this democracy. The workshop spies and the union aktiv were themselves workers, and they received rewards for buying into the system. The worker-promotion movement permitted a key segment of the rank and file—the capable and ambitious—to rise into positions of authority and relative comfort.[68] We must not forget that these were workers, too. As for the silent majority, the Stepans the Indifferent, who stayed away from factory meetings or ritually held up their hands to vote at the proper moment, they also made their accommodation with the regime. In terms of an economic theory of democracy, such workers calculated that they could promote their interests by delegating their political rights to the appropriate Communist authorities. While Communist and union activists wore themselves to the bone fulfilling all the expec-

---

66. Ibid.
67. See Filtzer, *Soviet Workers and Stalinist Industrialization*, 21; Ward, *Russia's Cotton Workers*, 181–88, 239.
68. Sheila Fitzpatrick, *Education and Social Mobility in the Soviet Union, 1921–1934* (Cambridge, 1979).

tations of proletarian democracy, the rank-and-file worker had time for a smoke and a drink, time for family and personal life.[69] It was entirely rational for a woman worker to stay away from meetings and organizations in order to deal with her private affairs, as long as someone else would carry the load. While some workers looked back to regret how little had changed with the transition to socialism, others must have accepted the small favors that came their way, a steady job, the promise of new housing, the opportunity to study, or the opportunity to take it easy on the job. We should not make the same mistake as the Communist trade unionists who assumed a single type of worker personality. For the truly committed Social Democrats, the working people's democracy may have looked hollow indeed; but for many other ordinary workers, even among the "extraordinarily cultured" workers in the printing trades, this socialist democracy perhaps was something they could live with.

Finally, we might consider a Communist hypothesis about workplace democracy, which evaluates worker disaffection toward socialist democratic forms as the result not of repression but of insufficient consciousness, inadequate urban culture, or incomplete sovietization.[70] The proletariat under socialism ought to possess a single, common interest: if workers criticized state or union policies, this hypothesis suggests, workers were merely insufficiently acculturated to perceive this common interest. But the disaffection of printers could not be blamed on their inadequate urbanization. As I have shown, printers of all political persuasions prided themselves on their urbanity, literacy, sophistication, and culture. The experience of printers, whether in open opposition, sullen compliance, or enthusiastic support, disproves any facile connection between social position and politics. It suggests that accepting difference and allowing political diversity—the Menshevik position, after all—might have been a more successful strategy for manufacturing consent than the Communists' utopian dream of forging a uniform and total proletarian.

69. See Anthony Downs, *An Economic Theory of Democracy* (New York, 1957).
70. See, for example, Avdeev, *Trudovye konflikty*, 7.

# CHAPTER 6

## NEW CULTURES OF CLASS

*We didn't come here to get a handout from the union, not favors, but work....*
— UNEMPLOYED WOMAN PRINTER, 1927

In the realm of culture and the everyday, the years of relative social peace from 1921 to 1928 offered the nascent socialist society a unique moment to explore alternative forms of social life and everyday practice. "Cultural revolution" meant teaching literacy and principles of hygiene. It also invoked radical experimentalism. "Bolshevism," wrote René Fülöp-Miller in 1926, "stands for a radical change of the whole of human life in all its fundamental aims and interests, in every one of its manifestations."[1] Cultural artifacts including cinema, music, and literature provide compelling material for the analysis of utopianism and experimentation, but while much has been written on the theory and the production of socialist culture, the consumption and use of this culture has received less attention. What was the relationship between socialist culture and the articulation of particular

1. René Fueloep-Miller, *The Mind and Face of Bolshevism: An Examination of Cultural Life in Soviet Russia*, trans. F. S. Flint and D. F. Tait from the 1926 German edition (New York, 1965), ix. For a recent discussion, see David-Fox, "What Is Cultural Revolution?"

worker identities among printers? This period of "high NEP" in fact offered printers and other workers unprecedented opportunities to choose cultural forms and participate in the elaboration of a socialist culture through their everyday practice. These practices helped to define their new socialist worker identities. Investigating the participation of individuals of incontrovertible working-class pedigree in the regime's cultural and identity projects allows us to see a new element of agency in the formation of socialist culture.

As precarious as the printing industry would remain in the mid-1920s, economic recovery provided a financial surplus and the mechanisms of choice to permit skilled urban workers to become consumers once again after the hungry years of war and Civil War. At the same time, this was also a period of increasing concern about the direction of the economy, anxiety about the survival of socialism in a hostile world, and conflict over political choices at home. Beyond the consumption of necessities—shelter and food—to what degree did the modest prosperity of NEP permit workers to participate in an urban consumer economy? How did printers' leisure activities reflect the competition of new forms of socialist culture with traditional practices of urban culture? Finally, how did these experiences and practices help to shape a new sense of class identity?

The anxieties, tensions, and possibilities of the NEP years led to the emergence of what I will argue was a double class identity among printers. Through some of their cultural practices, printers adhered to the official class profile of the total proletarian. These printers looked to labor as the source of identity and they elaborated a class identity of collectivism, productivism, sobriety, and inclusivity. A second, unofficial class identity also derived its essence from labor, but was expressed in cultural practices of rough behavior and exclusionary masculinity. The official class looked forward to a radiant egalitarian future, but the unofficial class often found its clearest expression in retrospective memories of class struggle in the conditions of tsarism.

## CLASS AND CONSUMPTION UNDER NEP

The disruption of supply in the years of Civil War had threatened workers' access to food and fuel, and the ensuing transformation of wooden housing stock into heat had resulted in the radical reduction in available housing in the main cities of Russia. "Issues of the stomach," as we have seen, continued to drive the political interests of printers as well. But in striving to secure for themselves items of primary necessity, and in demanding assistance in these areas from the regime, workers also exercised choices that helped to indicate and to shape their sense of class identity and their role in the new society. Goods, in the words of Mary Douglas and Baron Isherwood, "are the visible part of culture." The selection and use of commodities help to identify and place individuals within their social world, provide patterns and rituals to stabilize meaning, and thus amount to much more than what economists would call their use value. "Commodities are good for thinking."² Workers' concern for material possessions, denounced by Communist ascetics as philistinism (*obyvatel'shchina*) should instead be seen as just as constitutive of socialist identity as were work and production.

In material terms, securing items of basic necessity continued to dominate the economic lives of urban workers in the mid-1920s. Elena Kabo's famous 1924 survey of Moscow worker budgets included thirteen households headed by printers, who spent on average 77 percent of their annual income on three basic sets of necessities: food (an average of 46 percent), clothing (an average of 17 percent), and housing and heat (an average of 14 percent).³ But the variation among families was significant: one household of five people spent 26 percent of its income on clothes, another of the same size spent only 6 percent. A family of four spent 18 percent of its income on housing, another only 12 percent. Even within the realm of items of primary necessity, workers had latitude for choice, and in exercising their choices, they created further evidence of their sense of priorities and their place in society. As Nikolai Gordon had perhaps mockingly proclaimed, for some comrades, but only for some, trousers were "necessary."⁴

Gordon did not name housing in his quip about the simple needs of printers, but the acquisition of adequate and equitable living conditions occupied an important place in printers' lives now that the economy had revived. The Printers' Union and its members paid close attention to the social composition of the housing units under their control and to the continuing shortage of adequate housing. In 1923, for example, the Moscow union reported that it controlled fifty-seven "house-communes." These were not communal homes in either the idealistic or nostalgic sense of a combination of private and shared space, but a general term for publicly owned housing. The house-commune could take many forms, of which the communal apartment was only one. These fifty-seven apartment buildings housed nearly 5,800 printers, or 30 percent of all union members; 6,800 family members brought the total of printers and dependents to 68 percent of the residents of these buildings. The Soviet government had determined that every resident was entitled to 16 square arshins of living space (an area roughly 9 feet square), but these printers occupied an average of 12.5 square arshins per *family*.⁵ Another 23 percent of residents belonged to other unions, and 9 percent were considered to be "nonworking" elements. Nonworkers, as alien to the identity of the union, paid dearly for their right to live

2. Douglas and Isherwood, *World of Goods*, 41–45.
3. Kabo, *Ocherki rabochego byta*, 150–51, 154–55.
4. TsGA SPb, f. 4804, op. 6, d. 24 (Fourth Petrograd Guberniia Printers' Congress, 8 September 1922), l. 11. See Chapter 3.
5. *Moskovskii pechatnik* 34 (5 December 1924): 9; see also Iuliia Obertreis, "'Byvshee' i 'izlishnee': Izmenenie sotsial'nykh norm v zhilishchnoi sfere v 1920–1930-e gg. Na materialakh Leningrada," in *Normy i tsennosti povsednevnoi zhizni: Stanovlenie sotsialisticheskogo obraza zhizni v Rossii 1920–1930-e gody*, ed. Timo Vikhavainen (St. Petersburg, 2000), 86.

among printers, and these "gold-ruble" tenants subsidized the union members, whose rents were pegged to their wage rank at the print shop.[6]

Consciousness of class and social position infused almost all discussions of the housing issue among printers. The presence of a self-employed barber in the apartment house controlled by the Sixteenth State Print Shop produced angry comments about his overcharging the workers and not being "one of us" [*nash*], resulting in a decision to double the rent he owed to the house administration and eventually to evict him. Describing a day in the life of this building, a worker correspondent contrasted the workers who left at seven a.m. and eight with the white-collar employees who left with their briefcases at ten: "The big shots among them get into their automobiles and cabs."[7]

As more and more workers returned to the cities after 1921, pressure for space in enterprise and union housing mounted. The waiting list in the building with the barber was thirty people long; a Moscow survey in late 1924 revealed that only 12 percent of printers occupied space close to the official norm; one-quarter of them had no lodgings at all but shared with friends or took rooms in the country beyond the city limits. The larger the family, the more likely they were to live in substandard accommodations. One respondent reported, "I've lived apart from my wife for a year and a half, because I don't have enough living space for both of us."[8] As enterprises acquired new apartment buildings, the right to a new room went first to those who were currently homeless or ill with tuberculosis, then to those living in cellars or in damp dilapidated housing, and finally to those whose current lodgings were far away from the enterprise. Of the four printer households that Kabo describes in detail, typesetter V. enjoyed the most comfortable housing. He lived with his wife, three children, and younger sister in a self-contained apartment in one of the union's house-communes, a clean, sunny, and well-ventilated space consisting of a kitchen, a foyer, and a single large room.[9]

Evictions and reallocations of space continued, but Moscow union officials admitted in 1924 that the real solution to the housing crisis would be to construct more housing units rather than to evict nonworkers from apartments they occupied. For this purpose they organized a housing cooperative in August 1924, whose members would finance construction of their own housing units. By December of that year, the Moscow printers' housing cooperative had five hundred

---

6. *Pechatnik* 4 (March 1923): 25; TsGAMO, f. 699, op. 1, d. 393 (meetings of administration of Printers' Union house-commune no. 1, 1923), l. 57.

7. *Nasha zhizn'*, 15 June, 7 July, and 11 October 1923; TsGAMO, f. 699, op. 1, d. 570 (general, factory committee, and conflict commission meetings at Sixteenth, 1924), l. 152; *Moskovskii pechatnik* 47–48 (5 December 1925): 13.

8. *Nasha zhizn'*, 26 October 1923, 16 August 1924; *Moskovskii pechatnik* 34 (5 December 1924): 8–9. Such comments indicate the authenticity of the 1927 film *Tret'ia meshchanskaia* (released in the United States as *Bed and Sofa*), about a one-room basement ménage-à-trois involving a construction worker, his wife, and the worker's Red Army buddy, a typesetter who could not get a job until he had housing and could not get a room unless he had a job.

9. *Zhizn' pechatnika*, 15 December 1923: 4; Kabo, *Ocherki rabochego byta*, 40, 45, 111, 121.

members, and they began to plan the construction of fifty buildings with two apartments each and fifty with four, with a goal of housing six hundred printer families. A year later, the Moscow union reported that one-quarter of its members now lived in cooperative housing, but a substantial number—43 percent—occupied a room in someone else's lodgings or slept in train stations. Many printers continued to lambaste the union for its failure to solve the housing problem: "Workers don't see any housing and they don't understand what they were fighting for." The union in Leningrad had done even less in the way of housing for its workers: "If you were to come to my apartment," complained one unemployed printer at the 1926 guberniia congress, "and see how we manage, you'd be horrified. Why don't you invite your guests to visit us, the way the French [union delegates] were invited to Moscow—it would be a good thing if they could see how we live, with five people in a nine-square-arshin room."[10]

In their discussion of housing entitlements and hopes for improvements, such workers demanded from the revolution a minimum of space that was dry, warm, and comfortable. More than that, they hoped that their house-communes and worker settlements would facilitate the formation of proletarian community life. Workers who lived close to their workplaces could play a greater role in the social and political life of the enterprise. Apartment buildings themselves could become the nucleus of the new proletarian culture. The Moscow union envisioned that enterprise-centered club life could extend to workers' apartments when they all lived together: communal kitchens, laundries, and dining rooms could help transform daily life; apartment buildings could sponsor their own wall newspapers, circles, and lending libraries. One such community had emerged in the center of Moscow, in a large 260-apartment building housing over 3,000 residents, mostly members of the printers' and food workers' unions. A cultural organization based in the building had constructed a supervised children's playground, a club room, and a cooperative shop. During the summer of 1924, the residents enjoyed weekly outdoor film showings (of "exclusively revolutionary content"), lectures, and excursions. Others advocated the creation of special worker settlements on the outskirts of the city, where, instead of living scattered and isolated across the whole metropolis, workers could live comfortably and inexpensively, keep a garden and a few chickens, and live with friends "as in a family."[11]

Real life in the common buildings was not always so peacefully collective, of course.[12] Kabo conceded that conflicts over internal order were frequent in such

10. *Moskovskii pechatnik* 32 (15 October 1924): 9; 34 (5 December 1924): 7; 4–5 (January 1926): 10, 11; *Pechatnik* 22 (23 October 1925): 6; TsGAMO, f. 699, op. 1, d. 704 (general meetings at Krasnyi Proletarii, 1925), l. 11; d. 849 (general, factory committee, and conflict commission meetings at Sixteenth, 1926), l. 35; TsGA SPb, f. 4804, op. 10, d. 4 (stenographic report of Leningrad Union Seventh Congress, 14 March 1926), l. 522; *Pravda*, 23 September 1924.

11. *Pechatnik* 9–10 (1 June 1924): 27; *Moskovskii pechatnik* 15 (7 January 1924): 10; 28 (15 August 1924): 14, 15; *Nasha zhizn'*, 16 August 1924.

12. *Nasha zhizn'*, 22 October 1925, 4 September 1926, 13 August 1925; TsGAMO, f. 699, op. 1, d. 728 (meetings of rates and conflict commission at Sixteenth, 1925), l. 5.

apartment buildings, something she attributed to the differing cultural levels of the workers who resided there.[13] Collectivism was neither explicitly valued nor blamed for the defects in apartment life. Rather, these house-communes replicated many of the features of modern urban life, including the effort to create a space and an environment in which worker values could develop apart from those of the old ruling class; self-government and self-management; and personal conflicts and rivalries that could stem from any number of factors, from crowding to envy to politics.

The experience of worker housing suggests the continuing appeal of individualism in the creation of a new socialist culture. Printers readily embraced the new apartment culture and many expressed a preference for living in homogeneous communities; the old bourgeoisie, from barbers to doctors, would live "elsewhere." In one case, they asked that all nonprinters, not just Nepmen, be evicted from their building. But their preference for living as families and not as collectives remained strong. Even when communal cooking facilities were available, housewives preferred to prepare meals on a burner in their own rooms.[14]

The role played by the preparation and consumption of food in revolutionary Russia also offers important insight into the developing culture of Soviet socialism. If the effects of the famine of the early 1920s gradually faded in the daily lives of urban workers, access to food was still of critical importance to the regime, as it had been in the years of the World War and 1917 revolution. By the end of the 1920s, administrative measures would be adopted to control and ration access to food.[15] Such a sensitive issue found its fullest discussion only in the secret protocols of the party and police, and perhaps this is one reason why the public discourse of Russian printers paid relatively little attention to issues of food and its consumption. At the same time, the provision and preparation of food, whether as a daily necessity or form of special celebration, belonged primarily to the women's sphere of activity, and the masculinist Printers' Union discourse found little room for serious consideration of such matters. "Obtaining groceries is more our responsibility than men's," wrote one woman activist to encourage working women to join the new cooperatives.[16] But food and its consumption did receive public discussion. Consideration of problems of food and food supply in the union peaked in 1924, when the normalization of the NEP economy undergirded a renewed public effort to construct a socialist way of life. The canteen system of dining, having faded at the end of the Civil War period, was revived, and a campaign was launched to promote cooperative retail enterprises as an alternative to the private market.

13. Kabo, *Ocherki rabochego byta*, 97.
14. TsGAMO, f. 699, op. 1, d. 570; Kabo, *Ocherki rabochego byta*, 150–51; *Zhizn' pechatnika*, 5 October 1923.
15. Elena Osokina, *Za fasadom "stalinskogo izobiliia": Raspredelenie i rynok v snabzhenii naseleniia v gody industrializatsii, 1927–1941* (Moscow, 1998).
16. *Moskovskii pechatnik* 24 (15 June 1924): 10.

The public canteen (*stolovaia*) offered numerous benefits for the creation of a new socialist lifestyle. First, it could reduce the costs of good nutrition for workers. Through mechanization of food preparation, hot and appetizing meals could be provided at a much lower cost to workers than the alternative of preparing food at home. The printers in Kabo's survey, whose position in the wage hierarchy permitted them better diets than the average Moscow worker, still spent between 33 and 66 percent of their incomes on food, averaging 645 rubles a year. A canteen dinner of two courses, including a meat course and vegetable, cost 25 to 30 kopecks: a nourishing hot meal every day of the year would thus add up to about 90 to 110 rubles per person. A worker who ate a hot dinner at noon instead of snacking on a sandwich at the workbench would also be more productive. The benefits of the canteen to women received special attention in the 1924 drive to expand the canteen network: time-budget studies undertaken in 1922 had shown that working women spent fourteen hours at home and at work; women who did not work outside the home devoted eleven and a half hours a day to their household chores. Neither category could therefore find any time to engage in the important business of self-improvement or public life. Even housewives could "declare war on domestic pots and pans" by buying the family meal from the canteen and serving it at home. The canteen offered important cultural advantages as well, teaching cleanliness, principles of nutrition, and manners. Women at the Voronezh Economic Council Print Shop praised the canteen because they could avoid "snacking on foul language." The noon meal in the factory canteen could be used also for collective cultural activities: reading aloud of newspapers, organized discussions, and radio broadcasts.[17]

Eating at home required shopping either in the private market or in a cooperative store. The Printers' Union cooperative, Potkopechatnik (*Potrebitel'skaia kooperatsiia pechatnikov*), struggled like other fledgling socialist institutions to learn the techniques of purchasing, pricing, and retailing. Cooperative officials in Leningrad admitted that prices there were sometimes higher than on the open market, the quality was worse, cooperative employees were inattentive and rude, and the lines were too long. One joined the cooperative out of political loyalty rather than household economy or convenience: "You go to work every day, and you can't help noticing around the gate to our plant a whole string of different street traders, with rolls, sandwiches, and everything you need to eat. These traders offer up these stale goods with their dirty hands and at high prices, and the comrades buy them because there's nowhere else to buy them. You go to the Mosselprom bakery, but there are no eggs or sausage there; you go to the state sausage store, and there are no rolls. Here they sell everything,

---

17. Kabo, *Ocherki rabochego byta*, 248–76; *Pravda*, 12 September 1923, 28 March 1924; *Moskovskii pechatnik* 21 (1 May 1924): 20; 4 (28 January 1925): 12; 37 (29 September 1925): 11; 29–30 (September 1924): 7; 15 (7 January 1924): 9; 8 (1 March 1925): 8; 13 (6 April 1925): 8; *Nasha zhizn'*, 9 December 1924; TsGAMO, f. 699, op. 1, d. 570, l. 121; *Pechatnik* 18–19 (1 May 1926): 25; 40 (2 October 1926): 6; 3 (31 January 1927): 9; 28 (10 October 1927): 10.

and they'll give you credit until payday." Correct socialist husbands patronized their local cooperative stores, as in the case of a printer at the First Model Print Shop, who waited two hours in line at Potkopechatnik to purchase food for the New Year holiday in 1924. When he returned home, he found that unbeknownst to him, his wife had also shopped for the holiday, but at the private market, spending far less than he did in the process.[18] Women were the canny shoppers because good household management depended on them.

And how did they eat? Tea, bread, soup (sometimes with meat), and potatoes constituted the staples of the proletarian diet. According to Kabo's sample of Moscow workers, printers enjoyed a superior diet, with more white bread and rolls than the average worker and fewer potatoes, more vegetables, fruits, candy, meat, eggs, and dairy products. Meat and fats were the items of greatest rarity in the everyday diet, saved for holidays and special occasions. The union's rest homes symbolized the good life for workers under socialism. If in 1923 rest homes provided ample if "not refined" food, including large quantities of milk products, by 1926 they could feature ham, sausage, butter, cheese, eggs, and cream. Herring and sliced bread with green onions constituted party food to celebrate a bachelor worker's new apartment; baked goods such as pies and pastries marked weddings, name days, and holidays. The printer Fedor Borovskii's tale of starving worker writers, modeled on *La Bohème,* replaced Mimi with fresh meat as the aspiring writers' love object and inspiration for their poems.[19]

Not only what they ate but how they ate marked the boundary between normal life and the good life. A happy home life was symbolized by a hissing samovar, with white rolls and vegetable pies on the table. Another story by Borovskii describes a celebration of moving day in exquisite detail. His hero laid out his table with a clean newspaper cover, on which he set a genuine vodka service: a small pink-flowered decanter and three matching small glasses on tall thin stems. Carefully skinned herring, black bread, and sliced scallions completed his presentation.[20]

Borovskii's moving-day hero not only was a connoisseur of food and vodka but also treasured things. A compositor, he was a man of substance, with his own iron bedstead and mattress, a table and two chairs, and an étagère on which he displayed his prized possessions: a thick bound book, two dozen journals, and several booklets in new covers. On the wall were hung framed oleographs and a brightly painted Chinese paper fan; in the window, an empty birdcage for decoration. Such items were bought and sold in outdoor markets

18. *Krasnyi pechatnik* 3 (September 1922): 25–27; *Pravda,* 5 July 1924; *Nasha zhizn',* 22 October 1925; *Moskovskii pechatnik* 27 (1 August 1924): 10; *Pechatnik* 7 (15 April 1924): 11; 11 (15 June 1924): 3; 26 (26 June 1926): 11; 14 (15 May 1927): 9; 6 (28 February 1927): 16; *Zhizn' pechatnika,* 17 January 1924.

19. Kabo, *Ocherki rabochego byta,* 248–76; F. Borovskii, "Bogema ogoltelykh," in his *Rabochie rasskazy* (Moscow, 1924), 87.

20. *Pechatnik* 8 (1 May 1924): 14–15; Borovskii, "Novosel'e," in his *Rabochie rasskazy,* 29.

like the one in Sukharevskii in Moscow or through pawnbrokers, such as the one who ultimately acquired all of the compositor's nice things as he and his workmates went through bottle after bottle of vodka at the moving-day party. The printers' cooperative also traded in commodities other than food products, offering firewood, dishes, hardware, cloth, and trousers, but never on Sundays, provoking further discontent. "During weekdays, there's no time to run to the co-op to buy a pair of pants. On a holiday you drag yourself to the co-op and it's all locked up. So you just have to go to a private trader at Sukharevka."[21]

Issues of commodities such as trousers, kerosene, and food speak to a concern with scarcity. Rising food prices toward 1927 in particular created the climate of panic and suspicion that would spark a return to rationing and provide a social basis for a renewed assault on private peasant producers.[22] Commodities also offer evidence about how workers would define their everyday socialist culture. "Pastry, theater, and trousers" were necessities. What about the birdcage and the étagère? Was the proletarian consumer to be a strict utilitarian or could a worker also acquire goods with purely aesthetic value? By the mid-1930s, the consumption habits of model Stakhanovites would be used to define and shape a new socialist consumer culture, but this culture was already under construction in the middle years of NEP. Prizes handed out in ceremonies, including those honoring veteran workers, indicated what workers should have valued in the 1920s. Newlyweds received a set of books and a portrait of Lenin in August 1924. Labor heroes in 1923 received clothing: a winter overcoat, a warm woolen jersey, and suits of clothes.[23] A muted discussion in the trade union press spoke of the desire of some women workers to wear jewelry and cosmetics. This discussion would become much more pointed and politicized by the end of the decade.[24]

Everyday life and material life were not just the residue or the object of production. Even the relatively limited evidence presented here about the consuming lives of printers suggests that whatever the scale of absolute abundance or scarcity, commodities were indeed good for thinking.[25] Consumers were citi-

---

21. Borovskii, "Novosel'e," 28–29; F. Borovskii, "Tovarishchi na novosel'e," in his *P'esy* (Moscow, n.d.), 87; *Nasha zhizn'*, 3 January 1925, 6 December 1927; *Pechatnik* 19 (2 July 1927): 10.
22. See Chapter 8, and Osokina, *Za fasadom*, 37–58.
23. *Moskovskii pechatnik* 28 (15 August 1924): 15; 14 (10 December 1923): 13; *Pechatnik* 35 (18 December 1927): 11; 3 (1 May 1922): 16; 2 (35) (January 1923): 26; 5 (23 April 1923): 14. On Stakhanovites, see Lewis H. Siegelbaum, *Stakhanovism and the Politics of Productivity in the USSR, 1935–1941* (Cambridge, 1988), chap. 6.
24. *Pechatnyi dvor*, 31 July 1924; *Zhizn' pechatnika*, 24 August 1926; *Krasnyi proletarii*, 15 April and 1 May 1927. On "flapper fashion," see Gorsuch, *Youth in Revolutionary Russia*, 131–35.
25. See also Lebina, *Povsednevnaia zhizn'*, esp. chap. 3. For a later socialist society, see Ina Merkel, "Consumer Culture in the GDR, or How the Struggle for Antimodernity Was Lost on the Battleground of Consumer Culture," in *Getting and Spending: European and American Consumer Societies in the Twentieth Century*, ed. Susan Strasser, Charles McGovern, and Matthias Judt (Cambridge, 1998), 281–99, and "Working People and Consumption under Really-Existing Socialism: Perspectives from the German Democratic Republic," *International Labor and Working-Class History* 55 (1999): 92–111.

zens, not philistines. They used goods to convey information about themselves and their aspirations, to mark off differences between themselves and others and among themselves. The working-class housewife became an artisan in her own right in the ways she managed the family budget and found food for the table.[26] Even the total proletarian was figured in consumerist terms: the books he bought to enrich his mind, the bicycle he rode to train his body, and the clean shirt he donned to wear to the club all served to distinguish him as a builder of a socialist way of life. The social contract demanded by workers with their regime would continue to be measured in terms of commodities, particularly when they began to disappear at the end of the 1920s. This was not *obyvatel'shchina*: it too was socialism.

## SOCIALIST LEISURE AND SOCIAL RECREATION

Commodities and the world of goods contained an ambivalent message about the content of socialism, about how to measure sufficiency, abundance, and excess. Asceticism had constituted an important strain of revolutionary culture, from Chernyshevskii's self-denying hero Rakhmetov in the 1860s to the austere and modest lifestyles of the Kremlin elite in the 1930s.[27] Workers insisted that socialism should also be about material things, not merely ideas. But if Communists could disagree on the importance of material culture, they found more room for accord in the realm of leisure and recreation. Socialism, they maintained, should bring about new and collective forms of social life.

The club in the mid-1920s remained the centerpiece of organized proletarian leisure. Workers' preference for private life at the end of the period of privation of War Communism was blamed on the inadequate development of collective and public social life as well on inadequate facilities. The worker club, first and foremost, followed by societies for physical culture and rest homes, received the lion's share of trade union attention during NEP. Ultimately, argued activists, a well-ordered club would provide for every minute of the leisure time of a worker and his family. Where else could a worker spend his free time so cheaply, especially in winter? wrote the factory paper at Pechatnyi Dvor: his room was cold and uncomfortable, but at the club he could read a newspaper, play chess or checkers, share the opinions of his comrades, drink an inexpensive glass of tea; he could learn to play an instrument, hear a lecture, or join an excursion to a museum. The 1923 Moscow Guberniia Union Congress resolved that the club, with its strictly Marxist worldview, would become for workers and their families the "site of a new approach to everyday life." While acknowledging that in the current transition to socialism, clubs had to compete

---

26. See Nancy Reagin, "Comparing Apples and Oranges: Housewives and the Politics of Consumption in Interwar Germany," in Strasser et al., *Getting and Spending*, 241–61.

27. Nikolai G. Chernyshevsky, *What Is To Be Done?* trans. Michael R. Katz (Ithaca, 1989); on lifestyles of the nomenklatura in the 1930s, see Osokina, *Za fasadom*, 127–37.

with other providers of leisure activities, the goal of the club was to become the "center of proletarian social life," satisfying workers' normal demands for rest and relaxation but also for culture.[28]

The total proletarian would find his needs as a member of mass socialist society completely addressed by the offerings of his club. Worker clubs should shun any offerings suited to individuals rather than the mass, such as training on solo instruments or in solo singing. The club would become a place of reeducation, a center of self-reliance, a place to connect leisure to production. Thus the club would be tied to the life of the enterprise, whose centrality as symbol of the socialist mode of production would animate the new socialist way of life. The enemy of the club as the center of proletarian social life was not only the array of NEP commercial and declassed leisure options but the family as well. Ultimately, the total proletarian's entire family would pass all of its leisure time under the club's benevolent socializing canopy: workers' wives were to be drawn to the club by special gender-specific activities, as well as meals and safe playgrounds for their children. Young people would also find in these workers' clubs proper and healthful socialist activities, more than enough to satisfy all of their cultural and recreational needs.[29]

John Hatch has provided a rich picture of Moscow workers' club life, drawing on union and club movement publications, and printers' clubs in Moscow, Leningrad, and around the country recapitulated the essential features of the movement.[30] Recreational, cultural, and educational circles constituted the staples of club activity. By far the most common circles were those devoted to drama and music. The Petrograd union reported in May 1923 that its nine clubs boasted five political circles, three theatrical circles and three in general education, two each in choral singing, literature, and music, and additional circles on godlessness, Marxism, sewing and knitting, children's games, and the German language. The Voronezh union organization admitted to less sweeping accomplishments. Without their own club as yet, they claimed Monday evenings at the House of Enlightenment for their union, and planned to add a literary circle to their existing chess group. The local club at Moscow's First Model shop had been a pioneer in the workers' theater movement: by 1924 it boasted both a studio offering a "left, avant-garde" approach to theater and a drama circle devoted to realistic and traditional dramatic productions; in addition, it offered numerous circles in music, sports, sewing, and politics.[31]

28. *Pechatnik* 17 (1 September 1925): 5; 9 (27 February 1926): 3; *Pechatnyi dvor*, 14 January 1923; *Moskovskii pechatnik* 13 (12 November 1923): 21; 29–30 (September 1924): 25.

29. *Moskovskii pechatnik* 10 (12 August 1923): 4; 11 (22 September 1923): 5; 18 (27 February 1924): 1; 4 (28 January 1925): 14.

30. John B. Hatch, "The Politics of Mass Culture: Workers, Communists, and the Proletcult in the Development of Workers' Clubs, 1921–1925," *Russian History* 13, no. 3 (1986): 119–48; John B. Hatch, "Hangouts and Hangovers: State, Class, and Culture in Moscow's Workers' Club Movement, 1925–1928," *Russian Review* 53, no. 1 (1994): 97–117; see also Lynn Mally, *Revolutionary Acts: Amateur Theater and the Soviet State* (Ithaca, 2000).

31. GARF, f. R-5525, op. 5, d. 21 (monthly and quarterly reports from guberniia branches, in-

Public performances evolved as a multifaceted staple of club life. Theatrical productions mounted by the local dramatic circles had been an early mainstay of clubs' cultural fare. Other presentations included socialist rituals such as holiday celebrations and the rite of red christening, or "Octobering" newborn infants into the proletarian family. Public events included living newspapers, in which the local drama circle would act out the events of the day; evenings of reminiscences organized around the commemoration of revolutionary holidays; and concerts featuring local brass bands and occasional guest artists. Club activists seeking to integrate workers' production, political, and social lives experimented throughout the 1920s with events that would attract workers' interest with promises of pathos, risk, and prizes. "Trade union bazaars" and "trade union roulette" offered workers the chance to demonstrate their knowledge about political or professional issues. Demonstration trials, such as the "Trial of the Drunk," taught norms of everyday life.[32] Literary evenings constituted another common public event, often conducted in the form of an organized debate. In December 1925, for example, the club at First Model invited Fedor Gladkov to a discussion of his recently published novel, *Cement*. Workers had prepared by reading the novel (the club library had purchased 116 copies), and some submitted written commentaries. Gladkov received sharp criticism from the mostly young assembled workers. The portrayal of Dasha, the fearless new proletarian woman, was unrealistic, said one participant, but others countered that a part of Dasha lived in every new woman. Some criticized Gladkov's simple language: "Literary works should educate!" But Comrade Gorbachev seemed to speak for the majority when he claimed that one could find the hero, Gleb, in every Soviet factory. "*Cement* is our native [*rodnaia*] book."[33]

For the energetic, club life promoted physical culture. Sports, like other club activities, were meant to be fun with a purpose. A few hundred workers in Leningrad and Moscow, mostly men, enlisted in the physical culture circles and pressured their unions to expand the availability of playing fields, ice rinks, and indoor facilities for physical fitness. As with drama circles and other forms of

---

cluding Leningrad, 1923), l. 47; op. 3, d. 9 (transcripts and resolutions of Central Committee plenum, 1921), l. 80; *Moskovskii pechatnik* 18 (27 February 1924): 28; *Zhizn' pechatnika*, 17 January 1924.

32. See Mally, *Revolutionary Acts*; *Pechatnyi dvor*, 15 March 1923; *Otchet pravleniia moskovskogo gubernskogo otdela 1923–1924*, 73; *Pechatnik* 5 (1 March 1925): 16; 49 (4 December 1926): 9; 1 (1 January 1926): 8; 40 (2 October 1926): 6; 27 (1 December 1925): 7; 9 (25 March 1927): 17; *Zhizn' pechatnika*, 1 April 1924; 16 February 1924; 20 July 1924; *Krasnyi proletarii*, 24 December 1926. On agitational trials, see Elizabeth A. Wood, "The Trial of the New Woman: Citizens-in-Training in the New Soviet Republic," *Gender and History* 13 (November 2001): 524–45; and "The Trial of Lenin: Legitimating the Revolution through Political Theater, 1920–23," *Russian Review* 61, no. 2 (2002): 235–48.

33. *Pechatnik* 50–51 (20 December 1925): 20. Such discussions, as Michael Gorham argues, provided important evidence in the "politics of voice" in early Soviet Russia: *Speaking in Soviet Tongues: Language Culture and the Politics of Voice in Revolutionary Russia* (DeKalb, Ill., 2003).

cultured leisure, tensions arose between those who played for exercise and relaxation and those for whom sport and competition became an all-consuming passion. The union press advertised the wide range of available physical activities, including precision marching, gymnastics, football, and skating, that could allow individual physical development. Participants, however, specialized in competitive team sports, and soon the physical culture pages of the union journals emphasized organized competitions among teams from different cities and different unions. One group of young printers was criticized for aspiring to be "professional footballists" rather than "physical culturists" in 1924, but by 1926, *Moskovskii pechatnik* was boasting of the competitiveness of the union's basketball team. Competitions in speed skating, hockey, and swimming matched union teams from all over the Soviet Union. And even the traditional Russian game of *gorodki,* wrote *Pechatnik,* would be more fun if the union would organize regular teams for the summer season.[34]

Yet despite the best face put on all these new forms of collective proletarian leisure, most workers demonstrated an emphatic preference for a more individualist form of modern leisure, the cinema. As Denise Youngblood and Peter Kenez, among others, have demonstrated, the cinema captured the imagination of Soviet citizens of all social strata.[35] If in 1924 club activists insisted the club should become an alternative to the boulevard theater and the cinema, club practitioners competed with private entertainments with their own similar alternatives of paid entertainments and films.[36] But clubs suffered from a limited repertory and conditions inferior to the NEP-era movie palaces. The wildly popular *Thief of Baghdad,* whose star, Douglas Fairbanks, inspired a cult of *Duglasovshchina,* ran in Moscow private cinemas for more than a year, but it was not shown once in a workers' club.[37] The trade union stayed largely silent about the enormous popularity of this unproletarian art form: in pages upon pages of club-related policy and reporting, issues related to the cinema rarely appear, and yet we know that together, cinema and drinking were the two most common forms of working-class leisure in the early Soviet cities.[38]

Club issues remained primarily prescriptive throughout this period. The Printers' Union press confirms that these clubs and their activities attracted only a minority of union members. It was only the activist Communist elite who espoused the vision of the club as a site of total leisure, and officials admitted that

34. *Pechatnik* 14 (15 December 1923): 16; 19 (15 October 1924): 10; 23 (1 November 1925): 8; 10 (6 March 1926): 7; 19 (2 July 1927): 20; 24 (25 August 1927): 16; 18 (25 June 1927): 15; *Nasha zhizn',* 11 October 1923; TsGA SPb, f. 4804, op. 10, d. 4, l. 462; *Moskovskii pechatnik* 11 (22 September 1923): 11; 14 (10 December 1923): 15; 15 (7 January 1924): 23; 18 (27 February 1924): 32; 34 (September 1926): 12.

35. Youngblood, *Movies for the Masses;* Peter Kenez, *Cinema and Soviet Society, 1917–1953* (Cambridge, 1992).

36. *Moskovskii pechatnik* 29–30 (September 1924): 25; 22 (7 June 1925): 3; *Pechatnik* 20 (15 May 1926): 7.

37. Youngblood, *Movies for the Masses,* 51, 158.

38. Gorsuch, *Youth in Revolutionary Russia,* 71–73; Lebina, *Povsednevnaia zhizn',* 245–48.

fewer than 15 percent of Printers' Union members had joined the clubs.[39] The activists blamed this lack of unanimous participation on the perennial lack of funds and of organizational cadres, and on the takeover of club space by rowdy and drunk hooligans, another sign of the low cultural level of the masses that immersion in club life could cure.[40] Criticism of the club project continually drew attention to deviant worker practices, to some extent dancing but most particularly drinking, a form of worker recreation that will be considered in its own right. The prevalence of these "deviant" practices, however, suggests a more fundamental stance of workers toward their new socialist culture. No matter how fervent their support of the economic, social, and cultural goals of the revolution, workers in the printing industry rejected a universal form of proletarian leisure that would occupy their entire nonworking waking life.

The failure of the club movement suggests that even if workers supported the general aims and content of socialist clubs, however sober, didactic, and socialist in content, they wanted their own local sources of recreation and relaxation. They may have wanted collective and social leisure, but not a single universal form of rest. A series of complaints about the exclusivity or inclusivity of clubs suggested that even among workers, distinctions ought to be preserved. The most successful clubs were those that catered to individual enterprises, where the work collective could meet after hours and socialize with those with whom they had already established social relations. Even the union agreed that printers should socialize only with other printers, claiming that their "cultural uniqueness" dictated a unique form of cultural and leisure activity: it was bad when you went to a club "and you couldn't tell where you were, among textile workers, among food workers, or somewhere else." The Voronezh union complained that its workers were "hidden" in other union clubs. Localism, rather than the cultural specifics of the printing trade, shaped these workers' club preferences. Even unionwide clubs failed to reach the desired public: here workers declined to attend, saying, "This club isn't ours, so it's no concern of ours." Workers at the Sixteenth State Print Shop in Moscow chafed at their inability to establish their own proprietary (*sobstvennyi*) club: at the neighboring Krasnyi Maiak club they felt snubbed and ignored, stepsons in the Krasnyi Maiak family. Their dream evening entertainment drew on the intimate and local knowledge of their shop's own personalities and politics.[41]

The worker club, its proponents hoped, would counteract the materialist and individualist recreational behavior that attracted the allegiance of a great num-

---

39. *Moskovskii pechatnik* 18 (27 February 1924): 4; 5 (8 February 1925): 3; *Pechatnik* 16 (1 September 1924): 4.

40. *Moskovskii pechatnik* 5 (8 February 1925): 12; 47–48 (5 December 1925): 21; TsGAMO, f. 699, op. 1, d. 849, l. 181; *Iskry*, May 1927.

41. *Pechatnik* 44 (30 October 1926): 3; 18–19 (1 May 1926): 20; 18 (1 October 1924): 14; *Otchet o rabote pravleniia gubotdela, 1926–1927* (Voronezh), 19; *Stenograficheskii otchet piatogo s"ezda soiuza*, 1924, 286; TsGAMO, f. 699, op. 1, d. 849, l. 95; *Otchet pravleniia moskovskogo gubernskogo otdela, 1923–1924*, 55; *Pechatnyi dvor*, 30 June 1924; *Nasha zhizn'*, 8 January 1927.

ber of Russian workers. Some of these particularly unworthy behaviors, particularly drinking, fighting, and dancing, received considerable attention in the union press; others, such as card-playing and gambling, appear only obliquely.

Drinking was too much a part of Russian culture, especially workplace culture, and too large a problem in terms of losses to health and productivity to be ignored. Laura Phillips and others have demonstrated the close links between drinking and class identity. Under tsarism, the monotony of the workplace was broken regularly by the many drinking rituals that had become part of working-class life: the taking on of an apprentice, a new hire's first paycheck, moving days, and funerals all demanded the accompaniment of drink. Workers around the world believed that drinking was in fact a healthy antidote to the poisons of industrial life.[42] And although the Soviet regime officially promoted a culture of sobriety, the evidence from the Printers' Union supports Phillips's contention that drinking on the job remained but a small sin in the eyes of managers, foremen, and fellow workers. Factory committees regularly discussed the misbehavior of workers whose binges kept them away from work or slowed production while they were drunk on the job. Committees were liberal with warnings, but workers would plead family difficulties or illness, or promise never to drink again. Others insisted that their drinking had not impaired their ability to do their jobs. Only chronic and flagrant drinking resulted in dismissal. At the Sokolova print shop, two factory committee members opposed harsh measures toward drunk workers: as long as a drinking worker stayed away and did not infect the shop with his behavior, he should be left alone. "Firing a person for drunkenness should not be looked at so simply," said one. "You won't eliminate drinking, especially among typesetters," said the other.[43]

Reports of drunk workers and excessive alcohol consumption scarcely appeared in the period of the Civil War, owing to economic scarcity rather than the influence of revolutionary asceticism. Official disapproval of drinking and the occasional exemplary firing did not keep printers from consuming alcohol, and the revival of the economy in 1922 brought drinking culture roaring back to life. The union press noticed workers' "rapid adaptation" to the new conditions of NEP, a "drinking craze . . . as though they were making up for lost time during the stormy years of revolution." Throughout the mid-1920s, the press and union organizations reported that alcohol consumption was ever increasing and had reached epidemic proportions.[44]

---

42. Phillips, *Bolsheviks and the Bottle*, 61–64; Steinberg, *Moral Communities*, 70–77; *Moskovskii pechatnik* 5 (5 August 1922): 8.

43. *Nasha zhizn'*, 14 February 1925; TsGAMO, f. 699, op. 1, d. 728, ll. 39, 46, 112, 113; d. 849, ll. 61, 64; TsGA SPb, f. 4804, op. 9, d. 44 (general and factory committee meetings at Sokolova, 1924–25), l. 10.

44. TsGAIPD SPb, f. 435, op. 1, d. 98 (Leningrad factory committee reelections, 1923), l. 190b.; TsGA SPb, f. 4804, op. 8, d. 95 (general and factory committee meetings at Pechatnyi Dvor, 1924), l. 60b.; d. 93 (general and factory committee meetings at Zinov'ev, 1924), l. 15; *Moskovskii pechatnik* 18 (27 February 1924): 19; 10 (15 March 1925): 10; *Nasha zhizn'*, 3 January 1925; TsGAMO,

Local committees may have proved reluctant to enforce strict penalties for drinking, but the union journals featured both hortatory editorials on the evils of drink and a substantial number of feuilletons and short stories—morality tales—that conveyed the same message but also described the everyday practices of shop floor and after-work drinking. The worker-correspondents who contributed these stories surely wrote what they knew, describing a context that would be familiar to their readers. For the protagonists of these tales, drink was a natural behavior, and even for those who did not drink on the job, payday called for spending time with one's workmates in the tavern. To refuse their company was to insult them. These accounts follow a stylized pattern of temptation and redemption that bears further analysis. The key in many of these stories was the inner conflict between the desire to join the drinking crowd and the recognition that to succumb to temptation would result in ruin. In one story, the press feeder Marzanchikov cursed his factory committee for its inability to pay the workers. "How can I feed my family, buy wood, pay the shoemaker . . . always tomorrow!" When payday finally came, however, his print shop brothers encouraged him to join them in celebrating this important day. Marzanchikov resolved to go straight home with his money, dreaming of wood, clothes, and dinner, but on the way he came across a new tavern. Fellow workers invited him to join them in a bottle, and Marzanchikov thought: just one bottle, his wife would never know. As in many of these stories, one bottle led to another. Stumbling home drunk, Marzanchikov dreamed of the shoes he would buy for his son, but instead he lost the rest of his money and his overcoat to robbers. He ended up in the hospital with typhus, his children left starving and cold at home.[45]

A variation on this theme provided a happy ending for printers strong enough to resist invitations to drink. The pressman Guliev submitted silently to a factory committee's reprimand for his drinking, but a taunt from a Komsomol member changed his course in life: "Think less about your vodka, our Emil, think about your young ones and how to feed them." Gradually Emil overcame the temptation to drink with his friends, and stayed away from the tavern. His friends shunned him and called him "woman" (*baba*) to his face, but his children now adored him. Family responsibilities play a particularly strong role in these accounts. In a long tale of tricksters and suffering, the happy-go-lucky compositor Tesemkin followed the slippery path from drink to dirty tricks to unemployment to poverty, finally realizing that his children had become sickly and wild and that he was a "bastard, not a father." Once he won his job back, he bought clothes for his children and resolved to stay sober.[46]

---

f. 699, op. 1, d. 728, l. 46; *Zorkii glaz,* 19 December 1925; *Iskry,* March 1926; *Pechatnik* 11 (25 October 1923): 6; 47 (20 November 1926): 15.

45. *Pechatnik* 14 (15 December 1923): 15; *Moskovskii pechatnik* 7 (22 February 1925): 5.

46. *Moskovskii pechatnik* 8 (February 1926): 6; *Pechatnik* 44 (30 October 1926): 5; 12 (1 July 1924): 10.

Two sets of choices predominate in these tales. One holds out the alternatives of convivial drinking in smoky bars against the prospect of material comfort: wood for heat, boots, apples for the kids, newspapers, and first-class cigarettes.[47] (The moving-day drinking party discussed earlier provides another example: from comfort and possessions, the protagonist ends, through drink, with nothing.)[48] The other poses two alternative masculinities. Drinking was a manly occupation, and those who refused to drink were teased by their fellows as "women" and "red little girls."[49] But these stories suggested that it could also be manly to *resist* temptation, that masculine strength lay in sticking to one's resolve. Practicing sobriety allowed a worker to fulfill his other manly role of provider for his family. These worker writers couched their morality tales in terms that might appeal to this alternative masculinity. In their tales, to succumb to the temptation of drink is to be weak; to resist is to be strong and to be a real man.

The practice of drinking thus opened a wide and conflictual terrain for the definition of new identities under socialism: comradeship clashed with family responsibilities. Drink also fostered other kinds of behaviors that became part of worker identity. Along with alcohol came a rise in fistfights and brawls, which always seemed to accompany the excessive consumption of drink. A letter from a former Petrograd printer now toiling in the "back of beyond" (*medvezhyi ugol*) reported how fistfights would arise between binders and compositors over the right to special work clothing. Unemployed workers drank away their jobless benefits and then turned to brawling, often in the union headquarters.[50] Observers argued that drink caused workers to lose their self-control, another reason to promote sobriety, but Phillips has suggested a more complicated explanation. Fighting was a socially learned behavior, and in fact belonged to the category of traditional and unstructured recreational activity.[51] Printers who drank and brawled were practicing two time-honored leisure activities of Russian lower-class masculine life.

The apparently dramatic increase in drunkenness among printers contributed to another nationwide epidemic, that of theft or embezzlement of

---

47. *Pechatnik* 42 (16 October 1926): 5; 44 (30 October 1926): 4; *Moskovskii pechatnik* 6 (February 1926): 5.

48. Borovskii, "Novosel'e."

49. Phillips, *Bolsheviks and the Bottle*, 32–35.

50. *Nasha zhizn'*, 28 March 1924; other reports in TsGAMO, f. 699, op. 1, d. 728, l. 45; *Moskovskii pechatnik* 13 (6 April 1925): 6; 6 (15 February 1925): 5; 24 (21 June 1925): 2, 14; 25 (28 June 1925): 19; 17 (April 1926): 7; 32–33 (August 1926): 5; *Pechatnik* 48 (27 November 1926): 10; 11 (25 October 1923): 6.

51. *Moskovskii pechatnik* 6 (February 1926): 3; Phillips, *Bolsheviks and the Bottle*, 79–80; see Daniel Brower, "Labor Violence in Russia in the Late Nineteenth Century," *Slavic Review* 41, no. 3 (1982): 417–31; Charters Wynn, *Workers, Strikes, and Pogroms: The Donbass-Dnepr Bend in Late Imperial Russia, 1870–1905* (Princeton, 1992); *Moskovskii pechatnik* 30–31 (12 August 1925): 8.

"A Physically Uncultured Outburst." Instead of practicing "physical culture," a printers' picnic ends in drink and fisticuffs. (*Moskovskii pechatnik* 26 [6 July 1925]: 12.)

public funds: *rastrata*. Anyone who had access to public money, from the plant manager to the worker who collected dues in the workshop, now had the opportunity to squander that money for personal consumption. The new material culture of the high NEP years provided ample temptation for workers to augment their budgets with illegal funds. A few incidents of this sort of theft had been reported in 1918, but the real explosion of rastrata began in 1925, and did not abate. By the mid-1920s, the theft of union funds could no longer be exonerated on the grounds of hunger. Now the union press alleged that responsible officials stole public money to fund drinking binges. The themes of crime and punishment figured often in fictional accounts that appeared in the worker press. In one such story, the factory treasurer Produvkin stopped by the tavern carrying 750 rubles in union dues and contributions to the mutual aid fund, the Friends of Children Society, Friends of the Air Fleet, and others. One bottle led to twelve, and having spent all his own money, Produvkin then drank up the union funds as well. The ubiquity of embezzlement also found its expression in the humor section of the union journal:

"Our secretary is a conscious person."

"What do you mean?"

"He stole our hard-earned money and he did so consciously."[52]

Some of these accounts of embezzlement provide our only glimpse into another area of proscribed working-class leisure, gambling. Several of the reported embezzlers spent the public money not only on women and drink but at casinos, gambling clubs, and the race track. Another fell into crime when he stumbled upon a card game while carrying the union's money. Print shop "hooligans" were chastised for playing cards and drinking at home rather than attending the union club; other clubs looked the other way when workers engaged in their favorite pastime, playing the card game Goats (*Kozly*). Card playing, prohibited during the Civil War, regained its legality during NEP. Kabo's time-budget study indicates that about 12 percent of working and nonworking men and women engaged in card playing, and that working men and housewives averaged thirty-six minutes a month playing cards or the lottery; working women spent an hour and a half.[53]

Union activists bemoaned workers' continuing preference for private and uncollective leisure pursuits, whether gambling, drinking, or cinema, and they blamed inadequate resources for their failure to win workers over to the cause of collective and universal proletarian culture. Discussions at congresses about club life and laments and social satires about uncultured workers conveyed the set of norms that the total proletarian should aspire to in his or her life beyond the workplace. But if we take the practices discussed here as evidence of the preferences of skilled and urban workers, then we should conclude that while printers demonstrated a strong desire for social leisure and recreation, this did not mean for them a collective leisure of uplifting and socially useful pursuits. They preferred to relax in small groups, with friends, with workmates. They liked to discuss literature from time to time at their own (not others') club and they liked to compete in sports activities, but in teams, not in anonymous collectives. Socialism gave printers the means and opportunity for a full social life, but as with their politics and with other forms of consumption, they also indicated that they wanted to be able to choose the form their social life would take.

---

52. *Moskovskii pechatnik* 18 (8 May 1925): 4; 41 (27 October 1925): 6–9; TsGA SPb, f. 4804, op. 9, d. 5 (meetings of Leningrad union board, December 1924–September 1925), l. 5; other examples in *Moskovskii pechatnik* 30–31 (12 August 1925): 13; *Pechatnik* 2 (15 January 1925): 5; 18–19 (1 May 1926): 16; 29–30 (25 October 1927): 22; 36 (25 December 1927): 25.

53. *Pechatnik* 17 (1 September 1925): 2; 18–19 (1 May 1926): 16; 17 (15 June 1927): 18; *Zorkii glaz*, 22 January 1927; *Moskovskii pechatnik* 40–41 (October 1926): 5; 26 (July 1926): 7; TsGA SPb, f. 4804, op. 10, d. 66 (general and factory committee meetings at Pechatnyi Dvor, 1926), l. 337; Aleksandr Chistikov, "Gosudarstvo protiv kartochnoi igry," in Vikhavainen, *Normy i tsennosti*, 310; Kabo, *Ocherki rabochego byta*, 206, 208; A. N. Chistikov, "Azartnye igry v SSSR serediny 20-kh godov," *Voprosy istorii*, 1994, no. 2: 138–42; see also Lebina, *Povsednevnaia zhizn'*, 253–55.

One size did not fit all. But to celebrate diversity and difference within the class or family of workers did not necessarily mean to deny the salience of an overarching worker identity. The middle years of the 1920s, this time of relative prosperity and constrained but active local politics, also offered printers a new opportunity to define through practice the meaning of their worker identity and their citizenship in a proletarian state.

## WHO IS A WORKER? WHAT IS A WORKER?

By 1927, ten years into the revolution, worker identity remained a complicated tangle of conflicting attributes, reflecting labor movement traditions, socialist ideals, and realities of scarcity, as well as state-sponsored ascription. Sheila Fitzpatrick has emphasized the constructedness of identities in the USSR and the importance of the state in creating and defining social identity. In a society in which proletarian identity was the normative class identity, individuals scrambled to position themselves on the right side of the class barrier. The regime struggled to stigmatize both those with the wrong identity and those who falsely claimed to possess the right identity. The importance of class identities had also become internalized in this process: "presentation of a *class* self in everyday life was part of the common social experience."[54] But this analysis skirts the issue of the canonical worker identity itself. Defining oneself as a worker in a workers' state did not turn out to be a simple matter either, a task that the growing prosperity and stability of NEP only complicated.

In their own words, printers elaborated on the characteristics and categories of working-class identity. They defined themselves in terms of work and suffering, but also by celebrating their rough culture of drink, bad language, rowdiness, and disrespect for authority, socialist or otherwise. They defined themselves in terms of whom they excluded from their midst, whether office workers or peasants. They also articulated identities quite conscious of gender differences and characteristics that distinguished adult workers from immature youths.

Work, so precarious in the years of the Civil War calamity and only now beginning to hold out the promise of permanence, remained a central category of self-identification. As explored and celebrated in the pages of the Printers' Union press as well as in public debate, worker identity began with the material fact of production reinforced by the nonmaterial fact of knowledge, the skill that the worker applied to the task. Unskilled workers drew the scorn of those with skills.[55] The symbolic power of skill involved more than an end product; it involved also the right to autonomy, agency, and power. Given a task, whether a statistical table to set or a newspaper to lay out, skilled printers prided them-

---

54. Fitzpatrick, "Ascribing Class" and "Problem of Class Identity," 28.
55. *Moskovskii pechatnik* 13 (6 April 1925): 6; 33–34 (6 September 1925): 12–13; 9 (8 March 1925): 10; 3 (21 January 1925): 10; *Nasha zhizn'*, 11 October 1923.

selves on their ability to manage the process of work. (Historians who rely on the statistical data in Soviet publications should be grateful for the pride these printers took in presenting data carefully and accurately.)

Unemployment challenged the very core of a worker's identity, and its cost amounted to much more than the deprivation of a paycheck. Unemployed printers could find work in other sectors of the economy, but such work undermined their sense of identity. A feuilleton set in the Leningrad labor exchange in 1924 depicted a crowded room, thick with cigarette smoke, packed with unemployed workers hoping to land a job even for a day or two. When invited to claim a post running a carousel, however, the successful applicant refused: "That's not my trade," she said. Service and selling lay well beyond the boundaries of the production crafts. Unemployment, according to one of the most vocally active of the unemployed printers, affected unskilled and skilled alike, and led to crimes by men, prostitution among women, hooliganism among the youth, and worst of all, the "danger of complete declassing." An angry jobless woman insisted in 1927 on her right to work: "We didn't come here to get a handout from the union, not favors, but work, and if the union remains deaf, then we have to force on them our demand to recognize our right to work and to existence. We don't want handouts—give us work!" A poignant story, "The Old Compositor," follows the last days at work of Pavel Martynov, who lamented that his "time was up" after forty years of working life. "His heart tightened when he thought about how he would never again explore the secrets of human thoughts, his fingers would never again slide in letter after letter. . . ." The proletarian has two black days in his life, wrote a contributor to *Moskovskii pechatnik*: the day of unemployment and the day his health no longer permits him to work.[56]

Yet this work that workers claimed was such an essential part of their personal identities also came at great personal cost. In the tributes to heroes of labor and in obituaries of departed workers, for example, workers' skills and devotion to their trade became almost secondary to the suffering, sacrifices, and injuries they sustained in the course of their working lives. The basic criterion for the "hero" award was longevity, thirty years or more in the trade, but it is striking how many citations also stressed injury and disease. M. S. Semenov lost his arm in an accident on the press at the *Izvestiia* plant, but continued to work as the manager of the enterprise's housing unit. Tuberculosis was the scourge of the profession, and "breathing the dust" that bred the disease could be a marker of class identity as well. Georgii Klement'ev died in 1924 in the "flower of his years," at age thirty-seven, having sacrificed his health by going to Siberia as an organizer despite his tuberculosis. He cared little about himself, but gave

---

56. *Pechatnik* 7 (15 April 1924): 10; 39 (25 September 1926): 5–6; GARF, f. R-5525, op. 8, d. 1 (stenographic report of Sixth All-Union Congress of Printers' Union, 27 November–4 December 1926), ll. 161, 156; op. 9, d. 131 (general meetings of unemployed union members, 1927), l. 35; TsGAMO, f. 699, op. 1, d. 787 (protocols of the Third Moscow Guberniia Union Conference, October 1926), l. 19; *Moskovskii pechatnik* 32 (15 October 1924): 6; 8 (1 March 1925): 6.

his all to his union and to the workers, and fell fatally ill when he attended a union plenum against the advice of his doctors.[57]

Such tributes emphasized the tragic nobility of the printer's work. Other traits in which workers seemed to take great pride were located further along the continuum from nobility to baseness. Printers also celebrated their roughness, their rudeness, their readiness and willingness to display their bad manners and to flout authority. Drinking, swearing, brawling, and insubordination could be seen as holdovers from the capitalist system, and both workers and regime sometimes attributed these behaviors to the legacy of past subalternity.[58] Ideally, as the experience of the socialist respect for human dignity and equality came to erase memories of subordination and rebellion, the regime expected that socialist workers would adopt new codes of civility, dignity, respect, and cooperation. The tension between these two visions of working-class behavior received considerable attention in the trade union press, in stories written by workers, and in recorded discussions in workshop and union meetings. Significantly, though, as Soviet printers constructed and represented their sense of socialist worker identity in the mid-1920s, their bad behavior seemed to enjoy pride of place.

Drink remained a defining characteristic of class identity. It was well known that printers loved to drink, admitted a worker-correspondent; in fact, printers retained "the palm of superiority" in this regard. A parody of the *Small Soviet Encyclopedia* defined a pressman as someone who, "according to data from the Health Commissariat, is in second place to textile workers in the consumption of alcohol. One could hope that he would soon surpass them." In appealing his dismissal for drunkenness, Kurbatov, a printer at the Sixteenth shop, explained that the work company he had joined were all inveterate drinkers, and he was led to know that if he did not drink with them, they would arrange for him to lose his job. The worse for Kurbatov. Because of his poverty, he refused to buy drinks for his mates in honor of his joining the enterprise, the time-honored custom of *prival'naia*, and his fellows arranged for him to be assigned to inferior presses. Eventually they hounded him out of the workplace. As a collective practice, drinking reinforced the ties of the work group. Tales of entire shops as well as work teams drinking together were common: it was good to drink in the shop, you didn't waste time going out, reasoned some workers.[59]

---

57. *Moskovskii pechatnik* 2 (16 February 1922): 2; 32 (15 October 1924): 10; *Izvestiia*, 15 June 1923; *Nasha zhizn'*, 8 March and 19 April 1923; *Pechatnik* 2 (1 February 1924): 4; 3 (36) (February 1923): 25.

58. Labor historians have increasingly emphasized the rough culture of working-class masculinity in capitalist societies: Steven Maynard, "Rough Work and Rugged Men: The Social Construction of Masculinity in Working-Class History," *Labour/Le Travail* 23 (1989): 159–69; Peter Way, "Evil Humors and Ardent Spirits: The Rough Culture of Canal Construction Laborers," *Journal of American History* 79 (1993): 1397–1428; Steve Meyer, "Rough Manhood: The Aggressive and Confrontational Shop Culture of U.S. Auto Workers during World War II," *Journal of Social History* 36 (2002): 125–47.

59. *Moskovskii pechatnik* 6 (February 1926): 2; 26 (6 July 1925): 12; 12 (29 March 1925): 6;

The use of bad language emerges as another defining trait of working-class identity.[60] At the Moscow Cooperative Print Shop, one correspondent castigated the language of the cleaner Vladina, from whom "daily you could hear such vulgar words that your hair would stand on end," but her co-workers spurred her on. Swearing was a competitive sport among the printers: one would start a stream of oaths, and others would compete with their own vulgar expressions. Like drinking, these swearing competitions involved the entire work crew, or at least its male members, married or single, men of all ages, "aristocrats" and "plebs." Closely related to foul language was *zvon,* or the ribald teasing that also permeated the workshops. Such teasing was frequently aimed at women, and served to mark the workplace as male space. But it could also be launched at anyone who might appear vulnerable. A short story published in the union journal in 1926 described the daily shop floor banter: jesting and horseplay began in the morning and by afternoon had spread to the entire composing room. Those on piece rates who had already finished their quota would devote themselves entirely to teasing and joking. Setting an article on "the women's question" or a textbook on anatomy would invariably set the discussion off on the theme of the sex life of one or another worker. "The laughter starts with general questions and ends with intimate details of family life—but all are devoted to sexual questions."[61]

Rudeness was a way of life, even a practice to celebrate. Workers spoke simply, from their proletarian souls: they never learned the rules of proper etiquette, nor did they particularly wish to. In 1927, when the factory newspaper *Nasha zhizn'* adopted a new format of small dense type, workers reacted negatively: the new look was too "polite," unworkerly; "We want a worker face to our newspaper!" wrote one. I speak my mind, wrote another worker to this newspaper, and for this I'm called rowdy. But I have documents to prove my thirty-two years at the workbench, and "I can't possibly have a nonproletarian psychology."[62] Rowdiness (*buzoterstvo*), in other words, was part of the worker's psychological package.

Rowdiness in social situations found its workplace analog in poor discipline, and the conflict between production discipline and workplace autonomy generated yet another point of tension in the socialist code of behavior. Printers

---

32–33 (August 1926): 15–16; *Nasha zhizn',* 8 January 1927; *Pechatnik* 11 (25 October 1923): 6; TsGAMO, f. 699, op. 1, d. 570, ll. 164–65; *Zorkii glaz,* 19 December 1925; *Iskry,* March 1926.

60. See S. A. Smith, "The Social Meanings of Swearing: Workers and Bad Language in Late Imperial and Early Soviet Russia," *Past and Present,* no. 160 (1998), 167–202.

61. *Pechatnik* 4 (March 1923): 21; *Moskovskii pechatnik* 11 (22 September 1923): 11; 12 (March 1926): 5; 32–33 (August 1926): 15–16; *Zhizn' pechatnika,* 1 June 1927, 21 January 1926. For prerevolutionary examples, see Steinberg, *Moral Communities,* 78–79; and Maksim Gor'kii's short story about bakers, "Twenty-six Men and a Girl" (1899), in *The Collected Short Stories of Maxim Gorky,* ed. Avrahm Yarmolinsky and Moura Budberg (Secaucus, N.J., 1988).

62. *Pechatnik* 6 (16 May 1923): 24; TsGAMO, f. 699, op. 1, d. 849, l. 100; d. 438 (general and factory committee meetings at Krasnyi Proletarii, 1923), l. 5; *Nasha zhizn',* 17 April 1924, 18 May and 23 December 1927.

also located their identity in independence and unwillingness to submit to authority, even when authority resided somehow in their own kind. The running column satirizing common work practices at Pechatnyi Dvor testified to this prevailing work culture.

> "Petrov, let's have a smoke."
> "No, thanks, I have an urgent job to do: I've just finished two hours in the toilet smoking with Sergeev, and now I must drink some tea."

> "Petrov, go to the mechanical room and call the repairman; the screw has broken."
> "I already went—they don't have time, they're too busy insulting one another."[63]

Printers who took piece rates too seriously were likewise mocked for chasing after the big ruble instead of settling for the relaxed camaraderie of the shop floor. One correspondent reprimanded workers who were so eager to preserve optimal working conditions for themselves that they hid the best tools and type trays after their shifts. In another story, a new worker became so obsessed with making sure he had the right tools on hand that instead of winning a promotion in rank, he was transferred to the rank of the "dangerously insane."[64] Slacking off was real and widespread, and it was behavior in which workers took great pride.

The complex portrait that worker-correspondents themselves drew of their class identity combined pride in skill with pride in goofing off, and emphasized both their central role in transmitting culture and deliberate rejection of polite, cultured behavior. These attributes helped to define the boundaries of a class identity that had less to do with ascribed or experienced social categories than with everyday behavior. Workers also endeavored to define their sense of identity by naming categories excluded from their midst. While they rarely invoked social origin ("peasant" or "proletarian") as a marker of worker identity, either positive or negative, they often drew a line that defined both office workers (*sluzhashchie*) and those engaged in market exchange relations as outside the community of workers. One correspondent lampooned the office workers who adopted aristocratic airs as they enjoyed their holidays at the union rest home. At dinnertime the "aristocrats" conversed with *merci* and *pardon,* as in "*Merci,* you are so kind," while from the proletarian end of the table came coarse and ribald bantering. Unemployed workers who went into business for themselves were considered to have "dirtied the union with their tendencies

---

63. *Pechatnyi dvor,* 15 March 1923.
64. GARF, f. R-5525, op. 4, d. 1 (stenographic report of Fourth All-Russian Congress of Printers' Union, 18–21 October 1922), l. 106; other exchanges in *Pechatnyi dvor,* 25 April, 5 October, and 15 November 1923; *Moskovskii pechatnik* 30–31 (12 August 1925): 16; 32 (20 August 1925): 5–8.

alien to workers." The binder Grachev was expelled from the union because he continued to pursue his old trade of innkeeper in addition to his job in a print shop: "Innkeepers have no place in a proletarian organization." Real workers did not ape the aristocracy; they did not turn carousels; and they did not sell from stalls in the marketplace.[65]

The Communist regime's official discourse emphasized the importance of social origins in class formation: real workers were hereditary proletarians, sons and daughters of workers before them. But printers in their own writings stressed their current occupation as the marker of class identity. They appealed to social *origins*, the categories of the regime, only when they needed to address higher authority. Petitioning to reinstate her husband in the job he had held for thirty-six years when he had been replaced by an office worker, the Leningrad resident Ekaterina Kuz'mina wrote to Mikhail Kalinin, "Our family is of purely proletarian origin." A pressman with thirty-three years in the industry wrote to *Moskovskii pechatnik* to complain that his factory committee would not hire his son by his first wife because she had ties to the village.[66] "Proletarian pedigree" also served as the butt of jokes: in discussing new names for the ritual of red christening, one local writer suggested that since both father and son were proletarians, they could name the newborn Proletarii Proletarych.[67] At times like these, workers seemed to reject the regime's definition of proletarian in favor of their own. Considering all of these public and private, formal and informal representations of class, we can conclude that class identity in this industry, and one might venture to say among Soviet workers more generally, was far more complex than the simple hereditary binaries promoted by the regime's social statisticians.

Yet in all the complex attributes of class identity as generated by these workers themselves, a certain commonality emerges with striking clarity. The worker celebrated in contemporary trade union discourse, whether respectable or rough, was a skilled male worker. Even though 25 percent of the workforce in printing were female by the mid-1920s, the behaviors most valued as worker behavior—skilled work, drinking, swearing, horseplay, and flouting of authority—were quintessentially masculine. In defining for themselves what it meant to be a worker, these Russian printers were defining women out of the working class. In fact, the presence of women on the shop floor, and to a lesser extent that of adolescent boys, provided a serious challenge to workingmen's

65. *Pechatnik* 4 (March 1923): 36; 10 (10 October 1923): 9; 3 (36) (February 1923): 27; *Nasha zhizn'*, 11 October 1923; *Moskovskii pechatnik* 23 (1 June 1924): 15; 29–30 (September 1924): 18; 32 (15 October 1924): 6; TsGAMO, f. 699, op. 1, d. 396 (meetings in print shops in Zamoskvorech'e district, 1923), l. 47.

66. GARF, f. R-5525, op. 7, d. 118 (materials on conflicts, 1925), l. 30; *Moskovskii pechatnik* 19 (16 May 1925): 13; another example in TsGA SPb, f. 4804, op. 8, d. 113 (meetings and correspondence on youth quota, 1924), ll. 24–24ob.

67. *Izvestiia*, 15 June 1923; *Moskovskii pechatnik* 6 (15 February 1925): 6; 21 (30 May 1925): 7; *Zhizn' pechatnika*, 20 October 1923.

self-identity, one that was met with a level of resistance that spoke to rigid differences on the shop floor and within the working class.

Trade union organizational practice tacitly divided union members into a core of fully employed, ethnically Russian males and certain special groups who required extra attention and concern to bring them closer to the proletarian ideal: women, youth, "nationalities," home workers, and seasonal workers.[68] The Printers' Union, however, concerned itself with only two of these categories, women and youth, who merited special organizers and special attention on the agendas of conferences and congresses. Official union solicitude, however, contrasted sharply with hostility on the shop floor. And despite the relative prosperity of the industry in the mid-1920s, cultural aversion to women and adolescent workers combined with a sense of economic competition to reinforce sharp divisions within the working class between the skilled men and the women and youths whom they branded as inferior.

The control of skill constituted a particularly contentious arena of class relations in the 1920s. Women had a difficult time acquiring the skills that could qualify them as real workers.[69] One lamentable cause, cited by men and women alike, was that many women themselves had no interest in learning new skills and raising their pay grades.[70] Conditioned to see themselves as temporary sojourners in the workforce, they were content to take jobs at low pay rates and skill levels, not realizing that their lack of versatility would target them for layoffs as economic pressures mounted. Some women asserted and activists agreed that their domestic burden was to blame. Women at one meeting explained their reluctance to take on more demanding work or extra work activities because of their double burden of housework and job. In other cases, it was women's allegedly "delicate physical characteristics" that impeded true equality and acquisition of skill.[71]

Most frequently of all, however, women cited the hostility of men or the indifference of male-dominated factory committees for their lack of training. At

---

68. See, for example, the records for the Leningrad branch of the Union of Soviet and Trade Employees, TsGA SPb, f. 6276, op. 13 (1928).

69. For a fuller discussion of the factors of gender and generation, see Koenker, "Men against Women" and "Fathers against Sons."

70. *Pechatnik* 6 (16 May 1923): 3. See also Wendy Z. Goldman, *Women, the State, and Revolution* (Cambridge, 1993), 122–26, for similar discussions by women in other industries.

71. *Pravda*, 14 September 1923; *Pechatnik* 23 (25 August 1927): 14; 2 (9 January 1926): 11; *Moskovskii pechatnik* 8 (July 1923): 13; 5 (8 February 1925): 11; 11 (22 March 1925): 9; 2 (15 January 1925): 14; 18 (27 February 1924): 24; 10 (12 August 1923): 19–20; 9 (12 July 1923): 21; TsGAMO, f. 699, op. 1, d. 570, l. 27; the double burden was also catalogued in *Zhizn' pechatnika*, 8 March 1924, and TsGAMO, f. 699, op. 1, d. 395 (meetings of activist women workers, 1923), l. 55; "Kodeks zakonov o trude RSFSR Izd. 1922 g.," in *Deistvuiushchee zakonodatel'stvo o trude soiuza SSSR i soiuznykh respublik: Sbornik deistvuiushchikh dekretov, postanovlenii i instruktsii*, ed. E. Danilova (Moscow, 1927), 1:14 (Article 130); GARF, f. R-5525, op. 5, d. 118 (protocols of general meetings of women, 1923), l. 3. In Scotland, the Monotype had been considered "preeminently suited for females" because keyboarding and typecasting were separated (Reynolds, *Britannica's Typesetters*, 70).

one print shop, men did not allow women to work on the presses because "they're not capable of thinking about production matters when not at work." Low-skilled women were dismissed and not trained because men said, "We don't want to work with women; it makes us uncomfortable." The heroine of a short story in a collection published by women printers begged her foreman to teach her to operate the printing press. No, he said, not worth it—better that women should stick to supplying the press with clean paper. "If you all become masters, what will our brothers do?" Again and again, women reported the same story. Training required women to work alongside a senior, experienced man. But the standard male attitude was negative: you'll just get married and quit work. So most workers refused to instruct them. Even when trained, women were directed to "women's jobs": to the auxiliary skills of feeding and removing paper from the press, rarely to typesetting or work on the press itself.[72]

Local rejection of official policies of gender equality in the Printers' Union was already evident by 1924, just a year after a loud official proclamation of women's equality in the industry. Grigorii N. Mel'nichanskii, an official of VTsSPS, admitted to printers in late 1924 that the policy of mobilizing women was in trouble. "I know you discuss the question in your conferences, and you adopt resolutions about involving women more in our work. But I also know that many comrades, after discussing these questions at official meetings, when they go off to the side they begin to mock them, to smile, to snigger, they say, all the same, nothing will come of such work."[73] Aleksandr Borshchevskii could draw general laughter from union men by answering a woman's serious complaint about child-care facilities with a retort about her age.[74]

By the beginning of 1926, the practice of reserving one factory committee place for a woman had been abandoned: mainstreaming women into regular union activities was now the norm. This retreat from tokenism was supposed to ensure that "fewer but better" women would serve on the committees.[75] At the same time, perhaps not coincidentally, union leaders launched an assault on the status of women folders (*fal'tsovshitsy*) as skilled workers. Women in this occupation were not in fact skilled, union men decided, and should be paid at the same level as common day laborers. A woman delegate to a 1926 Leningrad union congress deplored this view: "We so-called unskilled hand folders can do

---

72. *Pravda*, 8 June and 17 October 1923, 4 January 1924; TsGAMO, f. 699, op. 1, d. 395, l. 84; d. 849, l. 84; *Pechatnitsa*, 8 March 1924, 9; *Pechatnik* 15 (1 August 1925): 14; 10 (7 April 1927): 10; 7–8 (8 March 1928): 4; *Moskovskii pechatnik* 8 (16 June 1923): 14–15; 9 (12 July 1923): 21–22; 7 (22 February 1925): 12; 38–39 (14 October 1925): 29.

73. *Stenograficheskii otchet piatogo s"ezda soiuza*, 1924, 17.

74. See Chapter 5; TsGAMO, f. 699, op. 1, d. 787, l. 48.

75. GARF, f. R-5525, op. 8, d. 1 (stenographic report of Sixth All-Union Congress of Printers' Union, 27 November–4 December 1926), l. 20; *Moskovskii pechatnik* 1 (January 1926): 11; Elizabeth A. Wood, "Class and Gender at Loggerheads: Who Should Organize the Female Proletariat and How?" in *Gender and Class in Modern Europe*, ed. Laura L. Frader and Sonya O. Rose (Ithaca, 1996), 294–310.

## Драма в тарифной сетке.

"Drama in the Tarif Grid." In an allusion to the popularity of melodramatic theater, a woman worker is bound hand and foot at the lowly seventh pay grade, while a male worker smokes contentedly at the top of the skilled worker ranks in the thirteenth grade. (*Pechatnik* 19 [1 October 1925]: 12.)

whatever is needed—we sew bindings, we fold, we can do any of the work and we can do all of it." Now these women, who had worked side by side with men for eight years, were told they had no skills. "This is very insulting."[76]

The experience of young male workers was very similar, even though culturally women and adolescents represented quite different kinds of "nonstandard" workers. Women, some men argued, could never become real workers because they could never become men. Boys, on the other hand, would inevitably become men, and they would become the skilled workers of tomorrow: the labor force of total proletarians could be replenished through no other source. Yet hostility on the part of adult workers toward their younger successors was a time-honored tradition of the craft. Practical training of apprentices

---

76. TsGA SPb, f. 4804, op. 10, d. 4, ll. 508, 517–18, 567–68; *Moskovskii pechatnik* 14 (April 1926): 3.

had always involved rituals of subordination. Over and over in the memoirs of Soviet printers we read about the distance they felt as teenagers from the real world of the trade they sought to learn. Rather than being initiated into the mysteries of their craft, they were called upon by bosses and senior workers alike to run errands (typically for vodka), to sort spilled type, to assist the owner with domestic tasks, and generally to provide unskilled labor for the enterprise. The majority of the adult printers who set the standards in the socialist print shops of the 1920s had spent their apprenticeship in the old style, and this experience surely affected their attitude toward training their own replacements. "The conditions of this apprenticeship," recalled the trade union newspaper *Trud*, created a "dismal picture of the past which can never be forgotten by those who passed through this oppressive [*tiazheluiu*] schooling."[77]

Communist officials claimed that socialism would reform this oppressive process by eliminating the competitiveness of market relations, which aided in the exploitation of the labor of trainees, and it would establish rational and scientific methods of training skilled workers, ideally in special well-lit schools, outfitted with superior equipment and staffed by expert vocational pedagogues.[78] The continuing economic troubles of the industry, however, limited the availability of vocational training to just one school each in Moscow and Leningrad. Most apprentices would learn their trades in the old way, as trainees on the shop floor, working under the hopefully kind supervision of a skilled senior worker. On-the-job training continued to apply the stigma of the apprentice as the lowest creature on the evolutionary ladder of factory status, and apprentices would wonder publicly whether studying the craft in the "real world" compensated for the insults, abuse, and indifference they endured. "It's hard to get along with the senior workers," said a youth delegate at a conference in April 1927.[79]

Left to their own devices, adult workers were extremely reluctant to admit apprentices to their enterprises at all. The persistence of unemployment among skilled workers created a harsh economic climate for aspiring printers. The market of early NEP still discriminated against training unskilled youths, who were seen as "nonproductive ballast." Consequently, as the cornerstone of its industrial youth policy, the Soviet regime intervened in the market and announced in May 1922 the introduction of a quota system for the employment of young people in industry.[80] The quota (*bronia*) stipulated that in the printing industry, 13

---

77. *Istoriia leningradskogo soiuza*, 59–76; Steinberg, *Moral Communities*, 68–74; Svavitskii and Sher, *Ocherk polozheniia*, 9–14, 43–49; Ivan Pavlov, *Zhizn' russkogo gravera*, ed. M. P. Sokol'nikov (Moscow, 1963), 40–43; Vechtomova, *Zdes' pechatalas'*, 22; *Trud*, 10 October 1922.

78. Scientific training made comparable headway in capitalist economies in the 1920s. Nolan, *Visions of Modernity*, 89–90; Daniel Nelson, *Managers and Workers: Origins of the New Factory System in the United States, 1880–1920* (Madison, 1975); Child, *Industrial Relations in the British Printing Industry*, 259–62; Baker, *Printers and Technology*, 357–58.

79. GARF, f. R-5525, op. 9, d. 144 (materials on work among youth, 1927), l. 22; op. 8, d. 144 (general meetings of worker youth, 1926), l. 4.

80. *Moskovskii pechatnik* 10 (1 November 1921): 5; M. M. Kucherenko, *Molodoe pokolenie*

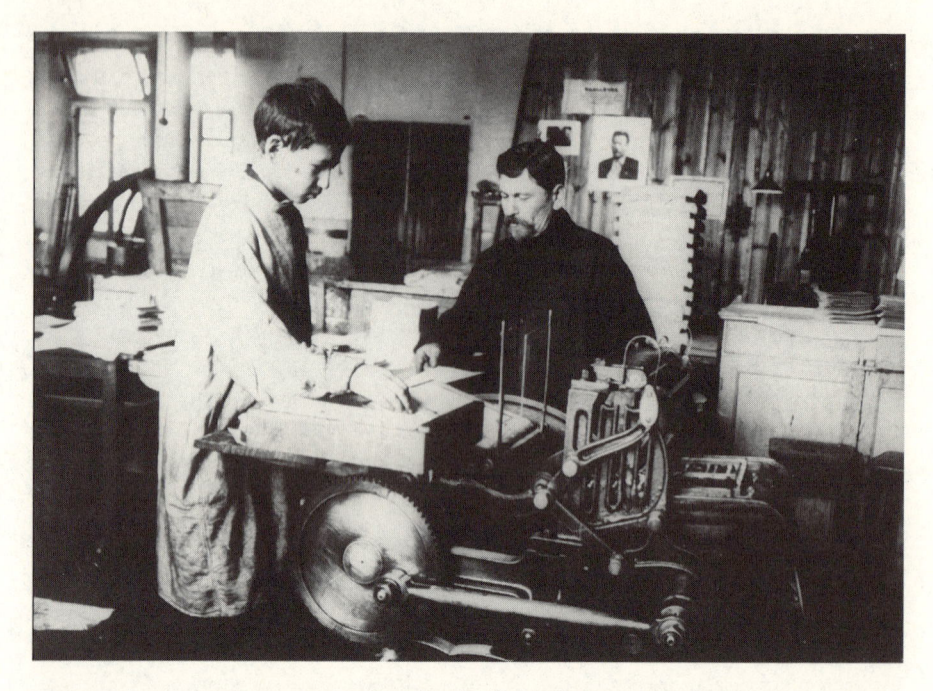

Master and apprentice, 1920s. A worker trains an apprentice at the *Pravda* print shop in the traditional one-to-one relationship. (Photo by Nikolai Petrov. Rossiiskii Gosudarstvennyi Arkhiv Kinofotodokumentov, 2-19305. Used with permission of the archive.)

percent of the labor force would be youths, and 25 percent of the youths would be female. This quota soon became the union's albatross as the ongoing industrial crisis in printing kept thousands of skilled printers out of work and idle in the labor exchange queue.

Preserving the youth quota led to a pattern in which the "reserved" youths, once trained, were denied full-time jobs in the industry because there was not enough work to sustain additional workers at adult pay rates. The graduated apprentices, having reached only the threshold of skill, imposed an unacceptable expense on their enterprises, so they fired the newly fledged workers while accepting new apprentices—at the low apprentice rate of pay—to fulfill the youth quota.[81] Suggestions to reduce the quota began to be heard at union congresses in late 1924. The union's youth organizer, Grigorii I. Barenboim, suggested a new limit of 7 percent, but a formal proposal to lower the youth quota at the 1924 union congress—which would have violated the policy of the cen-

---

*rabochego klassa SSSR: Protsess formirovaniia i vospitaniia, 1917–1979 gg.* (Moscow, 1979), 61; *Sobranie uzakonenii i rasporiazhenii rabochego i krest'ianskogo pravitel'stva* (Moscow, 1922), no. 39, st. 447.

81. *Moskovskii pechatnik* 13 (6 April 1925): 12; 46 (21 November 1925): 10; 35 (20 December 1924): 1–2; GARF, f. R-5525, op. 9, d. 144, l. 55; *Pechatnik* 9 (August 1923): 6.

tral government—went down to defeat by a vote of 94–64. This split vote was a remarkable division of opinion in an era in which socialist unanimity was already the order of the day, and thus testifies to the passion with which the Printers' Union confronted the challenge posed by preparing their successors. For the time being, the union deferred its desire to protect its control over the trade and accepted the ideological dictates of the regime.[82]

Despite official policy, within a year the union unilaterally took action to limit the influx of new workers, but such reforms failed to stem the hemorrhage of unemployable workers. By 1926, print shop managers were demanding that the quota be reduced still further and that the intake of new apprentices immediately be halted. Union activists from the shop floor still insisted that the union think ahead, because a new generation would eventually be needed. In short-term reality, however, even skilled adult workers could not find jobs, and cutting back on the costly training of apprentices seemed to offer an immediate solution to the unemployment crisis. The general opinion of Leningrad workers, wrote the Leningrad youth organizer in 1927, was that the quota needed to be reduced even further. "Individual workers speak out even more openly, saying that under current conditions we need to refuse to prepare new skilled workers."[83]

The formal decisions and discussions about the quota at union congresses impart a bland institutional patina to the fact of pervasive conflict between generations over access to jobs in the printing industry. Union officials constantly acknowledged their members' "hatred toward the young generation." The union youth specialist, L. Shekhmeister, felt compelled to explain to union members in 1927 that the recruitment of apprentices would not proceed at the expense of adult workers. Therefore, he reminded workers that they should treat the recruits with a friendly (*druzheliubnoe*) attitude. The marginalization of youth was captured in an entry in the "Printers' Encyclopedia" on the union journal's humor page in 1928: "Apprentice: a person for whom the print shop has become an impregnable fortress. Access to it is possible only under cover of the bronia."[84]

Was it their own remembered experience of bygone capitalism that convinced shop administrators of the idleness of apprentices, or was it the perceived reality of the socialist shop floor? Some argued that socialism had made a neg-

---

82. *Moskovskii pechatnik* 35 (20 December 1924): 2; TsGA SPb, f. 4804, op. 8, d. 56 (stenographic report of Petrograd Guberniia Fourth Congress, 15–17 December 1924), l. 11; d. 113, l. 61; *Shestoi moskovskii gubs"ezd*, 1924, 26–30; *Stenograficheskii otchet piatogo s"ezda*, 1924, 112, 123–24, 279–80, 319–20.

83. *Pechatnik* 10 (15 May 1925): 2; 16 (15 August 1925): 2; 17 (1 September 1925): 13; 50–51 (20 December 1926): 6–18, from the stenographic record of the Sixth All-Union Congress. The full report is in GARF, f. R-5525, op. 8, d. 1; *Moskovskii pechatnik* 36–37 (September 1926): 7; 28–29 (July 1926): 3; TsGA SPb, f. 4804, op. 10, d. 4, ll. 410, 425–26, 456, 512–13, 529; Ekimov to Shekhmeister, 14 December 1927, in GARF, f. R-5525, op. 9, d. 144, l. 60.

84. *Moskovskii pechatnik* 17 (April 1926): 2; *Pechatnik* 4 (March 1923): 22; 21 (25 July 1927): 5; 23 (15 August 1928): 26.

ative contribution to the training of the next generation. Adults accused apprentices of being indifferent to training (in many of the same terms they applied to women). Good-for-nothing trainees knew that the law prohibited their firing before the completion of their training, and so they felt invulnerable to discipline; other apprentices had entered the industry not out of any desire or aptitude but because their fathers had arranged their positions. Young printers' indifference to acquiring skills thus translated into rude and undisciplined behavior on the shop floor, for which they often sought immunity on account of their special status as the "next generation."[85]

Reflecting a growing concern in Soviet society about social deviancy, so-called hooliganism among apprentices included absenteeism, tardiness, loud and rowdy behavior, fighting, and rejection of all criticism. Hooligan jargon fostered nicknames, "aliases," that would further distinguish the unruly minority from the respectable mainstream, and printing apprentices took pride in their own "hooligan's alias" of "factory rabbits" (*fabzaichat*), a pun on the term for the vocational training school, *fabzavuch*. In the premier training school in the country, Moscow's Borshchevskii school, the director ruefully admitted that "we do have hooligans, our school graduates hooligans of the highest caliber." It was difficult to discipline young people, explained the chairman of the trade union, Nikolai Derbyshev, because responsible adults could not communicate with them: "That language of youth, it's a completely different [*drugoi*] language."[86] The cultural divide between generations, as perceived from the top down and reinforced by the scarcity of positions, thus remained a serious impediment to socialist unity.

Soviet Russia was not alone in facing the challenge from a distinctive culture among worker youth. The First World War had disrupted traditional family authority structures across Europe and North America, and the rise of a mass consumer society in the industrialized world had provided adolescents and young adults with unprecedented social and financial autonomy. Adults responded with alarm to the new flaunting of defiance, fashion, amorality, and dance-hall sexuality. The scientific study of the "youth problem" took off in the 1920s.[87] But these were capitalist societies, and the alienation and challenge of youth

---

85. TsGAMO, f. 699, op. 1, d. 570, l. 40; *Moskovskii pechatnik* 15 (7 January 1924): 17; 15 (23 April 1925): 11; 4–5 (January 1926): 9; *Pechatnik* 29 (17 July 1926): 13; *Krasnyi proletarii*, 26 August and 4 September 1926; *Iskry*, 15 January 1929; *Leningradskii pravdist*, 8 December 1930; TsGAIPD SPb, f. 435, op. 1, d. 29 (party meetings in Petrograd enterprises, 1921), l. 212.

86. *Pechatnik* 12 (7 November 1923): 11; *Moskovskii pechatnik* 34 (December 1924): 14; 35 (20 December 1924): 11; 5 (8 February 1925): 12; 25 (1 July 1925): 12; 28 (21 July 1925): 9; 16 (April 1926): 7; 47–48 (5 December 1925): 4; 8 (1 March 1925): 13; TsGAMO, f. 699, op. 1, d. 849, l. 176; *Zorkii glaz*, 22 January 1927; *Stenograficheskii otchet piatogo s"ezda*, 1924, 80.

87. Gorsuch, *Youth in Revolutionary Russia*, 25–26; Paula S. Fass, *The Damned and the Beautiful: American Youth in the 1920s* (Oxford, 1975), 20; Randy D. McBee, *Dance Hall Days: Intimacy and Leisure among Working-Class Immigrants in the United States* (New York, 2000), 69; Joanna Bourke, *Working-Class Cultures in Britain, 1890–1960: Gender, Class, and Ethnicity* (London, 1994), 45.

could be blamed on the inherent contradictions of the capitalist order. The total proletarian paradigm had no room for divisions by gender or by age. It was not only the fact of youth defiance and "hooliganism" that alarmed trade unionists, but the deviation this behavior represented from the imagined socialist ideal.

The picture of relations between apprentices and adult skilled workers in Soviet Russia reveals a polarized landscape of tension and hostility. Few intermediate layers of identity, such as marital status or seniority, could soften the sharp chasm between adults and youth, at least rhetorically. Male adult workers regarded young workers as annoying, bothersome, and unwelcome. How much was this perception due to economic pressure? How much of it was a cultural aversion? Economic tension was considerable, as the expenses involved in supporting the less productive apprentices could be seen to affect directly the material well-being of the adult males. But youths were also perceived as alien: they spoke a different jargon and failed to respect established rules of precedence. Badly trained apprentices, and potentially all apprentices, sowed doubt on the competence, the manliness of adult printers. Male printers' hostility to sharing their work space with women was often expressed in terms of skill: skill was something men could possess, the ability to earn a skilled wage was a marker of masculinity. Women could therefore never become skilled.[88] The years of apprenticeship were also recalled in hues of feminized subordination: masters beat their apprentices as they did their wives; apprentices minded the owners' children, helped the cook in the kitchen, and even milked the cow. Only the acquisition of skill—completion of the apprenticeship—permitted them to leave these womanly roles behind and become men.[89]

## THE DOUBLE NATURE OF CLASS IN THE PROLETARIAN STATE

The economic prosperity of the middle 1920s offered Soviet printers a level of affluence that was comfortable only in comparison with the starvation years of the Civil War period. Nonetheless, their standard of living provided sufficient surplus to begin to construct for themselves the material and cultural elements of their identity as socialist workers, as socialist citizens. Fundamental to this identity, as expressed in the everyday encounters and statements examined above, was skill and workplace experience. Printers articulated clear understandings of their distinctive place in society as workers, as members of a class whose value to society derived from the skilled labor they performed. They also expressed their sense of group affinity through the language of class, the language of the common experience of work, of the suffering that work brought to them, and through social and cultural life that became an extension of their workplace communities.

---

88. This argument is developed more fully in Koenker, "Men against Women."
89. Pavlov, *Zhizn' russkogo gravera*, 40–46; *Pechatnik* 18 (25 June 1927): 21; *Moskovskii pechatnik* 17 (April 1926): 2.

The relation of this work-based class identity to the new political citizenship of socialism, however, remained complicated and fraught. Printers in the mid-1920s articulated two distinct class identities. One class could be labeled "official class," the new socialist class, the ruling class of the total proletarian state. Official class began with labor as the source of identity and raised the centrality of production and productivism to a cardinal tenet of the new society. Socialist workers were builders, makers, and producers. This class included skilled men but also the entire proletarian family of printers, stepsons as well as sons, women as well as men, adolescents as well as adults. Official class was all-encompassing and collectivist: from the collective camaraderie of the workplace, socialist workers would adjourn to their proletarian clubs for food, education, entertainment, intelligent recreation, and new rituals appropriate for the new socialist ruling class. The official class scorned stimulants, particularly alcohol, and all behaviors that did not serve a constructive purpose in building socialist society, whether gambling, fighting, dancing, or romantic love. The official class was triumphant, confidant, and a militant representative of the new socialist order.

The alternative working class could be labeled indigenous, natural, or "unofficial class." This class too began with labor as its source of identity: the daily rhythms and rituals of the workplace provided the unofficial working class with its symbols and codes for interaction, its source of pride and location within the larger society. But unlike official class, the alternative class valued consumption as well as production. Work was not only an end in itself: it was also the mechanism by which the worker turned labor into commodities for personal consumption. This goal now appeared within reach during the middle years of NEP, but it had animated printers throughout their revolutionary years and in the early years of Soviet power: they agitated for decent wages in 1917 and for food in 1921. But by the mid-1920s they wanted more than the living minimum favored by proletarian asceticism: they wanted ample food, warm and comfortable housing, clothing, books, the cinema, and decorative art on the walls of their apartments. Unofficial class, however, was in other ways more restrictive than official class: the tenacious resistance of the rank and file to opening the union up to women and youths strongly suggests that this indigenous class identity rested exclusively with men, particularly with skilled men. And while these men drew their identity from their work collectives, those collectives themselves were restricted to fellows like themselves. When they left the workplace, these pillars of the alternative working class chose entertainment and leisure that was independent and unstructured, whether located within the family circle, the local tavern, the street, or the cinema. The unofficial class was as devoted to the practice of drinking as the official class was committed to sobriety.

The complicated distinctions between these two versions of the working class can be seen in the ways printers commemorated their past. All printers took pride in their long revolutionary pedigree, and the history of the union provided many rich examples of struggle, sacrifice, and victories in the name of the working class. Throughout the 1920s, printers commemorated the anniversaries of their collective endeavors: their 1903 general strike, the 1905 revolution, particular moments in the union's struggle against tsarist repression, the 1917 revolution, the struggle between the Mensheviks and Bolsheviks, and the victory of the red union in 1920.

The official class history privileged the triumph of the red Bolshevik union over the independent union championed by the Mensheviks and Socialist Revolutionaries. A spate of reminiscences published in 1925 to commemorate the fifth anniversary of the final defeat of the Mensheviks, both in the union journals and in the anniversary volume, *Materials on the History of the Trade Union of Workers in Printing Production,* featured articles by the union's leaders recalling the war between reds and yellows for hegemony in the Printers' Union. The theme of red victory over the pseudo-workers of the independent union was echoed in some of the factory newspapers.[90] This official story of fratricidal strife, when workers labeled one another betrayers of the working class, however, was seldom told by anyone outside the union leadership.

The alternative memory of class focused instead on collective struggles against "real" capitalists and "real" counterrevolutionaries. When rank-and-file printers published their memories of the past, they dwelled on the underground struggle under tsarism: defiant celebrations of May Day and the year 1905 as a turning point in the revolutionary movement.[91] Memories of 1917 tended to focus on the common struggle against the old regime and against newly empowered capitalists. The events of October 1917 came in two distinct versions: Nikolai Gordon sniped that the Menshevik union leadership refused to support the Soviet seizure of power, but A. Popov instead recalled the human tragedy of the street fighting in Moscow, recounting his first sight of two comrades shot down by "the enemy," with their last words asking to be remembered to their wives. The unofficial story stressed the role played by printers in serving the revolution: discovering an unused military printing press on a railway siding that helped to send the first proclamations of the decrees on land and peace to the front-line troops, the seizure from its capitalist owner of the bourgeois daily *Petrogradskaia gazeta* and its conversion to a socialist newspaper. Class here was constructed as against capital, against tsarist bureaucrats, not against other workers. Recollections of the Civil War, similarly, stayed clear of the bitter political struggle within the union and instead recalled mobile printing presses

---

90. Gordon in *Materialy,* 87–115; *Pechatnik* 10 (15 May 1925): 5; Borshchevskii in *Materialy,* 127–94; Derbyshev in *Materialy,* 124–26; Tikhanov in *Moskovskii pechatnik* 22 (15 May 1924): 10; 25 (28 June 1925): 3; *Nasha zhizn',* 30 April 1925, 5 November 1927.

91. *Moskovskii pechatnik* 16–17 (1 May 1925): 3–7; 21 (30 May 1925): 12–13; 42–43 (1 November 1925); *Pechatnik* 2 (15 January 1925): 6–8; 2 (9 January 1926): 7; 5 (30 January 1926): 2–5; 35 (28 August 1926); *Pechatnyi dvor,* April 1925; *Biiskii pechatnik* (Biisk, 1927), 4, 17; *Vospominaniia rabochikh 16-i tipolitografiia Mospoligraf (b. Levenson)* (Moscow, 1925); *Moskovskie pechatniki v 1905 g.* (Moscow, 1925).

serving the Ninth Red Army, the defense of Petrograd against "Germans and white Finns" in 1919, printing subversive postage stamps in occupied Kiev, and struggles against White generals on the fronts of the Civil War.[92]

Significantly, "volume 1" of the collective history of the Leningrad union, published in 1925, covered only the years 1904–7; subsequent volumes never appeared.[93] The prerevolutionary years constituted politically safe terrain, when class differences among printers could be ignored. But printers also acquired, in this retelling, a wistful remembrance of the bad old days when one knew who was a friend and who was an enemy. Printers suffered from economic exploitation, the lack of political rights, and a dangerous and unhealthy trade, but they suffered together. In this version of their history, the alternative version, victimhood was an important element of the printers' identity, an element that was reinforced by Civil War memories of suffering and hardship as well. In unofficial class consciousness, work emerged as both ennobling and destructive, and class was constituted as much defensively as triumphantly. This representation of class as tragedy—so firmly entrenched in the collective memory—turned out to be hard to reconcile with the official version of militancy and power.

The two kinds of class identity among printers were not mutually exclusive. Many printers embraced both positions, or parts of them, at the same time. Official printers dutifully adopted positions favoring the uplifting of women and adolescents at their congresses, but privately some sniggered and made fun of women, and some of them demanded the right for men to maintain their monopoly on skill by denying younger workers entry into the trade. Official policy condemned the consumption of vodka and punished printers for drinking on the job, but the Communist leadership engaged in drinking binges just as surely as did the rank and file. There were also individuals who genuinely embraced the official class culture, who preferred intelligent sober leisure at the club, who spent their evenings inventing better ink for their printing presses, and who denounced the alternative culture as a holdover of the past life of repression and resignation.

The complexity of class identity among Soviet workers echoes the messiness of class analysis for any society. It is not possible to explain why some printers adopted the official culture and others the alternative culture any more than it is possible to use sociological characteristics to explain why some printers became Bolsheviks, some became Mensheviks, and others remained outside the political arena altogether. Does class, then, becomes useless as a source of solidarity or method of analysis? William Reddy suggests that since we cannot precisely map individuals' shared intentions or behavior in terms of their economic

---

92. *Pechatnik* 45–46 (7 November 1926): 6, 7, 9–12, 14; 31 (7 November 1927): 17, 19–23, 30; 28 (8 December 1925): 5–6; *Moskovskii pechatnik* 8 (1 March 1925): 4; *Nasha zhizn'*, 5 November 1927; *Biiskii pechatnik*, 4–6.

93. *Istoriia leningradskogo soiuza.*

position, class holds no utility for the historian. In terms of theories of social class, this imprecision can be traced to the fact that Soviet workers, like others, occupied multiple class positions: they were bossed by their superiors and they bossed their inferiors. They possessed multiple assets, or capital: organizational capital in the form of access to state power; educational capital in the form of skill; cultural capital in the ways they organized their daily lives and in the stories they told about themselves and their pasts. But these stories were themselves multivocal: the writings in which printers worked out their identity as workers conveyed multiple meanings and interpretations, producing a heteroglossity that undermined a unified class identity rather than cemented it.[94] In the mid-1920s, Soviet power revealed an unsettling indeterminacy about class identity. Yet at the same time, there can be no doubt that the language of class and a set of identities that revolved around membership in the community of workers continued to structure the way printers wrote and spoke about themselves in society.

94. Reddy, *Money and Liberty in Modern Europe*, 1–33; Wright, "Rethinking, Once Again, the Concept of Class Structure," in Wright, *Debate on Classes*, 269–348; Bourdieu, *Distinction*; Steinberg, *Fighting Words*, 15.

# PART III

## THE TWISTING ROAD TO THE FIRST FIVE-YEAR PLAN, 1927–1930

# CHAPTER 7

## THE INDUSTRY WITHOUT A PLAN

Unemployment and Conflict
in the First Five-Year Plan

*Of course, we know that since October 1917, the boss is a comrade, but it also happens that this very comrade turns obligatorily into "Ivan Ivanych" and loves to inspire fear and trembling when he appears.*

—WORKER-CORRESPONDENT,
AUGUST 1928

In the economic and social history of the Soviet Union, the end of the Civil War and beginning of the New Economic Policy can be clearly dated to the end of 1920 and beginning of 1921. The end of the New Economic Policy is not so easily fixed. The Five-Year Plan was approved in principle as early as 1925, but this plan was intended to be compatible with other elements of a continuing mixed economy. The end came gradually, but increasing administrative direction of the economy led in the winter of 1929-30 to an all-out assault on the resistant peasantry, resulting in forced collectivization, massive expulsions, and resettlement.[1] The state assumed a much more activist role in the economy than it had done during NEP, summoning up new chimeras of class struggle and class enemies and eliminating sources of doubt and opposition, as in the wholesale purge of the trade union leadership. The roots of many of these processes could be ob-

---

1. For an overview, see Siegelbaum, *Soviet State and Society between Revolutions*, 188–203; see also Osokina, *Za fasadom*, chap. 1.

served earlier in the 1920s, but the accumulating tensions of the first decade of the revolutionary experiment all came to a head in 1929 and 1930, resulting in sweeping and massive changes in Communist practice and politics.

The enormity of the structural transformation and social dislocation during the years from 1928 to 1932 has commanded the attention of generations of historians of the Soviet Union. These years have acquired a fixed place in the periodization of Soviet history as the Stalin Revolution, the Cultural Revolution, or the Great Turn. As with any revolution, the causes and interpretations of this change are multiple, complex, and contested. Economic interpretations have centered on the question whether a mixed economy such as NEP was viable, whether for recovery or for growth. The relationship between town and country is crucial in this analysis: could Russia's traditional agrarian economy provide the capital for industrial growth, could the struggling industrial economy provide the consumer goods that peasants would be willing to trade for? These economic questions underpinned many of the theoretical debates among Communists in the 1920s. When a serious grain shortage loomed in 1927, many people concluded that the mixed economy was no longer working, and the time had come for a more aggressive approach to generating capital for industrial expansion.[2]

On the political side of the debate, historians have argued that economic realities mattered less to the Communist Party than maintaining the superiority of the city over the countryside, or that Stalin's maneuvering for political power trumped economic theory. Many historians now believe that NEP as an economic system was flawed but workable, and that the choice to abandon the mixed economy and gradual economic growth represented a political decision on the part of the Communist Party. Here too, however, explanations for these political choices are multiple. The familiar argument about Stalin's maneuvering for power remains persuasive. Some historians cite the importance of a new sense of urgency about economic development prompted by threats from abroad. Others cite a more complicated organizational struggle for control over the direction of the development of socialism. These interpretations have been more recently joined by cultural explanations: Communist ideology may not have predetermined the abandonment of NEP, but Communist political culture predisposed the party to choose voluntarist and authoritarian solutions to the perceived economic crisis. "Class war" remained a fundamental tenet of Communist political culture and provided a ready-made explanation for why the economic recovery had begun to stall. Likewise, Katerina Clark has argued that antimarket attitudes also predisposed the cultural intelligentsia to favor the command system over the market-driven NEP.[3]

2. Carr and Davies, *Foundations*, vol. 1; R. W. Davies, *The Soviet Economy in Turmoil, 1929–1930* (London, 1989); Alexander Erlich, *The Soviet Industrialization Debate, 1924–1928* (Cambridge, Mass., 1960); Stephen F. Cohen, *Bukharin and the Bolshevik Revolution* (New York, 1974); Isaac Deutscher, *Stalin* (New York, 1966); Nove, *Economic History of the U.S.S.R.*
3. Ward, *Russia's Cotton Workers*; Siegelbaum, *Soviet State and Society between Revolutions*;

The experience of the printing industry complicates these explanations, because from its vantage point, there was no great break or great turn. There was also no plan. Rather, the printing industry and the Printers' Union responded to continuing economic difficulties with the same kinds of policies as before: efforts to improve the central direction of the industry and attempts to intensify and accelerate the mechanisms to raise productivity and discipline on the level of the shop floor. As before, workers resisted these mechanisms, and conflict between the center's visions of productivism and printers' defense of their shop floor autonomy remained endemic. Labor relations between red directors and printers continued to be adversarial. The trade union found itself pulled increasingly toward workerism: by defending the interests of its members, it could channel dissent and minimize conflict. The revival of the printing industry by 1930 only reinforced workers' ability to negotiate the conditions of their employment, so long as they did so individually and not collectively. The Menshevik alternative of an independent trade union operating outside state control remained dead and buried, but printers continued to practice the same kind of workerist evasion, accommodation, and resistance they had been practicing since 1918.

## THE PRINTING INDUSTRY AT THE END OF THE NEW ECONOMIC POLICY

By 1927, the industry lay enveloped in a deep economic crisis, whose causes were loudly debated, but everyone recognized that this was a crisis of *socialist* industry: state-owned enterprises produced virtually all printed output by 1928.[4] According to one report, unemployment stood at over 26,000 printers on 1 October 1927, a figure that represented 19.5 percent of union members. The number of employed printers had fallen to 83,000 in October 1928. Printers' wages reflected this crisis. While printers' absolute wages remained at the top of the industrial wage hierarchy from 1925 to March 1928, these wages had risen relatively slowly during these years: their average wages were only 34 percent higher in 1928 than in 1925, placing them in last place among industrial groups in terms of the rate of growth. Figures on output offered a slightly brighter picture: production in the industry in 1927–28 had returned to the level of two years before, and had soared by another 50 percent in 1929. The production of newspapers led the way: the industry had printed 7 million newspapers a day in 1924–25 (up from a prewar figure of 3.5 million). By May 1930, printers were turning out 16.5 million papers a day. But if newspaper output had increased by 57 percent in 1929, production in the industry as a

---

Fitzpatrick, *Education and Social Mobility;* David R. Shearer, *Industry, State, and Society in Stalin's Russia, 1926–1934* (Ithaca, 1996); Hiroaki Kuromiya, *Stalin's Industrial Revolution: Politics and Workers, 1928–1932* (Cambridge, 1988); Sheila Fitzpatrick, *The Cultural Front: Power and Culture in Revolutionary Russia* (Ithaca, 1992); Katerina Clark, *Petersburg: Crucible of Cultural Revolution* (Cambridge, Mass., 1995).

4. Alan M. Ball, *Russia's Last Capitalists: The Nepmen, 1921–1929* (Berkeley, 1987), 148.

whole had risen only 19 percent.[5] These gains in production at a time when the labor force remained stagnant and unemployment high reflected some successes in the drive for productivity, but the unspoken price of productivity gains was the continuing reduction in the labor force.

The tone of discussions about the industry remained gloomy until the end of the decade. Industry and union leaders worried about three serious obstacles to their economic well-being: a continuing shortfall in the supply of printers' ink and paper, excessively high costs of production, and signs that planned investment from the First Five-Year Plan would bypass the printing industry despite its critical need for new presses and typesetting machines. Union officials blamed the poor quality of Soviet ink for raising the cost of printing in 1927: whole press runs had to be repeated because of defective ink, doubling the cost of production. The crisis in the paper industry loomed even larger. Officials spoke of a "paper famine" and anxiously debated solutions. In August 1929, the paper industry was moved from the class of light industry to category A, qualifying it for the highest priority in state investment. But still the paper industry lagged behind its assigned targets.[6]

In the meantime, printing officials sought other ways to reduce their costs of production in order to be able to offer their products—books and office supplies—at a more affordable price for the Soviet consumer. In addition to the well-publicized rationalization campaigns, industry leaders looked to other areas for cost-cutting: eliminating the role of commission agents and other middlemen was a favorite goal and one compatible with the antimarket ethos of socialist industrialists. "Running through all the work of these agents is the red thread of embezzlement, managerial incompetence, loss-making contracts, bribes, swindling, forgery, and more." Reducing the size of unproductive office staffs and trust bureaucracies also found support.[7]

Above all, union and industrial officials sought to position themselves more effectively in the competition for state investment resources. The printing industry was officially classified as light industry, category B in the planning process, but Printers' Union officials sought preferential status as the main conduit of cultural revolution. The party had decided in 1927 that industrialization could not be achieved without culture, reminded a union official in March

5. *Trud*, 21 February 1928, 27 January 1929, 5 May 1930; *Pechatnik* 6 (25 February 1929): 13; wages from VTsSPS data in *Pechatnik* 34 (5 December 1928): 8; GARF f. R-5525, op. 11, d. 1 (stenographic report of Seventh All-Union Congress of Printers' Union, 28 January–7 February 1929); *Izvestiia*, 30 November 1929.

6. *Trud*, 1 February, 26 December, and 29 December 1929, 26 January 1927, 25 March 1930; TsGAMO, f. 699, op. 1, d. 1059 (protocols of Fourth Moscow Guberniia Conference, 1928), ll. 56–79; *Ekonomicheskaia zhizn'*, 29 January and 9 August 1929; *Izvestiia*, 8 February 1929; GARF, f. R-5525, op. 11, d. 1, ll. 21, 129–30; d. 14 (meeting of Printers' Union Central Committee plenum, 29 September 1929), l. 2; *Pechatnik* 31 (20 November 1929): 3; 36 (25 December 1929): 9.

7. *Ekonomicheskaia zhizn'*, 9 August 1927; *Trud*, 10 September 1927, 30 June 1928; *Pechatnik* 27 (30 September 1927): 4–5.

1930, "and we are that culture."[8] It was critically important, therefore, for the industry to speak to the leaders with one voice, to consolidate its activities under one regulatory umbrella, something union leaders had been advocating throughout the NEP period. But as the stakes mounted in this struggle for resources, so did conflicts among union and industry officials about the form this regulatory organization should take.

In principle, union and managerial officials alike favored centralization under a single administrative head, but those who controlled local units resisted ceding their autonomy to any central body, no matter how efficient in principle. Instead of creating one head, attempts to centralize only proliferated the number of supervisory agencies competing to be that head.[9] In 1927, the printing industry found itself accountable to two masters: the Committee on Press Affairs (part of the People's Commissariat of Labor) and the Printing Committee of the Supreme Economic Council (Vesenkha). Union and industry officials argued throughout 1929 about which of the two candidates should assume the role of single administrative center. By November 1929, a commission convened by the Council of People's Commissars (Sovnarkom) concluded that the Committee on Press Affairs should assume all regulatory, planning, and administrative functions, but still the head of Mospoligraf insisted that this committee be subordinated to Vesenkha, his institutional master, rather than Sovnarkom. In December 1929, as the battle for the collective farm was raging in the countryside, a new high-level commission was appointed to study the organization of the industry. At the same time, Vesenkha itself split into factions on the issue of the printing industry. In the thirteenth year of the revolution (as the union journal *Pechatnik* now dated itself), the industry still paid lip service to the principle of centralized management but hung on tenaciously to the practice of local autonomy.

The debate over industrial organization was complicated by the assault within the party on the "right deviation" in the trade unions, an issue that will be considered in more detail in Chapter 8. As something of a compromise, a new All-Russian Association of the Printing Industry emerged in February 1930, a successor to the Vesenkha Printing Committee, whose function consisted of planning rather than management. Partisans of the older committees were reluctant to cooperate; the trusts in Moscow and Leningrad also held back from participating in the new body. Within the union's central committee, the new leadership fought valiantly for a Vesenkha center, while the discredited rightists, Borshchevskii and Rozov among them, sang the praises of decentralized industry. In the end, the goal of the single administrative center remained unattained.[10] As David Shearer has argued about the metal industry in the First

---

8. GARF, f. R-5525, op. 12, d. 15 (meetings of Printers' Union Central Committee presidium, 1930), ll. 63–64.

9. Ibid., op. 18, d. 47 (meetings of bureau of party fraction of Printers' Union Central Committee, 1927).

10. Ibid., op. 11, d. 1, ll. 126–99; d. 14, ll. 2, 9; op. 12, d. 7 (stenographic report of Printers'

Five-Year Plan, the bureaucratic struggle for resources operated independently of high-level political conflicts. Ideological centrists such as Borshchevskii readily reversed their positions in favor of protecting the autonomy and resources of their particular constituencies.[11]

The debate over the organization of the industry always returned to the economic position of printers. The high level of unemployment among printers offered a stark and very human indicator of the extent of the industry's crisis, and it lent urgency to the discussions about industrial organization. Economic recovery brought a reduction in joblessness for skilled printers by 1929, but meanwhile the union's effort to manage the unemployment crisis came to dominate union discussions about the nature and obligations of socialist labor relations.

The number of unemployed printers had stabilized between 1927 and 1929 at about 20 percent of the labor force. For many of those who had lost work, unemployment had been chronic: a March 1928 survey indicated that over half had been out of work longer than one year. Among press feeders, nearly a quarter of the unemployed had been without work for three years or more; in other words, since at least 1925.[12]

When recovery began, only skilled male printers in Moscow and Leningrad initially benefited. Moscow's unemployed level fell from 9,000 workers on 1 July 1927, to 7,200 workers a year later. In Leningrad, where 6,300 printers were out of work on 1 October 1927, this figure had dropped dramatically to 2,740 unemployed by 1 October 1929. Women figured disproportionately among the unemployed, and even more so when the rate began to fall: in Leningrad, women constituted 49 percent of the jobless in 1927 (while representing about one-quarter of the industry's workforce); by 1929, nearly three-quarters of all the unemployed printers in Leningrad were women. In Moscow, women represented about half of the unemployed workers through 1930, although they accounted for only one-third of union members there. Provincial centers also reported much higher levels of unemployment than the two capitals.[13]

---

Union Central Committee plenum, 5–11 February 1930), ll. 57–59; d. 38 (stenographic report of Leningrad Oblast Congress of Paper Makers and Printers, 14–17 February 1930), l. 6; d. 15, ll. 22–25, 63–67; *Trud*, 3 February and 16 April 1929, 27 December 1930; *Ekonomicheskaia zhizn'*, 10 April, 6 July, and 14 August 1929, 26 July 1930; *Izvestiia*, 16 July, 8 August, and 13 December 1929, 28 April 1930; *Pechatnik* 36 (25 December 1927): 3; 31 (20 November 1929): 2–3; 36 (25 December 1929): 9; 6 (1930): inside back cover.

11. Shearer, *Industry, State, and Society in Stalin's Russia*.

12. *Trud*, 10 May 1928; *Pechatnik* 3 (1930): 10. Figures for unemployment in the industry vary from source to source; some factored in the Section of Press Workers, and other errors creep into the reports along the way. *Pechatnik* reported 26,352 unemployed in April 1928, the highest figure on record, but still calculated at 20 percent of the membership (9–10 [25 March 1928]: 11–12). *Trud* reported 23,000 unemployed union members in February 1929 (5 February 1929), compared to *Pechatnik*'s 17,400.

13. *Pechatnik* 30 (22 October 1928): 5; 3 (1930): 10–11; *Otchet leningradskogo oblastnogo otdela 1927–1929*, 50–51; *Trud*, 5 February 1929.

Solving or at least coping with this crisis therefore remained a critical task for the union as the First Five-Year Plan got under way. The industry's high unemployment rate threatened the union's own status within the trade union movement and in industry. For printers themselves, joblessness threatened the very core of their identity as workers. Unemployment, as union members dared to note in 1929, was supposed to be a feature of capitalist economies, not socialist ones.[14] Consequently, the union debated the issue from the very highest levels of authority to every shop floor in the industry. Three kinds of solutions emerged from these discussions. Structural solutions would promote the long-term health of the industry, but they represented a double-edged sword. Industrial revival that would expand the industry would require even greater efficiencies in the printing industry and more productive labor. This was the promise of rationalization, whose goal was to economize on one of the most expensive inputs in the printing process, the wages of labor. Rationalization would also require greater intensity of labor, which might well be resented and resisted by printers on the shop floor. A second set of solutions favored social welfare centered at the point of production, calling for a variety of work-sharing schemes. A third set of solutions were merely palliative, the provision of social welfare and benefits for the unemployed. Each of these approaches, as shall be seen, added new tension to the inherently conflictual relations between socialist managers and socialist workers. And each provided opportunities for printers to assert their sense of values about the place of workers in the republic of labor.

The Printers' Union itself insisted the only permanent solution to the unemployment crisis was to move workers out of the industry altogether. Printers over the age of fifty would be transferred as quickly as possible to state insurance pension schemes. Unemployed printers would be sent to jobs in other industries, their retraining subsidized from union funds. Many of the unemployed pursued this path, but some complained that having completed six months of training for new jobs, they were no more employable than they had been as printers, or that their new skill level and status were significantly lower than those they had enjoyed as printers. At local meetings of the unemployed, a few bold and angry printers offered a different set of structural solutions. Industry itself needed to be reorganized, starting with the introduction of a free press: the Leningrad censor was "worse than tsarist censorship" in hindering production through lengthy delays in approval. According to a worried party account of the meeting in which this issue was raised, the proposal of a free press received not only applause but even two or three votes.[15]

---

14. TsGAMO, f. 4660, op. 1, d. 31 (general meetings of unemployed union members, 1929), ll. 6, 10.

15. *Trud,* 21 February and 3 July 1928; *Pechatnik* 12 (20 April 1928): 5; 9–10 (25 March 1928): 12; 6 (25 February 1929): 13; 33 (23 November 1928): 12; 20 (12 July 1928): 6; GARF, f. R-5525, op. 11, d. 1, l. 222; TsGAMO, f. 4660, op. 1, d. 31, ll. 10, 23, 90, 900b.; d. 129 (general meetings of unemployed union members, 1930), l. 66; TsGAIPD SPb, f. 435, op. 1, d. 68 (meetings of bureau of party fraction of Leningrad union, 1927), l. 99.

Far more popular than retraining for new occupations were proposals by employed and unemployed alike to share the work they had. In these discussions, fairness and equity came to dominate the agenda. In 1926 the Leningrad union had already begun to shorten the workweek and to extend workers' vacations by adding unpaid leave. Leningrad printers endorsed the measure. "They prefer to take two days off at their own expense rather than throw their comrades out of the enterprise and onto the street." Solidarity acquired real meaning in this context: favored printers—those with jobs—willingly shared with those who had none. Industrial managers disapproved of job sharing and tried to argue that workers themselves opposed cutting their own income in order to spread work around. To this objection an unemployed worker at the union's 1926 congress retorted, "I don't know what factory he represents, but all the workers in my shop favor shortening the workweek and would even shorten the workday instead of the week." Workers also pressed for an elimination of overtime and a return to time pay instead of piece rates. While some workers could use piece rates to earn big rubles, their gain meant misery for the unemployed. Workers also denounced the practice of hiring temporary workers from the labor exchange rather than providing full-time work and benefits to the workers employed.[16]

Other proposals for work sharing produced a different kind of conflict, among workers themselves. Many in the industry felt that families should also share work. Although the term itself does not appear, the principle of the family wage received significant support, as it did under different circumstances in the postwar United States.[17] Printers expressed widespread support for the practice of laying off family members (particularly women) when one was already employed. This notion, however, ran counter to other principles of socialist equality, and many union voices still defended a woman's absolute right to work. Work in production liberates women, claimed a woman activist at a union congress in 1928: women should not have to be dependent on men, "since there is not one woman who is guaranteed against being left alone, without the help of a man or a husband." A male union official concurred: "There's no place in this worker-peasant state for women to be regarded as some lower form of existence. It's nobody's business whether she has a husband or not."[18]

---

16. *Pechatnik* 40 (2 October 1926): 2; 11 (13 March 1926): 9; GARF, f. R-5525, op. 8, d. 1 (stenographic report of Sixth All-Union Congress of Printers' Union, 27 November–4 December 1926), ll. 161–76; op. 9, d. 131 (general meetings of unemployed union members, 1927), l. 24; TsGAMO, f. 699, op. 1, d. 787 (protocols of the Third Moscow Guberniia Union Conference, October 1926), l. 49; d. 1110 (meetings of unemployed union members—Section of Press Workers, 1928), ll. 11, 15.

17. See Martha May, "The Historical Problem of the Family Wage: The Ford Motor Company and the Five-Dollar Day," *Feminist Studies* 8 (Summer 1982): 399–424; Alice Kessler-Harris, "Gender Ideology in Historical Reconstruction: A Case Study from the 1930s," *Gender and History* 1 (Spring 1989): 31–49; Lawrence B. Glickman, *A Living Wage: American Workers and the Making of a Consumer Society* (Ithaca, 1997).

18. *Moskovskii pechatnik* 12 (29 October 1923): 24; GARF, f. R-5525, op. 10, d. 41 (protocols

Other voices, however, including many female ones, insisted that fairness should be based on the needs of families, and in most cases, women should step aside. There were many printers who echoed the sentiment of one Dudin at a meeting of Leningrad unemployed in 1927: lay off the wives whose husbands work. A meeting of unemployed Leningrad printers in January 1927 urged the union to fire duplicate wage earners, so-called doubles (*dvoiniki*). At a similar meeting in Moscow a year later, a woman worker noted that at the First Model plant, whole families were employed; most of the them should be laid off and replaced by the unemployed. Other women wanted to differentiate between women workers who could be supported by their husbands and those who themselves were the sole support of their children, or single women who were "desperately needy."[19]

These voices demanded fairness, even though many recognized that no single solution would be fair to all. The state's own vision of fairness privileged bureaucratic solutions, the creation of institutions that would monitor the unemployed and apply clear rules for assigning them to jobs that became available. As early as 1918, the Soviet government had delegated the responsibility for allocating jobs to labor exchanges that functioned under local trade union councils. The exchanges monitored the flow of unemployment, paid benefits, and assigned workers to jobs in a rational and orderly way. In the biggest cities, exchange sections served particular industrial trade unions. Moscow printers registered at the exchange on Rakhmanovskii Alley in central Moscow, and unemployment in the industry soon became known as the "Rakhmanovskii trust." Short stories in the union journal painted baleful vignettes of life with the trust, where "anthill" became the favorite metaphor for the chaotic and crowded labor exchange office. Here each day toward noon, the head of the section would appear with his packet of openings, and lucky printers whose skills met the required qualifications would be sent to work for a day, a week, or with luck permanently. To remain eligible for these openings, printers had to stay registered with the exchange and be tested from time to time on the level of their skills. The common complaint of the long-term unemployed, especially women and young men, was that their recently learned skills were atrophying from disuse. To take a job outside the industry, however temporary, was to lose one's place in the queue for the jobs in printing; but to refuse an offer of temporary work was also to risk disqualification.[20]

---

of oblast congresses, K–N, 1928), ll. 71, 73. For further discussion, see Koenker, "Men against Women," 1457–60.

19. GARF, f. R-5525, op. 9, d. 131, ll. 24, 36; op. 10, d. 41, ll. 65, 72; TsGA SPb, f. 4804, op. 11, d. 158 (meetings of Leningrad unemployed, 1926–29); TsGAIPD SPb, f. 435, op. 1, d. 74 (meetings of bureau of party fraction of Leningrad union, 1929); TsGAMO, f. 4660, op. 1, d. 31, ll. 5, 6, 9.

20. Rogachevskaia, *Likvidatsiia bezrabotitsy,* 68; *Pechatnik* 4 (15 February 1924): 6; 7 (15 April 1924): 10; 25 (15 November 1925): 9; 23 (5 June 1926): 1; 9 (25 March 1927): 10; 18 (25 June 1927): 8; 28 (10 October 1927): 16; 36 (25 December 1927): 12; 22 (3 August 1928): 17;

As unemployment leveled off in 1928 and 1929, new arguments about fairness and equity emerged with respect to the labor exchanges. Now that print shops were hiring again, workers bitterly charged that managers and exchange officials used their positions to send their friends and family to places in the industry. Vladislav Perkovskii explained how favoritism worked: An enterprise sent an order for a worker who was impossible to find. "We need a proofreader who knows English, Armenian, and Tibetan." If no such specialist existed, the enterprise could hire whomever it liked, bypassing the labor exchange queue. *Pechatnik* tended to publicize abuses by enterprises in which white-collar employees benefited from favoritism: this target resonated with the prevailing language of class struggle and the dangers of the bourgeoisie.[21] In private meetings, however, the target of workers' anger was much closer to home. The labor exchange chief was said to favor women workers who dressed attractively. Communist Party members emerged in these discussions as some of the chief practitioners of nepotism and favoritism, and unemployed workers resented the fact that party members received favorable treatment in both jobs and assignments for retraining. At Pechatnyi Dvor, only seven compositors were working full-time by 1929; all were members of the Communist Party. When an unemployed comrade asked one of them how he managed to get such a position, the other replied, "You join the party, you fool, and then you're taken on full-time."[22]

The laments of the unemployed extended as well to the paltry benefits they received. Those who registered as unemployed union members on the labor exchange received small subsidies through social insurance for up to twenty-seven months, with extra amounts for dependents. In October 1927, the average unemployed printer could count on a payment of just under 17 rubles, at a time when the average monthly wage in the industry was nearing 91 rubles. As one printer bitterly pointed out, "You might be able to feed a puppy on this, but not a family." The unemployed were also eligible for travel expenses to look for work in other cities and for free abortions (a concession, perhaps, to the large number of women among the unemployed), but they were cut off from other benefits subsidized by the union: free dental care, free eyeglasses, concert and theater tickets, passes to rest homes and spas.[23]

---

*Moskovskii pechatnik* 12 (29 October 1923): 10; 32 (15 October 1924): 6; 12 (29 March 1925): 1; TsGAMO, f. 699, op. 1, d. 1110, ll. 4, 9, 16; f. 4660, op. 1, d. 31, l. 60; GARF, f. R-5525, op. 12, d. 38; op. 10, d. 41, l. 72; TsGA SPb, f. 4804, op. 12, d. 4 (meetings of Leningrad conferences and union activists, April 1928–December 1929).

21. TsGAMO, f. 4660, op. 1, d. 31, l. 6; *Pechatnik* 18 (22 June 1928): 12; 22 (12 August 1929): 18; 17 (12 June 1928): 14; 12–13 (1930): 19. An exception is *Pechatnik* 3 (22 January 1928): 21.

22. TsGAMO, f. 699, op. 1, d. 1059, ll. 25, 30; d. 1110, l. 23; f. 4660, op. 1, d. 31, ll. 23, 520b., 90, 90ob., 80, 83; TsGA SPb, f. 4804, op. 11, d. 158, l. 87; GARF, f. R-5525, op. 11, d. 1, l. 225; TsGAIPD SPb, f. 435, op. 1, d. 74, l. 33ob.

23. *Pechatnik* 9 (25 March 1927): 5; 12 (20 April 1928): 4; 34 (5 December 1928): 8; *Trud*, 10 May 1928; TsGAMO, f. 699, op. 1, d. 787, l. 50; d. 1110, ll. 4, 12, 14; f. 4660, op. 1, d. 31, ll. 4, 5, 7, 11, 12, 22, 61; d. 129, l. 11; GARF, f. R-5525, op. 9, d. 131, l. 22; op. 11, d. 1, ll. 221–22.

The unemployment crisis threatened every worker in the industry, whether among the 80 percent with jobs or the 20 percent without. Even those with work had been working reduced hours for much of the second half of the 1920s, and they knew that their jobs were far from secure. It was not enough to be just a good worker in 1928, or even a male head of household: it was even better to have a few well-placed friends, to be a member of the Communist Party, and to keep your mouth shut at political meetings. Competition for the scarce resource of work highlighted continuing conflicts in socialist society: between deserving proletarians and white-collar employees and bureaucrats who constructed a world of protectionism and nepotism; between suffering proletarians and cost-conscious managers who took advantage of the reserve army of the unemployed to fire expensive workers and replace them with cheap temporary workers; between the rank and file and the union leadership who seemed to ignore the suffering of the unemployed; and between the nonparty printers and the Communists, who occupied the positions that most oppressed the unemployed. The discourse of unemployment provided fuel for both the political struggles within the union at the end of the 1920s and printers' own sense of class identity, as the next two chapters will show.

## THE EMERGENCE OF PLANNING

Union and industry officials hoped to solve the industrial crisis through the application of planning and central regulation, which would redress the industry's lack of capital investment, the shortages of raw materials, and the inefficiencies of its publishing branches. But many of the solutions embedded in the planning game targeted deficiencies that arose from within the workforce: lack of discipline, waste, incompetence, and inefficiency. Complementary to the planning process itself, with its short- and long-term targets and goals, therefore, came a series of programs and campaigns that aimed to transform the behavior of the Soviet worker. Discipline rather than planning became the hallmark of the First Five-Year Plan in the printing industry. At the level of the shop floor, however, workers and enterprises often managed to resist the orders issued from above. Increased efforts at centralization and command were met by an intensified workerism among printers and union officials alike.

The First Five-Year Plan targeted heavy industry and construction as its main goals for development. Consumer goods and services, while included in the planning process, received much lower priority and hence much less investment. Secondary industries such as printing not only received minimal new investment, it turns out, but scarcely participated in the planning process at all. Much ink was spilled in the union press about the plan for the printing industry, but in fact the industry had no plan. In place of an overall blueprint for the development of the industry, individual units, from the Mospoligraf trust to print shops belonging to individual agencies, elaborated sets of targets, or control figures, that became labeled as "plans." The two big regulators of the industry, the Committee on Press Affairs and the Printing Committee of Vesenkha, each worked out its own plan for the industry, but as the trade union newspaper *Trud* pointed out, two plans in the industry meant no plan.[24]

The rivals for printers' hegemony grandly announced their goals in the press. Five agencies offered wildly disparate targets for growth and estimates for investment to make it happen. The Committee on Press Affairs first called for a capital investment of 30 million rubles over five years, then revised the estimate to 400 million two years later. A special commission appointed to resolve the organizational problems in the industry recommended a target increase in production that was three times higher than Vesenkha's independent proposal. Each "plan" came with equally fanciful estimates of the labor and capital requirements to meet its targets. Delegates to the 1929 All-Union Congress of the Printers' Union charged that such figures were pulled out of the air, and when the Vesenkha administrator was asked where his figures had come from, he could not say.[25]

More specific but just as dubious were annual and monthly targets for production. Individual enterprises worked out goals for gross output, productivity, size of the wage bill, and reducing costs. For example, Mospoligraf pledged that in 1929 it would increase output by 21.3 percent, increase output per worker by 17.7 percent, and lower costs by 5.4 percent. Other targets included number of printed sheets, number of letters set in type, percentage of idle presses, and rate of absenteeism. None of these goals could be taken wholly at face value, nor could reports of their fulfillment. Delegates to the February 1930 Central Committee plenum admitted that the control figures and performance statistics were inflated. At the *Pravda* print shop, the chairman of the production commission could not report on the success of the plan because he had lost it.[26] In short, the industrial plan (*promfinplan*) was just another of a series of so-called scientific methods for rationalizing production that in fact relied on enthusiasm, exhortation, political pressure, and lies.

The Russian-born economist Wassily Leontief would win a Nobel Prize in economics for developing the theory that underlay the scientific basis of central planning. What distinguished the "plan" of the First Five-Year Plan, however, was not science but the rapidity and intensity of campaigns to stimulate productivity and output, of which the "plan" was only one among many. Understanding how workers in the printing industry coped with the acceleration of the First Five-Year Plan period requires us to distinguish the barrage of rationalization and productivity schemes from the way this assault was weathered on the shop floor. Printers exerted their workerist defense of shop floor autonomy by resisting and subverting each new scheme to advance production.

24. *Pechatnik* 17 (12 June 1928): 5; *Trud*, 1 February 1929, 24 March 1930; *Ekonomicheskaia zhizn'*, 14 August 1929.
25. *Izvestiia*, 30 September 1928, 28 April 1930; *Trud*, 3 February and 19 May 1929, 5 May and 26 August 1930; *Ekonomicheskaia zhizn'*, 14 August 1929, 7 May 1930.
26. *Pechatnik* 28 (14 October 1929): 9; 17 (12 June 1928): 5; 6 (1930): 9–11; GARF, f. R-5525, op. 12, d. 7, l. 33.

A number of systems to spur productivity had already been implemented earlier in the 1920s. Production conferences, bringing together workers and management for the purpose of solving production problems, continued to serve as the "headquarters" of the industrial project, although without much effectiveness, as has been seen. Then in December 1928, the newspaper *Pravda* launched a "review" (*smotr*) of production conferences, whose purpose was to mobilize support for the conferences among the workforce. Spurred by promises of prizes for the best reviews, special commissions busily hammered together suggestion boxes and passed out questionnaires asking their comrades: "What did you do in the production conference?" and "Why don't you belong to a production commission?" In Voronezh, results were mixed: the Kommuna print shop launched its review with suggestion boxes, departmental discussions, and articles in the factory newspaper; by January, this effort had yielded ninety-nine suggestions. But at the neighboring Okrano print shop, the review went perfunctorily, basically ignored by an overworked cadre of activists. The review commission at Kommuna blamed the failures of the production commissions on lack of interest in them by plant managers and factory committees alike.[27]

The review may have highlighted the problems of the production commissions, but it did not solve them. Workers continued to complain that management paid no attention to their suggestions for cost-saving modifications; rather their proposals "marinated" in the offices of the administration. Consequently, in the middle of 1930, VTsSPS jettisoned the seven-year-old experiment in participatory production planning and replaced the production commissions with—production *conferences,* which would be based on a truly voluntary principle, in which a paid staff member would organize the "volunteer" activists.[28] The history of all the prior efforts to engage workers in these processes, whether mobilized from above or motivated by local enthusiasm, suggests that this reform would merely pour old wine into new bottles, a vintage that had been none too potable even when new.

Several other mechanisms also promoted worker participation in solving the problems of production. Beginning in 1927, trade unions had encouraged ambitious workers to invent new production processes by setting up bonus funds within enterprises for rewarding innovation. The road to fame and reward, however, was a rocky one. *Pechatnik* duly reported the development of new methods for printing labels, for better lighting systems, and for safety switches to stop presses. But more often, inventors, like production commissions, found their ideas ignored by management and scorned by their fellow workers as well.

27. *Pechatnik* 11 (17 April 1927): 15; 17 (15 June 1927): 11; 23 (15 August 1927): 7; 7–8 (8 March 1928): 17; 12 (20 April 1928): 10; 15 (22 May 1928): 8; 5 (1 October 1928): 1; 34 (5 December 1928): 18; 35 (18 December 1928): 15; 36 (25 December 1928): 2; 2 (20 January 1929): 16; 4–5 (15 February 1929): 19; 6 (25 February 1929): 19; 7 (12 March 1929): 9; 8 (25 March 1929): 8, 12; 9 (30 March 1929): 2–3; 11 (20 April 1929): 16; 2 (1930) 15 (1930); *Pechatnyi dvor,* 8 August 1928.

28. *Pechatnik* 2 (1930): 10; 16 (1930): 8; 23–24 (1930): 2, 5; 15 (1930): 11.

In a *Pechatnik* feuilleton, one Dobrikov ("Good Guy") developed a new idea for a reverse transfer, but when he proposed his plan at a production conference, his envious fellow workers either denied its utility or claimed that someone other than Dobrikov had come up with the idea. Poor Dobrikov lost interest and hope in production, took to drink, and had to suffer the teasing of his comrades: "Hey, what have you invented lately?"[29] While the topic of worker invention would remain on the production agenda, stories such as this one suggest that many workers resisted this effort to transform the pace and culture of the shop floor.

Production contests (*konkursy*) emerged at about the same time as still another mechanism for promoting workers' enthusiasm and engaging them in the work of rationalizing the production process. Contests had been a fixture on the Soviet scene since the early 1920s, but like many other production schemes, their use began to escalate in 1927. First, amidst great fanfare, came local contests for the best apprentice. At a time when the union had stopped taking on new apprentices altogether, such contests might have been intended to raise the morale of those who remained in training and whose future job prospects still looked bleak. Throughout that year and across the country, local unions mounted similar contests for best typesetter, best female typesetter, and best hand typesetter. Local contests, however, began to be marked by signs of torpor and resistance. A contest at the Sokolova print shop in 1928 enjoyed popularity among the workers, but also summoned fears that such events would eventually raise production norms. "You go to the contest, show some speed, and they'll just add it to your norm," said Leningrad printers. And then there was the contest for "long-suffering," which perhaps indicated popular impatience with the ubiquity of contests. In this case, the event took place at a six-and-a-half-hour all-city union conference, "imprisonment in strict isolation without amnesty."[30]

The grand campaign to rationalize industry took a great leap forward in October 1927 with the promise by the Central Executive Committee of Soviets of a gift package of benefits to honor the achievements of ten years of revolution: the construction of more housing for workers, debt relief for peasants, old-age pensions, and the end of the death penalty, among other things. The first item on the list was a seven-hour workday with no reduction in pay. Ostensibly a marker of the success of the revolutionary project, this highly publicized new policy was surely part of a political maneuver to co-opt the increasingly vocal opposition to the party line. Autumn 1927 marked the climaxes of several left oppositions, including that of Lev Trotskii, and these movements received significant support among industrial workers fed up with their stagnating eco-

---

29. *Pechatnik* 15 (22 May 1928): 17; 10 (7 April 1927): 17; 19 (5 July 1928): 16; 14 (1930): 15.
30. *Iskry*, May 1927; *Pechatnik* 10 (7 April 1927): 10; 14 (15 May 1927): 14, 15, 22; 17 (15 June 1927): 14; 9–10 (25 March 1928): 21; 11 (8 April 1928): 6, 12–13; 15 (22 May 1928): 5, 15; 17 (12 June 1928): 23; 31 (1 November 1928): 21; *Ekonomicheskaia zhizn'*, 22 April 1928.

nomic positions.³¹ Planners also envisioned that the seven-hour workday would facilitate the introduction of second and third shifts in industry. But fundamentally, the seven-hour day offered workers a false bargain: it could be implemented only after enterprises demonstrated they could maintain and even increase productivity. The seven-hour day in printing meant greater efficiencies and intensity at work as payment for the extra hour of rest.³²

With the seven-hour workday as the radiant goal, industry experts embarked yet again on campaigns to organize work more rationally and scientifically. At the turn of the century throughout the industrial world, the stopwatch symbolized the efforts of the scientific managers championed by Frederick W. Taylor. Now photography joined the stopwatch as a key tool of the rationalizing trade. Rationalizing work began at the First Model Print Shop in autumn 1927 with a photographic record of the workday on every machine. By September 1928, the Pechatnyi Dvor print shop reported that all production processes had been photographed, and 70 percent of the binding and hand typesetting departments had been assessed by time-and-motion study. Armed with these measurements, rationalizers could determine how to revise production processes to make them more efficient. At Leningrad's Second Transpechat' print shop, for example, rationalizers learned that workers spent less than half their workday in actual production. In the typesetting department, printers spent only 49 percent of their day in setting type and 6 percent in resting and smoking. In the press department, only 35 percent of the workday was spent on actual press work.³³

The scientific data from the time-and-motion process would also assist in establishing scientific norms for output and allocation of labor. Artisans were accustomed to setting norms approximately, *na glaz* (by eye): this system allowed room for individual workers to haggle over their norms in order to increase bonuses for overfulfillment.³⁴ For their part, however, workers worried about the effect on their own daily practices: when the man with the watch showed up, should they devote maximum energy to their task or try to stretch their work out? Would norms be based on maximum or average rates? A feuilleton concluded that photography came courtesy of the "Rakhmanovskii trust." Those that did not shape up would find themselves clients there; and if all work-

---

31. *Direktivy KPSS*, vol. 1, 744–53; for the oppositions in the printing industry, see Chapter 8. Also see Catherine Merridale, *Moscow Politics and the Rise of Stalin: The Communist Party in the Capital* (London, 1990), chap. 1; Isaac Deutscher, *The Prophet Unarmed: Trotsky, 1921–1929* (New York, 1959), chap. 5; Daniels, *Conscience of the Revolution*.

32. *Ekonomicheskaia zhizn'*, 26 November 1927; *Pechatnik* 1 (1 January 1928): 7; 9–10 (25 March 1928): 10; Carr and Davies, *Foundations*, 1 (2): 495–99; Ward, *Russia's Cotton Workers*, 204–9; Chase, *Workers, Society, and the Soviet State*, 243–46.

33. *Trud*, 2 December 1927; *Pechatnik* 24–25 (1 September 1928): 21; 28–29 (12 October 1928): 19.

34. *Pechatnik* 19 (5 July 1928): 15; 9–10 (25 March 1928): 13; 20 (12 July 1928): 10; 21 (31 July 1929): 17. See also Lewis H. Siegelbaum, "Soviet Norm Determination in Theory and Practice, 1917–1941," *Soviet Studies* 36 (1984): 45–68.

ers submitted to the new norms, many of them would also become redundant in the new streamlined printing industry. Printers generally resisted the new methods. Workers at the Sixteenth shop did not trust the norm-determination process, claiming the men who timed their motions based their norms on the work of only a single model worker or that they noticed only the major elements of a job and not all the minor ones.[35]

Nothing exposed the frailty of the scientific norm process as much as the "match" incident at the Twelfth Mospoligraf print shop in Moscow. Workers and management here had been negotiating long and fruitlessly over new technical norms. At long last, only one conflict remained to be resolved: how much time should be allotted for washing colored ink off rollers? This was a task the shop would seldom if ever have to confront. After a further impasse, the union mediator Golov came up with a brilliant idea. As he recounted to the union's party fraction, he said, "The devil with it. Let's decide this five-minute disagreement by matches." Workers and management would draw matches, and the new norm would be set by the side that drew the longer match. The workers' side won, but the incident created a furor in the party and the trade union. The union presidium ruled that Golov's behavior was "completely impermissible" and dismissed him from his post.[36] Production norms, however individually trivial, were far too important to be decided by lot.

An intense campaign to emphasize workplace discipline accompanied the time-and-motion campaign. Despite the best efforts of the Taylorists, rationalization in the industry could not proceed without the participation and support of the workers themselves. Absenteeism and tardiness were endemic in Russian and Soviet print shops, but managers proved reluctant to deal harshly with disciplinary cases, even when the law stipulated that anyone absent for more than three days should be fired. Rates and conflict commissions gave second, third, and fourth chances to workers who were guilty of these infractions; foremen took it for granted that the workday began ten to fifteen minutes after the announced time, and that the quitting process also took a quarter hour or more. The link between productivity and the seven-hour workday drew new attention to these chronic problems, and *Pechatnik* launched a massive assault on worker indiscipline in its pages in March and April 1929, at a time when enterprises were still trying to reorganize work in order to qualify for the shorter workday. Now for the first time, printers' treasured practices of horseplay and teasing—*zvon*—came under official fire. If at one time zvon had served to chide a bad

---

35. *Pechatnik* 15 (22 May 1928): 30–31; 19 (5 July 1928): 15; 11 (20 April 1929): 11; 21 (31 July 1929): 17; 25–26 (11 September 1929): 4.

36. *Trud*, 15 August 1929; *Pechatnik* 24 (31 August 1929): 14; GARF, f. R-5525, op. 18, d. 51 (meetings of bureau of fraction of Printers' Union Central Committee, 1929); TsGAMO, f. 4660, op. 1, d. 5 (conferences and meetings in Moscow print shops to elect delegates to First Oblast Congress, 1929), l. 20b; GARF, f. R-5525, op. 11, d. 17 (meetings of Printers' Union Central Committee presidium, 1929), l. 180. The incident would also be used against Borshchevskii in the purge of the rightists later that year (op. 18, d. 51).

worker into improving his work, under socialism zvon seemed too similar to the bantering and insults of the street traders and too often led to fistfights and other breakdowns in factory discipline. The tsarist print shop may have been a marketplace of swearing and insult competitions, argued activists, but the Soviet print shop would be a temple of silence.[37]

Yet despite this noisy campaign to raise worker discipline, bad behavior continued. By 1929 and into 1930, all indicators suggested that absenteeism and lateness had continued to rise, despite punitive legal measures, despite the exhortation of union and party officials, and despite the bargain of the seven-hour workday. The combination of the leisurely pace of traditional work culture and the turnaround in the demand for skilled printing workers seriously undermined the regime's efforts to promote efficiency in the workplace. If we reprimand our workers for drinking on the job, admitted one factory committee chairman, they will just move to another workplace. There remained also an undercurrent of overt resistance to this new work ethic. One Leningrad print shop manager who tried to punish his workers for their indiscipline found himself assaulted late at night by those workers. And the union's central committee discussed in February 1930 the political meaning of zvon that was aimed against "leading workers who have voluntarily reduced their wages and actively participated in socialist emulation."[38] Trade union culture the world over frowns upon "tall poppies" who stand out from the others as well as the "strikebreakers" who cooperate with management. Whether the offender was the Voronezh union leader Melamed or a stalwart of socialist competition, the rank and file in the printing industry found ways to reject this behavior.

The enduring penchant for contests and competitions took a new turn with the inauguration of the "socialist emulation" (*sotsialisticheskoe sorevnovanie*) campaign in the spring of 1929. Inspired by V. I. Lenin and adopted by Komsomol activists, the emulation project in the printing industry was a strictly top-down affair, as union officials passed along central trade union directives to their membership. Workshops and enterprises were now exhorted to compete with one another to reach the goals of the rationalization effort: lower costs, higher productivity, more proletarian discipline, less absenteeism, less waste.[39] In the initial wave of reported enthusiasm, enterprises issued challenges to one another. Early in the campaign, the Leningrad print shop Pechatnyi Dvor challenged its Moscow counterpart, First Model, to a competition. The winner would be the enterprise that best fulfilled the promises of the contest, which in-

37. TsGAMO, f. 4660, op. 1, d. 120 (protocols of Second Moscow Oblast Congress, 13–15 December 1930, pt. 1), l. 65ob.; *Zorkii glaz*, 8 March 1929; *Pechatnik* 28–29 (12 October 1928): 38; 1 (1 January 1929): 38; 8 (25 March 1929): 13; 9 (30 March 1929): 7; 10 (10 April 1929): 11; 11 (20 April 1929): 9; 13 (17 May 1929): 19; 16 (14 June 1929): 11.

38. TsGAMO, f. 4660, op. 1, d. 120, l. 66; GARF, f. R-5525, op. 12, d. 7, l. 11; *Pechatnik* 15 (22 May 1928): 10; 27 (25 September 1929): 4.

39. The socialist emulation campaign was launched in an editorial in *Pechatnik* 11 (20 April 1929): 1. See Siegelbaum, *Stakhanovism*, 40–41.

cluded increasing their output by 10 percent over that stipulated in the plan, lowering production costs by 12 percent instead of the planned 8.8 percent, and reducing stoppages by 50 percent. Through these efforts, the contestants pledged to save the enterprise 75,000 rubles in the next seven months. The initial challenge received great fanfare, with multiple articles not only in the union journal, *Pechatnik*, but also in the daily national press. Soon after, Leningrad's Sokolova print shop entered into a similar agreement with Moscow's Krasnyi Proletarii, with even more ambitious goals. Not to be outdone, enterprises all across the country joined the campaign, some even throwing their challenges out beyond the ranks of the industry. The Dunaev lithographic plant in Moscow challenged a military unit to a friendly competition, although they lacked common points on which to measure success. The military man said, "Your job is to raise productivity, lower costs, improve quality. Our job is to improve our military preparation, raise our political literacy, and strengthen the defense of the country. Whoever does a better job will be the winner."[40]

The leading instruments for these emulation exercises became shock workers and shock brigades, volunteers who pledged personally to fulfill the requirements of the emulation agreement and to set a positive example for their more sluggardly comrades. From shock brigades came shock departments, and then the Iskra Revoliutsii print shop in Moscow became the first to claim the honor of "shock enterprise" for its efforts in the emulation campaign. But despite the publicity generated by the press and by an All-Union Congress of Shock Workers in November 1929, the excitement quickly subsided, as it so often did in the course of these campaigns.[41] Rank-and-file workers looked skeptically on the whole project: at First Model, "Some groups of politically backward workers say that this is not socialist emulation, but compulsion." By late summer, the correspondent from First Model admitted the emulation campaign had slowed to a snail's pace. The total number of shock workers at Pechatnyi Dvor by December 1929 was a mere twelve; Krasnyi Proletarii boasted 950 shock workers, but they existed only on paper. Labor discipline was worse now than before: workers arrived late, they took hours off for smoke breaks, and they wasted time in endless conversations. *Pechatnik*'s editors repeatedly urged the two enterprises to provide reports of concrete results from the competition, to no avail. In December the First Model factory committee reviewed the competition, acknowledged they had failed, and gave notice that they would start the contest again.[42]

40. *Pechatnik* 12 (20 April 1929): 2; 13 (17 May 1929): 3; 14–15 (31 May 1929): 4; 16 (14 June 1929): 7; 17 (23 June 1929): 5; 24 (31 August 1929): 11; *Pravda*, 21 April 1929; *Trud*, 23 April 1929; *Izvestiia*, 23 April 1929; *Ekonomicheskaia zhizn'*, 23 April 1929; *Leningradskaia pravda*, 12 May 1929.

41. GARF, f. R-5525, op. 11, d. 12 (meeting of Printers' Union Central Committee plenum, 20 June 1929), ll. 4–400b.; *Pechatnik* 10 (10 April 1929): 11; 17 (23 June 1929): 3; 19 (13 July 1929): 7; 4 (1930): 4–6; 7–8 (1930): 9.

42. GARF, f. R-5525, op. 11, d. 12, l. 6; *Pechatnik* 19 (13 July 1929): 7; 23 (20 August 1929): 6; 28 (14 October 1929): 11; 35 (15 December 1929): 24; 4 (1930): 5.

Elsewhere, too, the emulation campaign quickly fell by the wayside. The contest between Sokolova and Krasnyi Proletarii foundered in the face of the "complete passivity of party members and union activists." The Sixteenth Print Shop's agreement with Moscow's Thirteenth State Print Shop generally consisted of such empty slogans as "Shame on absentees," but it had a more destructive side as well. The Sixteenth's factory committee chairman personally persuaded one press worker, Volodin, to work alone on two presses as his contribution to the contest. But Volodin, it turned out, was a habitual drunk; he was drunk when he agreed to the terms of the contest and he was drunk when he attempted to carry out his promise, ruining 5,000 printed sheets in the process.[43] The balance sheet on socialist emulation by 1930 was printed in the stark black of failure: at the *Leningradskaia pravda* shop, productivity actually fell. Absenteeism was rising at the Sixteenth. Cases of outright and bold resistance reinforced these signs of passive noncooperation with the socialist emulation campaign. As usual, opposition was labeled "backward" and "unconscious" by union leaders, but the signs of resistance were unmistakable. The so-called backward workers were calling socialist emulation "a new form of exploitation of workers. The Trotskyists say it's merely a new campaign." Workers refused to participate in the competition because it was compulsory and artificial.[44]

In any event, by 1929 the "continual workweek" had become the new darling of the rationalization campaign. Under this scheme, machines would never rest: workers would work four days out of every five, with rest days falling throughout the seven-day calendar week. The Printers' Union again announced its plans to comply and promised to implement the five-day week in its largest plants by the end of the 1929–30 fiscal year. Workers would be divided into five groups, each with its own day off. At the same time, union leaders warned that the continual workweek would not solve the industry's most critical problems, which were not underutilization of machinery but a shortage of paper.[45] Increasingly, while paying lip service to the need to rationalize and improve individuals' discipline, the union was blaming outside forces for its economic woes.

The pattern by now should be painfully clear. A new campaign would be launched from above and officially embraced by the union and workers. Worker-correspondents were cued to write articles extolling the success of the campaign in their enterprises. The rank and file, from day laborer to factory

---

43. TsGAMO, f. 4660, op. 1, d. 51 (report on work of factory committee at Krasnyi Proletarii for September–December 1929), l. 10; *Pechatnik* 22 (12 August 1929): 5; 27 (25 September 1929): 3; 34 (5 December 1929): 19; *Nasha zhizn'*, 7 November 1929.

44. *Pechatnyi dvor*, 1 October 1930; GARF, f. R-5525, op. 11, d. 12, l. 5; *Pechatnik* 17 (23 June 1929): 9, for evidence of more Trotskyist opposition; 18 (30 June 1929): 5; 27 (25 September 1929): 9; 1 (1930): 11; 17–18 (1930): 13.

45. GARF, f. R-5525, op. 11, d. 17, ll. 168, 186ob.; *Pechatnik* 22 (12 August 1929): 1; 29–30 (31 October 1929): 20–21; Davies, *Soviet Economy in Turmoil*, 84–86.

committee chairman, paid little attention to the campaign, and it quickly lost the small bit of momentum it had acquired with its inauguration. Yet still the cheerleaders of rationalization pressed forward. A new variant of the emulation movement emerged in 1930 as the "public tugboat" (*obshchestvennyi buksir*). Printers knew about tugboats: this was the term given to wives who tried to haul their husbands home on payday before they had a chance to drink away their earnings. Now exemplary enterprises were called upon to serve as tugboats for those who lagged behind, to pull them forward to social responsibility and plan fulfillment.[46]

Finally, the Printers' Union in the Belorussian city of Gomel' proposed a new scheme to marry military methods to rationalization, echoes of Trotskii's plan to militarize labor in 1920. The Gomel' printers called their scheme a "production maneuver," declaring a ten-day "assault" on their target figures in September 1930. The old factory troika of trade union, party, and management leaders transformed themselves into a "headquarters" of the maneuver. Every worker completed a daily report accounting for that day's production, problems, and innovations. "Spies" roamed the workshops, reporting on defects such as an empty type case that stood in the way of compositors. The canteen was reorganized to provide hot breakfasts without queues. At the end of the "maneuver," the plan had been overfulfilled by 108 percent, 31 presses were repaired, and 5 more newly reoutfitted. The central union newspaper *Trud* championed the event with long and detailed reports from the front, although *Rabochaia gazeta* wrote critically about the episode, saying the Gomel' printers were just "playing at soldiers." The Printers' Union central leadership took a cautious approach, first criticizing the use of spies and military orders, but eventually recommending that the scheme be applied throughout the industry. Here as in other incidents, the union's caution reflected its loyalty to its worker base rather than support for the activist few. In reports about Gomel"s maneuver, worker enthusiasm, whipped up by rallies, spies, breakfast, and daily report sheets, provided the key to success, but one fact received much less publicity. The best workers in each department were rewarded with prizes: "educational opportunities," "production excursions" to Moscow, passes to a winter rest home, clothing, and cash.[47] Twelve years of socialist construction had not eliminated the need for material incentives to interest workers in their work.

The economic leverage of printers received a sharp and sudden boost at the end of 1929 and beginning of 1930. The unemployed continued to complain about their second-class treatment, and protectionism in the labor exchange continued to be denounced: these were familiar responses to the perceived glut

---

46. *Pechatnik* 17–18 (1930): 12; *Zorkii glaz*, 24 August 1929; Steinberg, *Moral Communities*, 79; Phillips, *Bolsheviks and the Bottle*, 110–11.

47. *Pechatnik* 21–22 (1930): 3, 19; 25–26 (1930): 12–14; GARF, f. R-5525, op. 12, d. 38, l. 57; *Trud*, 27 October, 27 November, 11 December, and 21 December 1930.

of unemployed printers. But union officials looked around and noticed that suddenly they faced an absolute shortage of skilled printers. Signs of this abrupt reversal could now be seen everywhere. On the Moscow labor exchange, skilled and semiskilled printers had all but disappeared; only the predominantly female bookbinders remained jobless because of changes in the production process. The Krasnyi Proletarii plant in Moscow, which had employed 1,170 workers in July 1927, operated by July 1930 at a strength of 1,860. Pechatnyi Dvor's labor force nearly doubled, and similar growth occurred everywhere.[48]

Union and industry officials belatedly realized the shortsightedness of their cutbacks in training programs for apprentices. One after another, independent training schools had been closed down in the second half of the 1920s because there were no job prospects for the young people being trained there. The intake of new apprentices into the profession had ceased entirely in 1927 and 1928: by October 1929, only 2 percent of the labor force in printing were younger than eighteen. The industry's plan, such as it was, called for an increase of forty thousand new workers by 1932, and officials realized that they possessed neither the young reserves to reach this goal nor the training facilities to prepare them. By the summer of 1930, union officials began to scramble to revive the training programs for apprentices that had been sacrificed to reduce unemployment. Predictably, blame for this lack of foresight fell again on the fact that the industry had no single administrative center: in the struggle between Vesenkha and the Committee on the Press, vocational training programs had been among the many casualties.[49]

Skilled printers now could command a premium on the expanding labor market, and individual managers competed for their services by offering more attractive rates—the big ruble—and better work conditions. Economic expansion, with or without a "plan," had produced market power for skilled printers. Managers turned a blind eye to the continuing violations of labor discipline, despite the endless campaigns against these practices. Turnover now became the scourge of this industry as it was in many others: workers took advantage of their newfound market power to turn print shops into revolving doors. In just six months in 1930, the First Model plant had hired 648 new workers (in a labor force of about 3,000), but had lost 410 workers—most of them by "personal request," because they had found better jobs elsewhere. The trade union responded with yet another campaign: public-minded workers pledged to "self-attach" themselves to their enterprises for the duration of the

48. GARF, f. R-5525, op. 11, d. 14, l. 3; d. 17, l. 188; *Zhizn' pechatnika,* 23 November 1929; TsGAMO, f. 4660, op. 1, d. 52 (report on work of factory committee at Krasnyi Proletarii, December 1929–July 1930), l. 1; *Pechatnik* 19 (2 July 1927): 11; 20 (12 July 1928): 9; 3 (1930): 11; 12–13 (1930): 4; 16 (1930): 2.

49. TsGA SPb, f. 4804, op. 14, d. 21 (meetings of Leningrad oblast board, 1930), l. 78ob.; *Pechatnik* 36 (25 December 1929): 19; 1 (1930): 2; 3 (1930): 11; 4 (1930): 7; 6 (1930): 16; 12–13 (1930): 8–9; 16 (1930): 13; 17–18 (1930): 2–3; 21–22 (1930): 8; 25–26 (1930): 17; GARF, f. R-5525, op. 12, d. 38 and d. 1 (stenographic report of First All-Union Congress of Paper and Print Workers, 22–24 December 1930), l. 60.

Five-Year Plan in order to eliminate the waste and costs of severance pay and retraining.[50]

In the face of every campaign to exhort workers to pledge their participation in the collective effort to advance the socialist economy, printers repeatedly responded with individual foot-dragging and evasion. The upturn in the market fortunes of printers gave skilled workers more protection to express their views individually, but collective resistance remained politically proscribed. These individual cases of resistance to acceleration, however, did produce a climate of antagonism on the shop floor. The basic conflict of interest between workers and managers continued to structure workplace relations, irrespective of grand socialist goals, campaigns for enthusiasts, or even the threat of unemployment.

## LABOR AND MANAGEMENT: THE IMPLACABLE FOES

Throughout the 1920s, the two models of labor relations continued to coexist. The productivist/statist model had been the choice of the Communist printers in their efforts to discredit and defeat their Menshevik opposition in the early 1920s, and this approach to worker-management relations continued to appeal to members of the trade union and party hierarchy. In this formulation, the good of the state commanded the highest priority, and expanding production and productivity would best guarantee the good of the state. Productivists understood that the needs of the state were best perceived from above, and they gave preference to the demands and interests of managers and officials who possessed this broader, "administrative" view.

The alternative workerist/independent model, favored by Mensheviks and defeated in the early 1920s, nonetheless continued to find favor among the now Communist trade union hierarchy and among the rank and file. In this model, the goal of production was consumption, including pleasure in work for its own sake, and workers asserted that their own well-being and not just that of the state constituted the highest good. Was this not a workers' state, a "republic of labor"? Decent wages, a comfortable pace of work, ample food, adequate housing, plentiful cultural opportunities, and respect and honor to workers constituted the terms of workers' sense of entitlement that had to be leveraged from the balance sheets of managers trying to satisfy the needs of the state as a whole. When the demands of workers and the needs of management clashed, the trade union had to negotiate the differences, but increasingly the Printers' Union oriented its efforts toward appeasing the needs of its worker constituency. In the

---

50. *Trud*, 23 August 1930; TsGA SPb, f. 4804, op. 14, d. 112 (general, factory committee, and party fraction meetings at Pechatnyi Dvor, 1930), l. 12; *Pechatnik* 7–8 (1930): 27; 14 (1930): 18; 19–20 (1930): 6; *Zhizn' pechatnika*, 16 August 1930; *Krasnoproletarets*, 11 June 1930; *Iskry*, 2 June 1930; TsGAMO, f. 4660, op. 1, d. 120, l. 66.

party discourse of the late 1920s, this line came to be labeled the "public" or *obshchestvennyi* line of policy.

In the republic of labor, the two lines—administrative/productivist and public/workerist—should have become one, and the trade union was only one of several institutions in which the two models were supposed to converge. The Communist Party served as another venue in which the two models would collapse into one, since all activists from every part of industry were represented in party cells and local committees. The institution of red directors also should have resolved the potential conflict between state interests and workers' demands. Since a red director had risen from the workers' ranks and was a member of the party, this figure represented within one personality the conflicting aims and needs of the society.

Despite all these social safeguards that were meant to preserve harmony between workers and management, hierarchies of unequal power relations remained at the heart of socialist labor relations. The fruits of this process were readily apparent in the behavior of managers in the crisis-riven printing industry and in the attitudes of rank-and-file workers toward them. An incident in the Leningrad union party fraction exemplifies the state of labor-management relations at the end of the 1920s. The director of the Leningrad Trade Union Council's print shop, Gershanovich, appeared before the party fraction in January 1927 after thirty-some workers at the plant had submitted a petition complaining about his "tactless" behavior. Gershanovich, they charged, had gone too far: yelling at workers, pulling them arbitrarily off one job and reassigning them to another. The local Communist Party cell had turned against him, and he found few friends in the union's party committee. A. N. Panteleev, the party man at the Sokolova shop, pointed out that when Gershanovich had worked there, he had had similarly poor relations with workers. Gershanovich explained that he had had an urgent job for a trade union customer, discipline in the enterprise was lax, and his behavior was therefore appropriately directorial. Nonetheless, Vasilii Volnukhin, a veteran of Pechatnyi Dvor and the union secretary, pointed out that the current party policy required a more "astute approach to the masses," and Gershanovich's relations constituted a violation of the party line. His mistake, said another, was that he had adopted a purely "administrative" line and lost sight of the obshchestvennyi line. He should behave more tactfully in the future.[51]

Gershanovich may have pleased the party with the results he achieved, but he alienated his workforce with his arbitrary and authoritarian approach to labor discipline. Workers in the printing trades were especially vocal about managers who resorted to immediate and arbitrary dismissal, a common enough opportunity in this period of high unemployment. One such manager was lampooned in *Pechatnik*'s humor page with a rhyme:

51. TsGAIPD SPb, f. 435, op. 1, d. 68, ll. 1–2.

> There lived an evil fellow
> A man deaf to honor and conscience,
> Though his work is secretarial [*sekretarskaia*]
> And his blood is proletarial [*proletarskaia*],
> He lives his life like a lord
> And behaves like a tsar.

"Of course, we know that since October 1917, the boss is a comrade," wrote a correspondent, "but it also happens that this very comrade turns obligatorily into 'Ivan Ivanych' [the name and patronymic implying hierarchy and respect] and loves to inspire fear and trembling when he appears." As these and many other examples suggest, proletarian blood was no guarantee against authoritarian behavior. Women workers were particularly vulnerable to the capricious behavior of these administrators, but anyone who criticized the director risked joining the Rakhmanovskii trust. Even worse, managers would replace the fired comrades with relatives and friends.[52]

Managers used their power to leverage other advantages for themselves and the enterprise. Many reports charged violations of the collective agreements intended to guarantee rates and working conditions: management felt unconstrained by these negotiated limits on their power. A manager who ruled his press department like a boss from the old days ensured productivity through compulsion: he invited workers to sign up for extra work, and whoever refused would be fired. Not surprisingly, "there exists among workers the widespread attitude toward the plant administration and managerial officials that they are incorrigible exploiters, whose only dream is to repress and silence the workers in any way possible."[53] In extreme cases, violence ensued. Printers at Pechatnyi Dvor dutifully denounced the phenomenon of *Bykovshchina,* named after a Leningrad leather worker who shot his foreman, a Communist Party member, in retaliation for his dismissal, but violence and murder occurred in the printing industry as well. In general, Russian urban society in the 1920s was surprisingly well armed. To be sure, the model Communist manager could still command respect from the workforce, but tributes to such paragons had become rare by the end of the 1920s.[54]

---

52. *Pechatnik* 10 (7 April 1927): 32; 3 (22 January 1928): 21; 13 (1 May 1928): 22; 22 (3 August 1928): 21; 26 (12 September 1928): 10, 14; 28–29 (12 October 1928): 12, 13; 4–5 (15 February 1929): 37; 6 (25 February 1929): 23; 7 (12 March 1929): 16; 17 (23 June 1929): 16; 23 (20 August 1929): 18; 12–13 (1930): 19; 21–22 (1930): 11; *Nasha zhizn'*, 24 October 1928.

53. TsGA SPb, f. 4804, op. 12, d. 4, l. 161; GARF, f. R-5525, op. 11, d. 1, l. 74; *Pechatnik* 19 (2 July 1927): 12; 32–33 (28 November 1927): 21; 12 (20 April 1928): 9; 34 (5 December 1928): 14; 17 (23 June 1929): 16; 31 (20 November 1929): 3; 34 (5 December 1929): 9; 35 (15 December 1929): 7.

54. TsGA SPb, f. 4804, op. 12, d. 101 (factory committee meetings at Pechatnyi Dvor, 1928), l. 172; see Vladimir Cherniaev, ed., *Piterskie rabochie i "diktatura proletariata": Oktiabr' 1917–1929. Sbornik dokumentov* (St. Petersburg, 2000), 402, on Bykovshchina; TsGAIPD SPb, f. 435, op. 1, d. 78 (meetings of the bureau of the party fraction, 1921–23), l. 13; *Pechatnik* 9 (25 March

Given these antagonistic relations between printers and managers, even when many of the managers had risen from the shop floor, one might expect that the regime's policy of one-man management, reintroduced on 5 September 1929, would find little support among the rank and file. The decree on management can be seen as part of the campaign to raise discipline: as interpreted in the printing industry, its main function was to weaken the power of the factory committee, which too often intervened to protect poor workers and bad work practices. Currently, said the partisans of the new approach, when management tried to fire a lazy worker, the factory committee would demand formal proof of the worker's incompetence, and usually succeeded in preventing the dismissal. Yet neither the trade union leaders nor the rank-and-file workers expressed much enthusiasm about ceding further authority to management, and just as in other branches of industry, one-man management existed more in principle than in reality. "We only pretend to implement one-man management," admitted a Ukrainian Printers' Union official.[55]

Labor relations in the printing industry by the late 1920s looked remarkably similar to the conflictual relations before the revolution, when workers and managers (even those who had risen from the ranks of the workers) played out their adversarial roles. The trade union, which under Communist leadership had put the squeeze on worker autonomy in the early years of the revolution, now backed the workers' side against the encroachments of authoritarian management. But despite the mounting hostility between labor and management, episodes of overt conflict in the form of strikes or other labor stoppages seldom appear in the records of the industry. Organized resistance, of course, carried a heavy penalty in the land of the Soviets. Some of the most vocal and long-term unemployed printers had essentially been blacklisted because of their political views: the high unemployment rate in the printing industry permitted little leeway for workers to exert organized leverage against the union or the party. The network of secret police spies who monitored popular opinion and reported on potential trouble spots to union and party leaders may not have been terribly efficient or accurate, but their presence surely discouraged workers from backing up their grumbling with calls for action.[56] Worker discontent was also defused through the extensive opportunities for socialist participation, whether the mind-numbing production conferences or the opportunity for individual advancement to supervisory positions or schooling.

---

1927): 11, 14; 12–13 (1 May 1927): 29; 27 (25 September 1928): 22; 34 (5 December 1928): 28; 36 (25 December 1928): 28; 17 (23 June 1929): 16; *Moskovskii pechatnik* 25 (June 1926): 10.

55. *Pechatnik* 31 (20 November 1929): 3; 34 (5 December 1929): 15; on one-man management, see Sarah Davies, *Popular Opinion in Stalin's Russia: Terror, Propaganda, and Dissent, 1934–1941* (Cambridge, 1997), 273–74; Kuromiya, *Stalin's Industrial Revolution*, 187–88; GARF, f. R-5525, op. 12, d. 7, ll. 16–17; TsGAMO, f. 4660, op. 1, d. 121 (protocols of Second Moscow Oblast Congress, 13–15 December 1930, pt. 2), l. 55.

56. See Davies, *Popular Opinion*; *Sotsialisticheskii vestnik* 1 (167) (12 January 1928): 11; 10/11 (200/201) (25 May 1929): 21; 12 (202) (14 June 1929): 14.

Socialist labor relations also aimed to reduce friction between the interests of labor and those of management by institutionalizing conflict resolution. Factory committees, rates and conflicts committees, and trade unions spent much of their time ameliorating petty conflicts and preventing individual grievances from mounting into collective protest. In the late 1920s, the campaign for collective agreements joined this panel of institutions for conflict minimization.

By 1927, the collective agreement governing issues of compensation and work rules had become an annual exercise requiring each enterprise to discuss and approve a contract adjusted to the special circumstances of that enterprise. The broad parameters of these agreements followed guidelines established by industry and union leaders on such major issues as the wage form, principles of wage differentiation, and the safety measures stipulated by the Labor Commissariat. But each enterprise had its own peculiarities of production, requiring individuation of the rates and norms schedules, and each plant had budget constraints that made certain stipulated benefits impossible to provide. The process of ratifying the agreements lasted for three or more months every autumn, and its progress, like that of so many other campaigns, was followed closely by the worker press. As in other campaigns, as well, the goals of these negotiations included raising workers' awareness about the specific issues and constraints of the production process.[57] The campaign also specifically endeavored to bring workers and management together to solve the burning problems in their industry. In this regard, the collective agreement campaigns served to put a public and cooperative face on labor relations. To the extent that the campaigns highlighted workers' success in changing the agreements in their favor, they also promoted the ideal of workerism that underlay the trade union view of socialism.

Yet despite the attempts to foster collaboration and inclusiveness, the tone of every campaign from 1927 through 1930 was far more adversarial than collegial. In 1927, when workers pressed for shorter hours in order to prevent layoffs, many managers insisted that reducing the labor force better served their economic interests. Workers wanted to limit the hiring of temporary workers, so that more of the unemployed could find full employment. Management preferred to hire a rotating cadre of temporary workers, since this tactic minimized their costs for benefits and severance pay. The issue of vacation time became particularly thorny in these years of unemployment as well: management wanted to spread workers' paid leaves out over the entire year, and extolled the virtues of "winter vacations"—skiing, skating, and brisk invigorating air. The charms of winter sport did not entice the workers at the Sixteenth Print Shop, and they voted against accepting vacations during winter. Other workers noted that none of the managerial personnel took their vacations in winter, but "in the twelfth year of the revolution, we have lost our right to a summer vacation." Signing the agreements every autumn became a protracted process, be-

---

57. TsGAIPD SPb, f. 435, op. 1, d. 68, ll. 75–77; *Pechatnik* 32–33 (28 November 1927): 4, 19; 35 (18 December 1927): 7–8; 1 (1 January 1929): 3–4; GARF, f. R-5525, op. 11, d. 1, l. 74.

cause management resisted concessions to workers' demands. Very often, disputed points in the agreement had to be worked out in meeting after meeting, or subjected to arbitration in special chambers or by conciliation boards. Drawing matches, as Golov found out, was not an option. Every year it was the same old story of protracted negotiations, said one Moscow union delegate in 1929. "The managers come out in a united front, trying to worsen our general conditions."[58] Nothing had in fact changed by the twelfth year of the revolution. Managers and workers played different roles, they were motivated by different interests. This had been the Mensheviks' critique all along, and nothing that the Communists had accomplished in the republic of labor had seemed to overcome these fundamental differences.

Work stoppages, as either bargaining tools or labor protests, remained hidden from the record: the undercurrent of endemic conflict did not translate into overt forms of labor protest in these years of economic recession. Only one strike appeared in the union press. Aimed against three remaining representatives of the minuscule private sector in Kazan', the strike whipped up the militant language of class struggle, but the event may have been publicized more to emphasize the concurrent class struggle in the countryside than to illustrate existing relations in industry.[59]

Ordinary conflict in the final years of NEP was neither so dramatic nor so quickly resolved. The local conflict commissions remained the first avenue of arbitration, and offered the union a useful vantage point from which to assess the extent and nature of worker complaints. Reporting on a review of thirty-three committees in 1927 and 1928, the union's central committee noted that nearly 80 percent of the committees' cases involved labor-management conflicts, and that their frequency had risen from 1927 to 1928. Fully half the conflicts in 1928 had involved issues of tarif grid assignments: managers took advantage of a new tarif system to push workers into lower pay categories in order to lower their costs and compete more effectively in the tight printing market. Disciplinary issues constituted a minority of the reported conflicts. Individual cases reported in the union journal confirm the pattern: conflicts arose overwhelmingly over rates and jobs, and they arose often. Workers, for their part, refused to accept the finality of management decisions. Facing a failure rate of 50 percent in the rates-conflict commissions, they appealed so frequently that in April 1929 the union adopted new stringent regulations concerning the appeal process and the statute of limitations for complaints.[60] With or without

58. *Pechatnik* 10 (7 April 1927): 2, 13; 1 (1 January 1928): 10; 4 (1 February 1928): 12; 28–29 (12 October 1928): 22; 33 (23 November 1928): 27; 36 (25 December 1928): 14; 1 (1 January 1929): 1; 2 (20 January 1929): 9; 3 (22 January 1929): 32; 4–5 (15 February 1929): 28; 34 (5 December 1929): 9; GARF, f. R-5525, op. 11, d. 1, ll. 83, 114; op. 10, d. 41, l. 83; *Pechatnyi dvor*, 11 December 1929; *Nasha zhizn'*, 15 January 1929.

59. TsGAIPD SPb, f. 435, op. 1, d. 68, ll. 6–7, 36; *Pechatnik* 36 (25 December 1929): 15; 1 (1930): 9.

60. GARF, f. R-5525, op. 11, d. 1, l. 89; *Pechatnik* 11 (17 April 1927): 14; 26 (12 September

strikes, labor relations in Soviet Russia at the start of the First Five-Year Plan remained fundamentally adversarial.

Every economic conflict carried political weight, and the conflicts arising over everyday work disagreements received careful attention among union and party members. They worried, as we shall see in Chapter 8, that Trotskyists and other political oppositionists were using workers' sense of economic injustice to launch broad attacks on the Communist regime. In this respect, the Printers' Union found itself in a position quite similar to that of 1921 and 1922, when the danger came from the Menshevik critique of union and regime policies. In both periods of crisis, while measures to repress dissent and opposition could be utilized, the Printers' Union also sought to appease its constituents by listening to their grievances and improving their economic positions. Productivism again yielded to workerism; pressure from workers themselves turned the administrative line into the public line.

As long as the industry remained economically depressed, managers could use the glut of skilled workers to exercise arbitrary power to hire, fire, promote, or demote, and the trade union could not significantly affect the conditions of its members. Only the sudden expansion in employment opportunities at the beginning of 1930 changed the nature of labor relations in favor of the workers. Reports of conflicts disappeared from the pages of the union press: now workers, with or without the support of their trade union, dictated the terms of their employment. By the end of 1930, managers could only complain that workers violated the terms of their collective agreements: absenteeism and drunkenness were on the rise. Allegations of shoddy work became common. Workers refused to accede to managers' requests, and simply changed jobs if they did not like their current conditions.[61] The big ruble had triumphed and enthusiasm had failed. Now only political intervention would be able to curb the market power of skilled workers in a tight labor market.

## THE MYSTERY OF THE FIRST FIVE-YEAR PLAN

Originally the Five-Year Plan was portrayed as a great triumph of the socialist way of economic development: the plan was epic in ambition and proportion, and its physical manifestations (the Dneprstroi hydroelectric dam, the giant steel mills in Magnitogorsk) generated the visual propaganda that created the aura of socialist superiority. A new cohort of economists and economic historians since the 1960s have questioned whether the benefits did outweigh the costs, and have exposed the tremendous waste, inefficiency, incompetence, and

---

1928): 15; 36 (25 December 1928): 9; 12 (20 April 1929): 17; 25–26 (11 September 1929): 22–23; 29–30 (31 October 1929): 16; 31 (20 November 1929): 17; 34 (5 December 1929): 6; *Nasha zhizn'*, 31 December 1929. See McAuley, *Labour Disputes*, chap. 2, for an overview of arbitration mechanisms.

61. *Pechatnik* 25–26 (1930): 10.

corruption that accompanied the industrialization effort.[62] Documents now detail the gruesome costs of collectivization and the massive resettlement of the rural population; new studies highlight the impoverished reality of consumer life "behind the facade of Stalinist abundance."[63] Work based on newly accessible archival sources has shed light on the politics of economic decision making, revealing fierce competition among regional satraps for labor and resources.[64] And yet the economy grew.

When we look at the experience of the printing industry, however, the mystery is not how the economy grew despite massive economic irrationality, but how the industry and party managed the multiple contradictions that characterized socialist labor relations and trade union politics. The union's persistent demand for more central control, a "single administrative center," clashed with the reluctance of local units to cede autonomy and resources. Workers demanded from the authoritative center policies that would guarantee them a livelihood, suggesting they too believed in the value of the command system. Yet in day-to-day behavior, printers acted as individual economic actors, bargaining about the value of their labor, declining to participate in schemes to raise productivity, changing jobs to find the best conditions and pay. The trade union wavered uncertainly between its official productivist stance, which favored administratively tough managers, and a workerist defense of the rights of the rank and file to soften the harsh consequences of rationalization and speedups. Printers expressed dissatisfaction with the productivists' goals through their complaints and their satires, and they resisted individual managerial initiatives with repeated success. Here were multiple recipes for conflict, yet organized and collective resistance did not arise. Why not?

The legacy of ten years of repressive assault on the Menshevik alternative of independent politics cannot be underestimated. There was no room in the Five-Year Plan to develop a coherent critique of Communist economic principles or industrial relations systems. A market-based alternative, although implemented by individuals in practice, found few supporters among printers, who resented the market-based programs of rationalization and cost effectiveness. Better forms of centralized control, structures that would consolidate resources and not squander them, remained attractive to printers' leaders and the rank and file.

62. James R. Millar, "Soviet Rapid Development and the Agricultural Surplus Hypothesis," *Soviet Studies* 22, no. 1 (1970): 77–93; Davies, *Soviet Economy in Turmoil*; William G. Rosenberg and Lewis H. Siegelbaum, eds., *Social Dimensions of Soviet Industrialization* (Bloomington, 1993).

63. V. Danilov, R. Manning, and L. Viola, eds., *Tragediia sovetskoi derevni: Kollektivizatsiia i raskulachivanie. Dokumenty i materialy v 5 tomakh, 1927–1939* (Moscow, 1999–2001); Osokina, *Za fasadom*.

64. Shearer, *Industry, State, and Society in Stalin's Russia*; James R. Harris, *The Great Urals: Regionalism and the Evolution of the Soviet System* (Ithaca, 1999); David J. Nordlander, "Origins of a Gulag Capital: Magadan and Stalinist Control in the Early 1930s," *Slavic Review* 57, no. 4 (1998): 791–812; Paul R. Gregory, ed., *Behind the Facade of Stalin's Command Economy: Evidence from the Soviet State and Party Archives* (Stanford, 2001).

In the absence of effective central control, printers held on to their ability to control the day-to-day terms of their work and employment. They did so through the workerist institutions of the trade union organization—factory committees and rates commissions—and by resisting shock brigade work and Taylorism. These institutions did not eliminate resistance and conflict, but they contained them within manageable limits. The Printers' Union, in supporting and encouraging the institutions and space to manage conflict, had tilted finally and decisively in favor of workerism as the necessary condition for whatever productivism they hoped to achieve. The traditions of trade unionism, with or without a Menshevik label, had prevailed.

# CHAPTER 8

## THE TWILIGHT OF THE SOCIALIST TRADE UNION

*Our factory committee didn't do anything and the new one won't do anything because the factory administrators are given too much power. Under these conditions, our factory committee can, so to say, only lick their boots.*

—WOMAN PRINTER AT A GENERAL MEETING OF THE SIXTEENTH PRINT SHOP, OCTOBER 1929

Between June 1929 and December 1930, virtually all the leaders of the national Union of Printers and its leading local organizations were replaced by new officials who in many cases had had no ties with the industry at all. This picture was replicated across the entire spectrum of the trade union movement.[1] This trade union purge could be understood as the inevitable fallout of the defeat of the "right deviation" at the end of 1928: once the trade union chair, Mikhail Pavlovich Tomskii, was swept away by the supporters of Stalin, all who had followed his lead were similarly doomed to defeat. "Democratic centralism" suggests that we need only examine Tomskii's role in the Communist Party Politburo and Central Committee to understand the total humiliation of the trade unions as defenders of workers' rights by the start of the 1930s. This examination would explore the principles for which the trade union stood and take a close look at the precarious position occu-

1. *Sotsialisticheskii vestnik* 12 (202) (14 June 1929): 4–5.

pied by trade union Communists, officials who had to defend the interests of their constituents and simultaneously carry out the general line of the party, even if interests and line no longer coincided. The trade unionists perhaps were doomed to defeat because their inherent workerism in fact stood in the way of rationalization, intensification of labor, and economic growth.[2]

There is more to this story. Stalin and his supporters labeled the trade unions as undemocratic, bureaucratic, and corrupt, but so did the working rank and file. On the printing industry's shop floor, in local trade union meetings, and in the factory press, printers exhibited strong disaffection from their union leadership, accusing them of suppressing union democracy and abandoning the interests of the working class for personal enrichment. Some scholars have argued that the Cultural Revolution and assault on the countryside represented an alliance between the hard-line industrializers and class-war zealots in the party leadership with a working rank and file that was fed up with the inequalities of the NEP and frustrated by a sense of the revolution delayed.[3] Did the interests of even the traditionally independent printers and the Stalinist center coincide? Could the trade union purge have been a response of the leadership to the political demands of workers?

Other scholars have said that the defeat of the opposition and stepping up of GPU surveillance and repression effectively silenced the dissident voices of independent workers and bludgeoned them into sullen passivity.[4] Exiled Menshevik commentators emphasized the political quiescence of urban workers during this time, but they also attributed this passivity to the dilution of the urban proletariat by the massive influx of peasants into the labor force.[5] The printing industry, however, experienced no such influx. In examining printers' response to the politics of Stalinism at the start of the First Five-Year Plan, we can safely leave peasantness out of the equation. Printers opposed their trade union and they did so vocally between 1928 and 1930, but their opposition did not stem from an embrace of Stalinist values of productivism, class war, and total proletarian culture. Rather, in rejecting both the existing trade union and its Stalinist alternative, printers at the end of the 1920s proved to be surprisingly vocal in their defense of an independent working-class politics. Trade union independence had been the platform of the Menshevik Party at the start of the decade. The transformation of "participatory dictatorship" in the first years of the Five-Year Plan revealed a continuing menshevism with a small *m* among

---

2. Carr and Davies acknowledge there was a grain of truth in this argument: *Foundations of a Planned Economy*, 1 (2): 563; see also S. Shvarts, "Agoniia profsoiuzov," *Sotsialisticheskii vestnik* 3 (217) (8 February 1930): 3–4; Manya Gordon, *Workers before and after Lenin* (New York, 1941), 98.

3. Fitzpatrick, *Education and Social Mobility*, 11; Vladimir Andrle, *Workers in Stalin's Russia: Industrialization and Social Change in a Planned Economy* (New York, 1988), 18.

4. Filtzer, *Soviet Workers and Stalinist Industrialization*, 87–89; Vladimir Brovkin, *Russia after Lenin: Politics, Culture, and Society, 1921–1929* (London, 1998), 183; Andrea Graziosi, "Stalin's Antiworker 'Workerism,' 1924–1931," *International Review of Social History* 40 (1995): 227.

5. This Menshevik view was developed in the pages of *Sotsialisticheskii vestnik* (e.g., 2/3 [6 Feb-

printers, a recapitulation of the politics of critical independence that had long characterized the industry's workers.

## THE STATE OF THE UNION BY 1928

Even during the period of its greatest prosperity, the Printers' Union had struggled to establish its legitimacy and authority among the industry's rank and file. Printers responded to participatory dictatorship by turning their backs on participation whenever possible, staying away from meetings and concentrating on their own private or work-centered lives. As the economic crisis of the industry grew worse in 1927 and 1928, the same sense of apathy or grudging routinized participation pervades the reports of union meetings. Well before the key events that brought down the trade union leadership in the 1929 purge, daring workers criticized their leaders for three sins: failure to defend their economic interests, corruption, and bureaucratic indifference.

The union's unemployed often led the criticism, both because they had most directly felt the brunt of the economic crisis and because, having lost their jobs already, they were immune to the threat of dismissal for speaking out. In Leningrad, unemployed printers demanded freedom of the press, but they also complained that the union had not organized sufficient benefits for them, such as subsidized meals.[6] In addition, delegates at provincial congresses and local representatives at factory meetings (those that chose to show up) spoke repeatedly about the union's failure to defend workers' wage levels, of refusing to defend the workers' side in collective agreement negotiations and in the rates commissions.[7] During the reelection of the factory committee at Moscow's Sixteenth Print Shop, one worker denounced the factory committee for permitting the shortening of the workweek (at less pay) while not reducing their own hours or pay. "Workers agitate about raising their wages, but when they're told [by the factory committee] that under current circumstances this isn't always possible, they become passive and lose interest in all other activities," admitted a factory committee representative at a Moscow conference in September 1928.[8]

In the shadow of depressed living standards, the embezzlement of union funds attracted particularly sharp criticism. Theft of public money accounted for many cases of expulsion from the union in 1927 and 1928. The former factory committee chair at Moscow's Glavnauka Print Shop, the treasurer of the

---

ruary 1928]: 21) and later incorporated in Solomon M. Schwarz, *Labor in the Soviet Union* (New York, 1951), 1–18.

6. TsGAIPD SPb, f. 435, op. 1, d. 68 (meetings of bureau of party fraction of Leningrad union, 1927), l. 100; TsGA SPb, f. 4804, op. 11, d. 158 (meetings of Leningrad unemployed, 1926–29), ll. 140–42; GARF, f. R-5525, op. 10, d. 41 (protocols of oblast congresses, K–N, 1928), l. 72.

7. GARF, f. R-5525, op. 10, d. 41, ll. 65–68, 83; *Pechatnik* 29–30 (25 October 1927): 9; *Nasha zhizn'*, 21 April 1928; TsGAMO, f. 699, op. 1, d. 1059 (protocols of Fourth Moscow Guberniia Conference, October 1928), ll. 12, 27, 28, 30, 40, 41, 44, 47.

8. *Nasha zhizn'*, 18 April 1927; *Pechatnik* 28–29 (12 October 1928): 5.

Moscow Training School, and the chair of the Voronezh Group Committee all lost their union positions because they had dipped into the union coffers.[9] The growth of theft was beginning to worry the masses, wrote the factory newspaper at the Zinov'ev Print Shop: are we really incapable of being honest people? Must we all fall victim to embezzlemania? Others blamed the union leadership, who seemed incapable of stopping the hemorrhage of union funds into personal pockets.[10]

Workers also took aim at central union and factory committee "bureaucratism": officials who had grown too distant from their worker origins, who became bogged down in endless oratory, who replaced "living contacts" with circular letters and ignored their responsibility to raise the activism of their constituents. In the bindery department at the Sixteenth Print Shop, workers called a meeting to replace their elected steward, Efimov, who had "forgotten he was elected by the mass and begun to act like a boss." A cartoon in *Pechatnik*, captioned "Some factory committee chairmen drag out their reports to extraordinary lengths," depicted one popular view of endless factory meetings. Generally, every election of a new factory committee summoned forth criticism of local and higher officials for inactivity, arrogance, and unresponsiveness.[11]

The sources here must be read with some care. In the spring of 1928, the party launched yet another campaign to involve workers in the tasks of governing and economic construction: self-criticism. Self-criticism would provide a healthy corrective for aberrations in trade union practice: defects in practical work, bureaucratic excesses, and abnormalities in daily life. But self-criticism, warned an editorial in *Pechatnik*, should not be used either for its own sake or for attacks on the entire system, which might unwittingly foster Menshevik or semi-Menshevik "theories and prescriptions." It was the proletarian duty of trade union leaders and worker-correspondents to admit mistakes and ferret them out among others. Self-criticism, however, quickly produced its antithesis, suppression of self-criticism, which appeared to nullify the opportunity for workers to discuss union and factory problems openly. Critics found their suggestions ignored and themselves left vulnerable to accusations of being troublemakers and rowdies. The Leningrad union branch denied, however, that it engaged in retaliation for self-criticism: that was a "Moscow disease." "There was suppression under Gordon," said one union representative in September 1929, "but there is none now." Elsewhere workers adjusted to the self-criticism program as they had to so many other campaigns, by ignoring it or subverting

---

9. *Pechatnik* 5 (23 February 1927): 7; 6 (28 February 1927): 7; 7–8 (10 March 1927): 21; 22 (5 August 1927): 2; 12–13 (1 May 1927): 28; 4 (12 February 1927): 9; 17 (15 June 1927): 6; 36 (25 December 1927): 6.

10. *Zorkii glaz*, 1 May 1927; TsGAMO, f. 699, op. 1, d. 1059, l. 27; *Pechatnik* 21 (31 July 1929): 20.

11. *Nasha zhizn'*, 6 December 1928; *Pechatnik* 5 (12 February 1928): 31; 7–8 (8 March 1928): 18; 11 (8 April 1928): 8–9; 14 (12 May 1928): 16–17; 16 (1 June 1928): 10–11; TsGA SPb, f. 4804, op. 12, d. 101 (factory committee meetings at Pechatnyi Dvor, 1928), l. 135.

## The Twilight of the Socialist Trade Union 249

### К перевыборам фабзавкомов

*Некоторые председатели фабзавкомов чрезвычайно затягивают свои отчеты.*

"Toward the Reelection of the Factory Committee: Some factory committee chairmen drag out their reports to extraordinary lengths." (*Pechatnik* 5 [12 February 1928]: 31.)

it. A *Pechatnik* correspondent satirized the effort in portraying the mutual self-criticism of two factory committee members who proceeded to implement the slogan in the Red Crab tavern: "You criticize me, and then I'll criticize you. It will be a division of labor. No one else will hear, and the proletarian slogan will be supported all the way."[12]

We must therefore ask ourselves to what extent the criticism of the trade union organization represented rote fulfillment of the self-criticism plan rather than genuine and spontaneous voices of outrage from below. Certain themes became much more common after the launching of the self-criticism campaign: the failure of union organizations to encourage activism among women or to promote the training of youth, and a series of complaints about insufficient cultural activism—poor club organizations, shortages of spaces in rest homes, and insufficient vigilance against religion and drinking.[13] These complaints were both politically correct and politically safe; once again the union could pay lip service to its commitment to organize women and young people, while everybody knew that these obligations, along with culture, remained at the bottom of the union's list of priorities. On the other hand, criticism of the union's defense of workers' interests, of corruption, and of bureaucratism remained constant, and appeared both in the invited columns of worker self-criticism and in the closed records of public and private meetings. Scripted or not, the union record before the trade union purge produces a picture of endemic dissatisfaction with the performance of union leaders and mid-level activists.

Criticism of the union leadership reached a new peak in the fall of 1928, when the Moscow and Leningrad union organizations held conferences to select delegates to the coming national congress. In response to the opening political report, Moscow delegates focused their recorded discussion on problems of union organization. From mismanaging the collective agreement campaign to moving too slowly on converting churches into clubs, the union leadership could do nothing right. Union officials scrambled to defend their records: "No need for self-criticism," said the head of the union's organizational bureau. The public account of the conference enumerated the areas of concern, but called these complaints "concrete and businesslike" suggestions, and the union chair, Solov'ev, smoothed over criticism by concluding that the productivist work of the union—rationalization, implementing the seven-hour workday, and expanding self-criticism—had received the full approval of the conference.[14]

Leningrad's conference assembled a month later, on 23 November 1928. After the report of the union chair, Rozov, delegates here too lashed out at defects

---

12. *Pechatnik* 15 (22 May 1928): 3; 28–29 (12 October 1928): 4, 10; 31 (1 November 1928): 10; 32 (7 November 1928): 15; TsGAIPD SPb, f. 435, op. 1, d. 74 (meetings of bureau of party fraction of Leningrad union, 1929), l. 81.

13. TsGAMO, f. 699, op. 1, d. 1059, ll. 10–15; 18, 26–27, 32, 36, 40–47; TsGA SPb, f. 4804, op. 12, d. 101, ll. 174–174ob.; d. 4 (meetings of Leningrad conferences and union activists, April 1928–December 1929), ll. 160–64.

14. TsGAMO, f. 699, op. 1, d. 1059, l. 44; *Pechatnik* 33 (28 November 1928): 12–13.

of the leadership: too much time spent on discussing culture, not enough about the collective agreement, norms, and rates. With unemployment still high, delegates complained about favoritism in hiring and in funding. Moscow always received priority in capital investment and allocations of paper, they claimed. (Not true, replied Borshchevskii, attending on behalf of the union central committee. "In Moscow they say the opposite.")[15] These protocols too could be interpreted as "businesslike," and most delegates offered concrete suggestions rather than sweeping criticisms. When the Leningrad union's party fraction met a few days later, however, the Communists were primarily concerned with a speech that had not been recorded in the protocols. Kuz'minskii, a compositor at the Sokolova print shop and "former oppositionist," had referred to bread lines, lack of food, higher rents, rationalization, and stricter labor discipline: "All this was repression of the working class," he had said. He had attracted some followers, admitted the party fraction, and had been able to propose a resolution at the November conference to the effect that if wages were not raised by 10 percent, he and his followers would break up the conference.[16]

Taken together, the evidence from the union record in 1928 suggests a strong degree of disaffection on the part of workers in the printing industry toward their union leadership. Yet it is difficult to conclude that the disapproval of the union mass brought about the purge of the trade union leaders. Even less does it indicate programmatic approval for Stalin or for any political opposition. There were no opportunities to channel this disaffection into alternative political programs. But at the very least, this public outpouring of criticism, however controlled, provided a backdrop for the more dramatic events taking place within closed party circles.

## THE TRADE UNION PURGE

The All-Union Central Council of Trade Unions, with the former printer Mikhail Tomskii at its head, had taken a cautious stance on plans for rapid industrialization, and rumors of Tomskii's disfavor had already reached the readers of the émigré *Sotsialisticheskii vestnik* by mid-1927.[17] A year later, Tomskii voted within the Politburo with the right opposition and drew Stalin's criticism for "capitulationism," but he retained his position as VTsSPS prepared to hold its Eighth All-Union Congress in late 1928.[18] In the meantime, the Stalinist and Komsomol press had begun the campaign of self-criticism with its accusations of bureaucratism and antidemocracy against the Central Trade Union Council.

---

15. TsGA SPb, f. 4804, op. 12, d. 4, ll. 160–64.
16. TsGAIPD SPb, f. 435, op. 1, d. 71 (meetings of bureau of party fraction of Leningrad union, 1928), ll. 103–1030b.; d. 106 (secret miscellaneous correspondence of party fraction of Leningrad union, 1928), ll. 26–260b.
17. *Sotsialisticheskii vestnik* 13 (155) (2 July 1927): 13.
18. Daniels, *Conscience of the Revolution*, 345–46; Carr and Davies, *Foundations of a Planned Economy*, 1 (2): 554–59, 2:64.

When the congress convened in December 1928, Tomskii came under withering public attack for excessive centralism and bureaucratism—the same charges printing industry workers had been leveling against their own leaders.[19] The real drama of the congress, however, took place within the Communist Party fraction, with the Politburo's proposal to add a trusted emissary of Stalin, Lazar' Kaganovich, to the Trade Union Council. Tomskii and Kaganovich stood on opposite sides of the right–left divide in the Politburo, but Kaganovich was also an old trade unionist and a longtime friend of many members of the Trade Union Council. Tomskii could not publicly oppose Kaganovich's appointment, but within the party fraction he and ninety-one of his supporters, a minority, voted against the nomination. One of those ninety-one was the Printers' Union chair, Aleksandr Borshchevskii.[20]

Although Tomskii briefly survived as nominal head of the Trade Union Council, by March 1929 he had disappeared from public view. At the same time, *Sotsialisticheskii vestnik*'s Moscow informant reported that one of Kaganovich's first steps in the VTsSPS was to put pressure on the Moscow Trade Union Council and on the central committees of trade unions to remove Tomskii's most outspoken supporters.[21] This episode in the history of Soviet trade unions remains largely unexplored. The records for the Printers' Union are incomplete, but pieced together, they indicate that the process by which the right deviation was purged from the trade union apparatus was far from direct and was characterized by personal rivalries within the union leadership as well as by politics. It also reflected an acute sensitivity to the attitudes of the union's rank and file.

Aleksandr Borshchevskii became the first victim of Kaganovich's purge. Soon after the national Trade Union Congress had sealed Tomskii's political fate, Borshchevskii opened the Seventh All-Union Congress of Printing Workers. He faced a barrage of criticism about the union's weak defense of workers' economic interests, its incompetent organization, and its failure to lead.[22] These had been the themes sounded in the Moscow and Leningrad conferences a few months before, and like those earlier criticisms, they corresponded to the kinds of grievances that had been chronic in enterprises throughout the 1920s. But now they added up to a vote of no confidence in the union's veteran Communist leader.

Toward the end of the congress, 129 members of its Communist party dele-

---

19. Carr and Davies, *Foundations of a Planned Economy*, 1 (2): 556–57; *Vos'moi s"ezd professional'nykh soiuzov (10–24 dekabria 1928 g.): Plenumy i sektsii. Polnyi stenograficheskii otchet* (Moscow, 1929); F. M. Vaganov, "Razgrom pravogo uklona v VKP(b) (1928–1930 gg.)," *Voprosy istorii KPSS*, 1960, no. 4: 71.

20. I am relying on Borshchevskii's account: GARF, f. R-5525, op. 18, d. 50 (fraction meeting at Seventh All-Union Congress of Printers' Union, 5 February 1929). A partial account appears in *Sotsialisticheskii vestnik* 7/8 (197/198) (12 April 1929): 20–21.

21. *Sotsialisticheskii vestnik* 7/8 (197/198) (12 April 1929): 20.

22. GARF, f. R-5525, op. 11, d. 1 (stenographic report of Seventh All-Union Congress of Printers' Union, 28 January–7 February 1929), ll. 46–116, 158–226.

gation met to discuss the selection of the next union central committee. Borshchevskii's political position had become fundamentally compromised by his defense of Tomskii at the national level, and now his own union's elected delegates withdrew their support. He did not defend his support of Tomskii and readily admitted his errors, but he faced criticism for lack of political backbone and excessive readiness to compromise: "Doesn't this smell, comrades, of those Menshevik sentiments from 1917?" asked one union leader. But others came to Borshchevskii's defense and argued that if he would only admit his mistake, he could continue as chair of the union.[23] This meeting reveals a conflict of opinion and personality rarely encountered in union documents, but it remains difficult to separate the relative influence of political ideology and personal loyalties (or rivalries) on the political decisions of the union's leaders. It must be inferred that the central Communist Party leadership wanted Borshchevskii removed: that was the hidden agenda transmitted from above. But the Communist leaders of the Printers' Union proved unwilling to obey party instructions unanimously.

Political disagreement combined with indecision when the party bureau of the union central committee met a few days later to choose Borshchevskii's replacement. Eight candidates emerged in the discussion as the bureau members—including Borshchevskii—evaluated their competence, their willingness to serve, and especially how they would be received by the workers. Central Committee members spoke most warmly of candidates within the trade union organization and opposed the nominations of industrial managers for the job. Representatives of union locals, however, put forward the names of experienced industrial administrators, men from outside the trade unionist orbit. Were they withdrawing support from the trade unionist line, or had the Stalin center already inserted its own agents—loyal productivists—among local Communists? The purge of the locals did not take place until later in 1929, and the officials who now favored choosing an industrial manager to lead them were themselves veteran unionists. The disagreement in February 1929 represented a genuine discussion about trade union leadership, in which veteran trade unionists took opposing sides. Borshchevskii continued to defend the trade unionist position: "Really, can it be that among 160,000 members of our union we can't find a chair of the Central Committee from among authoritative trade union figures but we have to go looking for him among the industrialists?" In the end, the bureau voted by a narrow margin to choose an industrialist, the current head of the Mospoligraf trust, over a Communist Party worker "who would be popular among workers" but had neither trade union nor industrial experience.[24]

The union's executive party organization had voted for a new chair who would represent the party line on labor-management relations, a representative

23. *Pechatnik* 14–15 (15 February 1929): 5; GARF, f. R-5525, op. 18, d. 50 (unnumbered), 5 February 1929.
24. GARF, f. R-5525, op. 18, d. 50, 5 February 1929.

from management, "known to the workers," but known also for upholding the principles of rationalization and productivity. And yet, two days later, when the bureau met to organize the new Central Committee presidium, it was Borshchevskii who reemerged as the chair of the union, with the same members of the apparatus and regional union bosses alongside. The fraction as a whole was told that having discussed the matter with the relevant party committees, and hearing Borshchevskii's confession of error in the vote against Kaganovich, he was now welcomed back as the union leader.[25] The Stalinist center had failed in this first attempt to purge the remnants of the Tomskii opposition. Trade union independence—"*tred-iiunionizm*"—remained dominant in the Printers' Union, at least for the moment. Yet we cannot know to what extent Borshchevskii's victory represented an overt rejection of the Stalin line, a concession to the perceived preferences of the rank and file, or a realization that competent leaders of Borshchevskii's caliber were difficult to find.

Borshchevskii's reappointment did not stop the criticism or the relentless pressure of the trade union purge. One by one over the next twelve months, Borshchevskii and the remnants of the Printers' Union leadership were stripped of power and denounced for adhering to the outmoded "trade union" line. When we look back from the standpoint of February 1930, the inevitability of defeat becomes clear. Yet the language used to engineer the trade unionists' ouster resonates with the kinds of grievances that had long been percolating up from the shop floor.

The campaign against the Moscow union branch, for example, was launched by a stream of articles in *Pechatnik* in July 1929. Criticism from worker-correspondents in various Moscow print shops followed familiar lines: representatives from the branch office rarely visited the local shops and could seldom be found in their offices either. "You invite them to attend a meeting at nine p.m. and they show up at midnight." The workers would complain about norms and rates, the branch officials would reply haughtily that the norms were correct. The union failed to lead the socialist emulation campaign. In conflicts between workers and management, the union representatives wavered from side to side. *Pechatnik* failed to address questions of "ordinary everyday life."[26] Note that these criticisms reflect both workerist goals (norms and rates and a defense of workers vis-à-vis management) and proletarian goals (socialist emulation). Even while mobilizing the journal to discredit the union's pro-worker line, the party leadership in effect acknowledged the authority of the pro-worker line.

The dishonesty of trade union officials also betrayed their working-class constituents, claimed worker-correspondents, and widespread crimes of embezzlement provided the occasion for the replacement of numerous local trade union

---

25. Ibid., 7 February 1929.
26. *Pechatnik* 20 (23 July 1929): 13; 22 (12 August 1929): 17; 23 (20 August 1929): 11–12; 24 (31 August 1929): 15; 25–26 (11 September 1929): 4–9; GARF, f. R-5525, op. 11, d. 12 (meeting of Printers' Union Central Committee plenum, 20 June 1929), l. 10.

boards.[27] Embezzlement was endemic among union officials, as we have seen, nor was the phenomenon confined to the trade union movement: the corrupt pensioners' home manager in Ilf and Petrov's *Twelve Chairs* who was systematically selling off his home's entire inventory must have struck a chord of recognition in Soviet Russia.[28] The fact that entire union organizations had to be replaced because of corruption could have meant that the union finally felt it needed to hold these officials collectively accountable in order to preserve member support. On the other hand, embezzlement may have been only an excuse to purge local activists and thereby undermine support from below for the union's central committee. In Moscow, exemplary bookkeeping practices protected the Central Committee from the plague of embezzlements, but here anonymous denunciations pointed to "disgraceful things," including "fictitious business trips with harems," drinking binges organized by Borshchevskii, and the illegal acquisition of "deficit goods."[29]

Ultimately the new Stalin party center indicted the Printers' Union leaders for their failure of political leadership. They allowed officials to settle production disputes by drawing matches. Borshchevskii had ignored the main issues of the day, including the tasks of the party in the struggle between town and country, a reference of course to the heightening grain collection and collectivization campaigns. He proved too tolerant of others' heterodox views—more Menshevik-style compromise, now labeled "opportunism." The Leningrad union Communists joined in the chorus on 18 September, agreeing that the Central Committee had discredited itself, but fortunately, things were just fine in Leningrad: "We have no Moscow disease here."[30] The union's journal, *Pechatnik*, needed to be tougher and more critical of failings in the union and industry, and not just offer "vegetarian" dishes. The journal needed more "sting" and more "teeth."[31] In 1929, of course, the only meat on the menu was served by the party: delegates who denounced Borshchevskii and *Pechatnik* wanted not open debate but a more aggressive pursuit of the party line, including a carnivorous assault on the peasantry. Vegetarianism signified avoidance of politics altogether.

For all their so-called workerism, the union leadership found few defenders among the worker rank and file. Printers reacted to the departure of Borshchevskii in 1929 with the same degree of disaffection that had met the ouster of Gordon in 1925. Only in Leningrad did printers rally around their union leader for one valiant last stand against the pressures of the central purge. Here

27. GARF, f. R-5525, op. 18, d. 49 (meetings of bureau of fraction of Printers' Union Central Committee, 1928), l. 39; op. 11, d. 17 (meetings of Printers' Union Central Committee presidium, 1929), ll. 46, 630b., 78, 177–79; *Pechatnik* 24 (31 August 1929): 2–3; 27 (25 September 1929): 22.

28. Il'ia Il'f and Evgenii Petrov, *Dvenadtsat' stul'ev* (Moscow, 1928).

29. GARF, f. R-5525, op. 18, d. 51 (meetings of bureau of fraction of Printers' Union Central Committee, 1929) (unnumbered), 26 September 1929.

30. TsGAIPD SPb, f. 435, op. 1, d. 74, l. 81.

31. GARF, f. R-5525, op. 11, d. 12, l. 10; *Pechatnik* 19 (13 July 1929): 20; 28 (14 October 1929): 3.

the union leader, Rozov, prided himself on his political toughness and his ability to follow the party line. "We're not vegetarians, we're not flowers," he had boasted in engineering the ouster of a rightist trade union leader.[32] But when the new union activists had finished removing Borshchevskii and his supporters from the central leadership, they discovered that apparently the Moscow disease had spread after all. Things were not well in the Leningrad organization either.[33] Rozov refused to yield, and turned his toughness against the inquisitors from the newly constituted central committee. The Leningrad organization resisted cooperation with the investigating team and rallied local union activists to oppose the center. One investigator acknowledged that it would be risky to raise the issue of removing the Leningrad leaders before they knew if the "member mass" would support the move.[34] Rozov remained, for the moment, in office. The support of the rank and file—or at least of the loyal local union organizations—may have made the decisive difference. Moreover, the fierce local patriotism of the Leningraders also played a role. Neither Rozov nor Gordon had enjoyed unalloyed popularity in Leningrad, but insofar as they represented Leningrad's independence from Moscow and the center, they seemed to have received considerable political backing.

With the lone exception of Leningrad, a new sweep in late 1929 brought about a wholesale turnover in union leadership.[35] In February 1930 the plenum of the Central Committee elected a new union chair to replace Borshchevskii, Boris Osipovich Magidov. Until now, the Printers' Union leaders had come from within the ranks of the profession; in its long history the union had nurtured abundant leadership material. Even if Rozov in 1926 had been appointed from outside to lead the Leningrad union, he was still "one of us," a printer. The forty-six-year-old Magidov, however, had joined the trade union movement in 1905 as a Bolshevik activist in the Gold and Silver Workers' Union, and after the 1917 revolution he served as a trade union official in the mining industry. Before taking over as head of the Printers' Union, he had served as chair of the Donetsk Trade Union Council and assistant chair of the Southern Bureau of the Miners' Union.[36] Under Magidov's leadership, the trade union faced the new tasks of socialist construction by continuing to eliminate the vestiges of oppo-

---

32. TsGAIPD SPb, f. 457, op. 1, d. 107 (party fraction of Leningrad Oblast Trade Union Council, 1929), l. 58ob.

33. GARF, f. R-5525, op. 18, d. 51, 2 October 1929.

34. Ibid., 18 November 1929.

35. Ibid., op. 11, d. 17, ll. 263ob., 268ob.; d. 36 (protocols of oblast congresses, 1929, Z–T), l. 210.

36. *Pechatnik* 5 (1930): inside front cover; Theodore H. Friedgut, *Iuzovka and Revolution*, vol. 2: *Politics and Revolution in Russia's Donbass, 1869–1924* (Princeton, 1994), 295, 299, 300, 321, 354, 357. On the Donbass connections of Stalin's inner circle, see Graziosi, "Stalin's Antiworker 'Workerism,'" 248–49. Magidov (1884–1972) served as head of the union until 1937 and was a member of the presidium of VTsSPS from 1941 to 1948. *Lichnye arkhivnye fondy v khranilishchakh SSSR* (Moscow, 1980), vol. 3; *Dokumenty po istorii i kul'ture evreev v arkhivakh Moskvy. Putevoditel'* (Moscow, 1997). My thanks to Angela Cannon for alerting me to these sources.

sition within its ranks and by orienting the union more directly toward the goals of production. The center turned once again to clean out the "right deviation" in Leningrad. Local reelections removed Rozov's earlier supporters and finally Rozov himself; a special congress in November 1930 featured Magidov's triumphant account of how he had set the union on the correct, productivist path.[37]

If trade union politics had not become such deadly business by 1930, Borshchevskii and his fellow purge victims might have appreciated the irony of the new leadership's efforts to change the direction of the trade union movement. The red union had driven out the Mensheviks in 1919 and 1920 in order to turn the union's face to production, only to find that the contradictions between productivism and trade unionism remained unbridgeable. Now Magidov's new central committee was equally unsuccessful in implementing the party line and winning the support of the trade union rank and file. In 1922 and 1923, trade union leaders blamed this failure on the residue of Menshevism; now in 1930, the new leaders found it difficult to clean up the mess left by the "right-left" bloc. Trotskyists had only dreamed of upsetting the course toward socialism, Magidov told a meeting of Leningrad printers in November 1930, but the rights actually succeeded in doing so. They supported only modest goals for industrial growth. They had failed to foresee the increase in demand for skilled printers.[38]

In his public appearances in late 1930, Magidov emphatically distanced himself from the work of the Printers' Union before September 1929, when Borshchevskii and the "opportunists" had been expelled. A small chorus of Magidov's supporters dutifully affirmed the "gross political mistakes" of the old leadership. Their line had been that of trade unionism, which they defined as "defending the interests of a small gang of skilled workers against the interests of the working class as a whole. Our *professional* union gives primacy to the interests of production."[39] But if one looked beyond the ritual denunciations of the discredited leadership, it was hard to find that any real change had taken place in the proficiency of the new union officials. The names of the local delegates at the 1930 congresses may have been new, but their criticisms continued along the same lines as before. The union offered no living leadership: they still relied on circulars published in the central press. Instructors rarely visited local enterprises: "If they're starting up some campaign or other, then they're compelled to show up at a plenary meeting of the factory commit-

---

37. TsGA SPb, f. 4804, op. 14, d. 21 (meetings of Leningrad oblast board, 1930), ll. 37–114; *Pechatnik* 19–20 (1930): 8; 25–26 (1930): 7; GARF, f. R-5525, op. 12, d. 38 (stenographic report of Leningrad Oblast Congress of Paper Makers and Printers, 14–17 February 1930), ll. 25–118.

38. GARF, f. R-5525, op. 12, d. 38, ll. 29, 31; d. 1 (stenographic report of First All-Union Congress of Paper and Print Workers, 22–24 December 1930), l. 47.

39. Ibid., d. 1, ll. 43, 97, 110ob., 114, 121ob., 124, 126, 129, 163ob., 174; TsGAMO, f. 4660, op. 1, d. 120 (protocols of Second Moscow Oblast Congress, 13–15 December 1930, pt. 1), ll. 29, 105–6, 112, 135, 181; GARF, f. R-5525, op. 12, d. 38, l. 37.

tee, speak a couple of warm words, and then disappear again for a month." At the Twenty-second Print Shop in Moscow, not one factory committee chair had served out a full term; either they were denounced as right deviationists, or called leftists, or had embezzled, or were incompetent. The new union chair had called for fewer meetings and more work, but as one delegate pointed out to much laughter, while the rules of the congress limited speeches to one hour, Magidov himself had spoken for two and a half. The union failed to quell sub rosa resistance to the party line, although they would not label the evidence as opposition. Instead, they cited "politically confused" headlines that appeared in the worker press: "We are against opportunists and socialism" instead of "against opportunists and social fascists"; "We demand the acquittal of our comrade wreckers" instead of their "conviction"; "Strengthen party poultry breeding [*kurovodstvo*]" instead of "party leadership" [*rukovodstvo*].[40]

Nor had the neoproductivists of the reformed union done very well in the economic sphere. The new central committee had failed to attain the goals of the industrial plan, nor did it seem to care to. They paid too little attention to helping locals negotiate their collective agreements. The new committee may have had the right party line, said one delegate, but not the right action.[41] Wages remained low, and worse, great disparities remained between conditions in different types of enterprises.

In the face of this barrage, the new union leadership merely fell back on the familiar tactic of scapegoating: instead of Menshevism, they now named the enemy "opportunism," defined as "the gap between resolutions and their implementation." The union still needed a systematic daily struggle with every manifestation of "opportunism" in theory and practice; it was too soon to throw out the slogan "Liquidate the opportunist dregs."[42] Menshevism at least had stood for a political program and a set of trade union values. "Opportunism" as used in 1930 had lost every last shred of political content.

Institutionally, the final months of 1930 ushered in a major reorganization of the trade union. This process appears to have played a small role in the work of the Printers' Union or the concerns of its members, but by October 1930, the deed was done: in the interests of improving the political and production work of all involved (in other words, to disinfect the union of the opportunist and trade unionist diseases), the autonomous Section of Journalists within the Printers' Union would be dissolved, and the new unified union would merge with the Union of Paper Workers.[43] The All-Union Congress that met on 24 De-

40. TsGAMO, f. 4660, op. 1, d. 120, ll. 143, 160, 209, 217, 249; d. 121 (protocols of Second Moscow Oblast Congress, 13–15 December 1930, pt. 2), l. 33; GARF, f. R-5525, op. 12, d. 1, ll. 1100b., 1310b., 202.

41. TsGAMO, f. 4660, op. 1, d. 121, ll. 7–8.

42. GARF, f. R-5525, op. 12, d. 1, ll. 244, 271–72.

43. *Leningradskaia pravda*, 27 October 1930; *Trud*, 22 December 1930. The journalists had always met in separate assemblies from the printers, and they published their own journal, *Zhurnalist*.

cember 1930, under the leadership of Magidov, thus represented the first meeting of the new combined union.

The officials who led the union into the 1930s reflected the complete transformation of the leadership. The presidium elected at the December 1930 congress consisted entirely of names new to the union leadership, some of them outsiders like Magidov, others newly promoted local leaders such as the new factory committee chair at Krasnyi Proletarii. The members of the oblast board in Moscow in 1930, with very few exceptions, had not served before 1930. Given the prevalence of some surnames, it is difficult to trace the continuity of board members with certainty, but not only did the members of the Moscow board in 1930 seem to be new to the board, but very few had been active anywhere in the industry before 1930.[44] The purge in Moscow, in other words, had claimed most of the trade union's party veterans. In Leningrad, Rozov had managed to hold onto his position until the beginning of 1930, and he was joined on the board there by a number of veteran party and trade union members from the Leningrad organization, particularly activists from the Pechatnyi Dvor print shop.[45] This reinforces the conclusion that Rozov had been able to resist the center's efforts to oust him because of the loyal support of the Leningrad organization, but as we have seen, the Leningrad resistance proved to be short-lived.

## WORKER POLITICS ON THE SHOP FLOOR OF THE FIVE-YEAR PLAN

The congresses and conferences in which the trade union purged its leaders drew the participation of a small number of union members.[46] The dramatic struggles between so-called right-wing opportunists and Stalinist Communists seemed to be taking place entirely apart from the day-to-day experience of the union rank and file. Yet the language of the party struggle invoked the "demands" and "interests" of the worker mass. What weight can actually be assigned to this "worker mass" in orchestrating the downfall of the old union leadership? Both the criticisms offered at official meetings and the worried concerns expressed at private party meetings offer ample evidence that the worker mass remained unhappy with its leadership. Was it possible that the purge of opportunism was at least partly a response to criticism from below? Did the overturn of the trade union leadership from top to bottom and the absence of local defenders represent the power of a grassroots Stalinism? In exploring the role of rank-and-file opposition, it is essential to distinguish between opposition to the trade union for its alleged faults and sins, opposition to the regime for its

---

44. GARF, f. R-5525, op. 12, d. 1, l. 5; the list of the board elected in December 1930 appears in TsGAMO, f. 4660, op. 1, d. 121, ll. 226–28. The analysis of continuity comes from a database I constructed of the names of members of the boards of Moscow and Leningrad and the central committees from 1918 to 1930.
45. GARF, f. R-5525, op. 12, d. 38, l. 23; TsGAMO, f. 699, op. 1, d. 1059, l. 67.
46. TsGAMO, f. 699, op. 1, d. 1059, l. 67; *Pechatnik* 4–5 (15 February 1929): 2.

antiworker policies, and broader opposition to Soviet socialism, by which I mean centralized and paternalist social ownership of the means of production.

Certainly the Printers' Union had given its members ample reason to lose confidence in its leadership. The union did not do a good job of defending its members' economic interests and seemed generally unresponsive to their needs. The reported problems of "no local ties," indifference, bureaucracy, favoritism, drinking parties, and corruption arose so frequently that they must have been genuine concerns. Diagnosis of the cause of these problems was more complicated: union members blamed individuals, but the party blamed political untrustworthiness. No one raised the possibility that the system itself guaranteed that the trade union could not serve two masters, the worker members and the "proletariat" at large. Instead, gaps between the leaders and the led were blamed on "Mensheviks" (in 1919 or 1922) and on opportunists in 1929, not on the persistent contradictions between the needs of the "working class as a whole" and the interests of particular groups of workers. The artificiality of this recourse to blaming political enemies, however, is proved by the fact that the chorus of discontent continued in the same key even after the "opportunists" across the country had been eliminated from their posts.

The unemployed had already registered their complaints, emboldened by the knowledge that they had no jobs that could be taken away in retribution for speaking out. "The party has become the new gentry," offered one speaker in 1927, and the unemployed were divided into two castes. Nonparty members remained unemployed, party members received jobs out of turn, and the unfairness created antagonism, an "abnormal phenomenon in a land of workers and peasants." Rozov, the Leningrad party chief, also noticed "abnormalities" in local enterprises: party members dared to speak out in favor of raising wages, and they received the support of "former oppositionists." In the lower Volga in 1929, workers (labeled "backward," of course, by the leadership) objected to the socialist emulation campaign: "They call it a new form of exploitation of the workers." In the aftermath of the purge of the union leadership in the fall of 1929, the new presidium conceded that a wave of anti-Soviet and antiparty outbursts (*vystupleniia*) was taking place. "And there are instances when the leadership of the organizations react to these counterrevolutionary acts with impermissible moderation." The presidium issued a stern warning to all union activists against smoothing over these protests or seeking to mediate them.[47]

Yet still the new leaders failed to mobilize their members for the tasks of socialist construction. Party members refused to accept assignments to help collectivize the countryside, preferring instead to resign from the party. Komsomol activists were dropping out of the party and ceasing their activism as soon as they finished their apprenticeships. There was flagrant opposition to shock work in individual enterprises. In one print shop, an enthusiast was told, "For such shock work you should get it in the neck."[48] Disaffection, opposition, and

47. GARF, f. R-5525, op. 10, d. 41, l. 72; TsGAIPD SPb, f. 435, op. 1, d. 71, l. 103; GARF, f. R-5525, op. 11, d. 12, l. 5, and d. 17, l. 2610b.
48. *Pechatnik* 3 (January 1930): 14; 5 (1930): 15.

covert resistance appeared to be widespread in the printing industry in 1929 and 1930. One can speculate, moreover, that the sudden shortage of skilled printers at the end of 1930 may have emboldened the disaffected, knowing that the party leaders could either repress dissent or promote production, but not both.

In fact, the response of workers on the print shop floor was complicated and contradictory. No less than the veteran Communists at the center of party politics, workers disagreed among themselves about the politics of revolution and the path to socialism. True believers in the total proletarian project did exist on the shop floor, rallying and chivvying their comrades toward support for the goals of the party leadership. The evidence from print shops also indicates the strong presence of a workerist opposition, sometimes linked to Trotskii, accusing the regime of failing to defend the interests of the working class. While these activists may have been particularly persecuted and therefore were few, their dissidence was met sympathetically by a much larger set of printers, many of them local activists, who tolerated the voices of opposition in their midst. Lenience toward the opposition became labeled as "rightist," "opportunism," and "tailism" (being dragged by the worker mass instead of leading as the party vanguard) or colloquially as "vegetarianism," and was attacked in the wholesale purge of the union cadres in 1929 and 1930. Finally, perhaps the largest number of printers turned their backs on politics altogether, drawing the wrath of the party zealots and the contempt of the oppositionists for their passivity and their "philistine" approach to life under socialism.[49]

Worker-correspondents served on the front line of party zealotry. While these activists received regular instructions on themes for discussion and they could publish only work that supported the party line, they were a self-selected group, and thus must have been willing, for ideological or selfish reasons, to express the party's point of view. One correspondent for the Sixteenth Print Shop's factory newspaper lashed out at workers who complained about tough discipline and Soviet power: this was an "unproletarian psychology, friends." As for the worker who allegedly spied on his comrades in order to enforce output rates, "it would be good if we had many such spies, who would honestly work alongside our leadership for the strengthening of our country."[50] Local party voices criticized the attitudes that discouraged shock work and party activism.[51] An open letter in the *Leningradskaia pravda* shop newspaper chastised one Volkov for anti-Soviet behavior: "I don't have grounds to call you a capitalist. . . . You work at the bench, that means you're a worker." But Volkov occupied himself too much in criticism and not enough in work; at a shop meeting he engaged in conversation instead of listening to the report. When called to order, Volkov

49. See *Sotsialisticheskii vestnik* 13 (179) (8 July 1928): 12.
50. *Nasha zhizn'*, 12 January 1928.
51. *Zhizn' pechatnika*, 11 December 1929; *Nasha zhizn'*, 21 and 30 April 1928, 15 January 1929, 23 March 1930; *Pechatnyi dvor*, 6 March 1930; *Zorkii glaz*, 8 March 1929, 24 November 1929; *Leningradskii pravdist*, 3 June and 26 December 1930; *Iskry*, 19 October and 24 December 1929.

said, "I'm not bothering you and I don't want to listen," thus "proving" his hostility to Soviet power and its institutions.[52]

Other voices spoke in terms of class war and of ridding the union of non-proletarian elements. A worker at First Model criticized the union leadership in August 1929, agreed that it was guilty of the right deviation, and argued that the only solution would be to promote real workers "from the bench" to positions in the union. An unemployed printer, Bakunin, called in October 1929 for the expulsion from the union of all workers who possessed houses and land so that "pure proletarians" could return to their jobs. Other speakers at such meetings spoke up not only for the principles of Lenin (which of course could be used in support of opposition) but to defend the current party line explicitly.[53] These party activists lashed out at all deviations from the total proletarian norm, whether it was outright opposition, toleration of opposition, or simply failure to be active at all.

Opposition itself came in many forms, from subtle and anonymous "mistakes" in headlines to bold statements against the party line. One source of opposition was the chronic conflict between workers and administrators over work rates and pay levels. The trade union tried to manage such disagreements, but dissidents sought to use this conflict to argue the bankruptcy of the Communist line. Trotskii's supporters, admitted the leadership, had made political capital out of the continuing economic troubles, and they used the periodic collective agreement campaigns to sow doubt and confusion among printers. An illegal Trotskyist proclamation that was circulated at the Sixteenth Print Shop led even some party members to vote against the party line on the collective agreement there.[54] At Krasnyi Proletarii, a group of young Communists admitted to drinking to Trotskii's health and seeing him off at the station when he was sent into exile in January 1928. Later, Trotskyists draped huge banners in each of the plant's two stairwells and sent leaflets to Komsomol members there, "with stamps, very politely," urging them to read the leaflets and pass them on.[55]

These critics argued from a socialist point of view ("from the left") that the Communist Party had betrayed the workers and subverted socialist democracy. "We need to elect someone who will defend *our* hides," insisted one unemployed printer in April 1929. The union compromises with the administrators, said another. Meeting in the aftermath of the dissolution of the Moscow union leadership in October 1929, workers at the Sixteenth Print Shop were asked to

---

52. *Zorkii glaz*, 1 May 1927.
53. TsGAMO, f. 4660, op. 1, d. 5 (conferences and meetings in Moscow print shops to elect delegates to First Oblast Congress, 1929), l. 3; also d. 31 (general meetings of unemployed union members, 1929), ll. 30, 60.
54. *Nasha zhizn'*, 15 January 1929.
55. *Krasnyi proletarii*, 9 March 1929, 6 December 1928; *Pechatnik* 35 (15 December 1929): 5; TsGAIPD SPb, f. 435, op. 1, d. 74, l. 133ob. See Leon Trotsky, *My Life* (New York, 1970), 540-41, and Daniels, *Conscience of the Revolution*, 371.

cast out their opportunist factory committee, too. They were skeptical. A woman from the cardboard department charged that the factory committee at the Sixteenth "didn't do anything and the new one won't do anything because the factory administrators are given too much power. Under these conditions, our factory committee can, so to say, only lick their boots." "This isn't a party, it's a den of thieves! Down with Soviet power," said an anonymous note passed up to the speaker during one of these meetings. Dissidents objected to the appointment of representatives from above: "I didn't elect you and I won't recognize you," said a worker at First Model. "We need to elect our people, and not the ones who are chosen for us."[56]

A few others risked even more flagrant opposition to the party line. At the Sixteenth Print Shop, drink gave the pressman Evdokimov the nerve to declare the Shakhty defendants not guilty in June 1928 and to turn on the Communist Party. "We should shoot all you Communists. You Communists don't have much time left to reign [*tsarstvovat'*]. They'll soon get you! They'll hang your commissars." (A month later Evdokimov denied he had said this, but had said "shoot all sham Communists." He was a proletarian and had spent the entire time of the revolution in the ranks of the printers, he said, as though to say no worker with his pedigree could utter such anti-Soviet words.)[57] Another such proletarian was the dissident Kuz'minskii in Leningrad. He had stirred up his fellow workers at the Sokolova print shop, attacking the party's policies and accusing it of repression. Not satisfied with just speaking out at meetings, the Leningrad union's party committee reported, he agitated among workers in their departments and invited them to his apartment for discussions, where he acquainted them with materials that would open their eyes to the incorrect line of the party. He played chiefly on the political struggles among the leadership but also on workers' lack of economic success. This same Kuz'minskii prided himself on his proletarian bearing. When scolded by a fellow worker for his hard-boiled (*otvaritel'nye*) and filthy abusive language, Kuz'minskii retorted that he didn't realize that with this worker he must avoid the workers' language and speak the language of the intelligentsia.[58]

The Pechatnyi Dvor Print Shop served as a special beacon of independence. Rozov had relied on the support of this shop in his successful resistance to the party's attempt to remove him in 1929, but their independence had attracted the worried attention of party leaders well before this. In early 1927, a general meeting of the printing plant's workers assembled to reconsider the recall of their Soviet deputy, Vasil'ev. In a "demagogic speech" he had denounced the regime: "We don't have a dictatorship of the proletariat, but a dictatorship of

---

56. TsGAMO, f. 4660, op. 1, d. 31, ll. 9, 29, 30; d. 22 (general meetings at Sixteenth, September–November 1929), l. 160b.; TsGA SPb, f. 4804, op. 11, d. 158, l. 470b.; *Pechatnik* 21 (31 July 1929): 16.

57. *Nasha zhizn'*, 9 June and 4 July 1928; *Krasnoproletarets*, 26 March 1930.

58. TsGAIPD SPb, f. 435, op. 1, d. 71, l. 1030b., and d. 106, ll. 26–260b.; *Iskry*, 15 December 1928.

thieves and embezzlers, and this means that Soviet power and we too are thieves and embezzlers." Vasil'ev defended his statements, saying they were constructed entirely from a speech of Stalin: if he, Vasil'ev, was a counterrevolutionary, he implied, then so was the general secretary. Although the general meeting voted to recall Vasil'ev as the plant's deputy ("If we printers elect such a demagogue to the soviet, then it's a sign that we're against the soviet"), the firebrand did not disappear from view. He was actually promoted to manager of the zincography department and continued to engage in politics, campaigning for the Leningrad Soviet in 1928 and forming a group of supporters, including some former Mensheviks. The print shop's party collective considered his case in April 1929, at the moment when the new trade union leadership was engaged in the purge of Tomskii supporters. Vasil'ev, they agreed, had always been a troublemaker, he supported whatever deviation was currently in fashion, and if earlier he was a Trotskii supporter, lately he had flagrantly adopted the right deviation. Only at the end of 1930 did Vasil'ev's party career come to an end. The enterprise's party collective voted to expel both Vasil'ev and another party member for criticizing the regime's agrarian policy. Meanwhile, worries about an oppositional mood in local print shops acquired special urgency in the autumn of 1929, when the central leadership attempted to depose Rozov and the Leningrad board. Factory committees in Leningrad received instructions to keep close watch on their workers, to provide information on their political mood and on the appearance of any "antisocial groupings, simultaneously feeling out their attitudes and trying to influence them."[59]

In fact, factory committees and union organizations preferred to ignore or to tolerate political dissidence within their ranks, especially when opposition was linked to defense of printers' economic interests. Excessive tolerance for political heterodoxy constituted another deviation from the proletarian norm. This was the crime of opportunism, also known as tailism or vegetarianism. Failure to lead had brought down Borshchevskii and the entire union leadership in 1929: their weak political work allowed a tailist mood among the workers. The toothless vegetarianism of *Pechatnik* had become part of the opportunist deviation. Tailism in local practice meant defense of workers' interests, or at least refusal to join those party forces that wished to mobilize workers for socialist campaigns to intensify production. When oppositionists agitated at the Sixteenth Print Shop in late 1928, local party members did not resist and did not reject the so-called narrow and selfish demands of some workers concerning the collective agreement: quintessential tailism, charged party activists.[60] The factory committee at the Sixteenth shop had to be replaced, said

---

59. TsGA SPb, f. 4804, op. 11, d. 99 (general and factory committee meetings at Pechatnyi Dvor, 1926–27), ll. 238–39; TsGAIPD SPb, f. 250, op. 1, d. 220 (bureau of party collective at Pechatnyi Dvor, 1929), ll. 114–114ob, 121; TsGAIPD SPb, f. 435, op. 1, d. 74 (bureau of fraction of Leningrad oblast union, 31 October 1929), l. 117; *Pechatnyi dvor*, 26 October 1930.

60. *Pechatnik* 28 (14 October 1929): inside front cover, 1; *Trud*, 7 June 1930; *Nasha zhizn'*, 15 January 1929; TsGAIPD SPb, f. 250, op. 1, d. 220, l. 152.

the new Moscow union leader, because it did not know how to cope with party directions on the current tasks of socialism, it was unable to mobilize its members toward the goals of the Five-Year Plan, and instead dealt with petty questions.[61]

Factory committees could be labeled tailist for tolerating the outbursts and anti-Soviet organizing of dissidents, as a case in Voronezh illustrates. Here Turbin, a factory committee member at the Kommuna print shop (now the only shop in town), circulated a petition to resist the terms of the collective agreement, harassed young bindery workers who tried to organize a shock brigade, and resisted the arrival of a stopwatch brigade in the shop: "Instead of using hours as your unit of measurement, why not just count blows of the lash!" Except for a few staunch Communists, no one objected to his anti-Soviet sentiments and he remained a factory committee member until December 1929. Apologizing, he was forgiven in view of his long service in production, but other factory committees and party cells were warned not to sleep through this *Turbinovshchina*. The "light hand of the party cell" in an unnamed provincial shop also permitted active criticism of management in 1928.[62]

Ultimately, tailism and opportunism came to include all behavior that did not actively support the goals and aims of the party and new union leadership. Apathy could be seen as just as harmful to the socialist cause as political deviation. Party activists remained acutely sensitive to the signs of worker mobilization and its absence, as they had been throughout the existence of socialism.[63] Total participation remained their ideal, and anything less compromised the successful construction of communism. But indifference had become the best and safest weapon with which workers could resist the regime's demands on them.

One of the clearest indicators of the disaffection of rank-and-file workers had always been their unwillingness to attend meetings. Union organizations reported publicly that participation in factory committee elections had risen to a healthy 75 or even 85 percent in 1928, but local reports contradicted this optimistic assessment.[64] At the Sixteenth Print Shop, no more than 5 or 6 percent of workers came to meetings to elect shop delegates, and even these grumbled "Hurry up" in the face of endless reports. A year later, less than one-third of the workers came to meetings to elect the factory committee. By late 1930, *Pechatnik* worried that an "unhealthy mood" prevailed toward political activism. At the Fourteenth Print Shop in Moscow, only 18 workers out of 100

---

61. TsGAMO, f. 4660, op. 1, d. 22, ll. 16–18; *Pechatnik* 34 (5 December 1929): 19.
62. *Sotsialisticheskii vestnik* 10/11 (200/201) (25 May 1929): 24.
63. *Pechatnik* 6 (28 February 1927): 4; 35 (18 December 1927): 4–5; 16 (1 June 1928): 11; 35 (18 December 1928): 11.
64. *Pechatnik* 11 (8 April 1928): 9; 14 (12 May 1928): 16; 16 (1 June 1928): 11; TsGAMO, f. 4660, op. 1, d. 52 (report on work of factory committee at Krasnyi Proletarii, December 1929–July 1930), ll. 1–2; *Pechatnyi dvor*, 1 October 1928; *Pechatnik* 9 (30 March 1929): 16; *Iskry*, 19 October 1929.

turned out for a meeting in one workshop, 20 of 80 in another. Two shop-level meetings had been canceled at the Sixteenth for lack of a quorum, five at Krasnyi Proletarii.[65]

Union officials continued to focus on the mechanics and organization of workplace activism in efforts to make meetings more attractive to members: shorter reports, better preparation, more delegates' meetings, fewer meetings, better activists.[66] Their urge to mobilize, however, faced stiff competition from the growing pressures of daily life. Dissidents blamed economic conditions for the loss of activism. Urban workers at the end of the 1920s had been so beaten down by the effort required to feed and shelter their families, wrote local correspondents to *Sotsialisticheskii vestnik*, that they had no time or energy for politics, either right or left. Others retreated to the comfort of the bottle. The party cell at the Sixteenth Print Shop's typesetting department was scolded because they ignored the party line, occupied themselves with drinking, or at the very least covered up other workers' drinking.[67]

Nor did the next generation of printers offer much hope for party activists eager to mobilize the Soviet working class. First of all, thanks to the cutbacks in the apprenticeship programs, very few young workers remained in Soviet print shops by the end of the 1920s. Their absence had served as one of the indictments against the old leadership, an expression of the hope that the new party leadership placed in the activism of youth.[68] But more important, even those young workers who found employment in the printing industry shared in the disaffection from politics that characterized the workforce as a whole. Great emphasis was placed on using enthusiastic youth as "light cavalry" to "add yeast" to the self-criticism project in 1928.[69] Far more common, however, was the incessant harping at young people for their lack of political activism, for "empty" shock brigades, indifference toward meetings, lack of concern for production, too much concern for private instead of production life, and dancing instead of defending the Soviet Union. "We are seeking," read one satiric notice in the *Krasnyi proletarii* lost-and-found section, "lost consciousness about the goals and tasks of the Komsomol. Please reply to the Komsomol cell, attention: some conscious Komsomols."[70]

One explanation for the disaffection of young people was their marginal-

---

65. *Nasha zhizn'*, 1 May 1927, 21 April 1928; *Pechatnik* 19–20 (1930): 7.
66. TsGAIPD SPb, f. 250, op. 1, d. 220, l. 310b.; *Pechatnik* 35 (18 December 1927): 4–5; 4 (1 February 1928): 7–8; 9–10 (25 March 1928): 16; 16 (1 June 1928): 11; 30 (22 October 1928): 22; 35 (18 December 1928): 11; 1 (1 January 1929): 8; 2 (20 January 1929): 5; 13 (17 May 1929): 10; 14–15 (31 May 1929): 26–27; 22 (12 August 1929): 7; 25–26 (11 September 1929): 20; 6 (1930): inside back cover.
67. *Sotsialisticheskii vestnik* 12 (202) (14 June 1929): 16; 22 (212) (21 November 1929): 16; *Nasha zhizn'*, 8–15 March 1929; *Pechatnik* 9 (1930): 20.
68. GARF, f. R-5525, op. 12, d. 38, l. 31.
69. *Zhizn' pechatnika*, 18 August 1928.
70. *Krasnyi proletarii*, 15 February 1927; *Iskry*, 20 December 1930; Koenker, "Fathers against Sons," 802–4.

ization by adult printers. But young would-be activists also faced the same constraints on truly independent activity as their elders, and responded in much the same way, by retreat into private life. The young stood outside public life, lamented the First Model factory newspaper in March 1929: "they marvel at revolutionary novels, but they've moved away from all that, they feel themselves free and with unlimited possibilities, they forget about the struggle that needs to be carried out to the end. Young people concern themselves only with ordinary things: to hang out, to dance a little, and for this they already have enough material security." It was no secret that not just the nonparty youth here but even Komsomols gathered in apartments, organized parties, took their girls to picnics at dachas, and engaged in continuous drinking. Others abandoned their Komsomol commitments as soon as they had completed their apprenticeships.[71]

## WORKING-CLASS POLITICS AND THE RISE OF STALIN

The purge of the Printers' Union leadership in 1929 terminated the possibility of an independent worker voice in this urban industry. However red the Printers' Union tried to be, however fervently they professed to concern themselves with production as well as labor, the structure and the tradition of the trade union movement required the leadership to respond to the interests of its members and not only to the state. In another socialist world, the trade union might have played a mediating role between the interests of workers and the goals of the workers' state: this was the vision of the leaders of the Menshevik trade union movement in the first years of the revolution. The total politics of the Communists, however, denied the possibility of a mediating role for any institution in society: a good Communist, a good class-conscious worker should be totally committed to the Communist Party line, which in 1928 meant the all-out assault for industrial growth. Any position less steadfast than this signified compromise, doubt, and a dangerous conciliation that undermined the cause of the socialist transformation.

The contradictory class position of workers, however, produced an alternative politics that complicated the Communist cause. Printers, as we have seen, accepted certain elements of the Communist project and rejected others. They accepted the division of society into classes and in their political grievances they defended their honor and their entitlements as printers, as workers, as the toilers whose labor produced the value on which society was built. This sensitivity to class could have made them receptive to the party's intensifying language of class war, and as we have seen, printers often articulated a class-based rhetoric of grievances in their complaints: against bureaucrats, against peasants, against bosses. The problem, though, included the contradictory class po-

---

71. *Zhizn' pechatnika,* 8 March and 6 April 1929; *Leningradskii pravdist,* 23 November 1930; *Iskry,* 23 August 1929.

sition of the bosses, whose job it was to enforce newly draconian measures of labor remuneration and labor discipline, but in the name of the proletarian state. Printers rejected the inevitability of proletarian labor relations that constrained their workplace culture even more tightly than remembered capitalism had done, and insofar as their trade union defended the regime's policies against the workers' perceived interests, printers rejected their trade union as well.

The Printers' Union leadership fell in 1929 because of a concerted campaign at the highest levels of the party leadership to root out and punish sources of opposition to the prevailing party line. But this campaign was made easier by the union's loss of authority and thus legitimacy among the tens of thousands of disaffected and alienated union members. Whether we measure the passive majority as a silent opposition or apolitical deserters from the socialist front, the records suggest that there was very little outright support for the trade union's policies. Printers declined to go to the barricades for Borshchevskii or, in the end, for Rozov. Their replacements, however, could only be worse. If Borshchevskii and Company had at least tried to maneuver the narrow passage between the goals of the party and the interests of their workers, the new leadership paid even less heed to mediating between workers and management or defending the interests of workers in the larger polity. Not surprisingly, then, they generated the same repertory of complaints from below: of bureaucracy, corruption, formalism, and indifference.

Political alternatives for workers, however, had now disappeared. Mensheviks had offered a plausible alternative to the disasters of Communist trade union politics in 1918, but Menshevism was no longer politically viable in the Soviet Union of 1929. Trotskyism could crystallize the discontent of the unemployed and underemployed in 1927, but Trotskyism too was now anathema to the socialist project. Trade unionists themselves had been disgraced and discredited as tailists and opportunists. By 1930 the Soviet system had no tolerance for an independent voice that could speak for workers or mediate between their interests and those of other parts of society. There was no room in the Soviet system for organized labor at all.

But there was room and a desperate need for labor, and this need provided a small space within which printers (and other workers) could carve out a kind of politics of daily life and daily work. The vibrant independent culture of printers had flourished because these workers honored debate as well as conformity. Menshevism had offered more space for political pluralism than had Boshevism; workerist trade unionism likewise tolerated heterodoxy more than the Communists' productivist variant. It was not necessarily inconsistent that a dissident such as Leningrad's Vasil'ev could be both a Menshevik and a Trotskyist—both positions offered critical distance from the reigning orthodoxy. Printers' experience of socialist trade unionism had taught them to practice infrapolitics and covert, petty resistance, and to seek solace for their grievances in arenas outside the realm of traditional politics. Mensheviks in Berlin grumbled that these potential shock workers for opposition had become trapped in the morass of the everyday. Communists in Moscow would continue to see danger in the disaffection of workers from the proletarian project. In withdrawing from active politics, printers and other workers like them ceded political primacy to the Stalinists, but their withdrawal was the result and not the cause of the turn to the hard-line politics of class war in the First Five-Year Plan.

# CHAPTER 9

## CLASS FORMATION OR THE UNMAKING OF THE WORKING CLASS?

*Individualism is developing here. The masses don't live for what our cultural work provides; they live for their own personal interests.*

— LENINGRAD UNION BOARD, 1930

*I don't believe the interests of the working class will be harmed if I color my fingernails with polish.*

— YOUNG WOMAN WORKER AT KRASNYI PROLETARII PRINT SHOP, 1927

In February 1930, *Pechatnik* published an alarming warning about the latest danger to confront the socialist project: the urban kulak. An ideological relative of the village kulak, then under ruthless assault by Communist collectivization brigades, the urban kulak chose different weapons to achieve the same goal of destroying Soviet industrialization. Where the rural kulak wielded sawed-off shotguns, axes, and pikes, the city kulak used more cultured and artful methods. He was a class enemy inside the very socialist enterprise that was supposed to lead the transformation effort. He possessed all the credentials of a genuine worker: he "worked all his life" and earned a decent wage as a skilled craftsman. He was a cultured worker, a familiar figure in the canon of proletarian self-improvement: he did not smoke or drink, he bought on subscription the collected works of Tolstoi, Dostoevskii, and Gor'kii. He attended church only occasionally, sometimes on holy days. But this cultured, urban skilled worker, who appeared to be the epitome of the total proletarian, betrayed his class in the ideology he shared with his village cousin: the ideology of selfishness, of stuffing himself (*zhrat'*). You could hear him express this ideology in loud animal roars or in snakelike whispers on the tram or in the bathhouse: "There is no meat. Wages are low. There's nothing to buy." These urban kulak oppositionists were no longer mere "spikes in the wheel" of socialist construction. No, under the conditions of triumphant socialism, these urban kulaks had placed a knife in the very back of the working class.[1] The article served in part as a warning to printers to be suspicious of the class credentials even of the most proletarian-appearing comrade, but it also signaled that class origin was no longer a guarantee of proper socialist ideology. In this way, the article served to undermine the stability of class identity altogether.

These so-called class enemies, in fact, claimed a superior working-class identity. In denouncing voluntary shock brigades at their print shop, they insisted that *they* stood on the high road of socialism and collectivism; they sarcastically denounced the claims of the "most senior" and "most highly skilled" Linotypists to either skill or socialism and accused them of joining the shock work movement out of motives of blatant self-advancement. Who was the more selfish—the shock worker or the anti–shock worker? Real proletarians, they implied, scorned the trumped-up production schemes of the regime, and they knew how to defend their collective.

This episode offers further evidence for the ability of skilled workers to manipulate socialist forms and to resist pressures to adopt more intensified work practices. In talking back to the worker-correspondent who attempted to shame them, the so-called urban kulaks dared to assert even in the very public forum of the union journal their right to control work processes. The episode also directly addresses the key concern of this chapter: the multiple meanings of proletarian identity in the years of transition to the Five-Year Plan. Both those who resisted socialist work schemes and those who defended them appropriated the images and language of the total proletarian to assert their claim to personify the Soviet working class. The urban kulak was skilled, sober, and a self-improver: how then could he denounce the regime, complain about its policies, and refuse to join in its productivity schemes? These proletarians who placed consumption over production could no longer be called proletarians; they must be some alien creature: hence the label "kulak." But for their part, these skilled workers were continuing to demand from their regime and their union a defense of their material expectations of socialism: meat, decent wages, and goods to spend them on. Even after the workerist leadership of the Printers' Union had disappeared into the dustbin of socialist oppositions, the interests they had been urged to defend continued to be upheld in infrapolitical actions such as these.

This episode also provides a link to the economic and political contexts of worker identity at the end of the 1920s. Materially, printers continued to enjoy

---

1. *Pechatnik* 5 (1930): 15; 31 (20 November 1929): 4.

a relatively high standard of living but with increasingly dim expectations that it would continue. The fear of unemployment and displacement from the industry would not abate until later in 1930, and the return to full employment in the industry would not be accompanied by a concomitant return to the material comfort of the mid-1920s. Getting and spending remained issues of paramount concern for printers. Politically, the struggle that eliminated the leaders of the so-called right deviation and produced the convulsive assault on the peasantry in the winter of 1929–30 also created a new vocabulary of politics, reflected aptly in the change of registers here from the inanimate "spike in the wheel" to the corporeal "knife in the back." This new language of mortal enemies permeated the political discourse of the period known as the Cultural Revolution, and in evaluating the evidence of worker culture and identity, we must be sensitive to both novelty and continuity in the ways in which printers participated in the elaboration of socialist culture.

## CLASS ON THE JOB

The relationship between class and craft remained complicated for Soviet printers at the end of the 1920s. To "become Soviet" meant to subordinate one's craft identity to an overarching proletarian ethic, and perhaps even to discard the particularities of the trade altogether. Once technology had succeeded in replacing all human labor with machines, the need for specialized skills would disappear.[2] Socialist tarif reform had relentlessly endeavored to equalize all skills and all jobs on a universal grid of knowledge and experience. Printers' well-known pride in their craft, while still celebrated in the chronicles of the union's past, also worked to keep the commanders of the leaden army aloof and separate from their proletarian brothers and sisters. At the same time, skilled work and production remained at the center of proletarian identity, a central attribute that defined the membership of printers in the working class and marked their distinctiveness as well.

The skilled work of printers and the distinctive jargon of their craft thus continued to be reflected in the ways in which printers talked about themselves and their place in the socialist society.[3] When printers joked among themselves, their craft provided the common language of humor. A particularly ribald story centered on the variety of fonts that printers needed to master and emphasized the important differences between the skilled initiates and the unskilled outsiders. Ivan Stepanych, a country boy who had never before encountered Latin text, could not make out the Latin words "minimum" and "maximum" in the copy he was working with. He saw the roman *m* and *n* as italicized Cyrillic letters, the lowercase *t* and *p*. What were these words "tipitit" and "takhitit"? he asked

---

2. A story in *Nasha zhizn'*, 9 June 1928, alludes to this utopian vision.
3. E.g., *Pechatnik* 1 (14 January 1927): 22; 7–8 (10 March 1927): 31; 18 (30 June 1929): 9; *Nasha zhizn'*, 8 March 1928; *Trud*, 18 July 1930.

all those around him. His confusion quickly earned him his permanent and somewhat obscene nickname, Tipitit Takhititovich. The "Printers' Encyclopedia" that appeared serially in *Pechatnik* in 1928 provided alternative definitions for many distinctive features of the work life of a printer. The vacuum cleaner "can successfully be replaced by the lungs of a typesetter." A hand (*ruchnoi*) typesetter "to the great distress of the boss is not always 'tame' [*ruchnym*]."[4] This was inside humor made intelligible only through knowledge of the printers' craft.

When printers wrote creatively about their lives, the distinctive work of printing continued to play a central role in their stories.[5] Especially poignant as the revolution entered its second decade was a sense of nostalgia for a world in which skill was even more valued and central to one's identity. Semen Lineikin (whose name derived from a typesetting tool) was an outstanding skilled typesetter with prerevolutionary credentials. He took satisfaction in his work for its own sake. He never chased after the big ruble. He trained his share of apprentices. But as printing work became more mechanized, there was less demand for Lineikin's specialized skill, and the new tarif reforms further reduced the difference between specialists as skilled as Lineikin and the rapidly trained younger generation. Lineikin did not begrudge a few rubles to raise the pay level of the least skilled workers, but still the attitude of one of his former pupils chafed at him. This lad, Tyrkin ("the bustler"), measured his own worth in terms of money, not skill: "I spit on skill," he boasted; "you don't need skill to pile up the rubles." When Lineikin discovered that his own skill grade and pay rank had been reduced to the same level as Tyrkin's, he complained to his boss, only to be told, "Yes, my fellow, the time is coming when narrow specialization will stop being a factor in production. All work processes will be done by machine, and people will just be the brains of the machine." Worst of all for Lineikin was to come home to his wife with 15 rubles less in his pay packet than before: would she remember that he was the same Lineikin, the highly skilled typesetter? The link between skill and manliness could hardly be made more emphatic. The story ends with a plaintive question that illustrates the ambiguity of the socialist victory. How could Lineikin oppose this injustice of the socialist wage system? "Behind the type case people were talking about an 'Italian strike' [a slowdown]—and he carried this thought with him to his own type case. No, this was nonsense. In the land of the Soviets there should be no place for 'Italian strikes,' he said almost aloud. I need to use other methods to restore my place in production." The story ended ambiguously: "But how?"[6]

How, indeed? What methods remained for workers to assert their control

---

4. *Pechatnik* 3 (31 January 1927): 25; 22 (3 August 1928): 33; 24–25 (1 September 1928): 48.
5. *Pechatnik* 36 (25 December 1928): 14; 29–30 (25 October 1927): 39; 31 (1 November 1928): 21; 6 (28 February 1927): 27; 25 (5 September 1927): 26.
6. *Nasha zhizn'*, 9 June 1928.

over their craft? Significantly, stories about work ceased to appear in the journals and factory newspapers after 1928, and fiction disappeared entirely from *Pechatnik* after 1929: even under the guise of fiction, perhaps too many uncomfortable questions were being raised about the socialist order. The disappearance of work and the printers' skills from public discourse helped to erode the printers' own distinctive self-image, collapsing them into the broader category of Soviet proletarians. Under socialism, work might fade as the key structuring principle of subjectivity, since now all of private and public life would be pursued according to socialist and humanist principles. Class identity would be sought and defined not only on the shop floor but at home in the family, on evenings and weekends with friends and sweethearts. Here too, on the domestic front of the Cultural Revolution, printers puzzled over the meanings of class and socialism.

## CLASS IN LOVE

Socialist theorists had long argued that patriarchal family relations were bourgeois; the proletarian marriage would be based on equality, respect, comfort, love, and monogamy.[7] But what did a worker marriage look like? The stories that appeared in their press and the indirect evidence of relations between men and women at work indicate that the companionate marriage supported by most socialist reformers remained more an ideal than a reality.

The drinking and abusive husband continued to be a stock character in the tragicomedy of worker life. The binder Ryshakov "taught his wife a lesson" when she refused to give him some of the housekeeping money for drink: he pawned her coat to get the money. His pal Dudyrkin, who had already drunk up half his monthly income, tried the same tactic and ended up hatless and coatless, clinging to every lamppost on the way home, but proud to have taught his wife a lesson, too. Another binder, in a real-life story, drank heavily and beat his pregnant wife so severely that she lost the child.[8]

Philandering husbands also appear with some regularity in the union press. Leaving aside the accusations that the union's central leadership had organized business trips with their "harems," rest home stays and trips to the south invited dreams of dalliance. In one story, old Nikolai Petrovich took a well-deserved two-week vacation in Essentuki, in the Caucasus, and came back so refreshed and rested that his mates teased him about all the chasing after women he must have done. In another story, Comrade Fedia took advantage of the free and easy life at the union rest home to make advances on a series of women, only to be put in his place by one after another. But like other husbands who strayed from the tedium of their domestic arrangements, he came to his senses

---

7. Gorsuch, *Youth in Revolutionary Russia*, 33–36, 113–14; Goldman, *Women, the State, and Revolution*, chap. 1.
8. *Pechatnik* 36 (25 December 1928): 11, 29; *Nasha zhizn'*, 11 June 1927.

and returned sheepishly but gratefully to home, wife, and children.[9] The authors here nodded to the prevailing assumptions about the unhappiness of worker marriages while at the same time offering models of true proletarian love. The total proletarian would perhaps not marry at all, but if he did, he would be a companion to his wife. The gap between norms and actual family situations contributed to the fragmentation of a singular class culture.

By contrast, wives in these vignettes and stories emerge as noble figures: sometimes as victims, sometimes as strong and stoic women dedicated to their families. A few emerged from their unhappy domestic relations with a new zeal for socialism and social change. At the start of "He Returned," Mariia Aleksandrovna sighed stoically as she patiently sewed and cooked for her young son while her husband began a new life with a younger woman. But she voicelessly took him back when her reprobate husband was inspired to return to his family nest after a glimpse of happy families reflected in the winter shop windows of the GUM department store. When the binder Struchkov finally drove his wife to leave him and was himself laid off for drinking, he found solace in more drink and he cursed her for abandoning him in his hour of need. But his wife was now safe in her native Tula village, recovering from his beatings and dreaming of bringing culture and enlightenment to the peasants. The housewife as shrew appears in only one vignette, which depicts a corrupt factory manager who abuses his authority so that he can buy a stylish chapeau at his wife's instruction. The model proletarian wife was submissive and forgiving, silent and strong. Only bourgeois housewives inverted the gender order and dominated their husbands in order to pursue a life of idle luxury.[10]

These familiar types had already been cast by the nature of prerevolutionary family relations, and the stories suggest that ten years of revolution were too little time to change customary practices. Young people, however, could more readily experiment with new forms of romance and courtship. For them, prescriptive models lay near at hand in the union press, complemented by accounts of the complicated path to socialist family construction, but they were also more likely to experiment and to assert their own form of family relations. Shop floor attitudes had dismissed girls as interested only in marriage and family, unlike their male counterparts, who had more important issues to deal with, such as politics and production. But the stories and articles that appeared in the press suggested that young men were just as interested in pursuing romance as young women. Young Kolia Bulkin burned with love for Natasha Chirkina, and when she threw him over for the print shop's star soccer player, Kolia could not control his feelings. As a good socialist, he knew love was just a "certain type of energy" that could be sublimated in work and great deeds, but he longed for

---

9. *Pechatnik* 2 (22 January 1927): 26; 19 (5 July 1928): 23; 5 (12 February 1928): 30.
10. A. Korolev, "Vernulsia," *Pechatnik* 5 (12 February 1928): 30; 36 (25 December 1928): 11; Dmitrii Borovskii, "Posledniaia kommandirovka zavtipa Fileichika," ibid. 32 (7 November 1928), literary supplement: 16–21; M. Frid'eva, "Smysl' zhizni," *Moskovskii pechatnik* 34 (5 December 1924): 4–5.

the chance to perform a great deed that could win Natasha back. In the end, he regained her love through his prowess at chess. Like their older married sisters, young women workers emerge as strong figures who exert a civilizing influence on their prospective mates.[11]

Young Communists, in particular, drew regular reminders from the party that their proletarian social life involved public service, not private satisfactions. Activists worried that marriage was taking Komsomol boys and girls away from their organization. Twenty-year-old Serezha at Krasnyi Proletarii was a "good worker" but shirked his Komsomol duties in favor of parties, where he enjoyed great success with the opposite sex. Marusia Perchuk looked like a good Komsomol—she paid her dues and regularly attended meetings—but she also organized parties and devoted her nights to dancing. At Pechatnyi Dvor, one correspondent chided the Komsomols for allowing love to dominate socialist feelings and obligations. Romantic life was even interfering with production, as young men and women used the traditional free and easy ways of the shop floor to flirt and engage in romantic horseplay.[12]

Despite Communist prescriptions, courtship and romance for these young workers appeared to be a matter of individual choice and initiative. While the marriages made in the Komsomol might not be matches of mutually committed social activists, they did appear to originate in a new milieu quite free from the strictures of family and patriarchal tradition. For the younger generation, companionate marriages based on equality might help to consolidate a class identity that extended from work to private life. If Komsomol romance represented the kind of proletarian marriage as it was coming to be, then currently existing workers' marriages reflected perhaps the unpleasant legacy of an older patriarchal order. This dissonance in time was also reflected in dissonance in the space of the proletarian home, where the boozing male breadwinner neglected his duties as husband and father, and the lonely housewife struggled with her triple burden of work, home, and children. Here class was male, and housewives remained excluded from it.

## CLASS AT REST

Socialist activists worried about the way young people were spending their time away from work, but "socialist leisure" affected all citizens in the new republic and was routinely recognized as a crucial site for the shaping of proletarian identities. At the end of the 1920s, cultural life retained its place on the agenda of trade union activism, and the club remained the official center of public activism and sociability. But despite the new emphasis on "cultural revolution,"

11. *Zhizn' pechatnika,* 7 November 1928; Iv. L-skii, "Obshchestvennik," *Pechatnik* 12–13 (1 May 1927): 44, 45; 32 (7 November 1928): 16–21; *Iskry,* 25 April 1929.
12. *Pechatnyi dvor,* 14 May and 31 July 1928, 26 October and 18 November 1930; *Krasnyi proletarii,* 18 May 1929; *Krasnoproletarets,* 29 July 1930; *Pechatnik* 32 (7 November 1928): 16.

the failures of clubs to provide for workers' total leisure and enlightenment occupied a large part of the trade union's genuine self-criticism.

"Clubs in Danger" served as the rubric for new discussion of the role of organized leisure at the start of the Five-Year Plan. Workers' clubs were becoming less popular by the end of the 1920s, a phenomenon that extended across many trade unions. Cultural officials frequently discussed the causes of this decline, and acknowledged that the club still failed to attract adults and families, that they remained the preserve of young people. There was no joy in the club, only boring reports, boring films, and tiresome familiar entertainers. Clubs had become formal "cathedrals of art" to which ordinary workers feared to come.[13] But should the trade union clubs give workers what they wanted or what they needed, and what in fact did "ordinary workers" want from their socialist clubs and cultural organizations?

Some activists argued that the cultural revolution required the club to become the centerpiece of proletarian culture, a culture practiced entirely in public, one based on production and on social and political responsibility. This line of argument became ever more strident during the first years of the Five-Year Plan and especially after the defeat of the right opposition within the trade union leadership. These activists envisioned an ideal club of the total proletarian and pointed proudly to evidence that workers themselves demanded and embraced the goal of cultured and productive leisure. In the club of the total proletarian, one would study ways to improve production, mobilize to carry out the various goals of the socialist and internationalist state, prepare one's body to defend that state, and improve one's cultural literacy in order better to understand the tasks that lay ahead on the road to communism.

Yet club life was noted mostly in its absence. Fewer and fewer circles remained active by the end of the 1920s, and the most popular ones were devoted more to recreation and self-improvement than to serious political study. For women workers, the favorite form of recreation remained handiwork circles, where they could fashion items for themselves and their families and enjoy the company of their fellow women workers and workers' wives. At the First Model club, sewing circle sessions lasted well into the night, sometimes breaking up after midnight. By contrast, mass cultural work (lectures and demonstrations) faltered for lack of an audience, and sports and physical culture activities likewise appealed only to a small minority of workers. Ping-pong became the rage in 1928, but in general, sports were becoming increasingly professionalized and less appealing to workers for their everyday leisure.[14]

13. V. Pletnev, "Kluby v opasnosti!" *Rabochii klub* 1 (January 1928): 5–14; *Pechatnik* 3 (31 January 1927): 9; 28 (10 October 1927): 19; 2 (12 January 1928): 3; 3 (22 January 1928): 24; 9–10 (25 March 1928): 32; 11 (8 April 1928): 14; 12 (20 April 1928): 21; 16 (1 June 1928): 28; 14–15 (31 May 1929): 31; 2 (1930): 16; 3 (1930): 13; *Pechatnyi dvor*, 17 March 1927; *Iskry*, January 1927; *Zhizn' pechatnika*, 28 July 1928; TsGAMO, f. 699, op. 1, d. 1059 (protocols of Fourth Moscow Guberniia Conference, 1928), l. 36; GARF, f. R-5525, op. 12, d. 7 (stenographic report of Printers' Union Central Committee plenum, 5–11 February 1930), l. 61.

14. TsGAMO, f. 4660, op. 1, d. 51 (report on work of factory committee at Krasnyi Proletarii

The proletarian club remained an unfulfilled dream, symbolized often by the image of the chess set or reading room "under lock and key." The surest way to attract adults to the club was to offer them an opportunity to drink, but such a club would then differ little from a bar or restaurant.[15] Nonetheless, there did exist a lively and popular club life in this union and others: the problem for cultural activists was that the chief participants were the young, and their interests focused primarily on the cinema and especially on dancing. Over and over, the club scene was described as devoid of adults. From Moscow to Biisk, wrote one correspondent, the mainstay of clubs was the youth. Adults and families were afraid of clubs: there were too many rowdy kids; there was too much disorder and not enough comfort. The club scene in Tambov exemplified the problem: here adult male workers retreated to their favorite taverns and women stayed home, since in their club the youth reigned supreme.[16]

Some of these young people participated in uplifting proletarian activities: they constituted 55 percent of the membership in circles in Leningrad in 1927, and they were the mainstay as well of physical culture groups. Many more, however, attended clubs for their cinema offerings. Clubs had turned into movie theaters for the young only, complained one delegate to the 1928 Leningrad oblast congress. Two years later the indictment remained the same: clubs had not turned their attention to production, their only activity was the cinema; movies now played at workers' clubs two and three nights a week.[17] And if movies might at least lure some adults to attend their clubs in the evening, a far greater peril to the cause of proletarian culture resulted when the workers' club turned into the young people's dance hall. They danced until five a.m. at the First Model club's party for apprentices; at Krasnyi Proletarii, most young people danced until four a.m., when the orchestra went home; but an accordionist remained, and half the group continued to dance until the trams started running again in the morning. At Komsomol dances, some young people observed the strictures against the waltz and the fox-trot, since "such dances lead to well-known bad results," but others eagerly sought the latest crazes, from the fox-trot to the Charleston to gypsy dances.

---

for September–December 1929), l. 12; Pletnev, "Kluby v opasnosti!" 8; *Pechatnik* 10 (7 April 1927): 14; 32–33 (28 November 1927): 28; 34 (10 December 1927): 13; 7–8 (8 March 1928): 36–37; 9–10 (25 March 1928): 32; 11 (8 April 1928): 14; 18 (22 June 1928): 24; 7 (12 March 1929): 22; 12–13 (1930): 11; *Zhizn' pechatnika*, 23 February 1928; 1 May 1928; TsGAMO, f. 699, op. 1, d. 1059, l. 30; TsGA SPb, f. 4804, op. 12, d. 4 (meetings of Leningrad conferences and union activists, April 1928–December 1929), l. 161; op. 13, d. 79 (factory committee meetings at Pechatnyi Dvor, 1929), l. 184.

15. *Pechatnik* 3 (31 January 1927): 9; 25 (5 September 1927): 20; 3 (22 January 1928): 23; TsGAMO, f. 699, op. 1, d. 1059, ll. 10–11, 45.

16. *Pechatnik* 11 (8 April 1928): 14–15; 2 (12 January 1928): 3; 13 (1 May 1928): 29; 5 (23 February 1927): 22; 2 (1930): 16; *Iskry*, January 1927; GARF, f. R-5525, op. 10, d. 41 (protocols of oblast congresses, K–N, 1928), l. 69; *Zhizn' pechatnika*, 20 February 1929.

17. TsGA SPb, f. 4804, op. 11, d. 187 (protocols and materials on work with youth, 1927), l. 28; GARF, f. R-5525, op. 10, d. 41, l. 69; op. 12, d. 38 (stenographic report of Leningrad Oblast Congress of Paper Makers and Printers, 14–17 February 1930), ll. 12–15; *Pechatnik* 12–13 (1930): 11.

Many of the commentators reported such events in tones of proletarian outrage, but as Anne Gorsuch points out, dancing among young people had universal appeal. The Charleston may have originated with the Western bourgeoisie, but dancing possessed an appeal that transcended class; it was fun, it brought young people together, and it helped to define their own unique generational culture. Dancing's widespread popularity among Komsomols and dropouts alike suggests that young printers, like others in the USSR, were "militant," as one account put it, in pursuing their dancing evenings.[18] As long as "workers" included the young, the worker club indeed was alive and well in socialist cities. The proletarian club of sober and purposeful leisure, however, was not.

Worker leisure possessed a distinct seasonality. In 1928, when printing industry employers attempted to save money by shifting some workers' paid vacations to the winter months, the rank and file dug in their heels, as we have seen.[19] Paid summer vacations had become one of the revolution's most successful benefits, providing printers with the opportunity and the means to escape and recuperate from the hazards of the industry. Summer leisure would offer cultural activists new realms in which to develop socialist and collective leisure behavior, but judging by the choices printers made about the use of their vacations, summertime had become personal time, time away from the collective, and occasionally time away from the family as well.

Printers had been accustomed to taking time off in the summer at their own expense, journeying outside the city limits for rest and relaxation. Before the revolution, compositors wandered by train, by foot, or by bicycle; they would boat down the Volga or explore the far North—"any place was beneficial that was not the dry and dusty composing room." By the end of the 1920s, printers continued to seek their rest as individuals, traveling to the countryside; now, however, they were encouraged to put their vacations to good social use by preparing to discuss political and social issues with the peasants among whom they rested.[20] This movement would take a much more organized form with the recruitment of the brigades of the Twenty-five Thousand, workers who left their jobs for assignment as full-time agitators in the village. But judging by the scolding that appeared in *Pechatnik*, voluntary agitation and propaganda were not popular alternatives for most vacationers.[21]

---

18. *Pechatnik* 9–10 (25 March 1928): 32; 13 (1 May 1928): 29; 15 (22 May 1928): 24; 12–13 (1930): 10; *Zhizn' pechatnika*, 24 March 1928; *Krasnyi proletarii*, 22 April 1929; *Pechatnyi dvor*, 21 January 1928; *Iskry*, 15 January 1929; Gorsuch, *Youth in Revolutionary Russia*, 124.

19. See Chapter 7.

20. *Istoriia leningradskogo soiuza*, 33–34; *Pechatnik* 18 (22 June 1928): 22; 20 (12 July 1928): 22; 24–25 (1 September 1928): 41; 18 (30 June 1929): 11; 23 (20 August 1929): 19; 19–20 (1930): 14–15.

21. *Pechatnik* 18 (30 June 1929): 11. On the Twenty-five Thousanders, see Lynne Viola, *The Best Sons of the Fatherland: Workers in the Vanguard of Soviet Collectivization* (Oxford, 1987). The Printers' Union contributed few volunteers for these brigades. GARF, f. R-5525, op. 11, d. 17 (meetings of Printers' Union Central Committee presidium, 1929), l. 264; op. 12, d. 38, l. 54; *Pechatnik* 25–26 (1930): 4, 6.

The union rest home continued to occupy pride of place in the repertory of organized summer leisure. Here workers could spend one or two weeks in rustic surroundings, replenish their organisms with nutritious food and ample rest, seek treatment from resident doctors, and engage in a wide variety of useful activities and games, from reading to radio to mushroom hunting. Rest homes remained a work in progress throughout the 1920s. Some residents grumbled about the food: "We're alive and well, but we don't know how; the cook tries to keep us thin." Others complained about the paucity of activities. Still others professed to be quite satisfied and grateful for the opportunity to get away from their work, wives, and family; but they complained that there were too few rest homes and passes to them had become a perquisite of status and favoritism. The Khimki home, the Moscow union's oldest, had places for 380 sojourners; Leningrad's Novyi Peterhof home could accommodate 150. The best that a worker could hope for was a place in a rest home or sanatorium every other year, while administrators and their wives seemed to receive a place every summer. The most coveted destinations were the all-union organization's sanatoria in the Crimea, about which most printers could only dream.[22] This resentment reflected a growing disparity between the promises of socialist equality and the realities of material shortages, but it is extremely important to note that the resentment coalesced around attitudes toward class and the value of manual labor, around the distinctions between those with unearned privileges and the powerless who went without.

To supplement the scarce opportunities for rest home stays, the union encouraged the development of outdoor summer clubs and organized excursions, and it dutifully embraced the new program of proletarian tourism launched in the summer of 1927.[23] Tourism offered organized itineraries both near and far, including ambitious travel by foot or boat to such destinations as the Volga River and the Caucasus Mountains. Unlike ordinary tourism, which had developed a following among the Russian middle class before the revolution and focused on entertainment, adventure, and escapism, proletarian tourism would offer workers training in socialist citizenship. They could experience at firsthand the Soviet Union's natural beauty, but they could also witness the "mighty process of socialist construction" through tours to building sites and factories; they could become acquainted with the Soviet Union's national minorities and learn about their culture and way of life.[24]

22. *Pechatnik* 17 (25 June 1927): 18; 22 (5 August 1927): 13; 12 (20 April 1928): 23; 17 (12 June 1928): 26; 19 (5 July 1928): 23; 23 (15 August 1928): 19; 24–25 (1 September 1928): 40; 26 (12 September 1928): 27; 18 (30 June 1929): 15; 19 (13 July 1929): 11; 14 (1930): 24; TsGAMO, f. 699, op. 1, d. 1141 (protocols of Eighth Moscow Guberniia Union Congress, September 1927), ll. 19, 43; TsGA SPb, f. 4804, op. 12, d. 4, l. 162.

23. *Pechatnik* 15–16 (1 June 1927): 32; 19 (2 July 1927): 23; 23 (15 August 1927): 10; 14 (12 May 1928): 27; 15 (22 May 1928): 22–23; 17 (12 June 1928): 29; 18 (22 June 1928): 20, 21; 20 (12 July 1928): 23, 26; 11 (20 April 1929): 22; 17 (23 June 1929): 18, 20–21; 22 (12 August 1929): 11–14; 17–18 (1930): 17; 22 (5 August 1927): 12–13; 11 (8 April 1928): 33.

24. *Pechatnik* 15–16 (1 June 1927): 31; 17 (15 June 1927): 17; 19 (2 July 1927): 21–22; 21 (25

All these summer activities provided a break from the everyday routine of work and family. It is also clear that summer provided a break from the routine of organization as well, and perhaps more ominously for the proletarian project, a chance to break away from the collective. Summer activities allowed printers to explore their own interests with groups of like-minded comrades, or to do nothing at all if they wished. Cultural activists lamented such behavior, but the rank and file celebrated the absence of organized activities at rest homes and the lack of compulsion. What was "too much free time" for the activist provided ample opportunity for card-playing and drinking among the ordinary residents of the rest home. For working women, summer rest homes provided a respite from caring for their children. For working husbands, sanatoria offered the opportunity to engage in idle romance. For those who wished for more autonomy, there were opportunities to rent a collective dacha for the season, as twenty-two young printers from the *Pravda* print shop did in 1929, or to go backpacking alone or in a small group through the vast Soviet land.[25]

Socialist leisure made vivid the paradox of total proletarian culture. The development of cultural opportunities for workers, intended to be collective and enlightening "intelligent leisure," produced an ever-increasing array of activities. The goal of proletarian culture was to produce a well-rounded amateur (*samodeiatel'nyi*) and the total proletarian would be expected to consume each and every cultural possibility. If a worker spent all of his or her time in clubs and circles, reading *and* sewing *and* swimming, the sum of these activities might drive out bad habits of dancing, drinking, and cards. "We need to find those forms that can realize the collective creativity of the mass, that will raise their initiative and all-around abilities," wrote a *Pechatnik* editorial.[26] But developing those forms and relying on workers' own initiative empowered these workers to choose their own paths to culture. Some chose reading, some the Prague Symphony, some the brass band, some a tent in Kareliia, and many the fox-trot. The development of proletarian culture fostered a proliferation of cultural practices and helped to fragment the cultural life of the working class. And a fragmented class was no class at all. Surveying the activities of young workers at the First Model print shop, the factory newspaper observed that only the most serious of them joined circles, that most preferred to dance, to stroll, or to foment trouble. "Individualism is developing here," it warned. In the Leningrad union, a board member called for even more concentrated cultural work: "The

---

July 1927): 13: 22 (5 August 1927): 11–13; 12 (20 April 1928): 23; 20 (12 July 1928): 26; 23 (15 August 1928): 18. On bourgeois tourism, see the programmatic statements of the newly created Society for Proletarian Tourism in *Na sushe i na more* 1 (January 1929): 2; 3 (March 1929): 10; *Turist-aktivist* 3 (March 1932): 7.

25. TsGAMO, f. 699, op. 1, d. 1059, l. 42; d. 1141, l. 32; *Pechatnik* 2 (22 January 1927): 25–26; 17 (15 June 1927): 18; 19 (5 July 1928): 23; 20 (12 July 1928): 24, 26; 19 (13 July 1929): 23; 25–26 (11 September 1929): 16; *Nasha zhizn'*, 20 October 1927.

26. *Pechatnik* 36 (25 December 1929): 15.

masses don't live for what our cultural work provides; they live for their own personal [*obyvatel'skie*] interests."[27] The long cultural revolution succeeded in giving voice to workers' own aspirations, but cultural revolutionaries had not expected that voice to be so heteroglossic.

## CRISIS IN CLASS IDENTITY: HOOLIGANISM

The assault on Communist heterodoxy at the end of the 1920s found expression in a class-war rhetoric in which militants of the Cultural Revolution targeted as their enemies the insidious forces of the hidden bourgeoisie, whether among engineers, office workers, peasants, or intellectuals. The power struggles at the highest levels of the Communist Party in which the printers' leaders became victims invoked the dangers of class enemies and their alarming toleration for dissent. But the total proletarian project managers must also have become alarmed by the continuing evidence of heterodoxy, diversity, and resistance to total socialism on the part of the project's main constituents, the urban working class. Printers' preservation of particularistic craft identity (and those of other distinct craft traditions) presented one danger to the architects of total socialism; their disharmonious private life and lack of uniformity in cultural preferences suggested others. The growing perception of an epidemic of working-class hooliganism offered further evidence of the failed formation of a uniform, homogeneous, and cultured proletariat.

In the autumn of 1928, *Pechatnik* featured a series of articles condemning various forms of worker indiscipline but in particular the phenomenon of hooliganism. "Hooliganism" was a generic term describing a variety of bad behaviors; in the late tsarist era it had come to represent audacious and rebellious behaviors by lower-class city dwellers.[28] It was not positively "class conscious," however, like joining trade unions or participating in political parties or strikes; rather it set workers apart from their betters in strident and troubling ways. Thus the meaning of "hooligan" in the dictatorship of the proletariat was fraught with contradictions. There was no question that workers engaged in hooligan behavior and that most hooligans were workers, but in the eleventh year of the revolution, the persistence of such behavior was cause for serious concern. In 1926 the printers' union had declared "war on hooliganism and drinking, to be punished by expulsion and criminal proceedings." Yet hooligans remained an integral part of working-class life, as one oppositional printer reminded those who condemned them. The union, he said, "conducts a battle against hooliganism, they're even thinking of introducing the death penalty for

---

27. *Zhizn' pechatnika*, 23 February 1928; TsGA SPb, f. 4804, op. 14, d. 21 (meetings of Leningrad oblast union board, 1930), l. 63ob.

28. *Pechatnik* 30 (22 October 1928): 25–29; 31 (1 November 1928): 21; see Joan Neuberger, *Hooliganism: Crime, Culture, and Power in St. Petersburg, 1900–1914* (Berkeley, 1993); Lebina, *Povsednevnaia zhizn'*, 57–67.

malicious hooligans. But the majority of hooligans are workers, and this means that our union is organizing a battle against workers."[29]

The line between normal worker behavior and hooliganism was very difficult to draw. Mikhail Tomskii himself had warned editors and journalists to use care when accusing someone of this crime, but labeling certain behaviors as "hooliganism" could help sharpen the distinction between good proletarians and bad workers, and help to instruct workers in appropriate class behavior. The tasks of the Five-Year Plan and the Cultural Revolution made this instruction more urgent than ever before. In the workplace, swearing, teasing, and playing tricks—what was once normal worker behavior—now drew the label of hooliganism. Hooligans—men *and* women, noted one report—defaced the walls of the washrooms at Pechatnyi Dvor with graffiti. At Krasnyi Proletarii, the merciless teasing of a woman greaser by a team of young hooligan workers threatened to undermine the success of socialist emulation.[30]

Hooliganism during off-work hours was an even more common complaint. Usually fueled by drink, hooligan workers engaged in brawling and fistfights, tried to crash the gates at club functions, or disrupted otherwise orderly group excursions. Hooligans took over rest homes and made the majority of peace-loving vacationers miserable. Time and again cultural activists blamed hooliganism for keeping adults away from the worker clubs. "The hooligan," jested the printers' encyclopedia, "is the only person who can have a good time and amuse himself even at the club."[31]

Hooliganism was a trait closely associated with youth. The union needed to do a better job of providing useful leisure activities for youth, said one unemployed pressman at the 1928 Moscow guberniia conference. "You go to the movies and it's all hooliganism and drinking." Nor did Komsomol membership offer much of a safeguard against hooliganism. *Pechatnik* reported the case of the "Hooligan with a Komsomol Card," who with two buddies beat up another apprentice at the Moscow training school so badly that the victim was confined to bed for three days. The factory committee and Komsomol cell encouraged such behavior with their silence, continued the report.[32] As with trade union lenience toward dissidents, tolerance toward hooligans implied complicity.

Indeed, hooligan behavior, like drink, was tolerated as a normal and com-

---

29. *Moskovskii pechatnik* 17 (April 1926): 3–4; TsGAMO, f. 699, op. 1, d. 787 (protocols of the Third Moscow Guberniia Union Conference, October 1926), l. 19.

30. *Pechatnik* 47 (20 November 1926): 5; 9 (25 March 1927): 12; *Zhizn' pechatnika*, 25 December 1929; *Pechatnyi dvor*, 22 September 1928; TsGA SPb, f. 4804, op. 12, d. 101 (factory committee meetings at Pechatnyi Dvor, 1928), l. 180; *Krasnoproletarets*, 4 November 1930; *Zorkii glaz*, 8 March 1927.

31. *Nasha zhizn'*, 23 November 1927; *Pechatnik* 3 (31 January 1927): 17; 10 (7 April 1927): 11; 19 (2 July 1927): 20; 11 (8 April 1928): 14; 14 (12 May 1928): 27; 23 (15 August 1928): 16, 26; 30 (22 October 1928): 29; 19 (13 July 1929): 11; 15 (1930): 11; *Zhizn' pechatnika*, 14 April 1928.

32. TsGAMO, f. 699, op. 1, d. 1059, l. 15; f. 4660, op. 1, d. 5 (conferences and meetings in Moscow print shops to elect delegates to First Oblast Congress, 1929), l. 2; *Pechatnik* 30 (22 October 1928): 29.

mon element of everyday life. Many of the articles criticizing hooligan actions also cited the indifference of managers, factory committees, party cells, and fellow workers as part of the problem of poor social discipline. A comrades' "trial of a hooligan" at the First Model Print Shop in 1928 presented the case of a lithographic pressman who had burst drunk and disorderly into his shop one night. He resisted the gatekeeper and a militiaman, let loose with "three-story" swearing, and invoked his right as a worker to behave as he pleased: "What are you defending against? What do I care about your authority [*vlast'*]—I am the authority!" In the dock, the accused admitted his guilt, and ventured that the shame of appearing in this way before his comrades was all the punishment he needed. The jury agreed: his hooliganism was confirmed, but he was given a suspended sentence.[33] Such public events did help to instill collective norms, but in this case it confirmed both the undesirability of hooliganism and its unimportance. Workers here managed to subvert the official position and to protect their own worker culture.

Eric Naiman writes that the discussion of the hooligan problem at this time in the national press was pervaded by images of infection and corruption.[34] By contrast, within the Printers' Union's press, hooliganism appeared to be common and everyday, not exceptional and diseased. "Hooliganism" was on everybody's lips in the second half of the 1920s, thanks to the national campaign to eradicate it from revolutionary culture. It became easy to apply to any and all behavior that deviated from the proletarian norm: hooligan nicknames, a hooligan face, hooligan language, hooligan pranks. But a term so broad that it included murder, gambling on checkers, failing to show respect when Nadezhda Krupskaia spoke on the radio, or drinking too much could hardly serve to designate a meaningful crime or signal inappropriate behavior. The premier printing trade school in the country, after all, had admitted to graduating "hooligans, hooligans of the highest caliber."[35] In the culture of workers, the hooligan was one of them. But he was not and he could never be a proletarian.

## CRISIS IN CLASS IDENTITY: THE 1929 PURGE CAMPAIGN

In the fall of 1929, the trade union joined a new effort to define proletarian identity, a task made particularly urgent because of the contemporaneous purge of the union leadership. Begun as a mechanism to counter the growing crisis of class identity, the purge campaign instead resulted in its affirmation. Officially, the purge aimed to eliminate "careerists, petty-bourgeois and bourgeois elements, and those with kulak origins," and to replace them as party and union officials with workers "from the bench"; in other words, real proletarians.[36]

---

33. *Pechatnik* 31 (1 November 1928): 21.
34. Naiman, *Sex in Public*, 262.
35. *Moskovskii pechatnik* 8 (1 March 1925): 13. See Chapter 6.
36. *Pechatnik* 24 (31 August 1929): 1. On the wider application of this campaign, see Merridale, *Moscow Politics and the Rise of Stalin*, 174.

More significantly, the purge process served to convey and reinforce norms of political behavior. As Oleg Kharkhordin writes, the aim of the purge process was not so much to punish party deviants as to admonish them and thereby to cure them of their illnesses. Public and private purge hearings throughout the 1920s served this purpose.[37] Now in 1929, excommunication and expulsion had been added to the repertory of political therapy. To set the tone, a traveling purge carnival toured the printers' clubs in Moscow, inviting workers to interview members of the union's office staff about their performance and their pedigrees and to participate in determining their fates. At the Krasnyi Maiak club of the *Pravda* print shop, 165 workers confronted 45 staff members with their questions and accusations. Anonymous denunciations accused clerks and typists of accepting rides from union leaders and of "hidden prostitution" (recall the "harem" of the Moscow board), but such denunciations were themselves denounced by workers in the audience. The telephone operator Kozlova identified her parents as a cook and a laundress, and subsequent debate confirmed her good public activism: she survived the purge. The typist Savost'ianova, daughter of a merchant who made 11,000 rubles a year and sister of a party member, did not survive, even though she renounced her father. A couple of weeks later, thirty-one more staff members faced workers at the Sixteenth Print Shop club. Among them was Nikolai Chistov, the prerevolutionary union leader and longtime Menshevik. As an old "revolutionary printer," announced the meeting's chair, Chistov would not be questioned but would recount his revolutionary past. Then the meeting moved on to interrogate others about their behavior and attitudes.[38] Was this "vegetarianism" or respect for the union's long revolutionary tradition? The lenience shown to the Menshevik Chistov suggests that printer solidarity remained strong even after ten years of the Communist-Menshevik conflict.

There is also ample evidence to suggest that workers themselves were highly indifferent to this purge process, seeing it as just another campaign launched from on high to encourage them to work harder. Only a handful of workers from the First Model shop turned out to purge union employees in August, responding to invitations to interrogate the staffers with the "silence of the grave." The first round of purge meetings in August had failed to attract an audience, and the union's purge commission had had to start all over again two months later.[39] Relatively few of the staff members received the harsh treatment meted out to Savost'ianova; most were confirmed to continue in their posts. Rather, the purpose of these meetings seemed to be to generate public discussion about norms of proletarian identity during this moment of crisis in the

---

37. Oleg Kharkhordin, *The Collective and the Individual in Russia: A Study of Practices* (Berkeley, 1999), chap. 2.
38. TsGAMO, f. 4660, op. 1, d. 42 (meetings of the commission on the purge of the union apparat, August–October 1928), ll. 7–8, 15–16; *Pechatnik* 31 (20 November 1929): 21.
39. *Nasha zhizn'*, 8 June 1929; *Pechatnik* 25–26 (11 September 1929): 8; TsGAMO, f. 4660, op. 1, d. 42, l. 1.

trade union movement. And local organizations' ritual compliance with the party's directive to hold public hearings of party members and union officials' fitness to serve pulled them inexorably into the game of labeling and ostracism.

What is particularly distinctive about these meetings is how personal such public discussions had become.[40] No longer shielded behind closed party doors but in public clubs and with reporters present, workers now were encouraged to consider the public and private behavior of their fellow workers. This parade of virtue and vice found particular resonance in the factory newspapers, and the discussions of personal characteristics in their pages provide a rich body of evidence about the meaning of proletarian identity at this time.

A review of production conferences in the Krasnyi Proletarii newspaper early in 1929 set the tone. Elsewhere this review had passed nearly without notice, but young Communists at Krasnyi Proletarii took their assignment seriously, offering "comradely criticism" of co-workers. They judged Mitfeeva to be a good worker, but she chattered too much on the job and distracted others from their work. Iliusha Kalinin too was a good worker, but this was not sufficient for a good proletarian: Komsomol officials did not know what he did in his free time, and Iliusha was therefore suspect. "He needs to shake off his individualist deviation [*uklon individual'shchika*] and get involved in public work, become interested in the life of our enterprise and go forward with the mass of youth."[41] Discipline on and off the job had become the identifying characteristic of the proletarian in socialist society, and it had become everybody's business—the business of the collective—to monitor and enforce this new proletarian discipline. Being a good worker was no longer enough, and those who deviated from prescribed norms now faced detailed and public shaming.

The open purge hearings later in 1929 also invited public scrutiny of individual behaviors. The goal of these hearings was not only to winnow out individual bad apples from the proletarian barrel but to provide instruction in proper values and to involve the maximum number of workers in this collective soul-searching. Still, the exercise lacked a sense of compulsion: at the First Model plant, with 400 party members (of 2,600 workers), only 200 individuals attended an open purge meeting on a cold payday in January 1930. Nonparty members shrugged off invitations to witness the spectacle, saying they could read the results in the newspapers.[42]

Once assembled, the purge meetings took on a standard form. Individual party members recited their political and proletarian biographies, beginning with party membership: when they joined the party, why they waited so long, any other parties they had belonged to in times past. Social origin now became a standard mark of identification, and the categories had become quite simpli-

---

40. Trotskii had disapproved of public interventions into private life in 1923, particularly the use of real names in accounts of family scandals: Trotsky, *Problems of Everyday Life*, 66; see also Kharkhordin, *Collective and the Individual*, 130.

41. *Krasnyi proletarii*, 5 February and 30 March 1929.

42. *Zhizn' pechatnika*, 21 January 1930.

Purge meeting at the Fifteenth State Print Shop in Moscow to review the Soviet apparat, 1929. Assistant Director Viktorov gives his report to assembled workers, who look more attentive than written accounts of such meetings suggest. (Rossiiskii Gosudarstvennyi Arkhiv Kinofotodokumentov, 2-36989. Used with permission of the archive.)

fied. Parents were "workers" or "peasants"; none were identified as practicing the printer's trade. Work history, too, was a standard element of the autobiography, and then typically the assembly or a smaller purge commission would ask a series of questions about political views and social behavior. In some cases, the political questioning was quite tough and the answers were evasive. One testifier admitted to admiring Trotskii as a personality but claimed no knowledge of his platform. Vasilii Ermilov was expelled from the party for having concealed his Communist Party membership when captured by Poles during the Civil War. But look on the bright side, said the purge commission: "If you hadn't hidden the fact that you were a Communist, you wouldn't be here today to be purged—you'd have been shot on the spot." But other respondents stood up for their heterodox views. When asked why he did not participate in the October seizure of power, Aleksandr Roslov replied, "I thought it was the ruin of the revolution." P. I. Tabakov admitted that he had demonstratively left the party in 1922 by tearing up his party card.[43]

43. Ibid.; *Krasnyi proletarii*, 4 January 1930; *Pechatnyi dvor*, 26 October 1930; *Nasha zhizn'*, 23 March 1930.

Resistance to authority and to capitalist oppression had of course been one of the defining elements of prerevolutionary proletarian identity. The complicated relationship between workers and their socialist bosses remained one of the most incendiary points of contention throughout the decade of socialist power, whether played out in labor relations on the shop floor, in the politics of the Communist Party, or in cultural representations of socialist working-class identity. Workers at the Sixteenth Print Shop seemed especially wedded to the old forms of resistance, with the result that several of their Communists were censured during the purge discussions there. The Communist cell as a whole was reprimanded for its failings, including the "substantial presence of prejudiced attitudes toward certain administrators who had been promoted from among the workers; these were viewed as 'bosses' who opposed the 'worker mass.'" M. S. Klimenov was warned for having signed a petition demanding reconsideration of the rate structure, and I. S. Il'intsev was likewise reprimanded for having said in a public meeting that the norms and rates were "dishonest." This was time-tested worker behavior, but under socialism it could warrant censure. It is true that the entire plant had remained a quiet bastion of Menshevism, a fact that had been one of the subtexts of this round of purges, and the Sixteenth had always reflected a level of insecurity about its revolutionary commitment. But there were no doubts about its *worker* identity. An experiment in the design of the factory newspaper, copying the sober and dense style of the prerevolutionary official government papers, drew loud protests: the look is too "European," we want a tabloid with loud headlines, a newspaper you can "converse with," a newspaper "with a worker's face."[44] The purge hearings of 1929 and 1930 bore vivid testimony to the fact that twelve years after the revolution workers still brought their own understandings of labor relations and worker identity to their everyday lives.

The commissions also scrutinized lifestyles: on the scale of Communist sins, personal defects such as alcoholism, sexual license, and religion ranked as less serious than careerism and party infighting, yet Communists needed to set a good example of appropriate proletarian behavior. Did these comrades drink, smoke, or play cards? Drinking a little was all right, but "systematic drinking" warranted expulsion. Did they harass women or engage in anti-Semitic taunting? Women workers accused First Model's Aleksandrov of rudeness and refusing to teach them new skills. But his mate defended him, blaming the women for their lack of interest. Did they permit icons in their households, go to church? Earlier, religion had ranked last on the list of the mistakes of party members; except for some Komsomol activists, religious belief among party members had been benignly ignored. The 1929 purge coincided with a militant campaign against religion, but most party members and questioners still

---

44. When other plants were choosing revolutionary names for themselves in the early 1920s, workers at the Sixteenth could not come up with a suitable name of their own. *Nasha zhizn'*, 1 December 1923, 18 May 1927, 27 January 1928.

shrugged off what was treated as casual religiosity. A worker received only a reprimand for having baptized his child in 1925. Even V. D. Naletov, who admitted to attending church up to 1926 and to keeping an icon in his apartment even after that, was permitted to remain in the party as long as he admitted his errors.[45]

Communists sought to secularize Christian charity; their goal was to reincorporate deviants into the body politic, not to excise them.[46] The purge proceedings placed party members in the public spotlight, but they also invited character witnesses to speak on behalf of the accused, and in the end, many were quite forgiving. A lithographer at First Model, Korovin, revealed a history of questionable political behavior: he had distributed literature for the Mensheviks before the revolution, and he had remained a Socialist Revolutionary throughout 1917. But others defended Korovin, citing his good public activism and his comradely relations with others. Forgiveness carried the day. Even most Communists at the Sixteenth Print Shop, who had cast off their residual Menshevism only to fall under the influence of the right opposition, received reprimands and not expulsions.[47]

Certification of political loyalty turned out to involve the same kind of bargaining and haggling that accompanied production relations on the shop floor. Certain levels of performance were expected and desired, but failure to comply could be explained away. Circumstances were almost always extenuating. Thus along with the quite detailed and possibly embarrassing spectacles of public shaming, these purge processes also allowed the workplace community to convey public forgiveness. In the end, norms of proletarian behavior remained guidelines rather than requirements. The totalist proletarian culture demanded total loyalty, total commitment, and total obedience to the collective will. But these workers rejected such proletarian absolutism, and their overall indifference to the entire purge process conveyed a dismissal of its normative goals. If some activists sought to subordinate individualism to the values of the collective, many others defined their own worker identity to include such individualist habits as drink, religion, and private life. The messy multiplicity of worker behavior survived the purge reviews.

## CLASS DIVIDED: WORKING WOMEN

The place of women workers in the Soviet working class remained problematic. Official efforts through the 1920s to recreate a definition of "worker" in which men and women counted equally were halfhearted at best, and by all accounts

---

45. Kharkhordin, *Collective and the Individual*, 36; *Pechatnik* 32–33 (30 November 1929): 22; *Zorkii glaz*, 28 July 1929; *Krasnyi proletarii*, 4 January 1930; *Zhizn' pechatnika*, 21 January, 5 February, and 19 February 1930; *Nasha zhizn'*, 23 March 1930.

46. See Kharkhordin, *Collective and the Individual*, 37–55, on the parallels between Communist purge institutions and Orthodox ecclesiastical courts.

47. *Zhizn' pechatnika*, 21 January 1930; *Nasha zhizn'*, 23 March 1930.

they had failed. Ten years of revolution seemed not to have changed the attitudes of men about who should belong to the working class, but there is considerable evidence that women were beginning to take the promises of October as genuine. They spoke out against the practices that marginalized them: "We promote women to trade union positions," said a woman delegate to the Seventh Leningrad Printers' Union Congress, "but we don't give them any training, and the women who serve in the factory committees always perform the most insignificant tasks." They complained about sexual harassment. They joined in the general indictments of the failures of the union leadership.[48]

Women emphasized their own attributes that made superior contributions to socialist production. At Krasnyi Proletarii, the factory administration tried to discriminate against women by claiming not that they were less skilled than men but less strong. A woman responded that this might be true, but women had compensating qualities: "If a man can lift fifty books, then I can lift thirty-five. But during the time that a man rolls a cigarette and smokes it, I can carry 135 books—and we're even." In another plant, women tried to upbraid male workers for smoking, and when the men responded with displeasure, the women formed their own work unit and earned the title of shock brigade. At the First Leningrad Oblast Congress in 1928, women continued to demand better training; they insisted that women with skills equal to men's not be fired first, and that more women be promoted to supervisory positions.[49]

As the leaders of the Communist Party Women's Section (Zhenotdel) had already discovered, however, the more insistently women spoke up for inclusion in the working class and its party, the sharper became the line that separated them from men.[50] The articulation of working-class identity provided no common language that could incorporate men and women in a single project. Instead, a proletarian double standard emerged to guarantee that men and women would not be seen as equals. Behaviors that were considered to be normal elements of male working-class life became anomalous when women engaged in them. Despite the official campaign against workplace horseplay, this behavior persisted among men, and it received elaborate affirmation in stories and feuilletons in the union press. When women teased their co-workers, their behavior was characterized as idle female gossip. Where men competed to insult one another with virtuoso swearing, women's emotional outbursts were commonly labeled "hysterics." If men called on their comrades to work with more care and

---

48. GARF, f. R-5525, op. 11, d. 1 (stenographic report of Seventh All-Union Congress of Printers' Union, 28 January–7 February 1929), l. 78; *Nasha zhizn'*, 1 May 1927, 27 March 1928, 8–15 March 1929; *Pechatnik* 29–30 (25 October 1927): 17; 5 (12 February 1928): 19; 19 (5 July 1928): 9; 6 (1930): 3–5; TsGA SPb, f. 4804, op. 11, d. 31 (meetings of Leningrad union board, 1927), l. 112; GARF, f. R-5525, op. 10, d. 41, ll. 66, 69, 86; TsGAMO, f. 699, op. 1, d. 1141, l. 21; *Zhizn' pechatnika*, 8 March 1929, 5 February 1930. For further detail, see Koenker, "Men against Women."

49. *Krasnyi proletarii*, 10 March 1928; *Pechatnik* 6 (1930): 3; 11 (17 April 1927): 16; GARF, f. R-5525, op. 10, d. 41.

50. Wood, *Baba and the Comrade*, esp. pt. 3; Clements, *Bolshevik Women*.

discipline, they were exhibiting conscious socialist work culture; when women did the same thing, they were being troublemakers and rowdies. Men engaged in continual haggling about pay rates, but when women raised the same issues, their discussions were dismissed as "womanish" (*babskie*) or trivial. Women's indifference to raising their skills was "proven" because they would not participate in production conferences, even though men shunned these meetings without invoking aspersions on their work capabilities.[51] Even when men and women behaved in quite similar ways, the male version of the behavior was considered to be aberrant, uncultured perhaps, but correctable; it was part of women's nature.

One case illustrates the proletarian double standard with great poignancy. It arose in retaliation against women workers for their accusations of sexual harassment by male supervisors. At the First Model plant, the misogyny of the foreman, Aleksandrov, had already earned him censure at the factory purge hearing in February 1930 for systematic discrimination against women. Aleksandrov's own behavior illustrated the double standard in action: when a man broke a machine part, Aleksandrov would smooth things over, but if a woman broke a part, she had demonstrated conclusively that women were incapable of performing the work. Soon after the hearing, two male correspondents contributed to *Pechatnik* a long exposé of the incorrect behavior of Aleksandrov and others toward women at this shop, concluding that the best lesson for all would be to fire Aleksandrov and replace him with a woman. The article ended, however, on a most curious note. Having dwelt extensively on the misogynistic climate at First Model, the authors continued, "All the above-stated pales before a fact that has been hidden from us by the women's organizer, a case that can only be compared with Chubarovism [*chubarovshchina*]. This involved insults toward a woman worker in the bindery department on the part of five women." With the assistance of the local prosecutor, these five were then fired. A subsequent account also lauded a worker-correspondent for bringing this group of women workers to justice for their Chubarovism in the workplace.[52] "Chubarovism" referred to a notorious episode that had taken place in Chubarov Alley in Leningrad in August 1926, a vicious mass rape of an unmarried woman worker by several dozen working men, many of them Komsomol members in a nearby factory.[53] The case had been widely publicized in the national press. Subsequently, "Chubarovism" had come to refer to any kind of "sexual hooliganism," not necessarily involving physical force.[54] On another level, Chubarovism symbolized violence by worker against worker, and this

---

51. Nemirovskii, "Zvon," *Pechatnik* 4 (1 February 1928): 30–31; 35 (18 December 1927): 13; 5 (12 February 1928): 19; 7 (12 March 1928): 17; 7 (12 March 1929): 16; 11 (20 April 1929): 9; 18 (30 June 1929): back cover; *Nasha zhizn'*, 30 April 1925, 24 October 1928; *Pechatnyi dvor*, 19 May 1924, 7 March 1927; *Zhizn' pechatnika*, 8 October 1929.
52. *Zhizn' pechatnika*, 5 February 1930; *Pechatnik* 6 (1930): 6; 7–8 (1930): 24.
53. Naiman, *Sex in Public*, chap. 7; see also Lebina, *Povsednevnaia zhizn'*, 64–65.
54. Personal communication from Eric Naiman, 22 January 2002.

perhaps is the sense in which the *Pechatnik* correspondents used the term in 1930. But far more central to the term and the original event was the idea of the sexual degradation of women. In applying this label to *women's* work shop behavior and in accusing the women's organizer of complicity, the male correspondents had inverted the guilt ascribed to the original rape. Horseplay was fine among men but it was criminal behavior for women. If women dared to punish men for asserting their male right to harass and abuse them, then men would retaliate by labeling women's behavior as not just deviant but sexually transgressive.

The context of these remarkable attacks requires some attention. The Printers' Union leadership had been conclusively purged by the beginning of 1930, and rank-and-file workers had lost their powerful defenders on the national scene: one might say the union movement had become emasculated. The union had vainly attempted to transform the printing industry in a way that would protect its members' workplace rights and their standard of living. Even though male hostility toward women had been a constant theme of trade union interchange in the postrevolutionary period, the sharpness and viciousness of attacks on women at work seemed only to increase by 1930. Men were now projecting their own powerlessness onto women. As the party leadership increasingly and forcefully asserted its mastery over the rest of society through the mechanisms of political denunciations and purges, male workers now sought to reassert their mastery over the subordinates closest at hand, and resistance to women could serve as a surrogate for resistance to management. Perhaps it is no accident that the trade union record links "Trotskyist-opportunist opposition" in 1930 with the support of women.[55]

The 1920s witnessed impassioned debates throughout Europe and North America about gender, women's roles, and sex in the aftermath of the traumatic World War and revolutionary upheavals. The debate in France, as Mary Louise Roberts writes, coalesced around three womanly types: the "modern woman," whose unconventional ways symbolized anxieties over gender; the "mother," who symbolized the essential role of women and the preservation of cultural continuity; and the "single woman," whose lack of a husband symbolized the demographic and psychic impact of the war. German socialists and Communists likewise grappled with the construction of a new gender order, torn between the prospects of a proletarian new woman, the militarized fighter for Communism, and the transformed mother and housewife. Eric Naiman suggests, however, that in Soviet Russia the battle over gender was much less multivocal; it focused on sex and the body, and particularly on the metonymic link between sex, women, and contamination.[56] This totalizing discourse of sex,

---

55. TsGAMO, f. 4660, op. 1, d. 121 (protocols of Second Moscow Oblast Congress, 13–15 December 1930, pt. 2), l. 194.
56. Mary Louise Roberts, *Civilization without Sexes: Reconstructing Gender in Postwar France, 1917–1927* (Chicago, 1994), 9–12; Eric D. Weitz, *Creating German Communism: From Popular*

which branded the feminine as dangerous and corrupting, clashed with another totalizing discourse, on the power of socialism to inexorably and inevitably effect the emancipation of women.

Judging by the pages of the union journal, the misogynist discourse of sex and contamination had triumphed over the discourse of emancipation. By 1929, "women's issues" received attention in *Pechatnik* only during the prescribed observation of 8 March. Women's organizers found themselves attacked for both too much activism and too little. A 1928 story in the 8 March issue of *Pechatnik*, titled "Brother Mariia," fittingly captures this defeat of the emancipationist discourse. Mariia Levchuk was a sexless Communist woman who dressed like a man, chain-smoked cigarettes, and even lived for a time in a male student hostel, just one of the boys. But she became irresistibly drawn to Bychkov (the bull), a proper young Komsomol boy. While doing his group's laundry on an assignment in the countryside, Bychkov encountered Mariia, who had gone to bathe. They embraced; she was transformed. In an instant she abandoned her free and coarse banter, and her blue eyes were now radiant and feminine (*zhenstvenny*). "I am a young woman," she announced, and she walked demurely away, no longer with a male gait but completely like a girl.[57] The unsexed woman worker-activist could not coexist with a sexed being. Bychkov's proletarian love had transformed the activist into a woman, and the activist had disappeared.

Discussions of working-class identity had failed to produce a proletarian model that could incorporate men and women equally. Yet the skyrocketing demands of the Five-Year Plan for labor required women to participate in production at an ever-increasing rate. The solution for incorporating women into the labor force without contaminating the resolutely male working class became to create strictly delineated spheres for men and for women in work. Women workers would become equal, perhaps, but separate. Hence *Pechatnik* began to publicize production contests for the best *woman* typesetter. Work spaces came to be increasingly separated by sex. Although women activists denounced the persistence of men's and women's typesetting departments at First Model as "the prewar, Sytin [bourgeois] division of labor," such segregation represented the wave of the future, not a relic of the past. Women shock workers formed their own brigades when men refused to work with them.[58] Wendy Goldman writes that this phenomenon was a legislated part of the Five-Year Plan, and Gosplan itself sent out a directive to managers to create separate work assignments for

---

*Protests to Socialist State* (Princeton, 1997), chap. 6; see also Karen Hagemann, *Frauenalltag und Männerpolitik: Alltagsleben und gesellschaftliches Handeln von Arbeiterfrauen in der Weimarer Republik* (Bonn, 1990); Naiman, *Sex in Public*.

57. T. Braz, "Brat Mariia," *Pechatnik* 7–8 (8 March 1928): 40–42. The story anticipates by eleven years the Hollywood film *Ninotchka*, in which the iron Communist Greta Garbo melts in the face of capitalist manhood.

58. *Pechatnik* 11 (8 April 1928): 12, 13; 6 (1930): 2–4; *Krasnyi proletarii*, 10 and 24 March 1928.

men and for women. Historians suggest that the dissolution of the Women's Section of the party marked the end of the road for socialist feminism.[59] The fate of women in the printing industry workplace demonstrates the economic pressures and the cultural prejudices that made this defeat possible.

## CLASS DIVIDED: WORKING YOUTH

Along with women, the young had received special and separate treatment from the union organization in its concern to inculcate proper class and proletarian values among members of the so-called next shift. They too had provoked hostility from adult male workers.[60] Far from picking up the baton of traditional worker values and charging ahead in the relay race of socialist construction, young people appeared at the end of the 1920s to have become a distinct category, dangerously aping the traits of the bourgeoisie, rejecting familiar working-class life.[61]

Instead of learning how to be good producers, the next generation seemed entirely absorbed by becoming good consumers. Rather than devoting their energies for the good of the collective, the next generation cared only about their personal lives, about their individual selves. In socialist discourse, the personal and consumption were realms of the female, not worthy of proper proletarian attention. Young men who strayed from production values risked losing their manhood through the feminizing practices of romance and clothes. Consumption also hovered dangerously close to bourgeois practice. Young women, including Komsomol girls, earned particular censure for their interest in fashion and cosmetics, and were seen as the repository of petty-bourgeois, unproletarian values. Girls left the Komsomol, in fact, because they rejected its dress code: simple clothes, no cosmetics, plain hair. The factory newspaper at First Model condemned "former Komsomol girls" for preferring silk dresses with fur trim and décolletage, powdered faces, hair waved by the best private hairdresser, and manicures. "Life for girls is divided into two parts: production and the Komsomol cell are one, and in counterweight to this stands a completely different world—domestic life with all its intrigues and influences, and quite often this world is dominant. All aspirations for public work, all energy and interest in broad public life are switched over to their tiny little world, which swallows up all their thoughts, strength, and feelings, and they scorn the common good, of

---

59. Wendy Z. Goldman, *Women at the Gates: Gender and Industry in Stalin's Russia* (Cambridge, 2002), chap. 5. The division of labor between the sexes also became increasingly evident in the iconography of the Soviet poster. See Victoria E. Bonnell, *Iconography of Power: Soviet Political Posters under Lenin and Stalin* (Berkeley, 1997), chap. 2; Wood, *Baba and the Comrade*; Clements, *Bolshevik Women*; Richard Stites, *The Women's Liberation Movement in Russia: Feminism, Nihilism, and Bolshevism, 1860–1930* (Princeton, 1978).

60. *Krasnyi proletarii*, 5 February and 30 March 1929; *Pechatnyi dvor*, 23 November 1928, 22 December 1928, 23 December 1930; *Zhizn' pechatnika*, 18 November 1930, 23 November 1929; *Zorkii glaz*, 23 February 1929; *Krasnoproletarets*, 20 June 1930.

61. Gorsuch, *Youth in Revolutionary Russia*.

which nothing remains."⁶² Such concern for their sexual allure may have been considered part of the essence of women, assigned to the realm of the biological and the sexual. But if married women workers were often portrayed as victims of the old patriarchal order and urged to transform themselves, young women who freely chose a lifestyle of fashion and romance earned only the scorn of the arbiters of proletarian values.

There was considerable concern, moreover, that it was not only young women who were choosing the life of the "I" over that of the collective. Laziness, pessimism, individualism, self-interest, hooliganism, and "Duglasovshchina"—emulating the Hollywood hero Douglas Fairbanks—had conquered many young male workers as well. They cared only about consumption and its display, symbolized by baggy Oxford trousers, Boston shoes, and checkered jackets and ties. Farewell Five-Year Plan and shock work: "At the critical moment of the Five-Year Plan, such bourgeois influence should not exist. 'Oxfords' slow down construction and deflect good kids from the Komsomol."⁶³ At the critical moment when all productive forces needed to be concentrated on socialist construction, any deviation toward individualism became a violation of proletarian values. Mikhail Vasil'ev was expelled from the Komsomol for expressing doubt about the Five-Year Plan and about collectivization: his personal "I," a worker-correspondent wrote in dismay, was more important to him than any Komsomol decision. Marusia Vorob'eva had dyed her hair: would the Five-Year Plan be better fulfilled, wondered her factory newspaper, if she was a redhead? Perhaps not, another young woman thought, but "I don't believe that the interests of the working class will be harmed if I color my fingernails with polish."⁶⁴ With official voices unable to reconcile the taste of youth for dressing well and looking good with the socialist productivist mission, many young workers thus cut themselves off from the production as well as the social collective, rejecting the old proletarian values of hard work and love of craft and driving another wedge into the imagined solidarity of the socialist working class.

It is worth noting that the factory newspaper of the Leningrad print shop Pechatnyi Dvor served as one of the most active sites of this debate over cosmetics and proper proletarian manners and dress. This debate occurred precisely at the moment when Pechatnyi Dvor was backing the renegade union leader Rozov against the attempts by the center to remove him from his post. Both in cultural life and in politics, workers here seemed especially active in the struggle to define their proletarian identity, an identity that included both proletarian asceticism and trade union autonomy. The enemy on one side was Oxford trousers and Boston shoes; on the other, the Stalinist party center. The

---

62. *Zhizn' pechatnika*, 8 March, 6 April, and 17 May 1929; 18 November 1930; *Pechatnyi dvor*, 8 January 1929; 5 June, 18 June, 26 October, and 18 November 1930; *Krasnyi proletarii*, 29 July 1930.

63. *Krasnyi proletarii*, 19 December 1928, 26 March 1930; *Pechatnyi dvor*, 27 April and 31 August 1929; 18 June, 19 September, and 1 October 1930; *Leningradskii pravdist*, 12 April 1930.

64. *Iskry*, 2 July 1930; *Pechatnyi dvor*, 5 June 1930; *Krasnyi proletarii*, 15 April 1927.

attitudes evidenced at Pechatnyi Dvor complicate the link between the class-war ideology of the period and support for the Stalinist hard line. Independently of party dictates as well as in response to them, Soviet workers continued to carve out their own sense of identity as workers, as proletarians, and as Soviet citizens.

## END OF CLASS?

Class formation in capitalist societies takes place in interactions with others: workers defined themselves in many respects by who they were not. This language of class distinction, of us and them, had been a part of worker discourse throughout the 1920s, although as seen in Chapter 6, many workers projected their sense of struggle only back to prerevolutionary encounters with the state and the capitalists. Now at the end of the 1920s, the language of class enemies had resurfaced as one of the key elements of the Cultural Revolution's assault on those who would hinder the progress of socialism. The highly publicized trial of alleged bourgeois saboteurs in the Shakhty mines in the spring of 1928 had provided a template for imagining class enemies, and the purge hearings that permeated the union appropriated this language as well.[65]

In discussing their own identities and place in society, printers also invoked a roster of class villains and enemies. Pompous plant administrators came in for regular lampooning in the union journal. Speakers at meetings of the unemployed targeted self-employed artisans and incompetent bureaucrats as "alien." Ties with "traders" were the most frequent cause for workers to be expelled from their party organizations during purge discussions. One printer questioned why the journalists at the newspaper *Leningradskaia pravda* refused to participate in the common organizational work at the plant, why they had chosen to be "alien." "Comrade co-workers, you are ours—honestly, ours. But why don't you want to be ours?"[66]

But such scripted attempts to draw sharp lines between them and us, class friend and class enemy, foundered on the very imprecision of the categories of proletarian and worker identity. As much of the evidence in this chapter indicates, the enemies were found more often within the workerist culture that was simultaneously the bearer of revolutionary legitimacy and the obstacle to the radiant future of communism. The hooligan, the petty bourgeois, the philistine (*obyvatel'*), and the woman were not capitalist relics but workers who did not

---

65. See the essays in Sheila Fitzpatrick, ed., *Cultural Revolution in Russia, 1928–1931* (Bloomington, 1978).

66. *Pechatnik* 32 (7 November 1928): 16–21; 16 (1 June 1928): 34; 18 (22 June 1928): 32; 34 (5 December 1928): 33; 36 (25 December 1928): 5; 2 (20 January 1929): 14; 10 (10 April 1929): 1; 11 (20 April 1929): 20–21; 34 (5 December 1929): 23; 36 (25 December 1929): 11; TsGAMO, f. 4660, op. 1, d. 31 (general meetings of unemployed union members, 1929), ll. 4–5, 11, 237; *Nasha zhizn'*, 12 January 1928; *Krasnyi proletarii*, 21 January 1930; *Pechatnyi dvor*, 23 December 1930; *Zorkii glaz*, 23 February 1929.

live up to the expected norms of proletarian behavior. In declaring war on meshchanstvo and philistinism, the factory newspaper *Krasnyi proletarii* wrote in December 1928:

> The old contempt for comrades who want to try to be cultured, who reject harmful habits like drinking, swearing, indifference to production, insensitivity in relations with their comrades—this has not yet died out.... Many comrades think culture means higher education, smart dress, having a circle of friends who are socially superior to them. And comrades neither feel nor see that this is an erroneous conception, they do not notice that there is a struggle to eliminate a previous identity [*lichnosti*], the nature of which was perverted by centuries of bourgeois culture—this is an antisocial identity, of not yet having reached consciousness of the fact that to work for society is to work for oneself. We need to fight meshchanstvo and obyvatel'stvo: miserliness, impoliteness, dissipation, wastefulness, egoism, religious lies, drunkenness, decadence, and intoxication, and replace them with a new person: one who has enthusiasm for construction, for solidarity and organization, for struggling to harness the forces of nature to benefit all of humanity and not individual groups.[67]

In many ways, this article was denouncing nothing less than the total *unproletarian*, the antithesis of the Communist ideal. Yet as we have seen, these behaviors remained among the treasured identities of many workers in the printing trades. Consumerism, far from a trait to be eradicated, was for many the goal of socialism, and the regime's failure to satisfy workers' material needs remained a dominant source of printers' discontent and dissent. And as the attack on the "urban kulak" with which this chapter began also illustrates, one could not be sure even that a so-called cultured worker stood on the side of the total proletarian. The complicated ideological and political battles within the party and trade union had made it impossible to determine what even constituted the "side" of the working class. Socialism's defeat of the bourgeoisie had brought the class war home and had turned the working class on itself. Without a really existing bourgeoisie to contain the inherent fissures in workers' cultural commonality, their common traits dissipated or even exploded. A humanistic socialism might have celebrated this diversity, but after thirteen years of revolution, there seemed to be little support from the official Communist Party for toleration of difference. Difference was outlawed, anathematized, and driven underground. Class remained among Soviet workers as a possible source of identity, unity, pride, and resistance, but it became much more complicated to understand and difficult to apply. The history of Soviet printers in the 1920s reveals this multiplicity of worker identities, their complicated social selves, and the poignancy of their efforts to find both common proletarian ground and room for the humanistic proletarian "I" in the building of socialism.

67. *Krasnyi proletarii*, 19 December 1928.

## CHAPTER 10

## SOVIET WORKERS AND THE SOCIALIST PROJECT

Epilogue and Conclusion

The years of the First Five-Year Plan, from 1928 to 1932, are frequently called the "Great Turn" or a "Second Russian Revolution," labels that emphasize the rupture represented by the economic mobilization and revolutionary language of this period in Soviet history. Yet such a periodization obscures important continuities from the 1920s to the 1930s and exaggerates the moderation of the NEP experience.

### THE PRINTERS IN THE YEARS OF INDUSTRIALIZATION

The marriage of the Paper Workers' and Printers' unions, blessed by Boris Magidov at the new union's first congress in December 1930, lasted only two years. The reasons for the original merger remain unclear. Economic rationality had been proposed as one justification for bringing these two sectors of the publishing industry together. Combining the two unions also may have appealed to the union leaders' own continuing calls for a "single authoritative center" for the printing industry. The merger, however, bucked a trend in the opposite direction. In January 1931 the VTsSPS declared that turning the trade unions' "face to production" would require the breaking up of gigantic trade unions into more manageable units: instead of twenty-three industrial unions, there would now be forty-four. Thus the union of metalworkers, with its 1.5 million members, was restructured into seven separate unions. In April 1932 the workers in the printing and paper industries again went their separate ways by order of the presidium of the VTsSPS.[1]

The trade unions continued to grow as the industrial labor force increased, and growth led again to a lack of responsiveness, "trade unionism," and "empiricism," according to VTsSPS's godfather, Lazar' Kaganovich. Consequently, a new round of restructuring was imposed in September 1934, creating 154 unions out of the previous 47.[2] Unions were divided both by production specialty and by geographic region. Out of the single Union of Workers in the Printing Industry of 1930 emerged three: the Union of Workers in Publishing (the old Section of Press Workers); the Union of Workers in the Printing Industry of the North, with Leningrad as its center; and the Union of Workers in the Printing Industry of the Center and South, headquartered in Moscow and chaired by Boris Magidov. In most respects, the Union of the Center and South became the successor to the old All-Union Union of Printers, with Leningrad's separate union consigning its printers ever more to the backwaters of the trade union movement.

Organizational schemes aside, the printing industry grew rapidly, if not evenly, during the 1930s. The official size of the labor force in printing had hovered around 60,000 workers through much of the 1920s, dipping in 1929 to 57,800, but thereafter the labor force expanded, as Table 1 indicates. In 1934, as before, the Moscow oblast dominated the industry, with 25,000 printing workers to Leningrad oblast's 12,400; the size of the Voronezh workforce remained under one thousand, with 853 workers in July 1934. The uneven growth through the mid-1930s reflects the second-class status of printing, as part of the group of less favored light industry. The growth of heavy industry demanded the products of printing enterprises—account books, reports, and newspapers that spread the word about the successes of the First Five-Year Plan—but the printing industry received no new investment until the Second and Third Five-Year plans. By 1937, reported Magidov, this investment had paid off: the Soviet Union was publishing 10,000 newspapers, in 37 million copies, and the labor force in printing had grown to 121,000.[3]

Historians of Soviet industrialization have noted how the growth of the industrial labor force defied the efforts of planners to channel newly mobilized labor into areas of greatest need. One mechanism for this channeling was wage policy, and the impact of wage planning on the printing industry reflects both

---

1. *Profsoiuzy SSSR*, 649–51; *Trud*, 25 April 1932; *Gosudarstvennyi arkhiv Rossiiskoi Federatsii: Putevoditel'*, vol. 3: *Fondy gosudarstvennogo arkhiva Rossiiskoi Federatsii po istorii SSSR*, ed. S. V. Mironenko (Moscow, 1997), 521.
2. *Trud*, 5 and 6 September 1934.
3. *Trud*, 20 September 1937.

Table 1. Number of workers (including apprentices) in the printing industry, 1929–1936

| Year | Number of workers |
| --- | --- |
| 1929 | 57,800 |
| 1930 | 65,100 |
| 1931 | 81,100 |
| 1932 | 86,200 |
| 1933 | 77,500 |
| 1934 | 76,300 |
| 1935 | 85,200 |
| 1936 | 97,600 |

Source: Tsentral'noe upravlenie narodno-khoziaistvennogo ucheta Gosplana SSSR, Otdel ucheta truda, *Trud v SSSR. Statisticheskii spravochnik*, ed. A. S. Popov (Moscow, 1936), 94.

an attempt to engineer industrial policy from above and the continued resistance of workers who controlled production at the level of the shop floor. Despite printers' continued cries of poverty, wages in the printing industry remained very high throughout the 1920s, averaging 90 rubles a month; only machine-building workers, at 93 rubles, earned more.[4] In 1931, toward the end of the Five-Year Plan that was supposed to favor heavy industry, printing workers still ranked second in earnings, behind the machine-building workers, although the differential between their wages had grown. For 1932, however, planners insisted this hierarchy would change: printers' wages would be suppressed, along with those in other light industries. Government funds would be used instead to increase the wages in extractive industries such as metallurgy and coal mining, which were planned to become the second and third highest paid industries in 1932. Printing was supposed to drop to eighth place among seventeen industries.[5] But wage trends did not respond as quickly to such decrees as the planners would have liked. In 1932, in fact, the printing industry ranked fifth overall in average wages, behind electricity, machine-building, metallurgy, and oil extraction. Only in 1935 did the printing industry find its planned level, eighth among the seventeen major industries.[6]

4. *Trud*, 11 April 1932; see also N. S. Maslova, *Proizvoditel'nost' truda i zarabotnaia plata v promyshlennosti SSSR (1928–1932 gg.)* (Moscow, 1983), 100; *Itogi vypolneniia pervogo piatiletnego plana razvitiia narodnogo khoziaistva SSSR* (Moscow, 1934), 179; TsUNKhU, *Trud v SSSR*, 97. On industrialization, see, for example, Nove, *Economic History of the U.S.S.R.*, and Gregory, *Political Economy of Socialism*.
5. *Trud*, 11 April 1932.
6. TsUNKhU, *Trud v SSSR*, 97.

The eventual decline in the status of the printing industry, as measured by its level of wages, reflected other transformations. Chief among them was the changing gender mix in the industry. According to Wendy Goldman, the First Five-Year Plan also incorporated a plan to regender the labor force, and an extensive list of occupations in which women were to dominate was drawn up, circulated, and discussed.[7] By 1 January 1934, women constituted 48 percent of the printing industry's labor force. While women did enter into many of the occupations formerly considered to be skilled and reserved for men, the work process as a whole was subdivided, so that skill was no longer so important. Apprenticeship was reduced during the 1930s to one year, but family connections remained important: children of printers entered the industry of their parents.[8] And the workplace remained segregated by gender: none of the prize-winning brigades noted in the factory histories named both men and women among their ranks. The occupation of press operator (*pechatnik*) remained male: only 9 percent of press operators in 1936 were female. On the other hand, the increasing numbers of women in the industry created new leadership opportunities for them: the factory committee chair at the end of the 1930s at the *Leningradskaia pravda* plant was a veteran activist, Valentina Slepenkina. The theme of the workplace as family persisted. One woman worker remembered Slepenkina fondly: "Valia Slepenkina, a person of generous spirit and unbelievable modesty, became a mother for us." For others, the shop was their "native home."[9]

Pride in the industry remained strong among printing workers. "We were ardent patriots of our enterprise," recalled S. Margolis. When the workers of the First Model Print Shop met with textile workers or leather workers in the 1930s, "we would say—how could you possibly compare yourselves with us printers! Think about it—you make slippers or women's handbags. We give the country books. Can you understand? We produce ideological output. Everywhere, in any corner of the country, you can find a poster or portrait printed in our enterprise! In any distant polar station, in any little hut forgotten in the woods."[10]

The steady stream of campaigns continued into the 1930s. In March 1932, the trade union newspaper *Trud* launched a campaign to create "cost-accounting brigades" that would monitor the efficiency of industrial enterprises. The recollections of these brigades cast some doubt on their efficacy; but continuing in the spirit of its light cavalry, brigades at Krasnyi Proletarii were extremely active. Every day, remembered A. L. Zhivotovskaia, her brigade held a production conference to discuss indicators and evaluate outcomes. The brigade even issued a daily newspaper, *Khozraschetchik* (Cost accounter), one of thirty-

---

7. Goldman, *Women at the Gates*, chap. 5.
8. *Leninskii zakaz*, 362–63; Vechtomova, *Zdes' pechatalas'*, 224; *Trud*, 26 September 1937.
9. Vechtomova, *Zdes' pechatalas'*, 188–89, 223; Goldman, *Women at the Gates*, 271; *Pervaia obraztsovaia tipografiia*, 74–75.
10. *Pervaia obraztsovaia tipografiia*, 74.

Women compositors, participants in a cost-accounting brigade in a Moscow print shop, 1931. Planners aimed to reduce the average level of wages in the printing industry by regendering occupations such as typesetting as female. (Rossiiskii Gosudarstvennyi Arkhiv Kinofotodokumentov, 280574. Used with permission of the archive.)

nine cost-accounting newspapers issued by brigades in this one enterprise! The tone of these papers continued the trend of the all-enterprise paper, *Krasno-proletarets,* shaming workers who had arrived late, taken days off, or talked during work by publishing their names.[11] Like many of the 1920s schemes to raise productivity, this one seemed to become an end in itself.

All of these initiatives paled before the crowning achievement of productivity campaigns, the Stakhanovite movement, which began in 1935. Printers did not lag behind. Ambitious Linotypists studied how to type with seven fingers instead of three; press operators learned how to operate multiple presses. By January 1937, 30 percent of the members of the Printers' Union of the Center and South had earned the title of Stakhanovite (slightly below the national average of 33 percent). In 1939, Leningrad's Pechatnyi Dvor shop boasted that 42 percent of its workers had been declared Stakhanovites. Gomel', home of the 1930 production maneuver, reported that 89.5 percent of the workers had become Stakhanovites by 1939.[12] Seen in the context of the many earlier cam-

11. *Fabrika knigi Krasnyi Proletarii,* 325–28.
12. Vechtomova, *Zdes' pechatalas',* 205–8; B. I. Saf'ian and Z. B. Marvits, *Ordenonosnyi*

paigns to produce shock workers or socialist emulation, these figures for Stakhanovite achievements must be considered skeptically. The experience of Soviet labor-management relations had taught workers and managers how to appear to respond to the campaign du jour without actually changing their approach to work.

Technological change proceeded more slowly: gains in productivity, as throughout the 1920s, were accomplished by reorganization of the work process, through campaigns, and through wage incentives, not through increased capitalization. Only gradually did Soviet-built equipment supply the expanding number of printing enterprises around the country. Large new physical plants were constructed for the newspaper *Pravda* and in republican capitals in central Asia; new buildings were added to existing large enterprises such as First Model and Krasnyi Proletarii. Soviet printers' technological reputation received a great boost when Krasnyi Proletarii's *Constitution of the Soviet Union* won the grand prize at an exhibition in Paris in 1936.[13]

The industrial news in the 1930s was all about production achievements and economic growth. Since the purge of the Tomskii trade union leadership, the entire union movement had been effectively made into a mouthpiece for the economic leadership. The All-Union Trade Union Council held its ninth congress in 1932; another one would not be held until 1949. The People's Commissariat of Labor, which had sponsored labor-management arbitration, was dissolved in 1933.[14] Then in 1937, at the height of the great purges, the trade union movement was brought back into the public spotlight. During August and September of that year, virtually all trade unions held congresses, loudly saluted their country's leaders, heard reports from the union chairmen about their accomplishments and failures, and proceeded in most cases to dismiss the old leaderships and appoint new ones. The Printers' Union of the North opened its congress on 28 August 1937 in Leningrad; the Union of the Center and South met two weeks later in Moscow, on 15 September. The proceedings of these two congresses seemed completely scripted from start to finish, and while the language of the published accounts reflected the hysterical tone of the concurrent purge mania, the themes that the delegates spoke to harked back to the printers' congresses in the late 1920s. The union leaders, A. M. Rymkevich in Leningrad and Magidov in Moscow, gave hopeful reports about the activities of their organizations. Magidov lauded the steady growth of wages in the indus-

---

"Pechatnyi Dvor": *Ocherki istorii tipografii imeni A. M. Gor'kogo* (Moscow, 1969), 41–47; *Trud*, 23 September 1937, 15 November 1939, 20 September 1937, 28 October 1939; Siegelbaum, *Stakhanovism*, 170.

13. *Pravda*, 22 July 1931, 17 November 1932, 24 May 1933, 12 February 1933, 5 May and 31 December 1934; Vechtomova, *Zdes' pechatalas'*, 190; V. N. Kirshin, *Orden na znameni: Kratkii ocherk istorii leningradskogo ordena otechestvennoi voiny I stepeni zavoda poligraficheskikh mashin* (Moscow and Leningrad, 1965), 102–8; *Trud*, 20 September 1937; *Leninskii zakaz*, 200, 210.

14. See Deutscher, *Soviet Trade Unions*, 127–28; Ruble, *Soviet Trade Unions*, 14–23.

try, cited concrete expenditures on social welfare, and pointed to the union's extensive international connections. (Recall the jokes in the 1920s about the "international situation.")[15]

The two leaders also admitted to problems within their organizations, and many of the complaints revisited old sore spots. Speakers from the floor responded with relish. The union leadership was too unresponsive to the rank and file; it did not visit, it did not instruct, it did not lead. The leadership actually stood in the way of campaigns such as Stakhanovism, and did nothing to eliminate rank-and-file opposition to its obstruction. The wage policy was incorrect. The union did not protect the health and safety of its members. The union leadership had failed to take care of its members' cultural needs. Even such a prominent enterprise as Pechatnyi Dvor felt ignored. "Our enterprise is labeled a giant of the printing industry. It is the biggest in the Soviet Union, and it would seem that the Central Committee of the union ought to show us some attention, take care that the workers' needs are satisfied. But we don't even have our own club." The union was blamed as well for allowing enemies of the people and Trotskyist, Bukharinite, and Baptist(!) agents to infiltrate factory committees and shop floors. Even the old call for a central management body received support: "We should seriously raise the question of whether all printing enterprises should be united under one economic management," said I. S. Karpov of Sverdlovsk, a sentiment voiced by "almost all the speakers."[16] Such inability to manage the affairs of the workers brought due punishment to the union leadership: Rymkevich and Magidov lost their positions.[17]

A second round of congresses in 1939 looked very much like the first one in 1937, as delegates from around the country gathered in Moscow or Leningrad to consider the accomplishments of industry and of their unions. The frenzied purge atmosphere had abated by 1939; discussions and criticism were more businesslike: there was no hint that war had begun in Europe or that Soviet forces had expanded the territory of the Northern Union westward into occupied Poland. Delegates voiced approval of some measures while criticizing others. The Northern Union boasted that forty-two of its fifty-four enterprises had overfulfilled their plan in the first half of 1939, but the union still did not do all it could to promote production. The center still paid too little attention to local organizations, said delegates from Arkhangel'sk, Gor'kii, and Simferopol'. The union provided too little in the way of child care facilities, forcing women to leave their jobs because they had no other way to care for their children.[18] Such failures and defects were nothing new in the long history of the union, which continued to try to balance its role as cheerleader of production with a

15. *Trud*, 2 and 20 September 1937.
16. Ibid., 2, 5, 20, 21, 23, 24, and 26 September 1937.
17. Ibid., 6 and 27 September 1937.
18. Ibid., 28 October, 15 and 16 November 1939.

defense of the printers' living standards and conditions. Only the names had changed.

## WORKERS AND THE SOCIALIST PROJECT IN SOVIET RUSSIA

In 1917, Russian workers decisively rejected autocracy, and through their electoral politics and labor activism they registered a strong preference for a democratic and socialist solution to the problem of Russian poverty and inequality. Democracy had been dealt a hard blow by the exigencies of the Civil War and the voluntarism of Bolshevik political culture, but even before the squeezing out of the last remnants of NEP-era free enterprise by 1930, socialism—the social ownership of the means of production—had triumphed in the Soviet Union.

The path had not been even. The economic and political crises of the Civil War had resulted in a contraction of the economy and in severe shortages of food, fuel, and commodities. Printers and their representatives responded in two contradictory ways, calling on the one hand for greater central authority and direction in order to solve their economic problems, and on the other hand, hoarding and protecting their scarce resources, whether fuel, food, or work itself, regardless of what central authorities might deem effective or necessary for the survival of socialism as a whole. The continuing political struggle between Communist and Menshevik variants of Social Democracy uniquely provided printers with a prominent platform on which to debate the direction that Russian socialism should take. The political struggle crystallized around issues of representative democracy, economic doctrine, and fairness and equity on the shop floor. It was part of the Communists' totalist vision that dissent and contradiction could not exist within the socialist order, and thus the struggle with the Mensheviks became imbued with the Leninist assumption of all or nothing, of *kto kogo*; there could be no compromise when it came to the ethos of Russian socialism. The Communists found it easier to anathematize and outlaw rival political parties than to coexist with them. But it was easier to repress rival political voices than to solve the economic issues that underlay the differing socialist approaches to Russia's transformation. In their struggle over the direction of their trade union, workers in the printing industry found themselves on the front lines of the battle for socialism.

Economic expediency triumphed in 1921, and moderate voices calling for a gradual march toward the socialist economy prevailed within the ranks of the Communist Party. The economy gradually recovered, although more slowly in the printing industry than in the country at large. Unemployment continued to characterize the industry until about 1925, when printers could begin to imagine the contours of a socialist culture from the vantage point of relative economic prosperity. Politically, the rout of the Mensheviks from their last strongholds inside individual print shops narrowed the range of acceptable arguments printers could employ to explain their situation, let alone try to change it. Dissent always summoned up memories of the anticommunist union of the immediate postrevolutionary period. But within the limits of what I have labeled the Communists' participatory dictatorship, printers engaged actively in efforts to control their workplaces and to elaborate their own vision of a socialist culture. Signs of disaffection and withdrawal were far more common than outright dissent or support for any of the oppositions to the Communist program that were mobilizing in the middle of the 1920s.

Continuing economic difficulties in the printing industry exacerbated disaffection, expressed in the mounting crisis of unemployment in 1926 and 1927. Planning would be their salvation, many believed, and printers and their union supported the idea of a strong central industrial authority that would efficiently coordinate the resources available to the industry and that could lobby for even greater resources. But at the same time, printers in their workplaces resisted centrally directed schemes to raise productivity and to change their work culture. The Printers' Union likewise appealed on one hand for greater resources and direction from the state and on the other sought to protect the livelihoods and incomes of their members, leading them down the road to what would be labeled "right opportunism." By the end of 1929 they could no longer negotiate this impossible compromise between centralism and trade unionism, and the union leaders were expelled from their posts. Quite independently, however, the economy began to revive with the pouring of investment into heavy industry and construction at a time when living standards were suppressed by extreme shortages of food and commodities. The printing industry, even without a plan, benefited from this economic upturn, and by 1930 it not only enjoyed full employment but faced new challenges of a labor shortage. How it would deal with these new terms of the labor market in the 1930s lies outside the limits of this study, but the evidence suggests that the trade union leaders would continue to apply the same concepts and methods to labor organization in the 1930s that they had learned from the experiences of the preceding thirteen years of the revolution.

This brief overview of the historical trajectory from 1918 to 1930 brings us back to the central question of this book: What did socialism mean to workers in Soviet Russia's printing trades? How do we understand socialist labor relations and "socialist workers" by the start of the First Five-Year Plan? Communist labor relations remained unable to resolve the dilemma that the Mensheviks had pinpointed back in 1917: the interests of workers and the interests of bosses remained fundamentally contradictory at many levels, both economically and culturally. The official solution of productivism placed the interests of the socialist state above those of socialist workers, but the state depended on those workers and their representatives to achieve their goals. Schemes and campaigns designed to provide workers with a sense of participation and ownership won some converts to the productivist cause, but as soon as their novelty wore off, and sometimes long before, workers ignored the appeals to enthusiasm and concentrated instead on control of their work rhythms and on protecting their economic interests. *Homo sovieticus* remained *Homo economicus*:

nothing spurred production like the promise of a just reward for effort. Within the constraints of the system, haggling over one's placement on the scale of wages offered better returns than participation in yet another socialist contest and was far less risky than organizing a collective defense of worker interests. For workers in the printing industry, socialism meant *both* a rational centralized economic authority *and* the recognition of their right to control their workplace lives and work processes. These two goals may have been mutually exclusive; certainly they were difficult to achieve together.

This book has deliberately taken the perspective of the workers' side of labor-management relations. The trade union in Soviet socialism attempted to occupy an impossible middle position between labor and management, but its history and its political functions drew it inevitably toward the workers' side of the table. This may have been its undoing politically, but when one has examined the role of the Printers' Union in the work lives of its members, it is difficult to see how the union could have behaved otherwise. Soviet socialism in the 1920s remained a complicated amalgam of participation and coercion. The Communists' class-based understanding of politics assumed that class interests were dominant, uniform, and indivisible. There was only one correct class position on any issue; anything else was false consciousness, backwardness, or deliberate sabotage. The function of trade union "democracy" was to use the forms of participation and debate to teach workers to recognize their true class interests and to shepherd them toward an understanding of their identities as total proletarians. The trade union, as its representatives announced many times, was a school for communism: its practices would teach workers how to become good Communist citizens. Participation was necessary. Guidance was also imperative: hence the appointment from above of suitable leaders, whether the chairman of the union's central committee or the "nonparty" token on the local factory committee. Democracy, in the sense of Western parliamentarianism, was thus extremely restricted, but nonetheless the efforts to promote a Communist trade union uniformity required that workers publicly discuss and voice their views.

The evolution of the Communist Printers' Union from 1918 to 1930 is quite stunning. The militant productivist and dictatorial trade union of the Civil War years had become the equivalent of its Menshevik opposite: an independent voice representing the interests of Soviet citizens as workers vis-à-vis those Soviet citizens who were managers. Forums such as the trade union conferences and congresses in each city, assemblies of women, meetings of unemployed, and scripted elections of the factory committees often generated dissent and debate that challenged the hegemonic view of the party and trade union. Having failed to secure the unanimous consent of the governed, the union had to respond to the voices of the rank and file. Leaders of potential oppositions were fired or arrested, but the union was also forced to replace discredited leaders, such as the drunkard Vasil'ev in Leningrad; it disobeyed the center's directives on apprentices when the skilled workers objected; it colluded with management to keep printers' wages high, even when central planners called for limiting the wage bill in the industry.

Socialism promised equality and equity: in the total proletarian state, neither skill nor age nor gender should divide the united workforce. Party and trade union officials pledged themselves in the early years of the revolution to making socialist equality a reality for men and women. The task seemed largely to be a matter of transforming women, of nurturing their public activism and proletarian consciousness, so that they could acquire both work skills and political acumen. The evidence is quite clear, however, that men resisted the encroachment of women into the traditionally masculine work space, and the union and its male members dragged their feet when it came to sharing their skills and training women. Workplace culture, with its swearing, drinking, and horseplay, remained resolutely masculine. By the end of the 1920s, a new generation of women had entered the workforce who had been bombarded with the promises of socialist equality every 8 March but whose own experiences had reinforced their awareness of their second-class status. It was at this point that official labor policy began to channel women into their own occupations, making official the prevailing social segregation of the sexes and preserving the linkage of masculinity and all-around skill.

Young people, especially young boys, also served as pupils in the school of communism, and the trade union officially worried about the proper occupational and political training of the next generation of socialist workers. Yet as was the case with women workers, official rhetoric diverged from actual practice. The union only reluctantly honored the regime's pledge to reserve a share of its job openings for apprentices; relations between old and young on the shop floor were frequently antagonistic and conflictual. To protect the jobs (and income) of its veteran workers, the union sought to solve its unemployment crisis by restricting and then eliminating the intake of apprentices into the industry. Only at the end of the decade did young people return to the printing industry, and they brought with them values quite different from those of their predecessors. Isolated from shop floor culture or treated as unwelcome intruders, they had been molded by their experience in socialist labor practices into a generation of politically indifferent but actively consumerist young men and women. Their culture may have reflected less the values of production and skill ("I spit on skill") than the identities they had developed outside production: a youth culture reflecting both the "hooligan" world of the club and the street and the "socialist" world of education and upward mobility.

Indeed, the world outside of work constituted an important terrain for workers' expectations of socialism. It was not enough to eliminate the discipline and exploitation of hostile capitalist bosses: socialism represented material ease and, in the future, abundance. Wages measured skill and effort; they also were exchanged for goods and services that made life better. "Concerns of the stomach" could be dismissed as representing low consciousness or fuel for demagogic socialist oppositions, but the insistence on higher standards of living remained fundamental to the labor politics of workers in the printing trades. When resources permitted, they demanded a variety of goods and services to consume: trousers in addition to food in the early years of the revolution; apartments, butter, vodka, movies, cosmetics, dances, and travel as the revolution progressed. The downturn of the economy and the onset of rationing at the end of the 1920s thus served as a particular slap in the face of workers imbued with cultural expectations.

Socialism, having transformed the material relations of production, could also create new forms of sociability and of social organization. Socialist theorists believed that the elimination of inequality and of difference combined with the traditional cooperative habits of the work process might produce a new collectivist approach to everyday life. In the Soviet Union, the collective, not the individual, would be the basic unit of society.[19] Whether this idea derived from the imagined communal harmony of the Russian peasant village, the utopian projects of the Enlightenment, or the syndicalist instincts of shared proletarian experience, its application in the 1920s posited the collective as the standard for social organization. Collective housing, collective dining, and collective recreation would reinforce the collectivism of the work process itself to transform all proletarians from the bourgeois "I" to the proletarian "we." Yet, as the experience of printers strongly suggests, workers did not embrace the collectivist utopia. Their sociability was based more on the appeal of familiar small-group attachments than on the abstraction of the collective "we." Their cooperative workplace experience did not extrapolate to a universal collectivism. Even the exceptional individuals who embraced the collective abnegation of the self and eagerly joined communal housing arrangements drew relatively constricted limits around the extent of the collective. Most workers still preferred to pursue individual or family-based cultural practices, from rejecting public dining arrangements in favor of the family primus to seeking individual recreation and leisure opportunities at the expense of proletarian mass culture. If anything, the worker's "I" had become more pronounced by the end of the 1920s: *individualizm* and *obyvatel'shchina* were creeping in everywhere.

The ambiguities surrounding collectivism and individualism are reinforced when we consider the role played by class both in printers' own political and social encounters and in the historian's attempt to make sense of the development of the Soviet social and political world. We cannot write the history of Soviet workers without considering the meaning of class for two important reasons: one is heuristic, in that class analysis provides us with categories and questions that let us compare the experience of Soviet workers with the experiences of workers in other societies at other times. The other relates quite forcefully to the saturation of class language in the discourse of the time, to the

---

19. See Robert C. Williams, "Collective Immortality: The Syndicalist Origins of Proletarian Culture, 1905–1910," *Slavic Review* 39, no. 3 (1980): 389–402; Kharkhordin, *Collective and the Individual*, 7, 76–79.

historical memory workers retained about class locations and class identities, and to the ways in which this language and this memory contributed to workers' ongoing efforts to understand their place in society.

The centrality of work in workers' sense of themselves cannot be ignored. Over and over, when printers told stories about themselves, whether the writer Fedor Borovskii, the party propagandist Ivan Lomskii, or the pseudonymous worker-correspondents, they wrote in the idiom of work. Work experience, work practices, and work conflicts provided the touchstone for the ways in which these workers thought about one another and about their relation to power. Work linked printers with other members of society who made their living in production of useful goods: man or woman, they were workers, not carousel turners. Work also generated conflict with bosses, however hard the regime tried to elide the distinction between managers and workers.

Work also, however, distinguished printers from other individuals who occupied different social positions. Their special importance for the socialist project, their unique skills and abilities that justified their relatively high wages, and their prerevolutionary history as proletarian fighters for socialism set them apart from other workers, even from other skilled workers. The industrial structure of the Soviet trade union movement further encouraged the development of loyalties and affiliations more narrow than the broad working class (but broader than Western craft unions). Consequently, while appropriating the universalist language of class, printers demonstrated more solidarity with other printers than with workers in other industries, and more loyalty to their individual cities or enterprises than to the industry as a whole. The solidarity of the small group, cemented by everyday reciprocities and exchange, came to challenge the theoretical power of class as a source of support and affiliation across the whole society.

This kind of localism, craft patriotism, and shop patriotism is intrinsic to the industrial experience. We speak of moments of class formation when the attraction of and need for greater solidarity overcomes localism. The language of class helps workers to form these bonds of solidarity at such moments. Printers in Soviet Russia spoke the language of class and deployed it repeatedly in order to articulate their identities. But the urgency of solidarity had disappeared with the victory of the socialist revolution. The state now embodied the victorious working class, linguistically and politically. Class solidarity could no longer serve as an external fulcrum from which to move their world. Instead, still without a strong alternate source of identity, elements of the working class hived off and fragmented into smaller units, toward more local sources of affinity and commonality. Gender, generation, and geography came to assert decisive sources of distinction that increasingly competed with class as a whole, particularly given the domination by adult male workers in the self-definition of class. Soviet social mobility also helped to erode the unity of class, as ambitious individuals—more often men than women, and the young rather than the old—rose through education and patronage to positions as supervisors, directors, and members of the growing stratum of intellectual and technical workers. By the 1930s, class antagonism had disappeared, claimed the party: the totalist project had allegedly triumphed.[20] Yet distinction and difference would continue to characterize Soviet society, and class would continue to provide a language with which to analyze the importance and identities of social aggregates in socialist society.

Finally, we must consider what this perspective from the urban working rank and file contributes to a key set of questions in the historiography of Russia and the Soviet Union on the social origins of the Stalinist paradigm of government and social relations. To what extent did the attitudes and practices of printers and their trade union contribute to those phenomena that historians label "Stalinist"? The definition of "Stalinism" invokes a debate with a very long pedigree, and it is impossible to summarize it here.[21] Many scholars have defined Stalinism in terms of what it was not: it was as different from Leninism, Trotskyism, and Bukharinism as Menshevism was from Bolshevism. Stalinism represented a choice, an alternative taken by the party in those critical years of 1929 and 1930. In this array of alternatives, Stalinism represented an authoritarian, antidemocratic, ultracentralist, and supervoluntarist approach to government and social relations. For some observers, Stalinism means above all the dark years of the purges and terror, and the deliberate destruction of any group or individual that could be said to be alien to the Soviet system. More recently, scholars have preferred to see Stalinism as a complex system, a "civilization" that combined many and contradictory practices of governmentality and social compacts. Sheila Fitzpatrick writes that Stalinism stands for "the complex of institutions, structures, and rituals that made up the habitat of *Homo Sovieticus* in the Stalin era." In this sense, it defines a period and not a policy, a period that was characterized by "Communist Party rule, Marxist-Leninist ideology, rampant bureaucracy, leader cults, state control over production and distribution, social engineering, affirmative action on behalf of workers, stigmatization of 'class enemies,' police surveillance, terror, and the various informal, personalistic arrangements whereby people at every level sought to protect themselves and obtain scarce goods."[22] Although Fitzpatrick suggests that this distinctive habitat manifested itself fully only in the 1930s, she acknowledges that elements of it were present in the 1920s as well.

As we assess printers' efforts to construct a socialist culture in the 1920s, their contribution to a "Stalinist civilization" becomes apparent, although not

---

20. Fitzpatrick, *Education and Social Mobility*, 235, citing Stalin.
21. Some useful discussions of this problem include Deutscher, *Stalin*, chap. 9; Moshe Lewin, "The Social Background of Stalinism," in *Making of the Soviet System*, 258–85; Robert C. Tucker, "Stalinism as Revolution from Above," in *Stalinism*, ed. Robert C. Tucker, 77–108 (New York, 1977); Stephen F. Cohen, "Bolshevism and Stalinism," in Tucker, *Stalinism*, 3–29.
22. Sheila Fitzpatrick, *Everyday Stalinism: Ordinary Life in Extraordinary Times: Soviet Russia in the 1930s* (New York, 1999), 3–4. Stephen Kotkin also sees Stalinism as a system, a "civilization": *Magnetic Mountain: Stalinism as a Civilization* (Berkeley, 1995).

without contradictions. Among particular features of this system was the hostility to the marketplace expressed by printers and their unions, a trait they shared with many Russian intellectuals during the revolutionary era.[23] Printers endorsed the view that only production work was meaningful work, that buying and selling were shamefully antisocial activities. Such attitudes provided the foundation for the administrative-command principles of the Stalin-era economy.

At the same time, however, while rejecting the market as an ideology, in their everyday practices they reflected a subtle understanding of market principles. They responded to monetary incentives of piece rates and bonuses; they worked together to restrict the labor market in order to preserve their jobs and their wages; and individually they engaged in constant haggling over the terms of their employment, from their position on the pay grade to the determination of norms. They also rejected the principle that production was an end in itself: for them, production was worthy because it was the means to create material goods and cultural services that could enrich their lives.

Another feature of the Stalinist system derives from the voluntarism of the Communists' worldview, their belief that will and energy could accelerate processes of long-term change. By the end of the 1920s, this voluntarism had translated into the quick-fix mentality of "eliminating the kulaks as a class" and achieving the "Five-Year Plan in four." Nikolai Gordon exemplified this trait within the Printers' Union.[24] The consistent yearning of the Printers' Union for a "strong administrative center" to solve the industry's problems also reflects confidence in voluntarism, as well as the belief that central authority is always more effective than the invisible hand of the marketplace. Despite the failures of the centralized system and despite the strong sense of affiliation with local cities and local enterprises, federalism never became an option. Yet at the same time, printers consistently bemoaned the consequences of centralization in their own union: excessive bureaucratism and the lack of "living ties" between the center and the locals.

The centralism and voluntarism of Stalinism led to a perverted form of democracy in which everyone participated but decisions were monopolized by the union center and by the Communist Party. Despite their consistent appeal to the center and their support for administrative solutions, printers at the local level favored the practice of genuine democracy: the opportunity to debate issues, elections in which the outcome was not foreordained, and accountability on the part of their elected leaders. This was one of the attractions of the Menshevik Printers' Union during the Civil War years, and printers remained largely alienated by the continuing antidemocratic practices of the Communist trade union and political institutions. The failure of factory meetings to gener-

23. Clark, *Petersburg*, xi, 17.
24. A satiric verse in *Pechatnik*, 9–10 (June 1924): 17, noted Gordon's power to command even the weather.

ate enthusiasm reveals only the tip of the iceberg of printers' disaffection from the political culture that would be perfected in the Stalinist 1930s. Printers' lukewarm response to the purge campaign of 1929 and 1930 offers additional evidence of a fundamental distance from authoritarian political culture, as does the preference by the rank and file to gloss over the internecine union struggles of the Civil War in their revolutionary reminiscences. Repression and constant monitoring by the party and the political police made any action beyond passive disaffection highly risky. Accommodation with the regime of the GPU did not necessarily signify approval.

Finally, we must confront an important and distinctive feature of the Stalin system, its totalist ambitions. While the regime never realized these ambitions and cannot therefore be called "totalitarian," I have suggested that Communist ideology before, during, and after Stalin reflected the power of the total-unity concept, a belief that a perfect, utopian world would ensue when difference was overcome. This belief in total unity made reasonable rather than contradictory the concepts of participatory dictatorship, central control, and the superiority of plan over market. The ideal socialist state would contain no contradictions, no ambiguity, and no conflict. The total proletarian ideal represented the totalist vision of socialist work culture, and those printers who supported its features of devotion to production, collective sociability, and everyday asceticism (simple clothes, no jewelry, and no tango) shared in these totalist aspirations. Nonetheless, the printers' own experiences as workers and as Soviet citizens disproved the validity of the totalist idea again and again: life itself was fraught with contradiction, ambiguity, and conflict. No wonder that only a minority of printers ever joined the Communist Party or became zealous nonparty activists. Liberalism, with its creed of the market, was never much of an option, even in 1917, but alternate socialist ideologies that could accommodate difference and ambiguity were forcefully routed from the Soviet political scene.

Yet the lesson of the attempt to build a socialist culture in Soviet Russia in these years—from the beginning of the revolutionary endeavor and well before the Great Turn to the 1930s—lies precisely in the contradictions and ambiguities that effort revealed. Above all, these contradictions lay in the inherently antagonistic relationship between what the Mensheviks called the work givers and the workers. At the point of production, the interests of management and of labor diverged. Management wanted power to enforce its standards of discipline and reduce costs. Workers wanted power to defend their lower standards of discipline and keep the price of their labor as high as possible. However red the directors, however much participation the regime cajoled from its labor force, management and labor at work occupied conflicting class positions. The trade union and Communist Party under socialism were meant to resolve this contradiction, but as we have seen, the tension persisted between productivism and workerism, between the administrative line and the public line, between those with the power to hire, fire, and punish and those without.

The total proletarian, the selfless, collectivist, productivist, cultured, self-improving, and zealous working person and builder of socialism, the worker whose goals and values marched in complete accord with the will of the party as a whole, was meant to resolve the contradiction between management and labor, boss and subaltern, collective and individual. This construct clashed with the realities of everyday life and human agency. Instead of the official version of class identity, which privileged the total proletarian and total political engagement, printers demonstrated a quite resilient alternate form of class identity, in which elements of the total proletarian coexisted with other behaviors linked with a lack of approved culture: political disaffection, materialism, consumerism, hooliganism, selfishness, drinking, swearing, fighting, and bullying of women by men. These contradictions can be seen as well in the conflict between productivism and consumerism: printers expressed pride in their skills as producers and drew on their qualities as producers to articulate their sense of class identity, yet at the same time, production remained a means to an end rather than the end itself. Their goal was not just the joy of work but the enjoyment of things that their work effort could buy: leisure both on and off the job, commodities, family life, and culture.

The total proletarian construct failed as well to resolve the contradiction between the collective "we" and the individual "I": both collectivism *and* individualism possessed meaning for Russian printers. Their socialism would offer space for the two to coexist. Contradictions emerged in the attempts to overcome gender barriers to class unity. Male workers and female workers both expressed a worker identity based on pride in work: it was women who said that carousel work was "not my trade" and "We don't want handouts—give us work." But longstanding workplace attitudes denying women the capability of learning skills as well as the rigid division of reproductive labor that created a double burden for women workers continued to ensure that the "proletarian" would be thought of in masculine terms. Contradictions emerged in political terms in the accommodation I have labeled participatory dictatorship: on one hand, the regime's compulsion to organize and to mobilize the total proletariat and its need to provide a veneer of democracy; on the other hand, its unwillingness to grant that proletariat the right to express division, doubt, uncertainty, and contradiction. Soviet workers, as represented by these printers, acknowledged ambiguity where the leaders wanted only certainty, but the certainty of the leadership created the conditions to which these workers learned to adjust. Thirteen years of socialist revolution taught them how to adapt to this habitat, whether by choice, compulsion, or indifference, and to make their own accommodation with the regime. They conceded much, but they preserved also an autonomy and authority rooted in the values of a rough and resilient sense of class identity.

# SELECTED BIBLIOGRAPHY

**Archival Materials**

Gosudarstvennyi Arkhiv Rossiiskoi Federatsii (GARF), Moscow.
    Fond R-5461. Tsentral'nyi sovet vserossiiskogo soiuza rabochikh pechatnogo dela, 1917–1919.
    Fond R-5525. Opisi 1–12, 18. Professional'nyi soiuz rabochikh poligraficheskogo proizvodstva, 1919–1930.
Tsentral'nyi Gosudarstvennyi Arkhiv Moskovskoi Oblasti (TsGAMO), Moscow.
    Fond 699. Opisi 1–2. Moskovskii gubernskii otdel vserossiiskogo soiuza rabochikh poligraficheskogo proizvodstva, 1917–1929.
    Fond 4660. Opis' 1. Moskovskii oblastnoi otdel vserossiiskogo soiuza rabochikh poligraficheskogo proizvodstva, 1929–1930.
Tsentral'nyi Gosudarstvennyi Arkhiv Sankt Peterburga (TsGA SPb), St. Petersburg.
    Fond 4804. Opisi 1–21. Leningradskii gubernskii otdel vserossiiskogo soiuza rabochikh poligraficheskogo proizvodstva, 1917–1930.
Tsentral'nyi Gosudarstvennyi Arkhiv Istoriko-Politicheskikh Dokumentov Sankt Peterburga (TsGAIPD SPb), St. Petersburg.
    Fond 16. Petrogradskii gubernskii komitet RKP(b), 1918–1927.
    Fond 250. Kollektiv RKP(b) Pervoi gosudarstvennoi tipografii (Pechatnyi Dvor), 1918–1930.
    Fond 435. Opis' 1. Fraktsii VKP(b) Leningradskogo gubernskogo otdela soiuza pechatnogo i kartonazhnogo proizvodstva, 1918–1929.
    Fond 457. Opis' 1. Fraktsii RKP(b) Petrogradskogo gubernskogo soveta professional'nykh soiuzov, 1918–1930.
    Fond 1196. Partiinaia organizatsiia tipografii imeni Evgenii Sokolovoi.

**Journals and Newspapers**

*Biulleten' moskovskogo obshchestva tipo-litografov.* Moscow. 1918.
*Ekonomicheskaia zhizn'.* Moscow. 1918–30.
*Gazeta pechatnika.* Moscow. 1918–19. Moskovskii soiuz rabochikh pechatnogo dela.
*Iskry.* Leningrad. 1925–30. Stengazeta tipografii im. Evgenii Sokolovoi.

*Izvestiia.* Moscow. 1917-30.
*Izvestiia petrogradskogo soveta rabochikh deputatov.* Petrograd. 1917.
*Krasnyi pechatnik.* Petrograd. 1921-22. Petrogradskii gubotdel vserossiiskogo soiuza rabochikh poligraficheskogo proizvodstva.
*Krasnyi proletarii.* Moscow. 1922-30. Stengazeta tipografii "Krasnyi proletarii." (From 1 September 1929 *Krasnoproletarets.*)
*Leningradskaia pravda.* Leningrad. 1918-30. (Until 1924, *Petrogradskaia pravda*).
*Moskovskii pechatnik.* Moscow. 1921-26. Moskovskii gubernskii otdel vserossiiskogo soiuza rabochikh poligraficheskogo proizvodstva.
*Nasha zhizn'.* Moscow. 1923-30. Mnogotirazhnaia gazeta 16-i tipografii.
*Pechatnik.* Moscow. 1917-19. Moskovskii profsoiuz pechatnikov.
*Pechatnik.* Moscow. 1922-30. Tsentral'nyi komitet vsesoiuznogo soiuza rabochikh poligraficheskogo proizvodstva.
*Pechatnitsa.* Moscow. 1924. Moskovskii gub'otdel vsesoiuznogo soiuza rabochikh poligraficheskogo proizvodstva. One issue.
*Pechatnoe delo.* 1917-18. Petrograd. Petrogradskii soiuz rabochikh pechatnogo dela.
*Pechatnyi dvor.* Leningrad. 1924-1930. Mnogotirazhnaia gazeta tipografii "Pechatnyi Dvor."
*Pravda.* Moscow. 1917-31.
*Professional'noe dvizhenie.* Moscow. 1919-24. Vserossiiskii tsentral'nyi i moskovskii sovety professional'nykh soiuzov.
*Rabochaia gazeta.* Petrograd. 1917.
*Rabochii klub.* Moscow. 1924-28.
*Revoliutsionnyi golos pechatnika.* Moscow. 1918.
*Revoliutsionnyi pechatnik.* Moscow. 1918-19.
*Revoliutsionnyi pechatnik.* Petrograd. 1917-19.
*Sotsialisticheskii vestnik.* Berlin. 1921-30.
*Trud.* Moscow. 1918-37.
*Trudovaia kopeika.* Moscow. 1917.
*Vestnik vserossiiskogo soiuza rabochikh pechatnogo dela.* Moscow. 1918-19. Soiuz rabochikh pechatnogo dela.
*Vpered!* Moscow, 1917. Menshevik party organ.
*Vserossiiskii pechatnik.* Moscow. 1919-22. Tsentral'nyi komitet vserossiiskogo soiuza rabochikh poligraficheskogo proizvodstva.
*Zhizn' pechatnika.* Moscow. 1923-30. Stengazeta Pervoi Obraztsovoi tipografii.
*Zorkii glaz.* Leningrad. 1924-30. Stengazeta 14-i tipografii (im. Zinov'eva), later tipografiia "Leningradskaia pravda." (From 20 January 1930 *Leningradskii pravdist.*)

**Books and Articles**

*Akademicheskaia tipografiia 1728-1928.* Leningrad: Akademii nauka SSSR, 1928.
Andrle, Vladimir. *Workers in Stalin's Russia: Industrialization and Social Change in a Planned Economy.* New York: St. Martin's Press, 1988.
Appadurai, Arjun, ed. *The Social Life of Things: Commodities in Cultural Perspective.* Cambridge: Cambridge University Press, 1986.

Arbuzov, S. *Polozhenie russkoi poligraficheskoi promyshlennosti.* Moscow: Gosizdat, 1921.
Ashin, Paul. "Wage Policy in the Transition to NEP." *Russian Review* 47, no. 3 (1988): 293–313.
Avdeev, P. N. *Trudovye konflikty v SSSR.* Moscow: Voprosy truda, 1928.
Aves, Jonathan. *Workers against Lenin: Labour Protest and the Bolshevik Dictatorship.* London: Tauris Academic Studies, 1996.
Avrich, Paul. *Kronstadt 1921.* New York: Norton, 1970.
Baker, Elizabeth F. *Printers and Technology: A History of the International Printing Pressmen and Assistants' Union.* New York: Columbia University Press, 1957.
Ball, Alan M. *Russia's Last Capitalists: The Nepmen, 1921–1929.* Berkeley: University of California Press, 1987.
Barnett, G. E. *Chapters on Machinery and Labor.* Cambridge: Harvard University Press, 1926.
Baron, Ava. "An 'Other' Side of Gender Antagonism at Work: Men, Boys, and the Remasculinization of Printers' Work, 1830–1920." In *Work Engendered: Toward a New History of American Labor,* ed. Ava Baron, 47–69. Ithaca: Cornell University Press, 1993.
——. "Contested Terrain Revisited: Gender and the Social Construction of Skill in the Printing Industry, 1850–1920." In *Women, Work and Technology: Transformations,* ed. Barbara Drygulski Wright et al., 58–83. Ann Arbor: University of Michigan Press, 1987.
——. "Questions of Gender: Deskilling and Demasculinization in the U.S. Printing Trade, 1830–1915." *Gender and History* 1 (Summer 1989): 178–99.
Berlanstein, Lenard, ed. *Rethinking Labor History.* Urbana: University of Illinois Press, 1993.
Bernshtam, M. S. "Nezavisimoe rabochee dvizhenie v 1918 g. Dokumenty i materialy." In *Narodnoe soprotivlenie kommunizmu v Rossii.* Paris: Issledovaniia noveishei russkoi istorii, 1981.
*Biiskii pechatnik, 1917–1927.* Biisk: Gazeta "Zvezda Altaia," 1927.
*Bolezni nashego pechatnogo dela.* Moscow: NKRKI, 1924.
Bonnell, Victoria E. *Iconography of Power: Soviet Political Posters under Lenin and Stalin.* Berkeley: University of California Press, 1997.
——. "The Iconography of the Worker in Soviet Political Art." In *Making Workers Soviet: Power, Class, and Identity,* ed. Lewis H. Siegelbaum and Ronald Grigor Suny, 341–75. Ithaca: Cornell University Press, 1994.
——. *Roots of Rebellion: Workers' Politics and Organizations in St. Petersburg and Moscow, 1900–1914.* Berkeley: University of California Press, 1983.
Borovskii, F. *P'esy.* Moscow: VTsSPS, n.d.
——. *Rabochie rasskazy.* Moscow: VTsSPS, 1924.
Borrero, Mauricio. "Communal Dining and State Cafeterias in Moscow and Petrograd, 1917–1921." In *Food in Russian History and Culture,* ed. Musya Glants and Joyce Toomre, 162–76. Bloomington: Indiana University Press, 1997.
Bourdieu, Pierre. *Distinction: A Social Critique of the Judgement of Taste.* Trans. Richard Nice. Cambridge: Harvard University Press, 1985.

*British Labour Delegation to Russia, 1920. Report.* London: TUC and Labour Party, 1920.
Brooks, Jeffrey. "Public and Private Values in the Soviet Press, 1921–28." *Slavic Review* 48, no. 1 (1989): 16–35.
———. *When Russia Learned to Read: Literacy and Popular Literature, 1861–1917.* Princeton: Princeton University Press, 1985.
Brovkin, Vladimir N. *Behind the Front Lines of the Civil War: Political Parties and Social Movements in Russia, 1918–1922.* Princeton: Princeton University Press, 1994.
———. *The Mensheviks after October: Socialist Opposition and the Rise of the Bolshevik Dictatorship.* Ithaca: Cornell University Press, 1987.
———. *Russia after Lenin: Politics, Culture, and Society, 1921–1929.* London: Routledge, 1998.
Brower, Daniel. "Labor Violence in Russia in the Late Nineteenth Century." *Slavic Review* 41, no. 3 (1982): 417–31.
Brown, Emily Clark. *Soviet Trade Unions and Labor Relations.* Cambridge: Harvard University Press, 1966.
Canning, Kathleen. *Languages of Labor and Gender: Female Factory Work in Germany, 1850–1914.* Ithaca: Cornell University Press, 1996.
Carr, E. H. *The Bolshevik Revolution, 1917–1923.* 3 vols. London: Macmillan, 1950–53.
———. *The Interregnum, 1923–1924.* London: Macmillan, 1954.
———. *Socialism in One Country, 1924–1926.* 3 vols. London: Macmillan, 1958–64.
Carr, E. H., and R. W. Davies. *Foundations of a Planned Economy, 1926–1929.* 2 vols. London: Macmillan, 1969.
Chase, William J. *Workers, Society, and the Soviet State: Labor and Life in Moscow, 1918–1929.* Urbana: University of Illinois Press, 1987.
Cherniaev, V. Iu., ed. *Piterskie rabochie i "diktatura proletariata": Oktiabr' 1917–1929. Sbornik dokumentov.* St. Petersburg: Russko-Baltiiskii informatsionnyi tsentr BLITS, 2000.
*Chetvertyi vserossiiskii s"ezd professional'nykh soiuzov (17–25 maia 1921 g.): Stenograficheskii otchet (raboty plenuma i sektsii).* Moscow: Izdanie RIO VTsSPS, 1922.
Child, John. *Industrial Relations in the British Printing Industry: The Quest for Security.* London: Allen & Unwin, 1967.
Chistikov, A. N. "Azartnye igry v SSSR serediny 20-kh godov." *Voprosy istorii.* 1994, no. 2: 138–42.
———. "Gosudarstvo protiv kartochnoi igry." In *Normy i tsennosti povsednevnoi zhizni 1920–1930-e gody,* ed. Timo Vikhavainen, 299–316. St. Petersburg: Zhurnal "Neva," 2000.
Clark, Florence E. *The Printing Trades and Their Workers.* Scranton: International Textbook Co., 1939.
Clark, Katerina. *Petersburg: Crucible of Cultural Revolution.* Cambridge: Harvard University Press, 1995.
Clements, Barbara. *Bolshevik Women.* Cambridge: Cambridge University Press, 1997.
Clowes, Edith W. "The Limits of Discourse: Solov'ev's Language of Syzygy and the Project of Thinking Total-Writing." *Slavic Review* 55, no. 3 (1996): 552–66.
Cockburn, Cynthia. *Brothers: Male Dominance and Technological Change.* London: Pluto, 1983.

Cohen, Lizabeth. *Making a New Deal: Industrial Workers in Chicago, 1919–1939*. Cambridge: Cambridge University Press, 1990.
Cohen, Stephen F. "Bolshevism and Stalinism." In *Stalinism,* ed. Robert C. Tucker, 3–29. New York: Norton, 1977.
——. *Bukharin and the Bolshevik Revolution*. New York: Knopf, 1973.
Dahrendorf, Ralf. *Class and Class Conflict in Industrial Society*. Stanford: Stanford University Press, 1959.
Dan, Fedor. *Dva goda skitanii (1919–1921)*. Berlin: Russische bücherzentrale Obrazowanie, 1922.
Daniels, Robert Vincent. *The Conscience of the Revolution: Communist Opposition in Soviet Russia*. New York: Simon & Schuster, 1960.
David-Fox, Michael. "What Is Cultural Revolution?" *Russian Review* 58, no. 2 (1999): 181–201.
Davies, R. W. *The Soviet Economy in Turmoil, 1929–1930*. London: Macmillan, 1989.
Davies, Sarah. *Popular Opinion in Stalin's Russia: Terror, Propaganda, and Dissent, 1934–1941*. Cambridge: Cambridge University Press, 1997.
*Deiateli SSSR i oktiabr'skoi revoliutsii*. 7th ed. Moscow: Entsiklopedicheskii slovar' russkogo bibliograficheskogo instituta Granata, 1927–29.
*Deistvuiushchee zakonodatel'stvo o trude soiuza SSSR i soiuznykh respublik: Sbornik deistvuiushchikh dekretov, postanovlenii i instruktsii*. Ed. E. Danilova. Moscow: Izd. NKT "Voprosy truda," 1927.
Depretto, Jean-Paul. *Les Ouvriers en U.R.S.S., 1928–1941*. Paris: Publications de la Sorbonne/Institut d'études slaves, 1997.
*Desiat' let bor'by i pobed iacheika VKP(b) tipografii Krasnyi Proletarii*. Ed. V. I. Baskakov. Moscow: Krasnyi proletarii, 1930.
Deutscher, Isaac. *The Prophet Unarmed: Trotsky, 1921–1929*. New York: Vintage, 1959.
——. *Soviet Trade Unions: Their Place in Soviet Labour Policy*. New York: Oxford University Press, 1950.
——. *Stalin*. New York: Oxford University Press, 1966.
*Direktivy KPSS i sovetskogo pravitel'stva po khoziaistvennym voprosam*. Moscow: Politicheskaia literatura, 1957.
Douglas, Mary, and Baron Isherwood. *The World of Goods: Towards an Anthropology of Consumption*. London: Routledge, 2001.
Downs, Anthony. *An Economic Theory of Democracy*. New York: Harper, 1957.
Drobizhev, V. Z. *Glavnyi shtab sotsialisticheskoi promyshlennosti: Ocherki istorii VSNKh, 1917–1932 gg*. Moscow: Mysl', 1966.
Engelstein, Laura. *Moscow, 1905: Working-Class Organization and Political Conflict*. Stanford: Stanford University Press, 1982.
Erlich, Alexander. *The Soviet Industrialization Debate, 1924–1928*. Cambridge: Harvard University Press, 1960.
*Fabrichno-zavodskaia promyshlennost' goroda Moskvy i moskovskoi gubernii, 1917–1927 gg*. Moscow, 1928.
*Fabrika knigi "Krasnyi proletarii": Istoriia tipografii byvsh. "T-va I. N. Kushnereva i K."* Moscow: Gizlegprom, 1932.
*Fabriki i zavody vsei Rossii. Svedeniia o 31,523 fabrikakh i zavodakh*. Kiev: L. M. Fish, 1913.

Ferro, Marc. "La Naissance du système bureaucratique en URSS." *Annales: Economies, Sociétés, Civilisations.* 1976: 243–60.
———. *La Révolution de 1917: Octobre, naissance d'une société.* Paris: Aubier, 1976.
Filtzer, Donald. *Soviet Workers and Stalinist Industrialization: The Formation of Modern Soviet Production Relations, 1928–1941.* Armonk, N.Y.: M. E. Sharpe, 1986.
Fitzpatrick, Sheila. "Ascribing Class: The Construction of Social Identity in Soviet Russia." *Journal of Modern History* 65, no. 4 (1993): 745–70.
———. "The Civil War as a Formative Experience." In *Bolshevik Culture: Experiment and Order in the Russian Revolution,* ed. Abbott Gleason, Peter Kenez, and Richard Stites, 57–76. Bloomington: Indiana University Press, 1985.
———. *The Cultural Front: Power and Culture in Revolutionary Russia.* Ithaca: Cornell University Press, 1992.
———. *Education and Social Mobility in the Soviet Union, 1921–1934.* Cambridge: Cambridge University Press, 1979.
———. *Everyday Stalinism: Ordinary Life in Extraordinary Times: Soviet Russia in the 1930s.* New York: Oxford University Press, 1999.
———. "The Problem of Class Identity in NEP Society." In *Russia in the Era of NEP: Explorations in Soviet Society and Culture,* ed. Sheila Fitzpatrick, Alexander Rabinowitch, and Richard Stites, 12–33. Bloomington: Indiana University Press, 1991.
———, ed. *Cultural Revolution in Russia, 1928–1931.* Bloomington: Indiana University Press, 1978.
Fitzpatrick, Sheila, Alexander Rabinowitch, and Richard Stites, eds. *Russia in the Era of NEP: Explorations in Soviet Society and Culture.* Bloomington: Indiana University Press, 1991.
Friedgut, Theodore H. *Iuzovka and Revolution,* vol. 2: *Politics and Revolution in Russia's Donbass, 1869–1924.* Princeton: Princeton University Press, 1994.
Fueloep-Miller, René. *The Mind and Face of Bolshevism: An Examination of Cultural Life in Soviet Russia.* 1926. Trans. F. S. Flint and D. F. Tait. New York: Harper & Row, 1965.
Galili, Ziva. *The Menshevik Leaders in the Russian Revolution: Social Realities and Political Strategies.* Princeton: Princeton University Press, 1989.
Genkina, E. B. "Vozniknovenie proizvodstvennykh soveshchanii v gody vosstanovitel'nogo perioda (1921–1925)." *Istoriia SSSR,* no. 3 (1958): 63–89.
Gimpel'son, E. G. *Rabochii klass v upravlenii sovetskim gosudarstvom: Noiabr' 1917–1920 gg.* Moscow: Nauka, 1982.
———. *Sovetskii rabochii klass, 1918–1920 gg.* Moscow: Nauka, 1974.
Goldman, Emma. *My Disillusionment in Russia.* New York: Thomas Y. Crowell, 1970.
Goldman, Wendy Z. *Women at the Gates: Gender and Industry in Stalin's Russia.* Cambridge: Cambridge University Press, 2002.
———. *Women, the State, and Revolution: Soviet Family Policy and Social Life, 1917–1936.* Cambridge: Cambridge University Press, 1993.
Goodrich, Carter L. *The Frontier of Control: A Study in British Workshop Politics.* New York: Harcourt, Brace & Howe, 1920.
Gordon, Manya. *Workers before and after Lenin.* New York: Dutton, 1941.
Gorham, Michael S. *Speaking in Soviet Tongues: Language Culture and the Politics of Voice in Revolutionary Russia.* DeKalb: Northern Illinois University Press, 2003.

Gorsuch, Anne E. *Youth in Revolutionary Russia: Enthusiasts, Bohemians, Delinquents.* Bloomington: Indiana University Press, 2000.

Gray, Robert Q. *The Labour Aristocracy in Victorian Edinburgh.* Oxford: Clarendon, 1976.

Graziosi, Andrea. "Stalin's Antiworker 'Workerism,' 1924–1931." *International Review of Social History* 40 (1995): 223–58.

Gregory, Paul R., ed. *Behind the Facade of Stalin's Command Economy: Evidence from the Soviet State and Party Archives.* Stanford: Hoover Institution Press, 2001.

Haimson, Leopold H. "The Problem of Social Identities in Early Twentieth Century Russia." *Slavic Review* 47, no. 1 (1988): 1–20.

——. "The Problem of Social Stability in Urban Russia, 1905–1914." *Slavic Review* 23, no. 4 (1964): 619–42; 24, no. 1 (1965): 1–22.

Haimson, Leopold H., with Eric Brian. "Changements démographiques et grèves ouvrières à St. Petersbourg, 1905–1914." *Annales: Economies, Sociétés, Civilisations* 4 (July–August 1985): 781–803.

Haimson, Leopold H., and Giulio Sapelli, eds. *Strikes, Social Conflict, and the First World War: An International Perspective.* Milan: Feltrinelli, 1992.

Haimson, Leopold H., and Charles Tilly, eds. *War, Strikes, and Revolution: Patterns in the Evolution of Industrial Labor Conflicts in the Late Nineteenth and Early Twentieth Centuries.* Cambridge: Cambridge University Press, 1988.

Hall, John R., ed. *Reworking Class.* Ithaca: Cornell University Press, 1997.

——. "The Reworking of Class Analysis." In *Reworking Class,* ed. John R. Hall, 1–37. Ithaca: Cornell University Press, 1997.

Hatch, John B. "Hangouts and Hangovers: State, Class, and Culture in Moscow's Workers' Club Movement, 1925–1928." *Russian Review* 53, no. 1 (1994): 97–117.

——. "The Politics of Mass Culture: Workers, Communists, and the Proletcult in the Development of Workers' Clubs, 1921–1925." *Russian History* 13, no. 3 (1986): 119–48.

Hinton, James. *The First Shop Stewards' Movement.* London: George Allen & Unwin, 1973.

Hobsbawm, Eric. *Labouring Men.* New York: Basic Books, 1964.

——. *Workers: Worlds of Labor.* New York: Pantheon, 1984.

Hoffmann, David L. *Peasant Metropolis: Social Identities in Moscow, 1929–1941.* Ithaca: Cornell University Press, 1994.

Hogan, Heather. *Forging Revolution: Metalworkers, Managers, and the State in St. Petersburg, 1890–1914.* Bloomington: Indiana University Press, 1993.

Howe, Ellic, ed. *The Trade: Passages from the Literature of the Printing Craft, 1550–1935.* London: Walter Hutchinson, 1943.

Hunter, Tera W. *To 'Joy My Freedom: Southern Black Women's Lives and Labors after the Civil War.* Cambridge: Harvard University Press, 1997.

Husband, William B. *Revolution in the Factory: The Birth of the Soviet Textile Industry, 1917–1920.* New York: Oxford University Press, 1990.

*Istoriia leningradskogo soiuza poligraficheskogo proizvodstva. Kniga pervaia: 1904–1907.* Leningrad: Leningradskii gubotdel soiuza rabochikh poligraficheskogo proizvodstva, 1925.

*Istoriia rabochikh Leningrada.* Vol. 2. Leningrad: Nauka, 1972.

*Itogi vypolneniia pervogo piatiletnego plana razvitiia narodnogo khoziaistva SSSR.* Moscow: Gosplan Soiuza SSR, 1934.

Johnson, Robert Eugene. *Peasant and Proletarian: The Working Class of Moscow in the Late Nineteenth Century.* New Brunswick: Rutgers University Press, 1979.

Kabo, E. O. *Ocherki rabochego byta. Opyt monograficheskogo issledovaniia domashnego rabochego byta.* Moscow: VTsSPS, 1928.

Kairovich, V. S. *Obzor deiatel'nosti Moskovskogo soiuza rabochikh pechatnogo truda (28 II 1916–1 I 1918).* Moscow, 1918.

Kaschuba, Wolfgang. "Popular Culture and Workers' Culture as Symbolic Orders: Comments on the Debate about the History of Culture and Everyday Life." In *The History of Everyday Life: Reconstructing Historical Experiences and Ways of Life,* ed. Alf Lüdtke, trans. William Templer, 169–97. Princeton: Princeton University Press, 1995.

Katznelson, Ira. "Working-Class Formation: Constructing Cases and Comparisons." In *Working-Class Formation: Nineteenth-Century Patterns in Western Europe and the United States,* ed. Ira Katznelson and Aristide R. Zolberg, 3–41. Princeton: Princeton University Press, 1986.

Kelley, Robin D. G. "'We Are Not What We Seem': Rethinking Black Working-Class Opposition in the Jim Crow South." *Journal of American History* 80, no. 1 (1993): 75–112.

Kenez, Peter. *Cinema and Soviet Society, 1917–1953.* Cambridge: Cambridge University Press, 1992.

Kharkhordin, Oleg. *The Collective and the Individual in Russia: A Study of Practices.* Berkeley: University of California Press, 1999.

Kir'ianov, Iu. I., V. Rozenberg, and A. N. Sakharov, eds. *Trudovye konflikty v sovetskoi Rossii, 1918–1929 gg.* Moscow: URSS, 1998.

Kirshin, V. N. *Orden na znameni: Kratkii ocherk istorii leningradskogo ordena otechestvennoi voiny I stepeni zavoda poligraficheskikh mashin.* Moscow and Leningrad: Mashinostroenie, 1965.

Koenker, Diane P. "Class and Consciousness in a Socialist Society: Workers in the Printing Trades during NEP." In *Russia in the Era of NEP: Explorations in Soviet Society and Culture,* ed. Sheila Fitzpatrick, Alexander Rabinowitch, and Richard Stites, 34–57. Bloomington: Indiana University Press, 1991.

———. "Factory Tales: Narratives of Industrial Relations in the Transition to NEP." *Russian Review* 55, no. 3 (1996): 384–411.

———. "Fathers against Sons/Sons against Fathers: The Problem of Generations in the Early Soviet Workplace." *Journal of Modern History* 73, no. 4 (2001): 781–810.

———. "Labor Relations in Socialist Russia: Class Values and Production Values in the Printers' Union." In *Making Workers Soviet: Power, Class, and Identity,* ed. Lewis H. Siegelbaum and Ronald Grigor Suny, 159–93. Ithaca: Cornell University Press, 1994.

———. "Men Against Women on the Shop Floor in Early Soviet Russia: Gender and Class in the Socialist Workplace." *American Historical Review* 100, no. 5 (1995): 1438–64.

———. *Moscow Workers and the 1917 Revolution.* Princeton: Princeton University Press, 1981.

———. "Rabochii klass v 1917 g.: Sotsial'naia i politicheskaia samoidentifikatsiia." In

*Anatomiia revoliutsii: 1917 god v Rossii: Massy, partii, vlast',* ed. V. Iu. Cherniaev, 203–16. St. Petersburg: Glagol', 1994.

———. "Urban Families, Working-Class Youth Groups, and the 1917 Revolution in Moscow." In *The Family in Imperial Russia: New Lines of Historical Research,* ed. David L. Ransel, 280–304. Urbana: University of Illinois Press, 1978.

Koenker, Diane P., and William G. Rosenberg. *Strikes and Revolution in Russia, 1917.* Princeton: Princeton University Press, 1989.

Koiranskii, B. B. *Trud i zdorov'e rabochikh tipografii.* Moscow: Moskovskii gubotdel VSRPP, 1925.

Kollontai, Alexandra. *Selected Writings of Alexandra Kollontai.* Ed. and trans. Alix Holt. London: Allison & Busby, 1977.

Kotkin, Stephen. *Magnetic Mountain: Stalinism as a Civilization.* Berkeley: University of California Press, 1995.

Kucherenko, M. M. *Molodoe pokolenie rabochego klassa SSSR: Protsess formirovaniia i vospitaniia, 1917–1979 gg.* Moscow: Mysl', 1979.

Kuromiya, Hiroaki. *Stalin's Industrial Revolution: Politics and Workers, 1928–1932.* Cambridge: Cambridge University Press, 1988.

———. "Workers' Artels and Soviet Production Relations." In *Workers in the Era of NEP: Explorations in Soviet Society and Culture,* ed. Sheila Fitzpatrick, Alexander Rabinowitch, and Richard Stites, 72–88. Bloomington: Indiana University Press, 1991.

Lebina, N. B. *Povsednevnaia zhizn' sovetskogo goroda 1920/1930 gody.* St. Petersburg: Zhurnal "Neva," 1999.

*Leningradskie profsoiuzy za desiat' let 1917–1927. Sbornik vospominanii pod redaktsii Istprofa L.G.S.P.S.* Leningrad: Leningradskii gubprofsovet, 1927.

*Leningradskii pechatnik, 1917–1927 gg.* Leningrad: Leningradskii gubotdel SRPP, 1927.

*Leninskii zakaz.* Moscow: Politicheskaia Literatura, 1969.

Levenson, A. A., T-vo skoropechatni. *Tovarishchestvo skoropechatni A. A. Levenson na vystavke pechatnogo dela i grafiki v Leipzige 1914 g.* Moscow: A. A. Levenson, 1914.

Lewin, Moshe. *The Making of the Soviet System: Essays in the Social History of Interwar Russia.* New York: Pantheon, 1985.

Lih, Lars T. *Bread and Authority in Russia, 1914–1921.* Berkeley: University of California Press, 1990.

Lipset, Seymour Martin, Martin A. Trow, and James S. Coleman. *Union Democracy: The Internal Politics of the International Typographical Union.* Glencoe, Ill.: Free Press, 1956.

Lüdtke, Alf. "Cash, Coffee-Breaks, Horseplay: *Eigensinn* and Politics among Factory Workers in Germany circa 1990." In *Confrontation, Class Consciousness, and the Labor Process: Studies in Proletarian Class Formation,* ed. Michael P. Hanagan and Charles Stephenson, 65–95. Westport, Conn.: Greenwood, 1988.

———. "Introduction: What Is the History of Everyday Life and Who Are Its Practitioners?" in *The History of Everyday Life: Reconstructing Historical Experiences and Ways of Life,* ed. Alf Lüdtke, trans. William Templer, 3–40. Princeton: Princeton University Press, 1995.

———, ed. *The History of Everyday Life: Reconstructing Historical Experiences and Ways of Life.* Trans. William Templer. Princeton: Princeton University Press, 1995.

Malle, Silvana. *The Economic Organization of War Communism, 1918–1921*. Cambridge: Cambridge University Press, 1985.
Mally, Lynn. *Culture of the Future: The Proletcult Movement in Revolutionary Russia*. Berkeley: University of California Press, 1990.
——. *Revolutionary Acts: Amateur Theater and the Soviet State*. Ithaca: Cornell University Press, 2000.
Mandel, M. David. *The Petrograd Workers and the Fall of the Old Regime*. London: Macmillan, 1983.
——. *The Petrograd Workers and the Soviet Seizure of Power*. London: Macmillan, 1984.
Maslova, N. S. *Proizvoditel'nost' truda i zarabotnaia plata v promyshlennosti SSSR (1928–1932 gg.)*. Moscow: Nauka, 1983.
*Materialy po istorii professional'nogo dvizheniia rabochikh poligraficheskogo proizvodstva (pechatnogo dela) v Rossii*. Comp. I. Skachkov. Ed. F. Smirnov, N. Gordon, and A. Borshchevskii. Moscow: TsK VSRPP, 1925.
McAuley, Mary. *Bread and Justice: State and Society in Petrograd, 1917–1922*. Oxford: Oxford University Press, 1991.
——. *Labour Disputes in Soviet Russia, 1957–1965*. Oxford: Oxford University Press, 1969.
*Men'sheviki v 1918 godu*. Ed. Z. Galili and A. Nenarokov. Moscow: Rosspen, 1999.
*Men'sheviki v 1919–1920 gg*. Ed. Z. Galili and A. Nenarokov. Moscow: Rosspen, 2000.
*Men'sheviki v 1921–1922 gg*. Ed. Z. Galili, A. Nenarokov, and D. Pavlov. Moscow: Rosspen, 2002.
Merridale, Catherine. *Moscow Politics and the Rise of Stalin: The Communist Party in the Capital*. London: Macmillan, 1990.
Mikhailov, N. V. "Samoorganizatsiia trudovykh kollektivov i psikhologiia rossiiskikh rabochikh v nachale XX v." In *Rabochie i intelligentsiia Rossii v epokhu reform i revoliutsii, 1861–fevral' 1917*, ed. S. I. Potolov et al., 149–65. St. Petersburg: Russko-Baltiiskii informatsionnyi tsentr BLITS, 1997.
Millar, James R. "Soviet Rapid Development and the Agricultural Surplus Hypothesis." *Soviet Studies* 22, no. 1 (1970): 77–93.
Montgomery, David. *The Fall of the House of Labor*. Cambridge: Cambridge University Press, 1987.
——. *Workers' Control in America*. Cambridge: Cambridge University Press, 1979.
More, Charles. *Skill and the English Working Class, 1870–1914*. New York: St. Martin's Press, 1980.
*Moskovskie pechatniki v 1905 g*. Moscow: Moskovskii gubotdel, 1925.
Musson, A. E. *The Typographical Association: Origins and History up to 1949*. London: Oxford University Press, 1954.
Naiman, Eric. *Sex in Public: The Incarnation of Early Soviet Ideology*. Princeton: Princeton University Press, 1997.
*Na novykh putiiakh. Itogi novoi ekonomicheskoi politiki 1921–1922 gg*. Vyp. 3: Promyshlennost'. Moscow: Soveta truda i oborony, 1923.
Netesin, Iu. N. "K voprosu o sotsial'no-demokraticheskikh korniakh i osobennostiakh rabochei aristokratii v Rossii." In *Bol'shevistskaia pechat' i rabochii klass Rossii v gody revoliutsionnogo pod"ema (1910–1914 gg.)*, 192–211. Moscow: Nauka, 1965.

Neuberger, Joan. *Hooliganism: Crime, Culture, and Power in St. Petersburg, 1900–1914.* Berkeley: University of California Press, 1993.
Nolan, Mary. *Visions of Modernity: American Business and the Modernization of Germany.* New York: Oxford University Press, 1994.
Nove, Alec. *An Economic History of the U.S.S.R.* Harmondsworth: Penguin, 1969.
Obertreis, Iuliia. "'Byvshee' i 'izlishnee': Izmenenie sotsial'nykh norm v zhilishchnoi sfere v 1920–1930-e gg. Na materialakh Leningrada." In *Normy i tsennosti povsednevnoi zhizni 1920–1930-e gody,* ed. Timo Vikhavainen, 75–98. St. Petersburg: Zhurnal "Neva," 2000.
Orlov, V. P. *Poligraficheskaia promyshlennost' Moskvy: Ocherk razvitiia, do 1917 goda.* Moscow: Iskusstvo, 1953.
Orlovsky, Daniel. "The Hidden Class: White-Collar Workers in the Soviet 1920s." In *Making Workers Soviet: Power, Class, and Identity,* ed. Lewis H. Siegelbaum and Ronald Grigor Suny, 220–52. Ithaca: Cornell University Press, 1994.
Osokina, Elena. *Za fasadom "stalinskogo izobiliia": Raspredelenie i rynok v snabzhenii naseleniia v gody industrializatsii, 1927–1941.* Moscow: Rosspen, 1998.
*Otchet gubernskogo otdela vserossiiskogo soiuza rabochikh poligraficheskogo proizvodstva s sentiabria 1920 g. po mart 1921 g.* Moscow: Izd. Mosk. Gub. SRPP, 1921.
*Otchet leningradskogo gubotdela professional'nogo soiuza rabochikh poligraficheskogo proizvodstva S.S.S.R. za 1926–1927 gg.* Leningrad: Leningradskii gubotdel PSRPP SSSR, 1928.
*Otchet leningradskogo oblastnogo otdela soiuza rabochikh poligraficheskogo proizvodstva SSSR s 1-go oktiabria 1927 g. po 1-e oktiabria 1929 g.* Leningrad: Izd. Len. Obl. Otd. PSRPP SSSR, 1929.
*Otchet moskovskogo gubernskogo otdela vserossiiskogo soiuza rabochikh poligraficheskogo proizvodstva s ianvaria 1922 g. po avgust 1922 g.* Moscow: MGSRPP, 1922.
*Otchet moskovskogo gubotdela professional'nogo soiuza rabochikh poligraficheskogo proizvodstva SSSR. VIII gubernskomu s"ezdu. Ianvar9 1926 g.–iiun' 1927 g.* Moscow: Mosk. Gubotdela Profsoiuza RPP SSSR, 1927.
*Otchet o deiatel'nosti pravleniia moskovskogo gubernskogo otdela soiuza rabochikh poligraficheskogo proizvodstva (s maia 1921 g. po fevral' 1922 g.).* Moscow: Moskovskii gubernskii otdel VSRPP, 1922.
*Otchet o deiatel'nosti pravleniia gubotdela soiuza rabochikh poligraficheskogo proizvodstva s 1 iiulia 1922 g. po 31 maia 1923 g.* Voronezh: Voronezhskii gubotdel, 1923.
*Otchet o deiatel'nosti pravleniia voronezhskogo gubotdela soiuza rabochikh poligraficheskogo proizvodstva s 1/VI 23 g. po 1/X 24 g.* Voronezh: VSRPP. Voronezhskii gubotdel, 1924.
*Otchet o rabote pravleniia gubotdela VI sozyva s 15/XI 1926 g. po 15/XI 1927 g., VII-mu Gubs"ezdu SRPP.* Voronezh: Voronezhskii gubotdel, 1927.
*Otchet pravleniia moskovskogo gubernskogo otdela vsesoiuznogo soiuza rabochikh poligraficheskogo proizvodstva oktiabr' 1923–oktiabr' 1924 gg.* Moscow: Moskovskii gubernskii otdel VSRPP, 1924.
*Otchet pravleniia moskovskogo gubernskogo otdela vsesoiuznogo soiuza rabochikh poligraficheskogo proizvodstva s 1 oktiabria 1924 g. po 1 oktiabria 1925 g.* Moscow: Izd. Mosk. Gub'otdela SRPP, 1925.

*Otchet pravleniia moskovskogo gub'otdela vserossiiskogo soiuza rabochikh poligraficheskogo proizvodstva ot 1 sentiabria 1922 g. po 1 sentiabria 1923 g*. Moscow: Izd. Moskovskogo gub'otdela VSRPP, 1923.

*Otchet pravleniia voronezhskogo gubernskogo otdela soiuza rabochikh poligraficheskogo proizvodstva za 1920 god*. Voronezh: 1-ia sovetskaia tipografiia, 1921.

*Otchet tsentral'nogo komiteta vserossiiskogo soiuza rabochikh poligraficheskogo proizvodstva s 1 iiunia po 1 sentiabria 1922 g*. Moscow: TsK VSRPP, 1922.

Pavlov, Ivan. *Zhizn' russkogo gravera*. Ed. M. P. Sokol'nikov. Moscow: Akademii khudozhestv SSSR, 1963.

*Pechatnyi dvor. Piatiletniaia rabota dlia knigi, 1918-1923*. Moscow and Petrograd: Gosizdat, 1923.

*Pechatnyi vestnik. Iubileinyi vypusk, 1905-1925. 16 aprelia 1925*. Leningrad: Izd. Leningradskogo gubernskogo otdela SRPP SSSR, 1925.

*Pechatnyi vestnik. 1905-1930 gg. Iubileinyi vypusk. 15 maia 1930 g*. Leningrad: Leningradskii oblastnoi otdel SRPP SSSR, 1930.

Perrot, Michelle. *Les Ouvriers en grève: France, 1871-1890*. 2 vols. Paris: Mouton, 1974.

*Pervaia obraztsovaia tipografiia imeni A. A. Zhdanova za 40 let sovetskoi vlasti*. Moscow: Pervaia obraztsovaia tipografiia imeni A. A. Zhdanova, 1957.

*Pervyi vserossiiskii s"ezd professional'nykh soiuzov, 7-14 ianvaria 1918. Polnyi stenograficheskii otchet s predisloviem M. Tomskogo*. Moscow: VTsSPS, 1918.

*Pervyi vserossiiskii s"ezd soiuzov rabochikh poligraficheskogo proizvodstva (2-7 maia 1919 g.). Protokoly i postanovleniia s"ezda (izvlechenie iz stenogramm)*. Moscow: VSRPP, 1919.

Phillips, Laura L. *Bolsheviks and the Bottle: Drink and Worker Culture in St. Petersburg, 1900-1929*. DeKalb: Northern Illinois University Press, 2000.

Pirani, Simon. "The Moscow Workers' Movement in 1921 and the Role of Non-Partyism." *Europe-Asia Studies* 56, no. 1 (2004): 143-60.

*Plenum tsentral'nogo komiteta vserossiiskogo soiuza rabochikh poligraficheskogo proizvodstva (7-11 dekabria 1920 g.). Doklady i rezoliutsii*. Moscow: VSRPP, 1921.

*Profsoiuzy SSSR. Dokumenty i materialy v chetyrekh tomakh (1905-1963 gg)*. Vol. 2. Moscow: VTsSPS Profizdat, 1963.

*Protokol zasedaniia IV-go gubernskogo s"ezda rabochikh i sluzhashchikh poligraficheskogo proizvodstva 21-23 oktiabria 1924 goda*. Voronezh: Pravlenie gubotdela VSRPP, 1924.

*Protokoly zasedaniia V-go gubernskogo s"ezda rabochikh i sluzhashchikh poligraficheskogo proizvodstva 24-25 oktiabria 1925 g*. Voronezh: Pravlenie Gubotdela SRPP, 1925.

Raleigh, Donald J. "Languages of Power: How the Saratov Bolsheviks Imagined Their Enemies." *Slavic Review* 57, no. 2 (1998): 320-49.

Rashin, A. G. *Zarabotnaia plata za vosstanovitel'nyi period khoziaistva SSSR (1922-1927)*. Moscow: VTsSPS, 1928.

Reddy, William M. *Money and Liberty in Modern Europe: A Critique of Historical Understanding*. Cambridge: Cambridge University Press, 1987.

Remington, Thomas F. *Building Socialism in Bolshevik Russia: Ideology and Industrial Organization, 1917-1921*. Pittsburgh: University of Pittsburgh Press, 1984.

Reynolds, Sian. *Britannica's Typesetters: Women Compositors in Edinburgh*. Edinburgh: Edinburgh University Press, 1989.
Roberts, Mary Louise. *Civilization without Sexes: Reconstructing Gender in Postwar France, 1917–1927*. Chicago: University of Chicago Press, 1994.
Roberts, Wayne. "The Last Artisans: Toronto Printers, 1896–1914." In *Essays in Canadian Working-Class History*, ed. Gregory S. Kealey and Peter Warrian, 125–42. Toronto: McClelland & Stewart, 1976.
Robin, Régine. "Stalinism and Popular Culture." In *The Culture of the Stalin Period*, ed. Hans Günther, 15–40. New York: Macmillan, 1990.
Rogachevskaia, L. S. *Likvidatsiia bezrabotitsy v SSSR, 1917–1930 gg*. Moscow: Nauka, 1973.
Rose, Sonya. "Class Formation and the Quintessential Worker." In *Reworking Class*, ed. John R. Hall, 133–68. Ithaca: Cornell University Press, 1997.
Rosenberg, William G. "Russian Labor and Bolshevik Power after October." *Slavic Review* 44, no. 2 (1985): 213–39.
———. "The Social Background to Tsektran." In *Party, State, and Society in the Russian Civil War: Explorations in Social History*, ed. Diane P. Koenker, William G. Rosenberg, and Ronald Grigor Suny, 349–73. Bloomington: Indiana University Press, 1989.
Rosenberg, William G., and Lewis H. Siegelbaum, eds. *Social Dimensions of Soviet Industrialization*. Bloomington: Indiana University Press, 1993.
Rozenfel'd, Ia. S. *Promyshlennaia politika SSSR (1917–1925 gg.)* Moscow: Planovoe khoziaistvo, 1926.
Ruble, Blair A. *Soviet Trade Unions: Their Development in the 1970s*. Cambridge: Cambridge University Press, 1981.
Rule, John. "The Property of Skill in the Period of Manufacture." In *The Historical Meanings of Work*, ed. Patrick Joyce, 99–118. Cambridge: Cambridge University Press, 1987.
Ruud, Charles A. *Russian Entrepreneur: Publisher Ivan Sytin of Moscow, 1851–1934*. Montreal: McGill–Queen's University Press, 1990.
Saf'ian, B. I., and Z. B. Marvits. *Ordenonosnyi "Pechatnyi Dvor": Ocherk istorii tipografii imeni A. M. Gor'kogo*. Moscow: Kniga, 1969.
*Sbornik dekretov i postanovlenii po narodnomu khoziaistvu (25 oktiabria 1917 g.–25 oktiabria 1918 g.)*. Moscow: Iuridicheskii otdel VSNKh, 1918.
Schapiro, Leonard. *The Communist Party of the Soviet Union*. 2nd ed. New York: Vintage, 1971.
———. *The Origin of the Communist Autocracy: Political Opposition in the Soviet State, First Phase, 1917–1922*. 2nd ed. Cambridge: Harvard University Press, 1977.
Schwarz, Solomon M. *Labor in the Soviet Union*. New York: Praeger, 1951.
Scott, James C. *Weapons of the Weak: Everyday Forms of Peasant Resistance*. New Haven: Yale University Press, 1985.
Scott, Joan W. "Statistical Representations of Work: The Politics of the Chamber of Commerce's *Statistique de l'industrie à Paris, 1847–48*." In *Work in France: Representations, Meaning, Organization, and Practice*, ed. Steven Laurence Kaplan and Cynthia J. Koepp, 335–63. Ithaca: Cornell University Press, 1986.
Seidman, Michael. *Workers against Work: Labor in Paris and Barcelona during the Popular Fronts*. Berkeley: University of California Press, 1991.

Sewell, William H., Jr. "Toward a Post-materialist Rhetoric for Labor History." In *Rethinking Labor History*, ed. Lenard R. Berlanstein, 15–38. Urbana: University of Illinois Press, 1993.

Shearer, David R. *Industry, State, and Society in Stalin's Russia, 1926–1934*. Ithaca: Cornell University Press, 1996.

Sher, V. V. *Istoriia professional'nogo dvizheniia rabochikh pechatnogo dela v Moskve*. Moscow: Nauka, 1911.

*Shestoi moskovskii gubernskii s"ezd rabochikh poligraficheskogo proizvodstva 23–26 oktiabria 1924 g*. Moscow: Mosk. Gubotdel VSRPP, 1924.

Shorter, Edward, and Charles Tilly. *Strikes in France, 1830–1968*. Cambridge: Cambridge University Press, 1974.

Siegelbaum, Lewis H. "Masters of the Shop Floor: Foremen and Soviet Industrialization." In *Social Dimensions of Soviet Industrialization*, ed. William G. Rosenberg and Lewis H. Siegelbaum, 113–37. Bloomington: Indiana University Press, 1993.

———. "Soviet Norm Determination in Theory and Practice, 1917–1941." *Soviet Studies* 36, no. 1 (1984): 45–68.

———. *Soviet State and Society between Revolutions, 1918–1929*. Cambridge: Cambridge University Press, 1992.

———. *Stakhanovism and the Politics of Productivity in the USSR, 1935–1941*. Cambridge: Cambridge University Press, 1988.

Siegelbaum, Lewis H., and Ronald Grigor Suny, eds. *Making Workers Soviet: Power, Class, and Identity*. Ithaca: Cornell University Press, 1994.

Sikorskii, N. M., ed. *Knigovedenie: Entsiklopedicheskii slovar'*. Moscow: Sovetskaia entsiklopediia, 1982.

Sirianni, Carmen. *Workers Control and Socialist Democracy: The Soviet Experience*. London: Verso, 1982.

Skachkov, I. "Ocherk po istorii professional'nogo dvizheniia rabochikh pechatnogo dela v Rossii (1903–1917 gg.)." In *Materialy po istorii professional'nogo dvizheniia rabochikh poligraficheskogo proizvodstva (pechatnogo dela) v Rossii*, comp. I. Skachkov, ed. F. Smirnov, N. Gordon, and A. Borshchevskii, 5–73. Moscow: TsK VSRPP, 1925.

Smith, S. A. "Craft Consciousness, Class Consciousness: Petrograd, 1917." *History Workshop Journal* 11 (1981): 33–56.

———. *Red Petrograd: Revolution in the Factories, 1917–1918*. Cambridge: Cambridge University Press, 1983.

———. "The Social Meanings of Swearing: Workers and Bad Language in Late Imperial and Early Soviet Russia." *Past and Present*, no. 160 (1998), 167–202.

———. "Workers against Foremen in St. Petersburg, 1905–1917." In *Making Workers Soviet: Power, Class, and Identity*, ed. Lewis H. Siegelbaum and Ronald Grigor Suny, 113–37. Ithaca: Cornell University Press, 1994.

Snowden, Mrs. Philip. *Through Bolshevik Russia*. London: Cassell, 1920.

Somers, Margaret. "Deconstructing and Reconstructing Class Formation Theory." In *Reworking Class*, ed. John R. Hall, 73–105. Ithaca: Cornell University Press, 1997.

Sorenson, Jay B. *The Life and Death of Soviet Trade Unions, 1917–1928*. New York: Atherton, 1969.

*Spisok fabrik i zavodov g. Moskvy i moskovskoi gubernii.* Moscow: Ministerstvo torgovli i promyshlennosti, Otdel promyshlennosti, 1916.
Steinberg, Marc W. *Fighting Words: Working-Class Formation, Collective Action, and Discourse in Early Nineteenth-Century England.* Ithaca: Cornell University Press, 1999.
Steinberg, Mark D. *Moral Communities: The Culture of Class Relations in the Russian Printing Industry, 1867–1907.* Berkeley: University of California Press, 1992.
———. *Proletarian Imagination: Self, Modernity, and the Sacred in Russia, 1910–1925.* Ithaca: Cornell University Press, 2002.
*Stenograficheskii otchet piatogo s"ezda soiuza rabochikh poligraficheskogo proizvodstva SSSR 20–24 dekabria 1924 g.* Moscow: TsK SRPP SSSR, 1925.
Stites, Richard. *Russian Popular Culture: Entertainment and Society since 1900.* Cambridge: Cambridge University Press, 1992.
———. *The Women's Liberation Movement in Russia: Feminism, Nihilism, and Bolshevism.* Princeton: Princeton University Press, 1978.
Strasser, Susan, Charles McGovern, and Matthias Judt, eds. *Getting and Spending: European and American Consumer Societies in the Twentieth Century.* Cambridge: Cambridge University Press, 1998.
Straus, Kenneth M. *Factory and Community in Stalin's Russia: The Making of an Industrial Working Class.* Pittsburgh: University of Pittsburgh Press, 1997.
Svavitskii, A., and V. V. Sher. *Ocherk polozheniia rabochikh pechatnogo dela v Moskve.* St. Petersburg: Imperatorskoe Russkoe tekhnicheskoe obshchestvo, XII Otdel, 1909.
Tikhanov, A. "Rabochie-pechatniki v gody voiny." In *Materialy po istorii professional'nogo dvizheniia v Rossii,* 3:112–40. Moscow: VTsSPS, 1924.
———. "Rabochie-pechatniki v 1917 g." In *Materialy po istorii professional'nogo dvizheniia v Rossii,* 4:157–99. Moscow: VTsSPS, 1925.
———. *Vserossiiskii soiuz rabochikh poligraficheskogo proizvodstva.* Moscow, 1921.
*Tretii gubernskii s"ezd moskovskogo gubernskogo soiuza rabochikh poligraficheskogo proizvodstva, 16–20 fevralia 1922 g.* Moscow: Moskovskii gubernskii otdel VSRPP, 1922.
*Tretii vserossiiskii s"ezd soiuza rabochikh poligraficheskogo proizvodstva (2–6 iiunia 1921 g.). Protokoly i postanovleniia s"ezda (izvlechenie iz stenogramm).* Moscow: TsK VSRPP, 1921.
*Tret'ya Vserossiiskaya Konferentsiya Professional'nykh Soyuzov, 1917.* Ed. Diane Koenker. Rpt. London: Kraus-Thompson, 1982.
Trotsky, Leon. *Problems of Everyday Life and Other Writings on Culture and Science.* New York: Pathfinder, 1973.
Tsentral'noe statisticheskoe upravlenie. *Trudy.* 35 vols. Moscow, 1917–26.
Tsentral'noe upravlenie narodno-khoziaistvennogo ucheta Gosplana SSSR. Otdel ucheta truda. *Trud v SSSR. Statisticheskii spravochnik.* Ed. A. S. Popov. Moscow, 1936.
Tucker, Robert C. "Stalinism as Revolution from Above." In *Stalinism,* ed. Robert C. Tucker, 77–108. New York: Norton, 1977.
*Tvorchestvo pechatnikov: Literaturnyi sbornik.* Comp. I. Lomskii and D. Zil'berberg. Ed. I. Ban'kovskii. Moscow: Moskovskii gubotdel soiuza RPP SSSR, 1925.

Vaganov, F. M. "Razgrom pravogo uklona v VKP(b) (1928–1930 gg.)." *Voprosy istorii KPSS*, 1960, no. 4: 62–80.

Vechtomova, E. A. *Zdes' pechatalas' "Pravda."* Leningrad: Lenizdat, 1969.

Viduetskaia, I. P. *A. P. Chekhov i ego izdatel' A. F. Marks.* Moscow: Nauka, 1977.

Vikhavainen, Timo, ed. *Normy i tsennosti povsednevnoi zhizni, 1920–1930-e gody.* St. Petersburg: Zhurnal "Neva," 2000.

*Vos'moi s"ezd professional'nykh soiuzov (10–24 dekabria 1928 g.). Plenumy i sektsii. Polnyi stenograficheskii otchet.* Moscow: VTsSPS. 1929.

*Vospominaniia rabochikh 16-i tipo-litografii Mospoligraf (b. Levenson).* Moscow: Iacheika VKP(b) i zavkom 16-i tipo-litografii Mospoligraf, 1925.

*Vtoraia moskovskaia gubernskaia konferentsiia rabochikh poligraficheskogo proizvodstva (stenograficheskii otchet) 12 maia 1921 g.* Moscow: Moskovskii gubernskii soiuz VSRPP, 1922.

*Vtoraia vserossiiskaia konferentsiia soiuza rabochikh pechatnogo dela (14–21 dekabria 1917).* Moscow: Soiuz rabochikh pechatnogo dela, 1918.

Vysshii sovet narodnogo khoziaistva. Glavnoe upravlenie poligraficheskoi promyshlennosti. *Vtoroi vserossiiskii s"ezd oblastnykh i gubernskikh poligraficheskikh otdelov (2–8 iiunia 1921 g.). Stenograficheskii otchet.* Moscow: VSNKh, 1922.

Vysshii sovet narodnogo khoziaistva. Poligraficheskii otdel. *Obzor deiatel'nosti za 1918–1920 gg. [K X-mu s"ezdu R.K.P.]* Moscow, 1921.

Ward, Chris. "Languages of Trade or a Language of Class? Work Culture in Russian Cotton Mills in the 1920s." In *Making Workers Soviet: Power, Class, and Identity*, ed. Lewis H. Siegelbaum and Ronald Grigor Suny, 194–219. Ithaca: Cornell University Press, 1994.

———. *Russia's Cotton Workers and the New Economic Policy: Shop Floor Culture and State Policy, 1921–1929.* Cambridge: Cambridge University Press, 1990.

Weitz, Eric D. *Creating German Communism: From Popular Protests to Socialist State.* Princeton: Princeton University Press, 1997.

Williams, Robert C. "Collective Immortality: The Syndicalist Origins of Proletarian Culture, 1905–1910." *Slavic Review* 39, no. 3 (1980): 389–402.

Wood, Elizabeth A. *The Baba and the Comrade: Gender and Politics in Revolutionary Russia.* Bloomington: Indiana University Press, 1997.

———. "Class and Gender at Loggerheads in the Early Soviet State: Who Should Organize the Female Proletariat and How?" In *Gender and Class in Modern Europe*, ed. Laura L. Frader and Sonya O. Rose, 294–310. Ithaca: Cornell University Press, 1996.

———. "The Trial of Lenin: Legitimating the Revolution through Political Theater, 1920–23." *Russian Review* 61, no. 2 (2002): 235–48.

———. "The Trial of the New Woman: Citizens-in-Training in the New Soviet Republic." *Gender and History* 13 (November 2001): 524–45.

Wright, Erik Olin. *The Debate on Classes.* London: Verso, 1989.

Wynn, Charters. *Workers, Strikes, and Pogroms: The Donbass-Dnepr Bend in Late Imperial Russia, 1870–1905.* Princeton: Princeton University Press, 1992.

Youngblood, Denise J. *Movies for the Masses: Popular Cinema and Soviet Society in the 1920s.* Cambridge: Cambridge University Press, 1992.

Zelnik, Reginald E. *Law and Disorder on the Narova River: The Kreenholm Strike of 1872.* Berkeley: University of California Press, 1995.

---. "On the Eve: Life Histories and Identities of Some Revolutionary Workers, 1870–1905." In *Making Workers Soviet: Power, Class, and Identity,* ed. Lewis H. Siegelbaum and Ronald Grigor Suny, 27–65. Ithaca: Cornell University Press, 1994.

Zerker, Sally F. *The Rise and Fall of the Toronto Typographical Union, 1832–1972: A Case Study of Foreign Domination.* Toronto: University of Toronto Press, 1982.

Zorev, L. K. *Pervaia Obraztsovaia.* Moscow: Kniga, 1967.

# INDEX

absenteeism, 34, 68, 206, 231, 233; penalties for, 136–37, 230
Aleksandrov (First Model foreman), 289, 292
All-Russian Association of the Printing Industry, 219
All-Union Central Council of Trade Unions (*Vsesoiuznyi tsentral'nyi sovet professional'nykh soiuzov*) (VTsSPS): and contracts, 88, 121; on dual unions, 55–57; and Printers' Union, 52, 60, 93; and production, 227, 251; and trade union organization, 74, 252, 300. *See also* Tomskii, Mikhail Pavlovich
All-Union Congress of Representatives of the Managerial Organs of the Printing Industry, 115
All-Union Congress of Shock Workers (November 1929), 232
All-Union trade union congresses: second (1919), 57; fifth (1922) 123; eighth (1928), 251–52
All-Union Trade Union of Workers in the Polygraphic Industry (*Vsesoiuznyi professional'nyi soiuz rabochikh poligraficheskogo proizvodstva*). *See* Printers' Union
apprenticeship: practices, 202–6; in printing industry, 25, 203, 235, 302
Arkhangel'sk, 305

Bakunin (unemployed printer), 262
Barenboim, Grigorii I. (Printers' Union youth organizer), 204
Bogomozov (oppositionist printer), 56
Bokov, P. M. (director at Krasnyi Proletarii Print Shop), 37, 85
Bolshevik party. *See* Communist party
bookbinding, 23, 41, 201–2
Borovskii, Fedor (worker author), 182, 311
Borshchevskii, Aleksandr Stepanovich (1886–1938) (Printers' Union leader): biography, 145–46; criticism of, 251, 255; in factory committee elections, 165; and Moscow identity, 195; politics of, 84, 147, 252; on printing industry, 219–20; in printing section, 52, 63; and purges, 253–54, 256–57, 264; support for, 268; on trade union unity, 59; and women workers, 153, 201
Borshchevskii Training School, Moscow, 203, 206, 248, 284
Bourdieu, Pierre, 8
British shop stewards' movement, 140–41
Budennyi, Semen, 77
Bureau of Congresses of the Printing Industry, 115
*Bykovshchina*, 238

censorship, 11, 161, 221
Chapaev, Vasilii, 77
Cheka, 73, 147–48, 239, 314; and dissent, 58, 66, 171, 246
Chernov, Viktor, 58
Chernyshevskii, Nikolai G., 184
Chicago, 132
Chistov, Nikolai I., 47n3, 153, 286
Chubarovism (*chubarovshchina*), 292
Chusov (Third State Print Shop manager), 119
Chusov (Trud i Kniga Print Shop manager), 118
cinema, 104, 179; popularity of, 168, 187, 279
Clark, Katerina, 216
class, language of, 7, 81, 87, 91–93, 95, 262–63, 310, 312
class analysis, 86, 92; and Russia, 80–81; and socialism, 6–10, 210–11, 311
class identities: exclusionary, 83, 188, 199, 297, 311; and housing, 99, 177–80; and leisure, 188; norms of, 194; and parties, 90;

class identities (*continued*)
  in purge, 287; at Sixteenth Print Shop, 289; under socialism, 176, 208, 272, 298, 315; and social origin, 199
clubs, 101, 187, 277; activities in, 102, 184–86, 280–81; criticism of, 188, 250, 278–79, 284
coal miners, 3
Cohen, Lizabeth, 132
Coleman, James S., 84
collective agreements, 27, 122, 125; demands in, 19, 40; during First Five-Year Plan, 240–41; during NEP, 120–21. *See also tarif*
collectivism, 18, 154, 171, 209, 310, 315; and class identity, 6, 10, 176, 272; in social life, 180, 184–85, 188, 282; in workplace, 70, 124–27, 208
Comintern Print Shop, Leningrad, 169
Commissariat of Labor, 52, 150, 240, 304
Committee on Press Affairs, 219, 226, 235
commodities, 176–77, 182–84. *See also* consumption
Communist International, 32
Communist party: and class identity, 308: criticisms of, 262; as customer, 113; and culture, 101–2; divisions within, 57–63, 67, 74–76; and factory committees, 164–76, 169–70; and favoritism, 224; and firing decisions, 151; and labor relations, 46–47, 52–53, 62; and Leningrad (Petrograd) Printers' Union, 51, 53–56, 61, 67, 113, 156–57; and Moscow Printers' Union, 53, 55, 57, 58–61, 66, 76; in 1917, 2; opposition to, 243, 251, 263, 288; political culture of, 18, 71, 216, 306, 313–14; and Printers' Union, 3, 45, 57, 60, 65, 117, 147, 253–55; and productivism, 46, 72; and repression, 171; and strikes, 67; support for, 61, 83–85, 90, 314; tactics, 61; and trade unions, 59, 63, 116, 155, 252, 267; on worker consciousness, 243; and workplace authority, 37, 39, 71;
Communist party congresses: Tenth (March 1921), 110; Fourteenth (December 1925), 155, 169
companies. *See under* workplace organization
compositors. *See* typesetters
conflict commissions, 38, 136–37, 172, 241
conflicts, 133–38, 314; about managers, 119–20, 237–38, 241, 289; trade unions and, 239–40. *See also* strikes; labor-management relations
consumerism: and printers, 310, 313, 315; under socialism, 183, 298; and youth, 295–96
consumption, 99–100, 177, 208; norms, 99, 181–82. *See also* commodities
control commissions, 132
cooperatives: consumer, 180–82; housing, 178–79

cosmetics, 183, 296
cost accounting (*khozraschet*), 34, 111–12, 218
Council for Labor and Defense, 110
Council of People's Commissars (*Sovet narodnykh komissarov,* Sovnarkom), 219
Council of Printing Congresses, 115–16
council of representatives (*sovet upolnomochennykh*), 38–39, 49–51, 54, 56
craft identities, 86, 273, 302; among printers, 19, 86–88, 311
Crimea, 281
cultural revolution, 5, 175, 218–19, 246, 277–78, 297
culture: in journals, 159; proletarian, 96, 179, 282; socialist, 4–5, 96–97, 100–105, 176, 180

Dan, Fedor, 71–72
dancing, 5, 104, 279–80, 282
Davydov, A. A. (Printers' Union leader), 115
democratic centralism, 145
Derbyshev, Nikolai Ivanovich (1879–1955) (Printers' Union leader), 52, 93, 115, 145, 147, 171, 206; at congresses, 146–49, 151
deskilling, 83
Deviatkin, Aleksandr F. (Menshevik and Printers' Union leader), 84
Dostoevskii, Fedor Mikhailovich, 271
Douglas, Mary, 176
drinking, 192, 210, 250, 267, 276; punishment for, 91, 136–37, 151; and worker culture, 96, 104–5, 189–92, 196, 208, 285, 315
dual unionism, 48, 54–56, 59
Dudarev, Dmitrii G. (manager at Fourteenth State Print Shop, Leningrad), 32, 67, 84–85
Dudin (unemployed printer), 223
Dudnik (union official), 154
*Duglasovshchina,* 187, 296
Dunaev lithography plant, Moscow, 232
Duncan, Isadora, 103

Efimov (steward at Sixteenth State Print Shop), 248
Eighth State Print Shop, Moscow, 65
embezzlement, 118, 147, 151; criticism of, 247, 254–55; growth of, 191–93
English trade union delegation, 58
Ermilov, Vasilii (purged printer), 288
Essentuki, 225
Evdokimov (pressman), 263
everyday life, 5, 96, 100, 179

factory committees: commissions of, 38, 162; criticisms of, 163–64, 172, 248, 264–65; and discipline, 189, 239; elections to, 163–66, 169–70; before 1917, 19; role of, 38,

42–43, 73–74, 162–64; and women workers, 200–201; and workplace authority, 37–38, 71–73
Fairbanks, Douglas, 187, 296
family, language of, 92–93
family life, 94, 275–77
family wage, 222–23
favoritism in hiring, 251
Fedorov Print Shop, Leningrad, 156
Fedotov, V. (Menshevik printer), 72
Ferro, Marc, 71
fiction: on class identities, 174, 195; on drinking, 190–92; on families, 275–76; on gender roles, 294; in journals, 3, 5, 159, 161, 275; on production schemes, 228; on unemployment, 223
Fifteenth State Print Shop, Moscow, 288
Fifth State Print Shop, Moscow, 135
First Five-Year Plan, 12, 110, 215, 218, 243
First Model Print Shop, Moscow (Pervaia Obraztsovaia Print Shop; formerly I. D. Sytin Print Shop): apathy in, 267; club, 185, 278–79; and Communist party, 166–67; consumers at, 182; cultural work, 101–2, 282; elections in, 70–72; and food supply, 73, 97–98; and hooliganism, 285; and housing, 99; management of, 112–13, and Mensheviks, 71, 85; mortality at, 69; before 1917, 30; in 1930s, 302, 304; opposition at, 262–63, and purge, 286–87, 290; and rationalization, 130, 229; and socialist emulation, 231–32; strikes in, 64–65; and trade union journals, 159; turnover at, 235; and unemployment, 223; and women workers, 289, 292, 294; and workplace authority, 38, 73
First State Print Shop, Leningrad. See Pechatnyi Dvor
fistfights, 151, 191–92, 196, 284, 315
Fitzpatrick, Sheila, 10, 81, 312
food consumption, 180–82, 184
food supply, 110, 183; in civil war, 64–66, 73–74, 97–98; and resistance, 68–69
Fordism, 132
Fourteenth State Print Shop, Leningrad (Zinov'ev Print Shop, *Leningradskaia pravda* Print Shop), 32, 67, 98, 166, 233, 297, 302; management of, 84, 113; on opposition, 156, 261
Fourteenth State Print Shop, Moscow, 149, 265
Fülöp-Miller, René, 175

Galaktionov, Ivan D. (manager), 38
gambling, 193
Gegel', Gustav (Communist printer), 57–58
Geller (unemployed printer), 153–54
gender, 3, 5, 9, 180, 293, 309; and class identity, 89, 199–200, 208, 291, 294, 315; and skill, 207, 302. *See also* masculinities; women workers
generation, and class, 5, 9. *See also* young workers; youth
Gershanovich (manager), 237
Girshfeld book bindery, Moscow, 52
Gladkov, Fedor Vasil'evich, 186
Glavnauka Print Shop, Moscow, 247
Godless (*Bezbozhnik*) print shop, Leningrad, 155
Goldman, Emma, 110
Goldman, Wendy Z., 294, 302
Golov (Printers' Union official), 230, 241
Gomel', 234, 303
Goodrich, Carter L., 140
Gorbachev (printer), 186
Gordon, Nikolai I. (Leningrad Printers' Union leader), 67, 84, 155, 209, 313; criticism of, 60, 171, 156–57, 166, 248, 255; and culture, 99–100, 103, 177; as leader, 39, 53–54, 61–62, 65, 76; on Moscow Printers' Union, 57–58; and Petrograd pride, 94; in printing section, 52; on regulation, 116; and schism, 54, 56–57, 60; and strikes, 67; support for, 256; on trade unions, 59, 74–75; and Zinov'ev, 147
Gor'kii, 305
Gor'kii, Maksim, 271
Gorsuch, Anne E., 280
Gosizdat (*Gosudarstvennoe izdatel'stvo*): firms of, 30–32, 38; as manager, 111, 113–14
Gosplan, 115, 294
*Gosudarstvennaia tipografiia*, St. Petersburg. *See* Pechatnyi Dvor
Gotlib, Ia. (unemployed printer), 155–57
Goznak plant, Moscow, 168
GPU. *See* Cheka
Grachev (purged printer), 199
Gray, Robert Q., 82

Haimson, Leopold H., 10
Hall, John R., 7
Hatch, John B., 185
heroes of labor, 88, 183, 195
hooliganism, 151, 154, 193; among printers, 283–85; among youth, 206–7, 284
housing: and class identity, 99; in Moscow, 98–99; norms of, 177–79; in Petrograd, 98, 251; trade union, 177–78
humor: on apathy, 277; on apprentices, 205; on drinking, 192–93; on labor-management relations, 164, 238, 249; in union journals, 3, 20, 159; and workplace, 228, 250, 273–74

identities, 6, 10, 94, 194; socialist, 176–78, 193, 184, 208

Ilf and Petrov (Il'ia Il'f and Evgenii Petrov), 255
Il'intsev, I. S. (dissident printer), 289
incentives. *See* wage form
indiscipline, 231, 233; and class identity, 197–98. *See also under* workplace culture
individualism, 6, 10, 296, 310, 315; in bargaining, 124, 133, 136, 138, 141, 229, 243; criticism of, 105, 185, 287, 296; in cultural life, 187, 282–83, 290; in social life, 180, 188
infrapolitics. *See under* resistance
international situation, 166–67, 305
International Typographical Union (USA), 83–84
Isherwood, Baron, 176
Iskra Revoliutsii Print Shop, Moscow, 232
Italian strike. *See under* strikes
Ivanov, Grigorii (Pechatnyi Dvor manager), 37–39
*Izvestiia* Print Shop, Moscow, 116, 195

jewelry, 183
journalists, 91, 258, 297
journals, 3, 5, 11, 19, 131, 285; functions of, 152, 158–61, 190; *Krasnaia Nov'*, 113; *Moskovskii pechatnik*, 128, 158–59, 161; *Pechatnik*, 51, 60, 120, 128, 158–59, 161, 167, 224, 230, 232, 254–55, 264, 275, 294; provincial, 152n20; readership of, 159–61; *Revoliutsionnyi pechatnik*, 51, 53; *Sotsialisticheskii vestnik*, 135, 171, 251–52; *Vestnik vserossiiskogo soiuza rabochikh pechatnogo dela*, 56

Kabo, Elena Osipovna, 177–79, 181–82
Kaganovich, Lazar' Moiseevich (1893–1991) (trade union leader), 252, 254, 300
Kagarlitskii, G. (Printers' Union official), 115
Kalinin, Iliusha (young printer), 287
Kalinin, Mikhail Ivanovich, 199
Kamenev, Lev Borisovich, 145
Kammermakher, Mark Samoilovich. *See* Kefali, Mark S.
Karpov, I. S. (Sverdlovsk printer), 305
Kaschuba, Wolfgang, 96
Kazan', 241
Kazatskii (Moscow printer), 69
Kefali, Mark S. (Mark Samoilovich Kammermakher) (Menshevik Printers' Union leader), 54, 59, 84
Kenez, Peter, 187
Kharkhordin, Oleg, 286
Khar'kov, 116, 147
*khozraschet*. *See* cost accounting
Kibbel', Fedor, Print Shop, Petrograd, 27–28
Kiev, 210

Klement'ev, Georgii (Printers' Union organizer), 195
Klimenov, M. S. (dissident printer), 289
Kollontai, Aleksandra, 80
Kommuna Print Shop, Voronezh, 114, 227, 265
Komsomol (Young Communist League): apathy in, 260, 266–67; and campaigns, 231, 251; and consumerism, 280, 295–96; and hooliganism, 184, 284, 292; in opposition, 262; and romance, 277
Korovin (dissident lithographer), 290
Kositskii (red congress delegate), 103
Kozlova (telephone operator), 286
*Krasnaia gazeta* Print Shop, Leningrad, 130
Krasnyi Maiak club, Moscow, 188, 286
Krasnyi Proletarii Print Shop (Ivan N. Kushnerev Print Shop, Twentieth Mospoligraf Print Shop), Moscow, 31, 145, 235; club, 279; and Communist party, 165; factory committee in, 167, 169, 259; hooliganism at, 284; management, 37, 112–13; in 1930s, 302, 304; and opposition, 89, 262, 287; and socialist emulation, 232–33; and women workers, 291; and youth, 277
Kronstadt revolt, 66
Krupskaia, Nadezhda, 285
Kurbatov (printer), 196
Kushnerev, Ivan N., Print Shop. *See* Krasnyi Proletarii Print Shop
Kuz'mina, Ekaterina (wife of printer), 199
Kuz'minskii (oppositionist printer), 251, 263
Kuznetsov, Vasilii (oppositionist printer), 166

labor aristocracy, 79, 82
Labor Code, 121
Labor Commissariat. *See* Commissariat of Labor
labor exchanges, 139, 150, 223, 229
labor relations, models of, 46–48, 75
labor-management relations, 4, 117, 236, 314. *See also* conflicts; strikes
language: of craft, 18, 273; of family, 92–93; on strikes, 66–67; on women, 294
language of class: in Communist-Menshevik conflict, 69–70, 91–93; during cultural revolution, 267, 283, 297; under socialism, 7, 95; theories of, 10
Lavrov, Mikhail F. (red director), 155
leather workers, 126, 302
leisure, 100, 277–78, 282; workers' preferences in, 105, 280
Lenin, Vladimir Il'ich, 37, 74, 79, 262
Leningrad (Petrograd) Printers' Union: during civil war, 51, 97; Communist victory in, 53–56; congresses, 154–56, 201, 291; criticisms of, 65, 154–56, 179, 248, 250–51; and culture, 103, 185, 282; leadership of,

157, 259, 304–5; and management, 38, 117, 237; in 1917, 27, 49–50; purge in, 255–57, 264; size of, 20, 146, 300. *See also* Gordon, Nikolai I.; Rozov, M. N.
Leningrad (St. Petersburg, Petrograd) printing industry, 20, 27, 34
*Leningradskaia pravda* Print Shop. *See* Fourteenth State Print Shop, Leningrad
Leningrad Trade Union Council Print Shop, 237
Leontief, Wassily, 226
Levenson, A. A., Print Shop. *See* Sixteenth State Print Shop, Moscow
light cavalry, 266
Lipset, Seymour Martin, 84
lithographers, 23, 40
Lloyd George, David, 69
Lomskii, Ivan (Printers' Union activist), 104, 311
Lozovskii, Aleksandr S. (Solomon Abramovich Dridzo) (trade union official), 59

Magidov, Boris Osipovich (1884–1972) (Printers' Union leader), 256–59, 299–300, 304–5
Main Committee on the Affairs of the Printing Industry, 115
management, 37, 90; red directors, 117–20, 237
Margolis, S. (First Model printer), 302
Marks, A. F., Print Shop. *See* Sokolova Print Shop, Leningrad
Marx, Karl, 8
masculinities, 5, 191, 199; and skill, 86–87, 89, 274, 309. *See also* gender
material culture, 182–84
Matikainen, V. M. (Leningrad Printers' Union leader), 156
McAuley, Mary, 98
Melamed, G. B. (Voronezh Printers' Union leader), 158, 231
Mel'nichanskii, Grigorii M. (Moscow trade union official), 57–58, 201
memory, 209–10
Menshevik party: on Communist tactics, 58–59, 69, 171; on cultural work, 101–2; defeats remembered, 209–10; and extraordinary congress, 1919, 56–57, 85; in factory committee elections, 165–67; at First Model Print Shop, 71–73, 85, 102, 166; as majority in Printers' Union, 2, 12, 45, 48–49, 51, 61; in Moscow Printers' Union, 50, 57, 65; at Pechatnyi Dvor, 264; and Petrograd Printers' Union, 54–55; printers' support for, 3, 39, 82–86, 90, 313; on role of trade unions, 46–47, 52–53, 75, 163, 241–43, 267, 306–7; on socialism, 68; on trade union democracy, 84; on trade union purge, 246

Menshevism: as label for false consciousness, 90, 93; as label for heterodoxy, 85, 154–55, 168, 253, 255, 258; as label for trade union independence, 244, 246–47, 257, 260; at Sixteenth State Print Shop, 289; as socialist opposition, 82, 157, 248, 268
*meshchanstvo*. *See* philistinism
metalworkers, 3, 126, 300
Miakin, F. A. (red director), 118
Mikhailov, Nikolai V., 81
Minchin, I. D. (Printers' Union official), 157
Mitfeeva (criticized printer), 287
Moscow Cooperative Print Shop, 197
Moscow Council of Trade Unions, 55, 57–58, 60, 252
Moscow Economic Council (Moscow Sovnarkhoz), 29, 31. *See also* Vesenkha
Moscow patriotism, 12, 94–95
Moscow Printers' Union, 50–52, 111, 117, 149, 153, 259; congresses, 154, 184; criticism of, 64–66, 153–54, 250, 254–55; structure, 146, 152
Moscow printing industry, 20, 27
Moscow Soviet of Workers' Deputies, 50–51, 60
Moscow Training School. *See* Borshchevskii Training School
Moscow Union of Workers in the Printing Trade (1917) (*Soiuz rabochikh pechatnogo dela*), 145
Mospechat' trust, 30–31, 111–12
Mospoligraf trust, 31, 111–13, 219, 226
Motor Print Shop, Moscow, 118
Murashov (punished printer), 137
Murzich (oppositionist printer), 154
music circles, 102, 184–85, 282

Naiman, Eric, 285, 293
Naletov, V. D. (reprimanded printer), 290
nationalization. *See under* printing industry
NEP (New Economic Policy), 210, 215–16
nepotism, 224
newspapers: factory, 3, 11, 130–31, 160, 197, 209, 285, 289, 298, 302; *Izvestiia*, 50, 135; *Leningradskaia pravda*, 297; *Petrogradskaia gazeta*, 209; *Petrogradskaia pravda*, 32, 113; *Pravda*, 32, 167, 227; *Russkoe slovo*, 50
norm-setting, 229–30

*obshchestvennyi buksir* (public tugboat), 234
*obyvatel'shchina*. *See* philistinism
Okrano Print Shop, Voronezh, 227
one-man management, 37, 117, 119, 239
opportunism, as label, 48, 255, 258, 260–61, 264–65, 307
oppositions. *See under* Communist party; First Model Print Shop; Fourteenth State Print

oppositions (*continued*)
    Shop, Leningrad; Komsomol; Krasnyi Proletarii Print Shop; Menshevism; Pechatnyi Dvor; Sixteenth State Print Shop; Sokolova Print Shop; Tomskii, Mikhail Pavlovich; Trotskii, Lev Davydovich; Trotskyist opposition; women workers; workerism; Zinov'ev, Grigorii Evseevich; Zinov'ev opposition
Orel, 148
Ostrogozhsk (Voronezh guberniia), 52

Panteleev, A. N. (Leningrad Communist), 237
peasant-proletarian dichotomy, 78–79, 92, 135
peasants, 79, 88, 199, 246
*Pechatnik. See under* journals
Pechatnyi Dvor (First State Print Shop, *Gosudarstvennaia tipografiia*, State Print Shop), Leningrad, 31–32, 235, 277, 303, 305; campaigns in, 229, 231–32; management in, 37–38, 113, 237–38; and oppositions, 154–55, 263, 297; politics in, 60, 85, 259; on proletarian manners, 284, 296; work culture in, 124, 128, 184,198; workplace authority in, 39, 132, 224
Penza, 69, 97
Perchuk, Marusia (Komsomol member), 277
Perepechko (Communist printer), 59
Perkovskii, Vladislav (dissident printer), 224
Petrograd Council of Trade Unions, 54–56, 60
Petrograd patriotism, 12, 94
Petrograd Printers' Union. *See* Leningrad Printers' Union
Petrograd printing industry. *See* Leningrad printing industry
Petrograd Union of Workers in the Printing Trade (1917) (*Soiuz rabochikh pechatnogo dela*), 27, 145
Petropechat' trust, 111–13
philistinism (*obyvatel'shchina, meshchanstvo*): criticized, 47–48, 177, 261, 298; and culture, 104–5, 184, 283, 297, 310
Phillips, Laura L., 189, 191
physical culture, 186–87, 278
piece rates, 40–42, 122–24, 154; contested, 125, 137, 141; results from, 126–27
Platform of the Ten, 74
Plekhanov, G. V., 78
*Poligraficheskii otdel. See* Printing Section
Popov, A. (worker memoirist), 209
Potkopechatnik (*Potrebitel'skaia kooperatsiia pechatnikov*), 181–82
*Pravda. See under* newspapers
*Pravda* Print Shop, 204, 226, 282, 286
press freedom, 49
press operators, 22, 41, 302

Priboi publishing house, Leningrad, 113
Printers' Union (*Vsesoiuznyi Professional'nyi Soiuz Rabochikh Poligraficheskogo Proizvodstva*, All-Union Trade Union of Workers in the Polygraphic Industry): *aktiv*, 149, 151–52, 161, 172; and apathy, 266; Central Committee, 11, 57–58, 99, 116–17, 145–49, 152, 158, 170, 219, 226, 305; and class, 87, 90–91; and conflicts, 135–36; and culture, 101–3, 218–19; and embezzlement accusations, 254–55; and factory committees, 163; and First Five-Year Plan, 226; histories of, 57, 209; and housing, 99; and industrial organization, 115–16, 313; leadership, 74, 253–54, 257, 259; membership in, 90, 149–51; and Menshevik party, 2, 45, 48–49, 51, 61; and merger with Union of Paper Workers, 258, 299; before 1917, 2, 101; purge in, 13, 252, 256, 268, 285–87, 289–90; rank and file criticism of, 148–49, 246–48, 250–51, 257–60; rank and file support for, 144–45, 247, 255; and rationalization, 230, 233–34, 307; role in management, 117; schism in, 48, 53–62; structure, 145–46, 148–49, 152, 258; and unemployment, 149–50, 221–22; and wages, 40–41, 88, 123–24; and youth quota, 204–5
Printers' Union, Leningrad. *See* Leningrad Printers' Union
Printers' Union, Moscow. *See* Moscow Printers' Union
Printers' Union, Petrograd. *See* Leningrad Printers' Union
Printers' Union, Voronezh. *See* Voronezh Printers' Union
Printers' Union conferences and congresses: second all-Russian conference (December 1917), 48–49; red congress (May 1919), 55, 84; extraordinary congress (August 1919), 56–57; fourth congress (October 1922), 146–48; fifth congress (December 1924), 146–49; sixth congress (November 1926), 149; seventh congress (February 1929), 116, 226, 252–53; congress of Union of Print and Paper Workers (December 1930), 258–59; congresses in 1930s, 304–5
Printers' Union of the Center and South, 300, 303–4
Printers' Union of the North, 300, 304–5
printing industry: and First Five-Year Plan, 225–26, 234; labor force in, 3, 20, 111, 235, 300–302, 307; management of, 112, 117–20; nationalization of, 26, 28–30, 111; during NEP, 111, 217–18; before 1917, 27; organization of, 21, 30; ownership of, 29–30; problems in, 114, 124, 131, 218; regula-

tion of, 114–16, 219, 243, 313; technology, 21, 83, 114, 304
Printing Section (*Poligraficheskii otdel*): functions of, 29, 32, 63; Moscow, 37, 63–64, 146; provincial, 52; Vesenkha, 29, 52, 62
prizes, 130, 183, 186, 227, 234, 304
production conferences, 128–30, 132, 227
production contests, 128–30, 228
productivism: and class identity, 176; Communist support for, 54, 61, 308; Menshevik support for, 73; in practice, 63, 66, 71, 115, 237, 242–44, 314; as principle of labor relations, 4, 46, 62, 72, 75, 117, 236, 307; and strikes, 50
productivity, 34, 140; incentives, 122–24, 127–28
proletarian culture. *See* socialist culture
proletarian identity. *See* identities: socialist
proletarian myth, 78–79
Proletkul't, 103
protest. *See* conflicts, oppositions, resistance, strikes
public tugboat (*obshchestvennyi buksir*), 234

railway workers, 3
Rakhmanovskii trust. *See* labor exchanges
rationalization: campaigns, 131–32, 228–30, 233–34; in 1930s, 302–3; and unemployment, 221. *See also* cost accounting; production conferences; production contests; regime of economy; seven-hour workday; shock brigades; socialist emulation; Stakhanovites; worker innovators
rationing, 41–42, 180
red directors. *See under* management
Reddy, William M., 7, 210
regime of economy, 131, 153, 168
resistance: and class analysis, 8–9; to Communist regime, 233, 258, 260–61; forms of, 144, 239, 262; through infrapolitics, 9, 68, 134, 171–72, 258. *See also* oppositions
rest homes, 91, 182, 224, 250, 275, 281–82, 284
revolution of 1917, 48–50, 209
Roberts, Mary Louise, 293
Robin, Régine, 96
Rose, Sonya, 8–9
Rosenberg, William G., 74
Roslov, Aleksandr (dissident printer), 288
rough culture, 196–97, 206
Rozov, M. N. (Leningrad Printers' Union leader), 219, 260, 268; as leader, 156–57, 250, 259, 263; purge of, 256–57, 264, 296
Rubin (Menshevik printer), 59
*Russkoe slovo* Print Shop, 50–51
Rymkevich, A. M. (Leningrad Printers' Union leader), 304–5

St. Petersburg printing industry. *See* Leningrad printing industry
Savost'ianova (purged office worker), 286
scissors crisis, 109, 123
Scott, Joan W., 9
Second Transpechat' Print Shop, Leningrad, 229
secret police. *See* Cheka
self-attachment campaign, 235–36
self-criticism campaign, 248, 250, 266
Semenov, M. S. (disabled printer), 195
seven-hour workday, 228–30
Seventh State Print Shop, Moscow, 113, 164
Sewell, William H., Jr., 9–10
Shearer, David R., 219
Shekhmeister, L. Ia. (Printers' Union youth organizer), 205
Shmidt, Vasilii Vladimirovich (Commissar of Labor), 63
shock brigades: forms of, 232, 266; resistance to, 244, 260–61, 265, 272, 296; women's, 291, 294, 303
Simferopol', 305
Sixteenth State Print Shop (formerly Levenson): apathy in, 265–66; conflict commission, 136–37; criticism in, 66, 240, 247–48; cultural life in, 159, 178, 188; history, 31; management, 112–13, 118; oppositions in, 261–64, 290; politics in, 70, 165; purge at, 286, 289; rationalization in, 129, 230, 233; and strikes, 64, 70
skill, 21, 273; acquisition of, 24–25; and class identity, 194–95, 198–99, 208, 274; and women workers, 200–202
Slepenkina, Valentina (factory committee chair at *Leningradskaia pravda* Print Shop), 302
Smolensk, 102
socialist culture, 4, 96, 187–88
socialist emulation: as campaign, 231–34; criticism of, 260; failures in, 254, 284
socialist identities. *See under* identities: socialist
Socialist Revolutionaries, 2, 49n9, 209
Society of Young Printers, Moscow, 101
*Soiuz rabochikh pechatnogo dela*, Moscow. *See* Moscow Union of Workers in the Printing Trade
*Soiuz rabochikh pechatnogo dela*, Petrograd. *See* Petrograd Union of Workers in the Printing Trade
Sokolov (Leningrad printer), 156
Sokolova, Evgeniia (Communist printer), 32
Sokolova, Evgeniia, State Print Shop (Twenty-Sixth State Print Shop, formerly A. F. Marks Print Shop), 32, 169; drinking at, 155, 189; management, 113, 237; oppositions in, 251, 263; and productivity campaigns, 228, 232–33

Solov'ev (Moscow Printers' Union chair), 250
Solov'ev, Vladimir, 79
Southeastern Railway Print Shop, Voronezh, 114
*sovet upolnomochennykh. See* council of representatives
Sovnarkom (Council of People's Commissars), 219
sport, 186–87, 278
Stakhanovites, 303–4
Stalin, Iosif, 216, 246, 251–52, 264
Stalinism, 170, 246, 259, 297, 312–14
standard of living, 24, 42, 177
State Print Shop, St. Petersburg. *See* Pechatnyi Dvor
*stavka. See* wage grid
Steinberg, Mark D., 18, 26, 81
strikes: issues in, 62, 64, 135; interpretations of, 46, 133–35, Italian, 134–35, 137, 274; language of, 66–67; in 1917, 28, 50–51; 1922 wave of, 67–68; political, 62, 64; in printing industry, 19, 135, 239, 241; under socialism, 35, 46, 134
supervisors, 26, 120; under socialism, 36–37
Supreme Economic Council. *See* Vesenkha
swearing, 5, 151, 197, 291, 315
Sytin, I. D. (printing entrepreneur), 30

Tabakov, P. I. (dissident printer), 288
Tambov, 279
tardiness, 91, 136, 206, 230–31
*tarif*, 40–42, 136; conflicts over, 52, 88, 170, 241; egalitarian, 273–74
Tashkent, 131
Taylor, Frederick W., 132, 229, 230
technology. *See under* printing industry
textile workers, 91, 302
theater, 105, 224; in clubs, 101–2, 167–69, 185–86
theft, 68, 73, 137. *See also* embezzlement
Third State Print Shop, Moscow, 119
Thirteenth State Print Shop, Moscow, 167, 233
Thirty-ninth State Print Shop, Moscow, 165
Tikhanov, Aleksandr Ia. (Printers' Union leader), 57, 62, 74, 84, 115
tobacco workers, 91
Tolstoi, Lev, 271
Tomskii, Mikhail Pavlovich (1880–1936) (chairman of VTsSPS), 28, 59, 62, 65, 84, 86, 284; in opposition, 123, 251, 254, 264; on Printers' Union, 57–58, 83; and purge, 245, 252–53
Tomskii Lithographic Plant, Leningrad (formerly Kibbel'), 28
total proletarian: as behavioral norm, 100, 151, 185, 193, 314–15; defined, 79–80; deviations from norm of, 262, 298; examples of, 82, 261; as goal, 105, 173; and official

class identity, 208; in practice, 81, 161, 176, 278, 282, 289
tourism, 281–82
Trade Union Debate, 74
trade union democracy, 59, 84; in United States, 83–84
trade unionism (*tred-iiunionizm*): as epithet, 257, 300; in printing, 90, 153, 244, 254
trade union journals. *See* journals
Trade Union of Paper and Print Workers. *See under* Printers' Union
Trade Union of Paper Workers, 258, 299
trade unions: and cultural work, 100–101; before 1917, 19; reorganization of, 300; roles of, 29, 46, 144, 151; as school for communism, 4, 143, 154, 308–9; under socialism, 4, 35–36, 116–17; and workplace democracy, 71
Transpechat' trust, 111, 145
Transport Workers' Union Central Committee (Tsektran), 74
Trauberg (red director), 120
Trotskii, Lev Davydovich (Bronshtein), 80, 131, 288; as oppositionist, 123, 145, 228; on trade unions, 47, 74–75, 143, 234; as Red Army commander, 52, 77
Trotskyist opposition, 233, 242, 257, 293; on shop floor, 82, 261–62, 264, 268, 305
Trow, Martin A., 84
Trud i Kniga Print Shop, Moscow, 118
trusts, 111
Tsektran (Transport Workers' Union Central Committee), 74
tuberculosis, 195–96
Turbin (Voronezh oppositionist), 265
turnover, 235
Twelfth Mospoligraf Print Shop, Moscow, 230
Twentieth State Print Shop, Moscow. *See* Krasnyi Proletarii Print Shop
Twenty-sixth State Print Shop, Leningrad. *See* Sokolova, Evgeniia, Print Shop
typesetters, 88; occupations, 21, 26; wages of, 25, 40

Ugorov (Leningrad Communist printer), 157
unemployment: and apprentices, 140, 203; during civil war, 33–34; and class identity, 153, 195, 221, 223–24; during NEP, 12, 35, 138–39, 217, 220, 306; remedies for, 153, 221–22, 224; and role of union, 147, 149–50; worker criticism of, 89, 141, 153–54, 156, 224, 247, 260
Union of Workers in Publishing, 300
Union of Workers in the Printing Industry of the Center and South. *See* Printers' Union of the Center and South
Union of Workers in the Printing Industry of the North. *See* Printers' Union of the North

Union of Workers in the Printing Trade (*Soiuz rabochikh pechatnogo dela*), Moscow (1917), 145
Union of Workers in the Printing Trade (*Soiuz rabochikh pechatnogo dela*), Petrograd (1917), 27, 145

vacations, 64, 240, 280–81
Vasil'ev, A. V. (factory committee chair at Krasnyi Proletarii), 165
Vasil'ev, Mikhail (purged Komsomol printer), 296
Vasil'ev, Petr (Leningrad Printers' Union official), 155, 308
Vasil'ev (oppositionist at Pechatnyi Dvor), 263–64, 268
Vesenkha (Supreme Economic Council, VSNKh): and collective agreements, 121; as manager, 30, 114, 235; on organization of printing industry, 29, 110–13, 115; Printing Committee, 219, 226; on productivity, 131. *See also under* Printing Section, Vesenkha
Viatka, 42
Viktorov (manager), 288
Vladina (worker), 197
vocational training, 203, 235. *See also* apprenticeship
Volkov (criticized printer), 261–62
Volnukhin, Vasilii (Leningrad printer), 237
Volodarskii Print Shop, Leningrad, 122
Volodin (printer), 233
Vorob'eva, Marusia (printer), 296
Voronezh Economic Council Print Shop, 181
Voronezh Group Committee, 248
Voronezh Printers' Union, 61, 157, 227; and clubs, 104, 185, 188; and congresses, 55–56; dissent in, 157–58; structure, 146, 158
Voronezh printing industry, 32–33, 113–14, 300
*Vsesoiuznyi professional'nyi soiuz rabochikh poligraficheskogo proizvodstva*. See Printers' Union
*Vsesoiuznyi tsentral'nyi sovet professional'nykh soiuzov*. See All-Union Central Council of Trade Unions
VSNKh. *See* Vesenkha
VTsSPS. *See* All-Union Central Council of Trade Unions

wage form, 39–42, 121; as collective pay, 43, 126; during NEP, 122–23; and productivity, 63, 124; as time pay, 40, 123. *See also* piece rates
wage grid (*stavka*), 40. *See also* tarif
wages: conflicts over, 66, 136; differentials in, 25, 26, 34, 40–43, 69, 88, 121–22, 138; equity in, 124–25; existence-based, 40–42; and family wage, 222–23; levels of, 121, 123, 126–27, 217, 300–301; negotiations over, 120–21
Ward, Chris, 80
white-collar workers: attitudes toward, 178, 198; and class identity, 92, 99; and trade unions, 90–91
Whitley Councils, 140
women workers: and activism, 173, 278; attitudes toward, 6, 200–201, 207, 289, 291–93, 309, 315; in bookbinding, 23; exclusion of, 95, 126, 199, 294; as housewives, 98, 181, 276; in 1930s, 302–3; in opposition, 12, 153, 291; policy towards, 19, 200; in press work, 22–23; and skill, 25, 86–87, 89, 201–2; in typesetting, 21–22; and unemployment, 89, 220, 222–23
work and class identities, 6, 194, 196, 208, 311
worker-correspondents, 11–12, 161, 261, 272; and campaigns, 131, 233
worker innovators, 130, 227
workerism, 44, 69; in labor relations, 46, 236–37, 240; as opposition, 254, 261; in Printers' Union, 239, 242–43
Workers' Opposition, 37, 74, 143
workplace authority: and factory committees, 70, 73; under socialism, 36–37; as workers' control, 125–27, 140–41
workplace culture, 26, 41, 44, 89, 126; and indiscipline, 124, 155, 198
workplace democracy, 171, 308, 313; and apathy, 167–69, 172, 265–66; during civil war, 37, 70–73; and factory committee elections, 162–63, 165–67, 170; limits on, 164, 168; workplace organization, 89; companies, 26, 125–26
workplace rituals, 18, 189, 196
Wright, Erik Olin, 8, 86, 92

Youngblood, Denise J., 187
Young Communist League. *See* Komsomol
young workers: apathy of, 266–67; attitudes toward, 6, 95, 202, 205–7, 295, 309; policy on, 200, 203–5
youth: at clubs, 101, 185, 279; in conflict, 309; and romance, 276–77, 294–95
youth problem in twentieth century, 206–7

*Zhenotdel* (Communist party Women's Section), 291, 295
Zhivotovskaia, A. L. (printer), 302
Zinov'ev, Grigorii Evseevich, 32, 39, 93; as oppositionist, 145, 147, 169; on trade unions, 74–75
Zinov'ev opposition, 145, 147, 155, 169
Zinov'ev Print Shop, Leningrad. *See* Fourteenth State Print Shop, Leningrad
*zvon*, 197, 230–31, 291